Sentence Skills
with Readings

Sentence Skills

with Readings

FIFTH EDITION

John Langan

Atlantic Cape Community College

Paul Langan

Connect
Learn
Succeed™

ISBN 978-0-07-803629-3
MHID 0-07-803629-1

ISBN 978-0-07-749816-0 (Annotated Instructor's Edition)
MHID 0-07-749816-X

Senior Vice President, Products & Markets: *Kurt L. Strand*
Vice President, General Manager, Products & Markets: *Michael Ryan*
Vice President, Content Production & Technology Services: *Kimberly Meriwether David*
Managing Director: *David Patterson*
Director: *Paul Banks*
Executive Brand Manager: *Kelly Villella-Canton*
Executive Director of Development: *Lisa Pinto*
Development Editors: *Lai T. Moy, Anne Stameshkin*
Editorial Coordinator: *Dana Wan*
Senior Marketing Manager: *Jaclyn Elkins*
Director, Content Production: *Terri Schiesl*
Content Project Manager: *Katie Fuller*
Buyer: *Susan K. Culbertson*
Designer: *Debra Kubiak*
Cover/Interior Designer: *Preston Thomas*
Cover Image: *Laptop:* © *Marnie Burkhart/Corbis* and © *Stockbyte/Getty Images*
Content Licensing Specialist: *Ann Marie Jannette*
Photo Research: *Emily Tietz, Editorial Image, LLC*
Compositor: *MPS Limited*
Typeface: *11/13 Times LT Std*
Printer: *R. R. Donnelley*

Library of Congress Cataloging-in-Publication Data

Cataloging-in-Publication Data has been requested from the Library of Congress.

www.mhhe.com

John Langan has taught and authored books on writing and reading skills for over thirty years. Before teaching, he earned advanced degrees in writing at Rutgers University and in reading at Rowan University. John now lives with his wife, Judith Nadell, near Philadelphia. In addition to his wife and Philly sports teams, his passions include reading and turning nonreaders on to the pleasure and power of books. Through Townsend Press, his educational publishing company, he has developed the nonprofit "Townsend Library"—a collection of more than 100 new and classic stories with wide appeal to readers of all ages.

Paul Langan has tutored adult students in basic reading and writing skills since he was a college undergraduate. Beginning as a community college student, he went on to graduate with honors from La Salle University and later earned a master's degree in reading, writing, and literacy from the University of Pennsylvania. In addition to editing and authoring a popular series of young adult novels, Paul has taught composition at Camden County College. A husband and father, he lives "a stone's throw" from Philadelphia and recently had a long-term hope fulfilled when the Phillies finally won the World Series.

BRIEF CONTENTS

CONTENTS

PART 2 Sentence Skills 71

SECTION 1 SENTENCES 72

CONNECT WRITING 2.0 PERSONAL LEARNING PLAN CORRELATION GUIDE

UNIT	TOPIC IN PERSONAL LEARNING PLAN
Writing Clear Sentences	Subjects and Verbs
Fixing Common Problems	Fragments Run-Ons

SECTION 4 PUNCTUATION AND MECHANICS   298

CONNECT WRITING 2.0 PERSONAL LEARNING PLAN CORRELATION GUIDE

UNIT	TOPIC IN PERSONAL LEARNING PLAN
Addressing Mechanics	Capitalization
	Abbreviations
	Numbers
Punctuating Correctly	Commas
	Apostrophes
	End Punctuation
	Quotation Marks
	Colons and Semicolons
	Parentheses
	Dashes
	Hyphens
Fixing Common Problems	Indirect and Direction Quotations

SECTION 5 WORD USE   387

CONNECT READING 2.0 PERSONAL LEARNING PLAN CORRELATION GUIDE

UNIT	TOPIC IN PERSONAL LEARNING PLAN
Using Words Effectively	Misspelled Words
	Commonly Confused Words
	Omitted Words
	Slang
	Euphemisms
	Clichés
	Sexist Words
	Biased Words
	Pretentious Words
	Wordy Phrases
	Empty Words
	Redundant Words
	Repetitive Words
	Unnecessary Passive Verbs

APPENDIXES

Preface

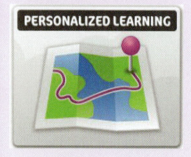

Adaptive Personalized Learning

Sentence Skills with Readings supports personalized learning. Powered by *Connect Writing 2.0*, students gain access to our groundbreaking Personal Learning Plan, which helps students become aware of what they already know and what they need to practice. A self-study tool, its cutting-edge, continually adaptive technology, and exclusive time-management features make students more productive and keep them on track as they prepare for their college courses.

With a baseline diagnostic that assesses student proficiencies in five core areas of grammar and mechanics, students can generate a unique learning plan tailored to their specific needs and the schedule of days per week they select for working on the site. Students receive a personalized program of lessons, videos, animations, and interactive exercises to improve their skills and immediate feedback on their work. With an engine that incorporates metacognitive learning theory and provides ongoing diagnosis for every learning objective, the personal learning plan continually adapts with each student interaction, while built-in time-management tools ensure that students achieve their course goals. This constantly assessing and adapting online environment increases student readiness, motivation, and confidence and allows classroom instruction to focus on thoughtful and critical writing processes.

A Personalized Learning icon (see the image at the beginning of this section) typically appears at the end of a chapter's introduction or at the end of the first A-head of a chapter that offers related content. Correlation guides to Connect Writing 2.0 Personal Learning Plan also appear in each section of Part II in the detailed table of contents; these guides show readers the related topics in the Connect Personal Learning Plan.

Mastering the Four Bases: Unity, Support, Coherence, Sentence Skills

By addressing a set of four skills for effective writing, *Sentence Skills with Readings* encourages new writers to see writing as a skill that can be learned and a process that must be explored. The four skills, or bases, for effective writing are as follows:

- **Unity:** Discover a clearly stated point, or topic sentence, and make sure that all other information in the paragraph or essay supports that point.

- **Support:** Support the points with specific evidence, and plenty of it.

- **Coherence:** Organize and connect supporting evidence so that paragraphs and essays transition smoothly from one bit of supporting information to the next.

- **Sentence skills:** Revise and edit so that sentences are error free for clearer and more effective communication.

The four bases are essential to effective writing. *Sentence Skills with Readings* introduces all four concepts but primarily emphasizes sentence skills.

UNITY

Discover a clearly stated point, or topic sentence, and make sure that all other information in the paragraph or essay supports that point.

SUPPORT

Support the points with specific evidence, and plenty of it.

COHERENCE

Organize and connect supporting evidence so that paragraphs and essays transition smoothly from one bit of supporting information to the next.

SENTENCE SKILLS

Revise and edit so that sentences are error free for clearer and more effective communication.

In addition to incorporating the Personalized Learning Plan, maintaining the four bases framework, and continuing to integrate many writing examples, *Sentence Skills with Readings* includes the following part-by-part changes.

Part 1: Effective Writing

- New Chapter 4 to provide guidance for using digital and electronic resources to enhance and simplify each stage of the writing process

- Updated examples to better reflect how today's students are producing and consuming writing

Part 2: Sentence Skills

- New Chapter 5, introducing students to the parts of speech—the building blocks of sentences—to help them better understand the "how and why" of the most common sentence errors

- Updated practice activities to reflect and ensure relevance to the interests and lives of today's students

- Updated guidelines for formatting a paper to best represent academic expectations

Part 3: Reinforcement of the Skills

- Updated practice materials to reflect and ensure relevance to the interests and lives of today's students

Part 4: Readings for Writing

- Three new reading selections that reflect the social and political concerns of the times:

  "Talkin' White" by Wayne Lionel Aponte

  "My Two Moms" by Zach Wahls

  "Don't Hang Up, That's My Mom Calling" by Bobbi Buchanan

- New sets of questions and assignments for each new reading

Appendixes

- Streamlined and condensed to focus on skills improvement, diagnosis, and achievement

Book-Specific Supplements for Instructors

The **Annotated Instructor's Edition** consists of the student text, complete with answers to all activities and tests and Teaching Tips.

The **Online Learning Center** (www.mhhe.com/langan) offers a number of instructional materials, including an instructor's manual, a test bank, and Power-Point® slides that may be tailored to course needs.

Create the perfect course materials with Create™

create Your courses evolve over time; shouldn't your course material? With McGraw-Hill's Create™, you can easily arrange your book to align with the syllabus, eliminate chapters you do not assign, combine material from other content sources, and quickly upload content you have written, such as your course syllabus or teaching notes, to enhance the value of course materials for your students. You control the net price of the book as you build it and have the opportunity to choose format: color, black-and-white, and eBook. When you build a Create™ book, you'll receive a complimentary print review copy in three to five business days or a complimentary electronic review copy (eComp) via e-mail in about one hour.

Go to www.mcgrawhillcreate.com and register today!

Customize *Sentence Skills with Readings* in Create™ with bonus content.

If you previously ordered *Sentence Skills* (without readings), you can easily order the updated content by asking your McGraw-Hill representative or Learning Solutions Consultant, or you can take this opportunity to get creative!

In addition to reorganizing and eliminating chapters in *Sentence Skills with Readings,* you have many other options to build the perfect book:

- Add your own materials (such as sample student paragraphs or essays) or add chapters from other McGraw-Hill textbooks.

- Customize the readings in Part Four by exchanging readings for those from other Langan titles.

- Customize with readings from other McGraw-Hill collections such as *Cornerstones* (nearly 400 readings with pedagogy for developing writers), *The Ideal Reader* (800 Composition-level readings by author, genre, mode, theme, and discipline), *Annual Editions* (5,500 articles from journals and periodicals), *Traditions* (readings in the humanities), *Sustainability* (readings with an environmental focus), and *American History and World Civilization Documents* (primary sources, including maps, charters, letters, memoirs, and essays).

McGraw-Hill Create™ *ExpressBooks* facilitate customizing your book more quickly and easily. To quickly view the possibilities for customizing your book, visit www.mcgrawhillcreate.com and enter "Sentence Skills with Readings" under the Find Content tab. Once you have selected the current edition of your chosen *Sentence Skills with Reading* book, click on the "View Related ExpressBooks" button or ExpressBooks tab to see options. ExpressBooks contain a combination of preselected chapters, articles, and readings that serve as a starting point to help you quickly and easily build your own text. These helpful templates are built using content available on Create™ and organized in ways that match various course outlines. We understand that you have a unique perspective. Use McGraw-Hill Create™ ExpressBooks to build the book you've only imagined!

Connect LMS Integration

Connect Writing integrates with your local learning management system (Blackboard, Desire2Learn, and others).

McGraw-Hill Campus™ is a new one-stop teaching and learning experience available to users of any learning management system. This complimentary integration allows faculty and students to enjoy single sign-on (SSO) access to all McGraw-Hill Higher Education materials and synchronized grade-book with our award-winning McGraw-Hill *Connect* platform. McGraw-Hill Campus provides faculty with instant access to all McGraw-Hill Higher Education teaching materials (eTextbooks, test banks, PowerPoint slides, animations and learning objects, and so on), allowing them to browse, search, and use any instructor ancillary content in our vast library at no additional cost to the instructor or students. Students enjoy SSO access to a variety of free (quizzes, flash cards, narrated presentations, and so on) and subscription-based products (McGraw-Hill *Connect*). With this integration enabled, faculty and students will never need to create another account to access McGraw-Hill products and services. For more information on McGraw-Hill Campus, please visit our website at **www.mhcampus.com** or contact your local McGraw-Hill representative to find out more about installations on your campus.

Tegrity

Tegrity Campus is a service that makes class time available all the time by automatically capturing every lecture in a searchable format for students to review when they study and complete assignments. With a simple, one-click start and stop process, users capture all computer screens and corresponding audio. Students replay any part of any class with easy-to-use browser-based viewing on a PC or Mac. Educators know that the more students can see, hear, and experience class resources, the better they learn. With Tegrity Campus, students quickly recall key moments by using Tegrity Campus's unique search feature. This search helps students efficiently find what they need, when they need it, across an entire semester of class recordings. Help turn all your students' study time into learning moments immediately supported by your lecture.

CourseSmart™

This text is available as an eTextbook at **www.CourseSmart.com**. At CourseSmart, your students can take advantage of significant savings off the cost of a print textbook, reduce their impact on the environment, and gain access to powerful tools for learning. CourseSmart eTextbooks can be viewed online or downloaded to a computer. CourseSmart offers free apps to access the textbooks on SmartPhones and iPads. The eTextbooks allow students to do full text searches, add highlighting and notes, and share notes with classmates. CourseSmart has the largest selection of eTextbooks available anywhere. Visit **www.CourseSmart.com** to learn more and to try a sample chapter.

ACKNOWLEDGMENTS

Reviewers who have contributed to this edition through their helpful comments include Karen Abele, *Sauk Valley College*; Glenda Bachman, *Northeastern Oklahoma A&M College*; Judy Covington, *Trident Technical College*; Anne Cox, *MT San Jacinto College–Menifee*; Ella Davis, *Wayne County Community College–Western*; Christie Firtha, *Barstow College*; Pamela Hudson, *Hawaii Community College;* George Rubio, *Santa Monica Community College*; Ken Tangvik, *Roxbury Community College*; and Bonnie Zobell, *San Diego Mesa College*.

I owe thanks as well for the support provided by Kelly Villella-Canton, Lisa Pinto, Anne Stameshkin, and Lai T. Moy at McGraw-Hill. My gratitude also goes to Paul Langan, who has helped this book become even more student-friendly than it was before.

Joyce Stern, assistant professor at Nassau Community College, contributed the ESL tips to the annotated instructor's edition. Professor Stern is assistant to the chair in the Department of Reading and Basic Education. An educator for over thirty years, she holds an advanced degree in TESOL from Hunter College, as well as a New York State Teaching Certificate in TESOL. She is currently coordinating the design, implementation, and recruitment of learning communities for both ESL and developmental students at Nassau Community College and has been recognized by the college's Center for Students with Disabilities for her dedication to student learning.

Donna T. Matsumoto, assistant professor of English and the Writing Discipline Co-ordinator at Leeward Community College in Hawaii (Pear City), wrote the teaching tips for the annotated instructor's edition. Professor Matsumoto has taught writing, women's studies, and American studies for a number of years throughout the University of Hawaii system, at Hawaii Pacific University, and in community schools for adults. She received a 2005 WebCT Exemplary Course Project award for her online writing course.

John Langan

Sentence Skills
with Readings

Effective Writing

PART 1

Introduction

Part One is a guide to the goals of effective writing and includes a series of activities to help you practice and master these goals. Begin with the introductory chapter, which makes clear the reasons for learning sentence skills. Then move on to Chapter 2, which presents all the essentials you need to know to become an effective writer. You will be introduced to the four goals of effective writing and will work through a series of activities designed to strengthen your understanding of these goals. Then, walk through the steps of the writing process—from prewriting to proofreading—in Chapter 3. Examples and activities are provided to illustrate each step, and after completing the activities, you'll be ready to take on the paragraph writing assignments at the end of the chapter. Finally, in Chapter 4, learn how online and electronic resources can help make the writing process both easier and more rewarding.

At the same time that you are writing papers, start working through the sentence skills in Parts Two and Three of the book. Practicing the sentence skills in the context of actual writing assignments is the surest way to master the rules of grammar, mechanics, punctuation, and usage.

Can you think of other careers, besides the one pictured here, in which good written communication skills are required? Why do you think writing is important to so many different types of careers?

Learning Sentence Skills

Why Learn Sentence Skills?

Why should someone planning a career as a nurse have to learn sentence skills? Why should an accounting major have to pass a competency test in grammar as part of a college education? Why should a potential physical therapist, graphic artist, or programmer have to spend hours learning the rules of standard English? Perhaps you are asking questions like these after finding yourself in a class with this book. On the other hand, perhaps you *know* you need to strengthen basic writing skills, even though you may be unclear about the specific ways the skills will be of use to you. Whatever your views, you should understand why sentence skills—all the rules that make up standard English—are so important.

Clear Communication

Standard English, or "language by the book," is needed to communicate your thoughts to others with a minimal amount of distortion and misinterpretation. Knowing the traditional rules of grammar, punctuation, and usage will help you write clear sentences when communicating with others. You may have heard of "Telephone," the party game in which one person whispers a message to the next person; the message is passed, in turn, along a line of several other people. By the time the last person in line is asked to give the message aloud, it is usually so garbled and inaccurate that it barely resembles the original. Written communication in some form of English other than standard English carries the same potential for disaster.

To see how important standard English is to written communication, examine the pairs of sentences on the following pages and answer the questions in each case.

1. Which sentence indicates that there might be a plot against Ted?
   a. We should leave Ted. These fumes might be poisonous.
   b. We should leave, Ted. These fumes might be poisonous.

2. Which sentence encourages self-mutilation?
   a. Leave your paper and hand in the dissecting kit.
   b. Leave your paper, and hand in the dissecting kit.

3. Which sentence indicates that the writer has a weak grasp of geography?
   a. As a child, I lived in Lake Worth, which is close to Palm Beach and Alaska.
   b. As a child, I lived in Lake Worth, which is close to Palm Beach, and Alaska.

4. In which sentence does the dog warden seem dangerous?
   a. Foaming at the mouth, the dog warden picked up the stray.
   b. Foaming at the mouth, the stray was picked up by the dog warden.

5. Which announcer was probably fired from the job?
   a. Outside the Academy Awards theater, the announcer called the guests names as they arrived.
   b. Outside the Academy Awards theater, the announcer called the guests' names as they arrived.

6. Below are the opening lines of two students' exam essays. Which student seems likely to earn a higher grade?
   a. Defense mechanisms is the way people hides their inner feelings and deals with stress. There is several types that we use to be protecting our true feelings.
   b. Defense mechanisms are the methods people use to cope with stress. Using a defense mechanism allows a person to hide his or her real desires and goals.

7. The following lines are taken from two English papers. Which student seems likely to earn a higher grade?
   a. A big problem on this campus is apathy, students don't participate in college activities. Such as clubs, student government, and plays.
   b. The most pressing problem on campus is the disgraceful state of the student lounge area. The floor is dirty, the chairs are torn, and the ceiling leaks.

continued

Teaching Tip
Read each sentence aloud so that students can "hear" the errors.

8. The following sentences are taken from reports by two employees. Which worker is more likely to be promoted?

   a. The spring line failed by 20 percent in the meeting of projected profit expectations. Which were issued in January of this year.

   b. Profits from our spring line were disappointing. They fell 20 percent short of January's predictions.

9. The following paragraphs are taken from two job application letters. Which applicant would you favor?

   a. Let me say in closing that their are an array of personal qualities I have presented in this letter, together, these make me hopeful of being interviewed for this attraktive position.

   sincerely yours'

   Brian Davis

   b. I feel I have the qualifications needed to do an excellent job as assistant manager of the jewelry department at Horton's. I look forward to discussing the position further at a personal interview.

   Sincerely yours,

   Richard O'Keeney

In each case, the first choice (*a*) contains sentence-skills mistakes. These mistakes include missing or misplaced commas, misspellings, and wordy or pretentious language. As a result of such mistakes, clear communication cannot occur—and misunderstandings, lower grades, and missed job opportunities are probable results. The point, then, is that all the rules that make up standard written English should be a priority if you want your writing to be clear and effective.

Success in College

Standard English is essential if you want to succeed in college. Any report, paper, review, essay exam, project, or assignment you are responsible for should be written in the best standard English you can produce. If you don't do this, it won't matter how fine your ideas are or how hard you work—most likely, you will receive a lower grade than you would otherwise deserve. In addition, because standard English requires you to express your thoughts in precise, clear sentences, training yourself to follow the rules can help you think more logically. The basic logic you learn to practice at the sentence level will help as you work to produce well-reasoned papers in all your subjects.

Success at Work

Knowing standard English will also help you achieve success on the job. Studies have found repeatedly that skillful communication, more than any other factor, is the key to job satisfaction and steady progress in a career. A solid understanding of standard English is a basic part of this vital ability to communicate. Moreover, we are living in an age of information—a time when people who use language skillfully have a great advantage over those who do not. Fewer of us are working in factories or at other types of manual labor. Many more of us are or will be working with information in various forms—accumulating it, processing it, analyzing it. No matter what kind of job you are preparing yourself for, you will need to know standard English to keep pace with this new economy. Otherwise, you are likely to be limited to low-paying jobs that offer few challenges or financial rewards.

"First off, there's no 'y' in resume . . ."

Success in Everyday Life

Standard English will help you succeed not just at school and work but in everyday life as well. It will help you communicate more effectively with friends and family, or express yourself more clearly when you write a letter of complaint to a company about a product. It will allow you to write letters and e-mails inquiring about bills—hospital, medical, utility, or legal—or about any kind of service. To put it simply, in our daily lives, those who can use and write standard English have more power than those who cannot.

Your Attitude toward Writing

Your attitude toward writing is an important part of learning to write well. To get a sense of just how you feel about writing, read the following statements. Put a check beside those statements with which you agree. (This activity is not a test, so try to be as honest as possible.)

_____ 1. A good writer should be able to sit down and write a paper straight through without stopping.

_____ 2. Writing is a skill that anyone can learn with practice.

_____ 3. I'll never be good at writing because I make too many mistakes in spelling, grammar, and punctuation.

_____ 4. Because I dislike writing, I always start a paper at the last possible minute.

_____ 5. I've always done poorly in English, and I don't expect that to change now.

Now read the following comments about these five statements. The comments will help you see if your attitude is hurting or helping your efforts to become a better writer.

Teaching Tip
You may want to provide additional statements such as "Good writers don't need any help" and "The teacher is the only one who can help me."

1. **A good writer should be able to sit down and write a paper straight through without stopping.**
    The statement is *false*. Writing is, in fact, a process. It is done not in one easy step but in a series of steps, and seldom at one sitting. If you cannot complete a paper all at once, you are like most of the other people on the planet. It is harmful to carry around the false idea that writing should be a fast and an easy matter.

Teaching Tip
Get students to talk about other skills they have mastered. Draw parallels to writing.

2. **Writing is a skill that anyone can learn with practice.**
    This statement is *absolutely true*. Writing is a skill, like driving or cooking, that you can master with hard work. If you want to learn to write, you can. It is as simple as that. If you believe this, you are ready to learn how to become a competent writer.

    Some people hold the false belief that writing is a natural gift that some have but others do not. Because of this belief, they never make a truly honest effort to learn to write—and so they never learn.

3. **I'll never be good at writing, because I make too many mistakes in spelling, grammar, and punctuation.**
    The first concern in good writing should be *content*—what you have to say. Your ideas and feelings are what matter most. You should not worry about spelling, grammar, and punctuation while working on content.

    Unfortunately, some people are so self-conscious about making mistakes that they do not focus on what they want to say. They need to realize that a paper is best done in stages and that the rules can and should wait until a later stage in the writing process. Through review and practice, you will eventually learn how to follow the rules with confidence.

4. **Because I dislike writing, I always start a paper at the last possible minute.**
    This practice is all too common. You feel you are *going to* do poorly, and then your behavior ensures that you *will* do poorly! Your attitude is so negative that you defeat yourself—not even allowing enough time to really try.

Again, what you need to realize is that writing is a process. Because it is done in steps, you don't have to get it right all at once. Just get started well in advance. If you allow yourself enough time, you'll find a way to make a paper come together.

5. I've always done poorly in English, and I don't expect that to change now.

How you may have performed in the *past* does not control how you can perform in the *present*. Even if you did poorly in English in high school, it is in your power to make this one of your best subjects in college. If you believe writing can be learned, and if you work hard at it, you *will* become a better writer.

In brief, your attitude is crucial. If you believe you are a poor writer and always will be, chances are you will not improve. If you realize you can become a better writer, chances are you will improve. Depending on how you allow yourself to think, you can be your own best friend or your own worst enemy.

Teaching Tip
Comment on other statements made in class.

How This Book Is Organized

- A good way to get a quick sense of any book is to turn to the table of contents. By referring to the Contents pages, you will see that the book is organized into three basic parts. What are they?

  Part One: Effective Writing

  Part Two: Sentence Skills

  Part Three: Reinforcement of the Skills

- In Part One, the final section of Chapter 3 includes activities in *the writing process*.

- Part Two deals with sentence skills. The first section is "Sentences." How many sections (skills areas) are covered in all? *five*

- Part Three reinforces the skills presented in Part Two. What are the three kinds of reinforcement activities in Part Three?

  Combined Mastery Tests

  Editing and Proofreading Tests

  Combined Editing Tests

- Helpful charts in the book include the *checklist of sentence skills* on the inside back cover.

- Finally, the four appendixes at the end of the book are

(A) ESL Pointers, (B) Sentence-Skills Diagnostic Test,

(C) Sentence-Skills Achievement Test,

(D) Answers to Introductory Activities and Practice Exercises

How to Use This Book

First, read and work through Part One, "Effective Writing"—a guide to the goals of effective writing followed by a series of activities to help you practice and master these goals. Your instructor may direct you to certain activities, depending on your needs.

Second, take the diagnostic test on pages 621–626. By analyzing which sections of the test give you trouble, you will discover which skills you need to concentrate on. When you turn to an individual skill in Part Two, begin by reading and thinking about the introductory activity. Often, you will be pleasantly surprised to find that you know more about this area of English than you thought you did. After all, you have probably been speaking English with fluency and ease for many years; you have an instinctive knowledge of how the language works. This knowledge gives you a solid base for refining your skills.

Your third step is to work on the skills in Part Two by reading the explanations and completing the practices. You can check your answers to each practice activity in this part by turning to the answer key at the back of the book (Appendix D). Try to figure out *why* you got some answers wrong—you want to uncover any weak spots in your understanding.

Your next step is to use the review tests and mastery tests at the end of each chapter in Part Two to evaluate your understanding of a skill in its entirety. Your instructor may also ask you to take the other reinforcement tests in Part Three of the book. To help ensure that you take the time needed to learn each skill thoroughly, the answers to these tests are *not* in the answer key.

The emphasis in this book is on writing clear, error-free sentences. The heart is practice material that helps reinforce the sentence skills you learn. A great deal of effort has been taken to make the practices lively and engaging and to avoid the dull, repetitive skills work that has given grammar books such a bad reputation. This text will help you stay interested as you work on the rules of English that you need to learn. The rest is a matter of your personal determination and hard work. If you decide—and only you can decide—that effective writing is important to your school and career goals and that you want to learn the basic skills you need to write clearly and effectively, this book will help you reach those goals.

A Brief Guide to Effective Writing

CHAPTER 2

This chapter and Chapter 3 will show you how to write effective paragraphs. The following questions will be answered in turn:

1. What is a paragraph?
2. What are the goals of effective writing?
3. How do you reach the goals of effective writing?

What Is a Paragraph?

A *paragraph* is a series of sentences about one main idea, or *point*. A paragraph typically starts with a point, and the rest of the paragraph provides specific details to support and develop that point.

Consider the following paragraph, written by a student named Greg Callahan.

Returning to School

Starting college at age twenty-nine was difficult. For one thing, I did not have much support from my parents and friends. My father asked, "Didn't you get dumped on enough in high school? Why go back for more?" My mother worried about where the money would come from. My friends seemed threatened. "Hey, there's the college man," they would say when they saw me. Another reason that starting college was hard was that I had bad memories of school. I had spent years of my life sitting in classrooms completely bored, watching clocks tick ever so slowly toward the final bell. When I was not bored, I was afraid of being embarrassed. Once a teacher called on me and then said, "Ah, forget it, Callahan," when he realized I did not know the answer. Finally, I soon learned that college would give me little time with my family. After work every day, I have just an hour and ten minutes to eat and spend time with my wife and daughter before going off to class. When I get back, my daughter is in bed, and my wife and I have only a little time together. Then the weekends go by quickly, with all the homework I have to do. But I am going to persist because I believe a better life awaits me with a college degree.

Teaching Tip Introduce students to the correction symbol ¶. Discuss how this symbol tells a writer to indent for a new paragraph.

Teaching Tip Ask students to underline the author's point as you read this paragraph aloud.

Teaching Tip
Have students
come up with
their own
examples of
bold state-
ments made
in school,
at work, or
among friends.

ESL Tip
In some
cultures, it is
considered
rude to state a
point directly.
Thus, non-
native speakers
may use circu-
lar reasoning
to address a
point and re-
state it in many
ways without
providing
support.

Teaching Tip
You may
want to do
this activity
with the entire
class. Copy
this partial
outline onto
the board
and then ask
students to fill
in the blanks.

The preceding paragraph, like many effective paragraphs, starts by stating a main idea, or point. A *point* is a general idea that contains an opinion. In this case, the point is that starting college at age twenty-nine was not easy.

In our everyday lives, we constantly make points about all kinds of matters. We express all kinds of opinions: "That was a terrible movie." "My psychology instructor is the best teacher I have ever had." "My sister is a generous person." "Eating at that restaurant was a mistake." "That team should win the playoff game." "Waitressing is the worst job I ever had." "Our state should allow the death penalty." In *talking* to people, we don't always give the reasons for our opinions. But in *writing*, we *must* provide reasons to support our ideas. Only by supplying solid evidence for any point that we make can we communicate effectively with readers.

An effective paragraph, then, must not only make a point but also support it with *specific evidence*—reasons, examples, and other details. Such specifics help prove to readers that the point is reasonable. Even if readers do not agree with the writer, at least they have in front of them the evidence on which the writer has based his or her opinion. Readers are like juries; they want to see the evidence so that they can make their own judgments.

Take a moment now to examine the evidence that Greg has provided to back up his point about starting college at twenty-nine. Complete the following outline of Greg's paragraph by summarizing in a few words his reasons and the details that develop them. The first reason and its supporting details are summarized for you as an example.

POINT: Starting college at age twenty-nine was difficult.

REASON 1: Little support from parents and friends

DETAILS THAT DEVELOP REASON 1: Father asked why I wanted to be dumped on again, mother worried about tuition money, friends seemed threatened

REASON 2: Bad memories of school

DETAILS THAT DEVELOP REASON 2: Boredom; fear of being embarrassed

REASON 3: Little time with family

DETAILS THAT DEVELOP REASON 3: About an hour to spend with them between work and school; only a little time before bed; homework on weekends

As the outline makes clear, Greg provides three reasons to support his point about starting college at twenty-nine: (1) he had little support from his friends or parents, (2) he had bad memories of school, and (3) college left him little time with his family. Greg also provides vivid details to back up each of his three reasons. His reasons and descriptive details enable readers to see why he feels that starting college at twenty-nine was difficult.

To write an effective paragraph, then, aim to do what Greg has done: begin by making a point, and then go on to support that point with specific evidence. Finally, like Greg, end your paper with a sentence that rounds off the paragraph and provides a sense of completion.

If you were to write a paragraph about the reasons you are in college, what point would you begin your paper with and what three reasons would you provide to support that point?

The Goals of Effective Writing

Now that you have considered an effective student paragraph, it is time to look at four goals of effective writing.

Goal 1: Make a Point

It is often best to state your point in the first sentence of your paper, just as Greg does in his paragraph about returning to school. The sentence that expresses the main idea, or point, of a paragraph is called the *topic sentence.* Your paper will be unified if you make sure that all the details support the point in your topic sentence. Activities on pages 14–17 will help you learn how to write a topic sentence.

Goal 2: Support the Point

To support your point, you need to provide specific reasons, examples, and other details that explain and develop it. The more precise and particular your supporting details are, the better your readers can "see," "hear," and "feel" them. The activities on pages 18–34 will help you learn how to be specific in your writing.

ESL Tip
Nonnative speakers may not be accustomed to writing a topic sentence that presents a strong or direct point.

ESL Tip
Rules for writing paragraphs may be different in other languages. Reading and analyzing the elements of a good paragraph can serve as a useful model for nonnative speakers.

Goal 3: Organize the Support

You will find it helpful to learn two common ways of organizing support in a paragraph—*listing order* and *time order.* You should also learn the signal words, known as *transitions,* that increase the effectiveness of each method. The activities on pages 34–41 will give you practice in the use of listing order and time order, as well as transitions, to organize the supporting details of a paragraph.

Goal 4: Write Error-Free Sentences

If you use correct spelling and follow the rules of grammar, punctuation, and usage, your sentences will be clear and well written. But by no means must you have all that information in your head. Even the best writers need to use reference materials to be sure their writing is correct. So when you write your papers, keep a good dictionary and grammar handbook—print or online—nearby (you can use Part Two of this book).

In general, however, save them for after you've gotten your ideas firmly down in writing. You'll see in the next part of this guide that Greg made a number of sentence errors as he worked on his paragraph. But he simply ignored them until he got to a later draft of his paper, when there would be time enough to make the needed corrections.

Activities in the Goals of Effective Writing

The following series of activities will strengthen your understanding of the four goals of effective writing and how to reach those goals. The practice will also help you prepare for the demands of your college classes.

Your instructor may ask you to do the entire series of activities or may select those activities most suited to your particular needs.

Activities in Goal 1: Make a Point

Effective writing advances a point, or main idea, in a general statement known as the *topic sentence.* Other sentences in the paragraph provide specific support for the topic sentence.

The activities in this section will give you practice in the following:

- Identifying the point
- Understanding the topic sentence
- Identifying topics, topic sentences, and support

Identifying the Point

Each group of sentences below could be written as a short paragraph. Circle the letter of the topic sentence in each case. To find the topic sentence, ask yourself, "Which is a general statement supported by the specific details in the other three statements?"

Begin by trying the example below. First circle the letter of the sentence you think expresses the main idea. Then read the explanation.

ACTIVITY 1

Teaching Tip
After students complete this activity, review the answers as a class. Encourage students to explain how they identified topic sentences.

EXAMPLE

    a. Online news sites are a good source of local, national, and world news.

    b. The ability to share news stories on social media sites and to click on related video links makes news consumption more interactive.

    (c.) Online news sites have a lot to offer.

    d. Some online news sites offer real-time coverage.

> **EXPLANATION:** Sentence *a* explains one important benefit of online news sites. Sentences *b* and *d* provide other specific advantages of online news sites. In sentence *c*, however, no one specific benefit is explained. Instead, the words "a lot to offer" refer only generally to such benefits. Therefore, sentence *c* is the topic sentence; it expresses the main idea. The other sentences support that idea by providing examples.

1. a. Even when Food City is crowded, there are only two cash registers open.
    b. The frozen foods are often partially thawed.
    (c.) I will never shop at Food City again.
    d. The market is usually out of sale items within a few hours.

2. a. Buy only clothes that will match what's already in your closet.
    b. To be sure you're getting the best price, shop in a number of stores before buying.
    c. Avoid trendy clothes; buy basic pieces that never go out of style.
    (d.) By following a few simple rules, you can have nice clothes without spending a fortune.

3. a. Once my son said a vase jumped off the shelf by itself.
    (b.) When my son breaks something, he always has an excuse.
    c. He claimed that my three-month-old daughter climbed out of her crib and knocked a glass over.
    d. Another time, he said an earthquake must have caused a mirror to crack.

4. (a.) Mars should be explored for many reasons.
   b. Astronauts could mine Mars for aluminum, magnesium, and iron.
   c. The huge volcano on Mars would be fascinating to study.
   d. Since Mars is close to Earth, we might want to have colonies there one day.
5. a. Instead of talking on the telephone, we send text messages.
   (b.) People rarely talk to one another these days.
   c. Rather than talking with family members, we sit silently, playing with our smartphones all evening.
   d. In cars, we ignore our traveling companions to listen to music.

Understanding the Topic Sentence

As already explained, most paragraphs center on a main idea, which is often expressed in a topic sentence. An effective topic sentence does two things. First, it presents the topic of the paragraph. Second, it expresses the writer's attitude or opinion or idea about the topic. For example, look at the following topic sentence:

Professional athletes are overpaid.

In the topic sentence, the topic is *professional athletes;* the writer's idea about the topic is that professional athletes *are overpaid.*

ACTIVITY 2

For each topic sentence that follows, underline the topic and double-underline the point of view that the writer takes toward the topic.

EXAMPLES

Living in a small town has many advantages.

Talking on a cell phone while driving should be banned in every state.

1. College textbooks are very expensive.
2. Cat owners and dog owners are two different types of people.
3. Public speaking is terrifying to many people.
4. The best things in life are free.
5. Disasters often bring out the best in people.
6. Serving on a jury can be an educational experience.
7. Our landlord is a strange man.
8. Loud car stereos should be made illegal.
9. The food in the cafeteria is unfit for humans to eat.
10. Divorce is not always the right answer to marriage problems.

ESL Tip
Tell nonnative speakers that every paragraph *says* something about the topic, *explains* something about it, and *provides* an example.

Identifying Topics, Topic Sentences, and Support

The following activity will sharpen your sense of the differences among topics, topic sentences, and supporting sentences. Each group of items below includes one topic, one main idea (expressed in a topic sentence), and two supporting details for that idea. In the space provided, label each item with one of the following:

> *T* — topic
> *MI* — main idea
> *SD* — supporting details

Teaching Tip
For added
practice, ask
students to
underline the
topic and
double under-
line the idea
about the topic
for the MI
sentences.

1. ___*T*___ a. Big-box stores like Target

   ___*MI*___ b. Big-box stores make shopping very convenient.

   ___*SD*___ c. It saves time to buy most or all of what you need in one store.

   ___*SD*___ d. Most big-box stores provide plenty of parking.

2. ___*SD*___ a. Children whose mothers smoke are more likely to have behavioral disorders.

   ___*MI*___ b. Children of smoking mothers suffer harmful effects.

   ___*SD*___ c. Research shows that secondhand smoke increases children's chances of getting lung diseases.

   ___*T*___ d. Mothers who smoke cigarettes.

3. ___*MI*___ a. Beethoven's deafness did not prevent him from composing magnificent music.

   ___*SD*___ b. His Ninth Symphony was written when he was totally deaf.

   ___*T*___ c. Beethoven's deafness.

   ___*SD*___ d. He wrote the famous Third Symphony, one of his most popular works, after his hearing had begun to fail.

4. ___*SD*___ a. Many refuges and parks have walkways where people in wheelchairs can pass through various bird environments.

   ___*MI*___ b. Bird watching can be enjoyed even by people with physical disabilities.

   ___*SD*___ c. Many birding hotspots feature an auto tour, allowing birds to be viewed from a vehicle.

   ___*T*___ d. Bird watching.

5. ___*SD*___ a. Career school graduates often become some of the best-paid professionals in the United States.

   ___*MI*___ b. Vocational training can have significant benefits in life.

   ___*T*___ c. Career schools.

   ___*SD*___ d. Many career school graduates eventually start their own successful businesses.

Activities in Goal 2: Support the Point

Effective writing gives support—reasons, facts, examples, and other evidence—for each main point. While main points are general (see page 13), support is *specific;* it provides the details that explain the main point.

To write well, you must know the difference between general and specific ideas. It is helpful to realize that you use general and specific ideas all the time in your everyday life. For example, in choosing a movie to stream, you may think, "Which should I watch: an action film, a comedy, or a romance?" In such a case, *movie* is the general idea, and *action film, comedy,* and *romance* are the specific ideas.

Or suppose you decide to begin an exercise program. You might consider walking, jumping rope, or lifting weights. In this case, *exercise* is the general idea, and *walking, jumping rope,* and *lifting weights* are the specific ideas.

Or if you are talking to a friend about a date that didn't work out well, you may say, "The dinner was terrible, the car broke down, and we had little to say to each other." In this case, the general idea is *the date didn't work out well,* and the specific ideas are the three reasons you named.

The activities in this section will give you practice in the following:

- Understanding general and specific ideas
- Recognizing specific details
- Providing specific details
- Selecting details that fit
- Providing details that fit
- Providing details in a paragraph

Understanding General and Specific Ideas

ACTIVITY 4

Each group of words consists of one general idea and four specific ideas. The general idea includes all the specific ideas. Underline the general idea in each group.

Teaching Tip
To appeal to your visual and kinesthetic learners, provide students with several related images or objects and ask them to identify the general category.

EXAMPLE

cooking   dusting   vacuuming   <u>chore</u>   washing dishes

1. hammer   drill   saw   screwdriver   <u>tool</u>
2. sprain   fracture   <u>injury</u>   scrape   cut
3. gold   <u>metal</u>   silver   aluminum   brass
4. gas   food   rent   taxes   <u>expense</u>
5. come here   stop   go   <u>command</u>   hurry
6. sneakers   boots   <u>footwear</u>   sandals   high heels

7. <u>entertainment</u>   television   concerts   movies   sporting   events

8. long lines   stuck doors   spam   slow waiters   <u>annoyances</u>

9. factory   <u>business</u>   hardware store   supermarket   restaurant

10. nail biting   tardiness   smoking   <u>bad habits</u>   interrupting

Review the answers as a class. Ask students to explain how they identified the general ideas.

In each item below, one idea is general and the others are specific. The general idea includes the specific ones. In the spaces provided, write in two more specific ideas that are covered by the general idea.

ACTIVITY 5

EXAMPLE

General: exercises

Specific: chin-ups, jumping jacks, ___*sit-ups*___ , ___*push-ups*___

Answers will vary. Some possibilities are shown.

1. General: college subjects
Specific: American history, ___*English*___ , ___*sociology*___
psychology,

2. General: cookies
Specific: gingersnap, ___*oatmeal*___ , ___*Fig Newton*___
chocolate chip,

Teaching Tip
After students complete Activity 5, review the answers as a class. Encourage students to explain how they identified the general ideas.

3. General: dogs
Specific: beagle, collie, ___*poodle*___ , ___*German shepherd*___

4. General: jobs
Specific: waitress, judge, ___*cook*___ , ___*editor*___

5. General: sports
Specific: tennis, baseball, ___*basketball*___ , ___*hockey*___

6. General: cooking methods
Specific: boil, steam, ___*bake*___ , ___*roast*___

7. General: seafood
Specific: clams, lobster, ___*shrimp*___ , ___*flounder*___

8. General: emotions
Specific: anger, embarrassment, ___*fear*___ , ___*love*___

9. General: disasters
Specific: plane crash, tornado, ___*fire*___ , ___*flood*___

10. General: circus performers
Specific: lion tamer, ___*clown*___ , ___*trapeze artist*___
human cannonball,

ACTIVITY 6 Read each group of specific ideas below. Then circle the letter of the general idea that tells what the specific ideas have in common. Note that the general idea should not be too broad or too narrow. Begin by trying the example item, and then read the explanation that follows.

EXAMPLE

Specific ideas: peeling potatoes, washing dishes, cracking eggs, cleaning out the refrigerator

The general idea is

   a. household jobs.

   (b.) kitchen tasks.

   c. steps in making dinner.

> **EXPLANATION:** It is true that the specific ideas are all household jobs, but they have in common something even more specific—they are all tasks done in the kitchen. Therefore, answer *a* is too broad, and the correct answer is *b*. Answer *c* is too narrow because it doesn't cover all the specific ideas. While two of them could be steps in making a dinner ("peeling potatoes" and "cracking eggs"), two have nothing to do with making dinner.

1. *Specific ideas:* "She's picking on me." "He teased me." "He started it." "Why does she get to stay up later than I do?"

   The general idea is

   a. complaints.

   (b.) kids' complaints.

   c. kids' complaints about bedtime.

2. *Specific ideas:* fleece-lined boots, wool scarf, mittens, ski jacket

   The general idea is

   a. clothing.

   (b.) winter clothing.

   c. winter footwear.

3. *Specific ideas:* horse, cow, tiger, elephant

   The general idea is

   a. living things.

   b. animals.

   (c.) four-legged animals.

4. *Specific ideas:* rain, hurricane, snow, wind

   The general idea is

   a. weather conditions.

   b. wet weather conditions.

   c. unusual weather conditions.

5. *Specific ideas:* dictionary, atlas, encyclopedia, almanac

   The general idea is

   a. books.

   b. nonfiction books.

   c. reference books.

6. *Specific ideas:* no smoking, speed limit 40 miles per hour, exit, gentlemen

   The general idea is

   a. signs.

   b. warning signs.

   c. road signs.

7. *Specific ideas:* "I didn't see the speed limit sign," "My car's speedometer was broken," "I was late for a wedding," "I didn't realize how fast I was going"

   The general idea is

   a. statements.

   b. excuses.

   c. excuses for driving too fast.

8. *Specific ideas:* go on a camping trip, take a trip to the seashore, visit a national park, go on a cruise

   The general idea is

   a. things to do.

   b. things to do on a vacation.

   c. things to do on a rainy Sunday afternoon.

9. *Specific ideas:* pretzels, cookies, tortilla chips, popcorn

   The general idea is

   a. foods.

   b. snack foods.

   c. health foods.

10. *Specific ideas:* bike, car, wheelbarrow, vacuum cleaner

The general idea is

a. common items.

b. things for riding.

c. things with wheels.

ACTIVITY 7

In the following items, the specific ideas are given, but the general ideas are un-stated. Fill in the blanks with the unstated general ideas.

EXAMPLE

General idea: _____ *car problems*

Specific ideas: flat tire   dented bumper

                     cracked windshield   dirty oil filter

Wording of answers may vary.

1. General idea: _____ *toys*

   Specific ideas: teddy bear   dollhouse

                 rocking horse   building blocks

2. General idea: _____ *performers*

   Specific ideas: violinist   actor

                 ballerina   singer

3. General idea: _____ *things that fly*

   Specific ideas: airplane   kite

                 bird   bee

4. General idea: _____ *beverages*

   Specific ideas: milk   tea

                 coffee   lemonade

5. General idea: _____ *tests*

   Specific ideas: SAT   midterm

                 final   pop quiz

6. General idea: _____ *things for passing from one level to another*

   Specific ideas: elevator   escalator

                 stairs   ladder

7. General idea: _____ *foods made from corn*

   Specific ideas: popcorn   caramel corn

                 corn chowder   corn muffins

8. General idea: _____ *containers (or carriers)*

   Specific ideas: suitcase   briefcase

                 shopping bag   backpack

9. *General idea:* _____ *annoyances* _____
   Specific ideas: mosquitoes   telemarketers
                        nosy neighbors   loud engines

10. *General idea:* _____ *free items (or lucky finds)* _____
    Specific ideas: food samples at the supermarket
                        a good chair on someone's curb on garbage pickup day
                        a twenty-dollar bill on a street corner
                        a free car wash for filling your tank with gas

Recognizing Specific Details

Specific details are examples, reasons, particulars, and facts. Such details are needed to support and explain a topic sentence effectively. They provide the evidence needed for us to understand, as well as to feel and experience, a writer's point.

Below is a topic sentence followed by two sets of supporting sentences. Put a check mark next to the set that provides sharp, specific details.

Topic sentence: Ticket sales for a recent Bruce Springsteen concert proved that the musician is still very popular.

_____ a. Fans came from everywhere to buy tickets to the concert. People wanted good seats and were willing to endure a great deal of various kinds of discomfort as they waited in line for many hours. Some people actually waited for days, sleeping at night in uncomfortable circumstances. Good tickets were sold out extremely quickly.

___✓___ b. The first person in the long ticket line spent three days standing in the hot sun and three nights sleeping on the concrete without even a pillow. The man behind her waited equally long in his wheelchair. The ticket window opened at 10:00 A.M., and the tickets for the good seats—those in front of the stage—were sold out an hour later.

EXPLANATION: The second set (*b*) provides specific details. Instead of a vague statement about fans who were "willing to endure a great deal of various kinds of discomforts," we get vivid details we can picture clearly: "three days standing in the hot sun," "three nights sleeping on the concrete without even a pillow," "The man behind her waited equally long in his wheelchair."

continued

Teaching Tip
Bring a movie script to class. Show students how the screenwriter includes specific details. If possible, show a clip from the film so that your students can "see" these details.

Instead of a vague statement that tickets were "sold out extremely quickly," we get exact and vivid details: "The ticket window opened at 10:00 A.M., and the tickets for the good seats—those in front of the stage—were sold out an hour later."

Specific details are often like a movie script. They provide us with such clear pictures that we could make a film of them if we wanted to. You would know just how to film the information given in the second set of sentences. You would show the fans in line under a hot sun and, later, sleeping on the concrete. The first person in line would be shown sleeping without a pillow under her head. You would show tickets finally going on sale, and after an hour you could show the ticket seller explaining that all the seats in front of the stage were sold out.

In contrast, the writer of the first set of sentences (*a*) fails to provide the specific information needed. If you were asked to make a film based on set *a*, you would have to figure out on your own just what particulars to show.

When you are working to provide specific supporting information in a paper, it might help to ask yourself, "Could someone easily film this information?" If the answer is yes, your supporting details are specific enough for your readers to visualize.

ACTIVITY 8   Each topic sentence below is followed by two sets of supporting details. Write *S* (for *specific*) in the space next to the set that provides specific support for the point. Write *G* (for *general*) next to the set that offers only vague, general support.

> **HINT**   Which set of supporting details could you more readily use in a film?

1. *Topic sentence:* Watching a rented movie at home is cheaper and more convenient than going to a movie theater.

   ___G___ a. Going to a first-run movie with the whole family costs us much more than it would to enjoy some pretty good movies at home. Also, food of all kinds at the theater is certainly more expensive than food we can easily make at home or even have delivered. It's not crowded at home, either. And if we have to leave our seats at the theater for some reason, we end up missing several minutes of the movie. But at home, we don't have that problem at all.

_____S_____ b. For the $44 it cost to take the family to a movie last night, we could have rented ten recent movies on demand. Instead of waiting in line for ten minutes to spend $5 per soda and $8 per box of popcorn, we could have had pizza delivered. And at the theater, when we left to take our son to the restroom, it took us five minutes to figure out what was happening on the screen when we got back. At home, we could have paused the movie for a few minutes.

2. *Topic sentence:* Young children can be difficult travel partners.

_____S_____ a. First, they constantly ask "Are we there yet?" even minutes after you have left your driveway. Then they always forget things—such as going to the bathroom or bringing their favorite toy—so that you have to stop or go back home. Worst of all is their constant arguing over such things as who is "making noises" or "looking at me in a funny way" and their pestering an adult to make the other child stop.

_____G_____ b. First, just a short time after you roll out of your driveway, they begin to ask about the trip. Then, they always want to stop for something that they need or something they have forgotten to do. Finally, the most annoying thing they do is get mad at each other for unimportant things. When this happens they often drag whichever adult is present into their arguments, pestering him or her over and over.

3. *Topic sentence:* I find life much easier in summer than in winter.

_____S_____ a. In the summer, I don't have to spend half an hour putting on sweaters, heavy socks, boots, coat, hat, and gloves. When I'm driving, I don't have to crawl at 10 miles per hour to avoid slipping off icy roads. And when I'm walking outside, I don't have to climb over snowbanks or wade through slush.

_____G_____ b. For one thing, I save a great deal of time in the summer every day because I don't have to put on heavy clothing to keep from freezing to death. The summer weather is very comfortable. In summer, also, it is much easier to get from place to place, whether I'm driving my car or going somewhere on foot.

4. *Topic sentence:* Eating chocolate is not as unhealthy as most people think.

_____G_____ a. As chocolate lovers know, eating chocolate in any form can make you feel better at certain times. It is a wonderful treat. Of course, snacking on too much of any food, especially sweets, can be bad for you. We all know that. But eating chocolate doesn't seem to have any lasting effect on your health. And that's definitely good news.

_S_   b. Chocolate can raise your spirits because it contains small amounts of a natural substance that doctors prescribe as an antidepressant. Of course, chocolate, like any fattening food, can make you gain weight if it is consumed to excess. However, because of its unique chemical makeup, the fat in chocolate won't raise your cholesterol, no matter how much you eat.

5. *Topic sentence:* Television sportscasters have some annoying habits.

_G_   a. They pile up overly dramatic words, acting like everything they say is the most important thing in the world. They make statements that are too obvious to need saying, but they announce each one as if it were an original or very deep thought everyone will be glad to hear. To top it all off, they keep making annoyingly off-the-wall comments about the players, especially at crucial moments in a game.

_S_   b. They never let a word stand on its own. A team isn't just in trouble; it's in *deep* trouble or *serious* trouble or *the worst kind* of trouble. And they'll say something that everyone knows, such as "He'd sure like to score now," as if it were amazing. And at two strikes with the bases loaded, they'll add a totally unrelated comment like "Johnny was born in Flint, Michigan, and collects butterflies."

ACTIVITY 9

At several points in each of the following paragraphs, you are given a choice of two sets of supporting details. Write *S* (for *specific*) in the space next to the set that provides specific support for the point. Write *G* (for *general*) next to the set that offers only vague, general support.

PARAGRAPH 1

Teaching Tip Direct students to the specific words used in the "S" paragraphs and the vague words used in the "G" paragraphs.

When my friends and I heard that a restaurant was opening up in town, we were excited that there would be a new place to go for dinner. But now that I have had my first meal there, I do not think I will be visiting that restaurant ever again. From the moment my friends and I walked in the door, our time at the restaurant was disappointing.

_G_   a. Reservations are not honored on time; the wait for our table was uncomfortably long. We saw many customers who had come before we did waiting impatiently, just as we were.

_S_   b. Even with a reservation, we had to wait in the lounge for forty-five minutes before getting our table. Others there said they had been waiting nearly an hour, and we saw two couples give up and leave in disgust.

The service was also a problem.

    _S_   c. Just to get a menu, we had to wait half an hour. After the soup, we had to wait another half hour for the main course—or, rather, for some of it, since the clam spaghetti ordered by one of my friends didn't arrive until the rest of us were nearly finished with our steaks. Dessert came faster, the only problem being that the waiter brought apple pie rather than the lemon sherbet we had ordered.

    _G_   d. We had to wait much too long even to get a menu; and after we had eaten our soup we had another lengthy wait for the main course. Unfortunately, the main dish ordered by one of my guests didn't arrive until long after the rest of us had been served and were almost done. We didn't have to wait nearly as long to get our dessert, but it was the wrong dessert—we had ordered something else.

The food was equally disappointing.

    _G_   e. The soup was not very tasty, to say the least. The clam spaghetti seemed rather skimpy; there were not enough clams in it. The steaks were done properly, but the meat did not seem to be of the highest quality. The dessert did not taste really fresh; in fact, it was quite stale.

    _S_   f. The soup was so bland that we couldn't be sure what was in it other than water and a few limp vegetables. The person who had the clam spaghetti counted precisely two clams in it. The steaks were rare, as requested, but so tough that we could hardly cut them. The pie was soggy and seemed to be at least a week old.

PARAGRAPH 2

Today's job market is more competitive than ever. To get a job in this economy, a person must have more than strong work skills; he or she must also possess strong interview skills. Here are a few steps you can take to strengthen the impression you make at a job interview. First, arrive early.

    _G_   a. By arriving a few minutes early for the job interview, you make your interviewer think some positive things about you. This can certainly affect what hiring decisions your potential employer makes. Also, if you are early, you will have the chance to do a few things to get ready, such as calm down, check your appearance, and prepare yourself to say the things you want to say to your interviewer.

_s_   b.   Arrive at least ten minutes early to show that you are serious about getting the job. Being early also shows that you will be a punctual and reliable employee. In addition, with the extra time, you can fix your shirt, comb your hair, and wipe any sweat from your palms or forehead. A few extra minutes can also help you review the things that you want to say to your interviewer—where you worked before, what skills you have, and why you think you can do the job.

Have a professional appearance when you go to an interview.

_G_   c.   Remember, you are up against strong competition, and you have only a short time to make an impression, so clothes are important. Don't wear clothes that seem to say you don't care what you look like. Make sure you have groomed yourself properly so that you send the right message to your potential boss.

_s_   d.   Remember, your interviewer may be speaking to thirty other job candidates. With so much competition and such little time to make an impression—twenty minutes, on average—it is important to show that you pay attention to detail. Wear clothing similar to what is worn at that job. Put on clean, wrinkle-free clothes; shine your shoes; and have your hair neat and clean.

Be sure to behave in a professional manner.

_s_   e.   When you talk to an interviewer, speak clearly. Do not mumble, whisper, or rush through your response. Also, as you talk, look directly at your interviewer. Keeping eye contact—not looking at the floor or the pictures on the wall—will show you are a confident speaker. In addition, sit with your back straight and your feet flat on the floor. Do not slouch forward or sit back in the chair. A relaxed posture suggests that you are not serious about the interview or your work.

_G_   f.   When you talk to an interviewer, be sure to speak in a manner that suggests you are a confident professional. Keep your eyes in the right place throughout the entire interview, and be conscious of your body language. All these factors will show the type of speaker and person you are. Also pay attention to your posture throughout the interview. You should make an effort to sit on your chair in a serious position. Appearing to be relaxed will weaken your effect on the interviewer.

Providing Specific Details

Each of the following sentences contains a general word or words set off in *italic* type. Substitute sharp, specific words in each case.

EXAMPLE

After the parade, the city street was littered with *garbage*.

After the parade, the city street was littered with multicolored confetti, dirty popcorn, and lifeless balloons.

1. It took me *a long time* to complete my chores.

   _____

   _____

2. When the relationship broke up, I felt *various emotions*.

   _____

   _____

3. In the accident, the car was *damaged*.

   _____

   _____

4. When the party started, there were *a lot of snacks* on the table.

   _____

   _____

5. *Different kinds of insects* invaded our home this summer.

   _____

   _____

6. Ray *has some unpleasant eating habits*.

   _____

   _____

7. Our new teacher *did some surprising things*.

   _____

   _____

ACTIVITY 10

Answers will vary.

Teaching Tip
To vary this activity select a vague sentence and ask students to call out a list of specific words. Then ask them to include these words in a revised sentence.

ESL Tip
Nonnative speakers might require some assistance finding sharp, specific words. Tell them to consult a dictionary or thesaurus.

8. *The weather has been dreadful* all weekend.

_____

_____

9. My dog can *do a wonderful trick.*

_____

_____

10. The children *acted up* when ordered to come in the house.

_____

_____

Selecting Details That Fit

ESL Tip
In some cultures, adding digressions or repeating ideas may be acceptable or even expected in writing. Remind all students that when writing in standard English, details must support their point.

All the details in your paper must clearly relate to and support your opening point. If a detail does not support your point, leave it out. Otherwise, your paper will lack unity. For example, circle the letter of the two sentences that do *not* support the topic sentence below.

Topic sentence: Vikram is a very talented person.

a. Vikram is always courteous to his professors.
b. He has created beautiful paintings in his art course.
c. Vikram is the lead singer in a local band.
d. He won an award in a photography contest.
e. He is hoping to become a professional photographer.

EXPLANATION: Being courteous may be a virtue, but it is not a talent, so sentence *a* does not support the topic sentence. Also, Vikram's desire to become a professional photographer tells us nothing about his talent; thus, sentence *e* does not support the topic sentence, either. The other three statements all clearly back up the topic sentence. Each in some way supports the idea that Vikram is talented—as an artist, a singer, or a photographer.

In each group below, circle the two items that do *not* support the topic sentence.

1. *Topic sentence:* Leaving car windows open during a rainstorm can damage a car.

   a. Any books or newspapers sitting on the car seats can be ruined.
   b. Wet carpets have a tendency to get moldy and eventually rot.
   c. Sitting on a wet seat can soak a passenger's clothing.
   d. Getting an instrument panel wet can cause short circuits.
   e. Water can permanently stain leather seats and dashboards.

2. *Topic sentence:* Rosa is a perfect employee.

   a. She always arrives at work on time.
   b. She saves most of her paycheck for bills.
   c. Rosa never misses a day of work.
   d. She is very polite to co-workers.
   e. She often tries to persuade her friends to get a job.

3. *Topic sentence:* Popcorn popped and served without fat is a healthy choice for a snack.

   a. Popcorn itself is very low in fat and in calories.
   b. It's high in complex carbohydrates, which are better for many people than the simple carbohydrates in sugary snacks.
   c. Many people love popcorn as much as other snacks that aren't as good for them.
   d. Unlike many snacks, popcorn helps digestion because it is a good source of fiber.
   e. Popcorn tastes best freshly made.

4. *Topic sentence:* It's hard being the little brother of an award-winning student and athlete.

   a. When you were both in grade school, your brother always managed to protect you from the school bullies.
   b. At the start of each school year, teachers and coaches exclaim, "We expect you to live up to your brother's standards!"
   c. When you get less than perfect grades, all you hear is "It's a shame you can't be more like your brother."
   d. Your brother leaves for college next year but promises to help you with your homework over Skype whenever you want.
   e. At family reunions, everyone crowds around your big brother to hear all the details of his latest accomplishments.

5. *Topic sentence:* In recent years, several factors have caused people to move out of large cities and into nearby suburbs.

   a. A loss of jobs within cities has forced people to seek work outside of the city.

   b. High city taxes have driven people out of the cities in search of cheaper living.

   (c.) Improved pollution-control methods have lowered air pollution in many cities.

   (d.) Big cities have more cultural and artistic resources than smaller cities and suburbs.

   e. The wish for open space and less-crowded neighborhoods has drawn many people to the suburbs.

Providing Details That Fit

ACTIVITY 12

Each topic sentence below is followed by one supporting detail. Add a second detail in each case. Make sure your detail supports the topic sentence.

1. *Topic sentence:* The movie rental chain is losing customers for many reasons.

   a. The chain stocks only limited copies of every movie, even the most popular titles.

   b. _____

2. *Topic sentence:* The little boy did some dangerous stunts on his bicycle.

   a. He rode down a flight of steps at top speed.

   b. _____

3. *Topic sentence:* Craig has awful table manners.

   a. He stuffs his mouth with food and then begins a conversation.

   b. _____

4. *Topic sentence:* There are many advantages to living in the city.

   a. One can meet many new people with interesting backgrounds.

   b. _____

5. *Topic sentence:* All high school students should have summer jobs.

   a. Summer jobs help teens learn to handle a budget.

   b. _____

Answers will vary.

Teaching Tip
You may want to ask your students to provide a third supporting detail for each topic sentence.

Add two supporting details for each of the topic sentences below.

1. *Topic sentence:* The managers of this apartment building don't care about their tenants.
   a. Mrs. Harris has been asking them to fix her leaky faucet for two months.
   b. _____
   c. _____

2. *Topic sentence:* None of the shirts for sale were satisfactory.
   a. Some were attractive but too expensive.
   b. _____
   c. _____

3. *Topic sentence:* After being married for forty years, Mr. and Mrs. Wong have grown similar in odd ways.
   a. They both love to have a cup of hot water with honey just before bed.
   b. _____
   c. _____

4. *Topic sentence:* It is a special time for me when my brother is in town.
   a. We always go bowling together and then stop for pizza.
   b. _____
   c. _____

5. *Topic sentence:* Our neighbor's daughter is very spoiled.
   a. When anyone else in the family has a birthday, she gets several presents too.
   b. _____
   c. _____

Providing Details in a Paragraph

The following paragraph needs specific details to back up its three supporting points. In the spaces provided on the next page, write two or three sentences of convincing details for each supporting point.

A Disappointing Show

Although I had looked forward to seeing my favorite musical group play live, the experience was disappointing. For one thing, our seats were terrible.

continued

_____

_____

_____

_____

_____

In addition, the crowd made it hard to enjoy the music. _____

_____

_____

_____

_____

Finally, the band members acted as if they didn't want to be there. _____

_____

_____

_____

_____

Activities in Goal 3: Organize the Support

Effective writing includes clearly organized support. In a paragraph, details are often arranged in a *listing order* or *time order* so readers can make sense of them. In addition, *transitions* or signal words help make the support easy to read and understand.

    The activities in this section will give you practice in the following:

- Understanding listing and time order
- Understanding transitions
- Using transitions
- Organizing details in a paragraph

Understanding Listing and Time Order

Listing Order The writer can organize supporting evidence in a paper by providing a list of two or more reasons, examples, or details. Often the most important or interesting item is saved for last because the reader is most likely to remember the last thing read.

Transition words that indicate listing order include the following:

one	second	also	next	last of all
for one thing	third	another	moreover	finally
first of all	next	in addition	furthermore	

The paragraph on page 11 about starting college uses a listing order: it lists three reasons that starting college at twenty-nine is not easy, and each of those three reasons is introduced by one of the transitions in the box above. In the spaces below, write in the three transitions:

For on thing _____ *Another* _____ *Finally* _____

The first reason in the paragraph about starting college is introduced with *for one thing*, the second reason by *another*, and the third reason by *finally*.

Time Order When a writer uses time order, supporting details are presented in the order in which they occurred. *First* this happened; *next* this; *after* that, this; and so on. Many paragraphs, especially paragraphs that tell a story or give a series of directions, are organized in time order.

Transition words that show time relationships include the following:

first	before	after	when	then
next	during	now	while	until
as	soon	later	often	finally

Read the paragraph below, which is organized in time order. Underline the six transition words that show the time relationships.

Della had a sad experience while driving home last night. She traveled along the dark, winding road that led toward her home. She was only 2 miles from her house when she noticed a glimmer of light in the road. The next thing she knew, she heard a sickening thud and realized she had struck an animal. The light, she realized, had been its eyes reflected in her car's headlights. Della stopped the car and ran back to see what she had hit. It was a handsome cocker spaniel with blond fur and long ears. As she bent over the still form, she realized there was nothing to be done.

Teaching Tip Discuss with your students what would happen if the most important detail were placed at the start of a paragraph.

ESL Tip Nonnative speakers often confuse *another* with *other*, or spell it as two words: *an other*. They may also write *firstable* (instead of *first of all*) because of how the word sounds in spoken English.

Teaching Tip Writers often rely too much on one transition word. Encourage students to use a variety of transitions.

ESL Tip
Nonnative
speakers must
learn that time
words will
require the
use of certain
verb tenses.
The time word
alone does
not signal time
order.

The dog was dead. Della searched the dog for a collar and tags. There was nothing. Before leaving, she walked to several nearby houses, asking if anyone knew who owned the dog. No one did. Finally, Della gave up and drove on. She was sad to leave someone's pet lying there alone.

The main point of the paragraph is stated in its first sentence: "Della had a sad experience while driving home last night." The support for this point is all the details of Della's experience. Those details are presented in the order in which they occurred. The time relationships are highlighted by these transitions: *while, when, next, as, before,* and *finally.*

Understanding Transitions

Transitions are words and phrases that indicate relationships between ideas. They are like signposts that guide travelers, showing them how to move smoothly from one spot to the next. Be sure to take advantage of transitions. They will help organize and connect your ideas, and they will help your readers follow the direction of your thoughts.

To see how transitions help, put a check mark beside the item in each pair that is easier to read and understand.

PAIR A

_____ One way to stay healthy is to eat low-calorie, low-fat foods. A good strategy is to walk or jog at least twenty minutes four times a week.

___✓___ One way to stay healthy is to eat low-calorie, low-fat foods. Another good strategy is to walk or jog at least twenty minutes four times a week.

PAIR B

_____ I begin each study session by going to a quiet place and setting out my textbook, pen, and notebook. I check my assignment book to see what I have to read.

___✓___ I begin each study session by going to a quiet place and setting out my textbook, pen, and notebook. Then I check my assignment book to see what I have to read.

> **EXPLANATION:** In each pair, the second item is easier to read and understand. In pair A, the listing word *another* makes it clear that the writer is going on to a second way to stay in shape. In pair B, the time word *then* makes the relationship between the sentences clear. The writer first sets out the textbook and a pen and notebook and *then* checks an assignment book to see what to do.

Using Transitions

As already stated, transitions are signal words that help readers follow the direction of the writer's thoughts. To see the value of transitions, look at the two versions of the short paragraph below. Check the version that is easier to read and understand.

_____ a. Where will you get the material for your writing assignments? There are several good sources. Your own experience is a major resource. For an assignment about childhood, for instance, you can draw on your own numerous memories of childhood. Other people's experience is extremely useful. You may have heard people you know or even people on TV or online talking about their childhood. Or you can interview people with a specific writing assignment in mind. Books, magazines, and blogs are good sources of material for assignments. Many experts, for example, have written about various aspects of childhood.

✓ b. Where will you get the material for your writing assignments? There are several good sources. First of all, your own experience is a major resource. For an assignment about childhood, for instance, you can draw on your own numerous memories of childhood. In addition, other people's experiences are extremely useful. You may have heard people you know or even people on TV or online talking about their childhood. Or you can interview people with a specific writing assignment in mind. Finally, books, magazines, and blogs are good sources of material for assignments. Many experts, for example, have written about various aspects of childhood.

EXPLANATION: Paragraph *b* is the easier one to read and understand. The listing transitions—*first of all, in addition,* and *finally*—make it clear when the author is introducing a new supporting point. The author's line of thinking is easier to follow and the three main sources of material for assignments are easier to identify: your own experience, other people's experience, and books, magazines, and blogs.

ACTIVITY 15

The following paragraphs use listing order or time order. In each case, fill in the blanks with appropriate transitions from the box preceding the paragraph. Use each transition once.

Teaching Tip
For this activity, read each paragraph aloud as your students fill in the blanks.

1.

after   before   later   then   when

On those miserable days when everything goes wrong, I like to fantasize about a day when everything would go right. On my fantasy day, I'd wake up early, a few minutes ____*before*____ the alarm would have gone off, and outside my window I'd see sparkling sunshine and blue sky. ____*After*____ dressing unhurriedly, I'd stroll to the bus stop, arriving just as the bus pulled up. I'd get a nice window seat, and ____*then*____ the bus would roll into town with no traffic tie-ups. When I arrived at work, my boss would greet me with a big smile and tell me he was giving me a raise. ____*Later*____, at lunchtime, he'd take me to a posh restaurant to celebrate. And ____*when*____ I arrived home that evening, my neighbor would be waiting for me with tickets to the game.

2.

third   finally   for one thing   second   in addition

Though not all migraine headaches are alike, they tend to have typical features. ____*For one thing*____, migraines are unpredictable—they may come every few days or weeks, or months may go by without an attack. A ____*second*____ feature is that, while a migraine can be set off by stress, it usually doesn't develop until after the stressful event is over. ____*Third*____, a migraine is one-sided: the pain is on the left or right side of the face or head, and for any individual it's usually on the same side. ____*In addition*____, the pain is throbbing and may be accompanied by nausea. ____*Finally*____, a coming attack is often signaled by an "aura": a period during which the individual may feel tired or depressed or may have difficulties with vision, such as seeing flashes of light or being unable to read.

3. | when   later   during |

_____*During*_____ the winter of 1928, a terrible flu epidemic raged across the United States. Many employees of Miles Laboratories, a pharmaceutical company in Elkhart, Indiana, were home sick. But _____*when*_____ the president of Miles Labs visited the office of the Elkhart newspaper, he found every employee healthy and at work. The paper's editor explained that, at the first hint of a cold symptom, he dosed staff members with a combination of aspirin and baking soda. The president was impressed with the idea. He _____*later*_____ asked his company chemists to come up with a tablet that combined the two ingredients. In 1931 the resulting product, Alka-Seltzer, was put on the market.

4. | another   last   first of all   also |

Date rape has become a serious issue for high school and college students. There are some basic strategies for protecting yourself from date rape and its consequences. _____*First of all*_____, double-date or group-date, especially if you are going out with someone you don't know very well. _____*Another*_____ thing to remember is not to drink alcoholic beverages. Alcohol can cloud your judgment and harm your memory. _____*Also*_____, avoid parties that are not chaperoned. At a party, stay with the crowd. Never allow anyone to lure you or force you into an empty room or hidden area. _____*Last*_____, if all of the precautions fail and you fall victim to date rape, go immediately to a hospital or rape crisis center and seek medical help and counseling.

Organizing Details in a Paragraph

The supporting details in a paragraph must be organized in a meaningful way. The two most common methods of organizing details are listing order and time order. The activities that follow will give you practice in both methods of organization.

ACTIVITY 16

Use *listing order* to arrange the scrambled list of sentences that follows. Number each supporting sentence 1, 2, 3, . . . so that you go from the least important item to what is presented as the most important item.

Note that transitions will help by making clear the relationships between some of the sentences.

Topic sentence: You can protect yourself and your valuables while traveling by keeping a few guidelines in mind.

_7_   Keep an immediate store of cash in your purse or wallet, but hide the rest of your money and your credit cards in a money belt.

_3_   Second, be aware of your surroundings and of the people around you.

_1_   The first rule is plain common sense: pack light.

_2_   The less you have to carry, the less you'll have to lose, and the less vulnerable you'll look to a would-be thief.

_6_   But the biggest favor you can do yourself is not to keep all your valuables in one place.

_4_   Don't discuss where you are staying, where you are going, or other personal details so that strangers can overhear you.

_8_   That way, if your purse or wallet is stolen, you won't lose everything.

_5_   In addition, make photocopies of your driver's license, credit cards, and other important documents, so you have all that information on hand in case the originals are stolen, and make sure any contacts and photos in your phone are backed up.

Use *time order* to arrange the scrambled sentences below. Number the supporting sentences in the order in which they occur in time (1, 2, 3, . . .).

Note that transitions will help by making clear the relationships between sentences.

Topic sentence: If you're interviewing for a job, following these steps will help you make a good impression.

___5___ One way to make sure you're on time is to do a "practice run" to figure out exactly how long it takes you to get to the office and find a parking spot or to walk from the bus or subway stop.

___8___ After the interview, be sure to send a thank-you note that says again how much you are interested in the job.

___3___ You can find out the company "look" by going by the office at the end of a workday and seeing what employees are wearing.

___1___ As soon as you've scheduled the interview, decide what outfit you will wear.

___4___ On the big day, do whatever is necessary to arrive for the appointment on time—even a few minutes early.

___7___ For example, if you are interviewing for a sales job, say, "As a psychology major, I've learned a lot about what makes people want to buy."

___2___ Choose an outfit that makes you look as though you already work for the company.

___6___ During the interview itself, express clearly how your abilities make you a good choice for the position.

The Writing Process

Steps in the Writing Process

Even professional writers do not sit down and write a paper automatically, in one draft. Instead, they have to work on it a step at a time. Composing a paper is a process that can be divided into the following steps:

- *Step 1:* Getting started through prewriting
- *Step 2:* Preparing a scratch outline
- *Step 3*: Writing the first draft
- *Step 4:* Revising
- *Step 5:* Editing and proofreading

These steps are described on the following pages.

Step 1: Getting Started through Prewriting

What you need to learn first are strategies for working on a paper. These strategies will help you do the thinking needed to figure out both the point you want to make and the support you have for that point.

There are several *prewriting strategies*—strategies you can use before writing the first draft of your paper:

- Freewriting
- Questioning
- Clustering
- Making a list

Freewriting

Freewriting is just sitting down and writing whatever comes into your mind about a topic. Do this for ten minutes or so. Write without stopping and without worrying at all about spelling, grammar, or the like. Simply get down on paper or screen all the information about the topic that occurs to you.

Here is the freewriting Greg did on his problems with returning to school. He had been given the assignment "Write about a problem you are facing at the present time." He felt right away that he could write about his college situation. He began prewriting as a way to explore and generate details on his topic.

EXAMPLE OF FREEWRITING

One thing I want to write about is going back to school. At age twenty-nine. A lot to deal with. I sometimes wonder if Im nuts to try to do this or just stupid. I had to deal with my folks when I decided. My dad hated school. He knew when to quit, I'll say that for him. But he doesn't understand Im different. I have a right to my own life. And I want to better myself. He teases me alot. Says things like didnt you get dumped on enough in high school, why go back for more. My mom doesnt understand either. Just keeps worring about where the money was coming from. Then my friends. They make fun of me. Also my wife has to do more of the heavy house stuff because I'm out so much. Getting back to my friends, they say dumb things to get my goat. Like calling me the college man or saying ooh, we'd better watch our grammer. Sometimes I think my dads right, school was no fun for me. Spent years just sitting in class waiting for final bell so I could escape. Teachers didnt help me or take an intrest, some of them made me feel like a real loser. Now things are different and I like most of my teachers. I can talk to the teacher after class or to ask questions if I'm confused. But I really need more time to spend with family, I hardly see them any more. What I am doing is hard all round for them and me.

Teaching Tip
Take a quick class poll. Ask students if they have trouble starting an assignment.

Teaching Tip
Point out that writers often want to correct their mistakes or pause during freewriting. Stress the importance of nonstop writing.

Look at this photo and freewrite for several minutes about a task you find difficult or challenging.

Teaching Tip
Get students to talk about why writers worry so much about being "correct." Offer a few reasons (for example, being a perfectionist, feeling insecure).

Notice that there are problems with spelling, grammar, and punctuation in Greg's freewriting. Greg is not worried about such matters, nor should he be. He is just concentrating on getting ideas and details down on paper. He knows that it is best to focus on one thing at a time. At this stage, he just wants to write out thoughts as they come to him, to do some thinking on paper or on screen.

You should take the same approach when freewriting: explore your topic without worrying at all about being "correct." At this early stage of the writing process, focus on figuring out what you want to say.

Questioning

Questioning means that you think about your topic by writing down a series of questions and answers about it. Your questions can start with words like *what, when, where, why,* and *how.*

Here are some questions that Greg might have asked while developing his paper, as well as some answers to those questions.

EXAMPLE OF QUESTIONING

Why do I have a problem with returning to school?	My parents and friends don't support me.
How do they not support me?	Dad asks why I want to be dumped on more. Mom is upset because college costs lots of money. Friends tease me about being a college man.
When do they not support me?	When I go to my parents' home for Friday night visits, when my friends see me walking toward them.
Where do I have this problem?	At home, where I barely see my wife and daughter, and where I have to let my wife do house things on weekends while I'm studying.
Why else do I have this problem?	High school was bad experience.
What details back up the idea that high school was bad experience?	Sat in class bored, couldn't wait to get out, teachers didn't help me. One embarrassed me when I didn't know the answer.

Clustering

Clustering is another prewriting strategy that can be used to generate material for a paper. It is helpful for people who like to do their thinking in a visual way.

In clustering, you begin by stating your subject in a few words in the center of a blank sheet of paper. Then as ideas come to you, put them in ovals, boxes, or circles around the subject, and draw lines to connect them to the subject. Put minor ideas or details in smaller boxes or circles, and use connecting lines to show how they relate.

Keep in mind that there is no right or wrong way of clustering. It is a way to think on paper about how various ideas and details relate to one another. The following is an example of clustering that Greg might have done to develop his idea.

EXAMPLE OF CLUSTERING

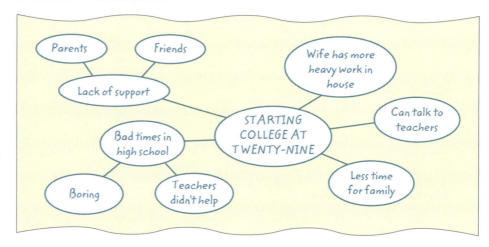

Making a List

In *making a list*—a prewriting strategy also known as *listing, list making,* and *brainstorming*—you make a list of ideas and details that could go into your paper. Simply pile these items up, one after another, without worrying about putting them in any special order. Try to accumulate as many details as you can think of.

After Greg did his freewriting about returning to school, he made up the list of details shown below.

EXAMPLE OF LISTING

parents give me hard time when they see me

Dad hated school

Dad quit school after eighth grade

Dad says I was dumped on enough in high school

Dad asks why I want to go back for more

continued

Mom also doesnt understand

keeps asking how Ill pay for it

friends give me a hard time too

friends call me college man

say they have to watch their grammar

my wife has more heavy work around the house

also high school was no fun for me

just sat in class after class

couldnt wait for final bell to ring

wanted to escape

teachers didnt help me

teachers didnt take an interest in me

one called on me, then told me to forget it

I felt like a real loser

I didnt want to go back to his class

now I'm more sure of myself

OK not to know an answer

talk to teachers after class

job plus schoolwork take all my time

get home late, then rush through dinner

then spend evening studying

even have to do homework on weekends

One detail led to another as Greg expanded his list. Slowly but surely, more supporting material emerged that he could use in developing his paper. By the time he had finished his list, he was ready to plan an outline of his paragraph and to write his first draft.

Notice that, in making a list, as in freewriting, details are included that will not end up in the final paragraph. Greg decided later not to develop the idea that his wife now has more heavy work to do in the house. And he realized that several of his details were about why school is easier in college ("now I'm more sure of myself," "OK not to know an answer," and "talk to instructors after class"); such details were not relevant to his point.

It is natural for a number of such extra or unrelated details to appear as part of the prewriting process. The goal of prewriting is to get a lot of information down on paper. You can then add to, shape, and subtract from your raw material as you take your paper through the series of writing drafts.

Important Points about Prewriting Strategies

ESL Tip
All prewriting activities, reading, and the writing of multiple drafts, provide opportunities for communication in the second language.

Some writers may use only one of the prewriting strategies described here. Others may use bits and pieces of all four strategies. Any one strategy can lead to another. Freewriting may lead to questioning or clustering, which may then lead to a list. Or a writer may start with a list and then use freewriting or questioning to develop items on the list. During this early stage of the writing process, as you do your thinking on paper, anything goes. You should not expect a straight-line progression from the beginning to the end of your paper. Instead, there probably will be a constant moving back and forth as you work to discover your point and decide just how you will develop it.

Keep in mind that prewriting can also help you choose from among several topics. Greg might not yet have decided which problem to write about. Then he could have made a list of possible topics—areas in his life in which he has had problems. After selecting two or three topics from the list, he could have done some prewriting on each to see which seemed most promising. After finding a likely topic, Greg would have continued with his prewriting activities until he had a solid main point and plenty of support.

Finally, remember that you are not ready to begin writing a paper until you know your main point and many of the details to support it. Don't rush through prewriting. It's better to spend more time on this stage than to waste time writing a paragraph for which you have no solid point and not enough interesting support.

Step 2: Preparing a Scratch Outline

Teaching Tip
Ask students what the word *scratch* means in "scratch outline."

A *scratch outline* is a brief plan for a paragraph. It shows at a glance the point of the paragraph and the main support for that point. It is the logical backbone on which the paper is built.

This rough outline often follows freewriting, questioning, clustering, or listing—or all four. Or it may gradually emerge in the midst of these strategies. In fact, trying to outline is a good way to see if you need to do more prewriting. If a solid outline does not emerge, then you know you need to do more prewriting to clarify your main point or its support. Once you have a workable outline, you may realize, for instance, that you want to do more listing to develop one of the supporting details in the outline.

In Greg's case, as he was working on his list of details, he suddenly discovered what the plan of his paragraph could be. He went back to the list, crossed out items that he now realized did not fit, and added the following comments.

EXAMPLE OF LIST WITH COMMENTS

Starting college at twenty-nine isn't easy—three reasons

parents give me hard time when they see me

Dad hated school

Dad quit school after eighth grade

Dad says I was dumped on enough in high school

Dad asks why I want to go back for more

Parents and friends don't support me

Mom also doesnt understand

keeps asking how Ill pay for it

friends give me a hard time too

friends call me college man

say they have to watch their grammar

~~my wife has more heavy work around the house~~

also high school was no fun for me

just sat in class after class

couldnt wait for final bell to ring

wanted to escape

teachers didnt help me

Bad memories of school

teachers didnt take an interest in me

one called on me, then told me to forget it

I felt like a real loser

I didnt want to go back to his class

~~now I'm more sure of myself~~

~~OK not to know an answer~~

~~talk to teachers after class~~

job and schoolwork take all my time

get home late, then rush through dinner

Not enough time with family

then spend evening studying

even have to do homework on weekends

Teaching Tip
Point out that a
scratch outline
can be pre-
pared quickly.

Under the list, Greg was now able to prepare his scratch outline.

EXAMPLE OF SCRATCH OUTLINE

> *Starting college at age twenty-nine isn't easy.*
>
> 1. *Little support from parents or friends*
> 2. *Bad memories of school*
> 3. *Not enough time to spend with family*

After all his preliminary writing, Greg sat back, pleased. He knew he had a promising paper—one with a clear point and solid support. Greg was now ready to write the first draft of his paper, using his outline as a guide.

Step 3: Writing the First Draft

ESL Tip
Remind non-
native speak-
ers that all
good writers
need to write
multiple drafts;
this process is
not an indica-
tion of poor
writing skills.

When you write your first draft, be prepared to put in additional thoughts and details that didn't emerge in your prewriting. Don't worry if you hit a snag; just leave a blank space or add a comment such as "Do later" and press on to finish the paper. Also, don't worry yet about grammar, punctuation, or spelling. You don't want to take time correcting words or sentences that you may decide to remove later. Instead, make it your goal to develop the content of your paper with plenty of specific details.

EXAMPLE OF FIRST DRAFT

> *Last fall, I finaly realized that I was stuck in a dead-end job. I wasnt making enough money and I was bored to tears. I figured I had to get some new skills which meant going back to school. Beginning college at age twenty-nine turned out to be much tougher than I thought it would be. My father didnt understand, he hated school. That's why he quit after eighth grade. He would ask, Didnt you get dumped on enough in high school? Then wondered why I wanted to go back for more of the same thing. My mother was worried about where the money were coming from and said so. When my friends saw me coming down*

continued

the st. They would make fun of me with remarks like Hey theres the college man. They may have a point. School never was much fun for me. I spent years just siting in class waiting for the bell to ring. So I could escape. The teachers werent much help to me. One time, a teacher called on me then told me to forget it. I felt like a real loser and didnt want to go back to his class. College takes time away from my family. ADD MORE DETAILS LATER. All this makes it very hard for me.

After Greg finished the draft, he was able to put it aside until the next day. You will benefit as well if you can allow some time between finishing a draft and starting to revise.

Step 4: Revising

Revising is as much a stage in the writing process as prewriting, outlining, and writing a first draft. *Revising* means rewriting a paper, building on what has been done, to make it stronger. One writer has said about revision, "It's like cleaning house—getting rid of all the junk and putting things in the right order." It is not just "straightening up"; instead, you must be ready to roll up your sleeves and do whatever is needed to create an effective paper. Too many students think that the first draft *is* the paper. They start to become better writers when they realize that revising a rough draft three or four times is often at the heart of the writing process.

Here are some quick hints that can help make revision easier:

- Ideally, set your first draft aside for a while. Although a few hours can be enough, a day or two is best. You can then come back with a fresh, more objective point of view.

- Work from typed or printed text. You'll be able to see the paper more impartially in this way than if you were just looking at your own familiar handwriting.

- Read your draft aloud. Hearing how your writing sounds will help you pick up problems with meaning as well as style.

- As you do all these things, add your thoughts and changes above the lines or in the margins of your paper. Your recorded comments can serve as a guide when you work on the next draft.

Teaching Tip
Ask students to think about why writers should put their draft aside for a while. Mention that a cake needs to cool before it is frosted.

Teaching Tip
Use these hints to help your students revise paragraphs they created for a previous activity.

Teaching Tip
Get students to talk about how they revise. Often students simply fix superficial features, such as spelling and punctuation.

Teaching Tip
Draw attention to the word *revision* (emphasize the root word *vision*). During this stage, writers are able to "see" their draft in a new light.

EXAMPLE OF SECOND DRAFT

> Starting college at age twenty-nine turned out to be really tough. I did not have much support from my parents and friends. My father hated school, so he asked, Didnt you get dumped on enough in high school? Why go back for more? My mother asking about where the money were coming from. Friends would be making fun of me. Hey theres the college man they would say as soon as they saw me. Another factor was what happened to me in high school. I spent years just siting in class waiting for the bell to ring. I was really bored. Also the teachers liked to embaras me. One teacher called on me and then said forget it. He must of relized I didnt know the answer. I felt like a real loser and didnt want to go back in his class for weeks. Finally I've learned that college takes time away from my family. I have to go to work every day. I have a little over one hour to eat dinner and spend time with my wife and daughter. Then I have to go off to class and when I get back my daughter is in bed asleep. My wife and I have only a little time together. On weekends I have lots of homework to do, so the time goes by like a shot. College is hard for me, but I am going to stay there so I can have a better life.

Teaching Tip
Ask students to provide additional changes and additions to Greg's second draft. Remind them that there is no right or wrong way to revise.

Notice the improvements made in the second draft:

- Greg started by clearly stating the point of his paragraph. He remembered the first goal in effective writing: *make a point*.

- To keep the focus on his own difficulties, he omitted the detail about his father quitting school. He remembered that the first goal in effective writing is also to *stick to one point* so the paper will have unity.

- He added more details so that he would have enough support for his reasons that college was hard. He remembered the second goal in effective writing: *support the point*.

- He inserted transitions to set off the second reason ("Another factor") and the third reason ("Finally") starting college at twenty-nine was difficult for him. He remembered the third goal in effective writing: *organize the support*.

Greg then went on to revise the second draft on the computer. He double-spaced the lines, allowing room for revisions, which he added during his third draft. Shown below are some of the changes that Greg made in longhand as he worked on his third draft.

Part of Third Draft

was difficult
Starting college at age twenty-nine ~~turned out to be really tough.~~
For one thing
I did not have much support from my parents and friends. My father

~~hated school, so he~~ asked, Didn't you get dumped on enough in
woried
high school? Why go back for more? My mother ~~asking~~ about where
make
the money were coming from. Friends would ~~be making~~ fun of me.

Hey theres the college man they would say as soon as they saw me.
reason that starting college was hard
Another ~~factor~~ was what happened to me in high school. I spent years
final
just siting in class waiting for the bell to ring. I was really bored. Also the

teachers liked to embaras me. . . .

After integrating these and other changes back into his file, Greg printed out the almost-final draft of his paper. He knew he had come to the fourth goal in effective writing: *aim for error-free sentences.*

Step 5: Editing and Proofreading

The next-to-last major stage in the writing process is *editing*—checking a paper for mistakes in grammar, punctuation, usage, and spelling. Students often find it hard to edit a paper carefully. They have put so much work into their writing, or so little, that it's almost painful for them to look at the paper one more time. You may simply have to *will* yourself to carry out this important closing step in the writing process. Remember that eliminating sentence-skills mistakes will improve an average paper and help ensure a strong grade on a good paper. Further, as you get into the habit of checking your papers, you will also get into the habit of using sentence skills consistently. They are an integral part of clear, effective writing.

The checklist of sentence skills on the inside back cover of the book will serve as a guide while you are editing your paper.

Here are hints that can help you edit the next-to-final draft of a paper for sentence-skills mistakes.

Teaching Tip Get students to talk about how they edit. Often students submit papers without carefully editing their work. They may expect their teachers to flag and correct their errors.

ESL Tip
Ask students to read their paragraph beginning with the last sentence. Nonnative speakers will find they can concentrate on the errors with missing articles, incorrect prepositions, verb tenses, etc., without being concerned about content.

ESL Tip
Nonnative speakers may make a lot of mistakes in grammar, sentence structure, mechanics, and punctuation. Some of their errors may be similar to those of native speakers; however, many are due to proficiency in the first language and their level of experience with second-language acquisition.

EDITING HINTS

1. Have at hand two essential tools: a good dictionary (see page 387) and a grammar handbook (you can use Part Two of this book).

2. If you're working off a handwritten draft, use a sheet of paper to cover your essay so that you expose only one sentence at a time. Look for errors in grammar and spelling. It may help to read each sentence out loud. If the sentence does not read clearly and smoothly, chances are something is wrong.

3. Pay special attention to the kinds of errors you tend to make. For example, if you tend to write run-ons or fragments, be especially on the lookout for these errors.

4. If you're working off an electronic draft, print it so you'll be able to see your writing more objectively than you can on a screen; edit with a pen with colored ink so that your corrections will stand out.

Shown below are some of the corrections in spelling, grammar, and punctuation that Greg made when editing his paper.

Part of Greg's Edited Draft

Starting college at age twenty-nine was difficult. For one thing, I did not have much support from my parents and friends. My father asked, "Didn't you get dumped on enough in high school? Why go back for more?" My mother *worried* about where the money *was* coming from. Friends would make fun of me. "Hey, there's the college man," they would say as soon as they saw me. . . .

All that remained for Greg to do was to enter in his corrections, print out the final draft of the paper, and proofread it (see the proofreading hints on the next page) for any typos or other careless errors. He was then ready to hand the paper in to his instructor.

Proofreading, the final stage in the writing process, means checking a paper carefully for errors in spelling, grammar, punctuation, and so on. You are ready for this stage when you are satisfied with your choice of supporting details, the order in which they are presented, and the way they and your topic sentence are worded. You will already have attempted to correct all grammar, spelling, and punctuation errors.

At this point in his work, Greg used his dictionary to do final checks on his spelling. He used a grammar handbook (such as the one in Part Two of this text) to be sure about grammar, punctuation, and usage. Greg also read through his paper carefully, looking for typing errors, omitted words, and any other errors he may have missed before. Proofreading is often hard to do—again, students have spent so much time with their work, or so little, that they want to avoid it. But if you do it carefully, this important final step will ensure that your paper is as good as possible.

Copyright © 2014 McGraw-Hill, a business unit of The McGraw-Hill Companies, Inc. All rights reserved.

PROOFREADING HINTS

1. One helpful trick at this stage is to read your paper out loud. You will probably hear awkward wordings and become aware of places where the punctuation needs to be improved. Make the changes needed for your sentences to read smoothly and clearly.

2. Another helpful technique is to use a sheet of paper to cover your paragraph, exposing just one line at a time and checking it carefully for errors.

3. A third strategy is to read your paper backward, from the last sentence to the first. This helps keep you from getting caught up in the flow of the paper and missing small mistakes—which is easy to do, since you're so familiar with what you mean to say.

Activities in the Writing Process

These activities will give you practice in some of the prewriting strategies you can use to generate material for a paper. Try to do two or more of these prewriting activities. If possible, try to complete these activities on a computer.

Freewriting

On a sheet of paper or on a computer, freewrite for several minutes about the best or most disappointing friend you ever had. Don't worry about grammar, punctuation, or spelling. Try to write, without stopping, about whatever comes into your head concerning your best or most disappointing friend.

ACTIVITY 1

Questioning

On another sheet of paper or in a separate file, answer the following questions about the friend you've started to write about.

1. When did this friendship begin and how long did it last?

2. Where did you meet your friend?

3. What is one reason you think highly or disapprovingly of this friend? Give one quality, action, comment, etc. Also, give some details to illustrate this quality.

4. What is another reason for your opinion of your friend? What are some details that support the second reason?

5. Can you think of a third reason? What are some details that support the third reason?

Clustering

In the center of a blank sheet of paper, write and circle the words *best friend* or *most disappointing friend.* Then, around the circle, add reasons and details about the friend. Use a series of boxes, circles, or other shapes, along with connecting lines, to set off the reasons and details. In other words, try to think about and explore your topic in a very visual way.

Making a List

On a separate sheet of paper or in a new file, make a list of details about the friend. Don't worry about putting them in a certain order. Just get down as many details about the friend as occur to you. The list can include specific reasons for your opinion of the person and specific details supporting those reasons.

Scratch Outline

On the basis of your prewriting, prepare a scratch outline made up of your main idea and the three main reasons for your opinion of your friend. Use the form below:

Teaching Tip
Remind students to look over their prewriting notes when creating a scratch outline.

_____ was my best *or* most disappointing friend.

Reason 1: _____

Reason 2: _____

Reason 3: _____

First Draft

Now write a first draft of your paper. Begin with your topic sentence, stating that a certain friend was the best or most disappointing one you ever had. Then state the first reason to support your main idea, followed by specific details supporting that reason. Next, state the second reason, followed by specific details supporting that reason. Finally, state the third reason, followed by support.

Don't worry about grammar, punctuation, or spelling. Just concentrate on getting down on paper the details about your friend.

ACTIVITY 6

Revising the Draft

Ideally, you will have a chance to put your paper aside for a while before writing the second draft. In your second draft, try to do all of the following:

ACTIVITY 7

1. Add transition words such as *first of all, another,* and *finally* to introduce each of the three reasons for your opinion of the friend you're writing about.

2. Omit any details that do not truly support your topic sentence.

3. Add more details as needed, making sure you have plenty of support for each of your three reasons.

4. Check to see that your details are vivid and specific. Can you make a supporting detail more concrete? Are there any persuasive, colorful specifics you can add?

5. Try to eliminate wordiness (see page 449) and clichés (see page 446).

6. In general, improve the flow of your writing.

7. Include a final sentence that rounds off the paper, bringing it to a close.

Teaching Tip Explain clichés to your students. Provide examples, such as "last but not least" and "sad but true." Ask them to provide other examples.

Editing and Proofreading

When you have your almost-final draft of the paper, proofread it as follows:

ACTIVITY 8

1. Using your dictionary, check any words that you think might be misspelled. Though the spell-checking features on most word-processing programs are useful tools, they often do not detect commonly misused words (see pages 416–33) such as *there, their,* and *they're.* Make sure you proofread your draft manually to avoid such errors.

2. Using Part Two of this book, check your paper for mistakes in grammar, punctuation, and usage.

3. Read the paper aloud, listening for awkward or unclear spots. Make the changes needed for the paragraph to read smoothly and clearly. Even better, see if you can get another person to read the draft aloud to you. The spots that this person has trouble reading are spots where you may have to do some rewriting.

4. Take a sheet of paper and cover your writing so that you can expose and carefully check one line at a time. Or read your writing backward, from the end of each paragraph to the beginning. Look for typing errors, omitted words, and other remaining errors.

Don't fail to edit and proofread carefully. You may be tired of working on your paper at this point, but you want to give the extra effort needed to make it as good as possible. A final push can mean the difference between a higher and a lower grade.

Ten Writing Assignments

Your instructor may ask you to do one or more of the following paragraph writing assignments. Be sure to check the rules for paper format on page 298.

WRITING ASSIGNMENT 1

Providing Examples

Teaching Tip
Writers may feel pressured to write a perfect first draft, which is unreasonable. Emphasize the importance of revision and editing.

Teaching Tip
Encourage students to use the five steps to complete these assignments, including prewriting and revision.

Listed below are three topic sentences followed by specific examples, the supporting details. On paper or on the computer, invent two additional examples to support each point. Try to make your examples as specific and as realistic as the ones shown.

Point: My friend Mac has several dangerous driving habits.

1. For one thing, he never signals when he's going to make a left-hand turn. The only warning a car behind Mac has is when he slows down suddenly.

2. . . .

3. . . .

Point: My apartment is in need of repairs.

1. When it rains, water runs down through the ceiling light fixture in the bedroom. The ceiling is always damp and soggy, and there is a musty odor that grows stronger every day.

2. . . .

3. . . .

Point: There are three kinds of everyday happenings that really annoy me.

1. First of all, I hate waiting in long lines at a store, especially when several employees are standing around nearby when they could be opening up another register.

2. . . .

3. . . .

WRITING ASSIGNMENT 2

A Great Snack

Everyone has a favorite snack. What is yours? Maybe it is a huge plate of tortilla chips coated with cheese, a bowl of vanilla ice cream sprinkled with semisweet chocolate chips, or a stack of chocolate graham crackers to dip in hot cocoa with marshmallows floating on top. Write a paragraph about preparing and eating your perfect snack, including any special way, place, or time you prefer to eat the snack.

Begin your paragraph with a statement that summarizes the details you plan to write about, such as this: "One of my favorite snacks is a ham and cheese sandwich with pickle chips, which must be made and eaten in just the right ways." Then go on to explain in detail just how you prepare your snack. For the sandwich example, you would include what kind of bread you use, how many slices of ham and cheese you put on, and exactly where you position the pickle chips. You would then go on to write about how you like to eat your creation. For instance, perhaps the best way to eat your favorite snack is late at night while sitting on your living room couch with a good book in your hand and the TV turned on with the sound turned down.

Your paragraph will be organized in time order, describing the steps involved in your enjoyment of the snack. Help your reader follow your supporting details by using time transition words, such as *first, next, then,* and *finally.*

WRITING ASSIGNMENT 3

A Special Photograph

Pictures have a magical power. They freeze moments in time, allowing us to look back to events that happened long ago. Find a photograph that has special meaning for you. Perhaps it is a photo of a family member who has passed away or a childhood picture of you and a close friend. Write a paragraph describing the picture and explaining its significance. Begin with your topic sentence, perhaps similar to one of the following:

> A photo I have of me with my first girlfriend, Dana, is very special for two reasons.

> A photograph of a funny scene during my tenth birthday party reminds me of the most fun—and the funniest—birthday party I ever had.

Since your readers will not actually see the picture, it is up to you to provide descriptive details so that they will know just what the picture looks like. You might use that description as a starting point for the specific details needed to support your topic sentence.

Teaching Tip Auditory learners need to verbalize their ideas. Ask students to pair up and talk about their topics before jotting down their ideas.

After describing the photo referred to in the first topic sentence, for example, you would go on to explain the two reasons mentioned. One reason might be that the photo was taken on a particularly wonderful date. A colorful description of that date will help readers see just how terrific it was. Your second reason might be that Dana is the person you ended up marrying, and that photo is the earliest one of you two together. A few more details about the photo—how you two posed, the expressions on your faces—may tell how the photo shows that you suspected even then you would end up together. (You may wish to attach or link to a copy of the photo to the draft of the paper you hand in.)

WRITING ASSIGNMENT 4

Your Position in the Family

ESL Tip
Create an error chart to help non-native speakers distinguish between global errors and local ones.

Psychologists have concluded that there are significant differences in being an only, oldest, middle, or youngest child. Which of these are you, and how did it influence the way you were brought up? Did you have more responsibilities than your brothers and sisters? If you were an only child, did you spend a lot of time with adults? Were you a spoiled youngest child? Jot down the advantages and disadvantages that come to mind.

Use the most important ideas on your list to develop a paragraph on how you think your position in your family affected you. Begin with your topic sentence, a statement such as this: "As the second of three children, I received less attention, was given more independence, and was pushed less to achieve than my brother and sister." Use specific examples to illustrate each part of your topic sentence. Try to make your examples interesting and colorful by including very specific, relevant details, such as how things looked and what was said.

WRITING ASSIGNMENT 5

An Embarrassing Moment

Each of us has been embarrassed at some time or other. Thankfully, we often look back at our embarrassing moments years later and smile. Write a paragraph about an embarrassing incident that happened to you which you can smile about today. The paragraph should provide lots of specific detail so that readers can feel and understand your embarrassment.

Begin your paragraph with a topic sentence that tells readers the general situation in which you were embarrassed, such as any of the following.

My first day on the job as a waiter ended with an embarrassing accident that still makes me cringe a little today.

When I met my girlfriend's parents, something happened that was so embarrassing it took me many months to be able to smile about it.

One of the most embarrassing moments in my life happened in high school when I was walking in the cafeteria with a platter of meat loaf on my tray.

You might find freewriting to be a useful way of quickly getting down on screen or paper the story you want to tell. Then you can use that freewriting as a starting point by adding, subtracting, and refining. As you tell events in the order in which they happened, help your readers follow your narrative by using time transitions like *first, next, then,* and *finally.*

WRITING ASSIGNMENT 6

Leaving Home

Sooner or later most young people leave the home they have grown up in to begin life on their own. While the feeling of independence may be thrilling, flying the coop also involves numerous problems. Write about one problem that many people are likely to meet when they live away from home for the first time. Your thesis statement should be similar to either of these:

When young adults move out on their own for the first time, they are likely to

experience a problem with _____.

When I moved out of my parents' home to live on my own for the first time,

one problem I experienced was _____.

Before beginning this paragraph, you may want to make a list of problems that young people on their own for the first time are likely to experience or problems that you experienced when you were first on your own. Select one of those problems to write about. Make sure you use adequate and relevant support to back up your point.

WRITING ASSIGNMENT 7

Life on the Job

Each of us has had a job that we have strong feelings about. Write a paragraph about the best or worst job you have ever had. You might begin with a general description of your job, explaining what it was and what you were supposed to do.

Here are some thesis statements that may help you think about your own paper.

I hated my government office job because the building was in bad condition, the rules were ridiculous, and many of the workers were unhappy.

I love my job as a waiter because my boss is friendly, the schedule is flexible, and the pay is good.

WRITING ASSIGNMENT 8

A Letter of Praise or Criticism

Most of us watch some television, listen to the radio, or read the newspaper. We have each seen, heard, or read things that we have found enjoyable or offensive. Write a letter to or comment on a post by a television network, radio station, or newspaper in which you compliment or criticize something that you saw, listened to, or read. Don't just say you liked or disliked your topic. Instead, give two or three detailed reasons that support your feelings either way.

WRITING ASSIGNMENT 9

The Most Important Qualities in a Person

TV ads, music videos, and many popular TV shows suggest that our culture values physical beauty, strength, and wealth. But are these the most important qualities a person can have? Can you think of others that are more important? For example, which is better: for a teenager to learn how to be cool or how to be kind? Think about the most important qualities a person can have and choose one that you think is very important. Write a paragraph in which you show why the trait you chose is so crucial.

A good prewriting strategy is to write a list of personal qualities that are important to you. Then choose the one that you feel most strongly about. Freewrite on some of these potential topics to see if they make strong subjects. In this way, you'll be able to determine whether a particular quality will work for this assignment.

Alternatively, write a paragraph titled "The Most Unpleasant Quality in People."

An Analysis of Spending Habits

Like many people, you probably would be happy if you could put more of your money aside for future needs, perhaps next year's tuition, another car, or even a new home. But—also like many people—you may find that by the end of each month there is nothing much left of your paycheck. Often a careful analysis of spending habits turns up several ways a person can find some cash to squirrel away. To prepare for this assignment, carefully analyze your own spending and shopping patterns. Then write a paragraph about one way you feel that you can change your spending habits in order to feed your bank account. Use at least three specific details.

Here's a sample scratch outline for this assignment:

Topic sentence: I now see that I can spend much less at the supermarket by being more disciplined.

(1) I can be more careful about using coupons.

(2) I can take better advantage of sales.

(3) I can buy less junk food.

If after analyzing your spending habits you feel that you have been doing a good job of making the most of your paycheck, write a paragraph instead about your success. A thesis statement for that paragraph might go like this: "An analysis of my spending habits shows that I have been doing a pretty good job of staying within my food budget."

CHAPTER 4

Writing with Digital and Electronic Resources

In the last decade, computers and online resources have become increasingly more important to the writing process. Almost all instructors require that papers be typed and printed (rather than handwritten), and most students use word-processing programs like Google Docs or Microsoft Word to compose, revise, and edit essays. Online resources provide a wide array of opportunities for brainstorming, learning more about topics, and sharing ideas with peers. Even if you don't currently own a computer or if you do but it needs maintenance, your school provides one or more computer labs with machines specifically for student use. These labs are sometimes staffed, and if they aren't, most computers have very user-friendly interfaces and Help programs.

Tips for Writing On-Screen

When using a computer to write, keep in mind the following best practices:

- If you are using your school's computer center, allow enough time. You may have to wait for a computer or printer to be free, or your school may have sign-up sheets in the lab or online. In addition, you may need several sessions at the computer and printer to complete your paper.

- When using word-processing programs like Microsoft Word or Google Docs *save your work frequently as you write your draft.* Most computers will occasionally auto-save your work every so often, but any file that is not saved may be lost if the program quits, the computer crashes, or the power is turned off.

- Always save and keep your work in three places—the hard drive you are working on; a backup device such as a flash drive or an external disk; and a server such as Dropbox, or iCloud.

- Print out your work or e-mail it to yourself at the end of every session. Then you will have not only your most recent draft to work on whether you're at a computer or not, but also another backup file in case something should happen to your hard drive, external disks, or servers.

- Before making major changes to your document, create a copy of it. For example, if your file is titled "Worst Job," create a new file called "Worst Job 2" or "Worst Job 013113" (using the date as reference). Then make all your changes in that new file. If the changes don't work out, you can always go back to the original file.

Using Digital and Electronic Resources at Each Stage of the Writing Process

Word processing programs like Microsoft Word or Google Docs make it easy for you to experiment with ideas and wording throughout your paper. They also allow you to create and save many versions.

Following are some ways to make use of digital and electronic programs at each stage of the writing process.

Prewriting

If you type fast, many forms of prewriting, especially freewriting, can be done effectively on the screen. A potentially useful thought is not likely to get lost. You may even find it helpful to dim the screen of your monitor so that you can't see what you're typing. If you temporarily can't see the screen, you won't have to worry about grammar, spelling, or typing errors (all of which do not matter in prewriting); instead, you can concentrate on getting down as many ideas and details as possible about your subject.

After you complete your prewriting, it's often very helpful to print out a copy of what you've done. A printout allows you to see everything at once and revise and expand your work with handwritten comments in the margins of the paper. Alternately, you can continue to work on-screen and track your changes there.

Preparing a Scratch Outline

If you have prepared a list of items during prewriting, you may be able to turn that list into an outline right on the screen. Delete the ideas you feel should not be in your paper (saving them at the end of the file in case you change your mind), and add any new ideas that occur to you. Then use the cut-and-paste or highlight-and-drag functions to shuffle your ideas around until you find the best order for your paper.

You can also create scratch outlines using web-based programs like Work-Flowy (also available as an app for most smartphones) and ThinkLinkr. Both tools can jumpstart brainstorming, take notes, and allow you to share and work on outlines with others. This can be useful when getting peer feedback or working on a group writing project.

Idea Gathering

At any point in the prewriting, outlining, or drafting process, you might experience writer's block or need some inspiration. One way to get ideas flowing is to do some Google searches based on key words in your topic. For instance, you could search for "worst jobs" and find some funny lists or sad stories on the topic. Maybe an anecdote by someone else will help you remember a specific detail from your own experience. It's easy to get caught up in web searching for hours, so restrict your search to ten or twenty minutes. Set an alarm so you won't go over your time limit.

If you are trying to find a new topic or can't think of one, try reviewing recent e-mails, text messages, and posts in Twitter, Facebook, or Tumblr. What have you been talking about with your friends, family, or classmates? Try writing about something that holds your interest outside of class.

Teaching Tip
If you're teaching in a writing lab or have access to a computer during class, do a Google search with your students. Pick a topic they're all familiar with—perhaps a controversial issue in recent news—and show them how to narrow down and refine a search.

Writing Your First Draft

Some people like to write out a first draft by hand and then type it into the computer for revision. If you feel comfortable composing directly on the screen, take advantage of the special features. For example, if you plan to use a freewrite in your paper, simply copy the it from your freewriting file and insert it where it fits into your paper. You can refine it then or later. Or if while typing you discover that a sentence is out of place, cut it from where it is and paste it where it would work better. And if you realize that an earlier sentence can be expanded, just go back to that point and type in the added material.

As you write a first draft, it can be tempting to break things up by visiting Facebook, answering e-mails, or watching something on Hulu. Avoid the temptation by hiding these other options. One way to do this is by drafting with a program like Typewriter, TextRoom, JDarkRoom, or FocusCopy. If you use a Mac, WriteRoom is a good option. Each of these programs turns your full screen into a blank sheet of paper or chalkboard removing all choice distractions like menus and font options. These programs also allow you to shield yourself from alerts about new messages or updates of any kind, so that you can focus on the writing itself.

When you're ready to start formatting your paper, you can copy and paste it into the word-processing program you normally use; TextRoom allows you to export text directly to Google Docs.

Revising

It is during revision that the virtues of word-processing programs and on-screen writing really shine. All substituting, adding, deleting, and rearranging can be done easily within an existing file. Also, you can choose to track your changes within a draft, instead of saving multiple versions, and leave comments and questions for yourself in the margins using a Comments (or similarly named) feature. You can concentrate on each change you want to make, because you never have to type from scratch or work on a messy draft. You can carefully go through your paper to check that all your supporting evidence is relevant and to add new support as needed here and there. Anything you decide to eliminate can be deleted quickly and neatly. Anything you add can be inserted precisely where you choose. You can undo edits easily too. If you change your mind, all you have to do is delete or cut and paste. Or, if you're using your word-processing program's Track Changes feature, you can reject the change with a click of the mouse. Revising on-screen let's you sweep through the paper, focusing on other tasks, such as improving word choice, increasing sentence variety, eliminating wordiness, and so on.

If you are like many students, you will find it convenient to print out a hard copy of your file at various points throughout the revision. You can then revise in longhand—adding, crossing out, and indicating changes—and later quickly make these changes in the document.

Teaching Tip For Microsoft Word, suggest that students use Track Changes to keep track of their revisions.

Editing and Proofreading

Word-processing programs and the Internet offer a number of useful tools for editing and proofreading. If you'd prefer to use an online text editor instead of what is part of your word-processing program, try DarkCopy. If you find editing or proofreading on-screen hard on your eyes, print your document. Mark any corrections on that copy, and then transfer them to your file.

If the word-processing software you're using includes spelling and grammar checks, by all means use them. The spell-check function tells you when a word is not in the computer's dictionary. Keep in mind, however, that the spell-checker cannot tell you how to spell a name correctly or inform you when you have mistakenly used, for example, *their* instead of *there*. To a spell-checker, *Thank ewe four the complement* is as correct as *Thank you for the compliment*. Also, use the grammar-checker with caution. Any errors it doesn't uncover are still your responsibility, and it may signal possible errors that don't exist in your paper.

A freshly printed paper, with its clean appearance and handsome formatting, looks so good that you may feel it is in better shape than it really is. Do not be fooled by your paper's appearance. Take sufficient time to review your grammar, punctuation, and spelling carefully.

Teaching Tip Remind students to use the spelling and grammar checks with caution.

ESL Tip
A good tip for native and nonnative speakers: proofread your writing to make sure the computer has provided you with the word that fits the context.

Teaching Tip
If you're teaching in a writing lab, give your students quick tips in identifying when it would be appropriate to insert an image and/or a link, and show them how to do so effectively.

Even after you hand in your paper, save the digital file. Your instructor may ask you to do some revising, and then the file will save you from having to type the paper again from scratch.

Occasionally, you may be asked to submit a paper in electronic form, either through e-mail or by uploading it onto a school server or FTP site or cloud. In these cases, always double-check that the file has been uploaded. Get confirmation from your instructor, not just from the system or destination itself. Submit a paper electronically only if your instructor specifically asks this of you.

Using Images and Links

Some writing assignments may require you to incorporate images or links. There are many rules, both legal and ethical, about when and how to use others' images and how to credit them. You probably know the saying "A picture speaks a thousand words." Remember this when selecting an image; aim to find one that illustrates or supports your paper's main idea.

Links should be used when they provide useful information that enhances the content of your paper. As with images, avoid links that might distract readers from the central point of your paper.

Incorporate visuals or links into a paper only with your instructor's approval and guidance.

Sentence Skills

PART 2

Introduction

Part Two explains the basic skills needed to write clear, error-free sentences. While the skills are presented within five traditional categories (sentences; verbs, pronouns, and agreement; modifiers and parallelism; punctuation and mechanics; word use), each section is self-contained so that you can go directly to the skills you need to work on. Note, however, that you may find it helpful to review Chapter 5, "Parts of Speech," and Chapter 6, "Subjects and Verbs," before turning to other skills. Typically, the main features of a skill are presented on the first pages of a section; secondary points are developed later. Numerous activities are provided so that you can practice skills enough to make them habits. The activities are varied and range from underlining answers to writing complete sentences involving the skill in question. One or more review tests at the end of each section offer additional practice activities. Mastery tests conclude each chapter, allowing you to immediately test your understanding of each skill.

Look at this photo and imagine you have been asked to write a paper about your ideal college experience. What kinds of people do you hope to meet? What classes will you take? What would you like to accomplish? Using any of the prewriting techniques (freewriting, questioning, clustering, making a list), spend time prewriting for a paper on this topic.

CHAPTER

5

Parts of Speech

Teaching Tip
As you begin
this section,
briefly provide
at least one
example of
each part of
speech so that
your students
will have refer-
ence points.

Words—the building blocks of sentences—can be divided into eight parts of speech. *Parts of speech* are classifications of words according to their meaning and use in a sentence.

This chapter will introduce and explain the eight parts of speech:

nouns	pronouns	verbs	prepositions
adjectives	adverbs	conjunctions	interjections

Nouns

A *noun* is a word that is used to name something: a person, a place, an object, or an idea. Here are some examples of nouns:

Nouns

woman	city	pancake	freedom
Alice Walker	street	diamond	possibility
Jonah Hill	Chicago	Ford	mystery

Teaching Tip
Ask students
to provide
several
examples of
common and
proper nouns.

Nouns that begin with a lowercase letter are known as *common nouns*. These nouns name general things. Nouns that begin with a capital letter are called *proper nouns*. While a common noun refers to a person or thing in general, a proper noun names someone or something specific. For example, *woman* is a common noun—it doesn't name a particular woman. On the other hand, *Alice Walker* is a proper noun because it names a specific woman.

Insert any appropriate noun into each of the following blanks.

1. The shoplifter stole a(n) _____ from the department store.

2. _____ threw the football to me.

3. Tiny messages were scrawled on the _____.

4. A _____ crashed through the window.

5. Give the _____ to Keiko.

Singular and Plural Nouns

A *singular noun* names one person, place, object, or idea. A *plural noun* refers to two or more persons, places, objects, or ideas. Most singular nouns can be made plural with the addition of *s*.

Some nouns, like *box*, have irregular plurals. You can check the plural of nouns you think may be irregular by looking up the singular form in a dictionary.

Singular and Plural Nouns

Singular	Plural
goat	goats
alley	alleys
friend	friends
truth	truths
box	boxes

For more information on nouns, see "Subjects and Verbs," pages 85–96.

Underline the three nouns in the following sentences. Some are singular, and some are plural.

1. Two bats swooped over the heads of the frightened children.

2. The artist has purple paint on her sleeve.

3. The lost dog has fleas and a broken leg.

4. Bella does her homework in green ink.

5. Some farmers plant seeds by moonlight.

Pronouns

A *pronoun* is a word that stands for a noun. Pronouns eliminate the need for constant repetition. Look at the following sentences:

The phone rang, and Malik answered the phone.

Lisa met Lisa's friends in the coffee shop at the mall. Lisa meets Lisa's friends there every Saturday.

The waiter rushed over to the new customers. The new customers asked the waiter for menus and drinks.

Now look at how much clearer and smoother these sentences sound with pronouns.

The phone rang, and Malik answered *it*.
(The pronoun *it* is used to replace the word *phone*.)

Lisa met *her* friends in the coffee shop at the mall. *She* meets *them* there every Saturday.
(The pronoun *her* is used to replace the word *Lisa's*. The pronoun *she* replaces *Lisa*. The pronoun *them* replaces the words *Lisa's friends*.)

The waiter rushed over to the new customers. *They* asked *him* for menus and drinks.
(The pronoun *they* is used to replace the words *the new customers*. The pronoun *him* replaces the words *the waiter*.)

Following is a list of commonly used pronouns known as personal pronouns:

Personal Pronouns

I	you	he	she	it	we	they
me	your	him	her	its	us	them
my	yours	his	hers		our	their

Fill in each blank with the appropriate personal pronoun.

1. André feeds his pet lizard every day before school. _____*He*_____ also gives _____*it*_____ flies in the afternoon.

2. The reporter interviewed the striking workers. _____*They*_____ told _____*him (or her)*_____ about their demand for higher wages and longer breaks.

3. Students should save all returned tests. _____*They*_____ should also keep _____*their*_____ review sheets.

4. The pilot announced that we would fly through some air pockets. ___He (or she)___ said that we should be past ___them___ soon.

5. Adolfo returned the calculator to Sheila last Friday. But Sheila insists that ___she___ never got ___it___ back.

There are several types of pronouns. For convenient reference, they are described briefly in the box below.

Teaching Tip
You may want to write a few sentences on the board that use different types of pronouns.

Types of Pronouns

Personal pronouns can act in a sentence as subjects, objects, or possessives.

> *Singular:* **I, me, my, mine, you, your, yours, he, him, his, she, her, hers, it, its**
>
> *Plural:*   **we, us, our, ours, you, your, yours, they, them, their, theirs**

Relative pronouns refer to someone or something already mentioned in the sentence.

> **who, whose, whom, which, that**

Interrogative pronouns are used to ask questions.

> **who, whose, whom, which, what**

Demonstrative pronouns are used to point out particular persons or things.

> **this, that, these, those**

Note: Do not use *them* (as in *them* shoes), *this here, that there, these here,* or *those there* to point out.

Reflexive pronouns end in *-self* or *-selves*. A reflexive pronoun is used as the object of a verb (as in *Cary cut **herself***) or the object of a preposition (as in *Jack sent a birthday card to **himself***) when the subject of the verb is the same as the object.

> *Singular:* **myself, yourself, himself, herself, itself**
>
> *Plural:*   **ourselves, yourselves, themselves**

Intensive pronouns have exactly the same forms as reflexive pronouns. The difference is in how they are used. Intensive pronouns are used to add emphasis. (*I **myself** will need to read the contract before I sign it.*)

Indefinite pronouns do not refer to a particular person or thing.

> **each, either, everyone, nothing, both, several, all, any, most, none**

Reciprocal pronouns express shared actions or feelings.

> **each other, one another**

For more information on pronouns, see "Pronoun Types," pages 232–46.

Verbs

Every complete sentence must contain at least one verb. There are three types of verbs: action verbs, linking verbs, and helping verbs.

Action Verbs

An *action verb* tells what is being done in a sentence. For example, look at the following sentences:

> Mr. Jensen *swatted* at the bee with his hand.
>
> Rainwater *poured* into the storm sewer.
>
> The children *chanted* the words to the song.

In these sentences, the verbs are *swatted, poured,* and *chanted.* These words are all action verbs; they tell what is happening in each sentence.

For more about action verbs, see "Subjects and Verbs," pages 85–96.

PRACTICE 4

Insert an appropriate word in each blank. That word will be an action verb; it will tell what is happening in the sentence.

1. The surgeon _____ through the first layer of skin.

2. The animals in the cage _____ all day.

3. An elderly woman on the street _____ me for directions.

4. The boy next door _____ our lawn every other week.

5. Our instructor _____ our papers over the weekend.

Linking Verbs

Some verbs are *linking verbs*. These verbs link (join) a noun to something that is said about it. For example, look at the following sentence:

The clouds *are* steel-gray.

In this sentence, *are* is a linking verb. It joins the noun *clouds* to words that describe it: *steel-gray.*

Other common linking verbs include *am, is, was, were, look, feel, sound, appear, seem,* and *become.* For more about linking verbs, see "Subjects and Verbs," pages 85–96.

In each blank, insert one of the following linking verbs: *am, feel, is, look, were.* Use each linking verb once.

PRACTICE 5

1. The important papers _____*were*_____ in a desk drawer.

2. I _____*am*_____ anxious to get my test back.

3. The bananas _____*look*_____ ripe.

4. The grocery store _____*is*_____ open until 11 P.M.

5. Whenever I _____*feel*_____ angry, I go off by myself to calm down.

Helping Verbs

Sometimes the verb of a sentence consists of more than one word. In these cases, the main verb is joined by one or more *helping verbs.* Look at the following sentence:

The basketball team *will be leaving* for the game at six o'clock.

In this sentence, the main verb is *leaving.* The helping verbs are *will* and *be.*

Other helping verbs include *do, has, have, may, would, can, must, could,* and *should*. For more information about helping verbs, see "Subjects and Verbs," pages 85–96, and "Irregular Verbs," pages 172–86.

see "Subjects and Verbs," pages 85–96, and "Irregular Verbs," pages 172–86.

PRACTICE 6

In each blank, insert one of the following helping verbs: *does, must, should, could, has been*. Use each helping verb once.

1. You ___*should (or must)*___ start writing your paper this weekend.

2. The victim ___*could*___ describe her attacker in great detail.

3. You ___*must (or should)*___ rinse the dishes before putting them into the dishwasher.

4. My neighbor ___*has been*___ arrested for drunk driving.

5. The bus driver ___*does*___ not make any extra stops.

Prepositions

A *preposition* is a word that connects a noun or a pronoun to another word in the sentence. For example, look at the following sentence:

A man *on* the bus was snoring loudly.

On is a preposition. It connects the noun *bus* to *man*. Here is a list of common prepositions:

Prepositions

about	before	down	like	to
above	behind	during	of	toward
across	below	except	off	under
after	beneath	for	on	up
among	beside	from	over	with
around	between	in	since	without
at	by	into	through	

The noun or pronoun that a preposition connects to another word in the sentence is called the *object* of the preposition. A group of words beginning with a preposition and ending with its object is called a *prepositional phrase*. The words *on the bus,* for example, are a prepositional phrase.

Now read the following sentences and explanations.

An ant was crawling *up the teacher's leg*.

The noun *leg* is the object of the preposition *up*. *Up* connects *leg* with the word *crawling*. The prepositional phrase *up the teacher's leg* describes *crawling*. It tells just where the ant was crawling.

The man *with the black mustache* left the restaurant quickly.

The noun *mustache* is the object of the preposition *with*. The prepositional phrase *with the black mustache* describes the word *man*. It tells us exactly which man left the restaurant quickly.

The plant *on the windowsill* was a present *from my mother*.

The noun *windowsill* is the object of the preposition *on*. The prepositional phrase *on the windowsill* describes the word *plant*. It describes exactly which plant was a present.
There is a second prepositional phrase in the previous sentence. The preposition is *from,* and its object is *mother*. The prepositional phrase *from my mother* explains *present*. It tells who gave the present. For more about prepositions, see "Subjects and Verbs," pages 85–96, and "Sentence Variety II," pages 282–97.

In each blank, insert one of the following prepositions: *of, by, with, in, without*. Use each preposition once.

PRACTICE 7

1. The letter from his girlfriend had been sprayed _____*with*_____ perfume.

2. The weed killer quickly killed the dandelions _____*in*_____ our lawn.

3. _____*Without*_____ giving any notice, the tenant moved out of the apartment.

4. Donald hungrily ate three scoops _____*of*_____ ice cream and an order of french fries.

5. The crates _____*by*_____ the back door contain glass bottles and old newspapers.

Adjectives

An *adjective* is a word that describes a noun (the name of a person, place, or thing). Look at the following sentence.

The dog lay down on a mat in front of the fireplace.

Now look at this sentence when adjectives have been inserted.

The *shaggy* dog lay down on a *worn* mat in front of the fireplace.

The adjective *shaggy* describes the noun *dog;* the adjective *worn* describes the noun *mat.* Adjectives add spice to our writing. They also help us identify particular people, places, or things.

Adjectives can be found in two places:

1. An adjective may come before the word it describes (a *damp* night, the *moldy* bread, a *striped* umbrella).

2. An adjective that describes the subject of a sentence may come after a linking verb. The linking verb may be a form of the verb *be* (he *is* **furious,** I *am* **exhausted,** they *are* **hungry**). Other linking verbs include *feel, look, sound, smell, taste, appear, seem,* and *become* (the soup *tastes* **salty,** your hands *feel* **dry,** the dog *seems* **lost**).

> **TIP** The words *a, an,* and *the* (called *articles*) are generally classified as adjectives.

For more information on adjectives, see "Adjectives and Adverbs," pages 247–56.

For more information on adjectives, see "Adjectives and Adverbs," pages 247–56.

PRACTICE 8

Write any appropriate adjective in each blank.

Answers will vary.

1. The _____ pizza was eaten greedily by the _____ teenagers.

2. Melissa gave away the sofa because it was _____ and _____.

3. Although the alley is _____ and _____, Jian often takes it as a shortcut home.

4. The restaurant throws away lettuce that is _____ and tomatoes that are _____.

5. When I woke up in the morning, I had a(n) _____ fever and a(n) _____ throat.

Adverbs

Teaching Tip Ask students to provide several examples of adverbs.

An *adverb* is a word that describes a verb, an adjective, or another adverb. Many adverbs end in the letters *-ly.* Look at the following sentence:

The canary sang in the pet store window as the shoppers greeted each other.

Now look at this sentence after adverbs have been inserted.

> The canary sang *softly* in the pet store window as the shoppers *loudly* greeted each other.

The adverbs add details to the sentence. They also allow the reader to contrast the singing of the canary and the noise the shoppers are making.

Look at the following sentences and the explanations of how adverbs are used in each case.

> The chef yelled **angrily** at the young waiter.

> (The adverb *angrily* describes the verb *yelled*.)

> My mother has an **extremely** busy schedule on Tuesdays.

> (The adverb *extremely* describes the adjective *busy*.)

> The sick man spoke **very** faintly to his loyal nurse.

> (The adverb *very* describes the adverb *faintly*.)

Some adverbs do not end in *-ly*. Examples include *very, often, never, always,* and *well*.

For more information on adverbs, see "Adjectives and Adverbs," pages 247–56.

Fill in each blank with any appropriate adverb.

PRACTICE 9

Answers will vary.

1. The water in the pot boiled _____.

2. Carla _____ drove the car through _____ moving traffic.

3. The famous actor spoke _____ to the young child.

4. The contestant waved _____ to his family in the audience.

5. Wes _____ studies, so it's no surprise that he did _____ poorly on his finals.

Conjunctions

A *conjunction* is a word that connects. There are two types of conjunctions: coordinating and subordinating.

Coordinating Conjunctions

Coordinating conjunctions join two equal ideas. Look at the following sentence:

> Kevin *and* Steve interviewed for the job, *but* their friend Anne got it.

In this sentence, the coordinating conjunction *and* connects the proper nouns *Kevin* and *Steve*. The coordinating conjunction *but* connects the first part of the sentence, *Kevin and Steve interviewed for the job,* to the second part, *their friend Anne got it.*

Following is a list of all the coordinating conjunctions. In this book, they are simply called *joining words*.

> ## Coordinating Conjunctions (Joining Words)
>
> | and | so | nor | yet |
> |-----|----|-----|-----|
> | but | or | for | |

For more on coordinating conjunctions, see information on joining words in "Run-Ons," pages 121–40, and "Sentence Variety I," pages 141–58.

PRACTICE 10

Write a coordinating conjunction in each blank. Choose from the following: *and, but, so, or, nor*. Use each conjunction once.

1. Either Jerome _____*or*_____ Alex scored the winning touchdown.

2. I expected roses for my birthday, _____*but*_____ I received a vase of plastic tulips from the discount store.

3. The cafeteria was serving liver and onions for lunch, _____*so*_____ I bought a sandwich at the corner deli.

4. Marian brought a volleyball net _____*and*_____ a pan of brownies to the company picnic.

5. Neither my sofa _____*nor*_____ my armchair matches the rug in my living room.

Subordinating Conjunctions

When a *subordinating conjunction* is added to a word group, the words can no longer stand alone as an independent sentence. They are no longer a complete thought. For example, look at the following sentence:

Karen fainted in class.

The word group *Karen fainted in class* is a complete thought. It can stand alone as a sentence. See what happens when a subordinating conjunction is added to a complete thought:

When Karen fainted in class

Now the words cannot stand alone as a sentence. They are dependent on other words to complete the thought:

When Karen fainted in class, we put her feet up on some books.

In this book, a word that begins a dependent word group is called a *dependent word*. Subordinating conjunctions are common dependent words. The following are some subordinating conjunctions.

> ## Subordinating Conjunctions
>
> | | | | | |
> |---|---|---|---|---|
> | after | before | since | when | wherever |
> | although | even if | though | whenever | whether |
> | as | even though | unless | where | while |
> | because | if | until | | |

Following are some more sentences with subordinating conjunctions:

After she finished her last exam, Irina said, "Now I can relax."
(*After she finished her last exam* is not a complete thought. It is dependent on the rest of the words to make up a complete sentence.)

Lamont listens to books on tape **while** he drives to work.
(*While he drives to work* cannot stand by itself as a sentence. It depends on the rest of the sentence to make up a complete thought.)

Since apples were on sale, we decided to make an apple pie for dessert.
(*Since apples were on sale* is not a complete sentence. It depends on *we decided to make an apple pie for dessert* to complete the thought.)

For more information on subordinating conjunctions, see information on dependent words in "Fragments," pages 97–120; "Run-Ons," pages 121–40; "Sentence Variety I," pages 141–58; and "Sentence Variety II," pages 282–97.

Write a logical subordinating conjunction in each blank. Choose from the following: *even though, because, until, when, before.* Use each conjunction once.

PRACTICE 11

1. The bank was closed down by federal regulators ___*because*___ it lost more money than it earned.

2. ___*When*___ Divya wants to look mysterious, she wears dark sunglasses and a scarf.

3. ___*Even though*___ the restaurant was closing in fifteen minutes, customers sipped their coffee slowly and continued to talk.

4. ___*Before*___ anyone else could respond to the bell, Leon rushed to the door and flung it open.

5. The waiter was instructed not to serve any food ___*until*___ the guest of honor arrived.

Interjections

An *interjection* is a word that can stand independently and is used to express emotion. Examples are *oh, wow, ouch,* and *oops*. These words are usually not found in formal writing.

"Hey!" yelled Maggie. "That's my bike."

Oh, we're late for class.

A Final Note

A word may function as more than one part of speech. For example, the word *dust* can be a verb or a noun, depending on its role in the sentence.

I *dust* my bedroom once a month. (verb)

The top of my refrigerator is covered with an inch of *dust*. (noun)

Subjects and Verbs

INTRODUCTORY ACTIVITY

Understanding subjects and verbs is a big step toward mastering many sentence skills. As a speaker of English, you already have an instinctive feel for these basic building blocks of English sentences. See if you can insert an appropriate word in each space below. The answer will be a subject.

1. The _____ will soon be over.

2. _____ cannot be trusted.

3. A strange _____ appeared in my backyard.

4. _____ is one of my favorite activities.

Now insert an appropriate word in the following spaces. Each answer will be a verb.

5. The prisoner _____ at the judge.

6. My sister _____ much harder than I do.

7. The players _____ in the locker room.

8. Rob and Marilyn _____ with the teacher.

Finally, insert appropriate words in the following spaces. Each answer will be a subject in the first space and a verb in the second.

9. The _____ almost _____ out of the tree.

10. Many _____ today _____ sex and violence.

11. The _____ carefully _____ the patient.

12. A _____ quickly _____ the ball.

Answers are on page 634.

Answers will vary.

Teaching Tip
You may want to use this activity to assess your students' understanding of subjects and verbs.

Teaching Tip
Bring a photo
of a DNA mol-
ecule to class.
Tell students
that just as
amino acids
are the build-
ing blocks of
DNA, subjects
and verbs
are the build-
ing blocks of
sentences.

ESL Tip
In all these
examples, the
verb follows
the subject
(S + V + O).
In some lan-
guages, the
word order is
V + S + O.

ESL Tip
Some lan-
guages do
not require
pronouns
as subjects.
Make students
aware that, in
English, a verb
always needs
a subject.

The basic building blocks of English sentences are subjects and verbs. Understanding them is an important first step toward mastering a number of sentence skills.

Every sentence has a subject and a verb. Who or what the sentence speaks about is called the *subject;* what the sentence says about the subject is called the *verb.* In the following sentences, the subject is underlined once and the verb twice:

People gossip.

The truck belched fumes.

He waved at me.

Alaska contains the largest wilderness area in the United States.

That woman is a millionaire.

The pants feel itchy.

A Simple Way to Find a Subject

To find a subject, ask *who* or *what* the sentence is about. As shown below, your answer is the subject.

Who is the first sentence about? People

What is the second sentence about? The truck

Who is the third sentence about? He

What is the fourth sentence about? Alaska

Who is the fifth sentence about? That woman

What is the sixth sentence about? The pants

It helps to remember that the subject of a sentence is always a *noun* (any person, place, or thing) or a pronoun. A *pronoun* is simply a word like *he, she, it, you,* or *they* used in place of a noun. In the preceding sentences, the subjects are persons (*People, He, woman*), a place (*Alaska*), and things (*truck, pants*). Note that one pronoun (*He*) is used as a subject.

A Simple Way to Find a Verb

To find a verb, ask what the sentence *says about* the subject. You should answer with a verb, as shown below.

What does the first sentence *say about* people? They gossip.

What does the second sentence *say about* the truck? It belched (fumes).

Teaching Tip
Have students brainstorm a list of nouns and verbs. Now ask them to create several sentences using these nouns (which will function as subjects) and verbs. Encourage everyone to be creative.

What does the third sentence *say about* him? He waved (at me).

What does the fourth sentence *say about* Alaska? It contains (the largest wilderness area in the United States).

What does the fifth sentence *say about* that woman? She is (a millionaire).

What does the sixth sentence *say about* the pants? They feel (itchy).

A second way to find the verb is to put *I, you, he, she, it,* or *they* in front of the word you think is a verb. If the result makes sense, you have a verb. For example, you could put *they* in front of *gossip* in the first sentence above, with the result, *they gossip,* making sense. Therefore, you know that *gossip* is a verb. You could use the same test with the other verbs as well.

Finally, it helps to remember that most verbs show action. In "People gossip," the action is gossiping. In "The truck belched fumes," the action is belching. In "He waved at me," the action is waving. In "Alaska contains the largest wilderness area in the United States," the action is containing.

Certain other verbs, known as *linking verbs,* do not show action. They do, however, give information about the subject of the sentence. In "That woman is a millionaire," the linking verb *is* tells us that the woman is a millionaire. In "The pants feel itchy," the linking verb *feel* gives us the information that the pants are itchy.

In each of the following sentences, underline the subject and double-underline the verb.

PRACTICE 1

> **HINT** To find the subject, ask *who* or *what* the sentence is about. Then, to find the verb, ask what the sentence *says about* the subject.

1. Rachel poured extra virgin olive oil into the skillet.
2. The company offered a fifty-dollar rebate on every energy-efficient refrigerator bought during the month of June.
3. The talk show host introduced ten-year-old Drake as a future *American Idol* star.
4. Taryn adjusted the volume on her smartphone as she entered the library.
5. The discarded cigarette butt burned a hole in the upholstery.
6. The bathroom upstairs is infested with cockroaches.
7. Royden tripped over the tangled cables behind my office desk.
8. The sports drink quenched my thirst.
9. The lawn trimmer tossed small rocks and other debris into the air.
10. Volunteers collected canned meats, beans, and peanut butter for the food bank.

PRACTICE 2

Follow the directions given for Practice 1. Note that all of the verbs here are link-ing verbs.

1. The best shows on television this week were the commercials.
2. In some countries, an after-dinner burp is a compliment to the cook.
3. Mirror sunglasses always look eerie, like a robot's eyes.
4. My voice sounds terrible in the morning.
5. Tamika became engaged to Hassan after just three dates.
6. Harold's new after-shave lotion smells like cleaning fluid.
7. Visitors often appear fearful at my German shepherd's bark of greeting.
8. To a female fly, a male's wing vibrations are a love song.
9. My head cold feels like a combination of fatal headache and torture by sneezing.
10. In some ways, the change from tadpole to frog seems as much of a miracle as the change from frog to prince.

PRACTICE 3

Follow the directions given for Practice 1.

1. One lonely neon light glowed in the distance.
2. The kite soared into the sky at the end of a taut, vibrating string.
3. Manuel caught a foul ball at the game.
4. The skaters shadowed each other's movements perfectly.
5. Fluorescent lights emphasized the lines in the tired man's face.
6. Tracy reads to her bedridden grandmother every night.
7. Marsha's oversized glasses slipped down her nose twenty times a day.
8. Carelessly, Jane gave the children too much candy.
9. The squirrel jumped from one tree branch to another.
10. Carpenters constructed a wooden wheelchair ramp next to the stone steps of the church.

More about Subjects and Verbs

Distinguishing Subjects from Prepositional Phrases

The subject of a sentence never appears within a prepositional phrase. A *prepositional phrase* is simply a group of words beginning with a preposition and ending with the answer to the question *what, when,* or *where.* Here is a list of common prepositions.

ESL Tip
Have nonnative speakers identify unfamiliar prepositions and check out their meanings in the dictionary (e.g. *beneath, among, through, toward*).

Common Prepositions

about	before	by	inside	over
above	behind	during	into	through
across	below	except	of	to
among	beneath	for	off	toward
around	beside	from	on	under
at	between	in	onto	with

When you are looking for the subject of a sentence, it is helpful to cross out prepositional phrases.

~~In the middle of the night~~, we heard footsteps ~~on the roof~~.

The magazines ~~on the table~~ belong ~~in the garage~~.

~~Before the opening kickoff~~, a brass band marched ~~onto the field~~.

The hardware store ~~across the street~~ went ~~out of business~~.

~~In spite of our advice~~, Sally quit her job ~~at Burger King~~.

Cross out prepositional phrases. Then underline subjects and double-underline verbs.

PRACTICE 4

1. Stripes ~~of sunlight~~ glowed ~~on the kitchen floor~~.
2. The black panther draped its powerful body ~~along the thick tree branch~~.
3. A line ~~of impatient people~~ snaked ~~from the box office to the street~~.
4. ~~At noon~~, every tornado siren in town wails ~~for fifteen minutes~~.
5. The tops ~~of my Bic pens~~ always disappear ~~after a day or two~~.
6. Joanne removed the lint ~~from her black socks with Scotch tape~~.
7. The mirrored walls ~~of the skyscraper~~ reflected the passing clouds.
8. Debris ~~from the accident~~ littered the intersection.
9. ~~Above the heads of the crowd~~, a woman swayed ~~on a narrow ledge~~.
10. The squashed grapes ~~in the bottom of the vegetable bin~~ oozed sticky, purple juice.

Verbs of More Than One Word

Many verbs consist of more than one word. Here, for example, are some of the many forms of the verb *help:*

Teaching Tip
For added practice, have students identify the many forms of the verb *talk*.

ESL Tip
Using correct verb tenses and forms is very confusing for nonnative speakers. Have students identify the verb tenses for each of the forms in the box.

Some Forms of the Verb *Help*

helps	should have been helping	will have helped
helping	can help	would have been helped
is helping	would have been helping	has been helped
was helping	will be helping	had been helped
may help	had been helping	must have helped
should help	helped	having helped
will help	have helped	should have been helped
does help	has helped	had helped

The following sentences contain verbs of more than one word:

Yolanda is working overtime this week.

Another book has been written about the Kennedy family.

We should have stopped for gas at the last station.

The game has just been canceled.

Teaching Tip
Introduce students to infinitives, which are verbs preceded by the preposition *to*. Remind students that an infinitive is not the main verb of a sentence.

TIPS

1. Words like *not, just, never, only,* and *always* are not part of the verb, although they may appear within the verb.

Yolanda is not working overtime next week.

The boys should just not have stayed out so late.

The game has always been played regardless of the weather.

2. No verb preceded by *to* is ever the verb of a sentence.

Sue wants to go with us.

The newly married couple decided to rent a house for a year.

The store needs extra people to help out during the holidays.

3. No *-ing* word by itself is ever the verb of a sentence. (It may be part of the verb, but it must have a helping verb in front of it.)

We planning the trip for months. (This is not a sentence, because the verb is not complete.)

We were planning the trip for months. (This is a complete sentence.)

Underline subjects and double-underline verbs. Be sure to include all parts of the verb.

1. Only Einstein could have passed that math test.
2. She could have been killed by that falling rock.
3. The children did not recognize their father in his Halloween costume.
4. The hunger strikers have been fasting for four days.
5. I could not see the tiny letters on the last row of the eye doctor's chart.
6. People may be wearing paper clothing by the year 2050.
7. He should have studied longer for the final.
8. Rosa has been soaking in the bathtub for an hour.
9. Long lines of southbound geese were flying overhead.
10. My little brother can ask the same stupid question five times in a row.

Compound Subjects and Verbs

A sentence may have more than one verb:

The dancer stumbled and fell.

Lola washed her hair, blew it dry, and parted it in the middle.

A sentence may have more than one subject:

Cats and dogs are sometimes the best of friends.

The striking workers and their bosses could not come to an agreement.

A sentence may have several subjects and several verbs:

Holly and I read the book and reported on it to the class.

Pete, Nick, and Eric caught the fish in the morning, cleaned them in the afternoon, and ate them that night.

Underline subjects and double-underline verbs. Be sure to mark *all* the subjects and verbs.

1. The trees creaked and shuddered in the powerful wind.
2. The little girl fell off the jungle gym and landed in the dirt.
3. On Sunday, I will vacuum the upstairs rooms and change the linens.
4. The late afternoon sun shone on the leaves and turned them to gold.
5. Sam and Billy greased their chapped lips with Vaseline.
6. The tall, masked man and his Native American friend rode off into the sunset.
7. My sister and I always race each other to the bathroom in the morning.
8. Nia breathed deeply and then began her karate exercises.

Teaching Tip
For added practice, ask students to cross out the prepositional phrases in this activity.

9. At the party, Phil draped a tablecloth around his shoulders and pretended to be Dracula.

10. The professional wrestler and his opponent strutted around the ring and pounded on their chests.

REVIEW TEST 1

Teaching Tip
You may want to use these review tests to assess what your students have learned.

Underline the subjects and double-underline the verbs. As necessary, cross out prepositional phrases to help find subjects. Underline all the parts of a verb, and remember that you may find more than one subject and more than one verb in a sentence.

1. The endings of most movies are happy.
2. I should have filled the car with gas before work.
3. The female of many animals is larger than the male.
4. Three buildings on our block are for sale.
5. Dozens of ants gathered around a scoop of pink ice cream on the sidewalk.
6. Many shoppers saw the pennies on the floor but would not pick them up.
7. Squirrels can collect thousands of nuts in one season.
8. Genetically modified fruits and vegetables should be banned in this country.
9. An extra key was placed under the big, empty planter by the front door.
10. Ved dieted for a year, lost a hundred pounds, and lowered his high blood pressure.

REVIEW TEST 2

Follow the directions given for Review Test 1.

1. A collection of watercolor paintings was damaged in the flood.
2. Everything in that linen store is on sale at 40 percent off.
3. My son is looking for dinosaur bones in the backyard.
4. According to surveys, most people talk to their dogs.
5. Jay and Elise were married two years ago and are divorced already.
6. At dinnertime, my cat meows and rubs against my leg.
7. The huge tree outside our kitchen window throws lovely shadows on the kitchen wall in the afternoon.
8. My parents and the Greens played bridge for hours and argued constantly.
9. Deanna chose a chocolate from the box, took one bite, and put the piece back.
10. Mona removed Ed's arm from her shoulders and ran from the theater with tears in her eyes.

NAME: _____

DATE: _____

Subject and Verbs

Underline subjects and double-underline verbs. Cross out prepositional phrases as necessary to help find subjects. (Be sure to underline all the parts of a verb. Also, remember that you may find more than one subject and one verb in a sentence.)

1. My cat sleeps ~~on the radiator~~.

2. An opened bag ~~of lemon cookies~~ hung ~~over the edge of the shelf~~.

3. Margie and Paul walked hand in hand ~~into the haunted house~~.

4. Those early Beatles records have become collectors' items.

5. Twenty people crammed themselves ~~into the tiny elevator~~.

6. The truck driver got out his jumper cables and attached them ~~to the battery of my car~~.

7. The man ~~in the gorilla suit~~ is my brother.

8. Vince always watches football ~~on television~~ but almost never goes ~~to a game~~.

9. Unable to find his parents ~~in the supermarket~~, Billy sat down and cried.

10. She opened the book, placed her finger ~~at the top of the page~~, and began to speed-read.

NAME: _____

DATE: _____

Subject and Verbs

Underline subjects and double-underline verbs. Cross out prepositional phrases as necessary to help find subjects. (Be sure to underline all the parts of a verb. Also, remember that you may find more than one subject and one verb in a sentence.)

1. Nancy burned her arm ~~on the charcoal grill~~.

2. I always keep a first-aid kit ~~in the trunk of my car~~.

3. He has been looking ~~for that book for at least a week~~.

4. The new office manager was hired ~~on Tuesday~~ and fired ~~on Wednesday~~.

5. My grandfather is often troubled ~~by arthritis~~.

6. Cheryl and her sister found a ten-dollar bill ~~in the wastebasket~~.

7. Fred ran ~~across the porch~~ and tripped ~~on a loose board~~.

8. Those violent cartoons ~~on Saturday morning television~~ are too scary ~~for small children~~.

9. All ~~of the leftover Christmas decorations~~ just went ~~on sale at half price~~.

10. Bonnie and Clyde strode ~~into the bank~~, waved their guns, and told everyone to lie down ~~on the floor~~.

NAME: _____

DATE: _____

Subject and Verbs

Underline subjects and double-underline verbs. Cross out prepositional phrases as necessary to help find subjects. (Be sure to underline all the parts of a verb. Also, remember that you may find more than one subject and one verb in a sentence.)

1. Tom reads the sports section every morning.

2. The name of that woman just flew out of my head.

3. Our dog whined pitifully during the violent thunderstorm.

4. That screen has at least twenty holes and needs to be replaced.

5. Her problems are starting to sound like TV reruns.

6. Three copies of that book have been stolen from the library.

7. The little girl with pigtails did graceful cartwheels in the yard.

8. My sixth-grade teacher never could understand my questions.

9. We bought a broken floor lamp at our neighbor's garage sale and then could not decide what to do with it.

10. The mud slides, flooded roads, and washed-out bridges were caused by last week's heavy rains.

NAME: _____

DATE: _____

Subject and Verbs

Underline subjects and double-underline verbs. Cross out prepositional phrases as necessary to help find subjects. (Be sure to underline all the parts of a verb. Also, remember that you may find more than one subject and one verb in a sentence.)

1. A low whistle suddenly pierced the silence.

2. Liz had spread her beach towel over the hot sand.

3. At the juice bar, Bob was sipping a strawberry-coconut milk shake.

4. Our old car has been repaired only three times in the last four years.

5. Annabelle's skin turned bright orange from the indoor tanning lotion.

6. Marsha and Ann begged their parents for permission to go to the concert.

7. The officer dismounted from his motorcycle, walked over to me, and asked for my license and registration.

8. Bananas, skim milk, and bran buds were the ingredients in the breakfast drink.

9. I listened to all the candidate's promises but did not believe a single one.

10. A doctor and nurse walked into the room, pulled down Mike's covers, and ordered him to roll over.

Fragments

INTRODUCTORY ACTIVITY

Every sentence must have a subject and a verb and must express a complete thought. A word group that lacks a subject or a verb and that does not express a complete thought is a *fragment*.

Listed below are a number of fragments and sentences. Complete the statement that explains each fragment.

1. Children.   *Fragment*

   Children cry.   *Sentence*

   "Children" is a fragment because, while it has a subject *(Children)*, it lacks a ____*verb*____ *(cry)* and so does not express a complete thought.

2. Dances.   *Fragment*

   Lola dances.   *Sentence*

   "Dances" is a fragment because, while it has a verb *(Dances)*, it lacks a ____*subject*____ *(Lola)* and so does not express a complete thought.

3. Staring through the window.   *Fragment*

   The cat was staring through the window.   *Sentence*

   "Staring through the window" is a fragment because it lacks a _____*subject*_____ *(The cat)* and part of the _____*verb*_____ *(was)* and because it does not express a complete thought.

4. When the dentist began drilling.   *Fragment*

   When the dentist began drilling, I closed my eyes.   *Sentence*

   "When the dentist began drilling" is a fragment because we want to know what happened when the dentist began drilling. The word group does not follow through and ____*express a complete thought*____

   Answers are on page 634.

Teaching Tip
You may want to use this activity to assess your students' understanding of fragments.

PERSONALIZED LEARNING

Teaching Tip
As you begin this section, provide at least one example of each fragment type so that students will have reference points.

What Fragments Are

Every sentence must have a subject and a verb and must express a complete thought. A word group that lacks a subject or a verb and does not express a complete thought is a *fragment*. Following are the most common types of fragments that people write:

1. Dependent-word fragments
2. *-ing* and *to* fragments
3. Added-detail fragments
4. Missing-subject fragments

Once you understand the specific kind or kinds of fragments that you might write, you should be able to eliminate them from your writing. The following pages explain all four types of fragments.

Dependent-Word Fragments

ESL Tip
Nonnative speakers may write dependent word fragments because they've often heard them spoken in English. In addition, some languages consider these acceptable in written expression.

Some word groups that begin with a dependent word are fragments. Here is a list of common dependent words:

Common Dependent Words

after	if, even if	when, whenever
although, though	in order that	where, wherever
as	since	whether
because	that, so that	which, whichever
before	unless	while
even though	until	who
how	what, whatever	whose

Whenever you start a sentence with one of these dependent words, you must be careful that a dependent-word fragment does not result. The word group beginning with the dependent word *after* in the selection below is a fragment.

After I stopped drinking coffee. I began sleeping better at night.

A *dependent statement*—one starting with a dependent word like *after*—cannot stand alone. It depends on another statement to complete the thought. "After I stopped drinking coffee" is a dependent statement. It leaves us hanging. We expect in the same sentence to find out *what happened after* the writer stopped drinking coffee. When a writer does not follow through and complete a thought, a fragment results.

To correct the fragment, simply follow through and complete the thought:

After I stopped drinking coffee, I began sleeping better at night.

Remember, then, that *dependent statements by themselves* are fragments. They must be attached to a statement that makes sense standing alone.*

Here are two other examples of dependent-word fragments.

Brian sat nervously in the dental clinic. While waiting to have his wisdom tooth pulled.

Maria decided to throw away the boxes. That had accumulated for years in the basement.

"While waiting to have his wisdom tooth pulled" is a fragment; it does not make sense standing by itself. We want to know in the same statement *what Brian did* while waiting to have his tooth pulled. The writer must complete the thought. Likewise, "That had accumulated for years in the basement" is not in itself a complete thought. We want to know in the same statement what *that* refers to.

HOW TO Correct Dependent-Word Fragments

In most cases, you can correct a dependent-word fragment by attaching it to the sentence that comes after it or to the sentence that comes before it:

After I stopped drinking coffee, I began sleeping better at night. (The fragment has been attached to the sentence that comes after it.)

Brian sat nervously in the dental clinic while waiting to have his wisdom tooth pulled. (The fragment has been attached to the sentence that comes before it.)

Maria decided to throw away the boxes that had accumulated for years in the basement. (The fragment has been attached to the sentence that comes before it.)

Another way of correcting a dependent-word fragment is to eliminate the dependent word and make a new sentence:

I stopped drinking coffee.

He was waiting to have his wisdom tooth pulled.

They had accumulated for years in the basement.

Do not use this second method of correction too frequently, however, for it may cut down on interest and variety in your writing style.

*Some instructors refer to a dependent-word fragment as a *dependent clause*. A *clause* is simply a group of words having a subject and a verb. A clause may be *independent* (expressing a complete thought and able to stand alone) or *dependent* (not expressing a complete thought and not able to stand alone). A dependent clause by itself is a fragment. It can be corrected simply by adding an independent clause.

Teaching Tip
You may want to teach your students about dependent and independent clauses. See the footnote.

Teaching Tip
Reiterate to your students that there are two ways to correct a dependent-word fragment: (1) join the fragment to a complete sentence or (2) get rid of the dependent word.

TIPS

1. Use a comma if a dependent-word group comes at the *beginning* of a sentence (see also page 144):

   > After I stopped drinking coffee, I began sleeping better at night.

   However, do not generally use a comma if the dependent-word group comes at the end of a sentence:

   > Brian sat nervously in the dental clinic while waiting to have his wisdom tooth pulled.

   > Maria decided to throw away the boxes that had accumulated for years in the basement.

2. Sometimes the dependent words *who, that, which,* or *where* appear not at the very start but *near* the start of a word group. A fragment often results.

   > Today I visited Faye. A friend who is in the hospital.

   "A friend who is in the hospital" is not in itself a complete thought. We want to know in the same statement *who* the friend is. The fragment can be corrected by attaching it to the sentence that comes before it:

   > Today I visited Faye, a friend who is in the hospital.

   (Here a comma is used to set off "a friend who is in the hospital," which is extra material placed at the end of the sentence.)

PRACTICE 1

Answers will vary.

Teaching Tip
Point out that a dependent-word group can start or end a sentence. For example, "Until I die" could appear in a sentence two ways: "I plan to eat chocolate until I die" or "Until I die, I plan to eat chocolate."

Turn each of the dependent-word groups into a sentence by adding a complete thought. Put a comma after the dependent-word group if a dependent word starts the sentence.

EXAMPLES

Before I begin college

Before I begin college, I want to brush up on my math and English skills.

_____

The horoscope forecast that I read

The horoscope forecast that I read predicted new love, but I am happily married.

_____

1. Before I log off from the lab's computer

_____

_____

2. Even though I cheated

_____

_____

3. Although my parents never went to college

_____

_____

4. The pills that the doctor prescribed

_____

_____

5. If I remember correctly

_____

_____

Underline the dependent-word fragment (or fragments) in each item. Then correct each fragment by attaching it to the sentence that comes before or the sentence that comes after—whichever sounds more natural. Put a comma after the dependent-word group if it starts the sentence.

PRACTICE 2

1. <u>Since she was afraid of muggers.</u> Barbara carried a small can of pepper spray on her key ring. A rape whistle on a chain was hidden under her coat.

   Since she was afraid of muggers, Barbara carried a small can of pepper spray on her

   key ring.

   _____

2. <u>When I began watching the movie.</u> I remembered that I had seen it before. I already knew who had murdered the millionaire.

   When I began watching the TV mystery movie, I remembered that I had seen it before.

   _____

   _____

3. Tulips had only begun to bloom. <u>When a freakish spring snowstorm blanketed the garden.</u> The flowers perished in the unseasonable cold.

   Tulips had only begun to bloom when a freakish spring snowstorm blanketed

   the garden.

   _____

4. Whenever I'm in the basement and the landline rings. I don't run up to answer it. If the message is important. The person will call back.

   Whenever I'm in the basement and the phone rings, I don't run up to answer it. If

   the message is important, the person will call back.

   _____

5. Since she is a new student. Carla feels shy and insecure. She thinks she is the only person. Who doesn't know anyone else.

   Since she is a new student, Carla feels shy and insecure. She thinks she is the only person

   who doesn't know anyone else.

   _____

-ing and *to* Fragments

When a word ending in *-ing* or the word *to* appears at or near the start of a word group, a fragment may result. Such fragments often lack a subject and part of the verb.

Underline the word groups in the examples below that contain *-ing* words. Each is an *-ing* fragment.

EXAMPLE 1

I spent all day looking at online job boards. Trying to find a job that suited me. The prospects looked bleak.

EXAMPLE 2

DeShawn surprised Amos on the nature hike. Picking blobs of resin off pine trees. Then she chewed them like bubble gum.

EXAMPLE 3

Mel took an aisle seat on the bus. His reason being that he had more legroom.

People sometimes write *-ing* fragments because they think the subject in one sentence will work for the next word group as well. In the first example above, they might think the subject *I* in the opening sentence will also serve as the subject for "Trying to find a job that suited me." But the subject must actually be *in* the sentence.

HOW TO   Correct *-ing* Fragments

1. Attach the fragment to the sentence that comes before it or the sentence that comes after it, whichever makes sense. Example 1 above could read "I spent all day on job boards, trying to find a job that suited me." (Note that here a comma is used to set off "trying to find a job that suited me," which is extra material placed at the end of the sentence.)

2. Add a subject and change the *-ing* verb part to the correct form of the verb. Example 2 could read "She picked blobs of resin off pine trees."

3. Change *being* to the correct form of the verb *be (am, are, is, was, were)*. Example 3 could read "His reason was that he had more legroom."

HOW TO   Correct *to* Fragments

As noted earlier, when *to* appears at or near the start of a word group, a fragment sometimes results.

> To remind people of their selfishness. Otis leaves handwritten notes on cars that take up two parking spaces.

The first word group in the example above is a *to* fragment. It can be corrected by adding it to the sentence that comes after it.

> To remind people of their selfishness, Otis leaves handwritten notes on cars that take up two parking spaces.

(Note that here a comma is used to set off "To remind people of their selfishness," which is introductory material in the sentence.)

Underline the *-ing* fragment in each of the following selections. Then make the fragment a sentence by rewriting it, using the method described in parentheses.

PRACTICE 3

Teaching Tip
For these activities, you may want to go over the answers as a class. Ask students to discuss the choices they made to correct these fragments.

EXAMPLE

The dog eyed me with suspicion. Not knowing whether its master was at home. I hesitated to open the gate.

(Add the fragment to the sentence that comes after it.)

Not knowing whether its master was at home, I hesitated to open the gate.

1. Julie spent an hour at her desk. Staring at a blank piece of paper. She didn't know how to start her report.

(Add the fragment to the preceding sentence.)

Julie spent an hour at her desk, staring at a blank piece of paper.

2. Rummaging around in the kitchen drawer. Tyrone found the key he had misplaced a year ago.

(Add the fragment to the sentence that comes after it.)

Rummaging around in the kitchen drawer, Tyrone found the key he had misplaced

a year ago.

3. I went back to get a carton of Tropicana. As a result, losing my place in the checkout line.

(Add the subject *I* and change *losing* to the correct form of the verb, *lost.*)

As a result, I lost my place in the checkout line.

PRACTICE 4

Underline the *-ing* or *to* fragment in each item. Then rewrite the item correctly, using one of the methods of correction described on pages 98–103.

Rewritten versions may vary.

1. Last night, my bedroom was so hot I couldn't sleep. Tossing and turning for hours. I felt like a blanket being tumbled dry.

Tossing and turning for hours, I felt like a blanket being tumbled dry. Or:

I tossed and turned for hours.

2. A sparrow landed on the icy windowsill. Fluffing its feathers to keep itself warm.

A sparrow landed on the icy windowsill, fluffing its feathers to keep itself warm. Or:

It fluffed its feathers to keep itself warm.

3. Alma left the party early. The reason being that she had to work the next day.

Alma left the party early, the reason being that she had to work the next day. Or:

The reason was that she had to work the next day.

4. Grasping the balance beam with her powdered hands. The gymnast executed a handstand. Then she dismounted.

Grasping the balance beam with her powdered hands, the gymnast executed a handstand.

_____

_____

5. To cover his bald spot. Walt combed long strands of hair over the top of his head. Unfortunately, no one was fooled by this technique.

To cover his bald spot, Walt combed long strands of hair over the top of his head.

_____

_____

Added-Detail Fragments

Added-detail fragments lack a subject and a verb. They often begin with one of the following words or phrases.

also	except	including
especially	for example	such as

Underline the one added-detail fragment in each of these examples:

EXAMPLE 1

Tony has trouble accepting criticism. Except from Emma. She has a knack for tact.

EXAMPLE 2

My apartment has its drawbacks. For example, no hot water in the morning.

EXAMPLE 3

I had many jobs while in school. Among them, busser, painter, and security guard.

People often write added-detail fragments for much the same reason they write *-ing* fragments. They think the subject and verb in one sentence will serve for the next word group as well. But the subject and verb must be in *each* word group.

HOW TO   Correct Added-Detail Fragments

1. Attach the fragment to the complete thought that precedes it. Example 1 could read "Tony has trouble accepting criticism, except from Emma." (Note that here a comma is used to set off "except from Emma," which is extra material placed at the end of the sentence.)

2. Add a subject and a verb to the fragment to make it a complete sentence. Example 2 could read "My apartment has its drawbacks. For example, there is no hot water in the morning."

3. Change words as necessary to make the fragment part of the preceding sentence. Example 3 could read "Among the many jobs I had while in school were busser, painter, and security guard."

PRACTICE 5

Underline the fragment in each selection below. Then make it a sentence by rewriting it, using the method described in parentheses.

EXAMPLE

My husband and I share the household chores. Including meals. I do the cooking, and he does the eating.

(Add the fragment to the preceding sentence.)

My husband and I share the household chores, including meals.

_____

1. My father has some nervous habits. For instance, folding a strip of paper into the shape of an accordion.

(Correct the fragment by adding the subject *he* and changing *folding* to the proper form of the verb, *folds*.)

For instance, he folds a strip of paper into the shape of an accordion.

_____

2. Marco stuffed the large green peppers. With hamburger meat, cooked rice, and chopped parsley. Next, using toothpicks, he reattached the stemmed pepper tops.

(Add the fragment to the preceding sentence.)

Marco stuffed the large green peppers with hamburger meat, cooked rice, and

chopped parsley.

3. My little brother is addicted to junk foods. For example, Bugles and Doritos. If something is good for him, he won't eat it.

(Correct the fragment by adding the subject and verb *he craves*.)

For example, he craves Bugles and Doritos.

Underline the added-detail fragment in each selection. Then rewrite that part of the selection needed to correct the fragment. Use one of the three methods of correction described on page 106.

Answers may vary.

Teaching Tip
For these activities, you may want to go over the answers as a class. Ask students to discuss the choices that they made to correct these fragments.

1. My husband keeps all his old clothes. For instance, his faded sweatshirt from high school. He says it's the most comfortable thing he owns.

For instance, he has his faded sweatshirt from high school.

2. My sister has some very bad habits. For example, borrowing my sweaters. She also returns them without washing them.

For example, she borrows my sweaters.

3. To improve her singing, Amber practiced some odd exercises. Such as flapping her tongue and fluttering her lips.

To improve her singing, Amber practiced some odd exercises, such as flapping her tongue and fluttering her lips.

4. When she spotted her ex-husband, Leona left the party. She did not want him to see how much she had changed. For example, put on forty pounds.

For example, she had put on forty pounds.

5. Stanley wanted a big birthday cake. With candles spelling out STAN. He wanted to see his name in lights.

Stanley wanted a big birthday cake with candles spelling out STAN.

Missing-Subject Fragments

ESL Tip
Some non-native speakers will omit subject pronouns just as they do in their native languages. Another ESL error is to omit verbs, especially a form of the verb *to be*.

In each example below, underline the word group in which the subject is missing.

EXAMPLE 1

One example of my father's generosity is that he visits sick friends in the hospital. <u>And takes along get-well cards with a few dollars folded in them.</u>

EXAMPLE 2

The weight lifter grunted as he heaved the barbell into the air. <u>Then, with a loud groan, dropped it.</u>

People write missing-subject fragments because they think the subject in one sentence will apply to the next word group as well. But the subject, as well as the verb, must be in *each* word group to make it a sentence.

HOW TO Correct Missing-Subject Fragments

1. Attach the fragment to the preceding sentence. Example 1 could read "One illustration of my father's generosity is that he visits sick friends in the hospital and takes along get-well cards with a few dollars folded in them."
2. Add a subject (which can often be a pronoun standing for the subject in the preceding sentence). Example 2 could read "Then, with a loud groan, he dropped it."

PRACTICE 7

Underline the missing-subject fragment in each selection. Then rewrite that part of the selection to correct the fragment. Use one of the two methods of correction described above.

Rewritten versions may vary.

1. Embarrassed, Sandra looked around the laundromat. <u>Then quickly folded her raggedy towels and faded sheets.</u>

   Then she quickly folded her raggedy towels and faded sheets.

   _____

Teaching Tip
You may want to complete this activity as an entire class.

2. Michael took his wool sweaters out of storage. <u>And found them full of moth holes.</u>

   Wally took his wool sweaters out of storage and found them full of moth holes.

   _____

3. My sister is taking a web design course. Also, is learning two computer languages. Technology doesn't frighten her.

    Also, she is learning two computer languages.

    _____

4. When someone comes to the door, my dog races upstairs. Then hides under the bed. Strangers really terrify him.

    Then he hides under the bed.

    _____

5. A tiny bug crawled across my paper. And sat down in the middle of a sentence. There was suddenly one comma too many.

    A tiny bug crawled across my paper and sat down in the middle of a sentence.

    _____

A REVIEW

HOW TO   Check for Fragments

1. Read your paper aloud from the *last* sentence to the *first*. You will be better able to see and hear whether each word group you read is a complete thought.

2. If you think any word group is a fragment, ask yourself, Does this contain a subject and a verb and express a complete thought?

3. More specifically, be on the lookout for the most common fragments.
   - Dependent-word fragments (starting with words like *after, because, since, when,* and *before*)
   - *-ing* and *to* fragments (*-ing* or *to* at or near the start of a word group)
   - Added-detail fragments (starting with words like *for example, such as, also,* and *especially*)
   - Missing-subject fragments (a verb is present but not the subject)

Teaching Tip
Encourage students to use this checklist to correct their fragments. Introduce students to the correction symbol "frag" for fragments.

COLLABORATIVE ACTIVITY

Editing and Rewriting

Working with a partner, read the short paragraph below and underline the five fragments. Then correct the fragments. Feel free to discuss the rewrite quietly with your partner and refer back to the chapter when necessary.

Teaching Tip
Ask students to work on the Collaborative Activities in pairs and share their answers for the Reflective Activity with the entire class.

¹Did you ever wonder how trainers get porpoises to do all those tricks, like leaping over a high bar or jumping through a hoop? ²Wild porpoises are first taught to eat fish from their trainer's hand. ³The trainer blows a *whistle when* ~~whistle.~~ ⁴When the animal accepts a fish. ⁵The porpoise associates the whistle with "correct" behavior. ⁶Once the porpoise touches a human hand to get a fish, it will touch other *things, like* ~~things.~~ ⁷Like a red target ball. ⁸For example, the trainer will hold the ball high above the water while leaning over a kind of pulpit. ⁹Seeing the *ball, the* ~~ball.~~ ¹⁰The porpoise leaps out of the *water because* ~~water.~~ ¹¹Because it knows it will be rewarded with a fish. ¹²A hoop can then be substituted for a ball, and the porpoise's behavior can be "shaped" so it will jump through the hoop. ¹³If the porpoise misses the hoop by *low, the* jumping too ~~low.~~ ¹⁴The fish reward is withheld. ¹⁵The intelligent mammal will associate "no fish" with "wrong" behavior. ¹⁶Very quickly, the porpoise will be leaping gracefully through the center of the hoop.

COLLABORATIVE ACTIVITY

Creating Sentences

Working with a partner, make up your own short fragments test as directed. Write one or more of your sentences about the photo to the right.

Answers will vary.

1. Write a dependent-word fragment in the space below. Then correct the fragment by making it into a complete sentence. You may want to begin your fragment with the word *before*, *after*, *when*, *because*, or *if*.

Fragment _____

Sentence _____

2. Write an *-ing* fragment in the space below. Then correct the fragment by making it into a complete sentence. You may want to begin your fragment with the word *laughing, walking, shopping,* or *texting.*

Fragment _____

Sentence _____

3. Write an added-detail fragment in the space below. Then correct the fragment by making it into a complete sentence. You may want to begin your fragment with the word *also, especially, except,* or *including.*

Fragment _____

Sentence _____

REFLECTIVE ACTIVITY

1. Look at the paragraph about porpoises that you revised. How has removing fragments affected the reading of the paragraph? Explain.

2. Explain what it is about fragments that you find most difficult to remember and apply. Use an example to make your point clear. Feel free to refer to anything in this chapter.

REVIEW TEST 1

Turn each of the following word groups into a complete sentence. Use the space provided.

EXAMPLES

Feeling very confident

Feeling very confident, I began my speech. _____

Until the rain started

We played softball until the rain started. _____

1. Before you leave work today

_____

2. When the game show came on

_____

Teaching Tip
You may want to use these review tests to assess what your students have learned.

Answers will vary.

3. Since I have to gain some weight

_____

4. While I was looking in the store window

_____

5. Will be in town next week

_____

6. Jason, who has a terrible temper

_____

7. Down in the basement

_____

8. Flopping down on the couch

_____

9. Who fixed my car

_____

10. To wake up early

_____

REVIEW TEST 2

Underline the fragment in each selection. Then correct the fragment in the space provided.

EXAMPLE

Sam received all kinds of junk mail. Then complained to the post office. Eventually, some of the mail stopped coming.

Then he complained to the post office.

1. Since she was afraid of re-injuring her elbow. Lenka refused to go swimming.

Since she was afraid of re-injuring her elbow, Lenka refused to go swimming.

_____

2. The first time I took a college course, I was afraid to say anything in class. I didn't open my mouth. Not even to yawn.

I didn't open my mouth, not even to yawn.

_____

3. Looking like a large dish of vanilla fudge ice cream. Our brown-and-white cat went to sleep on the table.

Looking like a large dish of vanilla fudge ice cream, our brown-and-white cat went to sleep on the table.

4. Mei read that a sure sign of age is forgetting things. She wanted to show the article to her doctor. But couldn't remember where it was.

She wanted to show the article to her doctor but couldn't remember where it was.

5. Dave insisted on wearing a silly hat. That his girlfriend hated. It had two horns like a Viking helmet.

Dave insisted on wearing a silly hat that his girlfriend hated.

6. A box of frozen vegetables slipped out of Mark's grocery bag. And split open on the sidewalk. Little green peas rolled in every direction, while hard white onions bounced down the street.

A box of frozen vegetables slipped out of Mark's grocery bag and split open on the sidewalk.

7. Even though Laurie isn't disabled. She used to park in "handicapped only" parking spaces. After receiving several tickets, however, she gave up this selfish habit.

Even though Laurie isn't disabled, she used to park in "handicapped only" parking spaces.

8. Thinking that the Halloween get-together was a costume party. Viktor came dressed as a boxer. Unfortunately, the other guests were dressed normally.

Thinking that the Halloween get-together was a costume party, Viktor came dressed as a boxer.

9. My doctor is using disposable equipment. Such as paper examining gowns and plastic thermometers. She says these are more hygienic.

My doctor is using disposable equipment, such as paper examining gowns and plastic thermometers.

10. Ryan painted his house lemon-yellow. <u>With orange shutters and a lime-green roof.</u> People say his house looks like a fruit salad.

Ryan painted his house lemon-yellow, with orange shutters and a lime-green roof.

_____

REVIEW TEST 3

In the space provided, write *C* in front of the five word groups that are complete sentences; write *frag* in front of the five fragments. The first two items are done for you.

frag   1. As I was driving my car to work last Monday morning.

C   2. I saw an animal die.

C   3. It was a beautiful, breezy fall day.

frag   4. With colorful leaves swirling across the road.

C   5. Suddenly, a squirrel darted out from the bushes.

frag   6. And began zigzagging in the path of approaching cars.

C   7. Soundlessly, the car in front of me hit the animal.

frag   8. Sending its tiny gray-brown body flying off the road in a flurry of leaves.

C   9. After the incident, I thought about how fragile life is.

frag   10. And how easily and quickly it can be taken away.

Now correct the fragments you have found. Attach each fragment to the sentence that comes before or after it, or make whatever other change is needed to turn the fragment into a sentence. Use the space provided. The first one is corrected for you.

Wording of answers may vary.

1. *As I was driving my car to work last Monday morning, I saw an animal die.*

_____

2. *It was a beautiful, breezy fall day, with colorful leaves swirling across the road.*

3. *Suddenly, a squirrel darted out from the bushes and began zigzagging in the path of approaching cars.*

4. *Soundlessly, the car in front of me hit the animal, sending its tiny gray-brown body flying off the road in a flurry of leaves.*

5. *After the incident, I thought about how fragile life is and how easily and quickly it can be taken away.*

REVIEW TEST 4

Write quickly for five minutes about the high school you attended. Don't worry about spelling, punctuation, finding exact words, or organizing your thoughts. Just focus on writing as many words as you can without stopping.

After you have finished, go back and make whatever changes are needed to correct any fragments in your writing.

NAME: _____

DATE: _____

Fragments

Each word group in the student paragraph below is numbered. In the space provided, write C if a word group is a complete sentence; write frag *if it is a fragment. You will find ten fragments in the paragraph.*

1. ___C___

2. ___frag___

3. ___C___

4. ___frag___

5. ___C___

6. ___frag___

7. ___frag___

8. ___C___

9. ___frag___

10. ___C___

11. ___frag___

12. ___frag___

13. ___C___

14. ___C___

15. ___frag___

16. ___C___

17. ___C___

18. ___frag___

19. ___C___

20. ___frag___

¹One of my favorite dishes to cook and eat is chili. ²The hotter the better. ³First, I chop onion, garlic, and sweet red and green peppers into small cubes. ⁴While I fry the vegetables in one pan. ⁵I brown some lean ground beef in another pan. ⁶Then combine the two mixtures. ⁷And add a can of shiny red kidney beans. ⁸Next, I decide what kind of seasonings to use. ⁹In addition to chili powder, hot pepper flakes, and Tabasco sauce. ¹⁰I sometimes add unusual ingredients. ¹¹Like molasses, cinnamon, chocolate, beer, red wine, or raisins. ¹²Stirring the bubbling pot and inhaling the spicy aromas. ¹³I occasionally taste the mixture to make sure it's good. ¹⁴I cook the chili over a flame for as long as possible. ¹⁵To give the flavors time to mellow and blend together. ¹⁶Also, longer cooking time produces spicier chili. ¹⁷My chili has been known to burn people's tongues and cause beads of perspiration to form on their brows. ¹⁸And has made friends reach desperately for a glass of water. ¹⁹However, no one has ever complained. ²⁰Or forgotten to ask for a second helping.

NAME: _____

DATE: _____

Fragments

Underline the fragment in each item. Then make whatever changes are needed to turn the fragment into a sentence.

EXAMPLE

In grade school, I didn't want to wear glasses, And avoided having to get them by memorizing the eye chart.

1. Nita's sons kept opening and closing the refrigerator door, To see just when the little light inside went out.

2. Even though there are a million pigeons in the city, You never see a baby pigeon. It makes you wonder where they are hiding out.

3. Frank likes to get to work early, And spread papers all over his desk. Then he looks too busy to be given any more work.

4. Brenda's doctor warned her to cut out sweets, Especially ice cream and candy.

5. Dragging her feet in the paper slippers, The patient shuffled along the corridor. She hugged the wall closely as nurses and visitors bustled past her.

6. The children ignored the sign, That the lifeguard had posted. They raced around on the slick cement bordering the pool.

7. Pete did not flunk out of college, After only two semesters. He proved he could pass more than just a football.

8. My neighbors' dog likes to borrow things. Today, I saw him trotting away from my back steps, Carrying one of my gardening shoes in his mouth.

9. Since cooking with a small toaster oven saves energy, I bought one to use for small meals and snacks.

10. My cousin e-mails me funny cards, Such as one with a picture of a lion hanging on to a parachute. It says, "Just thought I'd drop you a lion."

NAME: _____

DATE: _____

MASTERY TEST 3

Fragments

Underline the fragment in each item. Then make whatever changes are needed to turn the fragment into a sentence.

1. As Ranjit twisted the front doorknob, It came off in his hand. He regretted the day he had bought the house as a "do-it-yourself special."

2. Large, spiky plants called *Spanish spears* bordered the path. The leaves brushed against my legs, And left little slash marks on my ankles.

3. Tim stockpiles canned and dried foods in his basement, In case of emergency. Some of his soup is eight years old.

4. At the amusement park, we piled into a boat shaped like a hollowed-out log. Then, gripping the boat's sides and screaming in fear, We plunged through clouds of spray down a water-filled chute.

5. At the lumberyard, Clarence loaded his compact car, With ten-foot planks of raw pine. The car's open hatchback bounced and vibrated as he drove away.

6. Before the newly painted parking stripes had dried, Cars had begun driving over them. As a result, the lot was crisscrossed with pale white lines.

7. My father used to take me to base-ball games. He would always bring along a newspaper, To read between innings.

8. When Lucas goes on vacation, he fills the bathtub with an inch of water, Then puts his houseplants in the tub. This way, they don't die of thirst.

9. Terry wears her iPhone headphones everywhere she goes. For example, to the bookstore. She can't survive for ten minutes without her favorite songs.

10. The perfect shell glittered on the ocean bottom. The diver lifted it off the sand, And placed it in the bag hanging from his shoulder.

NAME: _____

DATE: _____

Fragments

Underline and then correct the five fragments in the following passage.

Did you know that one in every five children is overweight? If you think that these kids will simply outgrow their "baby fat," You're wrong. The number of overweight children in this country has doubled in the past twenty years, Creating a health epidemic. Too many children spend hours watching television, And playing video games when they should be outside playing. They consume sugary, high-calorie snacks, When they should be eating fresh fruits and low-fat yogurt. These children are at a higher risk for high cholesterol, high blood pressure, and type 2 diabetes. They are also more likely to miss school, endure teasing from their peers, and develop low self-esteem. These problems often follow them through adolescence and into adulthood. Sadly, overweight kids have a 70 percent greater chance of becoming overweight adults. Everyone, however, can make a difference, By being a positive role model. So live a healthy life. Turn off your television and take a twenty-minute walk.

NAME: _____

DATE: _____

Fragments

Underline and then correct the ten fragments in the following passage.

This summer, I discovered that nature offers some surprises to people. Who take the time to look and listen. After I began an exercise program of walking quickly a half hour a day, I soon slowed down because the world around me was so interesting. For one thing, *I became* becoming aware of the richness of the bird and animal life around me. I saw a robin with strands of newspaper in his mouth. And realized it was building a nest in a nearby tree. A family of quail exploded from hiding as I skirted a brushy field. I began to connect the birdsongs I heard with individual birds. For instance, I now know the lonely call of a mourning dove. And the happy buzz of a chickadee. After it rained, I discovered that creatures I have never seen before live in my neighborhood. In the mud beside my walking paths were various tracks. Among them, paws, hooves, and scaly feet. I also found that little dramas were taking place all the time. And that there are some grim moments in nature. I saw a swarm of maggots covering a dead mouse. I also came upon a fat snake spread across the path. I prodded it with a stick. To see if it would move. It shocked me by coughing up an entire frog. My walks have taught me there is a great deal to discover. When I open my eyes and ears.

Run-Ons

CHAPTER 8

INTRODUCTORY ACTIVITY

A run-on occurs when two sentences are run together with no adequate sign given to mark the break between them. Shown below are four run-on sentences and four correctly marked sentences. Complete the statement that explains how each run-on is corrected.

1. A man coughed in the movie theater the result was a chain reaction of copycat coughing.   *Run-on*

   A man coughed in the movie theater. The result was a chain reaction of copycat coughing.   *Correct*

The run-on has been corrected by using a ___*period*___ and a capital letter to separate the two complete thoughts.

2. I heard laughter inside the house, no one answered the bell.   *Run-on*

   I heard laughter inside the house, but no one answered the bell.   *Correct*

The run-on has been corrected by using a joining word, ___*but*___, to connect the two complete thoughts.

3. A car sped around the corner, it sprayed slush all over the pedestrians.   *Run-on*

   A car sped around the corner; it sprayed slush all over the pedestrians.   *Correct*

The run-on has been corrected by using a ___*semicolon*___ to connect the two closely related thoughts.

4. I had a campus map and a smartphone, I still could not find my classroom building.   *Run-on*

   Although I had a campus map and a smartphone, I still could not find my classroom building.   *Correct*

The run-on has been corrected by using the dependent word ___*although*___ to connect the two closely related thoughts.

Answers are on page 635.

Teaching Tip
You may want to use this activity to assess your students' understanding of run-ons.

ESL Tip
Nonnative
speakers do
not always
know about
sentence
boundaries
in English. In
an attempt
to combine
simple sen-
tences, they
may write run-
ons. They need
to learn to use
appropriate
connectors
and correct
punctuation.

ESL Tip
Nonnative
speakers may
use *now* or
then as a
conjunction to
connect simple
sentences.

What Are Run-Ons?

A *run-on* is two complete thoughts that are run together with no adequate sign given to mark the break between them. As a result of the run-on, the reader is confused, unsure of where one thought ends and the next one begins. Two types of run-ons are fused sentences and comma splices.

Some run-ons have no punctuation at all to mark the break between the thoughts. Such run-ons are known as *fused sentences:* they are fused or joined together as if they were only one thought.

FUSED SENTENCE

Rosa decided to stop smoking she didn't want to die of lung cancer.

The exam was postponed the class was canceled as well.

In other run-ons, known as *comma splices*, a comma is used to connect or "splice" together the two complete thoughts.* However, a comma alone is not enough to connect two complete thoughts. Some connection stronger than a comma alone is needed.

COMMA SPLICE

Rosa decided to stop smoking, she didn't want to die of lung cancer.

The exam was postponed, the class was canceled as well.

Comma splices are the most common kind of run-on. Students sense that some kind of connection is needed between thoughts, so they put a comma at the dividing point. But the comma alone is not sufficient. A stronger, clearer mark is needed between the two thoughts.

A Warning: Words That Can Lead to Run-Ons

People often write run-ons when the second complete thought begins with one of the following words. Be on the alert for run-ons whenever you use them in your writing.

I	we	there	now
you	they	this	then
he, she, it		that	next

Notes:
1. Some instructors feel that the term *run-ons* should be applied only to fused sentences, not to comma splices. Other instructors, and for our purposes in this book, the term *run-on* applies equally to fused sentences and comma splices. The bottom line is that you do not want either fused sentences or comma splices in your writing.
2. Some instructors refer to each complete thought in a run-on as an *independent clause*. A *clause* is simply a group of words having a subject and a verb. A clause may be *independent* (expressing a complete thought and able to stand alone) or *dependent* (not expressing a complete thought and not able to stand alone). A run-on is two independent clauses that are run together with no adequate sign given to mark the break between them.

Correcting Run-Ons

Here are four common methods of correcting a run-on:

1. Use a period and a capital letter to separate the two complete thoughts. (In other words, make two separate sentences of the two complete thoughts.)

   Rosa decided to stop smoking. She didn't want to die of lung cancer.

   The exam was postponed. The class was canceled as well.

2. Use a comma plus a joining word (*and, but, for, or, nor, so, yet*) to connect the two complete thoughts.

   Rosa decided to stop smoking, for she didn't want to die of lung cancer.

   The exam was postponed, and the class was canceled as well.

3. Use a semicolon to connect the two complete thoughts.

   Rosa decided to stop smoking; she didn't want to die of lung cancer.

   The exam was postponed; the class was canceled as well.

4. Use subordination (put a dependent word at the beginning of one word group).

   Because Rosa didn't want to die of lung cancer, she decided to stop smoking.

   When the exam was postponed, the class was canceled as well.

Teaching Tip
You may want to review semi-colons with your students.

Teaching Tip
You may want to provide several more examples of subordination for your students.

The following pages will give you practice in all four methods of correcting run-ons. The use of subordination will be explained further on page 149, in a chapter that deals with sentence variety.

Method 1: Period and a Capital Letter

One way of correcting a run-on is to use a period and a capital letter at the break between the two complete thoughts. Use this method especially if the thoughts are not closely related or if another method would make the sentence too long.

Locate the split in each of the following run-ons. Each is a *fused sentence*—that is, each consists of two sentences fused or joined together with no punctuation at all between them. Reading each sentence aloud will help you "hear" where a major break or split in the thought occurs. At such a point, your voice will probably drop and pause.

Correct the run-on by putting a period at the end of the first thought and a capital letter at the start of the second thought.

PRACTICE 1

Teaching Tip
For this activity, read each sentence aloud as your students make corrections.

EXAMPLE

Craig was not a success at his job. *H*/his mouth moved faster than his hands.

1. Michael gulped two cups of strong coffee. *H*/his heart then started to flutter.

2. Elena defrosted the freezer in her usual impatient way. *S*/she hacked at the thick ice with a screwdriver.

3. The engine was sputtering and coughing. *A*/a strong smell of gas came from under the hood.

4. A bright yellow Volkswagen Beetle pulled up beside me. *I*/it looked like a deviled egg on wheels.

5. The phone in the next apartment rings all the time. *T*/the new tenants keep complaining about the sound.

6. Numbered Ping-Pong balls bounced in the machine. *W*/we clutched our raffle tickets tightly.

7. The store clerk watched the girls closely. *T*/they must have looked like shoplifters to her.

8. It's hard to discuss things with Lauren. *S*/she interprets almost everything as criticism.

9. Kate's books look like accident victims. *T*/they have cracked spines and torn covers.

10. I got to the sale too late. *T*/the last ceiling fan had been sold just five minutes before.

PRACTICE 2

Locate the split in each of the following run-ons. Some of the run-ons are fused sentences, and some of them are *comma splices*—run-ons spliced or joined together only with a comma. Correct each run-on by putting a period at the end of the first thought and a capital letter at the start of the next thought.

1. Human teenagers must be descended from cockroaches, *B*/both like to stay out late and eat junk food.

2. Only the female mosquito drinks blood. *T*/the male lives on plant juices.

3. Sonja has the experience to be an excellent marriage counselor. *S*/she's already been married four times.

4. My uncle's final words probably express everyone's feeling about death. *H*/he said, "Wait a minute."

5. I remember every rainbow I've ever seen. *O*/one actually circled the sun.

6. The beach was once beautiful. *N*/now it is covered with cans, plastic six-pack rings, and cigarette butts.

7. In eighteenth-century Russia, smoking carried a death penalty. *T* the same is true of chain-smoking today.

8. The business school near our home just closed down. *I* it ran out of money.

9. The frankfurter or hot dog did not begin in Germany, *I* in fact, it first appeared in China.

10. The man about to become vegan had a last request. *H* he wanted a grilled cheese sandwich.

Write a second sentence to go with each sentence below. Start the second sentence with the word given in the margin.

Answers will vary.

EXAMPLE

It   My wireless all-in-one printer is so convenient. *It allows me to print, scan, copy, and fax documents.*

Then   1. The oysters were placed on the grill until their shells popped open.

It   2. I need to update the operating system on my computer. _____

She   3. Ashlee sent me several urgent texts last night. _____

They   4. Students who take studio art classes spend hours on their projects.

There   5. After the recent oil spill, people were afraid to swim in the ocean.

Method 2: Comma and a Joining Word

Another way of correcting a run-on is to use a comma plus a joining word to connect the two complete thoughts. Joining words (also called *coordinating conjunctions*) include *and, but, for, or, nor, so,* and *yet.* The meaning of the four most common joining words is explained below.

and   in addition, along with

Serena was watching *Monday Night Football,* and she was doing her homework.

(*And* means *in addition:* Serena was watching *Monday Night Football; in addition,* she was doing her homework.)

Teaching Tip Caution students against using the word *and* too often to join complete thoughts.

ESL Tip
Nonnative speakers need to learn the usage of coordinating conjunctions and the required punctuation. The comma precedes the conjunction.

Teaching Tip
You might also tell students that clauses that can be logically joined with *for* are easily combined with a semicolon.

but   however, except, on the other hand, just the opposite

I voted for the mayor two years ago, but I would not vote for him today.

(*But* means *however:* I voted for the mayor two years ago; *however,* I would not vote for him today.)

for   because, the reason that, the cause for something

Saturday is the worst day to shop, for people jam the stores.

(*For* means *because:* Saturday is the worst day to shop *because* people jam the stores.) If you are not comfortable using *for,* you may want to use *because* instead of *for* in the activities that follow. If you do use *because,* omit the comma before it.

so   as a result, therefore

Our son misbehaved again, so he was sent upstairs without dessert.

(*So* means *as a result:* our son misbehaved again; *as a result,* he was sent upstairs without dessert.)

| PRACTICE 4 | Insert the comma and the joining word (*and, but, for, so*) that logically connects the two thoughts in each sentence. |

Teaching Tip
For this activity, read each sentence aloud as your students make corrections.

EXAMPLE

I hate to see animals in cages, *so* a trip to the zoo always depresses me.

1. We knew the old desk had a secret drawer, *but* no one could find it.

2. I had to retype my term paper, *for* my little boy had scrawled on it with a purple crayon.

3. Last year my nephew needed physical therapy, *so* the whole family pitched in to work with him.

4. My new hybrid is a pleasure to drive, *and* it gets terrific mileage.

5. A cat food commercial came on, *and* Marie started to sing along with the jingle.

6. It rained a lot this summer, *so* we have not had to water our lawn.

7. I heard the grinding of the garbage truck, *so* I ran downstairs and grabbed the trash bags.

8. Ella wanted to take a break, *but* the boss wanted the inventory list right away.

9. The map was faded, *and* an ink stain had blotted out an entire country.

10. The two little boys had a giggling fit, *so* their father hustled them out of the church.

Add a complete, closely related thought to each of the following statements. When you write the second thought, use a comma plus the joining word shown at the left.

PRACTICE 5

Answers will vary.

EXAMPLE

but   I was sick with the flu, _but I still had to study for the test._

so   1. I couldn't resist the banana cream pie _____

_____

but   2. We tried to follow the directions _____

_____

and   3. Jamal took three coffee breaks before lunch _____

_____

for   4. The car seat was drenched _____

_____

but   5. I don't usually pick up hitchhikers _____

_____

Method 3: Semicolon

A third method of correcting a run-on is to use a semicolon to mark the break between two thoughts. A *semicolon* (;) is made up of a period above a comma and is sometimes called a *strong comma*. The semicolon signals more of a pause than a comma alone but not quite the full pause of a period.

Occasional use of semicolons can add variety to sentences. For some people, however, the semicolon is a confusing mark of punctuation. Keep in mind that, if you are not comfortable using it, you can and should use one of the first two methods of correcting a run-on sentence.

Semicolon Alone

Here are some earlier sentences that were connected with a comma plus a joining word. Now they are connected with a semicolon. Notice that a semicolon, unlike a comma, can be used alone to connect the two complete thoughts in each sentence.

Serena was watching *Monday Night Football;* she was doing her homework as well.

I voted for the mayor two years ago; I would not vote for him today.

Saturday is the worst day to shop; people jam the stores.

Teaching Tip
Write "Complete thought; complete thought" on the board, and then circle the semicolon. Stress that both thoughts in the sentence must be complete.

ESL Tip
The semicolon is often used differently in other languages. Non-native speakers would benefit from comparing its usage in their native language.

Insert a semicolon where the break occurs between the two complete thoughts in each of the following sentences.

EXAMPLE

She had a wig on; it looked more like a hat than a wig.

1. Alan had to go up the ramp backward; his wheelchair's strongest gear is reverse.
2. A cockroach is almost indestructible; it can live for weeks with its head cut off.
3. Pat read the funny birthday cards; she laughed aloud in the quiet store.
4. My brother captured the fluttering moth; it bumped around inside his hands.
5. Alex couldn't finish the book; it was giving him nightmares.

Semicolon with a Transition

A semicolon is sometimes used with a transitional word and a comma to join two complete thoughts:

I figured that the movie would cost me about ten dollars; however, I didn't consider the high price of food and drinks.

Fred and Martha have a low-interest mortgage on their house; otherwise, they would move to another neighborhood.

Sharon didn't understand the instructor's point; therefore, she asked him to repeat it.

TIP   Sometimes transitional words do not join complete thoughts but are merely interrupters in a sentence (see page 125).

My parents, moreover, plan to go on the trip.

I believe, however, that they'll change their minds.

Transitional Words

Here is a list of common transitional words (also known as *adverbial conjunctions*).

Common Transitional Words

however	moreover	therefore
on the other hand	in addition	as a result
nevertheless	also	consequently
instead	furthermore	otherwise

For each item, choose a logical transitional word from the box above and write it in the space provided. In addition, put a semicolon *before* the transition and a comma *after* it.

PRACTICE 7

Answers may vary.

ESL Tip
Nonnative speakers may need to learn the meanings of transitional words. Some may also use the wrong preposition (e.g., "*in* the other hand") or the wrong article (e.g., "as *the* result").

EXAMPLE

It was raining harder than ever ___*; however,*___ Bobby was determined to go to the amusement park.

1. Most people can do without food for a month ___*; on the other hand,*___ they need two quarts of water a day to survive.

2. Jean's son was sick ___*; therefore,*___ she did his chores for him.

3. Linda felt safe living near a fire hydrant ___*; however,*___ she wished that the neighborhood dogs didn't like it so much.

4. The bride's father apologized to the waiting guests ___*; furthermore,*___ he promised to return all the wedding gifts.

5. Andrea thinks gift-wrapping paper is a waste of money ___*; consequently,*___ she wraps presents in newspaper.

Punctuate each sentence by using a semicolon and a comma.

PRACTICE 8

Teaching Tip
Introduce students to the correction symbol "r-o" for a run-on and "cs" for a comma splice.

EXAMPLE

A band rehearses in the garage next door*; as a result,* I'm thinking of moving.

1. The hostess told us there would be a twenty-minute wait*; however,* she then seated the couple who came in after us.

2. Ricki knows nothing about computers*; as a result,* she decided to sign up for a programming course.

3. All too many children are emotionally abused*; moreover,* many are physically abused as well.

4. I insisted that my wife stop smoking*; otherwise,* I would have suffered the effects of the secondhand smoke from her cigarettes.

5. We packed the groceries carefully*; nevertheless,* the bread was squashed and two eggs were broken.

Method 4: Subordination

ESL Tip
Nonnative
speakers may
write depen-
dent clauses as
complete sen-
tences because
they hear them
used in spoken
English. Some
languages
consider
dependent
clauses accept-
able in written
form.

A fourth method of joining related thoughts is to use subordination. *Subordination* is a way of showing that one thought in a sentence is not as important as another thought. Here are three sentences in which one idea is subordinated to (made less emphatic than) the other idea:

Because Rosa didn't want to die of lung cancer, she decided to stop smoking.

The wedding reception began to get out of hand when the guests started to throw food at each other.

Although my brothers wanted to watch a *Community* rerun, the rest of the family insisted on turning to the network news.

Dependent Words

Notice that, when we subordinate, we use dependent words like *because, when,* and *although.* Following is a brief list of common dependent words (see also the list on page 98). Subordination is explained in full on pages 130–31.

> ### Common Dependent Words
>
> | after | before | unless |
> |---|---|---|
> | although | even though | until |
> | as | if | when |
> | because | since | while |

PRACTICE 9   Choose a logical dependent word from the box above and write it in the space provided.

Teaching Tip
Read each
sentence
aloud as
your students
provide the
answers.

EXAMPLE

Although going up a ladder is easy, looking down can be difficult.

1. _After_ an emotional reunion between a mother and son, the talk-show host took a moment to thank the show's sponsor, a maker of chewing gum.

2. You should have looked at the label _before_ you washed that wool sweater.

3. _When_ the instructor announced that there were only ten minutes left in the test, students began writing even more quickly to finish their essay answers.

4. _If_ you open the windows, the paint fumes will disappear more quickly.

5. The directions say to continue on the main highway _until_ a large red barn and a small road appear on the right.

Rewrite the five sentences below so that one idea is subordinate to the other. In each case, use one of the dependent words from the box on the previous page.

> **HINT** As in the example, use a comma if a dependent statement starts a sentence.

EXAMPLE

I hate to see animals in cages; a trip to the zoo always depresses me.

Because I hate to see animals in cages, a trip to the zoo always depresses me.

Answers may vary.

1. I had a campus map and a smartphone; I still could not find my classroom building.

   Even though I had a campus map, I still could not find my classroom. building.

2. A cat food commercial came on; Marie started to sing along with the jingle.

   When a cat food commercial came on, Marie started to sing along with the jingle.

3. The phone in the next apartment rings constantly; I'm beginning to get used to the sound.

   Since the phone in the next apartment rings constantly, I'm beginning to get used to the sound.

4. Michael gulped two cups of strong coffee; his heart began to flutter.

   After Michael gulped two cups of strong coffee, his heart began to flutter.

5. A car sped around the corner; it sprayed slush all over the pedestrians.

   As a car sped around the corner, it sprayed slush all over the pedestrians.

COLLABORATIVE ACTIVITY

Editing and Rewriting

Working with a partner, carefully read the short paragraph below and underline the five run-ons. Then correct them. Feel free to discuss the corrections quietly with your partner and refer back to the chapter when necessary.

Wording of answers may vary.

Teaching Tip Ask students to work on the Collaborative Activities in pairs and share their answers for the Reflective Activity with the entire class.

¹People do funny things when they get on an elevator. ²They try to move into a corner or against a wall. ³They all face forward *forward, and their* their hands are kept in front or at their sides. ⁴Most of all, they avoid eye contact with the other passengers, preferring to stare at the floor numbers or tiny TV screens. ⁵Nobody teaches these people how to behave on an elevator *elevator; however,* however, everyone seems to obey the same rules. ⁶Psychologists have a theory about elevator behavior that they feel explains these actions. ⁷Elevators are small, enclosed spaces *spaces. They* they force people into contact with one another. ⁸The contact is a violation of a person's "personal space" *space." This* this is the invisible shield we all carry with us. ⁹We get nervous when a stranger stands too close to us *us. We* we want to put that invisible shield back. ¹⁰Therefore, an elevator isn't the place to try to get to know someone.

COLLABORATIVE ACTIVITY

Creating Sentences

Working with a partner, make up your own short run-ons test as directed.

1. Write a run-on sentence. Then rewrite it, using a period and capital letter to separate the thoughts into two sentences.

Answers will vary.

Run-on _____

_____

Rewrite _____

_____

2. Write a sentence that has two complete thoughts. Then rewrite it, using a comma and a joining word to correctly join the complete thoughts.

Two complete thoughts _____

_____

Rewrite _____

_____

3. Write a sentence that has two complete thoughts. Then rewrite it, using a semicolon to correctly join the complete thoughts.

Two complete thoughts _____

_____

Rewrite _____

_____

REFLECTIVE ACTIVITY

1. Look at the paragraph about elevators that you revised. Explain how run-ons interfered with your reading of the paragraph.

2. In your own written work, which type of run-on are you more likely to write: comma splices or fused sentences? Why?

3. Which method of correcting run-ons are you most likely to use in your own writing? Which are you least likely to use? Why?

REVIEW TEST 1

Some of the run-ons that follow are *fused sentences*, having no punctuation between the two complete thoughts; others are *comma splices*, having only a comma between the two complete thoughts.

Correct the run-ons by using one of the following three methods:

- Period and a capital letter
- Comma and a joining word (*and, but, for, so*)
- Semicolon

Use whichever method seems most appropriate in each case.

Teaching Tip
You may want to use these review tests to assess what your students have learned.

EXAMPLE

                               and

    Haru pulled the cellophane off the cake, the icing came along with it.

Answers will vary.

                      but
1. The runner was called safe, even she couldn't believe it.

                                               A
2. I looked all over for my new shirt. all I could find was the empty bag.

                                         but
3. Patrick tried to fold the road map neatly, he gave up and stuffed it into the glove compartment.

                                           ;
4. First we can't wait to go on vacation, then we can't wait to come home again.

                                so
5. One step was sagging, Martina hired a carpenter to fix the porch.

                                         . T
6. I ran toward the supermarket, the manager had just locked the doors.

                                  but
7. Ted tried to assemble the barbecue, the instructions were impossible to understand.

8. I reached into the pretzel bag, all that was left was salt.

                            so
9. Tina was starving, she bought a limp sandwich from the vending machine.

                              S
10. Bev was bored. she drew rocket ships in the margins of her notebook.

REVIEW TEST 2

Correct the run-on in each sentence by using subordination. Choose from among the following dependent words.

after	before	unless
although	even though	until
as	if	when
because	since	while

EXAMPLE

    Dexter hated going to a new stylist, he was afraid of butchered hair.

    Because Dexter was afraid of butchered hair, he hated going to a new stylist.

_____

Answers will vary.

1. The fan started throwing beer cans onto the field security guards hustled him away.

    Because the fan started throwing beer cans onto the field, security guards hustled

    him away.

2. I had three cups of coffee, my eyes looked like huge globes.

   After I had three cups of coffee, my eyes looked like huge globes

3. The boy didn't want to talk to his mother, he pretended to be asleep.

   Because the boy didn't want to talk to his mother, he pretended to be asleep.

4. The check arrived in the mail we didn't really believe that we had won the contest.

   Until the check arrived in the mail, we didn't really believe that we had won the contest.

5. I forgot to put an SD card in my phone, the only pictures we have of our vacation are the ones in our memory.

   Since we forgot to put an SD card in my phone, the only pictures we have of our vacation are the ones in our memory.

6. I left school this afternoon hailstones as big as marbles were falling from the sky.

   When I left school this afternoon, hailstones as big as marbles were falling from the sky.

7. The plumber comes quickly our kitchen will look like a swamp.

   Unless the plumber comes quickly, our kitchen will look like a swamp.

8. The man circled the crowded parking lot in their car, his wife ran into the store to return a sweater.

   While the man circled the crowded parking lot in their car, his wife ran into the store to return a sweater.

9. The boy was wearing headphones nearly everyone on the bus could hear the beat of his playlist.

   Even though the boy was wearing headphones, nearly everyone on the bus could hear the beat of his playlist.

10. The computer went dead a message appeared on the screen saying, "System error."

    Before the computer went dead, a message appeared on the screen saying, "System error."

REVIEW TEST 3

On separate sheet of paper or in a new file, write six sentences, each having two complete thoughts. In two of the sentences, use a period and a capital letter between the thoughts. In another two sentences, use a comma and a joining word (*and, but, or, nor, for, so, yet*) to join the thoughts. In the final two sentences, use a semicolon to join the thoughts.

REVIEW TEST 4

Write quickly for five minutes about something that makes you angry. Don't worry about spelling, punctuation, finding exact words, or organizing your thoughts. Just focus on writing as many words as you can without stopping.

After you have finished, go back and make whatever changes are needed to correct any run-on sentences in your writing.

Run-Ons

In the space provided, write R-O *beside run-on sentences and* C *beside sentences that are punctuated correctly. Some of the run-ons have no punctuation between the two complete thoughts; others have only a comma.*

    Correct each run-on by using (1) a period and a capital letter, (2) a comma and a joining word, or (3) a semicolon. Do not use the same method of correction in every sentence.

Methods of
correction will
vary.

EXAMPLES

_____R-O_____ I applied for the job, *but* I never got called in for an interview.

_____R-O_____ Carla's toothache is getting worse, *; S* she should go to a dentist soon.

_____R-O_____ 1. This year's company picnic was not a success, *for* it attracted more bears than people.

_____R-O_____ 2. Chang is allergic to anything green, *. E* even houseplants make him sneeze.

_____R-O_____ 3. I was falling asleep in a hurry, I couldn't keep my eyes open any longer.

_____R-O_____ 4. Don't try to hand-feed the sharks, *Y* you could end up feeding them more than your hand.

_____C_____ 5. These days, getting married is a risky business, for over half of all marriages end in divorce.

_____R-O_____ 6. We quickly switched from one news program to another, *but* each one had the same story.

_____R-O_____ 7. An accident had happened on the bridge, *. T* traffic was backed up in both directions.

_____R-O_____ 8. On long car trips, my little brother drives me crazy, *. H* he insists on reading all the road signs out loud.

_____R-O_____ 9. Harold always finishes the ice cream, *, and* then he puts the empty carton back in the freezer.

_____C_____ 10. It was too hot indoors to read, so I took my book onto the front porch.

NAME: _____

DATE: _____

MASTERY TEST 2

Run-Ons

In the space provided, write R-O beside run-on sentences. Write C beside the one sentence that is punctuated correctly. Some of the run-ons have no punctuation between the two complete thoughts; others have only a comma.

Methods of correction will vary.

Correct each run-on by using (1) a period and capital letter, (2) a comma and joining word, or (3) a semicolon. Do not use the same method of correction for every sentence.

_____R-O_____ 1. I work for about two hours on my homework. I then spend about an hour watching television.

_____R-O_____ 2. Sheets of heavy rain were pounding against my car windshield, so I pulled over to the side of the road.

_____R-O_____ 3. A bus pulled away slowly from the curb. An elderly woman ran after it, waving her hand for it to stop.

_____R-O_____ 4. Our apartment gets really cold at night; the landlord refuses to turn up the heat.

_____R-O_____ 5. The little boy was struggling with the top of the candy bag. It suddenly tore open and spilled Skittles all over the floor.

_____R-O_____ 6. Dozens of restaurants open in the city every year, but almost that many go out of business.

_____C_____ 7. I got out of the shower to answer my phone, but it stopped ringing as soon as I touched it.

_____R-O_____ 8. The breakfast cereal is "new and improved"; it doesn't taste any different to me.

_____R-O_____ 9. The line at the cash register wasn't moving. The cashier seemed to have gone home.

_____R-O_____ 10. Several homeless men live under the bridge, so their sleeping bags and shopping carts are always there.

Run-Ons

In the space provided, write R-O beside run-on sentences. Write C beside the one sentence that is punctuated correctly. Some of the run-ons have no punctuation between the two complete thoughts; others have only a comma.

Correct each run-on by using (1) a period and capital letter, (2) a comma and joining word, or (3) a semicolon. Do not use the same method of correction for every sentence.

Methods of correction will vary.

_____R-O_____ 1. Americans spend millions of dollars each year on bottled water, *but* critics argue that tap water is equally safe to drink.

_____R-O_____ 2. Isaiah is confident that the trucking company will hire him *;* he has a valid CDL license and a clean traffic abstract.

_____R-O_____ 3. The mechanic said that many hybrid cars have transmission problems, *so* I am glad that I purchased a gasoline-powered subcompact car, which is equally fuel efficient.

_____R-O_____ 4. This summer brought record-breaking drought conditions, *. M* many farmers are being forced to plant fewer crops or irrigate their fields.

_____R-O_____ 5. Sydney decided to use recycled plastic to build an outdoor deck, *so* her children asked her to build a doghouse with the extra lumber.

_____R-O_____ 6. Mark worried when the canned chili sauce he ate while on his camping trip was recalled for botulism, *but* he did not experience any symptoms of food poisoning.

_____R-O_____ 7. Parents who sign up their children for martial arts hope that the study will provide physical exercise, self-confidence, and personal discipline, *. T* their children, however, say that they are simply having fun.

_____C_____ 8. The Ladies Professional Golf Association (LPGA) was founded in 1950, making it the oldest female professional sports organization in the United States.

_____R-O_____ 9. Witnesses reported that the bank robber was a woman, *but* security cameras revealed that the thief was a man carrying a handbag and wearing a wig and lipstick.

_____R-O_____ 10. Today, the average American teenager works sixteen hours per week *;* parents and educators are concerned that these part-time jobs leave little time for homework or sleep.

NAME: _____

DATE: _____

Run-Ons

In the space provided, write R-O beside run-on sentences. Write C beside the one sentence that is punctuated correctly. Some of the run-ons have no punctuation between the two complete thoughts; others have only a comma.

Methods of correction will vary.

Correct each run-on by using (1) a period and a capital letter, (2) a comma and joining word, or (3) a semicolon. Do not use the same method of correction for every sentence.

_____R-O_____ 1. Flora carried heavy trays all day long*;* her feet felt like hundred-pound lead weights.

_____C_____ 2. The young man paced anxiously while the laundry circled lazily in the dryer.

_____R-O_____ 3. The musician strummed her most popular song*, and* the crowd waved their phones and chanted the words along with her.

_____R-O_____ 4. That man has a million-dollar company*, but* he prefers to wear a stained T-shirt and torn jeans.

_____R-O_____ 5. I finished writing the paper for my English class*, so* I started reading and taking notes on a chapter in my psychology text.

_____R-O_____ 6. The detective burst into the crowded party*;* he announced that he knew the murderer's identity.

_____R-O_____ 7. Chicken and dumplings were cooking on the stove*. W*e set the table for dinner.

_____R-O_____ 8. Sid is trying to smoke less*;* he cut all his cigarettes in half and can smoke only one of those an hour.

_____R-O_____ 9. It was a beautiful springtime day full of sunshine and soft breezes*, but* the park was strangely empty.

_____R-O_____ 10. Raoul sat on his sofa staring out at the cold, gray snow*. H*e wondered what it would be like to live in Hawaii.

Sentence Variety I

This chapter will show you how to write effective and varied sentences. You'll learn more about two techniques—subordination and coordination—that you can use to expand simple sentences, making them more interesting and expressive. You'll also reinforce what you learned in Chapters 7 and 8 about how subordination and coordination can help you correct fragments and run-ons in your writing.

Four Traditional Sentence Patterns

Sentences in English are traditionally described as *simple, compound, complex,* or *compound-complex.* Each is explained below.

The Simple Sentence

A simple sentence has a single subject-verb combination.

> Children play.
>
> The game ended early.
>
> My car stalled three times last week.
>
> The lake has been polluted by several neighboring streams.

A simple sentence may have more than one subject:

> Afton and Julia drove home.
> The wind and sun dried my hair.

or more than one verb:

> The children smiled and waved at us.
> The lawn mower smoked and sputtered.

or several subjects and verbs:

> Manny, Moe, and Jack lubricated my car, replaced the oil filter, and cleaned the spark plugs.

PRACTICE 1 On a separate sheet of paper or in a separate file, write

Three sentences, each with a single subject and verb

Three sentences, each with a single subject and a double verb

Three sentences, each with a double subject and a single verb

In each case, underline the subject once and the verb twice. (See pages 85–96 if necessary for more information on subjects and verbs.)

The Compound Sentence

A compound, or "double," sentence is made up of two (or more) simple sentences. The complete statements in a compound sentence are usually connected by a comma plus a joining word (*and, but, for, or, nor, so, yet*).

A compound sentence is used when you want to give equal weight to two closely related ideas. The technique of showing that ideas have equal importance is called *coordination*.

Following are some compound sentences. Each sentence contains two ideas that the writer considers equal in importance.

The rain increased, so the officials canceled the game.

Jackson wanted to go shopping, but Walt refused to drive him.

Hollis was watching television in the family room, and April was upstairs on the phone.

I had to give up wood carving, for my arthritis had become very painful.

PRACTICE 2 Combine the following pairs of simple sentences into compound sentences. Use a comma and a logical joining word (*and, but, for, so*) to connect each pair.

 HINT For a review of joining words, see pages 81–84.

EXAMPLE

- The children wanted to eat pizza.

- I picked up fried chicken on the way home.

  The children wanted to eat pizza, but I picked up fried chicken on the way home.

1.
- I am majoring in digital media arts.
- I hope to find a job doing video-game animation.

   I am majoring in digital media arts, for I hope to find a job doing video-game animation.

2.
- My children were spending too much time in front of the TV and computer.
- I signed up my entire family for a one-year gym membership.

   My children were spending too much time in front of the TV and computer, so I signed up my entire family for a one-year gym membership.

3.
- Nicole's skin was blemished and sun damaged.
- She consulted with a dermatologist about skin cancer concerns.

   Nicole's skin was blemished and sun damaged, so she consulted with a dermatologist about skin cancer concerns.

4.
- Riley insists on buying certified-organic fruits and vegetables.
- I cannot distinguish organic from conventionally grown produce.

   Riley insists on buying certified-organic fruits and vegetables, but I cannot distinguish organic from conventionally grown produce.

5.
- I was recently promoted to shift manager at work.
- I need to drop down to part-time status at school next semester.

   I was recently promoted to shift manager at work, so I need to drop down to part-time status at school next semester.

Answers may vary.

ESL Tip
Review definitions and usage of all coordinating conjunctions.

ESL Tip
Nonnative speakers may require a lot of practice combining sentences. Additional practice may be taken from their own writing.

Teaching Tip
Remind students to insert a comma before a coordinating conjunction.

PRACTICE 3

On a separate sheet of paper or in a separate file, write five compound sentences of your own about the photo below. Use a different joining word (*and, but, for, or, nor, so, yet*) to connect the two complete ideas in each sentence.

ESL Tip
Nonnative speakers may confuse *even though* and *even if*. See the chart for the difference in meaning.

ESL Tip
Students need to understand the meaning of each dependent word. Grouping them in a chart might be helpful (e.g., by category: contrast, concession, result, reason, time, condition, purpose, place, etc.).

The Complex Sentence

A complex sentence is made up of a simple sentence (a complete statement) and a statement that begins with a dependent word.* Here is a list of common dependent words:

Dependent Words

after	if, even if	when, whenever
although, though	in order that	where, wherever
as	since	whether
because	that, so that	which, whichever
before	unless	while
even though	until	who
how	what, whatever	whose

---

*The two parts of a complex sentence are sometimes called an independent clause and a dependent clause. A *clause* is simply a word group that contains a subject and a verb. An *independent clause* expresses a complete thought and can stand alone. A *dependent clause* does not express a complete thought in itself and "depends on" the independent clause to complete its meaning. Dependent clauses always begin with a dependent, or subordinating, word.

A complex sentence is used when you want to emphasize one idea over another in a sentence. Look at the following complex sentence:

Because I forgot the time, I missed the final exam.

The idea that the writer wants to emphasize here—*I missed the final exam*—is expressed as a complete thought. The less important idea—*Because I forgot the time*—is subordinated to the complete thought. The technique of giving one idea less emphasis than another is called *subordination*.

Following are other examples of complex sentences. In each case, the part starting with the dependent word is the less emphasized part of the sentence.

Teaching Tip
Ask students what idea is being emphasized in each of these complex sentences.

While Aisha was eating breakfast, she began to feel sick.

I checked my money *before* I invited Pedro for lunch.

When Jerry lost his temper, he also lost his job.

Although I practiced for three months, I failed my driving test.

Use logical dependent words to combine the following pairs of simple sentences into complex sentences. Place a comma after a dependent statement when it starts the sentence.

PRACTICE 4

EXAMPLES

- I obtained a credit card.
- I began spending money recklessly.

When I obtained a credit card, I began spending money recklessly.

- Alan dressed the turkey.
- His brother greased the roasting pan.

Alan dressed the turkey while his brother greased the roasting pan.

Answers may vary.

1. • The movie disgusted Dena.
   • She walked out after twenty minutes.

   Because the movie disgusted Dena, she walked out after twenty minutes.

   _____

2. • The house had been burglarized.
   • Dave couldn't sleep soundly for several months.

   After the house had been burglarized, Dave couldn't sleep soundly for several months.

   _____

ESL Tip
Nonnative speakers may begin one clause with a dependent word and the next with a coordinating conjunction, e.g., *"Because the movie disgusted Dena, but she walked out."* Remind students they don't need to use two connectors.

3. • My vision begins to fade.
   • I know I'd better get some sleep.

   When my vision begins to fade, I know I'd better get some sleep.

   _____

4. • The family would need a place to sleep.
   • Fred told the movers to unload the mattresses first.

   Since the family would need a place to sleep, Fred told the movers to unload

   the mattresses first.

5. • The hurricane hit the coast.
   • We crisscrossed our windows with strong tape.

   When the hurricane hit the coast, we crisscrossed our windows with strong tape.

   _____

PRACTICE 5

Rewrite the following sentences, using subordination rather than coordination. Include a comma when a dependent statement starts a sentence.

EXAMPLE

Answers may vary.

The hair dryer was not working right, so I returned it to the store.

Because the hair dryer was not working right, I returned it to the store.

_____

Teaching Tip
For this activity, read each sentence aloud as your students provide the answers.

1. The muffler shop advertised same-day service, but my car wasn't ready for three days.

   Although the muffler shop advertised same-day service, my car wasn't ready for

   three days.

2. The hypertension medication produced dangerous side effects, so the government banned it.

   Because the hypertension medication produced dangerous side effects, the government

   banned it.

3. Phil lopped dead branches off the tree, and Michelle stacked them into piles on the ground below.

   While Phil lopped dead branches off the tree, Michelle stacked them into piles on the ground below.

4. Anne wedged her handbag tightly under her arm, for she was afraid of muggers.

   Anne wedged her handbag tightly under her arm because she was afraid of muggers.

5. Ellen counted the cash three times, but the total still didn't tally with the amount on the register tape.

   Although Ellen counted the cash three times, the total still didn't tally with the amount on the register tape.

Combine the following simple sentences into complex sentences. Omit repeated word. Use the dependent word *who, which,* or *that.*

PRACTICE 6

HINTS

   a. The word *who* refers to persons.
   b. The word *which* refers to things.
   c. The word *that* refers to persons or things.

ESL Tip
Relative clauses may be missing or incorrectly formed; or punctuation may be wrong because non-native speakers haven't learned to distinguish between restrictive and nonrestrictive clauses.

Use commas around the dependent statement only if it seems to interrupt the flow of thought in the sentence. (See page 366.)

EXAMPLES

- Clyde picked up a hitchhiker.
- The hitchhiker was traveling around the world.

   Clyde picked up a hitchhiker who was traveling around the world.

- Larry is a sleepwalker.
- Larry is my brother.

   Larry, who is my brother, is a sleepwalker.

ESL Tip
In some lan-
guages the
relative clause
precedes
the noun it
modifies.

Teaching Tip
Suggest that
students circle
the coordinat-
ing conjunc-
tion in each
sentence. You
might want to
mention that
who, which,
and *that*
are relative
pronouns.

1. • The boy was in a motorcycle accident.
   • The boy limps.

   The boy who limps was in a motorcycle accident.

   _____

2. • Raquel is a champion weight lifter.
   • Raquel is my neighbor.

   Raquel, who is my neighbor, is a champion weight lifter.

   _____

3. • The two screws were missing from the assembly kit.
   • The two screws held the bicycle frame together.

   The two screws that held the bicycle frame together were missing from the assembly

   kit.

4. • The letter is from my ex-wife.
   • The letter arrived today.

   The letter that arrived today is from my ex-wife.

   _____

5. • The tall hedge muffled the highway noise.
   • The hedge surrounded the house.

   The tall hedge that surrounded the house muffled the highway noise.

   _____

PRACTICE 7   On a separate sheet of paper or in a separate file, write eight complex sentences, using, in turn, the dependent words *unless, if, after, because, when, who, which,* and *that.*

The Compound-Complex Sentence

A compound-complex sentence is made up of two (or more) simple sentences and one (or more) dependent statements. In the following examples, a solid line is under the simple sentences and a dotted line is under the dependent statements.

When the power went out, Jack was listening to music, and Linda was reading in bed.

After I returned to school following a long illness, the math teacher gave me makeup work, but the history instructor made me drop her course.

Read through each sentence to get a sense of its overall meaning. Then insert a logical joining word (*and, or, but, for,* or *so*) and a logical dependent word (*because, since, when,* or *although*).

1. ___*Since*___ he had worked at the construction site all day, Tom decided not to meet his friends at the diner, ___*for*___ he was too tired to think.

2. ___*When*___ the satellite feed failed for a second time, some people in the audience hissed, ___*and*___ others shouted for a refund.

3. Nothing could be done ___*until*___ the river's floodwaters receded, ___*so*___ the townspeople waited helplessly in the emergency shelter.

4. ___*When*___ you are sent damaged goods, the store must replace the items, ___*or*___ it must issue a full refund.

5. Sears had the outdoor grill I wanted, ___*but*___ the clerk wouldn't sell it to me ___*because*___ it was the floor sample.

On a separate sheet of paper or in a separate file, write five compound-complex sentences.

Review of Subordination and Coordination

Subordination and coordination are ways of showing the exact relationship of ideas within a sentence. Through subordination we show that one idea is less important than another. When we **subordinate,** we use dependent words like *when, although, while, because,* and *after.* (A list of common dependent words has been given on page 143.) Through **coordination** we show that ideas are of equal importance. When we coordinate, we use the words *and, but, for, or, nor, so,* and *yet.*

PRACTICE 10

Use subordination or coordination to combine the following groups of simple sentences into one or more longer sentences. Be sure to omit repeated words. Since various combinations are possible, you might want to jot down several combinations on a separate sheet of paper or in a separate file. Then read them aloud to find the combination that sounds best.

Keep in mind that, very often, the relationship among ideas in a sentence is clearer when subordination rather than coordination is used.

Teaching Tip
Students may find this activity challenging, so encourage them to work in pairs. Ask them to talk about the relationship among the ideas in each group of simple sentences.

EXAMPLE

- My car does not start on cold mornings.
- I think the battery needs to be replaced.
- I already had it recharged once.
- I don't think charging it again would help.

Because my car does not start on cold mornings, I think the battery needs to be replaced. I already had it recharged once, so I don't think charging it again would help.

COMMA HINTS

a. Use a comma at the end of a word group that starts with a dependent word (as in "Because my car does not start on cold mornings, . . .").

b. Use a comma between independent word groups connected by *and, but, for, or, nor, so, yet* (as in "I already had it recharged once, so . . .").

Answers will vary.

1. • I needed butter to make the cookie batter.
   • I couldn't find any.
   • I used vegetable oil instead.

   I needed butter to make the cookie batter, but I couldn't find any, so I used vegetable oil instead.

2. • Tess had worn glasses for fifteen years.
   • She decided to get LASIK surgery.
   • She would be able to see without glasses or corrective lenses.
   • She would save money in the end.

   Although Tess had worn glasses for fifteen years, she decided to get LASIK surgery. She would be able to see without glasses or corrective lenses, and save money in the end.

3. • The children at the day care center took their naps.
   • They unrolled their sleeping mats.
   • They piled their shoes and sneakers in a corner.

   When the children at the day care center took their naps, they unrolled their sleeping mats, and they piled their shoes and sneakers in a corner.

4. • Jerry dialed the police emergency number.
   • He received a busy signal.
   • He dropped his phone and ran.
   • He didn't have time to turn back.

   When Jerry dialed the police emergency number, he received a busy signal. He dropped his phone and ran because he didn't have time to turn back.

5. • Louise disliked walking home from the bus stop.
   • The street had no overhead lights.
   • It was lined with abandoned buildings.

   Louise disliked walking home from the bus stop because the street had no overhead lights, and it was lined with abandoned buildings.

6. • The rain hit the hot pavement.
    • Plumes of steam rose from the blacktop.
    • Cars slowed to a crawl.
    • The fog obscured the drivers' vision.

    When the rain hit the hot pavement, plumes of steam rose from the blacktop.

    Cars slowed to a crawl, for the fog obscured the drivers' vision.

    _____

    _____

7. • His car went through the automated car wash.
    • Harry watched from the sidelines.
    • Floppy brushes slapped the car's doors.
    • Sprays of water squirted onto the roof.

    While his car went through the automated car wash, Harry watched from the
    sidelines. Floppy brushes slapped the car's doors, and sprays of water squirted onto
    the roof.

    _____

8. • The pipes had frozen.
    • The heat had gone off.
    • We phoned the plumber.
    • He couldn't come for two days.
    • He had been swamped with emergency calls.

    Since the pipes had frozen and the heat had gone off, we phoned the plumber. He
    couldn't come for two days because he had been swamped with emergency calls.

    _____

    _____

9. • My car developed an annoying rattle.
    • I took it to the service station.
    • The mechanic looked under the hood.
    • He couldn't find what was wrong.

    When my car developed an annoying rattle, I took it to the service station.

    The mechanic looked under the hood, but he couldn't find what was wrong.

    _____

    _____

10. • The childproof cap on the aspirin bottle would not budge.
   • The arrows on the bottleneck and cap were lined up.
   • I pried the cap with my fingernails.
   • One nail snapped off.
   • The cap still adhered tightly to the bottle.

The childproof cap on the aspirin bottle would not budge even though the arrows on the bottleneck and cap were lined up. When I pried the cap with my fingernails, one nail snapped off, and the cap still adhered tightly to the bottle.

REVIEW TEST 1

Combine each group of short sentences into one sentence. Various combinations are possible. Choose the combination that reads most smoothly and clearly and that sounds most appropriate in the context of the surrounding sentences. Complete this test on a separate sheet of paper or in a separate file.

Here is an example of a group of sentences and some possible combinations.

EXAMPLE
   • Martha moved in the desk chair.
   • Her moving was uneasy.
   • The chair was hard.
   • She worked at the assignment.
   • The assignment was for her English class.

Martha moved uneasily in the hard desk chair, working at the assignment for her English class.

Moving uneasily in the hard desk chair, Martha worked at the assignment for her English class.

Martha moved uneasily in the hard desk chair as she worked at the assignment for her English class.

While she worked at the assignment for her English class, Martha moved uneasily in the hard desk chair.

> **HINT**   In combining short sentences into one sentence, omit repeated words where necessary.

Answers will vary.

OUR FIRST CAMPING TRIP

* My husband and I went camping for the first time.
* It was an experience.
* The experience is one we will never forget.

Possible answers:

My husband and I went camping for the first time, and it was an experience that we will never forget.

* We borrowed a tent.
* We borrowed a propane stove.
* We borrowed them from my brother-in-law.

We borrowed a tent and a propane stove from my brother-in-law.

* We arrived at the campground.
* We chose a spot.
* The spot was where we could pitch our tents.

When we arrived at the campground, we chose a spot where we could pitch our tents.

* We had forgotten to bring the directions for setting up the tent.
* We had to put up the tent using a trial-and-error process.
* The process took us four hours.

Because we had forgotten to bring the directions for setting up the tent, we had to put up the tent using a trial-and-error process, which took us four hours.

* The tent suddenly collapsed.
* It was nearly dark.
* We had to put it up again.

When it was nearly dark, the tent suddenly collapsed, so we had to put it up again.

* Later, we had difficulty making dinner.
* The stove at first refused to light.
* The food wouldn't cook.

Later, we had difficulty making dinner because the stove at first refused to light, and the food wouldn't cook.

* We finished cleaning up.
* We were exhausted.
* We crawled into our sleeping bags.

After we finished cleaning up, we were exhausted, so we crawled into our sleeping bags.

- A brief rain awoke us that night.
- We were so tired.
- We soon fell asleep again.

A brief rain awoke us that night, but we were so tired that we soon fell asleep again.

- Morning came.
- We were damp and miserable.

When morning came, we were damp and miserable.

- We had learned the important lesson.
- It was that "roughing it" was too rough for us.

We had learned the important lesson that "roughing it" was too rough for us.

REVIEW TEST 2

Combine each group of short sentences into one sentence. Various combinations are possible. Choose the combination that reads most smoothly and clearly and that sounds most appropriate in the context of surrounding sentences. In combining short sentences into one sentence, omit repeated words where necessary. Complete this test on a separate sheet of paper or in a separate file.

MY DISHWASHING JOB

Possible answers:

Answers will vary.

- I had one of the worst experiences of my life.
- This happened when I showed up for my first night of work.
- It was work as a restaurant dishwasher.

I had one of the worst experiences of my life when I showed up for my first night of work as a restaurant dishwasher.

- I was to load the dirty dishes and silverware into the dishwashing machine.
- The dishes were cleaned and dried.

I was to load the dirty dishes and silverware into the dishwashing machine, where the dishes were cleaned and dried.

- Business at the restaurant started to pick up.
- This happened when dinnertime began.
- The dishes came in faster and faster.

When dinnertime began, business at the restaurant started to pick up, and the dishes came in faster and faster.

- I tried to scrape and load the dishes as fast as I could.
- I couldn't keep up.

I tried to scrape and load the dishes as fast as I could, but I couldn't keep up.

- The counter was piled high with dishes.
- The busboys began to stack pans of them on the floor.

When the counter was piled high with dishes, the busboys began to stack pans of them on the floor.

- I was hot and sweaty.
- My arms were spotted with bits of food.
- My fingertips were burned from grabbing the clean dishes out of the machine.

I was hot and sweaty, my arms were spotted with bits of food, and my fingertips were burned from grabbing the clean dishes out of the machine.

- Then my boss burst through the double doors of the kitchen.
- He told me to hurry up.
- He told me the dining room was almost out of clean dishes.

Then my boss burst through the double doors of the kitchen and told me to hurry up because the dining room was almost out of clean dishes.

- My back was aching.
- My head was splitting.
- I smelled like the garbage can next to me.
- This happened when the restaurant was ready to close.

When the restaurant was ready to close, my back was aching, my head was splitting, and I smelled like the garbage can next to me.

- It took all my courage to return to this job the next night.
- I stuck it out.
- I needed the money.

It took all my courage to return to this job the next night, but I stuck it out since I needed the money.

- I hope never to have to be a dishwasher again.
- I did become an expert one.
- I did this after I had been on the job for a few days.

Although I hope never to have to be a dishwasher again, I did become an expert one after I had been on the job for a few days.

SCORE
Number Correct

_____ /5

_____ %

Sentence Variety I

Combine each group of short sentences into one sentence. Various combinations are possible. Choose the combination that reads most smoothly and clearly and that sounds most appropriate in the context of surrounding sentences. Complete this test on a separate sheet of paper or in a separate file.

HINT In combining short sentences into one sentence, omit repeated words where necessary.

KIDS AND MUD

- Two toddlers sit on the ground.
- They play in the wet and gooey mud.

- They keep busy for hours.
- They build all sorts of things.

- Kids can turn mud into cakes.
- They can turn twigs into candles.
- They do so when they are allowed to use their imagination.

- They don't need expensive toys.
- They don't even need a television.

- What they need is some wet dirt.
- They also need patient parents.
- Patient parents won't yell about their muddy clothes.

Possible answers:

Two toddlers sit on the ground where they play in the wet and gooey mud.

They keep busy for hours, and they build all sorts of things.

When they are allowed to use their imagination, kids can turn mud into cakes, and they can turn twigs into candles.

They don't need expensive toys, and they don't even need a television.

What they need is some wet dirt and patient parents who won't yell about their muddy clothes.

157

NAME: _____

DATE: _____

Sentence Variety I

Follow the instructions provided for Mastery Test 1.

> **HINT** In combining short sentences into one sentence, omit repeated words where necessary.

THE DO-IT-YOURSELF SPECIAL

Possible answers:

- Kevin and Tyra decided to move out of their cramped apartment.
- They went to a real estate agent.
- The real estate agent was Kevin's high school friend.

Kevin and Tyra decided to move out of their cramped apartment, so they went to a real estate agent who was Kevin's high school friend.

- They looked at lots of houses.
- All the houses were too expensive.

They looked at lots of houses, but all the houses were too expensive.

- Finally, they found a house.
- They could afford the house.
- The house needed a lot of work.

Finally, they found a house that they could afford, but the house needed a lot of work.

- For example, the front steps had a railing.
- The railing was made of rusty pipes.
- The floors tilted a bit.
- The kitchen walls were covered in a crazy pattern of multicolored tiles.

For example, the front steps had a railing that was made of rusty pipes, the floors tilted a bit, and the kitchen walls were covered in a crazy pattern of multicolored tiles.

- There was a great deal of work to be done.
- Kevin and Tyra bought the do-it-yourself special.
- They knew it was a place they could call home.

Although there was a great deal of work to be done, Kevin and Tyra bought the do-it-yourself special because they knew it was a place they could call home.

Standard English Verbs

INTRODUCTORY ACTIVITY

Underline what you think is the correct form of the verb in each pair of sentences below.

That station once (play, <u>played</u>) top-forty hits.
It now (play, <u>plays</u>) talk radio.

When Sherry was a little girl, she (hope, <u>hoped</u>) to become a movie star.
Now she (hope, <u>hopes</u>) to be accepted at law school.

At first, my father (juggle, <u>juggled</u>) with balls of yarn.
Now that he is an expert, he (juggle, <u>juggles</u>) raw eggs.

On the basis of the preceding examples, complete the following statements.

1. The first sentence in each pair refers to an action in (<u>past time</u>, the present time), and the regular verb has an ___*-ed or -d*___ ending.
2. The second sentence in each pair refers to an action in (past time, <u>the present time</u>), and the regular verb has an ___*-s*___ ending.

Answers are on page 637.

Many people have grown up in communities where nonstandard verb forms are used in everyday life. Such nonstandard forms include *they be, it done, we has, you was, she don't,* and *it ain't.* Community dialects have richness and power but are a drawback in college and the world at large, where standard English verb forms must be used. Standard English helps ensure clear communication among English-speaking people everywhere, and it is especially important in the world of work.

This chapter compares the community dialect and the standard English forms of a regular verb and three common irregular verbs.

PERSONALIZED LEARNING

Regular Verbs: Dialect and Standard Forms

The chart below compares community dialect (nonstandard) and standard English forms of the regular verb *talk*.

Teaching Tip
Get students to talk about their own community dialects. Help them to see that there is value in these dialects.

ESL Tip
Nonnative speakers may use a single form of a verb ending in the past and present tenses. Generally, they will omit the -s (present) or the -ed (simple past). Remind students that they can't always depend on spoken English for correct verb forms.

Talk

Community Dialect		Standard English	
(Do not use in your writing.)		**(Use for clear communication.)**	
Present Tense			
I talks	we talks	I talk	we talk
you talks	you talks	you talk	you talk
he, she, it talk	they talks	he, she, it talks	they talk
Past Tense			
I talk	we talk	I talked	we talked
you talk	you talk	you talked	you talked
he, she, it talk	they talk	he, she, it talked	they talked

One of the most common nonstandard forms results from dropping the endings of regular verbs. For example, people might say "Rose work until ten o'clock tonight" instead of "Rose works until ten o'clock tonight." Or they'll say "I work overtime yesterday" instead of "I worked overtime yesterday." To avoid such nonstandard usage, memorize the forms shown above for the regular verb *talk*. Then do the activities that follow. These activities will help you make it a habit to include verb endings in your writing.

Present Tense Endings

The verb ending -s or -es is needed with a regular verb in the present tense when the subject is *he, she, it,* or any one person or thing.

He	He lifts weights.
She	She runs.
It	It amazes me.
One person	Their son Ted swims.
One person	Their daughter Terry dances.
One thing	Their house jumps at night with all the exercise.

All but one of the ten sentences that follow need -s or -es endings. Cross out the nonstandard verb forms and write the standard forms in the spaces provided. Mark the one sentence that needs no change with a *C*.

EXAMPLE

_____ends_____   The sale ~~end~~ tomorrow.

___wears___ 1. Lucille ~~wear~~ a wig to cover up her thinning gray hair.

___says___ 2. My horoscope ~~say~~ that today is a good day for romance.

___subscribes___ 3. Huang ~~subscribe~~ to three podcasts to keep up with current events.

___believes___ 4. My mother ~~believe~~ in always trying her best.

___sees___ 5. A dog ~~see~~ only tones of gray, black, and white.

___distributes___ 6. At Thanksgiving, our church ~~distribute~~ turkeys to the needy.

___C___ 7. Andrea breaks her carrots in half before eating them.

___feeds___ 8. Chris ~~feed~~ chopped-up flies and mosquitoes to his tropical fish.

___overcooks___ 9. That diner ~~overcook~~ all its food.

___polishes___ 10. He ~~polish~~ his shoes using a melted wax crayon and an old towel.

Teaching Tip
For these activities, read several sentences aloud so that students can "hear" the verb errors.

Rewrite the short selection below, adding present tense -s verb endings wherever needed.

Jon work for a company that deliver singing telegrams. Sometimes he put on a sequined tuxedo or wear a Cupid costume. He compose his own songs for birthdays, anniversaries, bachelor parties, and other occasions. Then he show up at a certain place and surprise the victim. He sing a song that include personal details, which he get in advance, about the recipient of the telegram. Jon love the astonished looks on other people's faces; he also enjoy earning money by making people happy on special days.

Jon works for a company that delivers singing telegrams. Sometimes he puts on a sequined tuxedo or wears a Cupid costume. He composes his own songs for birthdays, anniversaries, bachelor parties, and other occasions. Then he shows up at a certain place and surprises the victim. He sings a song that includes personal details, which he gets in advance, about the recipient of the telegram. Jon loves the astonished looks on other people's faces; he also enjoys earning money by making people happy on special days.

Past Tense Endings

The verb ending -d or -ed is needed with a regular verb in the past tense.

Yesterday we finished painting the house.

I completed the paper an hour before class.

Fred's car stalled on his way to work this morning.

All but one of the ten sentences that follow need -d or -ed endings. Cross out the nonstandard verb forms and write the standard forms in the spaces provided. Mark the one sentence that needs no change with a C.

EXAMPLE

jumped   The cat ~~jump~~ on my lap when I sat down.

turned   1. The first time I baked a pound cake, it ~~turn~~ out to be a ton cake.

bounced   2. The line drive slammed into the fence and ~~bounce~~ into the stands for a ground-rule double.

paged   3. Bettina ~~page~~ through the book, looking for the money she had hidden there.

crushed   4. Mario ~~crush~~ the sunglasses in his back pocket as he flopped on the sofa.

c   5. The sweating workers shoveled hot tar onto the road and then smoothed it out.

washed   6. The surgeons ~~wash~~ their hands before they entered the operating room.

cracked   7. The detective ~~crack~~ the case after finding a key witness.

collected   8. When she was a teenager, Rita ~~collect~~ pictures of her favorite bands.

pulled   9. As they struggled, the mugger ~~pull~~ the chain from Val's neck.

lacked   10. Ken knew he ~~lack~~ the ability to make the varsity team, but he tried out, anyway.

Rewrite the selection below, adding past tense -d or -ed verb endings where needed.

Brad hate working long hours, but he need money to support his growing family and to pay for school. He start working at the auto body shop when he graduate from high school because he like cars, but the job bore him. He wish that he could spend more time at home with his wife and new baby girl. He also want to dedicate more time to his homework. Brad knew that he had made his own choices, so he decide to appreciate his job, his family, and his chance to move ahead in life.

Brad hated working long hours, but he needed money to support his growing family and to pay for school. He started working at the auto body shop when he graduated from high school because he liked cars, but the job bored him. He wished that he could spend more time at home with his wife and new baby girl. He also wanted to dedicate more time to his homework. Brad knew that he had made his own choices, so he decided to appreciate his job, his family, and his chance to move ahead in life.

Three Common Irregular Verbs: Dialect and Standard Forms

The following charts compare the nonstandard and standard dialects of the common irregular verbs *be, have,* and *do.* (For more on irregular verbs, see the next chapter, beginning on page 172.)

Teaching Tip Encourage students to talk about what happens when they use nonstandard English in college.

Be

Community Dialect (Do not use in your writing.)		Standard English (Use for clear communication.)	
Present Tense			
I be (*or* is)	we be	I am	we are
you be	you be	you are	you are
he, she, it be	they be	he, she, it is	they are
Past Tense			
I were	we was	I was	we were
you was	you was	you were	you were
he, she, it were	they was	he, she, it was	they were

Have

Community Dialect		Standard English	
(Do not use in your writing.)		**(Use for clear communication.)**	
Present Tense			
~~I has~~	~~we has~~	I have	we have
~~you has~~	~~you has~~	you have	you have
~~he, she, it have~~	~~they has~~	he, she, it has	they have
Past Tense			
~~I has~~	~~we has~~	I had	we had
~~you has~~	~~you has~~	you had	you had
~~he, she, it have~~	~~they has~~	he, she, it had	they had

Do

Community Dialect		Standard English	
(Do not use in your writing.)		**(Use for clear communication.)**	
Present Tense			
~~I does~~	~~we does~~	I do	we do
~~you does~~	~~you does~~	you do	you do
~~he, she, it do~~	~~they does~~	he, she, it does	they do
Past Tense			
~~I done~~	~~we done~~	I did	we did
~~you done~~	~~you done~~	you did	you did
~~he, she, it done~~	~~they done~~	he, she, it did	they did

> **TIP** Many people have trouble with one negative form of *do*. They will say, for example, "She don't listen" instead of "She doesn't listen," or they will say "This pen don't work" instead of "This pen doesn't work." Be careful to avoid the common mistake of using *don't* instead of *doesn't*.

Underline the standard form of the irregular verb *be, have,* or *do.*

1. My brother Ron (be, <u>is</u>) a normal, fun-loving person most of the time.

2. But he (have, <u>has</u>) a hobby that changes his personality.

3. He (be, <u>is</u>) an amateur actor with our community theater group.

4. When he (do, <u>does</u>) a part in a play, he turns into the character.

5. Once the company (done, <u>did</u>) a play about Sherlock Holmes, the detective.

6. In the show, Ron (<u>was</u>, were) a frightened man stalked by a murderer.

7. The role (<u>had</u>, have) a strange effect on my brother.

8. At home, he (were, <u>was</u>) nervous and jittery.

9. I (done, <u>did</u>) my best to calm him.

10. However, he remained convinced that he (<u>was</u>, were) being followed.

Teaching Tip
For these activities, ask students if the subject of each sentence is singular or plural.

Cross out the nonstandard verb form in each sentence. Then write the standard form of *be, have,* or *do* in the space provided.

___*is*___ 1. That sports supply store, Sprinters, ~~be~~ the largest in the area.

___*has*___ 2. It ~~have~~ all the latest equipment.

___*has*___ 3. In addition, a special section ~~have~~ sneakers at reasonable prices.

___*are*___ 4. The salespeople ~~is~~ very knowledgeable about sports and equipment.

___*are*___ 5. They ~~is~~ willing to help a customer find any item in the store.

___*do*___ 6. They also ~~does~~ their best to order any machine available.

___*do*___ 7. The owners of Sprinters ~~does~~ a good job promoting local teams, too.

___*has*___ 8. The store ~~have~~ posters of local teams in the windows.

___*does*___ 9. It ~~do~~ special promotions on game days.

___*are*___ 10. My friends and I ~~be~~ loyal and satisfied customers of Sprinters.

Fill in each blank with the standard form of *be*, *have*, or *do*.

My friend Tyrell ___*is*___ a real bargain hunter. If a store ___*has*___ a sale, he runs right over and buys two or three things, whether or not they ___*are*___ things he needs. Tyrell ___*does*___ his best, also, to get something for nothing. Last week, he ___*was*___ reading the paper and saw that the First National Bank's new downtown offices ___*were*___ offering gifts for new accounts. "Those freebies sure ___*do*___ look good," Tyrell said. So he went downtown, opened an account, and ___*had*___ the manager give him a Big Ben alarm clock. When he got back with the clock, he ___*was*___ smiling. "I ___*am*___ a very busy man," he told me, "and I really need the free time."

REVIEW TEST 1

Underline the standard verb form.

1. We (<u>pay</u>, pays) more for car insurance since the accident.

2. Two years ago, my brother and his wife (adopt, <u>adopted</u>) a special-needs child.

3. The baby (grasp, <u>grasps</u>) his mother's long hair in his tiny fist.

4. The original Frisbees (was, <u>were</u>) tin pie plates from a baking company.

5. Greta (don't, <u>doesn't</u>) approve of her brother's deer hunting.

6. My stepmother likes to work in the yard whenever the sun (be, <u>is</u>) shining.

7. Jenni looks like a squirrel when she (<u>chews</u>, chew) a big wad of gum.

8. My little sister (<u>has</u>, have) an unusual ailment—an allergy to homework.

9. Anjelica (grease, <u>greases</u>) the casserole dish with melted chicken fat.

10. My brother (own, <u>owns</u>) a World War II flyer's leather jacket that belonged to our grandfather.

Cross out the nonstandard verb forms in the sentences that follow. Then write the standard English verb forms in the space above, as shown.

EXAMPLE

played

For most of yesterday morning, the children ~~play~~ quietly in the sandbox.

dunks
1. Usually, Tara ~~dunk~~ her chicken wings in sweet-and-sour sauce.

lock (or locked)
2. My parents ~~locks~~ themselves in the bathroom during arguments.

asked
3. A suspicious-looking man ~~ask~~ if I wanted to buy a new microwave oven for fifty dollars.

bites (or bit)
4. My sister ~~bite~~ the erasers off her pencils.

rides (or rode)
5. Theo ~~ride~~ a bicycle to work in order to save money on gas.

doesn't
6. The school ~~don't~~ allow anyone to use the darkroom without an appointment.

bounced
7. For the third time in the movie, a car ~~bounce~~ headlong down a cliff and burst into flames.

gives
8. The mail carrier ~~give~~ us a pink slip when we have a package waiting at the post office.

were
9. The ceilings ~~was~~ ringed with water marks from the leaky roof.

has (or had)
10. Instead of a keyhole, each hotel room door ~~have~~ a slot for a magnetic card.

NAME: _____

DATE: _____

Standard English Verbs

Underline the correct words in the parentheses.

1. "Jim works nonstop," my father (claim, <u>claims</u>). "He (push, <u>pushes</u>) himself tirelessly."

2. Because my engine (leak, <u>leaks</u>) oil, I (<u>park</u>, parks) my car in the street rather than in the driveway.

3. Perspiration (drip, <u>dripped</u>) off Alanya's forehead as she (mix, <u>mixed</u>) sand into the new cement.

4. Every time our upstairs neighbor (do, <u>does</u>) his workout, we hear him grunt as he (lift, <u>lifts</u>) his barbell.

5. Lee (were, <u>was</u>) so famished that she (swallow, <u>swallowed</u>) the mouthful of hamburger without chewing it.

6. Aunt Lucinda, who (<u>is</u>, be) an entrepreneur, buys every new business start-up guide she (have, <u>has</u>) read about online.

7. You (frighten, <u>frightened</u>) me to death a minute ago when I (turn, <u>turned</u>) around and saw you standing in the doorway.

8. Before Sharon (take, <u>takes</u>) a bath, she (silence, <u>silences</u>) the phone's ringer.

9. Why is it that, whenever I (<u>drop</u>, drops) my toast, it (fall, <u>falls</u>) on the buttered side?

10. I just (finish, <u>finished</u>) reading a horror story about some creatures from outer space that (<u>invade</u>, invades) earth disguised as video games.

NAME: _____

DATE: _____

Standard English Verbs

Cross out the nonstandard verb form and write the correct form in the space provided.

EXAMPLE

seems	The job offer ~~seem~~ too good to be true.
breaks	1. Chung ~~break~~ into a rash when he eats strawberries.
feels	2. It ~~feel~~ strange to get up before the sun rises.
threaded	3. Before he sewed the button back on his sweater, Carlos ~~thread~~ the needle.
did	4. The driver of the huge moving van ~~do~~ a double take as a the tiny Smart car passed him on the turnpike.
asked	5. The bartender flattered my aunt when he ~~ask~~ her to prove she was of drinking age.
stopped	6. As Catrick strolled casually passed the used-books store window, she ~~stop~~ in to browse through a few classics that caught her eye.
intend	7. I ~~intends~~ to pay all my bills the minute I obtain some extra cash.
knocked	8. He's so lazy that, if opportunity ~~knock~~, he'd say no one was at home.
pretend	9. Whenever we see my sister and her family coming down the front walk, we ~~pretends~~ we aren't at home.
has	10. Kenny ~~have~~ an antique car that looks like an overturned bathtub.

NAME: _____

DATE: _____

Standard English Verbs

PART 1

Fill in each blank with the appropriate standard verb form of be, have, *or* do *in the present or past tense.*

A small town in New England ___*has*___ the best kind of dogcatcher—the
                                    1
kind who ___*does*___ not want to hurt an animal. In this town, it ___*is*___ the law
              2   3
to shoot on sight dogs that ___*are*___ running loose. It turned out that the local
                                   4
police ___*did*___ not want to enforce this law, so they asked the dogcatcher. He
            5
answered, "I ___*have*___ never shot a dog in my life, and I ___*am*___ not going
                  6   7
to start shooting them now." Instead, he ___*was*___ seen on several occasions
                                              8
picking up stray dogs and putting them in his car to return them to their homes.

He ___*has*___ often taken dogs to his own house until he can find their owners.
        9
This man ___*is*___ certainly worthy of being called a dog's best friend.
             10

PART 2

Fill in each blank with the appropriate form of the regular verb shown in parentheses. Use the present or past tense as needed.

Ben's mother always (*clip*) ___*clips*___ the dollar-off coupons from the news-
                                  11
paper and (*save*) ___*saves*___ them for him. Every time he (*visit*) ___*visits*___, his
                        12   13
mother (*refuse*) ___*refuses*___ to let him go without those little pieces of paper that
                        14
advertise "$1 off on 3 cans" or "Save $1 on large economy size." Last week, she
even (*hand*) ___*handed*___ him some coupons for dog food, although he has never
                    15
(*own*) ___*owned*___ a dog in his life. Whenever he (*remember*) ___*remembers*___ to take
            16   17
some of her coupons to the market, they have usually already (*expire*) ___*expired*___.
                                                                              18
But he never (*turn*) ___*turns*___ them down, because he (*know*) ___*knows*___ that his
                          19   20
mother's coupons are her way of saying "I love you."

170

NAME: _____

DATE: _____

SCORE
Number Correct

_____/20

_____%

MASTERY TEST 4

Standard English Verbs

PART 1

Fill in each blank with the appropriate standard verb form of be, have, *or* do *in the present or past tense.*

My grandmother ____was____ an eccentric character. She ____had____ the idea
1   2

that my name was Joe (which it ____was____ not), and she insisted on calling me
3

that. She ____was____ also a miser; she ____did____ not hide money, though—only
4   5

candy. Under her bed ____was____ a suitcase full of saltwater taffy and licorice.
6

Once, when she thought she ____was____ alone, I saw her count the candy pieces
7

and then put them back. I'll never forget one thing she ____did____. When I brought
8

my girlfriend home for the first time, Grandma ____was____ sure we were married;
9

she kept asking us if we ____had____ any children yet.
10

PART 2

Fill in each blank with the appropriate form of the regular verb shown in parentheses. Use the present or past tense as needed.

A funny thing (*happen*) __happened__ recently at the Port Authority Bus Ter-
11

minal in New York City. This terminal (*serve*) __serves__ 168,000 riders every
12

day, so commuters (*expect*) __expect__ all sorts of delays. In fact, unless some-
13

one who (*ride*) __rides__ a bus buys a ticket online ahead of time, he or she
14

can spend the first twenty minutes of the trip just waiting in line to buy a ticket.

To reward these long-suffering commuters, the Port Authority (*ask*) __asked__ a
15

sculptor to create a statue in their honor. When the statue (*arrive*) __arrived__, it
16

(*turn*) __turned__ out to be three cast bronze commuters waiting in line. Then the
17

statues were (*place*) __placed__ in front of a gate, and a few commuters actually
18

(*line*) __lined__ up behind the bronze figures. "The line (*seem*) __seemed__ to be
19   20

moving about as fast as usual," one commuter said.

171

CHAPTER

11

Irregular Verbs

INTRODUCTORY ACTIVITY

Teaching Tip
You may want to use this activity to assess your students' understanding of irregular verbs.

You may already have a sense of which common English verbs are regular and which are not. To test yourself, fill in the past tense and past participle of the verbs below. Five are regular verbs and so take *-d* or *-ed* in the past tense and past participle. For these verbs, write *R* under *Verb Type* and then write their past tense and past participle verb forms. Five are irregular verbs and will probably not sound right when you try to add *-d* or *-ed*. For these verbs, write *I* under *Verb Type*. Also, see if you can write in their irregular verb forms.

PRESENT	VERB TYPE	PAST	PAST PARTICIPLE
fall	I	fell	fallen
1. scream	R	screamed	screamed
2. write	I	wrote	written
3. steal	I	stole	stolen
4. ask	R	asked	asked
5. kiss	R	kissed	kissed
6. Choose	I	chose	chosen
7. ride	I	rode	ridden
8. chew	R	chewed	chewed
9. think	I	thought	thought
10. dance	R	danced	danced

Answers are on page 637.

A Brief Review of Regular Verbs

Every verb has four principal parts: present, past, past participle, and present participle. These parts can be used to build all the verb tenses (the times shown by a verb).

Most verbs in English are regular. The past and past participle of a regular verb are formed by adding *-d* or *-ed* to the present. The *past participle* is the form of the verb used with the helping verb *have, has,* or *had* (or some form of *be* with passive verbs, which are explained on page 212). The *present participle* is formed by adding *-ing* to the present.

Here are the principal forms of some regular verbs:

Present	Past	Past Participle	Present Participle
laugh	laughed	laughed	laughing
ask	asked	asked	asking
touch	touched	touched	touching
decide	decided	decided	deciding
explode	exploded	exploded	exploding

List of Irregular Verbs

Irregular verbs have irregular forms in the past tense and past participle. For example, the past tense of the irregular verb *grow* is *grew*; the past participle is *grown.*

Almost everyone has some degree of trouble with irregular verbs. When you are unsure about the form of a verb, you can check the following list of irregular verbs. (The present participle is not shown on this list, because it is formed simply by adding *-ing* to the base form of the verb.) Or you can check a dictionary, which gives the principal parts of irregular verbs.

PRESENT	PAST	PAST PARTICIPLE
arise	arose	arisen
awake	awoke *or* awaked	awoke *or* awaked
be (am, are, is)	was (were)	been
become	became	become
begin	began	begun
bend	bent	bent
bite	bit	bitten
blow	blew	blown
break	broke	broken
bring	brought	brought

continued

Teaching Tip
You may want to ask students to use all the verb forms of a word in one sentence. For example, "I saw Ertan laughing, so I laughed, but there was nothing to laugh about."

Teaching Tip
Ask students to circle the unfamiliar irregular verb forms on this list. Then suggest that they write these verbs on flash cards to help them memorize the verb forms.

PRESENT	PAST	PAST PARTICIPLE
build	built	built
burst	burst	burst
buy	bought	bought
catch	caught	caught
choose	chose	chosen
come	came	come
cost	cost	cost
cut	cut	cut
do (does)	did	done
draw	drew	drawn
drink	drank	drunk
drive	drove	driven
eat	ate	eaten
fall	fell	fallen
feed	fed	fed
feel	felt	felt
fight	fought	fought
find	found	found
fly	flew	flown
freeze	froze	frozen
get	got	got *or* gotten
give	gave	given
go (goes)	went	gone
grow	grew	grown
have (has)	had	had
hear	heard	heard
hide	hid	hidden
hold	held	held
hurt	hurt	hurt
keep	kept	kept
know	knew	known
lay	laid	laid
lead	led	led
leave	left	left
lend	lent	lent
let	let	let
lie	lay	lain
light	lit	lit
lose	lost	lost
make	made	made
meet	met	met

ESL Tip
Nonnative speakers may confuse the forms of *feel* and *fall; thought* and *taught;* and *live* and *leave.*

PRESENT	PAST	PAST PARTICIPLE
pay	paid	paid
ride	rode	ridden
ring	rang	rung
rise	rose	risen
run	ran	run
say	said	said
see	saw	seen
sell	sold	sold
send	sent	sent
shake	shook	shaken
shrink	shrank or shrunk	shrunk or shrunken
shut	shut	shut
sing	sang	sung
sit	sat	sat
sleep	slept	slept
speak	spoke	spoken
spend	spent	spent
stand	stood	stood
steal	stole	stolen
stick	stuck	stuck
sting	stung	stung
swear	swore	sworn
swim	swam	swum
take	took	taken
teach	taught	taught
tear	tore	torn
tell	told	told
think	thought	thought
wake	woke or waked	woken or waked
wear	wore	worn
win	won	won
write	wrote	written

ESL Tip
Chinese does not contain any irregular verbs.

Cross out the incorrect verb form in each of the following sentences. Then write the correct form of the verb in the space provided.

PRACTICE 1

EXAMPLE

began   When the mud slide started, the whole neighborhood ~~begun~~ going downhill.

Teaching Tip
For this activity
read several
sentences
aloud so that
students can
"hear" the
verb errors.

___took___   1. The boys ~~taked~~ sodas into the darkened theater.

___chosen___ 2. The fire department has finally ~~chose~~ two women for its training
                 program.

___caught___ 3. The daredevil ~~catched~~ a bullet in his teeth.

___stolen___ 4. Someone has ~~stole~~ the GPS device from my car.

___saw___   5. After I ~~seen~~ my new haircut, I cried.

___gone___   6. I have ~~went~~ to the lost-and-found office several times, but my
                 leather gloves haven't turned up yet.

___fallen___ 7. The stunt man has ~~fell~~ off hundreds of horses without injuring
                 himself.

___sworn___   8. Steve has ~~swore~~ to control his temper.

___shrunk___ 9. The bacon strips in the pan had ~~shrank~~ into blackened stubs.

___spoken___ 10. Why haven't you ~~spoke~~ up about your problems?

PRACTICE 2

For each of the italicized verbs in the following sentences, fill in the three missing
forms in the order shown in the box:

> a. Present tense, which takes an *-s* ending when the subject is *he, she, it,* or
>   any *one person or thing* (see page 160)
> b. Past tense
> c. Past participle—the form that goes with the helping verb *have, has,* or
>   *had*

EXAMPLE

Teaching Tip
For this activ-
ity, read each
sentence aloud
as your stu-
dents provide
the answers.

My little nephew loves to *break* things. Every birthday he (a) ___breaks___ his
new toys the minute they're unwrapped. Last year he (b) ___broke___ five toys in
seven minutes and then went on to smash his family's new china platter. His
mother says he won't be happy until he has (c) ___broken___ their hearts.

1. My husband always seems to *lose* things. He (a) ___loses___ his glasses about
   three times a day. Once he (b) ___lost___ one of his running shoes while he
   was out jogging. He has (c) ___lost___ so many car keys that we keep one taped
   inside the bumper of our car.

2. Jamie is often asked to *bring* her gorgeous sister to parties. Poor Jamie
   (a) _____*brings*_____ Vanessa and then fades into the wallpaper. Last week she
   (b) _____*brought*_____ Vanessa to a pool party. Jamie felt as if she had (c) _____*brought*_____ a
   human magnet instead of a sister, since all the guys clustered around Vanessa
   the entire night.

3. Small babies can be taught to *swim*. They don't (a) _____*swim*_____ like adults, but
   they do float and keep their heads above water. Babies are accustomed to a
   watery environment, since they (b) _____*swam*_____ inside their mothers' bodies in a
   bath of fluid. Babies who have (c) _____*swum*_____ in pools shortly after birth seem
   to become more confident swimmers as children.

4. My brother actually likes to *go* to the dentist. He (a) _____*goes*_____ at least every
   three months for a checkup. He (b) _____*went*_____ last week just to have his teeth
   flossed. He has (c) _____*gone*_____ to his dentist so regularly that Dr. Ross has been
   able to afford a new sports car.

5. The vast crowd in the stadium waits for the concert to *begin*. The fans don't
   care if it (a) _____*begins*_____ late, since they are having a great time eating, drinking,
   and listening to music on their iPhones. In fact, if the concert (b) _____*began*_____ on
   time, they would feel cheated. Once it has (c) _____*begun*_____, the stadium will vi-
   brate from the screams of the fans and the roar of the music.

6. My little boy likes to *hide* from me. I usually find him, since he (a) _____*hides*_____ in
   obvious places, like under the bed or inside the closet. Once, however, he
   (b) _____*hid*_____ in an unusual place. I searched all over until I discovered that he
   had (c) _____*hidden*_____ inside an empty garbage can.

7. I like to *choose* unusual items when I order from a restaurant menu. My friends
   always (a) _____*choose*_____ something safe and familiar, but I'm more adventurous.
   Once I (b) _____*chose*_____ stuffed calves' brains, which were delicious. I have
   (c) _____*chosen*_____ items like squid, sea urchins, and pickled pigs' feet just to see
   how they would taste.

8. Last month I had to *speak* before the PTA members at my daughter's school. I can (a) _____*speak*_____ comfortably to small groups, but this was a meeting of hundreds of people in an auditorium. Before I gave my report, I (b) _____*spoke*_____ to the principal and told him how nervous I was. He assured me that, even though he had (c) _____*spoken*_____ in public many times over the years, he still got butterflies in his stomach.

9. Sheila has to *take* her dog to the veterinarian. Whenever she (a) _____*takes*_____ him, though, he howls in the waiting room or lunges at the other pets. The last time Sheila (b) _____*took*_____ Bruno, he had an accident on the linoleum floor. This time, however, Sheila has (c) _____*taken*_____ the precaution of keeping Bruno away from his water bowl for several hours.

10. Greg hates to *wake* up. When he does (a) _____*wake*_____ up, he is groggy and miserable. Once he (b) _____*woke*_____ up and yelled at his pet hamster for looking at him the wrong way. He has (c) _____*woken*_____ up this way so often that his family won't speak to him until noon.

Troublesome Irregular Verbs

ESL Tip
These verbs are especially important for ESL students because they function as auxiliaries in forming tenses, the negative, and questions.

Three common irregular verbs that often give people trouble are *be, have,* and *do.* See pages 163–66 for a discussion of these verbs. Three sets of other irregular verbs that can lead to difficulties are *lie-lay, sit-set,* and *rise-raise.*

Lie-Lay

The principal parts of *lie* and *lay* are as follows:

Present	Past	Past Participle
lie	lay	lain
lay	laid	laid

To lie means *to rest* or *recline*. *To lay* means *to put something down.*

<table>
<tr><td>

TO LIE

Ming *lies* on the couch.

This morning he *lay* in the tub.

He has *lain* in bed all week with the flu.

</td><td>

TO LAY

I *lay* the mail on the table.

Yesterday I *laid* the mail on the counter.

I have *laid* the mail where every one will see it.

</td></tr>
</table>

Underline the correct verb.

> **HINT**   Use a form of *lie* if you can substitute *recline*. Use a form of *lay* if you can substitute *place*.

1. Unknowingly, I had (lain, laid) my coat down on a freshly varnished table.
2. Like a mini solar panel, the cat (lay, laid) in the warm rays of the sun.
3. He was certain he had (lain, laid) the tiles in a straight line until he stepped back to look.
4. (Lying, Laying) too long in bed in the morning can give me a headache.
5. I (lay, laid) on the doctor's examining table, staring into the bright bars of fluorescent light on the ceiling.

Teaching Tip
For this activity, read each sentence aloud as your students provide the correct answers.

Sit-Set

The principal parts of *sit* and *set* are as follows:

Present	Past	Past Participle
sit	sat	sat
set	set	set

To sit means *to take a seat* or *to rest*. *To set* means *to put* or *to place.*

<table>
<tr><td>

TO SIT

I *sit* down during work breaks.

I *sat* in the doctor's office for three hours.

I have always *sat* in the last desk.

</td><td>

TO SET

Tony *sets* out the knives, forks, and spoons.

His sister already *set* out the dishes.

They have just *set* out the silverware.

</td></tr>
</table>

Underline the correct form of the verb.

> **HINT**   Use a form of *sit* if you can substitute *rest*. Use a form of *set* if you can substitute *place*.

1. Dillon had (sat, set) his iPod shuffle on the counter for only a few seconds before someone walked off with it.

2. Zena (sat, set) her heavy backpack down on the floor, and then she proceeded to take out her calculus textbook, graphing calculator, and class notes.

3. The cardiologist told me to (sit, set) down before she went over my X-ray results.

4. I (sat, set) a candle on the mantel in the living room to remember my younger sister, who died of leukemia last month.

5. Nigel was (sitting, setting) the weights down on the floor when he heard his spine crack.

Rise-Raise

The principal parts of *rise* and *raise* are as follows:

Present	Past	Past Participle
rise	rose	risen
raise	raised	raised

To rise means *to get up* or *to move up*. *To raise* (which is a regular verb with simple *-ed* endings) means *to lift up* or *to increase in amount*.

TO RISE	TO RAISE
The Buddhist monks *rise* at dawn.	I'm going to *raise* the stakes in the card game
The crowd *rose* to applaud the batter.	I *raised* the shades to let in the sun.
Dracula has *risen* from the grave.	I would have quit if the company had not *raised* my salary.

Underline the correct verb.

PRACTICE 5

> **HINT** Use a form of *rise* if you can substitute *get up* or *move up*. Use a form of *raise* if you can substitute *lift up* or *increase*.

Teaching Tip
For this activity, read each sentence aloud as your students provide the correct answers.

1. When food prices (<u>rise</u>, raise), people living on Social Security suffer.

2. They have (risen, <u>raised</u>) their daughter to be a self-sufficient person.

3. As the crowd watched, the Iraq War veteran (rose, <u>raised</u>) the flag.

4. The reporters (<u>rose</u>, raised) as the president entered the room for the press conference.

5. The promising weather report (rose, <u>raised</u>) our hopes for an enjoyable camping trip.

REVIEW TEST 1

Cross out the incorrect verb form. Then write the correct form of the verb in the space provided.

Teaching Tip
You may want to use these review tests to assess what your students have learned.

sang   1. The famous recording artist first ~~sung~~ in his hometown church choir.

bitten   2. After Renee was ~~bit~~ by the parrot, her finger was sore for a week.

took   3. Last August, Carmen ~~taked~~ her family to Yellowstone National Park.

run   4. The plane would have ~~ran~~ off the runway if the pilot hadn't been so skillful.

burst   5. He heard a frightening hissing sound before the pipes ~~bursted~~.

wrote   6. I couldn't believe I got a B on the first paper I ~~writed~~ in college.

lay   7. Stefano ~~laid~~ in a lounge chair, staring up at the moon through his new binoculars.

gone   8. The class clown had ~~went~~ too far, and the students waited to see what the teacher would do.

risen   9. The sun had already ~~rose~~ by the time I got home from the party.

swam   10. As we approached the quiet pond, a beaver slid into the water and ~~swum~~ toward its underwater lodge.

REVIEW TEST 2

Write short sentences that use the form requested for the following irregular verbs.

EXAMPLE

Past of *ride:* _The Lone Ranger rode into the sunset._

1. Past of *drink* _drank_

2. Present of *bring* _bring (or brings)_

3. Past participle of *grow* _grown_

4. Present of *swim* _swim (or swims)_

5. Past participle of *write* _written_

6. Past of *give* _gave_

7. Present of *do* _do (or does)_

8. Past participle of *begin* _begun_

9. Past of *go* _went_

10. Present of *know* _know (or knows)_

NAME: _____

DATE: _____

Irregular Verbs

Underline the correct word in the parentheses.

1. My girlfriend and I (saw, seen) a bad car accident yesterday.

2. Tina (weared, wore) her favorite jeans until the patches were paper-thin.

3. Gianni (hurt , hurted) his hand when he tried to open the mayonnaise jar.

4. That Cutlass (cost , costed) more than I was willing to pay.

5. We should have (took, taken) the dog to the vet sooner.

6. Ralph has (drawed, drawn) blueprints for the cabin he hopes to build.

7. Simone (sended, sent) Mike their divorce papers in the mail.

8. Ever since Indira (became , become) a supervisor, she hasn't talked to us.

9. Max (catched, caught) pneumonia when he went camping in the mountains.

10. I (knew, knowed) the answer—I just couldn't think of it.

11. I must have (drove, driven) around the development for half an hour looking for my brother's new house.

12. Within a month, the baby had (grew, grown) two inches and gained three pounds.

13. Before my grandfather died, he (gave, given) me his gold pocket watch and army medals.

14. That gray-haired lumberjack has (arose, arisen) every day at dawn for the past fifty years.

15. When I heard that my car still hadn't been repaired, I (lost, losted) my temper.

16. As soon as you have (ate, eaten) all your ice cream, you may have some spinach.

17. Sarita (choose, chose) soft blue carpeting for her bedroom.

18. After raking the leaves, Julio (lay, laid) down under a tree and fell sound asleep.

19. The dummy (sang, sung) in a clear voice, but the ventriloquist's lips never moved.

20. Valerie had (rode, ridden) the roller coaster five times before she started complaining that everything was going around in circles.

NAME: _____

DATE: _____

MASTERY TEST 2

Irregular Verbs

Cross out the incorrect verb form. Write the correct form in the space provided.

swore   1. Paul ~~sweared~~ loudly when the wasp stung him.

bit   2. I ~~bited~~ down on salt-water taffy and lost a filling.

driven   3. As the car groaned and lurched from side to side, we realized that Lamont had never ~~drove~~ with a manual shift before.

thrown   4. Because Jenna had ~~throwed~~ away the receipt, she couldn't return the business suit.

slid   5. Though the runner ~~slided~~ head first, he was still tagged out at home plate.

rang   6. Barry ~~rung~~ the bell for fifteen minutes and then decided that no one was home.

drank   7. After I ran three miles in ninety-degree heat, I ~~drunk~~ a whole quart of iced tea.

hid   8. Lenny ~~hided~~ his daughter's graduation present so well that even he couldn't find it.

known   9. If I had ~~knew~~ better, I would never have left my car door unlocked.

kept   10. Maria broke her engagement but ~~keeped~~ all the wedding presents.

caught   11. I stayed away from sick people and took extra vitamin C all winter, but I ~~catched~~ a cold, anyway.

slept   12. On his first day of summer vacation, Danny ~~sleeped~~ until two in the afternoon.

shrank   13. My new cotton sweater ~~shrinked~~ so much that it now fits my daughter.

written   14. Mac was instantly sorry he had ~~writed~~ such an angry e-mail, but there was no way to get it back.

lit   15. The hostess turned on soft music and ~~lighted~~ candles on the table before her guests arrived.

run   16. I had ~~runned~~ out of cash before payday, so I had to ask my parents for a loan.

made   17. Nobody believed the criminal's claim that Martians had ~~maked~~ him rob the bank.

spoke   18. After the politician was invited to say a few words, he ~~speaked~~ for half an hour.

shut   19. Something private must be going on in the meeting, because a committee member just got up and ~~shutted~~ the door.

left   20. The group of diners ordered the most expensive steaks, drank the best champagne, kept two waitresses busy all night, and then ~~leaved~~ only a 10 percent tip.

NAME: _____

DATE: _____

SCORE
Number Correct

_____/10

_____%

MASTERY TEST 3

Irregular Verbs

In the space provide, write the correct form of the verb shown in the margin.

1. When I was little, my parents _____*taught*_____ me how to find my way home if I got lost. **teach**

2. My best friend _____*lent*_____ me twenty dollars so I could buy Dad a birthday gift. **lend**

3. It took eight months before Andy's garage was finally _____*built*_____. **build**

4. I used to fidget in class so much that I _____*wore*_____ a hole in my trousers. **wear**

5. Yren has read every novel J.R.R.Tolkien has _____*written*_____. **write**

6. Frowning, the building inspector stood where the grocery store's sign had _____*fallen*_____. **fall**

7. We _____*saw*_____ the other car coming, but we couldn't stop in time. **see**

8. Rina and Marvin _____*sent*_____ texts to their families, saying that they were eloping. **send**

9. I don't think he's heard a single word I have _____*spoken*_____. **speak**

10. I must have _____*slept*_____ twelve hours before I finally woke up. **sleep**

185

NAME: _____

DATE: _____

MASTERY TEST 4

Irregular Verbs

In the space provided, write the correct form of the verb shown in the margin.

burst

1. As soon as little Davy stuck a pin in it, the balloon ____*burst*____.

go

2. When the alarm rang, Flavia shut it off and ____*went*____ back to sleep.

bring

3. Yesterday, my cousin ____*brought*____ over his entire baseball card collection.

hurt

4. You really ____*hurt*____ my feelings when you told me you didn't like my new outfit.

keep

5. Whenever she rode in a car, my mother ____*kept*____ reminding the driver when a turn was coming up or a light was changing.

shake

6. After the collision, we were badly ____*shaken*____ up, but we had no broken bones.

spend

7. Josh ____*spent*____ a fortune on fishing equipment, but all he ever caught was a cold.

shrink

8. When she saw the giant tomato reaching for her in her dream, Amy ____*shrank*____ back in horror.

buy

9. Because stick shifts made her nervous, Mei Lin ____*bought*____ a car with an automatic transmission.

stick

10. Why have I ____*stuck*____ with this broken-down car for so long?

Subject-Verb Agreement

INTRODUCTORY ACTIVITY

As you read each pair of sentences below, place a check mark beside the sentence that you think uses the underlined word correctly.

There <u>was</u> many applicants for the position. _____
There <u>were</u> many applicants for the position. ___✓___

The pictures in that magazine <u>is</u> very controversial. _____
The pictures in that magazine <u>are</u> very controversial. ___✓___

Everybody usually <u>watch</u> the lighted numbers in an elevator. _____
Everybody usually <u>watches</u> the lighted numbers in an elevator. ___✓___

On the basis of the examples above, complete the following statements.

1. In the first two pairs of sentences, the subjects are ___*applicants*___ and
   ___*pictures*___. Since both these subjects are plural, the verb must be plural.

2. In the last pair of sentences, the subject, *Everybody,* is a word that is always (<u>singular</u>, plural), so that verb must be (<u>singular</u>, plural).

Answers are on page 638.

Teaching Tip
You may want to use this activity to assess your students' understanding of subject-verb agreement.

ESL Tip
Some common
agreement
problems:
1. Third-person
singular in the
present tense
(ends in -s/-es).
2. Subject and
verb don't
agree when
words come in
between them.
3. Verb in a
relative clause
does not agree
with the noun
that the clause
modifies.
4. Subject and
verb do not
agree when a
gerund or in-
finitive is used
as the subject.
5. Subject and
verb do not
agree when
the subject be-
gins with *there*
or *here.*
6. Verb does
not agree with
compound
subject (e.g.,
"Andy and
Jorge *plays*
soccer").

A verb must agree with its subject in number. A *singular subject* (one person or thing) takes a singular verb. A *plural subject* (more than one person or thing) takes a plural verb. Mistakes in subject-verb agreement are sometimes made in the following situations:

1. When words come between the subject and the verb
2. When a verb comes before the subject
3. With indefinite pronouns
4. With compound subjects
5. With *who, which,* and *that*

Each situation is explained on the following pages.

Words between the Subject and the Verb

Words that come between the subject and the verb do not change subject-verb agreement.

The breakfast cereals in the pantry are made mostly of sugar.

In the example above, the subject (*cereals*) is plural, so the verb (*are*) is plural. The words *in the pantry,* which come between the subject and the verb, do not affect subject-verb agreement. To help find the subject of certain sentences, you should cross out prepositional phrases (explained on pages 88–89):

One ~~of the corrupt law enforcers~~ was jailed for a month.

The posters ~~on my little brother's wall~~ include R&B stars, athletes, and models in bathing suits.

Following is a list of common prepositions.

Common Prepositions

about	before	by	inside	over
above	behind	during	into	through
across	below	except	of	to
among	beneath	for	off	toward
around	beside	from	on	under
at	between	in	onto	with

Underline the subject. Then lightly cross out any words that come between the subject and the verb. Finally, double-underline the correct verb in parentheses.

EXAMPLE

The price of the speakers (is, are) too high for my wallet.

1. The leaders of the union (has, have) called for a strike.

2. One of Omar's pencil sketches (hangs, hang) in the art classroom.

3. Three days of anxious waiting finally (ends, end) with a phone call.

4. The members of the car pool (chips, chip) in for the driving expenses.

5. The woman with the teased, sprayed hairdo (looks, look) as if she were wearing a plastic helmet.

6. The addition of heavy shades to my sunny windows (allows, allow) me to sleep during the day.

7. Several houses in the old whaling village (has, have) been designated as historical landmarks.

8. The stack of baseball cards in my little brother's bedroom (is, are) two feet high.

9. Gooey puddles of egg white (spreads, spread) over the stove as Mike cracks the shells against the frying pan.

10. The box of Raisinets (sells, sell) for eight dollars at the theater's candy counter.

Verb before the Subject

A verb agrees with its subject even when the verb comes *before* the subject. Words that may precede the subject include *there, here,* and, in questions, *who, which, what,* and *where.*

Inside the storage shed are the garden tools.

At the street corner were two panhandlers.

There are times I'm ready to quit my job.

Where are the instructions for the Blu-Ray player?

> **TIP** If you are unsure about the subject, ask *who* or *what* of the verb. With the first sentence above, you might ask, "What are inside the storage shed?" The answer, garden *tools,* is the subject.

Teaching Tip Suggest to your students that they work in pairs to complete this activity.

Teaching Tip Remind students that the object in a prepositional phrase is not the subject in the sentence.

Underline the subject in each sentence. Then double-underline the correct verb in parentheses.

1. Lumbering along the road (was, <u>were</u>) six heavy <u>trucks</u>.

2. There (<u>is</u>, are) now wild <u>coyotes</u> wandering the streets of many California suburbs.

3. Lining the country lanes (is, <u>are</u>) <u>rows</u> of tall, thin poplar trees.

4. At the back of my closet (is, <u>are</u>) the high platform <u>boots</u> I bought ten years ago.

5. Helping to unload the heavy sofa from the delivery truck (<u>was</u>, were) a skinny young <u>boy</u>.

6. Nosing through the garbage bags (<u>was</u>, were) a furry <u>animal</u> with a hairless tail.

7. Here (<u>is</u>, are) the rug <u>shampooer</u> I borrowed last month.

8. Along the side of the highway (<u>was</u>, were) a sluggish little <u>stream</u>.

9. Where (<u>is</u>, are) the <u>box</u> of kitchen trash bags?

10. On the door of his bedroom (<u>is</u>, are) a <u>sign</u> reading "Authorized personnel only."

Indefinite Pronouns

The following words, known as *indefinite pronouns,* always take singular verbs.

Indefinite Pronouns

(*-one* words)	(*-body* words)	(*-thing* words)	
one	nobody	nothing	each
anyone	anybody	anything	either
everyone	everybody	everything	neither
someone	somebody	something	

Both always takes a plural verb.

Write the correct form of the verb in the space provided.

is, are

1. Neither of those last two books on the list _____*is*_____ required for the course.

remembers, remember

2. Nobody _____*remembers*_____ seeing a suspicious green car cruising the street.

fits, fit

3. Both of these belts _____*fit*_____ perfectly.

has, have

4. Somebody _____*has*_____ been playing with my Xbox.

wanders, wander

5. Nobody _____*wanders*_____ into those woods during hunting season without wearing bright-colored clothing.

needs, need

6. Each of those dogs _____*needs*_____ to be inoculated against rabies.

keeps, keep

7. One of my friends _____*keeps*_____ a pet iguana in her dorm room.

sneaks, sneak

8. Everyone _____*sneaks*_____ stationery and pens out of our office.

is, are

9. Either of those motels _____*is*_____ good enough for me.

eats, eat

10. One of my children _____*eats*_____ raw onions as if they were apples.

Teaching Tip
Tell students to underline the indefinite pronoun to help them determine whether the verb should be singular or plural.

Teaching Tip
You may want to provide additional examples of compound subjects joined by *either . . . or, neither . . . nor,* and *not only . . . but also.*

Compound Subjects

Subjects joined by *and* generally take a plural verb.

Yoga and biking are Alex's ways of staying in shape.

Ambition and strong work ethic are the keys to her success.

When subjects are joined by *or, either . . . or, neither . . . nor, not only . . . but also,* the verb agrees with the subject closer to the verb.

Either the restaurant manager or his assistants deserve to be fired for the spoiled meat used in the stew.

The nearer subject, *assistants,* is plural, so the verb is plural.

PRACTICE 4

Write the correct form of the verb in the space provided.

seem,
seems

1. The Pilates and spinning classes _____ *seem* _____ to help me stay in shape, but the key to fitness is a sensible diet.

is, are

2. Either the tongue ring or the dragon tattoo _____ *is* _____ responsible for Zack's appeal.

is, are

3. A double shot of espresso and two pumps of hazelnut syrup _____ *are* _____ all I need to start my morning.

help, helps

4. The lecture podcasts and study guides _____ *help* _____ me prepare for exams.

impress,
impresses

5. Neither Mick Jagger nor my favorite rock band, the Rolling Stones, _____ *impresses* _____ my ten-year-old daughter, who prefers Justin Bieber.

Who, Which, and That

When *who, which,* and *that* are used as subjects, they take singular verbs if the word they stand for is singular, and they take plural verbs if the word they stand for is plural. For example, in the sentence

Hannah is one of those people who are very private.

the verb is plural because *who* stands for *people*, which is plural. On the other hand, in the sentence

Hannah is a person who is very private.

the verb is singular because *who* stands for *person*, which is singular.

PRACTICE 5

Write the correct form of the verb in the space provided.

roams,
roam

1. The dogs that _____ *roam* _____ around this area are household pets abandoned by cruel owners.

begins,
begin

2. A sharp pain that _____ *begins* _____ in the lower abdomen may signal appendicitis.

thunders,
thunder

3. The heavy trucks that _____ *thunder* _____ past my car make me feel as though I'm being blown off the road.

fears,
fear

4. The canyon tour isn't for people who _____*fear*_____ heights.

tastes,
taste

5. This drink, which _____*tastes*_____ like pure sugar, is supposed to be 100 percent fruit juice.

COLLABORATIVE ACTIVITY

Editing and Rewriting

Working with a partner, read the short paragraph below and mark off the five mistakes in subject-verb agreement. Then use the space provided to correct the five agreement errors. Feel free to discuss the rewrite quietly with your partner and refer back to the chapter when necessary.

Sometimes I just don't understand people. For instance, my neighbors, Adolfo and Janelle, go to the gym almost every day. Adolfo rides an exercise bike, Janelle runs on the treadmill, and they both take Zumba classes. Neither of them <u>like</u> to pay for the gym membership. But, as Janelle says, "Fitness and good health <u>is</u> very important to us both." Now, I think it's great that anyone <u>are</u> trying to stay fit and healthy. But this is the part of their activities that <u>don't</u> make sense to me. In order to get to the gym, these fitness nuts drive half a mile. Then they come home and take the elevator three stories up to their apartment. Wouldn't walking and climbing stairs <u>burns</u> calories as well as the exercise they do in an expensive gym?

Neither . . . likes _____   *part . . . that doesn't* _____

Fitness and good health are _____   *walking and climbing . . . burn* _____

anyone is _____

Teaching Tip Ask students to work on the Collaborative Activities in pairs and share their answers for the Reflective Activity with the entire class.

COLLABORATIVE ACTIVITY

Creating Sentences

Working with a partner, write sentences as directed. With each item, pay special attention to subject-verb agreement.

1. Write a sentence in which the words *in the cafeteria* or *on the table* come between the subject and verb. Underline the subject of your sentence and circle the verb.

2. Look at the photo in this box and write a sentence that begins with the words *there is* or *there are*. Underline the subject of your sentence and circle the verb.

3. Write a sentence in which the indefinite pronoun *nobody* or *anything* is the subject.

4. Write a sentence with the compound subjects *manager* and *employees*. Underline the subject of your sentence and circle the verb.

REFLECTIVE ACTIVITY

1. Look at the paragraph about Adolfo and Janelle that you revised. Which rule involving subject-verb agreement gave you the most trouble? How did you figure out the correct answer?

2. Explain which of the five subject-verb agreement situations discussed in this chapter is most likely to cause you problems.

REVIEW TEST 1

Answers will vary.

Teaching Tip
You may want to use these review tests to assess what your students have learned.

Complete each of the following sentences, using *is, are, was, were, have,* or *has*. Underline the subject of each of these verbs.

EXAMPLE

The hot dogs in that diner ___*are hazardous to your health.*___

1. Either of those small keys _____

_____

2. The practical joker in our office _____
   _____

3. The celebrity and his bodyguard _____
   _____

4. He was the kind of customer who _____
   _____

5. The memos posted on the office door _____
   _____

6. There's always someone who _____
   _____

7. The old boiler, along with the rusty water tanks, _____
   _____

8. The air freshener hanging from her rearview mirror _____
   _____

9. The first few times that I tried to roller-skate _____
   _____

10. The spectators outside the courtroom _____
    _____

REVIEW TEST 2

Underline the correct word in the parentheses.

1. The number of commercials between television shows (is, are) increasing.
2. Lani and Paco (works, work) overnight at the motel's registration desk.
3. A report on either book (counts, count) as extra credit.
4. Both the mattress and the box spring on this bed (is, are) filled with rusty, uncoiling springs.
5. Nobody in that class ever (argues, argue) with the professor.
6. Remembering everyone's birthday and organizing family reunions (is, are) my sister's main hobbies.

7. Lying like limp little dolls on the bed (was, <u>were</u>) the exhausted children.

8. The woman at the cellphone store who (<u>takes</u>, take) appointments wears a photo ID tag around her neck.

9. The illegal dogfights which (occurs, <u>occur</u>) regularly in our town are being investigated by the SPCA.

10. Sewn into the sweater's seam (was, <u>were</u>) an extra button and a small hank of matching yarn for repairs.

REVIEW TEST 3

There are eight mistakes in subject-verb agreement in the following passage. Cross out each incorrect verb and write the correct form above it. In addition, underline the subject of each of the verbs that must be changed.

What are the <u>factors</u> that ~~makes~~ *make* a third-grade child aggressive and destructive? On the other hand, what experiences help a third-grader make friends easily and earn good grades in school? Years of research on a group of children from infancy through elementary school ~~has~~ *have* provided an answer, or at least a new theory. A <u>psychologist</u> from one of our leading universities ~~claim~~ *claims* that <u>success</u> in the early grades ~~are~~ *is* the direct result of a close relationship with the mother. <u>Babies</u> who have this relationship with a mother ~~seems~~ *seem* to gain the strength and self-esteem they need for future success in the classroom and in life. A strong, secure <u>bond</u> between a mother and child ~~are~~ *is* formed when mothers respond quickly and consistently to their babies' needs. Both the <u>speed</u> and the <u>attention</u> ~~is~~ *are* important in earning a baby's trust. The researcher points out that there ~~are~~ *is* no <u>evidence</u> of a link between day care arrangements and weaker mother-baby attachments. It is the quality of the relationship, not the actual hours spent, that causes a child to feel secure.

Subject-Verb Agreement

Underline the correct verb in the parentheses. Note that you will first have to determine the subject of each sentence. To help you determine the subjects in certain sentences, you may find it helpful to cross out prepositional phrases.

1. Neither of the dogs rescued from the greyhound kennel (<u>is</u>, are) likely to be adopted.

2. One of my roommates in college (<u>wants</u>, want) to become a software engineer so that she can create cutting-edge video games.

3. The cost of all my utilities, which include electricity, water, cable, and phone, (<u>is</u>, are) ridiculous.

4. High-speed chases and grisly car accidents (seems, <u>seem</u>) to be the focus on many reality television shows.

5. Not one of the red tag specials advertised on the store's website (<u>was</u>, were) left on the shelf.

6. Once a year, Jackie and her friends (takes, <u>take</u>) a weekend trip to Las Vegas for shopping, dining, and gambling.

7. The online articles that the librarian located for the student (was, <u>were</u>) originally published in print.

8. Squeaking from underneath the refrigerator (<u>was</u>, were) a tiny mouse caught in a forgotten, rusty, spring-based trap.

9. Neither Dad nor my brother Miguel (<u>wants</u>, want) to talk about his experiences as a combat soldier in the Iraq War.

10. There (<u>was</u>, were) a laptop left in one of the carrels at the library.

11. A kleptomaniac will steal anything that (<u>is</u>, are) not nailed down.

12. A few girls at my daughter's high school (plans, <u>plan</u>) to try out for the football team.

13. Not only the air ducts but also the plumbing in the abandoned building (<u>is</u>, are) infested with rats.

14. Everyone in my history class (<u>believes</u>, believe) that the professor grades unfairly, but nobody is willing to approach her.

NAME: _____

DATE: _____

Subject-Verb Agreement

In the space provided, write the correct form of the verb shown in the margin.

comes, come   1. All the wrinkles in a drip-dry shirt ____*come*____ out with a cool iron.

Is, Are   2. ____*Are*____ all the bracelets Toshiko wears made of real gold?

does, do   3. Alcoholic beverages and allergy pills ____*do*____ not make a good combination.

was, were   4. No one ____*was*____ willing to take the blame for the spilled paint.

is, are   5. Under the sofa ____*is*____ a year's supply of dust.

was, were   6. Neither of the jackets I was looking for ____*was*____ in the closet.

sees, see   7. Krista and Eve ____*see*____ better with contact lenses than they saw with glasses.

is, are   8. Three of the books Sandy borrowed from the library ____*are*____ overdue.

was, were   9. A complete list of complaints and demands ____*was*____ read at the beginning of the tenants' meeting.

is, are   10. At the intersection of Pleasant Grove Lane and Valley View Road ____*is*____ the future location of the new shopping mall.

NAME: _____

DATE: _____

SCORE
Number Correct

_____/10

_____%

MASTERY TEST 3

Subjects-Verb Agreement

Cross out the incorrect form of the verb. In addition, underline the subject that goes with the verb. Then write the correct form of the verb in the space provided. Mark the one sentence that is correct with a C.

are   1. There ~~is~~ some unpleasant <u>surprises</u> among this month's bills.

do   2. Those <u>piles</u> of dirty laundry ~~does~~ not belong to me.

have   3. The <u>lilies</u> that we planted last year ~~has~~ grown to over six feet tall.

have   4. My <u>counselor</u> and my English <u>instructor</u> ~~has~~ agreed to write job recommendations for me.

believes   5. Almost <u>every</u> child who celebrates Christmas in my neighborhood under the age of ten ~~believe~~ in Santa Claus.

C   6. Neither Gale nor Jerry plans to look for a job this summer.

stay   7. Many gas <u>stations</u> on that highway ~~stays~~ open all night.

is   8. The <u>mayor</u>, along with the council members, ~~are~~ helping carry sandbags for flood control.

was   9. Lying across all the lanes of the highway ~~were~~ a jackknifed <u>tractor-trailer</u>.

have   10. Emil's <u>parents</u>, who have been seeing a marriage counselor, ~~has~~ decided to get a divorce.

NAME: _____

DATE: _____

Subject-Verb Agreement

Cross out the incorrect form of the verb. In addition, underline the subject that goes with the verb. Then write the correct form of the verb in the space provided. Mark the one sentence that is correct with a C.

hangs

1. At the back of my mother's closet ~~hang~~ an old-fashioned muskrat fur coat with padded shoulders.

gets

2. Anyone who punches in late more than once ~~get~~ an official warning from the personnel department.

contain

3. Many scenes in the G-rated movie ~~contains~~ R-rated material.

are

4. His toy soldiers and stamp collection ~~is~~ the only things that mean anything to him.

was

5. Leaning against the lamppost with his hands in his pockets ~~were~~ a dangerous-looking character.

C

6. When I was seven, being alone in the house and hearing the walls creak in the wind were the scariest things in my life.

seems

7. Something ~~seem~~ odd about Uncle Rico this evening; he's forgetting everything people are saying.

burst

8. The plastic trash bags that never ~~bursts~~ on TV always break in my kitchen.

act

9. Thick white fur and black skin ~~acts~~ like a greenhouse, trapping heat and keeping a polar bear warm in the coldest weather.

are

10. When ~~is~~ Lew and Marian going to return the camping equipment they borrowed from us?

Consistent Verb Tense

INTRODUCTORY ACTIVITY

Underline the two mistakes in verb tense in the following selection.

When Computer Warehouse had a sale, Katya decided to buy a new laptop. She planned to set up a home office and hoped to connect to the Internet right away. When she arrived home, however, Katya discovers that, due to her building's location in a dead zone, setting up her wireless connection was complicated and confusing. After two hours of frustration, Katya gave up and calls a technician for help.

Now complete the following statement:

Verb tenses should be consistent. In the selection above, two verbs have to be changed because they are mistakenly in the (*present, past*) ___present___ tense, while all the other verbs in the selection are in the (*present, past*) ___past___ tense.

Answers are on page 639.

Teaching Tip
You may want to use this activity to assess your students' understanding of consistent verb tense.

ESL Tip
Nonnative speakers need to know that time is expressed by the verb in English.

Keeping Tenses Consistent

PERSONALIZED LEARNING

Do not shift tenses unnecessarily. If you begin writing a paper in the present tense, don't shift suddenly to the past. If you begin in the past, don't shift without reason to the present. Notice the inconsistent verb tenses in the following example:

Smoke spilled from the front of the overheated car. The driver opens up the hood, then jumped back as steam billows out.

The verbs must be consistently in the present tense:

Smoke spills from the front of the overheated car. The driver opens up the hood, then jumps back as steam billows out.

Or the verbs must be consistently in the past tense:

> Smoke <u>spilled</u> from the front of the overheated car. The driver <u>opened</u> up the hood, then <u>jumped</u> back as steam <u>billowed</u> out.

<table>
<tr><td>PRACTICE 1</td><td>In each item, one verb must be changed so that it agrees in tense with the other verbs. Cross out the incorrect verb and write the correct form in the space at the left of each sentence.</td></tr>
</table>

EXAMPLE

learned   I donated blood at the American Red Cross after I ~~learn~~ that someone in the U.S. will need blood every two or three seconds.

prepares   1. Bill, a devoted single father, cooks his children breakfast, drives them to school, takes them to soccer practice, ~~prepared~~ dinner at night, and helps them with their homework.

filled   2. Before starting his shift, the cab driver stopped at the ATM to withdraw fifty dollars and ~~fills~~ his car up with gas.

found   3. Worried that I would be late for class, I leaned my bike against the bike rack instead of locking it up. When I returned to it a few hours later, I ~~find~~ that it had been stolen.

began   4. After the labor union voted to enforce mandatory drug testing, my co-workers ~~begin~~ to talk about ways to cheat on the test, such as eating poppy seeds and drinking detox teas.

are   5. Some people argue that Americans are too materialistic. After all, there ~~were~~ more shopping malls than high schools in this country.

separated   6. Don and I divorced five years ago. He remarried the following year but ~~separate~~ from that wife a year later.

send   7. In the workplace, employees are discouraged from making personal phone calls. Many of them, however, ~~sent~~ personal e-mails while at work.

sells   8. Madeline spends her weekends going to garage sales, auctions, and thrift stores. She collects military antiques, which she ~~sold~~ for a profit online.

said   9. Last month, Tommy wanted to adopt a shelter cat, but the property manager at his apartment building ~~says~~ that he would be violating his lease agreement.

likes   10. When my dog is left home alone, he ~~liked~~ to pull dirty laundry from the hamper and rummage through the wastebaskets.

Change the verbs where needed in the following selection so that they are consistently in the past tense. Cross out each incorrect verb and write the correct form above it, as shown in the example. You will need to make ten corrections.

Teaching Tip
You may want to use these review tests to assess what your students have learned.

Making a foul shot that won a basketball game was a special moment for me. For most of the year, I sat on the bench. The coach put me on the team after the tryouts and then ~~forgets~~ *forgot* about me. Then my chance ~~appears~~ *appeared* near the end of the Rosemont High School game. The score was tied 65 to 65. Because of injuries and foul-outs, most of the substitutes, except me, were in the game. Then our last first-stringer, Larry Toner, got an elbow in the eye and ~~leaves~~ *left* the game. The coach looked at me and said, "Get in there, Watson." The clock showed ten seconds to go. Rosemont had the ball when, suddenly, one of their players ~~misses~~ *missed* a pass. People ~~scramble~~ *scrambled* for the ball; then our center, Kevin, grabbed it and ~~starts~~ *started* down the court. He looked around and saw me about twenty feet from the basket. I caught his pass, and before I could decide whether to shoot or pass, a Rosemont player ~~fouls~~ *fouled* me. The referee's whistle blew, and I had two free throws with two seconds left in the game. My stomach ~~churns~~ *churned* as I stepped to the foul line. I almost couldn't hold the ball because my hands were so damp with sweat. I shot and missed, and the Rosemont crowd ~~sighs~~ *sighed* with relief. My next shot would mean a win for us or overtime. I looked at the hoop, shot, and waited for what seemed like forever. The ball ~~circles~~ *circled* the rim and dropped in, and then the buzzer sounded. Everyone on the team slapped me on the back and the coach ~~smacks~~ *smacked* my rear end, saying, "All right, Watson!" I'll always remember that moment.

Change verbs as necessary in the following selection so that they are consistently in the past tense. Cross out each incorrect verb and write the correct form above it. You will need to make ten corrections in all.

According to an old Greek myth, the goddess of the harvest had one child, a beautiful daughter. One day, as the daughter was gathering flowers, the god of the underworld drove by in his chariot. He ~~sees~~ *saw* her and fell madly in love with her. He ~~reaches~~ *reached* out, grabbed the frightened girl, and pulled her into the chariot beside him. The daughter's screams were useless as the two drove below the surface of the earth. Soon they reached the land of the dead, where he ~~forces~~ *forced* her to become his wife. Not long afterward, the goddess ~~realizes~~ *realized* her daughter was missing. She searched for her all over the world. When she could not find the girl, she became so grief-stricken that she ~~neglects~~ *neglected* her duties, and all over the earth, the crops weakened and died. Finally she threatened that nothing would grow until her daughter was returned to her. Zeus, king of the gods, then commanded that the daughter ~~has~~ *had* to be released—but only if she had not eaten anything. The god of the underworld agreed to let her go, but he ~~tricks~~ *tricked* her into eating six pomegranate seeds before she ~~leaves~~ *left*. Because the girl had eaten the food of Death, she had to live in Death's kingdom six months of the year, one for each of the seeds. In this way, the Greeks said, the seasons came into being. When the daughter was permitted to rejoin her mother, she brought spring and summer with her—and the crops ~~begin~~ *began* to grow. But when fall came, she ~~is~~ *was* forced to return to the land of the dead, and all growing things on earth died with her.

NAME: _____

DATE: _____

Consistent Verb Tense

In each item, one verb must be changed so that it agrees in tense with the other verbs. Cross out the inconsistent verb and write the correct form in the space provided.

wiped   1. Before the toothbrush was invented, people ~~wipe~~ their teeth with a rag that had chalk on it.

stop   2. On my commute to my 8:30 A.M. class, I always ~~stopped~~ at Ben's Bagel Bakery and get an onion bagel with cream cheese.

discovered   3. I stepped on a horseshoe crab at the beach and ~~discover~~ it had sky-blue blood.

washed   4. Sally ~~washes~~ her permanent-press curtains and hung them on the rods while they were still wet.

turns   5. While Miguel is dieting, he avoids pasta, ~~turned~~ down pastries, and passes up chocolate milk shakes.

frightened   6. Leo enjoyed his first airplane flight, although the trip ~~frightens~~ him so much at first that he held onto the armrests.

smoke   7. Whenever I ~~smoked~~ more than ten cigarettes a day, my eyes burn and my hands start to shake.

found   8. Lidia reached for the economy brand of ketchup but ~~finds~~ that it cost as much as the name brand.

observed   9. For my sociology project, I went to a Laundromat, ~~observe~~ the people there, and took notes on their behavior.

pulled   10. Mrs. Frank sat wearily on her suitcase and stared off into space as the bus ~~pulls~~ into the station.

NAME: _____

DATE: _____

Consistent Verb Tense

In each item, one verb must be changed so that it agrees in tense with the other verbs. Cross out the inconsistent verb and write the correct form in the space provided.

collected

1. After I got my promotion, my friends ~~collect~~ three hundred dollars, rented a hall, and threw a party in my honor.

argue

2. Every year when Halloween comes, we ~~argued~~ about who gets to greet the trick-or-treaters at the door.

ended

3. When the strike finally ~~ends~~ and the teachers went back to work, everyone rejoiced except the students.

pokes

4. Uncle Paulie, who collects antique bottles, visits every garage sale in the neighborhood and ~~poked~~ around in people's attics for hidden treasures.

purchased

5. Leticia decided to become a CIA agent, so she ~~purchases~~ a trench coat and began speaking in whispers whenever she was in public.

was

6. Everything was strangely peaceful on our street; not a person was in sight and not a car ~~is~~ moving.

look

7. When I wake up with my contacts still in my eyes, my head pounds, my eyes ~~looked~~ like road maps, and they have trouble focusing.

brushed

8. I was really nervous before my first date. I ~~brush~~ my hair and looked in the mirror a dozen times.

collapses

9. At Thanksgiving, we consume a twenty-pound turkey and three kinds of pie for dessert. Then, everyone ~~collapsed~~ on the floor and moans in agony.

fixed

10. My little brother borrowed my dad's toolbox so he could play home repairman. Then he ~~fixes~~ all the kitchen chairs by removing the screws that held them together.

206

Additional Information about Verbs

The purpose of this special chapter is to provide additional information about verbs. Some people will find the grammatical terms here a helpful reminder of earlier school learning about verbs. For them, these terms will increase their understanding of how verbs function in standard English. Other people may welcome more detailed information about terms used elsewhere in the text. In either case, remember that the most common mistakes people make when using verbs have been treated in earlier sections of the book.

Verb Tense

Verbs tell us the time of an action. The time that a verb shows is usually called *tense.* The most common tenses are the simple present, past, and future. In addition, there are nine other tenses that enable us to express more specific ideas about time than we could with the simple tenses alone. Following are the twelve verb tenses and examples of each tense. Read them to increase your sense of the many different ways of expressing time in standard English.

Tenses	Examples
Present	I *work*.
	Tanya *works*.
Past	Howard *worked* on the lawn.
Future	You *will work* overtime this week.
Present perfect	Gail *has worked* hard on the puzzle.
	They *have worked* well together.
Past perfect	They *had worked* eight hours before their shift ended.
Future perfect	The volunteers *will have worked* many unpaid hours.
Present progressive	I *am* not *working* today.
	You *are working* the second shift.
	The dryer *is* not *working* properly.
Past progressive	She *was working* outside.
	The plumbers *were working* here this morning.
Future progressive	The sound system *will be working* by tonight.
Present perfect progressive	Married life *has been working* out well for that couple
Past perfect progressive	I *had been working* overtime until recently.
Future perfect progressive	My sister *will have been working* at that store for eleven straight months by the time she takes a vacation next week

ESL Tip
Nonnative speakers may need to learn the usage and forms of verb tenses. This chart can be expanded to include the function and form of verb tenses in English.

Teaching Tip
Ask students to provide another example for each of the verb tenses.

The perfect tenses are formed by adding *have, has, had,* or *will have* to the past participle (the form of the verb that ends, usually, in *-ed*). The progressive tenses are formed by adding *am, is, are, was, were,* or *will be* to the present participle (the form of the verb that ends in *-ing*). The perfect progressive tenses are formed by adding *have been has been, had been,* or *will have been* to the present participle.

Certain tenses are explained in more detail on the following pages.

Present Perfect (*have* or *has* + past participle)

The present perfect tense expresses an action that began in the past and has recently been completed or is continuing in the present.

> The city *has* just *agreed* on a contract with the sanitation workers.
>
> Tony's parents *have lived* in that house for twenty years.
>
> Bernadette *has enjoyed* vampire novels since she was a little girl.

Past Perfect (*had* + past participle)

The past perfect tense expresses a past action that was completed before another past action.

> Bella *had learned* to dance by the time she was five.
>
> The class *had* just *started* when the fire bell rang.
>
> Bad weather *had* never *been* a problem on our vacations until last year.

Present Progressive (*am, is,* or *are* + -*ing* form)

The present progressive tense expresses an action still in progress.

> I *am taking* an early train into the city every day this week.
>
> Karl *is playing* softball over at the field.
>
> The vegetables *are growing* rapidly.

Past Progressive (*was* or *were* + -*ing* form)

The past progressive expresses an action that was in progress in the past.

> I *was spending* only fifty dollars a week on groceries before I had a child.
>
> Last week, the store *was selling* many items at half price.
>
> My friends *were driving* over to pick me up when the accident occurred.

ESL Tip
A comparison between the simple present and present perfect, and the simple past and present perfect, may be helpful.

ESL Tip
A comparison between the simple past and the past perfect might assist non-native speakers in using the past perfect tense.

ESL Tip
Remind students that the present progressive is generally not used with certain verbs (see Appendix A). Students should review the form of this verb tense because they often leave out the correct form of *to be*.

PRACTICE 1

For the sentences that follow, fill in the present or past perfect or the present or past progressive of the verb shown. Use the tense that seems to express the meaning of each sentence best.

EXAMPLE

Teaching Tip
Students may find this activity challenging, so encourage them to work in pairs.

park   This summer, Mickey _____ *is parking* _____ cars at a French restaurant.

watch   1. The police _____ *had watched* _____ the house for months before they made the arrests.

write   2. She _____ *has written* _____ to the newspaper several times, but the editors never publish her comments.

take   3. I _____ *am taking* _____ a course in adolescent psychology; maybe it will help me understand my teenagers.

lift   4. The fog _____ *had lifted* _____ well before the morning rush hour began.

improve   5. For the last two years, our community group _____ *has improved* _____ our street by cleaning up trash and planting trees.

protest   6. The waitresses _____ *are protesting* _____ against the skimpy new uniforms that they are being told to wear.

dread   7. I _____ *have dreaded* _____ heights ever since one of my brothers pushed me off a wall when I was six.

vow   8. This semester, he _____ *has vowed* _____ to stick to an organized study schedule.

peek   9. Some students _____ *were peeking* _____ at their notes when the professor entered the exam room.

get   10. You _____ *are getting* _____ some gray hairs; why don't you let me pull them out?

Verbals

Verbals are words formed from verbs. Verbals, like verbs, often express action. They can add variety to your sentences and vigor to your writing style. The three kinds of verbals are *infinitives, participles,* and *gerunds.*

Infinitive

An infinitive is *to* plus the base form of the verb.

> I started *to practice.*
> Don't try *to lift* that table.
> I asked Russ *to drive* me home.

ESL Tip
Nonnative speakers may need to study commonly used verb forms (see Appendix A).

Participle

A participle is a verb form used as an adjective (a descriptive word). The present participle ends in *-ing.* The past participle ends in *-ed* or has an irregular ending.

> *Favoring* his *cramped* leg, the *screaming* boy waded out of the pool.
> The *laughing* child held up her *locked* piggy bank.
> *Using* a shovel and a bucket, I scooped water out of the *flooded* basement.

Gerund

A gerund is the *-ing* form of a verb used as a noun.

> *Studying* wears me out.
> *Playing* basketball is my main pleasure during the week.
> Through *jogging,* you can get yourself in shape.

In the space beside each sentence, identify the italicized word as a participle (*P*), an infinitive (*I*), or a gerund (*G*).

PRACTICE 2

ESL Tip
Nonnative speakers may have difficulty distinguishing between *-ed* and *-ing* forms when they are used as adjectives. Explain the difference— e.g., "I am *interesting*" as opposed to "I am *interested*" (see Appendix A).

_P_ 1. The aroma of *baking* sourdough bread lured diners into the restaurant.

_G_ 2. My professor told us that *reusing* our old papers is plagiarism.

_I_ 3. Caitlin wants *to enlist* in the U.S. Army once she graduates from high school.

_G_ 4. Online *investing* requires skill and knowledge, but novice investors are often overly eager to play the stock market.

_I_ 5. Community volunteers tried *to paint* over the graffiti left by vandals.

_P_ 6. Some marine scientists suggest that the *decaying* flesh of another shark is an effective shark repellent.

_P_ 7. *Whispering* softly, my co-worker cautioned me that our manager was in a foul mood.

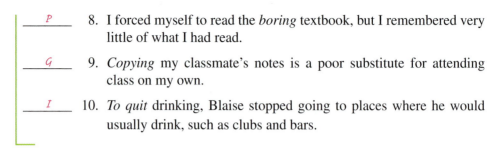

_____P_____ 8. I forced myself to read the *boring* textbook, but I remembered very little of what I had read.

_____G_____ 9. *Copying* my classmate's notes is a poor substitute for attending class on my own.

_____I_____ 10. *To quit* drinking, Blaise stopped going to places where he would usually drink, such as clubs and bars.

Active and Passive Verbs

When the subject of a sentence performs the action of a verb, the verb is in the *active voice.* When the subject of a sentence receives the action of a verb, the verb is in the *passive voice.*

The passive form of a verb consists of a form of the verb *be* plus the past participle of the main verb. Look at the active and passive forms of the verbs below.

ACTIVE

Uma *ate* the vanilla pudding.

(The subject, *Uma,* is the doer of the action.)

The plumber *replaced* the water heater.

(The subject, *plumber,* is the doer of the action.)

PASSIVE

The vanilla pudding *was eaten by* Uma.

(The subject, *pudding,* does not act. Instead, something happens to it.)

The water heater *was replaced by* the plumber.

(The subject, *heater,* does not act. Instead, something happens to it.)

In general, active verbs are more effective than passive ones. Active verbs give your writing a simpler and more vigorous style. The passive form of verbs is appropriate, however, when the performer of the action is unknown or is less important than the receiver of the action—for example,

My house was vandalized last night.
(The performer of the action is unknown.)

Troy was seriously injured as a result of your negligence.
(The receiver of the action, *Troy,* is being emphasized.)

Change the following sentences from the passive to the active voice. Note that you may have to add a subject in some cases.

PRACTICE 3

EXAMPLES

The moped was ridden by Morgan.

Morgan rode the moped.

The production's ensemble cast was given a standing ovation.

The audience gave the production's ensemble cast a standing ovation.

(Here a subject had to be added.)

1. Carla's long hair was snipped off by the beautician.

   The beautician snipped off Carla's long hair.

2. The teachers' strike was protested by the parents.

   The parents protested the teachers' strike.

3. The silent alarm was tripped by the alert bank teller.

   The alert bank teller tripped the silent alarm.

4. The escaped convicts were tracked by relentless bloodhounds.

   Relentless bloodhounds tracked the escaped convicts.

5. The new PET scanner was donated to the hospital.

   A famous entertainer donated the new PET scanner to the hospital.

6. A gallon glass jar of pickles was dropped in the supermarket aisle by a stock clerk.

   A stock clerk dropped a gallon glass jar of pickles in the supermarket aisle.

7. The deer was struck as it crossed the highway.

   A car struck the deer as it crossed the highway.

8. I was referred by my doctor to a specialist in hearing problems.

   My doctor referred me to a specialist in hearing problems.

9. One wall of my living room is covered by family photographs.

   Family photographs cover one wall of my living room.

10. The town was gripped by fear during the accident at the nuclear power plant.

    Fear gripped the town during the accident at the nuclear power plant.

Teaching Tip
Encourage students to underline the passive verb in each sentence.

Teaching Tip
Point out to students that a passive verb often makes a sentence wordy.

REVIEW TEST 1

On a separate sheet of paper or in a separate file, write three sentences apiece that use

1. Present perfect tense

2. Past perfect tense

3. Present progressive tense

4. Past progressive tense

5. Infinitive

6. Participle

7. Gerund

8. Passive voice (when the subject is unknown or is less important than the receiver of an action—see page 212)

NAME: _____

DATE: _____

Additional Information about Verbs

Part A

*In each space, write the **present perfect tense** form of the verb shown.*

occur   1. In the past few years, several shark attacks ___*have occurred*___ off the shores of Maui.

grow up   2. Millions of children ___*have grown up*___ reading the *Hunger Games* books.

testify   3. Thousands of people ___*have testified*___ in support of children's health care legislation.

Part B

*In each space, write the **past perfect tense** form of the verb shown.*

finish   4. Miho ___*had finished*___ taking her English and math placement tests before she received a call from the hospital about her father.

write   5. After two months, I ___*had written*___ only three pages of my term paper.

Part C

*In each space, write the **present progressive tense** form of the verb shown.*

take   6. I ___*am taking*___ insulin to control my diabetes, but my endocrinologist says that I can control the disease through exercise and diet.

organize   7. Gayle ___*is organizing*___ several Take Back the Night events at the Women's Center in March.

Part D

*In each space, write the **past progressive tense** form of the verb shown.*

raise   8. The students in Mr. Pascual's sixth-grade class ___*were raising*___ money for their trip to Washington, D.C., by recycling cans and bottles.

play   9. Until last year, my daughter ___*was playing*___ with Bratz dolls, but now all she wants to do is play *Plants vs. Zombies*.

Present   10. The mayor ___*was presenting*___ a speech at the neighborhood board meeting when the civil defense siren sounded.

215

NAME: _____

DATE: _____

Additional Information about Verbs

Part 1

In the space provided, identify the italicized word as a participle (P), *an infinitive* (I), *or a gerund* (G).

___P___ 1. Karen worries that her toddler will swallow *chipped* paint, which might contain lead.

___P___ 2. Mark, who works twice as hard as his teammates, joined the collegiate *wrestling* team as a walk-on.

___I___ 3. My seventeen-year-old son wants *to buy* a car, but he expects his parents to pay for the insurance and gasoline.

___G___ 4. Over fifty college students have died of alcohol *poisoning* since 2010.

___P___ 5. The Tex-Mex restaurant in town is known for its *sizzling* fajita steaks.

Part 2

Change the following sentences from the passive to the active voice. Note that you may have to add a subject in some cases.

1. The celebrities on the red carpet were photographed by the clamoring paparazzi.

   The paparazzi clamored to photograph the celebrities on the red carpet.

2. A five-day extension on the research project was given to students by the professor.

   The professor gave students a five-day extension on the research project.

3. Blood was drawn by a phlebotomist to randomly test employees for illegal drug use.

   The phlebotomist drew blood to randomly test employees for illegal drug use.

4. Thousands of dollars have been gambled away by Keith playing online video poker.

   Keith has gambled away thousands of dollars playing online video poker.

5. "Gently used" prom and bridal dresses were donated by women of all ages to high school girls in need of gowns.

   Women of all ages donated their "gently used" prom and bridal dresses to high school

   girls in need of gowns.

Pronoun Reference, Agreement, and Point of View

INTRODUCTORY ACTIVITY

Read each pair of sentences below, noting the underlined pronouns. Then circle the correct letter in each of the statements that follow.

1. a. Neither of the finalists in the talent competition showed their anxiety as the envelope was being opened.

   b. Neither of the finalists in the talent competition showed her anxiety as the envelope was being opened.

2. a. At the mall, they are already putting up holiday decorations.

   b. At the mall, shop owners are already putting up holiday decorations.

3. a. I go to the steak house often because you can get inexpensive meals there.

   b. I go to the steak house often because I can get inexpensive meals there.

In the first pair, (a, b) uses the underlined pronoun correctly because the pronoun refers to *Neither,* which is a singular word.

In the second pair, (a, b) is correct because otherwise the pronoun reference would be unclear.

In the third pair, (a, b) is correct because the pronoun point of view should not be shifted unnecessarily.

Answers are on page 639.

Teaching Tip
You may want to use this activity to assess your students' understanding of pronoun reference, agreement, and point of view. Introduce students to the term *antecedent.*

Pronouns are words that take the place of nouns (words for persons, places, or things). In fact, the word *pronoun* means "for a noun." Pronouns are shortcuts that keep you from unnecessarily repeating words in writing. Here are some examples of pronouns:

> Meena shampooed *her* dog. (*Her* is a pronoun that takes the place of *Meena's*.)
>
> As the door swung open, *it* creaked. (*It* replaces *door*.)
>
> When the motorcyclists arrived at the rest stop, *they* removed *their* helmets. (*They* replaces *motorcyclists; their* replaces *motorcyclists'*.)

This chapter presents rules that will help you avoid three common mistakes people make with pronouns. The rules are as follows:

1. A pronoun must refer clearly to the word it replaces.
2. A pronoun must agree in number with the word or words it replaces.
3. Pronouns should not shift unnecessarily in point of view.

Pronoun Reference

Teaching Tip
Ask students to underline the pronouns in these sentences and circle their antecedents.

A sentence may be confusing and unclear if a pronoun appears to refer to more than one word, as in this sentence:

> I locked my suitcase in my car, and then it was stolen.

What was stolen? It is unclear whether the suitcase or the car was stolen.

> I locked my suitcase in my car, and then my car was stolen.

A sentence may also be confusing if the pronoun does not refer to any specific word. Look at this sentence:

> We never buy fresh vegetables at that store because they charge too much.

Who charges too much? There is no specific word that *they* refers to. Be clear.

> We never buy fresh vegetables at that store because the owners charge too much.

Here are additional sentences with unclear pronoun reference. Read the explanations of why they are unclear and look carefully at the ways they are corrected.

UNCLEAR

Lilli told Gina that she had gotten a job interview.

(*Who* had gotten a job interview: Lilli or Gina? Be clear.)

My older brother is an electrician, but I'm not interested in it.

(There is no specific word that *it* refers to. It would not make sense to say, "I'm not interested in electrician.")

Our instructor did not explain the assignment, which made me angry.

(Does *which* mean that the instructor's failure to explain the assignment made you angry or that the assignment itself made you angry? Be clear.)

CLEAR

Lilli told Gina, "I got a job interview."

(Quotation marks, which can sometimes be used to correct an unclear reference, are explained in Chapter 27.)

My older brother is an electrician, but I'm not interested in becoming one.

I was angry that our instructor did not explain the assignment.

Rewrite each of the following sentences to make clear the vague pronoun reference. Add, change, or omit words as necessary.

EXAMPLE

Lana thanked Denise for the gift, which was very thoughtful of her.

Lana thanked Denise for the thoughtful gift.

1. At the gas station, they told us one of our tires looked soft.

   When we pulled into the gas station, the attendant told us one of our tires looked soft.

2. Nora dropped the heavy platter on her foot and broke it.

   Nora broke the heavy ashtray when she dropped it on her foot.

3. Vicki asked for a grade transcript at the registrar's office, and they told her it would cost three dollars.

   Vicki asked for a grade transcript at the registrar's office, and the clerk told her it would cost three dollars.

PRACTICE 1

Answers will vary. Rewritten sentences may have meanings different from the answers provided.

Teaching Tip
Ask students to underline the pronouns in these sentences and circle their antecedents.

4. Don't touch the freshly painted walls with your hands unless they're dry.

Don't touch the freshly painted walls with your hands unless the walls are dry.

5. Maurice stays up half the night watching *Chiller Theater,* which really annoys his wife.

Maurice's habit of staying up half the night watching Chiller Theater really annoys his wife.

6. Robin went to the store's personnel office, where they are interviewing for sales positions.

Robin went to the store's personnel office to be interviewed for a sales position.

7. Leon told his brother that he needed to lose some weight.

Leon told his brother, "You need to lose some weight."

8. I wrote to the insurance company, but they haven't answered my letters.

I wrote to the insurance company but haven't received an answer.

9. Because my eyes were itchy and bloodshot, I went to the doctor to see what he could do about it.

I went to the doctor to see what he could do about my itchy, bloodshot eyes.

10. I took the loose pillows off the chairs and sat on them.

I took the loose pillows off the chairs and sat on the pillows.

Pronoun Agreement

A pronoun must agree in number with the word or words it replaces. If the word a pronoun refers to is singular, the pronoun must be singular; if the word is plural, the pronoun must be plural. (Note that the word a pronoun refers to is known as the *antecedent.*)

Britta agreed to lend me her Billie Holiday albums.

The gravediggers sipped coffee during their break.

In the first example, the pronoun *her* refers to the singular word *Britta;* in the second example, the pronoun *their* refers to the plural word *gravediggers.*

Write the appropriate pronoun (*they, their, them, it*) in the blank space in each of the following sentences.

PRACTICE 2

EXAMPLE

My credit cards got me into debt, so I shredded ___them___.

1. Even though I should replace my disposable contact lenses every week, I often forget to change ___them___ out.

2. Several legislators proposed a bill to establish a registry of convicted murderers, but these lawmakers still need to determine the cost of ___their___ proposal.

3. Many educators had to change the way that ___they___ teach in order to comply with the No Child Left Behind Act.

4. After I promised my children that I would take them to the movies on Friday, I had to tell ___them___ that the hospital needed me to work an additional shift.

5. Less than a week after I placed a backorder for my textbook, the bookstore called to say that ___it___ had arrived.

ESL Tip
Nonnative speakers may have difficulty with pronoun agreement. In Spanish, for example, the pronoun agrees with the noun it modifies, not the word it replaces. A Spanish speaker might say. "Petra agreed to lend me *their* albums."

Indefinite Pronouns

The following words, known as *indefinite pronouns,* are always singular.

Indefinite Pronouns

(-one words)	(-body words)	
one	nobody	each
anyone	anybody	either
everyone	everybody	neither
someone	somebody	

Either of the apartments has *its* drawbacks.

One of the girls lost *her* skateboard.

Everyone in the class must hand in *his* paper tomorrow.

In each example, the pronoun is singular because it refers to one of the indefinite pronouns. There are two important points to remember about indefinite pronouns.

Point 1

The last example above suggests that everyone in the class is male. If the students were all female, the pronoun would be *her.* If the students were a mixed group of males and females, the pronoun form would be *his or her.*

Everyone in the class must hand in *his or her* paper tomorrow.

Some writers still follow the traditional practice of using *his* to refer to both men and women. Many now use *his or her* to avoid an implied sexual bias. Perhaps the best practice, though, is to avoid using either *his* or the somewhat awkward *his or her.* This can often be done by rewriting a sentence in the plural:

All students in the class must hand in *their* papers tomorrow.

Here are some examples of sentences that can be rewritten in the plural.

A young child is seldom willing to share her toys with others.
Young children are seldom willing to share their toys with others.

Anyone who does not wear his seat belt will be fined.
People who do not wear their seat belts will be fined.

A newly elected politician should not forget his or her campaign promises.
Newly elected politicians should not forget their campaign promises.

Point 2

In informal spoken English, *plural* pronouns are often used with indefinite pronouns. Instead of saying

Everybody has *his or her* own idea of an ideal vacation.

we are likely to say

Everybody has *their* own idea of an ideal vacation.

Here are other examples:

> Everyone in the class must pass in *their* papers.
>
> Everybody in our club has *their* own idea about how to raise money.
>
> No one in our family skips *their* chores.

In such cases, the indefinite pronouns are clearly plural in meaning. Also, the use of such plurals helps people avoid the awkward *his or her*. In time, the plural pronoun may be accepted in formal speech or writing. Until that happens, however, you should use the grammatically correct singular form in your writing.

Underline the correct pronoun.

EXAMPLE

> Neither of those houses has (its, their) own garage.

1. Girls! Did everyone remember to bring (her, their) insect repellent?

2. Anyone can pass our men's physical education course if (he, they) will laugh at all the instructor's jokes.

3. Each of the lead actresses had (her, their) own dressing room.

4. Neither of the Mets' relief pitchers was able to get (his, their) curve ball across.

5. If any student wants to apply for the scholarship offered by the women's college, (she, they) will need two recommendations.

6. Either type of recording system has (its, their) drawbacks.

7. Each ballerina stretched for an hour to prepare for (her, their) audition.

8. Three boys were suspected, but nobody would confess to leaving (his, their) fingerprints all over the window.

9. All women leaving the room should pick up (her, their) lab reports.

10. During the fire, any one of those men could have lost (his, their) balance on that narrow ledge.

Pronoun Point of View

Pronouns should not shift their point of view unnecessarily. When writing a paper, be consistent in your use of first-, second-, and third-person pronouns.

Type of Pronoun	Singular	Plural
First-person pronouns	**I (my, mine, me)**	**we (our, us)**
Second-person pronouns	**you (your)**	**you (your)**
Third-person pronouns	**he (his, him)** **she (her)** **it (its)**	**they (their, them)**

> **TIP**   Any person, place, or thing, as well as any indefinite pronoun like *one, anyone, someone,* and so on (page 221), is a third-person word.

For instance, if you start writing in the first-person *I*, don't jump suddenly to the second-person *you*. Or if you are writing in the third-person *they*, don't shift unexpectedly to *you*. Look at the examples.

INCONSISTENT

One reason that *I* like living in the city is that *you* always have a wide choice of sports events to attend.

(The most common mistake people make is to let a *you* slip into their writing after they start with another pronoun.)

Someone who is dieting should have the help of friends; *you* should also have plenty of willpower.

Students who work while *they* are going to school face special problems. For one thing, *you* seldom have enough study time.

CONSISTENT

One reason that *I* like living in the city is that *I* always have a wide choice of sports events to attend.

Someone who is dieting should have the help of friends; *he* or *she* should also have plenty of willpower.

Students who work while *they* are going to school face special problems. For one thing, *they* seldom have enough study time.

Cross out inconsistent pronouns in the following sentences and write the corrections above the errors.

EXAMPLE

                                         me

I work better when the boss doesn't hover over ~~you~~ with instructions.

1. When we drive through the Pennsylvania countryside, ~~you~~ *we* see some of the horse-drawn buggies used by the Amish people.

2. One of the things I like about the corner store is that ~~you~~ *I* can buy homemade sausage there.

3. In our family, we had to learn to keep our bedrooms neat before ~~you~~ *we* were given an allowance.

4. No matter how hard we may be working, the minute ~~you~~ *we* relax, the supervisor will be watching.

5. People shouldn't discuss cases outside of court if ~~you~~ *they* serve on a jury.

6. As I read the daily papers, ~~you~~ *I* get depressed by all the violent crime occurring in this country.

7. I never eat both halves of a hamburger bun, because ~~you~~ *I* save calories that way.

8. If someone started a bakery or donut shop in this town, ~~you~~ *he or she* could make a lot of money.

9. Sara likes to shop at the factory outlet because ~~you~~ *she* can buy discount clothing there.

10. I can't wait for summer, when ~~you~~ *I* can stop wearing heavy coats and itchy sweaters.

PRACTICE 4

Teaching Tip
Ask students to underline the antecedents in these sentences, which might include pronouns.

REVIEW TEST 1

Underline the correct word in the parentheses.

1. John spent all morning bird-watching and didn't see a single (one, <u>bird</u>).

2. Of the six men on the committee, no one was prepared to give (<u>his</u>, their) report, so the deadline was extended.

3. If a student in that women's college wants to get a good schedule, (<u>she</u>, you) must enroll as soon as possible.

4. Neither of the delis near our office has a very wide choice of sandwiches on (<u>its</u>, their) menu.

Teaching Tip
You may want to use these review tests to assess what your students have learned.

5. My father has cut down on salt because it can give (you, <u>him</u>) high blood pressure.

6. Well, gentlemen, if anyone objects to the plan, (<u>he</u>, they) should speak up now.

7. I put my wet umbrella on the porch until (it, <u>the umbrella</u>) was dry.

8. I don't like that fast-food restaurant, because (they, <u>the employees</u>) are inefficient.

9. Doctors make large salaries, but (you, <u>they</u>) often face the pressure of dealing with life and death.

10. After eight hours in the cramped, stuffy car, I was glad (it, <u>the trip</u>) was over.

REVIEW TEST 2

Cross out the pronoun error in each sentence and write the correction in the space provided at the left. Then circle the letter that correctly describes the type of error that was made.

EXAMPLES

People   ~~Anyone~~ turning in their papers late will be penalized.

Mistake in: a. pronoun reference   (b.) pronoun agreement

Paul   When Clyde takes his son Paul to the park, ~~he~~ enjoys himself.

Mistake in: (a.) pronoun reference   b. pronoun point of view

_We_   From where we stood, ~~you~~ could see three states.

Mistake in: a. pronoun agreement   (b.) pronoun point of view

_we_   1. In our company, ~~you~~ have to work for one year before getting vacation time.

   Mistake in: a. pronoun agreement   (b.) pronoun point of view

nurses   2. Amy signed up for a nursing program because she heard that ~~they~~ are in demand.

   Mistake in: (a.) pronoun reference   b. pronoun agreement

_we_   3. We did not eat much of the fruit; ~~you~~ could tell that it was not fresh.

   Mistake in: a. pronoun agreement   (b.) pronoun point of view

the counselors 4. Eric visited the counseling center, because ~~they~~ can help him straighten out his schedule.

   Mistake in: (a.) pronoun reference b. pronoun agreement

his or her 5. Every student who was in the chemistry lab has ~~their~~ own memories of the fire.

   Mistake in: a. pronoun reference (b.) pronoun agreement

HINT You may want to rewrite item 5 in the plural, using the lines below.

Students who were in the chemistry lab have their own memories of the fire.

_____

---

the cheese slices (or the hamburgers) 6. After LaTanya put cheese slices on the hamburgers, the dog ate ~~them~~.

   Mistake in: (a.) pronoun reference b. pronoun point of view

they 7. If people feel that they are being discriminated against in jobs or housing, ~~you~~ should contact the appropriate federal agency.

   Mistake in: a. pronoun agreement (b.) pronoun point of view

the neighbor's 8. Amineh told her neighbor that ~~her~~ house needed a new coat of paint.

   Mistake in: (a.) pronoun reference b. pronoun agreement

his 9. One of the actors forgot ~~their~~ lines and tried to ad-lib.

   Mistake in: (a.) pronoun agreement b. pronoun point of view

he or she 10. If anyone wants a tryout, ~~they~~ should be at the gym at four o'clock.

   Mistake in: a. pronoun reference (b.) pronoun agreement

HINT You may want to rewrite item 10 in the plural, using the lines below.

If players want a tryout, they should be at the gym at four o'clock.

_____

NAME: _____

DATE: _____

Pronoun Reference, Agreement, and Point of View

Underline the correct word in the parentheses.

1. Each of my daughters had to get (her, their) own lunch before leaving for school.
2. Lonnell needed his writing folder from the file cabinet, but he couldn't find (it, the folder).
3. In our office we have to work for six months before (we, you) get a raise.
4. Shoppers seem to like the new store because (you, they) rarely have to wait in line.
5. Although I liked my chemistry teacher, I never really understood (it, chemistry).
6. The bellhop discovered that someone had left (his, their) expensive suit in one of the hotel closets.
7. If you want to lose weight by exercising, (one, you) should begin with a sensible program of light workouts.
8. Every player on the Rangers' bench pulled on (his, their) helmet and jumped onto the ice as soon as the fight broke out.
9. John's neighbor called to tell him that someone had parked in (his, John's) spot.
10. Whenever I go to that post office, (they, the clerks) act as if I'm troubling them when I ask for stamps.
11. On the first day of school, students spend most of the time getting (your, their) schedule in order and finding classrooms.
12. The cat sat staring at the bird in the cage, and (the bird, it) was very upset.
13. Elise treated Ariana to lunch at the restaurant that (she, Elise) likes best.
14. As we walked toward the accident site, (they, police officers) told us to stay out of the way.
15. Dae-Ho watches movies of all kinds, because he's interested in (it, making movies) as a possible career.
16. A person has to be self-confident to go to a party where (you, he or she) doesn't know anyone.
17. Felice stopped at the bakery to pick up the cake she'd ordered, but (he, the baker) was not finished decorating it.
18. I don't know anybody who has (their, his or her) report finished yet.
19. When I got my bike out of the garage, I noticed that (it, the garage) really needed cleaning.
20. There was a pretty bow on my present, but I threw (it, the bow) into the trash.

SCORE
Number Correct

_____ /10

_____ %

MASTERY TEST 2

Pronoun Reference, Agreement, and Point of View

In the space provided, write PE *for sentences that contain pronoun errors. Write* C *for the three sentences that use pronouns correctly. Then cross out each pronoun error and write a correction above it.*

EXAMPLE

Corrections may vary.

_____PE_____ Each of the boys explained ~~their~~ *his* project.

_____PE_____ 1. Drew told his boss, ~~that he needed more time to finish the report~~ *"I need more time to finish the report."*

_____C_____ 2. Each musician carried his or her own instrument onto the bus.

_____C_____ 3. In this course, people can sit in class for weeks before the instructor calls on them.

_____PE_____ 4. Harold refuses to take his children to amusement parks because he doesn't like ~~them.~~ *amusement parks*

_____PE_____ 5. Everyone who parks on that street has had ~~their~~ *his or her* car windows smashed.

_____PE_____ 6. Carl says he has problems taking lecture notes because ~~they~~ *the instructors* all talk too fast.

_____PE_____ 7. I hate standing in bakery lines where ~~you~~ *I* have to take a number.

_____C_____ 8. "Anyone even suspected of cheating," warned the instructor at the boys' school, "forfeits his chance of passing this test."

_____PE_____ 9. ~~The ace pilots flew in formation over the crowded stadium, which was breathtaking.~~ *The ace pilots' flight in formation over the crowded stadium was breathtaking.*

_____PE_____ 10. He avoids foods that might give ~~you~~ *him* heartburn.

NAME: _____

DATE: _____

MASTERY TEST 3

Pronoun Reference, Agreement, and Point of View

Corrections may vary.

In the space provided, write PE *for sentences that contain pronoun errors. Write* C *for the two sentences that use pronouns correctly. Then cross out each pronoun error and write a correction above it.*

____PE____   1. Irena called Ellen to tell her that the instructor had read ~~her~~ *Ellen's* paper to the class.

____PE____   2. Danny's favorite toy is the robot ~~you~~ *he* must wind up.

____C____   3. Neither contestant answered her bonus question about the Civil War battles correctly.

____PE____   4. Jesse won't go for the job interview because he says ~~they~~ *the employers* hire only college graduates.

____PE____   5. If you send in your ticket order in advance, ~~one~~ *you* can be sure of getting good seats.

____PE____   6. With rain in the forecast, just about everybody in the stadium had an umbrella by ~~their~~ *his or her* side.

____PE____   7. The old man asked me to move my suitcase off the bench so he could sit on ~~it~~ *the bench*.

____PE____   8. Hana is really a generous person, but she keeps ~~it~~ *her generosity* hidden.

____C____   9. Whenever we take our children on a trip, we have to remember to bring snacks and toys to keep them occupied.

____PE____   10. One of the men in our cab company just got ~~their~~ *his* license revoked.

230

NAME: _____

DATE: _____

Pronoun Reference, Agreement, and Point of View

In the space provided, write PE *for sentences that contain pronoun errors. Write* C *for the sentence that uses pronouns correctly. Then cross out each pronoun error and write a correction above it.*

Corrections may vary.

_____PE_____ 1. After Erica put the candles on her twin sons' birthday cakes, the dog ate
~~them~~. *the candles*

_____PE_____ 2. None of the women in the class was eager to have ~~their~~ presentation put on *her* video.

_____PE_____ 3. The cheeseburgers we were served were so thick that ~~you~~ could hardly bite *we* into them.

_____PE_____ 4. The citizens protested at City Hall because ~~they~~ had raised taxes for the sec- *the legislators* ond year in a row.

_____PE_____ 5. Tina knew Edward was still angry, but he wouldn't talk about ~~it~~. *his anger*

_____PE_____ 6. Devon asked Spencer, ~~to try out his new motorbike~~. *"Why don't you try out my new motorbike?"*

_____PE_____ 7. Carol was told to sign on the dotted line with her ballpoint pen, but she couldn't find ~~it~~. *her pen*

_____C_____ 8. Either the dog or the cat had spilled water from its dish all over the kitchen floor.

_____PE_____ 9. Davy complained to his brother that ~~he~~ always got asked to walk the puppy. *Davy*

_____PE_____ 10. The grounder took a bad hop and bounced over the shortstop's head; ~~this~~ *the error* resulted in two runs scoring.

CHAPTER

16

Pronoun Types

INTRODUCTORY ACTIVITY

In each pair, place a check mark beside the sentence that you think uses pronouns correctly.

✓ Ali and *I* enrolled in a computer course.

_____ Ali and *me* enrolled in a computer course.

✓ The police officer pointed to my sister and *me*.

_____ The police officer pointed to my sister and *I*.

_____ Elle prefers men *whom* take pride in their bodies.

✓ Elle prefers men *who* take pride in their bodies.

_____ The players are confident that the league championship is *theirs'*.

✓ The players are confident that the league championship is *theirs*.

_____ *Them* concert tickets are too expensive.

✓ *Those* concert tickets are too expensive.

_____ Our parents should spend some money on *themself* for a change.

✓ Our parents should spend some money on *themselves* for a change.

Answers are on page 640.

This chapter describes some common types of pronouns: subject and object pronouns, relative pronouns, possessive pronouns, demonstrative pronouns, and reflexive pronouns.

Subject and Object Pronouns

Pronouns change their form depending on the place they occupy in a sentence. Here is a list of subject and object pronouns:

Teaching Tip
Encourage students to memorize these subject pronouns and object pronouns.

Subject Pronouns	Object Pronouns
I	me
you	you (*no change*)
he	him
she	her
it	it (*no change*)
we	us
they	them

Subject Pronouns

Subject pronouns are subjects of verbs.

They are getting tired. (*They* is the subject of the verb *are getting*.)
She will decide tomorrow. (*She* is the subject of the verb *will decide*.)
We women organized the game. (*We* is the subject of the verb *organized*.)

Several rules for using subject pronouns, and mistakes people sometimes make, are explained below.

ESL Tip
In some languages, subject pronouns are omitted—e.g., in Spanish, "Yo tengo quince años" is often written as "Tengo quince años."

Rule 1

Use a subject pronoun in a sentence with a compound (more than one) subject.

INCORRECT	CORRECT
Dwayne and *me* went shopping yesterday.	Dwayne and *I* went shopping yesterday.
Him and *me* spent lots of money.	*He* and *I* spent lots of money.

If you are not sure which pronoun to use, try each pronoun by itself in the sentence. The correct pronoun will be the one that sounds right. For example, "*Me* went shopping yesterday" does not sound right; "*I* went shopping yesterday" does.

Rule 2

Use a subject pronoun after forms of the verb *be*. Forms of *be* include *am, are, is, was, were, has been, have been,* and others.

> It was *I* who telephoned.
>
> It may be *they* at the door.
>
> It is *she.*

The sentences above may sound strange and stilted to you, since this rule is seldom followed in conversation. When we speak with one another, forms such as "It was me," "It may be them," and "It is her" are widely accepted. In formal writing, however, the grammatically correct forms are still preferred. You can avoid having to use a subject pronoun after *be* simply by rewording a sentence. Here is how the preceding examples could be reworded:

> *I* was the one who telephoned.
>
> *They* may be at the door.
>
> *She* is here.

Rule 3

Use subject pronouns after *than* or *as* when a verb is understood after the pronoun.

> You read faster than I (read). (The verb *read* is understood after *I.*)
>
> Tom is as stubborn as I (am). (The verb *am* is understood after *I.*)
>
> We don't go out as much as they (do). (The verb *do* is understood after *they.*)

> ## TIPS
>
> **1.** Avoid mistakes by mentally adding the "missing" verb at the end of the sentence.
>
> **2.** Use object pronouns after *as* or *than* when a verb is not understood after the pronoun.
>
> > The law applies to you as well as me.
> >
> > Our boss paid Monica more than me.

Object Pronouns

Object pronouns (*me, him, her, us, them*) are the objects of verbs or prepositions. (Prepositions are connecting words like *for, at, about, to, before, by, with,* and *of.* See also page 78.)

> Nika chose *him.* (*Him* is the object of the verb *chose.*)
>
> We met *them* at the ball park. (*Them* is the object of the verb *met.*)

Don't mention UFOs to *us*. (*Us* is the object of the preposition *to*.)

Between you and *me*, I don't trust that woman. (*Me* is the object of the preposition *between*.)

People are sometimes uncertain about what pronoun to use when two objects follow the verb.

INCORRECT

I spoke to George and *he*.

She pointed at Hana and *I*.

CORRECT

I spoke to George and *him*.

She pointed at Hana and *me*.

> **TIP** If you are not sure what pronoun to use, try each pronoun by itself in the sentence. The correct pronoun will be the one that sounds right. For example, "I spoke to he" doesn't sound right; "I spoke to him" does.

Underline the correct subject or object pronoun in each of the following sentences. Then show whether your answer is a subject or an object pronoun by circling the *S* or *O* in the margin. The first one is done for you as an example.

S (O)   1. I left the decision to (<u>her</u>, she).

(S) O   2. At a sale, my mother and (<u>I</u>, me) get bargain-hunting fever.

S (O)   3. As he gazed at (she, <u>her</u>) and the children, he knew he was happy.

S (O)   4. The panhandler asked my brother and (I, <u>me</u>) for some change.

S (O)   5. Without (she, <u>her</u>) and (he, <u>him</u>), this club would be a disaster.

(S) O   6. Suki can change a tire faster than (<u>I</u>, me).

(S) O   7. (<u>We</u>, Us) athletes always have to stay in shape.

(S) O   8. It was (<u>she</u>, her) who noticed that the phone was turned off.

S (O)   9. The bad feelings between you and (I, <u>me</u>) have lasted too long.

(S) O   10. Before the wedding, Romeo and (<u>he</u>, him) tried, without much luck, to put on the cummerbunds that came with the tuxedos.

PRACTICE 1

Teaching Tip
After students complete this activity, go over the answers in class.

For each sentence, in the space provided, write an appropriate subject or object pronoun. Try to use as many different pronouns as possible. The first one is done for you as an example.

1. Dina ran after Kris and ____*me*____ to return the keys she had borrowed.

2. That video equipment belongs to Barry and _*me (or him, or her, or them)*_.

PRACTICE 2

Answers will vary.

3. Sally and _____*I (or he, etc.)*_____ decided to open a bookstore together.

4. Henry has worked at the welding shop longer than _____*I (or she, etc.)*_____.

5. Take that box of candy from the shelf and give it to _____*me (or him, etc.)*_____.

6. Why do you and _____*I (or she, etc.)*_____ always get stuck with the cleaning up?

7. I really envy _____*them*_____ for their ability to get along with people.

8. The police caught Val and _____*him (or them, etc.)*_____ as they were trying to break into the boarded-up store.

9. My neighbor and _____*I (or she, etc.)*_____ are soap-opera addicts.

10. Neither Ron nor _____*(or he, she)*_____ is afraid of walking through the cemetery at night.

Relative Pronouns

Teaching Tip
Remind students that *whose* is often confused with the contraction *who's*.

ESL Tip
Nonnative speakers may confuse *who* and *that* because they use one word for both meanings in their native language.

Relative pronouns do two things at once. First, they refer to someone or something already mentioned in the sentence. Second, they start a short word group that gives additional information about this someone or something. Here is a list of relative pronouns, followed by some example sentences:

Relative Pronouns	
who	which
whose	that
whom	

The only friend *who* really understands me is moving away.

The child *whom* Ben and Arlene adopted is from South Korea.

Chocolate, *which* is my favorite food, upsets my stomach.

I guessed at half the questions *that* were on the test.

In the example sentences, *who* refers to *friend*, *whom* refers to *child*, *which* refers to *chocolate*, and *that* refers to *questions*. In addition, each of these relative pronouns begins a group of words that describes the person or thing being referred to. For example, the words *whom Ben and Arlene adopted* tell which child the sentence is about, and the words *which is my favorite food* give added information about chocolate.

Points to Remember about Relative Pronouns

Point 1

Whose means *belonging to whom.* Be careful not to confuse *whose* with *who's,* which means *who is.*

Point 2

Who, whose, and *whom* all refer to people. *Which* refers to things. *That* can refer to either people or things.

> I don't know *whose* book this is.
>
> He mistakenly sat on the blue chair, *which* is broken.
>
> Let's build a house *that* is energy-efficient.

Point 3

Who, whose, whom, and *which* can also be used to ask questions. When they are used in this way, they are called *interrogative* pronouns:

> *Who* murdered the secret agent?
>
> *Whose* fingerprints were on the bloodstained knife?
>
> To *whom* have the detectives been talking?
>
> *Which* suspect is going to confess?

> **TIP** In informal usage, *who* is generally used instead of *whom* as an interrogative pronoun. Informally, we can say or write, "*Who* are you rooting for in the game?" or "*Who* did the instructor fail?" More formal usage would use *whom:* "*Whom* are you rooting for in the game?" and "*Whom* did the instructor fail?"

Point 4

Who and *whom* are used differently. *Who* is a subject pronoun. Use *who* as the subject of a verb:

> Let's see *who* will be teaching the course.

Whom is an object pronoun. Use *whom* as the object of a verb or a preposition:

> Dr. Martinez is the instructor *whom* I like best.
>
> I haven't decided for *whom* I will vote.

You may want to review the material on subject and object pronouns found on pages 233–35.

Here is an easy way to decide whether to use *who* or *whom.* Find the first verb after the place where the *who* or *whom* will go. See if it already has a subject. If it does have a subject, use the object pronoun *whom.* If there is no subject, give it one by using the subject pronoun *who.* Notice how *who* and *whom* are used in the sentences that follow:

> I don't know *who* sideswiped my car.

> The suspect *whom* the police arrested finally confessed.

In the first sentence, *who* is used to give the verb *sideswiped* a subject. In the second sentence, the verb *arrested* already has a subject, *police.* Therefore, *whom* is the correct pronoun.

PRACTICE 3   Underline the correct pronoun in each of the following sentences.

1. Alexandre Dumas, (who, which) wrote *The Three Musketeers,* once fought a duel in which his pants fell down.

2. The power failure, (who, which) caused the stage to go black, happened during the singer's performance of "You Light Up My Life."

3. The football coach wasn't very encouraging toward Mark, (who, whom) he advised to get extra health insurance.

4. A national animal-protection society honored a high school student (who, whom) refused to dissect a frog in her biology class.

5. Several of the students (who, which) were taking College Survival Skills dropped out before the end of the semester.

PRACTICE 4   On a separate sheet of paper or in a separate file, write five sentences using *who, whose, whom, which,* and *that.*

Teaching Tip
For Practice 4, suggest that students write sentences that are specific to their own lives.

Possessive Pronouns

Possessive pronouns show ownership or possession.

> Clyde shut off the engine of *his* motorcycle.

> The keys are *mine.*

Here is a list of possessive pronouns:

> ## Possessive Pronouns
>
> | | |
> |---|---|
> | my, mine | our, ours |
> | your, yours | your, yours |
> | his | their, theirs |
> | her, hers | |
> | its | |

Points to Remember about Possessive Pronouns

Point 1

A possessive pronoun *never* uses an apostrophe. (See also page 334.)

ESL Tip
Remind nonnative speakers that in standard English, the possessive pronoun agrees with the possessor, not the object it modifies.

INCORRECT	CORRECT
That coat is *hers'*.	That coat is *hers*.
The card table is *theirs'*.	The card table is *theirs*.

Point 2

Do not use any of the following nonstandard forms to show possession.

INCORRECT	CORRECT
I met a friend of *him*.	I met a friend of *his*.
Can I use *you* car?	Can I use *your* car?
Me sister is in the hospital.	*My* sister is in the hospital.
That magazine is *mines*.	That magazine is *mine*.

Cross out the incorrect pronoun form in each of the sentences that follow. Write the correct form in the space at the left.

PRACTICE 5

EXAMPLE

___*My*___   ~~Me~~ stomach is growling, so I will have a light snack before dinner.

___*hers*___   1. Is this Kindle Fire ~~hers'~~?

___*mine*___   2. The sushi without horseradish is ~~mines~~.

Teaching Tip
For this acti-
vity, read
each sentence
aloud to help
your students
"hear" the
pronoun
errors.

_____ours_____ 3. My husband came home and told me that the new Chevrolet Suburban SUV in the driveway is ~~ours'~~ .

_____its_____ 4. The wireless router has a dozen cables running from ~~it's~~ parts.

_____their_____ 5. Marisa and Jo often remind ~~they~~ children that they need to budget their money if they want to go to Disney World next summer.

Demonstrative Pronouns

ESL Tip
Nonnative
speakers tend
to confuse
these words.
You might
want to use
gestures to
illustrate the
difference in
meaning and
show how they
parallel *here*
and *there*.

Demonstrative pronouns point to or single out a person or thing. There are four demonstrative pronouns:

Demonstrative Pronouns	
this	these
that	those

Generally speaking, *this* and *these* refer to things close at hand; *that* and *those* refer to things farther away.

Teaching Tip
You may want
to tell your
students what
the word *de-
monstrative*
means.

Is anyone using *thi*s spoon?

I am going to throw away *these* magazines.

I just bought *that* silver Prius at the curb.

Pick up *those* toys in the corner.

> **TIP**   Do not use *them, this here, that there, these here,* or *those there* to point out. Use only *this, that, these,* or *those.*

INCORRECT

Them tires are badly worn.

This here book looks hard to read.

That there candy is delicious.

Those there squirrels are pests.

CORRECT

Those tires are badly worn.

This book looks hard to read.

That candy is delicious.

Those squirrels are pests.

Cross out the incorrect form of the demonstrative pronoun and write the correct form in the space provided.

EXAMPLE

Those   ~~Them~~ clothes need washing.

This   1. ~~This here~~ waitress will take your order.

Those   2. ~~Them~~ sunglasses make you look really sharp.

These   3. ~~These here~~ phones are out of order.

Those   4. ~~Them~~ batteries won't fit my camera.

that   5. I didn't know ~~that there~~ gun was loaded.

Look at the photo above and write four sentences about it using _this, that, these,_ and _those._

_____

_____

_____

_____

Reflexive Pronouns

Reflexive pronouns are pronouns that refer to the subject of a sentence. Here is a list of reflexive pronouns:

Reflexive Pronouns

myself	herself	ourselves
yourself	itself	yourselves
himself		themselves

Sometimes the reflexive pronoun is used for emphasis:

> You will have to wash the dishes *yourself.*
> We *ourselves* are willing to forget the matter.
> The president *himself* turns down his living room thermostat.

Points to Remember about Reflexive Pronouns

Point 1

In the plural, *-self* becomes *-selves.*

> Aliyah soaks *herself* in lavender bath oil.
> They treated *themselves* to a vacation in Bermuda.

Point 2

Be careful that you do not use any of the following incorrect forms as reflexive pronouns.

INCORRECT	CORRECT
He believes in *hisself.*	He believes in *himself.*
We drove the children *ourself.*	We drove the children *ourselves.*
They saw *themself* in the fun house mirror.	They saw *themselves* in the fun house mirror.
I'll do it *meself.*	I'll do it *myself*

Cross out the incorrect form of the reflexive pronoun and write the correct form in the space at the left.

EXAMPLE

themselves   She believes that God helps those who help ~~themself~~.

ourselves   1. We painted the kitchen ~~ourself~~.

himself   2. The mayor ~~hisself~~ spoke to the striking bus drivers.

themselves   3. Marian's sons don't like being left by ~~theirselves~~ in the house.

yourself   4. You must get the tickets ~~yourselfs~~.

ourselves   5. Bill and I cooked the dinner ~~ourself~~.

Underline the correct word in the parentheses.

EXAMPLE

Tomas and (<u>I</u>, me) have already seen the movie.

1. It looks as if (<u>this</u>, this here) Blu-ray player is out of order.

2. I exercise twice as much as (<u>she</u>, her), and I'm in worse shape.

3. The only thing for Jack and (I, <u>me</u>) to eat was cold rice.

4. That folding umbrella you just picked up is (our's, <u>ours</u>).

5. Since Paula and (<u>he</u>, him) are engaged, we should give them a party.

6. Why do our parents always embarrass (we, <u>us</u>) kids by showing those old home movies?

7. The manager (hisself, <u>himself</u>) plans to take a cut in salary.

8. They knew the stolen clock radios were (<u>theirs</u>, their's), but they couldn't prove it.

9. If you put (them, <u>those</u>) vegetables in the microwave, they'll defrost in a few minutes.

10. My nephews couldn't stop giggling after they saw (theirselves, <u>themselves</u>) in their Halloween costumes.

REVIEW TEST 2

Cross out the pronoun error in each sentence and write the correct form above it.

EXAMPLE

You and ~~me~~ *I* have to stick together.

1. I asked the dentist's receptionist for appointments for my sister and ~~I~~ *me*.

2. I can't tell if ~~them~~ *those* potatoes are cooked all the way through or not.

3. Since the fault is ~~your's~~ *yours*, you owe me the cost of the repairs.

4. When the will was read, my cousin and ~~me~~ *I* had inherited a thousand dollars each.

5. After we got our income tax refund, we rewarded ~~ourself~~ *ourselves* and the kids with a vacation.

6. Demetri's car had ~~it's~~ *its* antenna broken off while it was parked outside the mall.

7. Nothing is more bothersome to ~~he~~ *him* than having to fix things around the house.

8. ~~This here~~ *This* town needs a tough sheriff.

9. Since I take better notes than ~~him~~ *he*, we studied from mine for the exam.

10. In small claims court, the judges ~~themself~~ *themselves* decide the cases and award damages.

REVIEW TEST 3

On a separate sheet of paper or in a separate file, write sentences that correctly use each of the following words or word groups.

EXAMPLE

Peter and him   *The coach suspended Peter and him.*

1. you and I   6. taller than I

2. yours   7. yourselves

3. Kathy and me   8. with Roberto and him

4. Otto and he   9. those

5. the neighbors and us   10. Lisa and them

Pronoun Types

Underline the correct word in parentheses.

1. (Them, <u>Those</u>) doves nest in our cedar tree every year.

2. I suspect that those dirty dishes are (<u>yours</u>, your's).

3. Horror movies don't scare my friends and (I, <u>me</u>) one bit.

4. The four boys finally had the house all to (themself, <u>themselves</u>).

5. Ling and (<u>I</u>, me) have been engaged for over three years.

6. (<u>That</u>, That there) woman is a helicopter pilot.

7. Without asking for permission, (<u>he</u>, him) and Nelson began cutting the cake.

8. My new Buick got (<u>its</u>, it's) first scratch when I parked too close to a fence.

9. Ray decided to buy (hisself, <u>himself</u>) a reward for sticking to his diet for one solid month.

10. The plumber showed Elaine and (I, <u>me</u>) the corroded lead pipes under the sink.

11. Terry's foul-shooting percentage isn't as good as (<u>mine</u>, mines).

12. Kurt needs some sleep right now more than he needs (we, <u>us</u>).

13. Marla is taking more courses this semester than (<u>I</u>, me).

14. I don't understand how (<u>this</u>, this here) formula is used.

15. Does anyone know how (<u>those</u>, them) screens got torn?

16. Any friend of the Newtons is a friend of (our's, <u>ours</u>).

17. The team members (theirselves, <u>themselves</u>) are selling candy door to door.

18. I wish (<u>those</u>, those there) babies would stop crying.

19. When you're finished with the calculator, return it to either Roberta or (I, <u>me</u>).

20. Those power tools are (<u>hers</u>, hers').

245

NAME: _____

DATE: _____

Pronoun Types

Cross out the incorrect pronoun in each sentence and write the correct form in the space provided at the left.

her	1. If we offered Sergio and ~~she~~ some money, would they accept it?
those	2. Every one of ~~those there~~ courses is filled.
they	3. We caught a lot more fish than ~~them~~.
Those	4. ~~Them~~ mountains in the distance are the Catskills.
himself	5. Jake ~~hisself~~ decided to confess to the robbery.
I	6. My dog and ~~me~~ usually eat our meals at the same time.
theirs	7. Our SUV can hold more people than ~~their's~~.
These	8. ~~These here~~ boots will hurt you until they're fully broken in.
ourselves	9. This will be the first time in weeks we've had dinner by ~~ourself~~.
yours	10. Those garden tools of ~~your's~~ are getting rusty.
me	11. The sweaters Gloria knitted for Ron and ~~I~~ came out two sizes too small.
me	12. Every woman at the party wore jeans except Michelle and ~~I~~.
us	13. The chief showed ~~we~~ rookie firefighters what to do when an alarm sounded.
this	14. You can't park here, because ~~this here~~ space is reserved for the supervisor.
hers	15. Are these binoculars ~~her's~~?
he	16. Matina and ~~him~~ have nothing to discuss.
he	17. Of all my grandchildren, Chris and ~~him~~ wear me out the fastest.
that	18. Check the pockets of ~~that there~~ bathrobe for your glasses.
its	19. His bicycle had ~~its'~~ tires slashed overnight.
themselves	20. They've decided to repair the engine by ~~themselves~~.

Adjectives and Adverbs

INTRODUCTORY ACTIVITY

Write in an appropriate word or words to complete each of the sentences below.

1. The teenage years were a _____ time for me.

2. The mechanic listened _____ while I described my car problem.

3. Basketball is a _____ game than football.

4. My brother is the _____ person in our family.

Now complete the following sentences.

The word inserted in the first sentence is an (adjective, adverb); it describes the word *time*.

The word inserted in the second sentence is an (adjective, adverb); it probably ends in the two letters __*ly*__ and describes the word *listened*.

The word inserted in the third sentence is a comparative adjective; it may be preceded by *more* or end in the two letters __*er*__.

The word inserted in the fourth sentence is a superlative adjective; it may be preceded by *most* or end in the three letters __*est*__.

Answers are on page 641.

Answers will vary.

Teaching Tip
You may want to use this activity to assess your students' understanding of adjectives and adverbs.

Adjectives and adverbs are descriptive words. Their purpose is to make the meaning of the words they describe more specific.

Adjectives

What Are Adjectives?

ESL Tip
Many non-native speakers experience difficulty with adjectives, e.g., word order or word form. Nonnative speakers may also have trouble distinguishing between *-ing* and *-ed* adjectives (see Appendix A for an explanation and some practice exercises).

Adjectives describe nouns (names of persons, places, or things) or pronouns.

> Charlotte is a *kind* woman. (The adjective *kind* describes the noun *woman*.)
>
> He is *tired*. (The adjective *tired* describes the pronoun *he*.)

An adjective usually comes before the word it describes (as in *kind woman*). But it can also come after forms of the verb *be* (*is, are, was, were,* and so on). Less often, an adjective follows verbs such as *feel, look, smell, sound, taste, appear, become,* and *seem*.

> The bureau is *heavy*. (The adjective *heavy* describes the bureau.)
>
> These pants are *itchy*. (The adjective *itchy* describes the pants.)
>
> The children seem *restless*. (The adjective *restless* describes the children.)

Describe this painting, using as many specific details as possible. How many adjectives did you use? Circle them.

Using Adjectives to Compare

For most short adjectives, add -*er* when comparing two things and -*est* when comparing three or more things.

> I am *taller* than my brother, but my father is the *tallest* person in the house.
>
> The farmers' market sells *fresher* vegetables than the corner store, but the *freshest* vegetables are the ones grown in my own garden.

For most *longer* adjectives (two or more syllables), add *more* when comparing two things and *most* when comparing three or more things.

> Backgammon is *more enjoyable* to me than checkers, but chess is the *most enjoyable* game of all.
>
> My mother is *more talkative* than my father, but my grandfather is the *most talkative* person in the house.

Points to Remember about Adjectives

Point 1

Be careful not to use both an -*er* ending and *more,* or both an -*est* ending and *most.*

INCORRECT	CORRECT
Football is a *more livelier* game than baseball.	Football is a *livelier* game than baseball.
Tod Traynor was voted the *most likeliest* to succeed in our high school class.	Tod Traynor was voted the *most likely* to succeed in our high school class.

Point 2

Pay special attention to the following words; each has irregular forms.

	COMPARATIVE (Two)	SUPERLATIVE (Three or More)
bad	worse	worst
good, well	better	best
little	less	least
much, many	more	most

Teaching Tip
For each sentence ask students to underline the word that the adjective describes. For added practice, ask students to create a sentence in which they compare two of their classmates. Then ask them to create a sentence in which they compare three of their classmates.

ESL Tip
Nonnative speakers may use *more* (comparative) *or the more* (superlative) to compare because they are translating from their native languages.

PRACTICE 1

Fill in the comparative or superlative forms for the following adjectives. The first two are done for you as examples.

Teaching Tip
You may
want to do
this activity
with the entire
class.

	COMPARATIVE (Two)	SUPERLATIVE (Three or More)
fast	faster	fastest
timid	more timid	most timid
kind	kinder	kindest
ambitious	more ambitious	most ambitious
generous	more generous	most generous
fine	finer	finest
likable	more likable	most likable

PRACTICE 2

Add to each sentence the correct form of the word in the margin.

EXAMPLE

bad

The _____worst_____ day of my life was the one when my house caught fire.

thick

1. I attempted to bite into the _____thickest_____ sandwich I had ever seen.

lazy

2. Each perfect summer day was _____lazier_____ than the last.

harsh

3. The judge pronounced the _____harshest_____ sentence possible on the convicted robber.

flexible

4. My new hairbrush is _____more flexible_____ than my old one and doesn't pull out as many hairs.

bad

5. I felt even _____worse_____ after I had taken the antimotion-sickness pills.

good

6. The _____best_____ seats in the stadium are completely sold out.

little

7. I'm looking for a cereal with _____less_____ sugar than "Candy Flakes."

vulnerable   8. The body's central trunk is _less vulnerable_ to frostbite than the hands and feet.

wasteful   9. Many people throughout the world feel that Americans are the _most wasteful_ people on earth.

shiny   10. My hair looked _shinier_ than usual after I began taking vitamins.

Adverbs

What Are Adverbs?

Adverbs describe verbs, adjectives, or other adverbs. An adverb usually ends in *-ly*.

> Charlotte spoke *kindly* to the confused man. (The adverb *kindly* describes the verb *spoke*.)

> The man said he was *completely* alone in the world. (The adverb *completely* describes the adjective *alone*.)

> Charlotte listened *very* sympathetically to his story. (The adverb *very* describes the adverb *sympathetically.*)

A Common Mistake with Adjectives and Adverbs

Perhaps the most common mistake that people make with adjectives and adverbs is to use an adjective instead of an adverb after a verb.

INCORRECT	CORRECT
Saad explains *thorough*.	Saad explains *thoroughly*.
I rest *comfortable* in that chair.	I rest *comfortably* in that chair.
She learned *quick*.	She learned *quickly*.

Underline the adjective or adverb needed.

1. She walked (hesitant, <u>hesitantly</u>) into the room.
2. I could have won the match (easy, <u>easily</u>) if I had concentrated more.
3. After turning the motorcycle (sharp, <u>sharply</u>), Marilyn tried to regain her balance.
4. The bus stopped (abrupt, <u>abruptly</u>), and the passengers were thrown forward.
5. The candidate waged an (<u>aggressive</u>, aggressively) campaign, and the voters turned against him.

ESL Tip
Nonnative speakers may have difficulty with the placement of adverbs describing frequency (e.g., *always, sometimes, never*). They may also make errors in the placement of a series of adverbs describing time and place (e.g., "I went *at 10 p.m.* to the movies" instead of "I went to the movies *at 10 p.m.*").

PRACTICE 3

Teaching Tip
You may want to do this activity with the entire class.

6. The man talked (regretful, <u>regretfully</u>) about the chances he had missed.

7. The instructor spoke so (quick, <u>quickly</u>) that we gave up taking notes.

8. The students eat so (messy, <u>messily</u>) that the cafeteria must be cleaned twice a day.

9. The boy was (<u>envious</u>, enviously) of his brother's new cowboy boots.

10. Maureen worked (terrible, <u>terribly</u>) hard at her job, yet she managed to find time for her children.

Well and *Good*

Two words often confused are *well* and *good*. *Good* is an adjective; it describes nouns. *Well* is usually an adverb; it describes verbs. *Well* (rather than *good*) is also used as an adjective when referring to a person's health. Here are some examples:

I became a *good* swimmer. (*Good* is an adjective describing the noun *swimmer*.)

For a change, two-year-old Rodney was *good* during the movie. (*Good* is an adjective describing Rodney and comes after *was*, a form of the verb *be*.)

Maryann did *well* on that exam. (*Well* is an adverb describing the verb *did*.)

I explained that I wasn't feeling *well*. (*Well* is used in reference to health.)

PRACTICE 4

Write *well* or *good* in the sentences that follow.

1. As a manager, I am always looking for _____*good*_____ employees—people who are reliable, work hard, and get along with others.

2. My friends assure me George, my blind date this Saturday night, is a _____*good*_____ man.

3. The army buddy who gave my uncle's eulogy knew him _____*well*_____.

4. Horacio told the therapist that he was feeling _____*well*_____, but he was still having nightmares and anxiety attacks.

5. I suspected that I was doing _____*well*_____ in my world civilization class, but I never thought that I would score a 98 percent on the final exam.

Cross out the adjective or adverb error in each sentence and write the correction in the space at the left.

Teaching Tip
You may want to use these review tests to assess what your students have learned.

EXAMPLES

frequently   My boss ~~frequent~~ tells me to slow down.

harder   For me, the country is a ~~more harder~~ place to live than the city.

well   1. I knew she wasn't feeling ~~good~~ when I saw her put her head in her hands.

better   2. It is ~~best~~ for me now to be in school than to have a full-time job.

softly   3. The mother pressed the baby against her shoulder and sang ~~soft~~ in his ear.

gratefully   4. After the two-week camping trip, Donna gazed ~~grateful~~ at her warm bathroom and clean towels.

dullest   5. That show is the ~~most dullest~~ one on television.

restlessly   6. Squirming ~~restless~~ in the seat next to her date, Carol felt uneasy during the violent movie scene.

kindest   7. My sister Ella is the ~~kinder~~ of the four children in our family.

imploringly   8. Clutching a box of chocolate-flavored cereal, the boy stood in the supermarket aisle and looked ~~imploring at~~ his mother.

well   9. He had done ~~good~~ on the first test, so he decided not to study for the next one.

suspiciously   10. Peering ~~suspicious~~ at the can of corn, the shopper peeled back the new price label that had been stuck over the old one.

REVIEW TEST 2

Write a sentence that uses each of the following adjectives and adverbs correctly.

1. nervous _____

2. nervously _____

3. good _____

4. well _____

5. carefully _____

6. most honest _____

7. easier _____

8. best _____

9. more useful _____

10. loudest _____

SCORE

Number Correct

_____/10

_____%

Adjectives and Adverbs

Part 1

Cross out the incorrect adjectival or adverbial form in each sentence. Then write the correct form in the space provided.

well   1. Clark runs ~~good~~ for a person who's thirty pounds overweight.

strangely   2. The car's brakes were acting ~~strange~~, so the mechanic checked the fluid.

beautifully   3. The girls sang ~~beautiful~~, but the faulty microphones spoiled the show.

really   4. That actor's inexperience is ~~real~~ obvious.

carefully   5. Janelle tiptoed ~~careful~~ past the guest room, not wanting to wake the sleeping children.

Part 2

Cross out the error in comparison in each sentence. Then write the correct form in the space provided.

glossiest   6. The ad tried to prove which model's hair was the ~~most glossiest~~ by using a light meter.

better   7. My sister does ~~more well~~ on standardized tests than I do.

more impatient   8. The longer Luis waited in line at the bank, the ~~impatienter~~ he got.

most awkward   9. My ~~awkwardest~~ moment came when I tried to introduce my wife to my boss and forgot both their names.

most productive   10. This has been the ~~most productivest~~ session we've had yet.

NAME: _____

DATE: _____

Adjectives and Adverbs

Part 1

Cross out the incorrect adjectival and adverbial form in each sentence. Then write the correct form in the space provided.

quickly 1. Sherry ate ~~quick~~ so she wouldn't miss the beginning of the early show.

well 2. Xavier decided he wasn't feeling ~~good~~ enough to bowl for the team.

terribly 3. I had a ~~terrible~~ high fever and a deep cough.

easily 4. Hakim makes friends ~~easy~~ because he is so sure of himself.

tightly 5. Paul gripped the handle ~~tight~~ and told the barman to let the mechanical bull loose.

Part 2

Add to each sentence the correct form of the word in the margin.

loud 6. During the spring thunderstorm, each booming clap of thunder was *louder* than the preceding one.

tried 7. After doing fifty push-ups, I was *more tired* than I had been in years.

cheap 8. You'll need binoculars if you sit in the *cheapest* seats in the stadium.

bad 9. The *worst* clashes of the war occurred in the hot jungles of some small South Pacific islands.

little 10. This semester, I'm making *less* money at my after-school job, but I have more free time.

Misplaced Modifiers

CHAPTER

18

INTRODUCTORY ACTIVITY

Because of misplaced words, each of the sentences below has more than one possible meaning. In each case, see if you can explain both the intended meaning and the unintended meaning.

1. The farmers sprayed the apple trees wearing masks.

   Intended meaning: *The farmers were wearing masks.*

   Unintended meaning: *The apple trees were wearing masks.*

2. The woman reached out for the faith healer who had a terminal disease.

   Intended meaning: *The woman had a terminal disease.*

   Unintended meaning: *The faith healer had a terminal disease.*

Answers are on page 641.

What Misplaced Modifiers Are
and How to Correct Them

Misplaced modifiers are words that, because of awkward placement, do not describe the words the writer intended them to describe. Misplaced modifiers often confuse the meaning of a sentence. To avoid them, place words as close as possible to what they describe.

ESL Tip
In some languages, the modifier may precede the noun or object.

MISPLACED WORDS	CORRECTLY PLACED WORDS
They could see the Goodyear blimp *sitting on the front lawn.*	Sitting on the front lawn, they could see the Goodyear blimp.
(The *Goodyear blimp* was sitting on the front lawn?)	(The intended meaning—that the Goodyear blimp was visible from the front lawn—is now clear.)
We had a hamburger after the movie, *which was too greasy for my taste.*	After the movie, we had a hamburger, which was too greasy for my taste.
(The *movie* was too greasy for your taste?)	(The intended meaning—that the hamburger was greasy—is now clear.)
My phone *almost rang* fifteen times last night.	My phone rang almost fifteen times last night.
(The phone *almost rang* fifteen times, but, in fact, did not ring at all?)	(The intended meaning—that the phone rang a little under fifteen times—is now clear.)

Other single-word modifiers to watch out for include *only, even, hardly, nearly,* and *often.* Such words should be placed immediately before the word they modify.

PRACTICE 1

Underline the misplaced word or words in each sentence. Then rewrite the sentence, placing related words together to make the meaning clear.

Teaching Tip
Help students identify the misplaced modifiers in each of these sentences.

EXAMPLE

Anita returned the milk to the supermarket <u>that was spoiled.</u>

Anita returned the milk that was spoiled to the supermarket.

_____

1. We noticed several dead animals <u>driving along the wooded road.</u>

   Driving along the wooded road, we noticed several dead animals.

   _____

2. Maya envisioned the flowers that would bloom <u>in her mind.</u>

   In her mind, Maya envisioned the flowers that would bloom.

   _____

3. I watched my closest friends being married <u>in my tuxedo.</u>

   In my tuxedo, I watched my closest friends being married.

   _____

4. Zoe carried her new coat on her arm, <u>which was trimmed with fake fur.</u>

   Zoe carried her new coat, which was trimmed with fake fur, on her arm.

5. We just heard that all major highways were flooded <u>on the radio.</u>

   We just heard on the radio that all major highways were flooded.

6. Fresh-picked blueberries <u>almost</u> covered the entire kitchen counter.

   Fresh-picked blueberries covered almost the entire kitchen counter.

7. Betty sunk into the hot bath <u>making sounds of contentment.</u>

   Making sounds of contentment, Betty sunk into the hot bath.

8. The salesman demonstrated the Roomba vacuum cleaner <u>with a grin.</u>

   With a grin, the salesman demonstrated the Roomba vacuum cleaner.

9. Natasha is delivering pizzas <u>dressed in a top hat and tails.</u>

   Dressed in a top hat and tails, Natasha is delivering pizzas.

10. The local drama group needs people to build scenery <u>badly.</u>

    The local drama group badly needs people to build scenery.

PRACTICE 2

Rewrite each sentence, adding the *italicized* words. Make sure that the intended meaning is clear and that two different interpretations are not possible.

EXAMPLE

I use a flash drive to back up my computer files. (Insert *that I keep on my key chain.*)

I use a flash drive that I keep on my key chain to back up my computer files.

1. I rolled down my car window only a few inches for the police officer. (Insert *using caution*.)

   Using caution, I rolled down my car window only a few inches for the police officer.

2. Gossip blogs publish unflattering photos of celebrities who are arrested for drunk driving or for possession of illicit drugs. (Insert *all over the world*.)

   Gossip blogs all over the world publish unflattering photos of celebrities who are arrested for drunk driving or for possession of illicit drugs.

3. The mongoose was brought to Hawaii to kill rats but has since destroyed much of the native plant life. (Insert *which resembles the ferret*.)

   The mongoose, which resembles the ferret, was brought to Hawaii to kill rats but has since destroyed much of the native plant life.

4. Led Zeppelin's fourth album sold 33 million copies. (Insert *almost*.)

   Led Zeppelin's fourth album has sold almost 33 million copies.

5. Elisa decided to undergo laser eye surgery to correct her astigmatism. (Insert *at the university medical center*.)

   Elisa decided to undergo laser eye surgery at the university medical center to correct her astigmatism.

REVIEW TEST 1

Teaching Tip
You may want to use these review tests to assess what your students have learned.

Write *M* for *misplaced* or *C* for *correct* in the space to the left of each sentence.

_____M_____ 1. Books don't sell well in bookstores with hard covers.

_____C_____ 2. Books with hard covers don't sell well in bookstores.

_____M_____ 3. Marilyn went to the door to let in the plumber wearing her pajamas.

_____C_____ 4. Wearing her pajamas, Marilyn went to the door to let in the plumber.

_____C_____ 5. Franco spent nearly three hours in the doctor's office.

_M_ 6. Franco nearly spent three hours in the doctor's office.

_M_ 7. I spent three days in a hospital watching reruns recovering from surgery.

_C_ 8. Recovering from surgery, I spent three days in a hospital watching reruns.

_C_ 9. Paula searched through the closet for something to wear on her date.

_M_ 10. Paula searched for something to wear on her date through the closet.

_M_ 11. Nick and Kate found six boxes of pictures of their vacation in the attic.

_M_ 12. Nick and Kate found six boxes of pictures in the attic of their vacation.

_C_ 13. In the attic, Nick and Kate found six boxes of pictures of their vacation.

_C_ 14. Mrs. Liu mistakenly put the milk container, which was leaking in the refrigerator.

_M_ 15. Mrs. Liu mistakenly put the milk container in the refrigerator, which was leaking.

_M_ 16. Susie whispered a silent prayer before the exam began under her breath.

_C_ 17. Susie whispered a silent prayer under her breath before the exam began.

_C_ 18. Under her breath, Susie whispered a silent prayer before the exam began.

_C_ 19. On the patio, we ate roast beef sandwiches dripping with gravy.

_M_ 20. We ate roast beef sandwiches on the patio dripping with gravy.

Underline the five misplaced modifiers in the passage below. Then, in the spaces that follow, show how you would correct them.

¹The tired hikers almost slept for ten hours in the trail shelter. ²Then Rick awakened and hurried out of his cot when he saw a black spider looking out of the corner of his eye. ³At this point, his brother Hal woke up with a start and sneezed several times. ⁴Because Hal was coming down with a cold, Rick agreed to prepare the breakfast. ⁵He first fetched a canteen of orange juice from a nearby stream, which had cooled overnight. ⁶Next, he started a fire and set about boiling water for coffee and frying up some bacon and eggs. ⁷Meanwhile, Hal sniffled, sipped some orange juice, and waited by the fire for a cup of coffee wearing a heavy sweatshirt and gloves. ⁸After both had eaten, Rick was ready to plan another day's hiking. ⁹But Hal was interested only in hiking to the bus on the nearby highway that could drop him a block from his house.

1. *The tired hikers slept for almost ten hours in the trail shelter.*

2. *Then Rick awakened and hurried out of his cot when, looking out of the corner of his eye, he saw a black spider.*

3. *He first fetched from a nearby stream a canteen of orange juice, which had cooled overnight.*

4. *Meanwhile, wearing a heavy sweatshirt and gloves, Hal sniffled, sipped some orange juice, and waited by the fire for a cup of coffee.*

5. *But Hal was interested only in hiking on the nearby highway to the bus that could drop him a block from his house.*

Misplaced Modifiers

Underline the misplaced word or words in each sentence. Then rewrite the sentence, placing related words together and making the meaning clear.

Wording of answers may vary.

1. Leroy stepped on the worm <u>without shoes on</u>.

   Without shoes on, Leroy stepped on the worm.

   _____

2. Ahad purchased an expensive ticket from a scalper <u>that turned out to be a fake</u>.

   Ahad purchased from a scalper an expensive ticket that turned out to be a fake.

   _____

3. I watched a woman board a bus <u>wearing a dress that was several sizes too small</u>.

   I watched a woman wearing a dress that was several sizes too small board a bus.

   _____

4. A tray of donuts had been placed on the counter, <u>which smelled delicious</u>.

   A tray of donuts, which smelled delicious, had been placed on the counter.

   _____

5. The student tried to study in the noisy library <u>with great concentration</u>.

   With great concentration, the student tried to study in the noisy library.

   _____

6. Craig was spotted by a teacher <u>cheating on an examination</u>.

   Craig was spotted cheating on an examination by a teacher.

   _____

7. I stayed at the cabin window watching the bear <u>in my pajamas</u>.

   In my pajamas, I stayed at the cabin window watching the bear.

   _____

8. Akira <u>almost</u> read the whole psychology assignment in two hours.

   Akira read almost the whole psychology assignment in two hours.

   _____

NAME: _____

DATE: _____

Misplaced Modifiers

Underline the misplaced word or words in each sentence. Then rewrite the sentence, placing related words together and making the meaning clear.

Wording of answers may vary.

1. I bought the used car from a friend with a bad exhaust system.

    I bought the used car with a bad exhaust system from a friend.

2. The news featured a man who played basketball in a wheelchair with no legs.

    The news featured a man with no legs who played basketball in a wheelchair.

3. Our neighbor received a reward for returning the puppy to its family, which had been missing for a week.

    Our neighbor received a reward for returning the puppy, which had been missing for a week, to its family.

4. We saw a commercial for a company that promises to remodel any bathroom on television.

    We saw on television a commercial for a company that promises to remodel any bathroom.

5. The hungry lions crept up behind the big game hunter who had fallen asleep without making a sound.

    Without making a sound, the hungry lions crept up behind the big game hunter who had fallen asleep.

6. Larissa watched her sons toss a baseball back and forth through her living room picture window.

    Through her living room picture window, Larissa watched her sons toss a baseball back and forth.

7. We were notified that we had won a trip to Disney World by text message.

    We were notified by text message that we had won a trip to Disney World.

8. I woke up this morning thinking I had a paper due in a cold sweat.

    I woke up in a cold sweat this morning thinking I had a paper due.

Dangling Modifiers

INTRODUCTORY ACTIVITY

Because of dangling words, each of the sentences below has more than one possible meaning. In each case, explain both the intended meaning and the unintended meaning.

1. Munching leaves from a tall tree, the children were fascinated by the eighteen-foot-tall giraffe.

   Intended meaning: *The giraffe was munching leaves.*

   Unintended meaning: *The children were munching leaves.*

2. Arriving home after ten months in the army, Michael's neighbors threw a block party for him.

   Intended meaning: *Michael was arriving home after ten months in the army.*

   Unintended meaning: *The neighbors were arriving home after ten months in the army.*

Answers are on page 642.

Teaching Tip
You may want to use this activity to assess your students' understanding of dangling modifiers.

Note
Some instructors might consider the first example a misplaced modifier, since the subject of the phrase *munching leaves from a tall tree*—the giraffe—does appear later in the sentence. However, correcting the error would involve changing words. Therefore, this type of error is classified as a dangling modifier in *Sentence Skills with Readings*.

What Dangling Modifiers Are and How to Correct Them

A modifier that opens a sentence must be followed immediately by the word it is meant to describe. Otherwise, the modifier is said to be *dangling,* and the sentence takes on an unintended meaning. For example, look at this sentence:

> While sleeping in his backyard, a Frisbee hit Bill on the head.

The unintended meaning is that the *Frisbee* was sleeping in his backyard. What the writer meant, of course, was that *Bill* was sleeping in his backyard. The writer should have placed *Bill* right after the modifier, revising the rest of the sentence as necessary:

> While sleeping in his backyard, *Bill* was hit on the head by a Frisbee.

The sentence could also be corrected by adding the missing subject and verb to the opening word group:

> While *Bill* was sleeping in his backyard, a Frisbee hit him on the head.

Other sentences with dangling modifiers follow. Read the explanations of why they are dangling, and look carefully at how they are corrected.

DANGLING	CORRECT
Having almost no money, my survival depended on my parents.	Having almost no money, *I* depended on my parents for survival.
(*Who* has almost no money? The answer is not *survival* but *I*. The subject *I* must be added.)	*Or:* Since *I* had almost no money, I depended on my parents for survival.
Riding his bike, a German shepherd bit Tony on the ankle.	Riding his bike, *Tony* was bitten on the ankle by a German shepherd.
(*Who* is riding the bike? The answer is not *German shepherd,* as it unintentionally seems to be, but *Tony*. The subject *Tony* must be added.)	*Or:* While *Tony* was riding his bike, a German shepherd bit him on the ankle.
When trying to lose weight, sugary snacks are best avoided.	When trying to lose weight, *you* should avoid sugary snacks.
(*Who* is trying to lose weight? The answer is not *snacks* but *you*. The subject *you* must be added.)	*Or:* When *you* are trying to lose weight, avoid sugary snacks.

These examples make clear two ways of correcting a dangling modifier. Decide on a logical subject and do one of the following:

1. Place the subject *within* the opening word group:

Since *I* had almost no money, I depended on my parents for survival.

In some cases an appropriate subordinating word such as *since* must be added, and the verb may have to be changed slightly.

2. Place the subject right *after* the opening word group:

Having almost no money, *I* depended on my parents for survival.

Sometimes even more rewriting is necessary to correct a dangling modifier. What is important to remember is that a modifier must be placed as close as possible to the word that it modifies.

Rewrite each sentence to correct the dangling modifier. If the sentence is correct, mark it with a *C*.

1. Foaming at the mouth, the shelter had the stray put to sleep.

    The shelter had the stray, which was foaming at the mouth, put to sleep.

2. Kicked carelessly under the bed, Marian finally found her slippers.

    Marian finally found her slippers, which had been kicked carelessly under the bed.

3. Rusty with disuse, I tried out the old swing set.

    I tried out the old swing set, which was rusty with disuse.

4. Having given up four straight hits, the manager decided to replace his starting pitcher.

    The manager decided to replace his starting pitcher, who had given up four straight hits.

5. Having frozen on the vines, the farmers lost their entire tomato crop.

    The farmers lost their entire tomato crop, which had frozen on the vines.

6. While I was pouring out the cereal, a small toy fell into my bowl of milk.

   c _____

   _____

7. Dancing on their hind legs, the audience cheered wildly as the elephants paraded by.

   The audience cheered wildly as the elephants, which were dancing on their hind legs,

   paraded by.

8. Burned beyond all recognition, Marta took the overdone meat loaf from the oven.

   Marta took the overdone meat loaf, which was burned beyond all recognition, from

   the oven.

9. Tattered, faded, and hanging in shreds, we decided to replace the dining room wallpaper.

   We decided to replace the dining room wallpaper, which was tattered, faded, and

   hanging in shreds.

10. When sealed in plastic, a person can keep membership cards clean.

    A person can keep membership cards clean by sealing them in plastic.

    _____

    _____

PRACTICE 2

Complete the following sentences. In each case, a logical subject should follow the opening words.

Answers will vary.

EXAMPLE

Checking my monthly credit card statement, *I discovered that the restaurant had charged me twice for my meal.*

1. Since starting college, _____.

2. After finishing the first semester, _____.

3. While listening to music, _____.

4. Before starting a family, _____.

5. At the age of sixteen, _____.

Write *D* for *dangling* or *C* for *correct* in front of each sentence. Remember that the opening words are a dangling modifier if they are not followed immediately by a logical subject.

Teaching Tip
You may want to use these review tests to assess how much your students have learned and how much they have understood what they've learned.

_____*D*_____ 1. Yellowed with age, the young researcher could hardly read the old newspaper clipping.

_____*C*_____ 2. The young researcher could hardly read the old newspaper clipping, which was yellowed with age.

_____*D*_____ 3. Tired and exasperated, the fight we had was inevitable.

_____*C*_____ 4. Since we were tired and exasperated, the fight we had was inevitable.

_____*C*_____ 5. After signing the repair contract, I had second thoughts.

_____*D*_____ 6. After signing the repair contract, second thoughts made me uneasy.

_____*D*_____ 7. At the age of twelve, several colleges had already accepted the boy genius.

_____*C*_____ 8. At the age of twelve, the boy genius had already been accepted by several colleges.

_____*D*_____ 9. While setting up the board, several game pieces were missing.

_____*C*_____ 10. While setting up the board, we noticed that several game pieces were missing.

_____*D*_____ 11. Walking to class, a gorgeous white car sped by me.

_____*C*_____ 12. As I was walking to class, a gorgeous white car sped by me.

_____*C*_____ 13. While waiting for the dentist to see her, Vicky became more nervous.

_____*D*_____ 14. While waiting for the dentist to see her, Vicky's nervousness increased.

_____*C*_____ 15. While she was waiting for the dentist to see her, Vicky became more nervous.

_____*D*_____ 16. Protected with slipcovers, my mother lets us put our feet on the living room furniture.

_____*C*_____ 17. My mother lets us put our feet on the living room furniture, since it is protected with slipcovers.

_____*D*_____ 18. Packed tightly in a tiny can, Jesmyn had difficulty removing the anchovies.

_____*C*_____ 19. Since they were packed tightly in a tiny can, Jesmyn had difficulty removing the anchovies.

_____*C*_____ 20. Packed tightly in a tiny can, the anchovies were difficult for Jesmyn to remove.

REVIEW TEST 2

Underline the five dangling modifiers in this passage. Then correct them in the spaces provided.

¹For years, students have been using the same methods of cheating on exams. One tried-and-true technique is the casual glance. ²Pretending to stare thoughtfully out the window, peripheral vision will be used to look at another student's paper. ³Another all-time favorite method, the pencil or pen drop, requires a helper. ⁴Dropping a pen and then diving for it, "Number seventeen" (or the number of some other question) is whispered. ⁵Then, making a similar pen drop, the answer is whispered by the helper. ⁶The most elaborate system, though, is writing up cheat sheets. ⁷Tucked up a shirtsleeve or hidden in a text message, pages of textbook material are condensed into tiny scraps of paper or several cell phone screens. ⁸No matter how smooth a cheater's style is, however, the time-tested methods are often ineffective. ⁹Having been a student at one time, the same ones are probably familiar to the instructor.

1. *Pretending to stare thoughtfully out the window, a student will use peripheral vision to look at another student's paper.*

2. *Dropping a pen and then diving for it, a cheater whispers "Number seventeen" (or the number of some other question).*

3. *Then, making a similar pen drop, the helper whispers the answer.*

4. *Pages of textbook material are either condensed in tiny scraps of paper that are tucked up a shirtsleeve, or in a text message that may take up several cell phone screens.*

5. *Having been a student at one time, the instructor is probably familiar with the same ones.*

SCORE
Number Correct

_____ /8

_____ %

MASTERY TEST 1

Dangling Modifiers

Underline the dangling modifier in each sentence. Then rewrite the sentence, correcting the dangling modifier.

1. Being made of clear glass, the children kept bumping into the sliding door.

   Since it was made of clear glass, the children kept bumping into the sliding door.

   _____

   Wording of answers may vary.

2. Still green, Helen put the tomato in sunlight to ripen.

   Since it was still green, Helen put the tomato in sunlight to ripen.

3. Though somewhat warped, my grandfather still enjoys playing his record collection from the sixties.

   Though it is somewhat warped, my grandfather still enjoys playing his record

   collection from the sixties.

4. Having turned crispy and golden, I removed the chicken from the pan.

   I removed the chicken, which had turned crispy and golden, from the pan.

   _____

5. Bigger than ever, Aunt Clara predicted that this year's watermelon entry would win first prize at the county fair.

   Aunt Clara predicted that this year's watermelon entry, which was bigger than ever,

   would win first prize at the county fair.

6. After changing the bait, the fish started to bite.

   After we changed the bait, the fish started to bite.

7. Coming home without a job, the news on television only made Jennifer feel depressed.

   Since she was coming home without a job, the comedies on television only made

   Jennifer feel depressed.

8. Having rehearsed his speech several times, Amal's presentation to the staff went smoothly.

   Since he had rehearsed his speech several times, Amal's presentation to the staff

   went smoothly.

271

NAME: _____

DATE: _____

Dangling Modifiers

Underline the dangling modifier in each sentence. Then rewrite the sentence, correcting the dangling modifier.

Rewritten
sentences may
vary.

1. Being too heavy to lift, Jo asked Bob to help her move the sofa.

   Since it was too heavy to lift, Jo asked Bob to help her move the sofa.

2. Parched and dry, the ice-cold Coke soothed my throat.

   The ice-cold Coke soothed my throat, which was parched and dry.

3. Clutching a handful of silverware and a flatscreen, our neighbor's watchdog surprised a burglar.

   Our neighbor's watchdog surprised a burglar, who was clutching a handful of

   silverware and a flatscreen.

4. Living in a tent for two weeks, the camping trip made us appreciate hot show-ers and dry towels.

   After we had lived in a tent for two weeks, the camping trip made us appreciate

   hot showers and dry towels.

5. Thrown on the floor in a heap, we could not tell if the clothes were clean or dirty.

   We could not tell if the clothes that were thrown on the floor in a heap were clean

   or dirty.

6. Afraid to look his father in the eye, Danny's head remained bowed.

   Afraid to look his father in the eye, Danny kept his head bowed.

7. Straining at the leash, I could see my neighbor's Great Dane getting ready for his walk.

   I could see my neighbor's Great Dane, which was straining at the leash, getting

   ready for his walk.

8. While lying in bed with a cold, my cat jumped on me and curled up on my stomach.

   While I was lying in bed with a cold, my cat jumped on me and curled up on

   my stomach.

Faulty Parallelism

CHAPTER

20

INTRODUCTORY ACTIVITY

Read aloud each pair of sentences below. Place a check mark beside the sentence that reads more smoothly and clearly and sounds more natural.

PAIR 1

_____ I use my computer to write papers, to chat with friends, and for playing games.

___✓___ I use my computer to write papers, to chat with friends, and to play games.

PAIR 2

_____ One option the employees had was to take a cut in pay; the other was longer hours of work.

___✓___ One option the employees had was to take a cut in pay; the other was to work longer hours.

PAIR 3

_____ Dad's favorite chair has a torn cushion, the armrest is stained, and a musty odor.

___✓___ Dad's favorite chair has a torn cushion, a stained armrest, and a musty odor.

Answers are on page 642.

Parallelism Explained

Words in a pair or a series should have parallel structure. By balancing the items in a pair or a series so that they have the same kind of structure, you will make the sentence clearer and easier to read. Notice how the parallel sentences that follow read more smoothly than the nonparallel ones.

Teaching Tip
Ask students to underline the nonparallel items in each sentence.

ESL Tip
Remind non-native speakers that when items in a series are combined with coordinating conjunctions (*and, or, but, nor, yet*), they should all be written in the same grammatical form (e.g., all infinitives, noun clauses, or objects).

NONPARALLEL (NOT BALANCED)

Shadana spends her free time reading, listening to music, and she works in the garden.

After the camping trip I was exhausted, irritable, and wanted to eat.

My hope for retirement is to be healthy, to live in a comfortable house, and having plenty of money.

Nightly, Alexei puts out the trash, checks the locks on the doors, and the burglar alarm is turned on.

PARALLEL (BALANCED)

Shadana spends her free time reading, listening to music, and working in the garden.

(A balanced series of *-ing* words: *reading, listening, working*)

After the camping trip I was exhausted, irritable, and hungry.

(A balanced series of descriptive words: *exhausted, irritable, hungry*)

My hope for retirement is to be healthy, to live in a comfortable house, and to have plenty of money.

(A balanced series of *to* verbs: *to be, to live, to have*)

Nightly, Alexei puts out the trash, checks the locks on the doors, and turns on the burglar alarm.

(Balanced verbs and word order: *puts out the trash, checks the locks, turns on the burglar alarm*)

Balanced sentences are not a skill you need to worry about when you are writing first drafts. But when you rewrite, you should try to put matching words and ideas into matching structures. Such parallelism will improve your writing style.

PRACTICE 1

The unbalanced part of each sentence is italicized. Rewrite this part so that it matches the rest of the sentence.

EXAMPLE

In the afternoon, I changed two diapers, ironed several shirts, and *was watching* soap operas. _watched_____

Teaching Tip
You may want to do these activities as an entire class.

1. As the home team scored the winning touchdown, the excited fans screamed, cheered, and *pennants were waved.*
   _waved pennants_____

2. Would you prefer to go for a walk outside or *staying indoors*?
   _to stay indoors_____

3. Before Pete could assemble the casserole, he had to brown the meat, dice the vegetables, and *a cream sauce had to be made.*

   make a cream sauce _____

4. Please feed the dog, *the heat must be turned down,* and lock the doors.

   turn down the heat _____

5. That restaurant specializes in *hamburgers that are overdone,* wilted salads, and mushy fries.

   overdone hamburgers _____

6. The old Ford sputtered, *was coughing,* and finally stopped altogether.

   coughed _____

7. The hospital patients can sometimes be cranky, *make a lot of demands,* and ungrateful.

   demanding _____

8. After eating a whole pizza, *two milk shakes,* and sampling a bag of chips, Ernest was still hungry.

   drinking two milk shakes _____

9. As soon as she gets up, she starts the coffee machine, turns on music, and *a frozen waffle is put into the toaster.*

   puts a frozen waffle into the toaster _____

10. The boss told Vern that he had only two options: to work harder or *leaving the company.*

    to leave the company _____

Complete the following statements. The first two parts of each statement are parallel in form; the part that you add should be parallel in form as well.

PRACTICE 2

EXAMPLE

Three things I could not live without are my cell phone, my laptop, and

my morning coffee. _____

1. The new reality TV show is disappointing: the premise is absurd, the cast members are uninteresting, and _____.

Answers will vary.

2. As a parent, I promise to love my child unconditionally, to provide for my child's needs, and _____.

3. As the students waited for the professor to arrive for class, they rummaged through their backpacks, silenced their phones, and _____.

4. During my first year in my own apartment, I learned how to fix leaky toilets and torn screens, how to survive on instant ramen and frozen pizzas, and

_____.

5. Online dating is popular, unpredictable, and _____.

COLLABORATIVE ACTIVITY

Editing and Rewriting

Working with a partner, carefully read the short paragraph below and mark the five instances of faulty parallelism. Then correct the instances of faulty parallelism. Feel free to discuss the rewrite quietly with your partner and refer back to the chapter when necessary.

Teaching Tip
Ask students to work on the Collaborative Activities in pairs and share their answers for the Reflective Activity with the entire class.

¹For the 10 percent of the American population that is left-handed, life is not easy. ²Using a pair of scissors or ~~to write~~ *writing* in a spiral notebook can be very difficult. ³The scissors and the notebook are two items designed for right-handers. ⁴Also, have you ever seen a "southpaw" take notes or ~~writing~~ *write* an exam at one of those right-handed half-desks? ⁵The poor "lefty" has to twist like a yoga devotee or ~~in the style of~~ *[delete]* a circus acrobat in order to reach the paper. ⁶But a recent study proves that being left-handed can be psychologically damaging as well as ~~tax a person physically.~~ *physically taxing.* ⁷A survey of 2,300 people showed that 20 percent more left-handers than right-handers smoked. ⁸Perhaps left-handed people smoke to relieve the tension or ~~they are forgetting~~ *to forget* the problems of living in a right-handed world.

COLLABORATIVE ACTIVITY

Creating Sentences

Working with a partner, make up your own short test on faulty parallelism, as directed.

1. Write a sentence that includes three things you want to do tomorrow. One of those things should not be in parallel form. Then correct the faulty parallelism.

   Nonparallel _____

   _____

   Parallel _____

   _____

2. Write a sentence that names three positive or three negative qualities of a person you know.

   Nonparallel _____

   _____

   Parallel _____

   _____

3. Write a sentence that includes three everyday things that annoy you.

   Nonparallel _____

   _____

   Parallel _____

   _____

REFLECTIVE ACTIVITY

1. Look at the paragraph about being left-handed that you revised on page 276. How does parallel form improve the paragraph?

2. How would you evaluate your use of parallel form in your writing? Do you use it almost never, at times, or often? How would you benefit from using it more?

REVIEW TEST 1

Teaching Tip
You may want
to use these
review tests to
assess what
your students
have learned
and to de-
termine how
much they
understand
what they've
learned.

Cross out the unbalanced part of each sentence. Then rewrite the unbalanced part so that it matches the other item or items in the sentence.

EXAMPLE

I enjoy watering the grass and ~~to work~~ in the garden.

working

1. The traffic cop blew his whistle, ~~was waving his hands~~, and nodded to the driver to start moving.

   waved his hands

2. Mike's letter of application was smudged, improperly spaced, and ~~it had wrinkles~~.

   wrinkled

3. Kendra spoke vividly and ~~with force~~ at the student government meeting.

   forcefully

4. I like Rihanna; ~~Beyoncé is preferred by my sister~~.

   my sister prefers Beyoncé

5. Darkening skies, ~~branches that were waving~~, and scurrying animals signaled the approaching storm.

   waving branches

6. The pitcher wiped his brow, straightened his cap, and ~~he was tugging at his sleeve~~.

   tugged at his sleeve

7. The driving instructor told me to keep my hands on the wheel, to drive defensively, and ~~the use of caution at all times~~.

   to use caution at all times

8. The customer made choking noises, turned red, and ~~was pointing to his throat~~.

   pointed to his throat

9. My sister eats pasta without sauce, cereal without milk, and ~~doesn't put mustard on hot dogs~~.

   hot dogs without mustard

10. The scratches on my car's hood were caused by rocks hitting it, ~~people who sat on it~~, and cats jumping on it.

    people sitting on it

REVIEW TEST 2

On a separate sheet of paper or in a separate file, write five sentences of your own that use parallel structure. Each sentence should contain three items in a series.

REVIEW TEST 3

There are six nonparallel parts in the following passage. The first is corrected for you as an example. Underline the other five and write corrections in the space provided.

[1]Consumers have several sources of information they can use in the never-ending war against poor services and merchandise that is shoddy. [2]For one thing, consumers can take advantage of the Better Business Bureau or Angie's List. [3]If you plan to contract the Fly-By-Night Company to paint your house or the replacement of siding, you should first consult its website, which includes reviews and reports, to learn about any complaints against that company. [4]Second, consumers can refer to helpful information available from the U.S. Government Printing Office. [5]You can learn, for instance, how to buy a house, shopping for health insurance, or protect yourself from auto repair rip-offs. [6]Finally, careful buyers can turn to *Consumer Reports*, an independent print and online magazine and one that is nonprofit that tests and rates a wide range of consumer products. [7]For example, if you are thinking about buying a certain car, *Consumer Reports* will give you information on its comfort level, safety features, fuel economy, and record for repair. [8]If consumers remember to look before they leap and are taking advantage of the above sources of information, they are more likely to get a fair return on their hard-earned dollars.

1. *shoddy merchandise* _____

2. *replace your siding* _____

3. *shop for health insurance* _____

4. *an independent nonprofit magazine* _____

5. *repair record* _____

6. *to take* _____

NAME: _____

DATE: _____

Faulty Parallelism

The unbalanced part of each sentence is italicized. Rewrite this part so that it matches the rest of the sentence.

1. The bus squeaked, grunted, and then *there was a hiss* as it shifted gears.

   hissed

2. *With grace* and skillfully, Charles took aim and tossed a quarter into the basket at the toll booth.

   Gracefully

3. Sue beats the blues by taking a hot bubble bath, cuddling up in a cozy quilt, and *eats her favorite snack.*

   eating her favorite snack

4. They didn't want a 15" flatscreen, but *a 52" flatscreen couldn't be afforded.*

   they couldn't afford a 52" flatscreen

5. We stayed at a country inn and dined on tender steak, baked Idaho potatoes, and *vegetables that were local.*

   local vegetables

6. When she learned she had won the gymnastic contest, Nikki gasped, screamed, and *all teammates were kissed by her.*

   kissed all her teammates

7. I avoid camping because I don't like to eat half-cooked food, sleep on rocks and twigs, or *the biting of insects.*

   get bitten by insects

8. Make sure you have proofread your paper, stapled it, and *there are numbers on the pages* before you turn it in.

   numbered the pages

9. Unless you are either very noisy or *persist,* you won't wake me up.

   persistent

10. Kerry uses his rollerblades to get to school, to go to the store, and *for going to football practice.*

    to go to football practice

NAME: _____

DATE: _____

Faulty Parallelism

Draw a line under the unbalanced part of each sentence. Then rewrite the unbalanced part so that it matches the other items in the sentence.

Rewritten parts may vary.

1. Michael was so hungry he could have eaten a horse—roasted, broiled, or in a stew.

   stewed

2. In the last game, Julio had one single, a two-base hit, and one triple.

   one double

3. Bill told us to help ourselves at the buffet and that we could fix our own drinks in the kitchen.

   to fix our own drinks in the kitchen

4. My grandfather must have foods that are easy to cook and digestible.

   easy to digest

5. The awards show was filled with splashy dance numbers, film clips that were boring, and long-winded speeches.

   boring film clips

6. My driving instructor told me to keep both hands on the wheel, to use caution at all times, and don't take my eyes off the road.

   not to take my eyes off the road

7. Jackie sucked in her stomach, stopped breathing, and was trying to pull the zipper up again.

   tried to pull the zipper up again

8. Phil was so sick that all he was good for was lying in bed and to look up at the ceiling.

   looking up at the ceiling

9. When she gets very angry, Gale works off her anger by cleaning out her desk drawers, windows getting washed, or scrubbing the bathtub.

   washing the windows

10. The movie about the serial killer was violent, it caused shock, and demeaning to women.

    shocking

CHAPTER

21

Sentence Variety II

Like Chapter 9, this chapter will show you several ways to write effective and varied sentences. You will increase your sense of the many ways available to you for expressing your ideas. The practices here will also reinforce much of what you have learned in this section about modifiers and the use of parallelism.

-ing Word Groups

Use an *-ing* word group at some point in a sentence. Here are examples:

The doctor, *hoping* for the best, examined the X-rays.

Jogging every day, I soon raised my energy level.

More information about *-ing* words, also known as *present participles,* appears on page 211.

PRACTICE 1

Combine each pair of sentences below into one sentence by using an *-ing* word and omitting repeated words. Use a comma or commas to set off the *-ing* word group from the rest of the sentence.

EXAMPLE

- The diesel truck chugged up the hill.
- It spewed out smoke.

Spewing out smoke, the diesel truck chugged up the hill.

Or *The diesel truck, spewing out smoke, chugged up the hill.*

1. - The sparrow tried to keep warm.
   - It fluffed out its feathers.

   Fluffing out its feathers, the sparrow tried to keep warm.

2. • I managed to get enough toothpaste on my brush.
   • I squeezed the tube as hard as I could.

   Squeezing the tube as hard as I could, I managed to get enough toothpaste on my brush.

   _____

3. • The building superintendent started up the enormous boiler.
   • He checked the glass-faced gauges.

   Checking the glass-faced gauges, the building superintendent started up the enormous boiler.

4. • The runner set her feet into the starting blocks.
   • She stared straight ahead.

   Staring straight ahead, the runner set her feet into the starting blocks.

   _____

5. • The produce clerk cheerfully weighed bags of fruit and vegetables.
   • He chatted with each customer.

   The produce clerk, chatting with each customer, cheerfully weighed bags of fruit and vegetables.

PRACTICE 2

On a separate sheet of paper or in a separate file, write five sentences of your own that contain *-ing* word groups.

-ed Word Groups

Use an *-ed* word group at some point in a sentence. Here are examples:

Tired of studying, I took a short break.
Mary, *amused* by the joke, told it to a friend.
I opened my eyes wide, *shocked* by the red "F" on my paper.

More information about *-ed* words, also known as *past participles,* appears on page 211.

Teaching Tip
For added practice, ask students to provide another possible answer for each pair of sentences.

ESL Tip
Sentence variety will improve expression in academic writing. Just remember that nonnative speakers may need more practice and direction in combining sentences.

PRACTICE 3

Combine each of the following pairs of sentences into one sentence by using an -*ed* word and omitting repeated words. Use a comma or commas to set off the -*ed* word group from the rest of the sentence.

EXAMPLE

- Tim woke up with a start.
- He was troubled by a dream.

Troubled by a dream, Tim woke up with a start.

Or *Tim, troubled by a dream, woke up with a start.*

Answers will vary.

1. • I dozed off.
   • I was bored with the talk show.

   Bored with the talk show, I dozed off.

2. • The old dollar bill felt like tissue paper.
   • It was crinkled with age.

   Crinkled with age, the old dollar bill felt like tissue paper.

3. • The students acted nervous and edgy.
   • They were crowded into a tiny, windowless room.

   Crowded into a tiny, windowless room, the students acted nervous and edgy.

4. • I waited for someone to open the door.
   • I was loaded down with heavy bags of groceries.

   Loaded down with heavy bags of groceries, I waited for someone to open the door.

5. • Ron bought a green-striped suit.
   • He was tired of his conservative wardrobe.

   Tired of his conservative wardrobe, Ron bought a green-striped suit.

On a separate sheet of paper or in a separate file, write five sentences of your own that contain *-ed* word groups.

-ly Openers

Use an *-ly* word to open a sentence. Here are examples:

Gently, he mixed the chemicals together.

Anxiously, the contestant looked at the game clock.

Skillfully, the quarterback rifled a pass to his receiver.

More information about *-ly* words, which are also known as *adverbs,* appears on page 251.

Combine each of the following pairs of sentences into one sentence by starting with an *-ly* word and omitting repeated words. Place a comma after the opening *-ly* word.

EXAMPLE

- I gave several yanks to the starting cord of the lawn mower.
- I was angry.

Angrily, I gave several yanks to the starting cord of the lawn mower.

_____

1. • Clarissa hung up on the telemarketer.
   • She was abrupt.

   Abruptly, Clarissa hung up on the telemarketer.

   _____

2. • The thief slipped one of the watches into her coat sleeve.
   • She was casual.

   Casually, the thief slipped one of the watches into her coat sleeve.

   _____

3. • I tugged on my shoes and pants as the doorbell rang.
   • I was swift.

   Swiftly, I tugged on my shoes and pants as the doorbell rang.

   _____

4. • The defense lawyer cross-examined the witnesses.

    • He was gruff.

    Gruffly, the defense lawyer cross-examined the witnesses.

    _____

5. • Estelle poked the corner of a handkerchief into her eye.

    • She was careful.

    Carefully, Estelle poked the corner of a handkerchief into her eye.

    _____

PRACTICE 6   On a separate sheet of paper or in a separate file, write five sentences of your own that begin with *-ly* words.

To Openers

ESL Tip
Nonnative
speakers may
need to know
that the infini-
tive in this case
stands for "in
order to."

Use a *to* word group to open a sentence. Here are examples:

To succeed in that course, you must attend every class.

To help me sleep better, I learned to quiet my mind through meditation.

To get good seats, we went to the game early.

The *to* in such a group is also known as an *infinitive,* as explained on page 211.

Combine each of the following pairs of sentences into one sentence by starting with a *to* word group and omitting repeated words. Use a comma after the opening *to* word group.

EXAMPLE

- I fertilize the grass every spring.
- I want to make it greener.

  To make the grass greener, I fertilize it every spring.

  _____

1. • We set bricks on the ends of the picnic table.
   • We did this to anchor the flapping tablecloth.

   To anchor the flapping tablecloth, we set bricks on the ends of the picnic table.

   _____

2. • Darryl scraped the windshield with a credit card.
   • He did this to break up the coating of ice.

   To break up the coating of ice, Darryl scraped the windshield with a credit card.

   _____

3. • We gave our opponents a ten-point advantage.
   • We wanted to make the basketball game more even.

   To make the basketball game more even, we gave our opponents a ten-point advantage.

   _____

4. • I offered to drive the next five hundred miles.
   • I wanted to give my wife a rest.

   To give my wife a rest, I offered to drive the next five hundred miles.

   _____

5. • Ashaki added Hamburger Helper to the ground beef.
   • She did this to feed the unexpected guests.

   To feed the unexpected guests, Ashaki added Hamburger Helper to the ground beef.

   _____

On a separate sheet of paper or in a separate file, write five sentences of your own that begin with *to* word groups.

Prepositional Phrase Openers

Use prepositional phrase openers. Here are examples:

> *From* the beginning, I disliked my boss.
>
> *In spite* of her work, she failed the course.
>
> *After* the game, we went to a movie.

> **TIP**   Prepositional phrases include *in, from, of, at, by,* and *with*. A full list is
> on page 88.

A full list is on page 88.

PRACTICE 9   Combine each of the following groups of sentences into one sentence by omitting repeated words. Start each sentence with a suitable prepositional phrase and put the other prepositional phrases in places that sound right. Generally, you should use a comma after the opening prepositional phrase.

EXAMPLE

- A fire started.
- It did this at 5 A.M.
- It did this inside the garage.

At 5 A.M., a fire started inside the garage.

Answers may vary.

1. • The old man wrote down my address.
   - He did this on the bus.
   - He did this with a stubby pencil.

   On the bus, the old man wrote down my address with a stubby pencil.

2. • Special bulletins interrupted regular programs.
   - They did this during the day.
   - The bulletins were about the election returns.

   During the day, special bulletins about the election returns interrupted regular programs.

3. • My clock radio turned itself on.

    • It did this at 6:00 A.M.

    • It did this with a loud blast.

    • The loud blast was of '90s music.

    At 6:00 A.M., my clock radio turned itself on with a loud blast of '90s music.

    _____

4. • The security guard looked.

    • He did this at the concert.

    • He did this in Aly's bag.

    • He did this for concealed bottles.

    At the concert, the security guard looked in Aly's pocketbook for concealed bottles.

    _____

5. • A plodding turtle crawled.

    • It did this on the highway.

    • It did this toward the grassy shoulder of the road.

    On the highway, a plodding turtle crawled toward the grassy shoulder of the road.

    _____

ESL Tip
Nonnative speakers should understand that these prepositional phrases tell *when, why,* and *where* and function like adverbs. If they modify the whole sentence, they can be placed in the beginning or at the end of a sentence. If they begin a sentence, they should be followed by a comma.

On a separate sheet of paper or in a separate file, write five sentences of your own, each beginning with a prepositional phrase and containing at least one other prepositional phrase.

PRACTICE 10

Teaching Tip
Encourage students to write about events in their own lives.

Series of Items

Use a series of items. Following are two of the many items that can be used in a series: adjectives and verbs. The section on parallelism (page 273) gives you practice in some of the other kinds of items that can be used in a series.

ESL Tip
Nonnative students may need to practice the order of adjectives (see Appendix A).

Adjectives in Series

Adjectives are descriptive words. Here are examples:

The *husky young* man sanded the *chipped, weather-worn* paint off the fence.

Husky and *young* are adjectives that describe *man; chipped* and *weather-worn* are adjectives that describe *paint.* More information about adjectives appears on page 248.

PRACTICE 11

Combine each of the following groups of sentences into one sentence by using adjectives in a series and omitting repeated words. Use a comma between adjectives only when *and* inserted between them sounds natural.

EXAMPLE

- I sewed a set of buttons onto my coat.
- The buttons were shiny.
- The buttons were black.
- The coat was old.
- The coat was green.

I sewed a set of shiny black buttons onto my old green coat.

1. • The child gazed at the gift box.
   - The child was impatient.
   - The child was excited.
   - The gift box was large.
   - The gift box was mysterious.

   Impatient and excited, the child gazed at the large, mysterious gift box.

   _____

2. • Juice spurted out of the caterpillar.
   - The juice was sticky.
   - The caterpillar was fuzzy.
   - The caterpillar was crushed.

   Sticky juice squirted out of the fuzzy crushed caterpillar.

   _____

3. • The car dangled from the crane.
   - The car was battered.
   - The crane was gigantic.
   - The crane was yellow.

   The battered car dangled from the gigantic yellow crane.

   _____

4. • Patty squeezed her feet into the shoes.
   • Patty's feet were swollen.
   • Patty's feet were tender.
   • Patty's feet were sunburned.
   • The shoes were tight.

   Patty squeezed her swollen, tender, sunburned feet into the tight shoes.

   _____

5. • The cook flipped the hamburgers on the grill.
   • The cook was tall.
   • The cook was white-aproned.
   • The hamburgers were thick.
   • The hamburgers were juicy.
   • The grill was grooved.
   • The grill was metal.

   The tall white-aproned cook flipped the thick, juicy hamburgers on the grooved metal grill.

On a separate sheet of paper or in a separate file, write five sentences of your own that contain a series of adjectives.

PRACTICE 12

Teaching Tip
Emphasize that verbs in a series need to be parallel.

Verbs in Series

Verbs are words that express action. Here are examples:

In my job as a cook's helper, I *prepared* salads, *sliced* meat and cheese, and *made* all kinds of sandwiches.

Basic information about verbs appears on pages 86–90.

PRACTICE 13

Combine each group of sentences below into one sentence by using verbs in a series and omitting repeated words. Use a comma between verbs in a series.

Teaching Tip
You may
want to have
students do
this activity in
pairs.

EXAMPLES

- At the gym, Elsa lifted free weights.
- She did several lateral pull-downs.
- She jumped on the elliptical machine for twenty minutes.

  At the gym, Elsa lifted free weights, did several lateral pull-downs, and jumped on the elliptical machine for twenty minutes.

1.
   - In the sports bar, Dave placed a bet on his favorite basketball team.
   - He took a swig from his bottle of beer.
   - He sat back to watch the NBA playoff semifinals.

     In the sports bar, Dave placed a bet on his favorite basketball team, took a swig from his bottle of beer, and sat back to watch the NBA playoff semifinals.

2.
   - The robber scanned the liquor store for a surveillance camera.
   - He fidgeted with his dark sunglasses and baseball cap.
   - He signaled to the clerk behind the counter that he had a handgun.

     The robber scanned the liquor store for a surveillance camera, fidgeted with his dark sunglasses and baseball cap, and signaled to the clerk behind the counter that he had a handgun.

3.
   - The phlebotomist pressed down on Logan's forearm.
   - She slid the needle into his arm.
   - She let out a heavy sigh as the needle missed his vein.

     The phlebotomist pressed down on Logan's forearm, slid the needle into his arm, and let out a heavy sigh as the needle missed his vein.

4.
   - The comedy hypnotist invited a volunteer to the stage.
   - He quickly brought her into a trance.
   - He offered her a clove of garlic, which she thought was a cashew nut.

     The comedy hypnotist invited a volunteer to the stage, quickly brought her into a trance, and offered her a clove of garlic, which she thought was a cashew nut.

5. • The paparazzo stalked the Hollywood actor on vacation.

    • He adjusted his lens.

    • He snapped hundreds of candid photos.

    The paparazzo stalked the Hollywood actor on vacation, adjusted his lens, and snapped hundreds of candid photos.

On a separate sheet of paper or in a separate file, write five sentences of your own that use verbs in a series.

PRACTICE 14

REVIEW TEST 1

On a separate sheet of paper or in a separate file, combine each group of sentences into one sentence. Combinations are possible. Choose the combination that reads most smoothly and clearly and that sounds most appropriate in the context of surrounding sentences.

Answers will vary.

Teaching Tip
You may want to use these review tests to assess what your students have learned and to determine how much they understand what they've learned.

> **HINT** In combining short sentences into one sentence, omit repeated words where necessary.

ENGLISH CLASS

• The teacher said, "Name three famous poets."

• She was looking at John.

• The teacher repeated the question when John didn't answer.

• She did this in an encouraging voice.

• John sat up straight.

• He did this quickly.

• John named Dickinson and Frost.

• He couldn't name a third poet.

• The teacher was feeling sorry for John.

• The teacher decided to give him a hint.

• She was smiling warmly.

• She asked, "What's taking you so long, fellow?"

Possible answers:
Looking at John, the teacher said, "Name three famous poets."

In an encouraging voice, the teacher repeated the question when John didn't answer.

John quickly sat up straight and named Dickinson and Frost, but he couldn't name a third poet.

Feeling sorry for John, the teacher decided to give him a hint.

Smiling warmly, she asked, "What's taking you so long, fellow?"

- Many long seconds passed, and then John blurted, "Longfellow."
- John was happy.

Many long seconds passed, and then John happily blurted, "Longfellow."

- John heard the other students laughing.
- The students were behind him.
- The laughing was loud.

John heard the other students laughing loudly behind him.

- One student called out, "What took you so long, fellow?"
- The student did so in a teasing tone.

In a teasing tone, one student called out, "What took you so long, fellow?"

- John realized why everyone was laughing.
- He was embarrassed.

John, embarrassed, realized why everyone was laughing.

- But John joined in the laughter.
- He had a good sense of humor.

But, having a good sense of humor, John joined in the laughter.

REVIEW TEST 2

On a separate sheet of paper or in a separate file, combine each group of sentences into one sentence. Various combinations are possible. Choose the combination that reads most smoothly and clearly and that sounds most appropriate in the context of surrounding sentences.

> **HINT**   In combining short sentences into one sentence, omit repeated words where necessary.

Answers will vary.

PRACTICAL JOKER

- My brother Mark was handing me what looked like a kaleidoscope.
- Mark is my older brother.
- He said to me, "Twist this tube and watch the patterns of glass."

Possible answers:
Handing me what looked like a kaleidoscope, my older brother Mark said to me, "Twist this tube and watch the patterns of glass."

- I twisted the tube.
- I said that I couldn't see anything.

Twisting the tube, I said that I couldn't see anything.

- Mark said, "You must be blind."
- As he said this, he was laughing loudly.

Laughing loudly, Mark said, "You must be blind."

- I knew that Mark was a practical joker.
- I looked in a mirror.
- I saw a black ring around my right eye.
- However, Mark outsmarted himself.
- He did this one Sunday evening.
- It was an evening when I took a shower to be ready for school the next day.
- Mark had unscrewed the showerhead.
- He had poured in a packet of dye.
- He replaced the showerhead.
- He waited for his victim to take a shower.
- While Mark was in the kitchen, my father headed for the bathroom.
- This was unfortunate.
- My father was wearing his robe.
- His robe was red-and-white striped.
- Soon, a shout pierced the bathroom walls.
- The shout was deafening.
- The shout was angry.
- My father burst through the door.
- He was splattered in navy blue.
- Mark did the sensible thing.
- Mark took off through the back door.
- He ran till he was out of sight.
- He didn't return until my father cooled off.

Knowing that Mark was a practical joker, I looked in a mirror and saw a black ring around my right eye.

One Sunday evening when I took a shower to be ready for school the next day, however, Mark outsmarted himself.

Mark had unscrewed the showerhead, poured in a packet of dye, replaced the showerhead, and waited for his victim to take a shower.

Unfortunately, while Mark was in the kitchen, my father headed for the bathroom wearing his red-and-white-striped robe.

Soon, an angry, deafening shout pierced the bathroom walls.

My father, splattered in navy blue, burst through the door.

Doing the sensible thing, Mark took off through the back door, ran till he was out of sight, and didn't return until my father cooled off.

NAME: _____

DATE: _____

Sentence Variety II

Combine each group of short sentences into one sentence. A variety of combinations is possible. Choose the combination that reads most smoothly and clearly and that sounds most appropriate in the context of surrounding sentences. Use a separate sheet of paper or computer file. The story continues in the next mastery test.

> **HINT** In combining short sentences into one sentence, omit repeated words where necessary.

BARGAIN FLIGHT

- Ramon missed his grandparents.
- He decided to visit them.
- His grandparents are in Florida.
- He decided to do this during the semester break.

Possible answers:
Since Ramon missed his grandparents, he decided to visit them in Florida during the semester break.

- Ramon needed to save money and time.
- He looked for a flight to Miami.
- He looked for a cheap flight.
- He looked for a direct flight.

Needing to save money and time, he looked for a cheap, direct flight to Miami.

- Florida Express Airline offered a fare.
- It was a no-frills fare.
- It was a nonstop fare.
- It was a hundred-dollar fare.

Florida Express Airline offered a no-frills, nonstop, hundred-dollar fare.

- Ramon was excited about the good deal.
- He bought a ticket.
- He packed his bags.

Excited about the good deal, he bought a ticket and packed his bags.

- However, Ramon began to have doubts about his bargain flight.
- He did this as he entered the terminal.
- The terminal was dingy.
- The terminal was little-used.

As he entered the dingy, little-used terminal, however, Ramon began to have doubts about his bargain flight.

Sentence Variety II

Follow the directions given for Mastery Test 1.

BARGAIN FLIGHT (Continued)

- An airline clerk charged Ramon fifty dollars to check in his suitcase.
- The clerk was rude.
- This happened at the counter.

Possible answers:
At the counter, a rude airline clerk charged Ramon fifty dollars to check in his suitcase.

- Ramon and the other passengers had to sprint onto the runway.
- They did this to board the plane.
- They did this when the boarding announcement was yelled out.

When the boarding announcement was yelled out, Ramon and the other passengers had to sprint onto the runway to board the plane.

- Ramon was sweaty and annoyed.
- He wedged himself into a narrow seat.
- The seat was worn.
- He did this after pushing his way down the crowded aisle.

Sweaty and annoyed, Ramon wedged himself into a worn, narrow seat after pushing his way down the crowded aisle.

- The flight attendant sold Ramon a snack.
- This happened once the plane took off.
- The snack was ten dollars.
- The snack was stale.

Once the plane took off, the flight attendant sold Ramon a stale ten-dollar snack.

- Ramon calculated that he hadn't saved any money on the flight.
- He swore he'd never take a bargain flight again.
- This had happened by the time the plane landed.

By the time the plane landed, Ramon calculated that he hadn't saved any money on the flight, and he swore he'd never take a bargain flight again.

Paper Format

INTRODUCTORY ACTIVITY

This chapter will discuss the guidelines for preparing a paper. Which of the paper openings below seems clearer and easier to read?

✓A

	Finding Faces	
	It takes just a little imagination to find faces in the objects	
	around you. For instance, clouds are sometimes shaped like faces.	
	If you lie on the ground on a partly	

B

	"finding faces"	
	It takes just a little imagination to find faces in the objects around	
	you. For instance, clouds are sometimes shaped like faces. If you lie	
	on the ground on a partly cloudy day, chances are you will be able	
	to spot many well-known faces	

What are three reasons for your choice?

In "A," the title is capitalized and centered and has no quotation marks around it; there is a blank line between the title and the body of the paragraph; the first line is indented; there are left and right margins around the body of the paper.

Answers are on page 644.

Guidelines for Preparing a Paper

Here are guidelines to follow in preparing a paper for an instructor.

1. Use full-size theme or printer paper, 8½ by 11 inches.

2. Leave wide margins (1 to 1½ inches) all around the paper. In particular, do not crowd the right-hand or bottom margin. This white space makes your paper more readable; also, it gives the instructor room for comments.

3. Center the title of your paper on the first line of the first page. Do not put quotation marks around the title. Do not underline the title. Capitalize all the major words in a title, including the first word. Short connecting words within a title, such as *of, for, the, in*, and *to,* are not capitalized.

4. Skip a line between the title and the first line of your text, and double-space lines. Indent the first line of each paragraph about five spaces (half an inch) from the left-hand margin.

5. Use punctuation marks. Use one space after each period.

6. If you break a word at the end of a line, break only between syllables (see page 389). Do not break words of one syllable.

7. Put your name, date, and course number where your instructor asks for them.

Remember these points about the title and the first sentence of your paper:

8. The title should be several words that tell what the paper is about. It should usually *not* be a complete sentence. For example, if you are writing a paper about your jealous sister, the title could simply be "My Jealous Sister."

9. Do not rely on the title to help explain the first sentence of your paper. The first sentence must be independent of the title. For instance, if the title of your paper is "My Jealous Sister," the first sentence should *not* be "She has been this way as long as I can remember." Rather, the first sentence might be "My sister has always been a jealous person."

Identify the mistakes in format in the following lines from a student paper. Explain the mistakes in the spaces provided. One mistake is described for you as an example.

PRACTICE 1

Teaching Tip

Have your students use these guidelines to revise a previously written paragraph.

ESL Tip

Guideline 5 might be important to learn for some nonnative speakers who are not accustomed to indenting for a new paragraph.

Teaching Tip
You may want
to complete
this activity as
an entire class

> ### "Too small to fight back"
>
> Until I was ten years old, I was at the mercy of my parents. Because they were bigger than I was, they could decide when we were going out, where we were going, and how long it would take to get there. I especially hated the long weekend trips that we would take even during

1. *Do not use quotation marks around the title.*

2. *Capitalize the major words in the title (Too Small to Fight Back).*

3. *Skip a line between the title and the first line of the paper.*

4. *Indent the first line of the paper.*

5. *Keep margins on both sides of the paper*

PRACTICE 2

As already stated, a title should tell in several words what a paper is about. Often a title can be based on the sentence that expresses the main idea of a paper.

Following are five main-idea sentences from student papers. Using each sentence as a base, write a suitable and specific title for each paper.

Answers will
vary.

EXAMPLE

Title: *Aging Americans as Outcasts*
Our society treats aging Americans as outcasts in many ways.

1. Title: *My First-Grade Teacher*
   I will never forget my first-grade teacher.

2. Title: *My Hardest Year*
   The first year of college was the hardest year of my life.

3. Title: *My Father's Sense of Humor*
   My father has a wonderful sense of humor.

4. Title: *Ways to Conserve Energy*
   There are several ways that Americans could conserve energy.

5. Title: *Violence in the Movies*
   In the past few years I have become concerned about the amount of violence in movies.

In four of the five sentences that follow, the writer has mistakenly used the title to help explain the first sentence. But as has already been stated, you must *not* rely on the title to help explain your first sentence.

Rewrite the sentences so that they stand independent of the title. Then write *Correct* under the one sentence that is independent of the title.

EXAMPLE

Title: Finishing a Marathon

First sentence: I managed to do this because I followed a strict training schedule.

Rewritten: *I managed to finish a marathon because I followed a strict training schedule.*

1. Title: Effective Communication

   First sentence: This is often the key to a healthy relationship.

   Rewritten: *Effective communication is often the key to a healthy relationship.*

2. Title: Reality TV Shows

   First sentence: They are popular for several reasons.

   Rewritten: *Reality TV shows are popular for several reasons.*

3. Title: My First Day of College

   First sentence: My first day of college was the most nerve-wracking day of my adult life.

   Rewritten: *Correct*

4. Title: The Best Vacation I Ever Had

   First sentence: It began when my friends from high school booked a one-week trip to Cancun, Mexico.

   Rewritten: *The best vacation I ever had began when my friends from high school booked a one-week trip to Cancun, Mexico.*

5. Title: Professional Athletes on Steroids

First sentence: Most say that they don't use them to enhance athletic performance.

Rewritten: _Most professional athletes say that they don't use steroids to enhance athletic performance._

REVIEW TEST 1

Use the space provided below to rewrite the following sentences from a student paper, correcting the mistakes in format.

> **"my first Blind Date"**
>
> It is an occasion I will not easily forget. I was only fifteen and had not gone out very much at all, but since I was so young, it hardly mattered. Then, one day, my mother came back from her doctor's appointment smiling from ear to ear. She informed me that I was going out on

	My First Blind Date
	My first blind date is an occasion I will not easily forget. I was only thirteen
	and had not gone out very much at all, but since I was so young, it hardly
	mattered. Then one day, my mother came back from her doctor's appointment
	smiling from ear to ear. She informed me that

SCORE
Number Correct

_____/5

_____%

Paper Format

Identify the five formatting mistakes in the student paper that follows. From the box below, choose the letters that describe the five mistakes, and write those letters in the spaces provided in the order in which they appear in the paper.

a. The title should not be underlined.

b. The title should not be set off in quotation marks.

c. There should not be a period at the end of the title.

d. All the major words in a title should be capitalized.

e. The title should just be several words and not a complete sentence.

f. The first sentence of a paper should stand independent of the title.

g. A line should be skipped between the title and the first line of the paper.

h. The first line of a paper should be indented.

i. The right-hand margin should not be crowded.

j. Hyphenation should occur only between syllables.

"Kicking the habit"

After twenty years, I finally quit smoking. I started smoking in high school as a way to fit in with my friends and look "cool." Back then, I could buy a pack of cigarettes for about a dollar from vending machines throughout the city. After I graduated and starting selling cars, I found myself smoking a pack a day, sometimes two packs. There were no anti-smoking laws back then, so I could smoke at work. Sometimes I smoked out of boredom, but other times I smoked to relieve stress. Although my wife begged me to stop, I kept on smoking. Last year, my dad died of lung cancer. He was asmoker for over sixty years. When I saw what smoking had done to him, I quit by going "cold turkey."

---

1. ___*b*___   2. ___*d*___   3. ___*g*___   4. ___*h*___   5. ___*i*___

NAME: _____

DATE: _____

Paper Format

Identify the five formatting mistakes in the student paper that follows. From the box below, choose the letters that describe the five mistakes, and write those letters in the spaces provided in the order in which they appear in the paper.

a. The title should not be underlined.

b. The title should not be set off in quotation marks.

c. There should not be a period at the end of the title.

d. All the major words in a title should be capitalized.

e. The title should just be several words and not a complete sentence.

f. The first sentence of a paper should stand independent of the title.

g. A line should be skipped between the title and the first line of the paper.

h. The first line of a paper should be indented.

i. The right-hand margin should not be crowded.

j. Hyphenation should occur only between syllables.

<u>cheating</u>

Teachers warn students about the dangers of it, but they should encourage their students to cheat at least once. When I was a senior in high school, I cheated on a take-home history test. Although I studied, I was not able to answer all the questions, so I looked online and copied down information from a few websites. I was so worried that I would be caught that I could not look directly at my teacher when I turned in my test. All week, I thought that he would confront me about my cheating. Instead, my teacher gave me an "A" on the test. I felt so guilty that I vowed never to cheat again, and I have never cheated since.

1. ___*a*___   2. ___*d*___   3. ___*f*___   4. ___*j*___   5. ___*i*___

Capital Letters

INTRODUCTORY ACTIVITY

You probably already know a good deal about the uses of capital letters. Answering the questions below will help you check your knowledge before you begin the chapter.

1. Write the full name of a good friend: _____

2. In what city and state were you born? _____

3. What is your present street address? _____

4. Name a country where you would like to travel: _____

5. Name a school that you attended: _____

6. Give the name of a store where you buy food: _____

7. Name a company where you or anyone you know works:

   _____

8. Which day of the week gives you the best chance to relax? _____

9. What holiday is your favorite? _____

10. Which brand of toothpaste do you use? _____

11. Give the brand name of candy you like: _____

12. Name a song or television show you enjoy: _____

13. Write the title of a magazine or blog you read:

    _____

Three capital letters are needed in the example below. Underline the words you think should be capitalized. Then write them, capitalized, in the spaces provided.

14on Super Bowl Sunday, my roommate said, 15"let's buy some snacks and invite a few friends over to watch the game." 16i knew my plans to write a term paper would have to be changed.

14. _____*On*_____   15. _____*Let's*_____   16. _____*I*_____

Answers are on page 644.

Answers will vary for 1–13.

Teaching Tip
You may want to use this activity to assess your students' understanding of capital letters.

Main Uses of Capital Letters

Capital letters are used with

1. First word in a sentence or direct quotation
2. Names of persons and the word *I*
3. Names of particular places
4. Names of days of the week, months, and holidays
5. Names of commercial products
6. Titles of books, magazines, articles, films, television shows, songs, poems, stories, papers, websites, podcasts, apps, blogs, and the like
7. Names of companies, associations, unions, clubs, religious and political groups, and other organizations

Each use is illustrated on the pages that follow.

First Word in a Sentence or Direct Quotation

Our company has begun laying people off.

The doctor said, "This may hurt a bit."

"My husband," said Sheryl, "is a light eater. When it's light, he starts to eat."

In the third example above, *My* and *When* are capitalized because they start new sentences. But *is* is not capitalized, because it is part of the first sentence.

Names of Persons and the Word *I*

At the picnic, I met Carson Wu and Mae Imbruglia.

Names of Particular Places

After graduating from Gibbs High School in Houston, I worked for a summer at a nearby Holiday Inn on Clairmont Boulevard.

But Use small letters if the specific name of a place is not given.

After graduating from high school in my hometown, I worked for a summer at a nearby hotel on one of the main streets.

Names of Days of the Week, Months, and Holidays

Memorial Day falls on the last Monday in May.

But Use small letters for the seasons—summer, fall, winter, spring.

In the early summer and fall, my hay fever bothers me.

Names of Commercial Products

The consumer magazine gave high ratings to Cheerios breakfast cereal, Breyer's ice cream, and Progresso chicken noodle soup.

But Use small letters for the *type* of product (breakfast cereal, ice cream, chicken noodle soup, and the like).

Titles of Books, Magazines, Articles, Films, Television Shows, Songs, Poems, Stories, Papers, Websites, Podcasts, Apps, Blogs, and the Like

My oral report was on *The Diary of a Young Girl* by Anne Frank.

While watching *Community* on television, I read the *New York Times* online and thumbed through *Cosmopolitan* magazine.

Names of Companies, Associations, Unions, Clubs, Religious and Political Groups, and Other Organizations

The National Rifle Association opposes the new bill placed before Congress.

My wife is Jewish; I am Roman Catholic. We are both members of the Green Party.

My parents have life insurance with Prudential, auto insurance with Allstate, and medical insurance with Blue Cross Blue Shield.

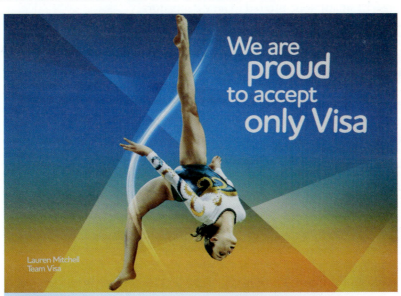

Write a paragraph describing the advertisement shown here so that a person who has never seen it will be able to visualize it and fully understand it. Once you have written your paragraph, check to make sure you have used capital letters properly throughout.

PRACTICE 1

In the sentences that follow, cross out the words that need capitals. Then write the capitalized forms of the words in the space provided. In each case, the number of spaces tells you how many corrections to make.

EXAMPLE

Rhonda asked, "~~why~~ should I bother to *eat* this ~~hershey~~ bar? I should just apply it directly to my hips." ____*Why*____ ____*Hershey*____

Teaching Tip
Consider making a game out of this activity. See how quickly your students can complete the activity correctly. You may want to ask them to create a set of game rules first.

1. My sister, an e-card addict, sends cards on the ~~fourth~~ of ~~july~~ and ~~veterans'~~ ~~day~~.
   ____*Fourth*____ ____*July*____ ____*Veterans'*____ ____*Day*____

2. My brother George said, "~~when~~ I get the urge to exercise, ~~I~~ lie down until it goes away."
   ____*When*____ ____*I*____

3. When Len's ~~toyota~~ ran out of gas on the ~~long island expressway~~, he hitched a ride to the nearest filling station.
   ____*Toyota*____ ____*Long*____ ____*Island*____ ____*Expressway*____

4. According to the latest issue of ~~entertainment weekly~~, ~~walking dead~~ has become one of the most popular shows in its time slot.
   ____*Entertainment*____ ____*Weekly*____ ____*Walking*____ ____*Dead*____

5. Alberta opened an account at the First ~~national bank~~ in order to get the free ~~samsung~~ smartphone offered to new depositors.
   ____*National*____ ____*Bank*____ ____*Samsung*____

6. Teresa works part time at the ~~melrose diner~~ and takes courses at the Taylor ~~business institute~~.
   ____*Melrose*____ ____*Diner*____ ____*Business*____ ____*Institute*____

7. In a story by Ray Bradbury called "~~a sound~~ of ~~thunder~~," tourists of the future can travel back in time to observe living dinosaurs.
   ____*A*____ ____*Sound*____ ____*Thunder*____

8. Stacy, whose ambition is to be an architect, studies at ~~pratt institute~~.
   ____*Pratt*____ ____*Institute*____

9. Last night there was a fire at the ~~sears~~ store on ~~ninth street~~.
   ____*Sears*____ ____*Ninth*____ ____*Street*____

10. For breakfast, I mixed a ~~slim-fast~~ shake and fried some ~~boca~~ sausage.
    ____*Slim—Fast*____ ____*Boca*____

Other Uses of Capital Letters

Capital letters are also used with

Teaching Tip
Ask students to create a sentence for each use of capital letters.

1. Names that show family relationships
2. Titles of persons when used with their names
3. Specific school courses
4. Languages
5. Geographic locations
6. Historical periods and events
7. Races, nations, and nationalities
8. Opening and closing of a letter

Each use is illustrated on the pages that follow.

Names That Show Family Relationships

Aunt Fern and Uncle Jack are selling their house.

I asked Grandfather to start the fire.

Is Mom feeling better?

But Do not capitalize words like *mother, father, grandmother, grandfather, uncle,* and *aunt* when they are preceded by *my* or another possessive word.

My aunt and uncle are selling their house.

I asked my grandfather to start the fire.

Is my mom feeling better?

Titles of Persons When Used with Their Names

I wrote an angry letter to Senator Dipka.

Can you drive to Dr. Stein's office?

We asked Professor Cholenko about her attendance policy.

But Use small letters when titles appear by themselves, without specific names.

I wrote an angry letter to my senator.

Can you drive to the doctor's office?

We asked our professor about her attendance policy.

Specific School Courses

My courses this semester are Accounting I, Introduction to Web Design, Business Law, General Psychology, and Basic Math.

But Use small letters for general subject areas.

This semester I'm taking mostly business courses, but I have a psychology course and a math course as well.

ESL Tip
In many languages, names of languages are not capitalized.

Languages

Yasmin speaks English and Spanish equally well.

Geographic Locations

I lived in the South for many years and then moved to the West Coast.

But Use small letters in giving directions.

Go south for about five miles and then bear west.

Historical Periods and Events

One essay question dealt with the Battle of the Bulge in World War II.

Races, Nations, and Nationalities

The census form asked whether I was Caucasian, African American, Native American, Latino, Asian/Pacific Islander, or Other.

Last summer I hitchhiked through Italy, France, and Germany.

The city is a melting pot for Arab, Vietnamese, and Mexican Americans.

Opening and Closing of a Letter

Dear Sir: Sincerely yours,

Dear Madam: All the best,

 TIP   Capitalize only the first word in a closing.

Cross out the words that need capitals in the following sentences. Then write the capitalized forms of the words in the spaces provided. In each case, the number of spaces tells you how many corrections to make.

PRACTICE 2

Teaching Tip
Consider making a game out of these activities. See how quickly your students can complete the activity correctly. You may want to ask them to create a set of game rules first.

1. My uncle david, who has cirrhosis of the liver, added his name to the national waiting list for organ transplants.

    Uncle   *David*

2. My daughter asked me to buy her a magenta pink motorola razr phone and bluetooth headset for her sixteenth birthday.

    Motorola   *Razr*   *Bluetooth*

3. united states president barack obama received the nobel peace prize in 2009.

  United *States* *President* *Barack*
  Obama *Nobel* *Peace* *Prize*

4. Terisa spoke to the class about her experience as a pacific islander from samoa who is now living on the east coast.

  Pacific *Islander* *Samoa* *East*
  Coast

5. Next semester, I want to register for principles of marketing and two other business courses.

  Principles *Marketing*

Unnecessary Use of Capitals

Many errors in capitalization are caused by adding capitals where they are not needed. Cross out the incorrectly capitalized letters in the following sentences and write the correct forms in the spaces provided. The number of spaces tells you how many corrections to make in each sentence.

PRACTICE 3

1. In our High School, the vice-Principal was in charge of Discipline.

  high *school* *principal* *discipline*

2. My Father settled in to watch his favorite *Dr. Who* rerun, the one in which Shakespeare is controlled by Witch aliens and writes a Play called *Love's Labors Won.*

  father *witch* *play*

3. A group called Project Bigfoot offers a thousand-dollar reward to anyone finding the S̶k̶u̶l̶l̶, H̶a̶i̶r̶, or B̶o̶n̶e̶s̶ of the legendary Bigfoot.

   skull _____   *hair* _____   *bones* _____

4. In Salt Lake City, Utah, there is a M̶o̶n̶u̶m̶e̶n̶t̶ to the sea gulls that saved the first S̶e̶t̶t̶l̶e̶r̶s̶' crops by eating a P̶l̶a̶g̶u̶e̶ of L̶o̶c̶u̶s̶t̶s̶.

   monument _____   *settlers'* _____   *plague* _____   *locusts* _____

5. "My brand-new M̶o̶t̶o̶r̶c̶y̶c̶l̶e̶ was crushed by a T̶r̶a̶c̶t̶o̶r̶-T̶r̶a̶i̶l̶e̶r̶ in the M̶o̶t̶e̶l̶ parking lot," moaned Damon.

   motorcycle _____   *tractor* _____   *trailer* _____   *motel* _____

COLLABORATIVE ACTIVITY

Editing and Rewriting

Working with a partner, read the short paragraph that follows and mark off the ten spots with missing capital letters. Then rewrite the passage, adding the necessary capital letters. Feel free to discuss the rewrite quietly with your partner and refer back to the chapter when necessary.

¹Some seventh-graders in a *Pittsburgh* p̶i̶t̶t̶s̶b̶u̶r̶g̶h̶ school have gone into the candy-making business. ²It all started one *January* j̶a̶n̶u̶a̶r̶y̶ when a parent showed the children how to make chocolates. ³T̶h̶e̶ *The* first week, the children made 775 chocolate-covered pretzels and sold the entire batch. ⁴Then the *Frick Foundation* f̶r̶i̶c̶k̶ ̶f̶o̶u̶n̶d̶a̶t̶i̶o̶n̶, a charitable organization, donated $2,100. ⁵With this money, the students bought candy molds and began taking orders for $800 worth of *Easter* e̶a̶s̶t̶e̶r̶ candy. ⁶They also produced red heart lollipops for Valentine's *Day* d̶a̶y̶. ⁷The children have even gotten good at packaging their products. ⁸They proudly tell their parents, "*We* w̶e̶ are learning how to keep our own financial records!" ⁹They are now planning a line of candies for Christmas, to be delivered by their own Santa *Claus* C̶l̶a̶u̶s̶. ¹⁰It is good to hear that one school in *America* a̶m̶e̶r̶i̶c̶a̶ has experienced the sweet smell of success.

COLLABORATIVE ACTIVITY

Creating Sentences

Working with a partner, write a sentence (or two) as directed. Pay special attention to capital letters.

1. Write about a place you like (or want) to visit. Be sure to include the name of the place, including the city, state, or country where it is located.

2. Write a sentence (or two) in which you state the name of your elementary school, your favorite teacher or subject, and your least favorite teacher or subject.

3. Write a sentence (or two) that mentions three brand-name products you often use. You may begin the sentence with the words "Three brand-name products I use every day are . . ."

4. Think of the name of your favorite musical artist or performer. Then write a sentence in which you include the musician's name and the title of one of his or her songs.

5. Write a sentence in which you describe something you plan to do two days from now. Be sure to include the date and day of the week in your sentence.

REFLECTIVE ACTIVITY

1. What would writing be like without capital letters? Use an example or two to help show how capital letters are important to writing.

2. What three uses of capital letters are most difficult for you to remember? Explain, giving examples.

REVIEW TEST 1

Cross out the words that need capitals in the following sentences. Then write the capitalized forms of the words in the spaces provided. The number of spaces tells you how many corrections to make in each sentence.

EXAMPLE

During halftime of the ~~saturday~~ afternoon football game, my sister said, "~~let's~~ get some hamburgers from ~~wendy's~~ or put a pizza in the oven."

____Saturday____   ____Let's____   ____Wendy's____

1. Mom played a ~~bob dylan~~ album, and the outside world faded away.

____Bob____   ____Dylan____

Teaching Tip
You may want to use these review tests to assess what your students have learned and to determine how much they understand what they have learned.

2. After uncle Bruce returned from his trip to florida, he showed us endless slides of the everglades and the miami Zoo.

Uncle	Florida	Everglades	Miami

3. As grandma turned on *dancing with the stars*, we slipped out of the living room and began a serious game of monopoly in the den.

Grandma	Dancing	Stars	Monopoly

4. This saint patrick's day, the local school band is going to march down fifth avenue.

Saint	Patrick's	Day	Fifth

Avenue

5. Jackie yelled, "you kids have seen that episode of *phineas and ferb* at least fifteen times!"

You	Phineas	Ferb

6. Last spring, in my introduction to anthropology course, we had to start fires without using matches or flints.

Introduction	Anthropology

7. After he watched a *top chef* marathon, Norman dreamed that michael voltaggio was his personal chef.

Top	Chef	Michael	Voltaggio

8. In namibia, a country in africa, a small herd of elephants survives in an area where it hasn't rained for five years.

Namibia	Africa

9. During our visit to the west coast, we ate dinner on the *queen Mary*, the old british luxury liner docked in Long Beach.

West	Coast	Queen	British

10. "Since last september," said Dmitri, "i've been repossessing cars for a collection agency. I've had to collect everything from a small toyota to a rolls-royce."

September	I've	Toyota	Rolls

Royce

REVIEW TEST 2

On a separate sheet of paper or in a file, write the following:

- Seven sentences demonstrating the seven main uses of capital letters

- Eight sentences demonstrating the eight other uses of capital letters

NAME: _____

DATE: _____

SCORE
Number Correct

_____/10

_____%

MASTERY TEST 1

Capital Letters

Cross out the two capitalization errors in each of the following sentences. Then write the corrections in the spaces provided.

sister *French*	1. My ~~Sister~~ Tanya is studying ~~french~~ this semester.
Western North *Carolina*	2. Zach Galifianakis's comedy routine focused on his childhood in ~~western north carolina~~ and his exploits performing stand-up at the back of a hamburger joint in New York City's Times Square.
You're *King*	3. I ordered a Big Mac, and the cashier said, "~~you're~~ at Burger ~~king~~, you know."
Milky *Way*	4. Alice found two ~~milky way~~ wrappers and a peach pit in the shag rug.
My *Way*	5. The Frank Sinatra version of "~~my way~~" was blasting from the diner's jukebox.
Dell *Macbook*	6. I traded in my ~~dell~~ laptop for a ~~macbook~~.
Mrs. *soda*	7. As soon as ~~mrs.~~ Werner pulled into the gas station, the children headed for the ~~Soda~~ machine.
Year's *Day*	8. Rita always breaks her New ~~year's~~ resolutions long before Valentine's ~~day~~.
Did *attic*	9. Terry said, "~~did~~ you read the *National Enquirer* story about the woman who was locked in an ~~Attic~~ for forty-seven years?"
Dr. *malpractice*	10. My little brother really annoyed ~~dr.~~ Thompson by asking "Is your ~~Malpractice~~ insurance paid up?"

NAME: _____

DATE: _____

Capital Letters

Cross out the two capitalization errors in each of the following sentences. Then write the corrections in the spaces provided.

Miracle
Gro

1. I fed my plants with ~~miracle-gro~~ so often that they died from overeating.

Chicago.
Inn

2. It would take eighteen hours to drive to ~~chicago~~, so Jin suggested that we stay one night in a Holiday ~~inn~~.

Fourth
July

3. Every ~~fourth~~ of ~~july~~, my dog howls when he hears the fireworks.

_It's_
Shoprite

4. "~~it's~~ so dull in this town," said Joe, "that sometimes we go down to the ~~shoprite~~ just to watch them restock the toothpaste."

Tigers
Detroit

5. The ~~tigers~~ played well in Florida but started losing when they got back to ~~detroit~~.

Visa
Target

6. To curb impulse buying, Toni cut up her ~~visa~~ and ~~target~~ charge cards.

Scope
Axe

7. During the argument, my brother accused me of needing ~~scope~~ mouthwash and I told him to buy some ~~axe~~ deodorant.

California
Ford

8. On his way to ~~california~~, the hitchhiker rode in a moving van, a 1972 ~~ford~~, and a 2012 Prius.

Entertainment
Weekly

9. Because I hadn't gotten the new ~~entertainment weekly~~, I didn't know when the new season for all my favorite fall shows started.

Red
Have

10. The ~~red~~ Cross poster urged, "~~have~~ a heart and give blood."

NAME: _____

DATE: _____

SCORE
Number Correct

_____/10

_____%

MASTERY TEST 3

Capital Letters

Cross out the two capitalization errors in each of the following sentences.
Then write the corrections in the spaces provided.

With
enemies

1. "~~with~~ friends like you, George," said Pat, "a person doesn't need ~~Enemies~~."

steak
Baltimore

2. Every payday, we treat ourselves to dinner at a ~~Steak~~ house on ~~baltimore~~ Pike.

lottery
Marv's

3. Bill bought three ~~Lottery~~ tickets and a pack of gum at ~~marv's~~ News.

aunt
peppers

4. When my ~~Aunt~~ was pregnant, she craved raw green ~~Peppers~~ sprinkled with salt.

German
mosquito

5. Next to my neighbor's ~~german~~ shepherd, my toy poodle looks like a ~~Mosquito~~.

Wheat
Thins

6. Every time I buy a box of ~~wheat thins~~, the price goes up fifty cents.

Empire
State

7. Kelly almost fell over backward trying to see the top of the ~~empire state~~ Building.

Time
_I_

8. When my issue of *time* arrives, ~~i~~ turn to the "Health" section first.

Mets
triple

9. An infielder for the New York ~~mets~~ team of 1962 once hit a ~~Triple~~ and was called out because he forgot to touch first base.

Prentices
apartment

10. The ~~prentices~~, who live in the next ~~Apartment~~, have a baby that cries all the time.

NAME: _____

DATE: _____

Capital Letters

Cross out the two capitalization errors in each of the following sentences.
Then write the corrections in the spaces provided.

Arizona State
University

1. Maxine begins classes at the ~~arizona state university~~ this fall.

grandmother
August

2. My ~~Grandmother~~ starts buying Christmas presents in ~~august~~.

networks
Thanksgiving

3. The press conference was streamed and carried live on all major ~~Networks~~ the evening before ~~thanksgiving~~.

DJ
Abbey Road

4. The ~~dj~~ promised to play a track from the Beatles album *~~abbey road~~* after the commercial.

Revolutionary
War

5. The history professor announced that there would be a quiz on Friday about the ~~revolutionary war~~.

Adele

6. "I've just gotten a request," said the dj, "to play some ~~adele~~ for the night crew at McNeil Industries."

English
Swiss

7. I suddenly realized that my lunch consisted of an ~~english~~ muffin, ~~swiss~~ cheese, and German potato salad.

summer
Chevy

8. Last ~~Summer~~, we drove to San Francisco in our ~~chevy~~ van.

chemicals
Streets

9. A tractor-trailer loaded with ~~Chemicals~~ had flipped over at the intersection of Oakdale and Cherry ~~streets~~.

cole
Dee-lish

10. I ordered two veggie burgers and a pound of ~~Cole~~ slaw from the ~~dee-lish~~ Delicatessen.

Numbers and Abbreviations

INTRODUCTORY ACTIVITY

This chapter will introduce you to the specific rules for using numbers and abbreviations in your writing. In each pair, write a check mark beside the sentence that you think uses numbers correctly.

✓ _____ I finished the exam by 8:55, but my grade was only 65 percent.

_____ I finished the exam by eight-fifty-five, but my grade was only sixty-five percent.

_____ 9 people are in my biology lab, but there are 45 in my lecture group.

✓ _____ Nine people are in my biology lab, but there are forty-five in my lecture group.

In each pair, write a check mark beside the sentence that you think uses abbreviations correctly.

_____ Both of my bros. were treated by Dr. Lewis after the mt. climbing accident.

✓ _____ Both of my brothers were treated by Dr. Lewis after the mountain climbing accident.

_____ I spent two hrs. finishing my Eng. paper and handed it to my teacher, Ms. Peters, right at the deadline.

✓ _____ I spent two hours finishing my English paper and handed it to my teacher, Ms. Peters, right at the deadline.

Answers are on page 644.

Teaching Tip
You may want to use this activity to assess your students' understanding of numbers and abbreviations.

PERSONALIZED LEARNING

Numbers

Rule 1

Spell out numbers that consist of no more than two words. Otherwise, use numerals—the numbers themselves.

> Last year Tina bought nine new albums on iTunes.
>
> Ray struck out fifteen batters in Sunday's softball game.

But

> Tina now has 114 albums in her collection.
>
> Already this season Ray has recorded 168 strikeouts.

You should also spell out a number that begins a sentence:

> One hundred fifty first-graders throughout the city showed flu symptoms today.

Rule 2

Be consistent when you use a series of numbers. If some numbers in a sentence or paragraph require more than two words, then use numerals throughout the selection.

> This past spring, we planted 5 rhodos, 15 azaleas, 50 summersweet, and 120 myrtle around our house.

Rule 3

Use numbers to show dates, times, addresses, percentages, exact sums of money, and parts of a book.

> John Kennedy was killed on November 22, 1963.
>
> My job interview was set for 10:15. (*But:* Spell out numbers before *o'clock.* For example: The time was then changed to eleven o'clock.)
>
> Lee's new address is 118 North 35th Street.
>
> Almost 40 percent of my meals are eaten at fast-food restaurants.
>
> The cashier rang up a total of $18.35. (*But:* Round amounts may be expressed as words. For example: The movie has a five-dollar admission charge.)
>
> Read Chapter 6 in your math textbook and answer questions 1 to 5 on page 123.

Teaching Tip
Write several sentences on the board in which you intentionally break these rules. Ask students to identify the mistakes.

Use the three rules to make the corrections needed in these sentences.

1. This semester, Mohammed is taking ~~5~~ *five* classes and two labs.

2. My dog Missy, an adorable Maltese, is ~~11~~ *eleven* years old—that's ~~77~~ *seventy-seven* in people years.

3. Every day Ilise gets up at ~~5~~ *five* o'clock to run ~~4~~ *four* miles.

4. During the summer, I like to stay up until ~~two-thirty~~ *2:30* A.M. playing video games and chatting on XBox LIVE with my gamer friends.

5. Americans waste over ~~fifteen~~ *15* percent of the food that they purchase from supermarkets and restaurants.

6. An adult human body has ~~two hundred and six~~ *206* bones.

7. Dr. Martin Luther King, Jr., was born on January ~~fifteenth~~ *15*.

8. Someone ate over ~~200~~ *two hundred* pickled jalapeno peppers at the State Fair of Texas.

9. My cousin went to Las Vegas to get married on July ~~seventh~~ *7*, ~~two-thousand-and-seven~~ *2007*, supposedly the luckiest day of the year.

10. Michel Hazanavicius's film *The Artist* won ~~5~~ *five* Academy Awards in ~~twenty-twelve~~ *2012*.

Abbreviations

While abbreviations are a helpful time-saver in note-taking, you should avoid most abbreviations in formal writing. Listed below are some of the few abbreviations that are acceptable in compositions. Note that a period is used after most abbreviations.

PERSONALIZED LEARNING

1. **Mr., Mrs., Ms., Jr., Sr., and Dr. when used with proper names:**

   Mr. Rollin   Ms. Peters   Dr. Coleman

2. **Time references:**

   A.M., or A.M., or a.m.   P.M., or P.M., or p.m.   B.C. or B.C.; A.D. or A.D.

3. **First or middle initial in a signature:**

   T. Alan Parker   Linda M. Evans

4. **Organizations, technical words, and trade names known primarily by their initials:**

   ABC   CIA   UNESCO   GM   AIDS   DNA

PRACTICE 2

Cross out the words that should not be abbreviated and correct them in the spaces provided.

1. My friend can't go into a ~~dept.~~ store without making an impulse ~~purch.~~

   _____department_____   _____purchase_____

2. Driving along ~~I-80~~ in ~~Penn.~~, we saw deer along the roadside.

   _____Interstate 80_____   _____Pennsylvania_____

3. The heaviest man who ever lived in ~~Amer.~~ weighed over nine hundred ~~lbs.~~ and was buried in a piano crate.

   _____America_____   _____pounds_____

4. This Swiss army knife has everything from a ~~pr.~~ of scissors to a six-~~in.~~ ruler.

   _____pair_____   _____inch_____

5. The first ~~appt.~~ my eye ~~dr.~~, Dr. C. I. Glass, could give me was for early next ~~mo.~~

   _____appointment_____   _____doctor_____   _____month_____

6. After I study in the ~~lib.~~ for fifteen ~~min.~~, I get bored and open ~~Fbook.~~

   _____library_____   _____minutes_____   _____Facebook_____

7. Only a ~~tsp.~~ of watery ~~Fr.~~ dressing was sprinkled over the limp lettuce salad.

   _____teaspoon_____   _____French_____

8. Mandy lost her ~~lic.~~ when she was arrested for ~~driv.~~ on the wrong side of the ~~rd.~~

   _____license_____   _____driving_____   _____road_____

9. How can I be expected to ~~fin.~~ my ~~assign.~~ by 9 P.M. if there isn't one ball-~~pt.~~ pen in the house?

   _____finish_____   _____assignment_____   _____point_____

10. The *CBS Evening News* suggested that, if we don't approve of the new speed ~~lim.~~, we should let our state ~~sen.~~ or ~~rep.~~ know.

    _____limit_____   _____senator_____   _____representative_____

Cross out the mistake or mistakes in numbers and abbreviations, and correct them in the spaces provided.

Teaching Tip
You may want to use this review test to assess what your students have learned and to evaluate how much they understand what they have learned.

1. The Liberty Bell cracked several ~~yrs.~~ after the ~~Amer.~~ Revolution.

   _____ *years* _____   _____ *American* _____

2. The power failure happened at exactly ~~five-twenty~~ A.M. and lasted for almost ~~2~~ hours.

   _____ *5:20* _____   _____ *two* _____

3. I mailed my letter at the ~~p.o.~~ on Grant and Carter ~~Sts.~~

   _____ *post office* _____   _____ *Streets* _____

4. Juan's insect collection includes ~~seventeen~~ grasshoppers, ~~eight~~ moths, and 148 fireflies.

   _____ *17* _____   _____ *8* _____

5. I didn't have time to study for my ~~chem.~~ test because I had to study for my ~~Span.~~ final.

   _____ *chemistry* _____   _____ *spanish* _____

6. I arrive at the Hartford ~~Ins.~~ ~~Build.~~ at ~~8~~ o'clock every morning.

   _____ *Insurance* _____   _____ *Building* _____   _____ *eight* _____

7. How can I write a ~~3~~-page paper on a poem that's only ~~14~~ lines along?

   _____ *three* _____   _____ *fourteen* _____

8. Every ~~Mon.~~ morning I wake up wishing it were ~~Fri.~~

   _____ *Monday* _____   _____ *Friday* _____

9. Tom found a great bargain today—a wool jacket and ~~2~~ pairs of pants for ~~ninety dollars and ninety-nine cents.~~

   _____ *two* _____   _____ *$90.99* _____

10. This is the ~~3rd~~ time since New Year's that I've tried to lose ~~10~~ ~~lbs.~~

   _____ *third* _____   _____ *ten* _____   _____ *pounds* _____

NAME: _____

DATE: _____

Numbers and Abbreviations

Cross out the mistake in numbers or abbreviations in each sentence and correct it in the space provided.

_____two_____   1. *Consumer Reports* rated ~~2~~ of twelve brands of bacon it tested as "unacceptable."

_____conditioner_____   2. When the air ~~cond~~. broke down, the supermarket employees packed shaved ice around the dairy products.

_____1861_____   3. After her husband died in ~~eighteen sixty-one~~, Queen Victoria went into mourning for twenty-five years.

_____page_____   4. One ~~pg~~. of the history textbook showed the stone tools of prehistoric people.

_____apartment_____   5. I managed to fit the entire contents of my ~~apt~~. into the back of my brother's station wagon.

_____one thousand_____   6. The team of six bank robbers got away with less than ~~1,000~~ dollars.

_____109_____   7. The telephone book lists ~~one hundred and nine~~ Richard Browns and 41 Dick Browns.

_____North Carolina_____   8. The six of us left Cleveland in a camper and headed for the Outer Banks of ~~N.C~~.

_____four_____   9. On page 122 of the tax guide is a sample form showing a typical joint return filed by a couple with 4 dependents.

_____room_____   10. By 9:30, every student in my ten o'clock psychology class was already in the examination ~~rm~~.

SCORE
Number Correct

_____/10

_____%

Numbers and Abbreviations

Cross out the mistake in numbers or abbreviations in each sentence and correct it in the space provided. Mark the one sentence that is correct with a C.

six

1. As soon as Karina finished ~~6~~ months of work, she will get one week's paid vacation.

chapters

2. Tonight, I have to read two ~~chaps.~~ in my English textbook.

room

3. The new puppy chewed the wooden legs on our dining ~~rm.~~ chairs.

sixteen

4. Sherry answered ~~16~~ of the twenty test questions correctly.

73

5. There's a smudge on page ~~seventy-three~~ that looks like chocolate syrup and one on page 90 that looks like coffee.

president

6. The ~~pres.~~ waved to the crowd as he left on the flight to California.

1969

7. When the astronauts landed on the moon in ~~nineteen sixty-nine~~, they had traveled over 244,000 miles.

hours

8. If I go without getting an e-mail for several ~~hrs.~~, I begin to feel nervous.

C

9. Half of all the people in the United States live in just eight of the fifty states.

New York

10. The flight from San Juan, Puerto Rico, to ~~N. Y.~~ was delayed for more than three hours.

CHAPTER

25

End Marks

INTRODUCTORY ACTIVITY

A sentence always ends with a period, a question mark, or an exclamation point. Each of these will be discussed in turn on the following pages. First, see if you can add the end mark needed in each of the following sentences.

1. All week I have been feeling under the weather.
2. What is the deadline for handing in the paper?
3. The man at the door wants to know whose car is double-parked.
4. That truck ahead of us is out of control!

Answers are on page 645.

Period (.)

PERSONALIZED LEARNING

Use a period after a sentence that makes a statement.

> More single parents are adopting children.
> It has rained for most of the week.

Use a period after most abbreviations.

Mr. Sanchez	B.A.	Dr. Patel
Ms. Peters	A.M.	Tom Ricci, Jr.

Question Mark (?)

Use a question mark after a *direct* question.

> When is your paper due?
>
> How is your cold?
>
> Lubna asked, "When are you leaving?"
>
> "Why doesn't everyone take a break?" Marisol suggested.

Do not use a question mark after an *indirect* question (a question not in the speaker's exact words).

> She asked when the paper was due.
>
> He asked how my cold was.
>
> Lubna asked when I was leaving.
>
> Marisol suggested that everyone take a break.

Is the exclamation point used correctly in this sign? If not, what should be done to fix the sign?

Exclamation Point (!)

Use an exclamation point after a word or sentence that expresses strong feeling.

> Come here!
>
> Ouch! This pizza is hot!
>
> That truck just missed us!

 TIP   Be careful not to overuse exclamation points.

Add a period, a question mark, or an exclamation point, as needed, to each of the following sentences.

1. Why can't I find my car keys when I'm rushing out the door*?*

2. My husband asked me if I wanted a back rub or a foot massage.

3. The pedestrian yelled to the speeding motorist, "Watch out, jerk*!*"

4. When Chandra told me that she had cheated on every exam so far, I was shocked.

PRACTICE 1

Teaching Tip
You may want to do this activity as an entire class.

5. Dr. Klein is not a medical doctor; he earned his doctorate in psychology.

6. Fred, who loved practical jokes and silly pranks, would often say, "Gotcha!"

7. Famous actors, musicians, and athletes have posed with milk mustaches in the popular "Got milk?" ads.

8. Ratsami asked me if I knew of anyone who could repair the roof that had been damaged in the storm.

9. Jordan answered my question by asking me, "What do *you* think?"

10. Ms. Caraway will replace Mr. Lee as the chief financial officer.

REVIEW TEST

Add a period, a question mark, or an exclamation point as needed to each of the following sentences.

1. Why do these mashed potatoes look green?

2. The group that donates the most blood wins free T-shirts.

3. Watch out so you don't step in that broken glass!

4. The artist throws buckets of paint at a huge canvas on the wall.

5. Did you know that Trina has a twin brother?

6. There's the man who stole my wallet!

7. The dinosaurs in that movie looked like overgrown lizards.

8. Have you read the new book by Gillian Flynn?

9. All that remained after the car accident was a bloodstain.

10. Be careful not to run over that turtle on the highway!

NAME: _____

DATE: _____

End Marks

Add a period, a question mark, or an exclamation point, as needed, to each of the following sentences.

> **HINT** End marks always go *inside* the quotation marks that appear in sentences in this test.

1. Andy wondered whether he would look better if he shaved off his beard.
2. "My hand's as swollen as a baseball glove," moaned Flora.
3. Suddenly, someone yelled, "Get off that wet cement!"
4. During the electrical storm, the nervous mother asked all her children to put on their rubber sneakers.
5. When Rob woke up, his tongue felt as though it were wearing a woolly sock.
6. "How many people here believe in ESP?" the speaker asked.
7. If I pay for the gas, will you do all the driving?
8. Hurry, grab the fire extinguisher!
9. Darlene slammed the phone down and yelled, "Don't call me again!"
10. Audrey asked, "Is the dinosaur the biggest animal that ever lived?"
11. Sylvia wondered if she would ever see Sam again.
12. On a bet, Pasquale drank a glassful of horseradish.
13. I yelled as my spoon touched something squishy in the coffee cup.
14. The TV evangelist exclaimed to his audience, "If you've been born again, raise your hand!"
15. Why does the same pair of jeans cost more in the women's department than in the men's?
16. Does a snake really shed its skin all in one piece?
17. Would someone give me a hand with this window?
18. Three people have asked me for a match already.
19. Will you please save my seat for me?
20. In the movies, it seems that only two minutes after a woman goes into labor, someone shouts, "It's a boy!"

NAME: _____

DATE: _____

End Marks

Add a period, a question mark, or an exclamation point, as needed, to each of the following sentences.

> **HINT** End marks always go *inside* the quotation marks that appear in sentences in this test.

1. The coach screamed, "That runner was safe!"
2. "For someone who claims to be so smart," Dora snapped, "Steve says some pretty unintelligent things."
3. The ad asked, "Are you ready for wall-to-wall sound?"
4. When she goes out, Edith worries about what her children are watching on TV.
5. The teenagers in the back row threw Milk Duds at the people in front.
6. The headline in the yellowing old newspaper read, "Horsecar Strikes Pedestrian."
7. "I can't believe you gave my favorite jacket to the Salvation Army!" Nick yelled.
8. When did our instructor say the paper would be due?
9. Please fill up the tank and check the oil.
10. It's strange that no one has ever told Vince that he needs to use mouthwash.
11. Ken put the money in a safe place and then couldn't find it.
12. Blair asked her mother, "If I don't keep my dentist appointment, will my teeth fall out?"
13. I was told I could pick up this suit on Wednesday afternoon.
14. Can we stop for lunch soon?
15. The zookeeper yelled, "Close the cage!"
16. He wondered whether the mail had arrived yet.
17. I wish my boss would stop looking over my shoulder and asking when the project will be done.
18. Emmet remarked, "Can this be the same hotel we stayed at five years ago?"
19. Jan, expecting the glass door to open automatically, got a painful surprise.
20. He is afraid of only two things: snakes and the IRS.

Apostrophe

INTRODUCTORY ACTIVITY

Carefully look over the three sets of statements below. Then see if you can answer the questions that follow each set.

1. She is my best friend.   =   She's my best friend.

   I am afraid of snakes.   =   I'm afraid of snakes.

   Do not watch too much TV.   =   Don't watch too much TV.

   They are a perfect match.   =   They're a perfect match.

   It is a terrible movie.   =   It's a terrible movie.

What is the purpose of the apostrophe in the examples above?

To indicate missing letters and shortened spellings

_____

2. the desk of the editor   =   the editor's desk

   the car of Giovanni   =   Giovanni's car

   the teeth of my cat   =   my cat's teeth

   the smile of the child   =   the child's smile

   the briefcase of my mother   =   my mother's briefcase

What is the purpose of the apostrophe in the examples above?

To show ownership or possession

_____

3. Several families were affected by the flood. One family's car floated
   away and was found in a field more than a mile away.

Why does the apostrophe belong in the second sentence but not the first?

Because families signals a plural noun, while family's indicates

ownership or possession.

Answers are on page 677.

Teaching Tip
You may
want to use
this activity to
assess your
students' un-
derstanding of
apostrophes.

The two main uses of the apostrophe are

1. To show the omission of one or more letters in a contraction
2. To show ownership or possession

Each use is explained on the pages that follow.

PERSONALIZED LEARNING

Apostrophe in Contractions

A contraction is formed when two words are combined to make one word. An apostrophe is used to show where letters are omitted in forming the contraction. Here are two contractions:

have + not = haven't (the *o* in *not* has been omitted)

I + will = I'll (the *wi* in *will* has been omitted)

ESL Tip
Remind nonnative speakers that contractions are used more often in spoken English.

The following are some other common contractions:

I + am	= I'm		it + is	= it's
I + have	= I've		it + has	= it's
I + had	= I'd		is + not	= isn't
who + is	= who's		could + not	= couldn't
do + not	= don't		I + would	= I'd
did + not	= didn't		they + are	= they're
let + us	= let's		there + is	= there's

TIP   The combination *will* + *not* has an unusual contraction: *won't*.

PRACTICE 1

Teaching Tip
Consider making a game out of this activity. You may want to ask students to create a set of game rules first.

Combine the following words into contractions. One is done for you.

they + will	= *they'll*		they + are	= *they're*
should + not	= *shouldn't*		can + not	= *can't*
does + not	= *doesn't*		who + is	= *who's*
is + not	= *isn't*		would + not	= *wouldn't*
will + not	= *won't*		are + not	= *aren't*

Write the contraction for the words in parentheses.

PRACTICE 2

EXAMPLE

He (could not) _couldn't_ come.

1. When you hear the whistle blow, (you will) _you'll_ know (it is) _it's_ quitting time.
2. Because he (had not) _hadn't_ studied the owner's manual, he (could not) _couldn't_ figure out how to start the power mower.
3. There (is not) _isn't_ a rug in this house that (does not) _doesn't_ have stains on it.
4. (I am) _I'm_ fine in the morning if (I am) _I'm_ left alone.
5. (Where is) _Where's_ the idiot (who is) _who's_ responsible for leaving the front door wide open?

Teaching Tip
See how quickly your students can complete the activity correctly. You may want to ask them to create a set of game rules first.

 TIP   Even though contractions are common in everyday speech and in written dialogue, usually it is best to avoid them in formal writing.

Write five sentences using the apostrophe in different contractions.

PRACTICE 3

1. _____
2. _____
3. _____
4. _____
5. _____

Four Contractions to Note Carefully

Four contractions that deserve special attention are *they're, it's, you're,* and *who's.* Sometimes these contractions are confused with the possessive words *their, its, your,* and *whose.* The following chart shows the difference in meaning between the contractions and the possessive words.

CONTRACTIONS	POSSESSIVE WORDS
they're (means *they are*)	their (means *belonging to them*)
it's (means *it is* or *it has*)	its (means *belonging to it*)
you're (means *you are*)	your (means *belonging to you*)
who's (means *who is*)	whose (means *belonging to whom*)

Possessive words are explained further on pages 334 and 337.

Underline the correct form (the contraction or the possessive word) in each of the following sentences. Use the contraction whenever the two words of the contraction (*they are, it is, you are, who is*) would also fit.

1. (It's, Its) the rare guest who knows when (it's, its) time to go home.

2. If (they're, their) going to bring (they're, their) vacation pictures, I'm leaving.

3. (You're, Your) a difficult kind of person because you always want (you're, your) own way.

4. I don't know (who's, whose) fault it was that the window got broken, but I know (who's, whose) going to pay for it.

5. Unless (it's, its) too much trouble, could you make it (you're, your) business to find out (who's, whose) been throwing garbage into my yard?

Apostrophe to Show Ownership or Possession

To show ownership or possession, we can use such words as *belongs to, owned by,* or (most commonly) *of.*

the knapsack *that belongs to* Lila

the grades *possessed by* Travis

the house *owned by* my mother

the sore arm *of* the pitcher

But the apostrophe plus *s* is often the quickest and easiest way to show possession. Thus, we can say

Lila's knapsack

Travis's grades

my mother's house

the pitcher's sore arm

Points to Remember

1. The *'s* goes with the owner or possessor (in the examples given, *Lila, Travis, mother,* and *pitcher*). What follows is the person or thing possessed (in the examples given, *knapsack, grades, house,* and *sore*

arm). An easy way to determine the owner or possessor is to ask the question "Who owns it?" In the first example, the answer to the question "Who owns the knapsack?" is *Lila*. Therefore, the *'s* goes with *Lila*.

2. A singular word ending in -*s* (such as *Travis*) also shows possession by adding an apostrophe plus *s* (Travis's).

Teaching Tip
Writers often misunderstand this rule (point 2). Provide a few more examples, such as "Ross's."

Rewrite the italicized part of each of the sentences below, using the *'s* to show possession. Remember that the *'s* goes with the owner or possessor.

PRACTICE 5

Teaching Tip
You may want to encourage students to work with a partner.

EXAMPLES

The motorcycle *owned by Clyde* is a frightening machine.

Clyde's motorcycle

The roommate of my brother is a sweet and friendly person.

My brother's roommate

1. The *rifle of the assassin* failed to fire.

   The assassin's rifle

2. The playboy spent *the inheritance of his mother* within six months.

   his mother's inheritance

3. *The throat of Ali* tightened when the doorbell rang.

   Ali's throat

4. The new salesman took *the parking space of Sam.*

   Sam's parking space

5. *The hat of the chef* fell into the pea soup.

   The chef's hat

6. A big man wearing sunglasses stayed near *the wife of the president.*

   the president's wife

7. *The hand of the mugger* closed over the victim's mouth.

   The mugger's hand

8. The *briefcase of Harry* was still there, but the documents were gone.

   Harry's briefcase

9. *The handbag of Sandy* had vanished from her locker.

Sandy's handbag

10. *The leash of the dog* was tangled around a fire hydrant.

The dog's leash

PRACTICE 6

Underline the word in each sentence that needs an *'s.* Then write the word correctly in the space at the left. One is done for you as an example.

ex-husband's   1. Julie is always upset after one of her ex-husband visits.

instructor's   2. My instructor worst habit is leaving her sentences unfinished.

astrologer's   3. The astrologer predictions were all wrong.

Ellen's   4. Ellen jeans were so tight that she had to lie flat in order to zip them.

lemonade's   5. The lemonade bitter flavor assaulted my taste buds.

sister's   6. My sister life is like a soap opera.

Brian's   7. Brian gold wedding band slid into the garbage disposal.

Nita's   8. Nita ten-year-old Volvo is still dependable.

Ted's   9. We didn't believe any of Uncle Ted stories.

hypnotist's   10. The hypnotist piercing eyes frightened Kelly.

PRACTICE 7

Add an *'s* to each of the following words to make it the possessor or owner of something. Then write sentences using the words. Your sentences can be serious or playful. One is done for you as an example.

1. Aaron   Aaron's

Aaron's girlfriend sends him more than forty text messages a day.

2. bus   bus's

_____

3. computer   computer's

_____

4. Ross   Ross's

_____

5. pizza   pizza's

_____

Apostrophe versus Possessive Pronouns

Do not use an apostrophe with possessive pronouns. They already show ownership. Possessive pronouns include *his, hers, its, yours, ours,* and *theirs.*

INCORRECT	CORRECT
The bookstore lost its' lease.	The bookstore lost its lease.
The racing bikes were theirs'.	The racing bikes were theirs.
The change is yours'.	The change is yours.
His' problems are ours', too.	His problems are ours, too.
His' skin is more tanned than hers'.	His skin is more tanned than hers.

Apostrophe versus Simple Plurals

When you want to make a word plural, just add an *s* at the end of the word. Do *not* add an apostrophe. For example, the plural of the word *movie* is *movies,* not *movie's* or *movies'.* Look at this sentence:

When Korie's cat began catching birds, the neighbors called the police.

The words *birds* and *neighbors* are simple plurals, meaning more than one bird, more than one neighbor. The plural is shown by adding -*s* only. (More information about plurals starts on page 337.) On the other hand, the *'s* after *Korie* shows ownership—that Korie owns the cat.

Teaching Tip
Writers often misunderstand this rule. Write a few simple plural words on the board and draw an "X" over these words to reinforce this concept.

ITY TEA'S & COFFEE'S

US NEW RESTAURANT

Are the apostrophes used correctly in this sign? If not, what should be done to fix the sign?

PRACTICE 8

In the spaces provided under each sentence, add the one apostrophe needed and explain why the other words ending in *s* are simple plurals.

Teaching Tip
You may want to complete this activity as an entire class. Call on students to provide answers.

EXAMPLE

Originally, the cuffs of mens pants were meant for cigar ashes.

cuffs: *simple plural, meaning more than one cuff*

mens: *men's, meaning "belonging to men"*

ashes: *simple plural, meaning more than one ash*

1. Phil thinks that the restaurants hamburgers taste better than sirloin steaks.

   restaurants: *restaurant's, meaning "the hamburgers of the restaurant"*

   hamburgers: *simple plural, meaning more than one hamburger*

   steaks: *simple plural, meaning more than one steak*

2. San Franciscos cable cars can go up hills at a sixty-degree angle.

   San Franciscos: *San Francisco's, meaning "the cable cars of San Francisco"*

   cars: *simple plural, meaning more than one car*

   hills: *simple plural, meaning more than one hill*

3. My twelve-year-old brothers collection of baseball cards is in six shoe boxes.

   brothers: *brother's, meaning "the collection of my brother"*

   cards: *simple plural, meaning more than one card*

   boxes: *simple plural, meaning more than one box*

4. Only women shaped like toothpicks look decent in this years fashions.

   toothpicks: *simple plural, meaning more than one toothpick*

   years: *year's, meaning "the fashions of this year"*

   fashions: *simple plural, meaning more than one fashion*

5. Pedros blood pressure rose when he drove around the mall for twenty minutes and saw that there were no parking spaces.

   Pedros: *Pedro's, meaning "the blood pressure of Pedro"*

   minutes: *simple plural, meaning more than one minute*

   spaces: *simple plural, meaning more than one space*

6. The write-ups of Rubys promotion made her co-workers jealous.

   write-ups: *simple plural, meaning more than one write-up*

   Rubys: *Ruby's, meaning "the promotion of Ruby"*

   co-workers: *simple plural, meaning more than one co-worker*

7. My sons backyard fort is made from pieces of scrap lumber, old nails, and spare roof shingles.

   sons: *son's, meaning "the fort of my son"*

   pieces: *simple plural, meaning more than one piece*

   nails: *simple plural, meaning more than one nail*

   shingles: *simple plural, meaning more than one shingle*

8. The mayors double-talk had reporters scratching their heads and scribbling in their notebooks.

   mayors: *mayor's, meaning "the double-talk of the mayor"*

   reporters: *simple plural, meaning more than one reporter*

   heads: *simple plural, meaning more than one head*

   notebooks: *simple plural, meaning more than one notebook*

9. Two cuts over the boxers left eye prompted the referee to stop the fight after six rounds.

   cuts: *simple plural, meaning more than one cut*

   boxers: *boxer's, meaning "the left eye of the boxer"*

   rounds: *simple plural, meaning more than one round*

10. As rock music blared over the cafeterias loudspeakers, Theresa tried to study for her exams.

    cafeterias: *cafeteria's, meaning "the loudspeakers of the cafeteria"*

    loudspeakers: *simple plural, meaning more than one loudspeaker*

    exams: *simple plural, meaning more than one exam*

Apostrophe with Plural Words Ending in *-s*

Plurals that end in *-s* show possession simply by adding the apostrophe, rather than an apostrophe plus *s*.

Both of my *neighbors'* homes have been burglarized recently.

The many *workers'* complaints were ignored by the company.

All the *campers'* tents were damaged by the hailstorm.

PRACTICE 9

Teaching Tip
Stress the difference between possession for singular words ending in s and plural words ending in s. You may want to write a few more examples on the board.

In each sentence, cross out the one plural word that needs an apostrophe. Then write the word correctly, with the apostrophe, in the space provided.

EXAMPLE

bosses'   My two ~~bosses~~ tempers are much the same: explosive.

stores'   1. Bobby wanted to look in all the ~~stores~~ windows.

friends'   2. Why are all my ~~friends~~ problems easier to solve than my own?

Cowboys'   3. Dad hopes that the Dallas ~~Cowboys~~ new quarterback will get them into the Super Bowl.

students'   4. The ~~students~~ insect collections were displayed in a glass case.

voters'   5. The poll showed that the ~~voters~~ wish was to replace all the politicians in office.

COLLABORATIVE ACTIVITY

Editing and Rewriting

Working with a partner, read the short paragraph below. Then rewrite the paragraph, adding ten apostrophes where needed to indicate contractions and possessives. Feel free to discuss the rewrite quietly with your partner and refer back to the chapter when necessary.

Teaching Tip
Ask students to work on the Collaborative Activities in pairs and share their answers for the Reflective Activity with the entire class.

¹If ~~youre~~ *you're* going to visit someone in the hospital, ~~dont~~ *don't* be gloomy. ²Other ~~peoples~~ *people's* problems ~~wont~~ *won't* help someone ~~whos~~ *who's* sick to feel better. ³But you ~~dont~~ *don't* have to limit yourself to "safe" topics like ~~todays~~ *today's* weather. ⁴You can even discuss the ~~patients~~ *patient's* condition, as long as neither of you gets upset. ⁵Also, ~~dont~~ *don't* stay too long. ⁶Patients are usually weak and ~~cant~~ *can't* talk for long periods. ⁷Leave before the patient gets tired.

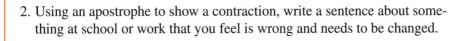

COLLABORATIVE ACTIVITY

Creating Sentences

Working with a partner, write sentences that use apostrophes as directed.

1. Write a sentence describing something a friend owns. For instance, you might mention a pet or a material possession.

   _____

2. Using an apostrophe to show a contraction, write a sentence about something at school or work that you feel is wrong and needs to be changed.

   _____

3. Write a sentence that correctly uses the word *teachers*. Then write a second sentence that correctly uses the word *teacher's*.

   _____

   _____

REFLECTIVE ACTIVITY

1. Look at the paragraph about the hospital visit that you revised. How has adding apostrophes affected the reading of the paragraph?

2. Explain what it is about apostrophes that you find most difficult to remember and apply. Use an example to make your point clear.

REVIEW TEST 1

In each sentence, cross out the two words that need apostrophes. Then write the words correctly in the spaces provided.

1. That ~~restaurants~~ menu ~~hasnt~~ changed its selections since ten years ago.

   ___*restaurant's*___   ___*hasn't*___

2. Steve ~~doesnt~~ begin writing his papers until the day before ~~theyre~~ due.

   ___*doesn't*___   ___*they're*___

3. My ~~fathers~~ habit is never to root for a team until he thinks ~~its~~ going to lose.

   ___*father's*___   ___*it's*___

Teaching Tip
You may want to use these review tests to assess what your students have learned and to determine how well they understand what they have learned.

4. The toddler knocked his ~~mothers~~ sewing box onto the floor; then he dropped her calculator into the ~~dogs~~ water bowl.

    _____*mother's*_____   _____*dog's*_____

5. Part of ~~Colins~~ nursing training consists of a stint in the local ~~hospitals~~ trauma center.

    _____*Colin's*_____   _____*hospital's*_____

6. "~~Youre~~ daring someone to steal that camera if you carry it to the concert," warned ~~Tinas~~ dad.

    _____*You're*_____   _____*Tina's*_____

7. Ever since my sister passed her ~~drivers~~ test, she keeps asking for the keys to our ~~parents~~ car.

    _____*driver's*_____   _____*parents'*_____

8. The store ~~wouldnt~~ exchange ~~Carols~~ birthday gift, since earrings cannot be returned.

    _____*wouldn't*_____   _____*Carol's*_____

9. I use ~~Sids~~ dry-cleaning service because he will clean ~~anyones~~ American flag free.

    _____*Sid's*_____   _____*anyone's*_____

10. When ~~Dannys~~ cut was being stitched up, he asked the doctor why she ~~didnt~~ use a sewing machine.

    _____*Danny's*_____   _____*didn't*_____

REVIEW TEST 2

Rewrite the following sentences, changing the underlined words into either a contraction or a possessive.

1. I wanted to buy <u>the house of my uncle</u> but <u>could not</u> get a mortgage.

    my uncle's house

    couldn't

2. <u>The issue of this week</u> of *Time* features a report on <u>the campaign of the president</u> to raise educational standards.

    This week's issue

    the president's campaign

3. The programs of next week always look better than what is on now.

    Next week's programs _____

    what's _____

4. The tires of the car are as smooth as the eggs of a hen.

    The car's tires _____

    hen's eggs _____

5. The voice of the instructor boomed in the ears of Marie as she sat in the front row.

    The instructor's voice _____

    Marie's ears _____

NAME: _____

DATE: _____

Apostrophe

In each sentence, cross out the word that needs an apostrophe. Then write the word correctly in the space provided.

nobody's   1. She is ~~nobodys~~ fool when money is involved.

duck's   2. The cartoon ~~ducks~~ beak had been taped shut.

Ronnie's   3. That was ~~Ronnies~~ third car accident this year.

hawk's   4. A ~~hawks~~ wings beat faster when it is about to dive at its prey.

safecracker's   5. The ~~safecrackers~~ eyes gleamed as the lock clicked open.

dentist's   6. My ~~dentists~~ worst habit is asking me questions when my mouth is stuffed with cotton.

It's   7. ~~Its~~ been estimated that the typical American consumes one hundred pounds of white sugar a year.

company's   8. When the insurance ~~companys~~ check arrived, I ran to the bank.

doctor's (or doctors')   9. The ~~doctors~~ waiting room was stuffy and crowded.

resort's   10. The ~~resorts~~ policy is to give a partial refund if the weather is poor.

Apostrophe

In the space provided under each sentence, add the one apostrophe needed and explain why the other word ending in s *is a simple plural.*

EXAMPLE

Joans hair began to fall out two days after she dyed it.

Joans: *Joan's, meaning "the hair belonging to Joan"*

Days: *simple plural, meaning more than one day*

1. The elderly womans long, knotty fingers show a lifetime of wear.

    womans: *woman's, meaning "the fingers of the woman"*

    fingers: *simple plural, meaning more than one finger*

2. Studies show that a rooms color can affect our moods.

    rooms: *room's, meaning "the color of the room"*

    moods: *simple plural, meaning more than one mood*

3. Kens homework is not yet done because of the two football games on TV today.

    Kens: *Ken's, meaning "the homework of Ken"*

    games: *simple plural, meaning more than one game*

4. The raccoons tracks led from a hole in the backyard fence to our garbage can.

    raccoons: *raccoon's, meaning "the tracks of a raccoon"*

    tracks: *simple plural, meaning more than one track*

5. In my mothers picture collection, my grandparents posed against a backdrop of painted scenery.

    mothers: *mother's, meaning "the picture collection belonging to my mother"*

    grandparents: *simple plural, meaning more than one grandparent*

NAME: _____

DATE: _____

Apostrophe

In each sentence, two apostrophes are missing or are used incorrectly. Cross out the two errors and write the corrections in the spaces provided.

can't

evening's

1. I ~~cant~~ understand why our neighbors disturb the ~~evenings~~ quiet with their electronic bug zapper.

sister's

hours

2. My ~~sisters~~ habit of tying up the phone for ~~hours'~~ drives my parents crazy.

who's

children's

3. I wonder ~~whos~~ responsible for making ~~childrens~~ clothes so expensive.

saloon's

doors

4. The gunslinger barged through the ~~saloons~~ swinging ~~door's~~.

Olympics

athlete's

5. Qualifying for the ~~Olympic's~~ is an amateur ~~athletes~~ crowning achievement.

store's

antics

6. The ~~stores~~ photographer used a variety of ~~antics'~~ to get the children to smile.

supermarket's

machines

7. While her mother paid the clerk, Michelle wandered over to the ~~supermarkets~~ gum-ball ~~machine's~~.

couldn't

burglar's

8. The suspect ~~couldn't~~ have committed the crime, for his shoe size did not match the ~~burglars~~ footprints.

o'clock

factory's

9. At twelve ~~oclock~~, the ~~factorys~~ whistle blows, and the shift changes.

Dewdrops

bicycle's

10. ~~Dewdrops'~~ glistened on the ~~bicycles~~ vinyl seat.

NAME: _____

DATE: _____

Apostrophe

In each sentence, two apostrophes are missing or are used incorrectly. Cross out the two errors and write the corrections in the spaces provided.

Sandy's	1. ~~Sandys~~ brown eyes filled with tears as she listened to ~~Jims~~ explanation.
Jim's	
son's	2. My ~~sons~~ toys were strewn all over the ~~Greenfields~~ driveway.
Greenfields'	
Fatima's	3. ~~Fatimas~~ Saint Bernard has a custom-built shelter as big as a ~~childs~~ playhouse.
child's	
morning's	4. Monday ~~mornings~~ *Press* omitted several popular comic ~~strip's~~.
strips	
Ben's	5. ~~Bens~~ behavior at the ~~Hernandezs~~ party surprised everyone.
Hernandez's	
jury's	6. When the ~~jurys~~ verdict was announced, both ~~defendants'~~ looked stunned.
defendants	
Omar's	7. When ~~Omars~~ phone bill comes in, ~~hes~~ likely to rip it into little pieces.
he's	
Helen's	8. ~~Helens~~ mistake was to trust the strength of the fraying hammock in her ~~fathers~~ yard.
father's	
firefighters	9. Two ~~firefighter's~~ rushed into the burning building to rescue the ~~familys~~ pet dog.
family's	
can't	10. When she ~~cant~~ handle her two toddlers, Jen takes them to her ~~mothers~~ house.
mother's	

Quotation Marks

INTRODUCTORY ACTIVITY

Teaching Tip
You may want to use this activity to assess your students' understanding of quotation marks.

Read the following scene and underline all the words enclosed within quotation marks. Your instructor may also have you dramatize the scene, with one person reading the narration and three others acting the speaking parts—Len, Tina, and Mario. The speakers should imagine the scene as part of a stage play and try to make their words seem as true-to-life as possible.

At a party that Len and his wife, Tina, hosted recently, an old friend named Mario had too much to drink and kept bothering Tina. "Listen, man," Len said, "what's this thing you have for my wife? There are lots of other women at this party."

"Relax," Mario replied. "Tina was my first girlfriend; I haven't seen her in years, and I like talking with her."

"Listen, Mario," Tina said. "Why don't you call your wife and tell her to join us? I need to talk to my husband now, and I need you to stop putting your arm around me."

"Look, there's no law that says I can't talk to you if I want to," Mario challenged.

"Mario, I'm only going to say this once," Len warned. "Lay off my wife, or leave."

Mario grinned at Len. "Why should I leave? I'm not done talking with Tina."

Len took out his phone. "I'm giving you a choice," Len said. "Leave now or I'll call your wife and she can assess the situation."

Mario left right away.

1. On the basis of this selection, what is the purpose of quotation marks?
   Quotation marks set off the exact words of a speaker.

2. Do commas and periods that come after a quotation go inside or outside the quotation marks?
   They go inside the quotation marks.

Answers are on page 669.

The two main uses of quotation marks are

1. To set off the exact words of a speaker or writer

2. To set off the titles of short works

Each use is explained on the pages that follow.

Quotation Marks to Set Off the Words of a Speaker or Writer

Use quotation marks when you want to show the exact words of a speaker or writer:

"Who left the cap off the toothpaste?" Amalia demanded. (Quotation marks set off the exact words that Amalia spoke.)

Ben Franklin wrote, "Keep your eyes wide open before marriage, half shut afterward." (Quotation marks set off the exact words that Ben Franklin wrote.)

"You're never too old," my Aunt Claire often tells me, "to learn something new." (Two pairs of quotation marks are used to enclose the aunt's exact words.)

Fernanda complained, "I look so old some days. Even makeup doesn't help. I feel as though I'm painting a corpse!" (Note that the end quotes do not come until the end of Fernanda's speech. Place quotation marks before the first quoted word of a speech and after the last quoted word. As long as no interruption occurs in the speech, do not use quotation marks for each new sentence.)

Complete the following statements that explain how capital letters, commas, and periods are used in quotations. Refer to the four examples as guides.

> **HINT**   In the four preceding examples, notice that a comma sets off the quoted part from the rest of the sentence. Also observe that commas and periods at the end of a quotation always go *inside* quotation marks.

- Every quotation begins with a ___*capital*___ letter.
- When a quotation is split (as in the sentence about Aunt Claire), the second part does not begin with a capital letter unless it is a ___*new*___ sentence.

- _Commas_ are used to separate the quoted part of a sentence from the rest of the sentence.
- Commas and periods that come at the end of a quotation go _inside_ quotation marks.

The answers are *capital, new, Commas,* and *inside.*

PRACTICE 1

Insert quotation marks where needed in the sentences that follow.

1. "This is the tenth commercial in a row," complained Niko.
2. The police officer said sleepily, "I could really use a cup of coffee."
3. My boss asked me to step into his office and said, "Joanne, how would you like a raise?"
4. "I'm out of work again," Miriam sighed.
5. "I didn't know this movie was R-rated!" Lorrine gasped.
6. "Why does my dog always wait until it rains before he wants to go out?" Donovon asked.
7. A sign over the box office read, "Please form a single line and be patient."
8. "Unless I run three miles a day," Marty said, "my legs feel like lumpy oatmeal."
9. "I had an uncle who knew when he was going to die," claimed Dan. "He saw the date in a dream."
10. The unusual ad on Craigslist read, "Young farmer would be pleased to hear from young lady with tractor. Send photograph of tractor."

Teaching Tip
In a computer lab, ask students to type out their answers for this activity. Introduce your students to the correction symbols for inserting quotation marks.

PRACTICE 2

Rewrite the following sentences, adding quotation marks where needed. Use a capital letter to begin a quotation, and use a comma to set off a quoted part from the rest of the sentence.

EXAMPLE

I can't eat another bite Jeremy told his grandmother.

"I can't eat another bite," Jeremy told his grandmother.

1. The firefighter asked the neighbors Is there anyone still in the building?

   The firefighter asked the neighbors, "Is there anyone else still in the building?"

2. You'll have to remove your sunglasses the security guard reminded the customers at the bank.

   "You'll have to remove your sunglasses," the security guard reminded the customers

   at the bank.

3. Upon eating a few drops of Horacio's homemade habanero sauce, Trudy yelped That's hot!

Upon eating a few drops of Horacio's homemade habanero sauce, Trudy yelped,

"That's hot!"

4. Good things come to those who wait Zhao told himself as he waited in line for hours to buy the new iPhone.

"Good things come to those who wait," Zhao told himself as he waited in line for hours

to buy an iPhone.

5. If at first you don't succeed my wife joked you should read the directions.

"If at first you don't succeed," my wife joked, "you should read the directions."

1. Write three quotations that appear in the first part of a sentence.

EXAMPLE

"Let's go shopping," I suggested.

a. _____

b. _____

c. _____

2. Write three quotations that appear at the end of a sentence.

EXAMPLE

Bob asked, "Have you had lunch yet?"

a. _____

b. _____

c. _____

3. Write three quotations that appear at the beginning and end of a sentence.

EXAMPLE

"If the bus doesn't come soon," Mary said, "we'll freeze."

a. _____

b. _____

c. _____

PRACTICE 3

Responses will vary.

Teaching Tip
After students complete this activity have them go over their answers with a partner.

Indirect Quotations

Teaching Tip
You may want
to provide
more exam-
ples of direct
and indirect
quotations.
Ask students
to help you
construct these
sentences.

An indirect quotation is a rewording of someone else's comments rather than a word-for-word direct quotation. The word *that* often signals an indirect quotation.

DIRECT QUOTATION	INDIRECT QUOTATION
George said, "My son is a daredevil."	George said that his son is a daredevil.
(George's exact spoken words are given, so quotation marks are used.)	(We learn George's words *in*directly, so no quotation marks are used.)
Carol's note to Arnie read, "I'm at the neighbors' house. Give me a call."	Carol left a note for Arnie that said she would be at the neighbors' house and he should give her a call.
(The exact words that Carol wrote in the note are given, so quotation marks are used.)	(We learn Carol's words *in*directly, so no quotation marks are used.)

PRACTICE 4

Rewrite the following sentences, changing words as necessary to convert the sentences into direct quotations. The first one is done for you as an example.

1. Luis asked Marian if she had had a bad day at work.

   Luis asked Marian, "Did you have a bad day at work?"

2. Marian said that it was the worst day of her life.

   Marian said, "It was the worst day of my life."

3. Luis said to tell him all about it.

   Luis said, "Tell me all about it."

4. Marian insisted that he wouldn't understand her job problems.

   Marian insisted, "You wouldn't understand my job problems."

5. Luis said he would certainly try.

   Luis said, "I will certainly try."

Rewrite the following sentences, converting each direct quotation into an indirect statement. In each case, you will have to add the word *that* or *if* and change other words as well.

EXAMPLE

The barber asked Reggie, "Have you noticed how your hair is thinning?"

The barber asked Reggie if he had noticed how his hair was thinning.

1. He said, "I need a vacation."

   He said that he needed a vacation.

2. Gretchen said, "Purple is my favorite color."

   Gretchen said that purple was her favorite color.

3. She asked the handsome stranger, "Could I buy you a drink?"

   She asked the handsome stranger if she could buy him a drink.

4. My brother asked, "Has anyone seen my frog?"

   My brother asked if anyone had seen his frog.

5. Françoise complained, "I married a man who falls asleep during horror movies."

   Françoise complained that she married a man who falls asleep during horror movies.

Quotation Marks to Set Off the Titles of Short Works

Titles of short works are usually set off by quotation marks, while titles of long works are italicized. Use quotation marks to set off the titles of short works such as articles in books, newspapers, or magazines; chapters in a book; short stories; poems; and songs. On the other hand, you should italicize the titles of books, newspapers, magazines, plays, movies, albums, and television shows. See the following examples.

QUOTATION MARKS

the article "The Toxic Tragedy"

the article "What to Watch For in the Second Presidential Debate"

ITALICS

in the book *Who's Poisoning America*

in the newspaper the *Washington Post*

continued

Teaching Tip
Bring newspapers, magazines, poetry books, and music CDs to class. Ask students to write out several long and short titles, using quotation marks and underlines as needed.

QUOTATION MARKS	ITALICS
the article "Pete Townshend on the Future of the Who"	in the magazine *Rolling Stone*
the chapter "Connecting with Kids"	in the book *Straight Talk*
the story "The Dead"	in the book *Dubliners*
the poem "Birches"	in the book *The Complete Poems of Robert Frost*
the song "Rolling in the Deep"	in the album *21*
the episode "Better Angels"	in the cable drama *The Walking Dead*
	the movie *Rear Window*

> **TIP**   In published work, the titles of long works are set off by italics. In handwritten papers, these titles should be underlined.

PRACTICE 6

Teaching Tip
After students complete this activity, have them go over their answers with a partner.

Use quotation marks or underlines as needed.

1. My recently divorced sister refused to be in the talent show when she was told she'd have to sing "Love Is a Many-Splendored Thing."

2. Disgusted by the constant dripping noise, Brian opened his copy of Handy Home Repairs to the chapter titled "Everything about the Kitchen Sink."

3. My little brother has seen Avengers at least eight times.

4. Before they bought new car tires, Nick and Fran studied the article "Testing Tires" in the February 2012 issue of Consumer Reviews.

5. Many people mistakenly think that Huckleberry Finn and The Adventures of Tom Sawyer are children's books only.

6. I just found out that the musical My Fair Lady is based on a play by George Bernard Shaw called Pygmalion.

7. The ending of Shirley Jackson's story "The Lottery" really surprised me.

8. I sang the song "Mack the Knife" in our high school production of The Threepenny Opera.

9. Unless he's studied the TV Guide listings thoroughly, my father won't turn on his television.

10. Stanley dreamed that both Time and Newsweek had decided to use him in their feature article "Person of the Year."

Other Uses of Quotation Marks

1. **To set off special words or phrases from the rest of a sentence (italics are also used for this purpose):**

   Many people spell the words "all right" as one word, "alright," instead of correctly spelling them as two words.

   I have trouble telling the difference between "principal" and "principle."

2. **To mark off a quote within a quote. For this purpose, single quotes (' ') are used:**

   Ben Franklin said, "The noblest question in the world is, 'What good may I do in it?' "

   "If you want to have a scary experience," Eric told Lynn, "read Stephen King's story 'The Mangler' in his book *Night Shift*."

Teaching Tip
Provide an example of a quotation within a quotation.

COLLABORATIVE ACTIVITY

Editing and Rewriting

Working with a partner, read the short passage below and circle the ten sets of quotation mark mistakes. Then, on separate paper, rewrite the passage, adding the ten sets of quotation marks. Feel free to discuss the rewrite quietly with your partner and refer back to the chapter when necessary.

¹Ava put aside her books to answer the phone. ²"Hello," she said.

³"Hey, Ava, take a break," said Lamar. ⁴"There's a great party going on here. ⁵Why don't you come over?"

⁶Ava hesitated. ⁷She was tired and bored; the party was tempting. ⁸She felt like a cartoon character with a devil perched on one shoulder and an angel on the other.

⁹"Go to the party," the devil said. ¹⁰"Forget this studying."

¹¹"Stay home," the angel whispered, "or you'll regret it tomorrow."

¹²Interrupting Ava's thoughts, Lamar urged, "Oh, come on, you can cram when you get home."

¹³Ava felt an imaginary stab from the devil's pitchfork. ¹⁴"I want to, Lamar," she said.

¹⁵Then she gave in to the imaginary angel. ¹⁶"But I can't. ¹⁷I really have to pass this test."

Teaching Tip
Ask students to work on the Collaborative Activities in pairs and then share their answers for the Reflective Activity with the entire class.

COLLABORATIVE ACTIVITY

Creating Sentences

Working with a partner, write sentences that use quotation marks as directed.

1. Write a sentence in which you quote a favorite expression of someone you know. Identify the person's relationship to you.

EXAMPLE

My brother Sam often says after a meal, "That wasn't bad at all."

_____

_____

2. Write a quotation that contains the words *Greg asked Esther.* Write a second quotation that includes the words *Esther replied.*

_____

_____

_____

3. Write a sentence that interests or amuses you from a book, magazine, or newspaper (print or online). Identify the title and author of the book, magazine, or newspaper article.

EXAMPLE

In her book At Wit's End, Erma Bombeck advises, "Never go to a doctor whose office

plants have died."

_____

REFLECTIVE ACTIVITY

1. Look at the paragraph about Ava and Lamar that you revised on page 355. How has adding quotation marks affected the reading of the paragraph?

2. What would writing be like without quotation marks? Using an example, explain how quotation marks are important to understanding writing.

3. Explain what it is about quotation marks that is most difficult for you to remember and apply. Use an example to make your point clear. Feel free to refer back to anything in this chapter.

REVIEW TEST 1

Place quotation marks around the exact words of a speaker or writer in the sentences that follow.

1. "Look at the dent in my car!" André cried.

2. My mother always says to me, "When in doubt, don't."

3. Franklin Roosevelt said, "The only thing we have to fear is fear itself."

4. "It's much too quiet in here," whispered Vince as he entered the library.

5. The sign on the manager's desk reads: "I'd like to help you out. Which way did you come in?"

6. Clutching his partner's hands in midair, the trapeze artist murmured, "We've got to stop meeting like this."

7. "I've got two tickets on the fifty-yard line!" the scalper shouted as the fans filed into the stadium.

8. Looking at the football fan who had removed his shirt in subzero weather, Lonnie said, "There's a guy whose elevator doesn't go to the top."

9. "I can't believe it," he muttered. "I put the hammer right there a minute ago, and now it's gone."

10. "Why doesn't anyone ever get hungry at the beach?" Dad asked. When we didn't answer, he explained, "Because of all the sand which is there."

Teaching Tip
You may want to use these review tests to assess what your students have learned and to determine how much they understand what they have learned.

REVIEW TEST 2

Go through the comics section of a newspaper or a graphic novel to find a scene that amuses you. Be sure to choose a scene in which two or more characters are speaking to each other. Write a full description that will enable people to visualize the scene clearly and appreciate its humor. Describe the setting and action in each panel, and enclose the words of the speakers in quotation marks.

NAME: _____

DATE: _____

Quotation Marks

Place quotation marks or underlines where needed.

1. The lifeguard shouted, "No ball playing in the water!"

2. Kathy insisted in a loud voice, "I'm not really overweight. I'm just six inches too short."

3. "If today were a blackboard," Terrence said, "I'd erase it and start over."

4. In her diet book, Miss Piggy advises, "Never eat anything at one sitting that you can't lift."

5. "Something is wrong with my satellite radio," Fred said to the mechanic. "It won't work unless the windshield wipers are turned on."

6. "You creep!" Zella yelled to the tailgater behind her. "I've got small children in this car!"

7. The first chapter in the book How to Train Your Dog is titled "Training the Master."

8. "Why do I skydive?" the elderly man repeated to the news reporter. "Well, I guess because I'm terrible at checkers."

9. "I'll only warn you this time," said the officer. "But next time you'd better drive more slowly or be prepared to open your wallet."

10. "When I was a child," said Cindy, "I thought that, if you swallowed a water-melon seed, a watermelon would grow in your stomach."

Quotation Marks

Place quotation marks or underlines where needed.

1. Darla said, "To err is human. That's why I do it so much."

2. At breakfast, Terry said, "I'll trade the sports section and a piece of bacon for the comics."

3. Danny's second-grade teacher asked, "How many months have twenty-eight days?"

4. "All twelve of them," Danny answered.

5. "And the winner," announced the host, "is Miss Mexico!"

6. "I'm not hungry," said Bertha. "I'm starved."

7. The bumper sticker on the car ahead of us read, "If you get any closer, introduce yourself."

8. "Where are you going?" asked Carrie sarcastically. "A Halloween party?"

9. "If you guys don't start hustling," warned the coach, "you're going to see football scholarships start vanishing into thin air."

10. The episode titled "Finding a Voice" on the television series Nova describes how some people with cerebral palsy are now speaking through the use of computers that have artificial voices.

NAME: _____

DATE: _____

Quotation Marks

Place quotation marks or underlines where needed.

1. "Minds are like parachutes," the teacher said. "They work only when they're open."

2. "If you refrigerate candles before using them," said the household hints book, "they'll last longer and won't drip."

3. In Psychology Today magazine, the author of the article called "The Techniques of the Artful Salesman" suggests that successful salespeople almost hypnotize their customers.

4. "When I wake up in the morning," said Elizabeth, "I sometimes have dream hangovers. For several hours, I can't shake the emotions I felt in my dream."

5. "My insomnia is terrible these days," said Yiyun. "I can't even sleep on the job."

6. I turned the radio up when Simon and Garfunkel's classic song "Bridge over Troubled Water" came on.

7. I read a horror story titled "Children of the Kingdom," in which giant slugs that eat people live in the sewers of New York City.

8. As the miser was taking a walk, a robber pressed a gun into his ribs and demanded, "Your money or your life!"

9. "Take my life," said the miser. "I'm saving my money for my old age."

10. The sign on Toshio's desk reads "In the rat race, only the rats win."

Quotation Marks

Place quotation marks or underlines where needed.

1. "When I saw <u>Raiders of the Lost Ark</u>," my great-grandfather said, "it reminded me of the old adventure serials we watched in the thirties and forties."

2. Before she asked her boss for a raise, Nadine said timidly, "Are you in a good mood, Mr. Huff?"

3. The newspaper headline read, "Good Humor Man Slays Ten."

4. The driver leaned out and handed six dollars to the toll collector, saying, "I'm paying for the car behind me, too."

5. "Did you know," he said to the expectant mother, "that it now costs $125,000 to raise a child to the age of eighteen?"

6. The TV announcer warned, "The latest figures indicate there will be a billion cars on the road by the year 2016. So if you want to cross the street, you'd better do it now."

7. My six-year-old nephew stared at me and asked, "How did you break your kneecap with that big, heavy cast on your leg?"

8. "I never go back on my word," he promised. "I might just go around it a little, though."

9. After Kay read a book called <u>Chocolate: The Consuming Passion</u>, she ran out and bought six Hershey bars.

10. Reassuring me that my diseased elm would recover, the tree surgeon said, "Don't worry. Its bark is worse than its blight."

Comma

INTRODUCTORY ACTIVITY

Teaching Tip
You may want to use this activity to assess your students' understanding of commas.

Commas often (though not always) signal a minor break or pause in a sentence. Each of the six pairs of sentences below illustrates one of six main uses of the comma. Read each pair of sentences and choose the rule that applies from the box on the next page. Each of these rules will be discussed in detail in the pages that follow.

_____a_____ 1. Joel watched the eleven o'clock news, a movie, a *Project Runway* rerun, and an hour-long infomercial.

Please endorse your check, write your account number on the back, and fill out a deposit slip.

_____b_____ 2. Even though I was warm indoors, I shivered at the thought of the bitter cold outside.

To start the car, press the accelerator and then turn the ignition key.

_____c_____ 3. The opossum, like the kangaroo, carries its young in a pouch.

Macy Gray, recording artist turned actress, played a supporting role in the movie *The Paperboy* (2012).

_____d_____ 4. I enrolled in the course, but my name was not on the class list.

A police cruiser blocked the busy intersection, and an ambulance pulled up on the sidewalk near the stunned victims.

_____e_____ 5. Omar asked, "Why is it so hard to remember your dreams the next day?"

"To prepare for the interview," said Ciara, "I researched the company online."

continued

_____*f*_____ 6. Mike has driven over 1,500,000 accident-free miles in his job as a long-distance trucker.

The Gates Trucking Company of 1800 Industrial Highway, Jersey City, New Jersey, gave Mike an award on January 26, 2007, for his superior safety record.

> a. Separate items in a series (list).
> b. Separate introductory material from the sentence.
> c. Separate words that interrupt the sentence.
> d. Separate complete thoughts in a sentence.
> e. Separate direct quotations from the rest of the sentence.
> f. Separate numbers, addresses, and dates in everyday writing.

Answers are on page 680.

Six Main Uses of the Comma

Commas are used mainly as follows:

1. Between items in a series
2. After introductory material
3. On both sides of words that interrupt the flow of thought in a sentence
4. Between two complete thoughts connected by *and, but, for, or, nor, so, yet*
5. Around a direct quotation to set it off from the rest of a sentence
6. For certain everyday material

You may find it helpful to remember that the comma often marks a slight pause, or break, in a sentence. These pauses occur at the points where the six main comma rules apply. Read aloud the sentence examples given on the following pages for each of the comma rules, and listen for the minor pauses that are signaled by commas.

At the same time, you should keep in mind that commas are far more often overused than underused. As a general rule, you should *not* use a comma unless a given comma rule applies or unless a comma is otherwise needed to help a sentence read clearly. A good rule of thumb is that, when in doubt about whether to use a comma, it is often best to leave it out.

After reviewing each of the comma rules that follow, you will practice adding commas that are needed and omitting commas that are not needed.

Teaching Tip
Provide at least one example of each comma use so that your students will have reference points. Stress this rule: "If in doubt, leave it out."

ESL Tip
Sometimes nonnative speakers may use a comma instead of a period. Review the rules for commas in English.

Comma between Items in a Series

Use a comma to separate items in a series.

> Magazines, paperback novels, and textbooks crowded the shelves.
>
> Hard-luck Jonathan needs a loan, a good-paying job, and a close friend.
>
> Pat sat in the doctor's office, checked her watch, and chewed gum nervously.
>
> Taye ate all the fresh, organic corn.
>
> More and more people entered the crowded, noisy stadium.

A comma is used between two descriptive words in a series only if *and* inserted between the words sounds natural. You could say,

> Taye ate all the fresh and organic corn.
>
> More and more people entered the crowded *and* noisy stadium.

But notice in the following sentences that the descriptive words do not sound natural when *and* is inserted between them. In such cases, no comma is used.

> The model wore a light sleeveless blouse. ("A light *and* sleeveless blouse" doesn't sound right, so no comma is used.)
>
> Dr. Van Helsing noticed two tiny puncture marks on his patient's neck. ("Two *and* tiny puncture marks" doesn't sound right, so no comma is used.)

PRACTICE 1

Place commas between items in a series.

1. Ling tossed her sunglasses, a bottle of water, and a recent issue of *Every Day with Rachael Ray* into her tote bag.

2. Stephen uses the computer to check e-mail, play games, look at friends' photos on Facebook download music, and send instant messages.

3. In the neighbors' backyard are an igloo-shaped doghouse, several plastic toys, trampled flowers, and a cracked ceramic gnome.

PRACTICE 2

For each item, cross out the one comma that is not needed. Add the one comma that is needed between items in a series.

1. A metal tape measure, a pencil, a ruler, and a hammer dangled, from the carpenter's pockets.

2. The fortune-teller uncovered the crystal ball, peered into it, and began, to predict my future.

3. That hair stylist is well known, for her flat blowouts, butchered haircuts, and brassy hair colorings.

Comma after Introductory Material

Use a comma to set off introductory material.

Fearlessly, Alyson picked up the slimy slug.

Just to annoy Tori, she let it crawl along her arm.

Although I have a black belt in karate, I decided to go easy on the demented bully who had kicked sand in my face.

Mumbling under her breath, the woman picked over the tomatoes.

TIPS

a. If the introductory material is brief, the comma is sometimes omitted. In the activities here, however, you should include the comma.

b. A comma is also used to set off extra material placed at the end of a sentence. Here are two sentences in which this comma rule applies:

I spent all day at the employment office, trying to find a job that suited me.

Lauren has trouble accepting criticism, except from Scott.

Place commas after introductory material.

PRACTICE 3

1. With shaking hands, the frightened baby-sitter dialed 911.
2. During the storm, snow drifted through cracks in the roof of the cabin.
3. Ashamed to ask for help, Betty glanced around nervously at the other students to see how they were filling out the computer questionnaire.

For each item, cross out the one comma that is not needed. Add the one comma that is needed after introductory material.

PRACTICE 4

1. In order to work at that fast-food restaurant, you have to wear a cowboy hat and six-shooters. In addition, you have to shout "Yippee!" every time, someone orders the special Western-style double burger.
2. Barely awake, the woman slowly rocked, her crying infant. While the baby softly cooed, the woman fell asleep.
3. When I painted the kitchen, I remembered to cover the floor with newspapers. Therefore, I was able to save the floor from looking, as if someone had thrown confetti on it.

Comma around Words
Interrupting the Flow of Thought

Teaching Tip
Ask volunteers
to read these
sentences
aloud. Encour-
age students
to listen for
pauses and
breaks.

Use a comma before and after words that interrupt the flow of thought in a sentence.

> The car, cleaned and repaired, is ready to be sold.

> Joanne, our new neighbor, used to work as a bartender at Rexy's Tavern.

> Taking long walks, especially after dark, helps me sort out my thoughts.

Usually, you can "hear" words that interrupt the flow of thought in a sentence. However, when you are not sure if certain words are interrupters, remove them from the sentence. If it still makes sense without the words, you know the words are interrupters and that the information they give is nonessential. Such nonessential information is set off with commas. In the following sentence,

> Indiglo, which is my friend's band, won the award for "Best Acoustic Band" at the local "Battle of the Bands" competition.

the words *which is my friend's band* are extra information, not needed to identify the subject of the sentence, *Indiglo*. Put commas around such nonessential information. On the other hand, in the sentence

> Indiglo which is my friend's band won the award for "Best Acoustic Band" at the local "Battle of the Bands" competition.

the words *which is my friend's band* supply essential information needed for us to identify the band as associated with the speaker. If the words were removed from the sentence, we would no longer know that the band that won the competition was friends with the speaker. Commas are not used around such essential information.

Here is another example:

> *The Help,* a novel by Kathryn Stockett, is one of the most moving books I've ever read.

Here the words *a novel by Kathryn Stockett* are extra information, not needed to identify the subject of the sentence, *The Help*. Commas go around such nonessential information. On the other hand, in the sentence

> Kathryn Stockett's novel *The Help* is the most moving book I've ever read.

the words *The Help* are needed to identify the novel. Commas are not used around such essential information.

Most of the time you will be able to "hear" words that interrupt the flow of thoughts in a sentence and will not have to think about whether the words are essential or nonessential.*

*Some instructors refer to nonessential, or extra, information that is set off by commas as a *nonrestrictive* clause. Essential information that interrupts the flow of thought is called a *restrictive* clause. No commas are used to set off a restrictive clause.

Add commas to set off interrupting words.

1. This all-purpose kitchen gadget, ladies and gentlemen, sells, for only $19.98!
2. Tigers, because they eat people, do not make good house pets.
3. A practical joker had laid a dummy, its straw-filled "hands" tied with rope, across the railroad tracks.

For each item, cross out the one comma that is not needed. Add the comma that is needed to completely set off interrupting words.

1. My brother, who likes only natural foods, would rather eat a soybean patty, than a cheeseburger.
2. That room, with its filthy rug, and broken dishwasher, is the nicest one in the building.
3. My aunt, who claims she is an artist, painted her living room ceiling, to look like the sky at midnight.

Comma between Complete Thoughts Connected by a Joining Word

Use a comma between two complete thoughts connected by *and, but, for, or, nor, so, yet.*

My parents threatened to throw me out of the house, so I had to start paying rent.

The polyester bedsheets had a gorgeous design on them, but they didn't feel as comfortable as plain cotton sheets.

The comma is optional when the complete thoughts are short:

Calvin relaxed but Robert kept working.

The soda was flat so I poured it out.

Be careful not to use a comma in sentences having *one* subject and a *double* verb. The comma is used only in sentences made up of two complete thoughts (two subjects and two verbs). In the sentence

Dawn lay awake that stormy night and listened to the thunder crashing.

there is only one subject (*Dawn*) and a double verb (*lay* and *listened*). No comma is needed. Likewise, the sentence

Teaching Tip
Ask volunteers to read these sentences aloud. Encourage students to listen for pauses and breaks.

ESL Tip
Nonnative speakers may put the comma after the joining word. Remind them that commas precede coordinating conjunctions.

The quarterback kept the ball and plunged across the goal line for a touchdown.

has only one subject (*quarterback*) and a double verb (*kept* and *plunged*); therefore, no comma is needed.

Place a comma before a joining word that connects two complete thoughts (two subjects and two verbs). The three sentences that have only one subject and a double verb do not need commas; mark these *C* as "correct."

1. Vince has to make sixty burgers an hour, or he'll lose his job at Burgerland.
2. The doctor assured me that my back was fine, but it still felt as rigid as an iron rod.
3. That new theater gets all the latest releases, and it provides free popcorn for customers who see ten or more movies a year.
4. My new toaster is more hi-tech than my old one, but it burns toast just as often.

C   5. Carol and Barbara pulled the volleyball net as tight as they could and then lashed it to a convenient pair of trees.

C   6. Ralph refuses to pay rent to his parents and will not do any chores at home.

7. Frieda wore a pair of wooden clogs while housecleaning, and the people in the apartment next door could hear her clomping up and down the stairs.
8. William kept the cookie in his mouth until its chocolate coating melted, and then he crunched the naked wafer into bits.
9. My little sister loves to call strangers on the telephone, but she hangs up as soon as anyone answers.

C   10. David hopes to make a few million dollars by the time he's thirty and then write a book about his experiences.

Comma with Direct Quotations

Use a comma to set off a direct quotation from the rest of a sentence.

"Please take a number," said the deli clerk.

Ertan told Henrietta, "I've just signed up for a knitting class."

"Those who sling mud," a famous politician once said, "usually lose ground."

"Reading this book," complained Stan, "is about as interesting as watching paint dry."

TIP A comma or a period at the end of a quotation goes inside quotation marks. See also page 349.

In each sentence, add the one or more commas needed to set off the quoted material.

PRACTICE 8

1. Frowning, the clerk asked, "Do you have a driver's license and two major credit cards for identification?"
2. In my high school yearbook, my best friend wrote, "2 Good 2 B 4 Gotten."
3. "The only thing that man couldn't talk his way out of," said Richie, "is a coffin."

Teaching Tip
For these activities read each sentence aloud as students add or delete commas.

In each sentence, cross out the one comma that is not needed. Add the comma that is needed to set off a quotation from the rest of the sentence.

PRACTICE 9

1. "Could you spare six dollars," the boy asked passersby, in the mall, "for train fare?"
2. "Man does not live by words alone," wrote Adlai Stevenson, "despite the fact, that sometimes he has to eat them."
3. "That actress," said Velma, "has promoted everything, from denture cleaner to shoelaces."

Comma with Everyday Material

Use a comma with certain everyday material as shown in the following sections.

Persons Spoken To

Sally, I think that you should go to bed.

Please turn down the stereo, Jo.

Please, sir, can you spare a dollar?

Teaching Tip
Ask volunteers to read these sentences aloud. Encourage students to listen for pauses and breaks.

Dates

My best friend got married on April 29, 2010, and he became a parent on January 7, 2013.

Addresses

Cheyenne's sister lives at Greenway Village, 342 Red Oak Drive, Los Angeles, California 90057.

 TIP   No comma is used before the zip code.

Openings and Closings of Letters

Dear Vanessa,	Sincerely,
Dear John,	Truly yours,

 TIP   In formal letters, a colon is used after the opening:

Dear Sir:

Dear Madam:

Numbers

Government officials estimate that Americans spend about 785,000,000 hours a year filling out federal forms.

PRACTICE 10   Place commas where needed.

1. I am sorry, sir, but you cannot sit at this table.
2. On May 6, 1954, Roger Bannister became the first person to run a mile in under four minutes.
3. Redeeming the savings certificate before June 30, 2010, will result in a substantial penalty.
4. A cash refund of one dollar can be obtained by sending proof of purchase to Seven Seas, P.O. Box 760, El Paso, TX 79972.
5. Leo, turn off that TV this minute!

Unnecessary Use of Commas

Remember that, if no clear rule applies for using a comma, it is usually better not to use a comma. As stated earlier, when in doubt, leave it out. Following are some typical examples of unnecessary commas.

INCORRECT

Sharon told me, that my socks were different colors. (A comma is not used before *that* unless the flow of thought is interrupted.)

The union negotiations, dragged on for three days. (Do not use a comma between a simple subject and verb.)

I waxed all the furniture, and cleaned the windows. (Use a comma before *and* only with more than two items in a series or when *and* joins two complete thoughts.)

Alexa carried, the baby into the house. (Do not use a comma between a verb and its object.)

I had a clear view, of the entire robbery. (Do not use a comma before a prepositional phrase.)

Teaching Tip
Read these sentences aloud. Pause where there are commas so that students can identify unnecessary commas.

Cross out the one comma that does not belong in each sentence. Do not add any commas.

PRACTICE 11

Teaching Tip
For this activity, read each sentence aloud as students add or delete commas.

1. A new bulletproof material has been developed, that is very lightweight.
2. The vet's bill included charges, for a distemper shot.
3. Since the firehouse, is directly behind Ken's home, the sound of its siren pierces his walls.
4. Hard sausages, and net-covered hams hung above the delicatessen counter.
5. The students in the 1980s dance class, were dressed in a variety of bright tights, baggy sweatshirts, and woolly leg warmers.
6. A woman in the ladies' room asked me, if she could borrow a safety pin.
7. Books, broken pencils, and scraps of paper, littered the reporter's desk.
8. The frenzied crowd at the game cheered, and whistled.
9. Splitting along the seams, the old mattress spilled its stuffing, on the ground.
10. To satisfy his hunger, Enrique chewed on a piece of dry, rye bread.

COLLABORATIVE ACTIVITY

Editing and Rewriting

Working with a partner, carefully read the short paragraph below and mark the ten places where commas are missing. Then, in the space between the lines, insert the ten additional commas needed. Feel free to discuss the rewrite quietly with your partner and refer back to the chapter when necessary.

Teaching Tip
Ask students to work on the Collaborative Activities in pairs and share their answers for the Reflective Activity with the entire class.

¹You may have heard of Robinson ~~Crusoe but~~ *Crusoe, but* there is an even stranger story of shipwreck and survival. ²In ~~1757 a~~ *1757, a* Scottish whaling ship sank in the icy polar seas of the Arctic. ³Only one ~~man Bruce~~ *man, Bruce* ~~Gordon survived~~ *Gordon, survived*. ⁴Without food or ~~shelter Gordon~~ *shelter, Gordon* spent his lonely first night huddled on the ice. ⁵The next ~~day the~~ *day, the* whaling ship—upside-down—rose to the surface of the sea and lodged tightly in the ice floes. ⁶~~Gordon using~~ *Gordon, using* some of the shipwreck ~~debris managed~~ *debris, managed* to break into a cabin window. ⁷He survived for a year in the freezing world of the upside-down ship by using some stored coal to build a fire. ⁸~~Eventually Bruce~~ *Eventually, Bruce* Gordon was rescued by a band of Inuit hunters. ⁹After living for more than five years in the native ~~village the~~ *village, the* shipwrecked sailor finally made it back to Scotland.

Creating Sentences

Working with a partner, write sentences that use commas as directed.

1. Write a sentence mentioning three items that can be found in this photo.

   _____

   _____

2. Write two sentences describing how you relax after getting home from school or work. Start the first sentence with *After* or *When.* Start the second sentence with *Next.*

   _____

   _____

3. Write a sentence that tells something about your favorite movie, book, television show, or song. Use the words *which is my favorite movie* (or *book, television show,* or *song*) after the name of the movie, book, television show, or song.

   _____

   _____

4. Write a sentence containing two complete thoughts about a person you know. The first thought should mention something that you like about the person. The second thought should mention something you don't like. Join the two thoughts with *but.*

   _____

   _____

5. Invent a line that Lily might say to her husband, Tom. Use the words *Lily said* in the sentence. Then include Tom's reply, using the words *Tom responded.*

   _____

   _____

6. Write a sentence about an important event in your life. Include in your sentence the day, month, and year of the event.

   _____

   _____

REFLECTIVE ACTIVITY

1. Look at the paragraph about Bruce Gordon that you revised. Explain how adding commas has affected the reading of the paragraph.

2. What would writing be like without the comma? How do commas help writing?

3. What comma rule is the most difficult for you to remember and apply? Explain, giving an example.

REVIEW TEST 1

Insert commas where needed. In the space provided under each sentence, summarize briefly the rule that explains the use of the comma or commas.

1. During the sudden downpour, people covered their heads with folded newspapers.

   Comma after introductory material

2. Helen's sister always stopped her from buying expensive items by saying, "You have champagne taste and a beer budget."

   Set off a direct quotation

3. The damp, musty, shadowy cellar was our favorite playground.

   Separate items in a series

4. My favorite pillow, a sad specimen leaking chunks of memory foam, is over ten years old.

   Set off words interrupting the flow of thought

5. Mary Ann started work as a file clerk on June 21, 2012, and quit on June 22.

   Set off everyday material

6. Phan agreed to sit in the window seat, but he kept his eyes tightly shut during the takeoff and landing.

   Separate two complete thoughts

7. The massive fullback, his uniform torn and bloodied, hobbled back to the huddle.

   Set off words interrupting the flow of thought

8. Martin Luther King wrote, "A man can't ride on your back unless it's bent."

   Set off a direct quotation

9. If you want to avoid that run-down feeling, you should look both ways before crossing the street.

   Comma after introductory material

10. My brother, who is a practical joker, once put a plastic shark in our bathtub.

   Set off words interrupting the flow of thought

REVIEW TEST 2

Insert commas where needed. One sentence does not need commas; mark this sentence *C* for "correct."

1. "Thelma and Louise," a corn snake that lived at the San Diego Zoo, was popular with visitors.

2. She wasn't popular because corn snakes, which are harmless, are rare.

3. In fact, corn snakes are among the most common North American snakes.

4. "Thelma and Louise" was a perfectly ordinary snake, except for one little thing.

5. She had, believe it or not, two heads.

6. Scientists say that two-headed snakes are born fairly often, but they usually don't survive long.

7. Because their two heads often want to go in different directions, such snakes are slow and clumsy.

8. The two-headed babies are quickly caught and eaten by hawks, raccoons, skunks, and other animals.

9. But in the safety of the zoo, Thelma and Louise lived a long life.

c 10. She even gave birth to fifteen normal babies.

REVIEW TEST 3

On a separate sheet of paper or in a separate file, write six sentences, each demonstrating one of the six main comma rules.

NAME: _____

DATE: _____

Comma

Add commas where needed. Then refer to the box below and write, in the space provided, the letter of the comma rule that applies in each sentence.

a. Between items in a series	d. Between complete thoughts
b. After introductory material	e. With direct quotations
c. Around interrupters	f. With everyday material

_____a_____ 1. Tasha makes her studying more bearable by having plenty of popcorn, pretzels, and Skittles close by.

_____b_____ 2. Because Jim is the company's top salesperson, he receives special attention from the boss.

_____e_____ 3. "You look different," said Nikki. "Have you lost weight?"

_____c_____ 4. My Uncle Al, who is hard of hearing, always asks me to repeat what I just said.

_____e_____ 5. "I really appreciate the ride," the hitchhiker said. "A hundred cars must have passed me."

_____d_____ 6. My little sister loves to ride on the back of my motorcycle, but my parents worry about her falling off.

_____f_____ 7. I have to pay $8,250 by June 30, 2015, before I officially own my car.

_____a_____ 8. Will emptied his piggy bank and sorted the nickels, dimes, and quarters into three shiny piles.

_____b_____ 9. Huddled under a large piece of plastic, we waited out the rain delay in the ball game.

_____d_____ 10. The vacationing boys slept in the car that night, for they'd spent too much on meals and souvenirs.

Comma

Cross out the one comma in each sentence that is not needed. Then add the one comma that is needed and in the space provided write the letter of the rule that applies for each comma you added.

a. Between items in a series	d. Between complete thoughts
b. After introductory material	e. With direct quotations
c. Around interrupters	f. With everyday material

_____c_____ 1. *Harry Potter and the Deathly Hallows,* the seventh and final book in the *Harry Potter* series, sold over eight million copies, on the first day of its release.

_____b_____ 2. Pretending to be a baby-sitter, the shoplifter slipped several DVDs, into her baby stroller.

_____a_____ 3. Emmett, who recently adopted a baby girl, rushed to the supermarket, to buy infant formula, baby wipes, and disposable diapers.

_____e_____ 4. "Before I leave on my business trip," Emily told her two children, "I want both of you to promise me, that you will *not* torment the dog or Dad."

_____c_____ 5. Brandie, a breast cancer survivor, religiously wears her pink, "awareness bracelet" to remember her victory over the disease.

_____b_____ 6. Recognizing the deadly effects of cigarette smoking, the Walt Disney Company has banned depictions of smoking, in its films.

_____d_____ 7. Kurt rehearsed the exact moment for months, but he still stumbled over his own words, when he asked Keisha to marry him.

_____a_____ 8. Everyone at the barbecue party enjoyed the mustard-coated, oil-drizzled Alaskan, Copper River sockeye salmon fillets roasted on cedar planks.

_____e_____ 9. Mahatma Gandhi, was wise when he said, "We must be the change we wish to see."

_____d_____ 10. The substitute teacher tried to enforce the class rules, yet students misbehaved by sending text messages, and playing games on their cell phones.

NAME: _____

DATE: _____

MASTERY TEST 3

Comma

Add commas where needed. Then refer to the box below and write, in the space provided, the letter of the comma rule that applies in each sentence.

a. Between items in a series	d. Between complete thoughts
b. After introductory material	e. With direct quotations
c. Around interrupters	f. With everyday material

_____*f*_____ 1. My friend Tina lives at 333 Virginia Avenue, Atlantic City.

_____*d*_____ 2. I went to her house one night recently, and the two of us watched television for several hours.

_____*c*_____ 3. Tina, who is always hungry, suggested we go to Tony's Grill for a pizza.

_____*b*_____ 4. Along with about a dozen other drivers, I parked in a tiny lot with a "No Parking" sign.

_____*c*_____ 5. I believed, foolishly enough, that my car would be safe there.

_____*a*_____ 6. We had our pizza, left the restaurant, and returned to the lot.

_____*d*_____ 7. A 2008 Chevy and a tow truck were parked in the lot, but my Honda and all the other cars had vanished.

_____*b*_____ 8. After walking twenty blocks back to Tina's house, I called the towing company.

_____*e*_____ 9. A recorded voice said, "Come to 26 Texas Avenue tomorrow morning with seventy-five dollars in cash."

_____*b*_____ 10. Whenever Tina craves pizza, I now buy a frozen pie at the local convenience store.

NAME: _____

DATE: _____

Comma

Add commas where needed. Then refer to the box below and write, in the space provided, the letter of the comma rule that applies in each sentence.

a. Between items in a series	d. Between complete thoughts
b. After introductory material	e. With direct quotations
c. Around interrupters	f. With everyday material

_____c_____ 1. Matt's first car, a 1960 Chevy Impala, had enormous tail fins.

_____e_____ 2. Kia called from upstairs, "Could you turn the TV down?"

_____a_____ 3. The broken-down farm housed a swaybacked horse, a blind cow, and two lame chickens.

_____b_____ 4. In Phil's job as toll collector, he takes quarters from over 5,500 drivers every day.

_____b_____ 5. Halfway through the film, the restless toddler in the audience began to cry.

_____a_____ 6. The combination of milk stains, peanut butter splotches, and jelly smears made the toddler's face look like a finger painting.

_____b_____ 7. Though public transportation saves her money, Aimee prefers driving to work.

_____e_____ 8. "Better to keep your mouth shut and be thought a fool," my father always says, "than to open it and remove all doubt."

_____c_____ 9. The fried eggs, as they sizzled in the rusty iron skillet, began to turn red.

_____d_____ 10. The road map must have been out of date, for the highway it showed no longer existed.

Other Punctuation Marks

INTRODUCTORY ACTIVITY

The main purpose of this chapter is to explain and illustrate five punctuation marks not previously discussed. They are the colon (:), semicolon (;), dash (—), hyphen (-), and parentheses ( ). Each sentence below needs one of these punctuation marks. See if you can insert the correct mark in each case.

1. The following items were on Ted's grocery list: soda, potato chips, chocolate chip cookies, ice cream, and carrots.

2. A life-size statue of her cat adorns the living room of Diana's penthouse.

3. Sigmund Freud (1856–1939), the pioneer of psychoanalysis, was a habitual cocaine user.

4. As children, we would put pennies on the railroad track; we wanted to see what they would look like after being run over by a train.

5. The stuntwoman was battered, broken, and barely breathing but alive.

Answers are on page 681.

Colon (:)

The colon is a mark of introduction. Use the colon at the end of a complete statement to do the following:

1. **Introduce a list.**

   My little brother has three hobbies: playing video games, racing his toy cars all over the floor, and driving me crazy.

2. **Introduce a quotation.**

   Janet's paper was based on a passage from George Eliot's novel *Middlemarch:* "If we had a keen vision and feeling of all ordinary human life, it would be like hearing the grass grow and the squirrel's heart beat, and we should die of that roar which lies on the other side of silence. As it is, the quickest of us walk about well wadded with stupidity."

3. **Introduce an explanation.**

There are two ways to do this job: the easy way and the right way.

Two minor uses of the colon are after the opening in a formal letter (*Dear Professor Taylor:*) and between the hour and the minute when writing the time (*The bus will leave for the game at 11:45.*).

Place colons where needed.

1. A comedian once defined mummies as follows:people who are pressed for time.
2. The manager boasted that his restaurant was full of good things: good food, good selections, and good prices.
3. In her book *The Plug-In Drug,* Marie Winn describes the effect of television on family life:"By its domination of the time families spend together, it destroys the special quality that distinguishes one family from another, a quality that depends to a great extent on what a family *does,* what special rituals, games, recurrent jokes, familiar songs, and shared activities it accumulates."

Semicolon (;)

The semicolon signals more of a pause than the comma alone but not quite the full pause of a period. Use a semicolon to do the following:

1. **Join two complete thoughts that are not already connected by a joining word such as *and, but, for,* or *so.***

The chemistry lab blew up; Professor Thomas was fired.

I once stabbed myself with a pencil; a black mark has been under my skin ever since.

2. **Join two complete thoughts that include a transitional word such as *however, otherwise, moreover, furthermore, therefore,* or *consequently.***

I cut and raked the grass; moreover, I weeded the lawn.

Preeta finished typing the paper; however, she forgot to bring it to class.

TIP The first two uses of the semicolon listed here are treated in more detail on pages 123–28.

ESL Tip
Some languages use a semicolon for other purposes.

3. Mark off items in a series when the items themselves contain commas.

This fall I won't have to work on Labor Day, September 7; Veterans Day, November 11; or Thanksgiving Day, November 26.

At the final Weight Watchers' meeting, prizes were awarded to Ashlee Johnson, for losing 20 pounds; Irving Ross, for losing 26 pounds; and Tara Mills, the champion loser, who had lost 102 pounds.

PRACTICE 2

Teaching Tip
You may want to ask students to complete this activity in pairs.

Place semicolons where needed.

1. Be sure to plug up all unused electrical outlets;otherwise, your toddler might get a severe shock.

2. In the old horror movie, the incredible shrinking man battled a black widow spider;he finally speared it with a straight pin.

3. Having nothing better to do, Laurie watched the *Today* show from 7:00 to 9:00 A.M.;a rerun of *Dexter,* from 9:00 to 10:00;and a marathon of *America's Next Top Model* from 12:30 to 4:00 P.M.

Dash (—)

A dash signals a degree of pause longer than a comma but not as complete as a period. Use the dash to set off words for dramatic effect.

I suggest—no, I insist—that you stay for dinner.

The convicted felon walked toward the flashing cameras—grinning.

A meaningful job, a loving wife, and a car that wouldn't break down all the time—these are the things he wanted in life.

PRACTICE 3

Teaching Tip
In a computer lab, ask students to form a dash on the keyboard by striking the hyphen twice (--).

Place dashes where needed.

1. Our dishwasher doesn't dry very well͟the glasses look as if they're crying.

2. After I saw two museums, three monuments, and the governor's mansion, there was only one other place I wanted to see my hotel room.

3. I hoped no, I prayed that the operation would be successful.

Hyphen (-)

Use a hyphen in the following ways:

1. With two or more words that act as a single unit describing a noun.

The elegant ladies nibbled at the deep-fried grasshoppers.

A white-gloved waiter then put some snails on their table.

> **TIP** Your dictionary will often help when you are unsure about whether to use a hyphen between words.

Teaching Tip
Ask students to help you create several more examples using hyphens. Point out that most word processing programs wrap text, so words are not divided at the end of a typed line.

2. **To divide a word at the end of a line of writing or typing.**

Although it had begun to drizzle, the teams decided to play the championship game that day.

> **TIPS**
>
> 1. Divide a word between syllables. Use your dictionary (see page 387) to be sure of correct syllable divisions.
> 2. Do not divide words of one syllable.
> 3. Do not divide a word if you can avoid dividing it.

Place hyphens where needed.

PRACTICE 4

1. Sideway Inn, a hole-in-the-wall diner located in the newly gentrified part of town, serves both comfort food and upscale, hoity-toity dishes.
2. Grandpa needs to throw out his console TV and rabbit-ear antenna and buy a new high-definition flatscreen.
3. The people in my hometown are honest, hard-working folks, but they aren't very friendly to out-of-towners.

Parentheses ( )

Use parentheses to do the following:

1. **Set off extra or incidental information from the rest of a sentence.**

The chapter on drugs in our textbook (pages 142–78) contains some frightening statistics.

The normal body temperature of a cat (101 to 102°) is 3° higher than the temperature of a human being.

Teaching Tip
Ask students to help you create several more examples using parentheses.

2. **Enclose letters or numbers that signal items in a series.**

Three steps to follow in previewing a textbook are to (1) study the title, (2) read the first and last paragraphs, and (3) study the headings and subheadings.

> **TIP** Avoid using parentheses too often in your writing.

PRACTICE 5

Add parentheses where needed.

1. The high ticket prices(fifty to ninety dollars)made Rodney think twice about going to the concert.

2. In the last election(the April primary), only 20 percent of eligible voters showed up at the polls.

3. When you come to take the placement test, please bring with you(1)two sharpened pencils and(2)an eraser.

Teaching Tip
You may want to ask students to complete this activity in pairs.

REVIEW TEST 1

Teaching Tip
You may want to use these review tests to assess what your students have learned and to determine how well they understand what they have learned.

At the appropriate spot or spots, place the punctuation mark shown in the margin.

EXAMPLE

;   The singles event was a success; I met several people I wanted to see again.

:   1. Fascinated, Corey read two unusual recipes in *The Joy of Cooking*: roasted saddle of moose and woodchuck smothered with onions.

—   2. Sam's Pizza Heaven is advertising a Friday-night special on lasagna all you can eat for $12.99.

-   3. Very few older cars have front-wheel drive.

()   4. The sign on my instructor's office door read, "Available only during office hours(2 to 4 P.M.)"

:   5. In *Walden,* Thoreau wrote: "I went to the woods because I wished to live deliberately, to front only the essential facts of life, and see if I could not learn what it had to teach, and not, when I came to die, discover that I had not lived."

;   6. Mosquitoes prefer to bite children rather than adults;they are also more attracted to blonds than to brunettes.

—   7. Please go to the White Hen it's that convenience store in the middle of the next block and get a carton of milk.

-   8. We can't afford to see first-run movies anymore.

()   9. Four hints for success in taking exams are(1)review your notes the night before,(2)be on time for the exam,(3)sit in a quiet place, and(4)read all directions carefully before you begin to write.

; 10. My neighbor's boxer, Dempsey, is a great watchdog;in fact, he can sit on my porch and watch me for hours.

REVIEW TEST 2

On a separate sheet of paper or in a new file, write two sentences for each of the following punctuation marks: colon, semicolon, dash, hyphen, parentheses.

NAME: _____

DATE: _____

Other Punctuation Marks

At the appropriate spot (or spots), place the punctuation mark shown in the margin.

; 1. There are several ways to save money on your grocery bills; for example, never go shopping on an empty stomach.

: 2. There are only two ways to get there: hike or hitch a ride.

— 3. "The cooking at this restaurant," said the dissatisfied customer, "lacks just one thing, good taste."

- 4. Pete's over the shoulder catch brought the crowd to its feet.

( ) 5. Call your local office of the IRS (Internal Revenue Service) if you think you're entitled to a refund.

— 6. Annabelle gave Harold back his engagement ring without the diamond.

: 7. That new ice cream place has great flavors: blueberry cheesecake, pineapple, bubble gum, and Oreo cookie.

— 8. Some teenagers there they go around the corner just stole that man's wallet.

- 9. I'm waiting for the day when someone invents zero calorie ice cream.

; 10. In a study, people were asked who in their family got the most smiles and touches; 44 percent said the family pet.

385

NAME: _____

DATE: _____

MASTERY TEST 2

Other Punctuation Marks

Add colons, semicolons, dashes, hyphens, or parentheses as needed. Each sentence requires only one of the five kinds of punctuation marks.

1. It's impossible for two blue-eyed parents to have a brown-eyed child.

2. People watch more television than most of us realize; the average TV is on for more than six hours a day.

3. My aunt loves giving blow-by-blow accounts of all her operations.

4. Electrical storms, inflation, and my little brother's jokes—these are the things that bother me the most.

5. My car was losing power; I asked a gas station attendant to check the battery.

6. To cure hiccups, try one of the following methods: put a paper bag over your head, hold your breath, or eat a teaspoonful of sugar.

7. A portion of the sociology text (pages 150–58) deals with the changing roles of women.

8. My mother likes to listen to audio books; she can do other things at the same time.

9. Our math instructor said: "Standard units of measurement used to be set by parts of the body; for example, King Henry I of England defined a yard as the distance from his nose to his outstretched thumb."

10. From my second-row seat at the movies, I could count the leading lady's eyelashes.

Dictionary Use

INTRODUCTORY ACTIVITY

The dictionary is an indispensable tool, as will be apparent if you try to answer the following questions *without* using the dictionary.

1. Which one of the following words is spelled incorrectly?

    fortuitous
    fortutious   macrobiotics   stratagem

2. If you wanted to hyphenate the following word correctly, at which points would you place the syllable divisions?

    h i/e r/o/g l y p h/i c s

3. What common word has the sound of the first *e* in the word *chameleon*?

    be
    _____

4. Where is the primary accent in the following word?

    o c / t o / g e / n a r / i / a n

5. What are the two separate meanings of the word *earmark*?

    (1) Identifying mark on the ear of a domestic animal

    (2) Identifying feature or characteristic

Your dictionary is a quick and sure authority on all these matters: spelling, syllabication, pronunciation, and word meanings. And as this chapter will show, it is a source for many other kinds of information.

Answers are on page 681.

Teaching Tip
You may want to use this activity to assess your students' familiarity with a dictionary.

But Dr Johnson ov wat yuse wil this dicshunary of yors be?

ESL Tip
Nonnative
speakers may
benefit from
using ESL dic-
tionaries that
contain sen-
tences utilizing
the words.

The dictionary is a valuable tool. To take advantage of it, you need to understand the main kinds of information that a dictionary gives about a word. Look at the information provided for the word *dictate* in the following entry from the *American Heritage Dictionary,* fourth paperback edition.*

Spelling and syllabication   **Pronunciation**   **Part of speech**

dic•tate (dĭk′tāt′, dĭk-tāt′) *v.* **-tat•ed, -tat•ing.**   **Meanings**
1. To say or read aloud for transcription.
2. To prescribe or command with authority.
—*n.* (dĭk′tāt′). **1.** A directive; command.
2. A guiding principle: *the dictates of*   **Example**
conscience. [< Lat. *dictāre.* < *dīcere, say*]
—**dic•ta′tion** *n.*   **Etymology**

Other form of the word

*© 2001 Houghton Mifflin Company. Reprinted by permission from *American Heritage Dictionary of the English Language,* Fourth Paperback Edition.

Spelling

The first bit of information, in the boldface (heavy type) entry itself, is the spelling of *dictate*. You probably already know the spelling of *dictate*, but if you didn't, you could find it by pronouncing the syllables in the word carefully and then looking it up in the dictionary.

Use your print, electronic, or online dictionary to correct the spelling of the following words:

responsable ___responsible___ delite ___delight___

thorogh ___thorough___ duble ___double___

akselerate ___accelerate___ carefull ___careful___

finaly ___finally___ luckyer ___luckier___

refiree ___referee___ dangrous ___dangerous___

shizophrenic ___schizophrenic___ accomodate ___accommodate___

prescripshun ___prescription___ envalope ___envelope___

hankercheif ___handkerchief___ prenatel ___prenatal___

marryed ___married___ progres ___progress___

alright ___all right___ jeneric ___generic___

fotographer ___photographer___ excelent ___excellent___

krucial ___crucial___ persue ___pursue___

Teaching Tip
Encourage students to explore several online dictionaries. Have students bring a dictionary to class. Ask them to look up a personal word, such as their first name, state, or ethnicity. Then ask them to look at the information provided for that word.

Syllabication

The second bit of information that the dictionary gives, also within the boldface entry, is the syllabication of *dic•tate*. Note that a dot separates each syllable (part) of the word. Use your dictionary to mark the syllable divisions in the following words. Also indicate how many syllables are in each word.

c o n•t a c t   (__2__ syllables)

m a g•n e t•i c   (__3__ syllables)

d e•h u•m a n•i z e   (__4__ syllables)

s e n•t i•m e n•t a l•i z e   (__5__ syllables)

Noting syllable divisions will enable you to *hyphenate* a word: divide it at the end of one line of writing and complete it at the beginning of the next line. You can correctly hyphenate a word only at a syllable division, and you may have to check your dictionary to make sure of the syllable divisions for a particular word.

Pronunciation

The third bit of information in the dictionary entry is the pronunciation of *dictate:* *(dik´tat´)* or *(dik-tat´)*. You already know how to pronounce *dictate,* but if you did not, the information within the parentheses would serve as your guide. Use your dictionary to complete the pronunciation exercises on the next page.

Vowel Sounds

You will probably use the pronunciation key in your dictionary mainly as a guide to pronouncing different vowel sounds (*vowels* are the letters *a, e, i, o,* and *u*). Here is the pronunciation key that appears in the front of the paperback *American Heritage Dictionary:*

> ă pat ā pay â care ä father ĕ pet ē be ĭ pit ī tie î pier ŏ pot ō toe
> ô paw, for oi noise oŏ took o͞o boot ou out th thin *th* this ŭ cut
> û urge yo͞o abuse zh vision ə about, item, edible, gallop, circus

This key tells you, for example, that the short *a* is pronounced like the *a* in *pat,* the long *a* is like the *a* in *pay,* and the short *i* is like the *i* in *pit.*

Now look at the pronunciation key in your own dictionary. The key is probably located in the front of the dictionary or at the bottom of every page. What common word in the key tells you how to pronounce each of the following sounds?

ĕ	*pet*	ō	*toe*
ī	*pie*	ŭ	*cut*
ŏ	*pot*	o͞o	*boot*

TIP Note that a long vowel always has the sound of its own name.

The Schwa (ə)

The symbol ə looks like an upside-down *e*. It is called a *schwa,* and it stands for the unaccented sound in such words as *about, item, edible, gallop,* and *circus.* More approximately, it stands for the sound *uh*—like the *uh* that speakers sometimes make when they hesitate. Perhaps it would help to remember that *uh,* as well as ə, could be used to represent the schwa sound.

Here are three of the many words in which the schwa sound appears: *social-ize* (sō´shə līz or sō´shuh līz); *legitimate* (lə jĭt´ə mĭt or luh jĭt´uh mĭt); *oblivious* (ə blĭv´ē əs or uh blĭv´ē uhs). Open your dictionary to any page, and you will almost surely be able to find three words that make use of the schwa in the pronunciation in parentheses after the main entry. Write three such words and their pronunciations in the following spaces:

1. _____   Answers will

2. _____   vary.

3. _____

Accent Marks

Some words contain both a primary accent, shown by a heavy stroke (′), and a secondary accent, shown by a lighter stroke (′). For example, in the word *vicissitude* (vĭ sĭs′ĭ tōōd′), the stress, or accent, goes chiefly on the second syllable (sĭs′) and, to a lesser extent, on the last syllable (tōōd′).

   Use your dictionary to add stress marks to the following words:

soliloquy (sə lĭl′ə kwē)

diatribe (dī′ə trīb′)

rheumatism (rōō′mə tīz′əm)

representation (rĕp′rĭ zĕn tā′shən)

Full Pronunciation

Use your dictionary to write out the full pronunciation (the information given in parentheses) for each of the following words:

1. germane ___*jər-mān′*___
2. jettison ___*jĕt′ĭ-sən*___
3. juxtapose ___*jŭk′stə-pōz′*___
4. catastrophic ___*kăt′ə-strŏf′ĭk*___
5. alacrity ___*ə-lăk′rĭ-tē*___
6. exacerbate ___*ĭg-zăs′ər-bāt*___
7. sporadic ___*spə-răd′ĭk*___
8. cacophony ___*kə-kŏf′ə-nē*___
9. intrepid ___*ĭn-trĕp′ĭd*___
10. oligarchy ___*ŏl′ĭ-gär′kē*___
11. raucous ___*rô′kəs*___
12. temerity ___*tə-mĕr′ĭ-tē*___
13. forensic ___*fə-rĕn′sĭk*___
14. megalomania ___*mĕg′ə-lō-mā′nē-ə*___
15. perpetuity ___*pûr′pĭ-tōō′ĭ-tē*___

Now practice pronouncing each word. Use the pronunciation key in your dictionary as an aid to sounding out each syllable. Do *not* try to pronounce a word all at once; instead, work on mastering *one syllable at a time.* When you can pronounce each of the syllables in a word successfully, then say them in sequence, add the accent, and pronounce the entire word.

> **TIP** Some online dictionaries offer spoken pronunciations of words. For example, if you go to www.merriam-webster.com, you will see a speaker icon next to each word entry. If you click on this icon, the word will be pronounced for you.

Other Information about Words

Parts of Speech

Teaching Tip
You may want to ask students to complete this activity in pairs.

ESL Tip
Nonnative speakers will benefit from learning related word forms; this will increase their vocabulary.

The dictionary entry for *dictate* includes the abbreviation *v.* This means that the meanings of *dictate* as a verb will follow. The abbreviation *n.* is then followed by the meanings of *dictate* as a noun.

At the front of your dictionary, you will probably find a key that will explain the meanings of abbreviations used in the dictionary. Use the key to fill in the meanings of the following abbreviations:

pl. = _____*plural*_____   adj. = _____*adjective*_____

sing. = _____*singular*_____   adv. = _____*adverb*_____

Principal Parts of Irregular Verbs

Dictate is a regular verb and forms its principal parts by adding *-d, -d,* and *-ing* to the stem of the verb. When a verb is irregular, the dictionary lists its principal parts. For example, with *begin* the present tense comes first (the entry itself, *begin*). Next comes the past tense (*began*), then the past participle (*begun*)—the form of the verb used with such helping words as *have, had,* and *was.* Then comes the present participle (*beginning*)—the *-ing* form of the word.

Look up the principal parts of the following irregular verbs and write them in the spaces provided. The first one has been done for you.

Teaching Tip
Consider doing these activities with your entire class.

PRESENT	PAST	PAST PARTICIPLE	PRESENT PARTICIPLE
see	*saw*	*seen*	*seeing*
go	*went*	*gone*	*going*
ride	*rode*	*ridden*	*riding*
speak	*spoke*	*spoken*	*speaking*

Plural Forms of Irregular Nouns

The dictionary supplies the plural forms of all irregular nouns (regular nouns form the plural by adding -s or -es). Give the plurals of the following nouns:

country   *countries*

volcano   *volcanoes*

curriculum   *curricula*

woman   *women*

See page 401 for more information about plurals.

Meanings

When a word has more than one meaning, the meanings are numbered in the dictionary, as with the verb *dictate.* In many dictionaries, the most common meanings are presented first. The introductory pages of your dictionary will explain the order in which meanings are presented.

Use the sentence context to try to explain the meaning of the underlined word in each of the following sentences. Write your definition in the space provided. Then look up and record the dictionary meaning of the word. Be sure you pick out the meaning that fits the word as it is used in the sentence.

1. The insurance company <u>compensated</u> Jean for the two weeks she missed work.

   Your definition: _____

   Dictionary definition: *made a payment to*

2. Justin is in excellent <u>condition</u> from running two miles a day.

   Your definition: _____

   Dictionary definition: *state of health*

3. The underworld chief attained power by <u>liquidating</u> his competitors.

   Your definition: _____

   Dictionary definition: *killing*

Answers for the students' definitions will vary.

Etymology

Etymology refers to the history of a word. Many words have origins in foreign languages, such as Greek (abbreviated Gk in the dictionary) or Latin (L). Such information is usually enclosed in brackets and is available in most quality dictionaries.

Teaching Tip
Have students look at the etymology of their chosen word.

A good dictionary will tell you, for example, that the word *cannibal* derives from the name of the man-eating tribe, the Caribs, that Christopher Columbus discovered on Cuba and Haiti.

The following are good dictionaries:

The Oxford English Dictionary
The American Heritage Dictionary
Random House College Dictionary
Merriam-Webster's Collegiate Dictionary
Webster's New World Dictionary

See if your dictionary says anything about the origins of the following words.

derrick *from Derrick, a seventeenth-century English hangman*

_____

berserk *from an Old Norse word meaning "a wild man"*

_____

boycott *after Charles C. Boycott, a landlord who was isolated from public services because he opposed land reform*

chauvinism *after Chauvin, a legendary French soldier famous for his devotion to Napoleon*

Usage Labels

As a general rule, use only standard English words in your writing. If a word is not standard English, your dictionary will probably give it a usage label such as *informal, nonstandard, slang, vulgar, obsolete, archaic,* or *rare.*

Look up the following words and record how your dictionary labels them. Remember that a recent hardbound desk dictionary will always be the best source of information about usage.

messed up *slang* _____

peppy *informal* _____

techie *informal* _____

ain't *nonstandard* _____

gross out (meaning *to fill with disgust*) *slang* _____

Synonyms

A *synonym* is a word that is close in meaning to another word. Using synonyms helps you avoid unnecessary repetition of the same word in a paper. A good dictionary will give you synonyms for words. (You might also want to own a *thesaurus,* a book that lists synonyms and antonyms. An *antonym* is a word approximately opposite in meaning to another word.)

Consult a dictionary that gives synonyms for the following words, and write some of the synonyms in the spaces provided.

frighten *alarm, panic, scare, startle, terrify*   Answers may

giant *colossal, enormous, huge, immense, tremendous*   vary.

insane *batty, crazy, cuckoo, deranged, lunatic, mad*

REVIEW TEST

Use your dictionary to answer the following questions.

1. How many syllables are in the word *magnanimous?* _____*four*_____

2. Where is the primary accent in the word *detrimental?* _____*third syllable*_____

3. In the word *tractable,* the second *a* is pronounced like

    a. short *a.*

    b. long *a.*

    c. short *i.*

    (d.) schwa.

4. In the word *officiate,* the second *i* is pronounced like

    a. short *i.*

    b. long *i.*

    (c.) long *e.*

    d. schwa.

5. In the word *sedentary,* the first *e* is pronounced like

    (a.) short *e.*

    b. long *e.*

    c. short *i.*

    d. schwa.

Teaching Tip
You may want to use this review test to assess what your students have learned.

There are five misspelled words in the following sentence. Cross out each misspelled word and write the correct spelling in the spaces provided.

Our ~~physical~~ education ~~instructer~~, Mrs. Stevens, ~~constently~~ tells us that people who ~~exersize~~ every day have a more positive ~~attitude~~ toward life than people who never work out.

6. *physical* _____

7. *instructor* _____

8. *constantly* _____

9. *exercise* _____

10. *attitude* _____

NAME:

DATE:

SCORE
Number Correct

_____/10

_____%

MASTERY TEST 1

Dictionary Use

Items 1–5

Use your dictionary to answer the following questions.

1. How many syllables are in the word *incongruous*? _____*four*_____

2. Where is the primary accent in the word *culmination*? _____*cul mi na' tion*_____

3. In the word *periphery,* the *i* is pronounced like
   a. long *i.*
   b. short *i.*
   c. long *e.*
   d. short *e.*

4. In the word *acquiesce,* the *i* is pronounced like
   a. long *i.*
   b. short *i.*
   c. long *e.*
   d. short *e.*

5. In the word *apostasy,* the first *a* is pronounced like
   a. long *a.*
   b. short *a.*
   c. short *o.*
   d. schwa.

Items 6–10

There are five misspelled words in the following sentence. Cross out each misspelled word and write in the correct spelling in the spaces provided.

~~Altho~~ there were legal suits filed against him, the ~~mayer~~ decided to run for reelection, but the ~~citizans~~ of our town were not ~~anxous~~ to give him a second ~~oportunity~~ at public office.

6. _____*Although*_____   8. _____*citizens*_____   10. _____*opportunity*_____

7. _____*mayor*_____   9. _____*anxious*_____

397

NAME: _____

DATE: _____

Dictionary Use

Items 1–5

Use your dictionary to answer the following questions.

1. How many syllables are in the word *pandemonium*? _____*five*_____

2. Where is the primary accent in the word *unremitting*? _____*un re mit' ting*_____

3. In the word *expatriate*, the *i* is pronounced like a
   a. long *i*.
   b. short *i*.
   c. long *e*.
   d. short *e*.

4. In the word *recapitulate*, the *i* is pronounced like a
   a. long *i*.
   b. short *i*.
   c. long *e*.
   d. short *e*.

5. In the word *frivolous*, the first *o* is pronounced like a
   a. long *o*.
   b. short *o*.
   c. short *u*.
   d. schwa.

Items 6–10

There are five misspelled words in the following sentence. Cross out each misspelled word and write in the correct spelling in the spaces provided.

We ~~regreted~~ that we could not attend your ~~anniversery~~ ~~celabration~~. Our car broke down on the freeway, ~~leaveing~~ us with no means of ~~transpertation~~.

6. ____*regretted*____   8. ____*celebration*____   10. ____*transportation*____

7. ____*anniversary*____   9. ____*leaving*____

Spelling Improvement

INTRODUCTORY ACTIVITY

See if you can circle the word that is misspelled in each of the following pairs:

(akward)	*or*	awkward
exercise	*or*	(exercize)
business	*or*	(buisness)
worried	*or*	(worryed)
(shamful)	*or*	shameful
(begining)	*or*	beginning
(partys)	*or*	parties
(sandwichs)	*or*	sandwiches
heroes	*or*	(heros)

Answers are on page 681.

Poor spelling often results from bad habits developed in the early school years. With work, such habits can be corrected. If you can write your name without misspelling it, there is no reason you can't do the same with almost any word in the English language. Following are seven steps you can take to improve your spelling.

PERSONALIZED LEARNING

Step 1: Use the Dictionary

Get into the habit of using the dictionary. When you write a paper, allow yourself time to look up the spelling of all the words you are unsure about. Do not underestimate the value of this step just because it is such a simple one. By using the dictionary, you can probably make yourself a 95 percent better speller.

ESL Tip
Many languages contain words that are similar in meaning to English but are spelled differently (cognates). However, there are some false cognates; for example, in French *librarie* sounds similar to *library,* but it means "bookstore."

Step 2: Keep a Personal Spelling List

Keep a list of words you misspell, and study those words regularly. When you accumulate additional words, you may want to use a back page of your English notebook.

> **TIP** When you have trouble spelling long words, try to break each word into syllables and see whether you can spell the syllables. For example, *misdemeanor* can be spelled easily if you can hear and spell in turn its four syllables: *mis–de–mean–or.* The word *formidable* can be spelled easily if you hear and spell in turn its four syllables: *for–mi–da–ble.* Remember, then, try to see, hear, and spell long words in terms of their syllables.

Teaching Tip
Using a word-processing program, ask students to intentionally misspell a word. Direct them to notice how the spell-checker corrects the word's spelling.

Step 3: Master Commonly Confused Words

Master the meanings and spellings of the commonly confused words on pages 000–000. Your instructor may assign twenty words for you to study at a time and give you a series of quizzes until you have mastered all the words.

Step 4: Use a Computer's Spell-Checker

Most word-processing programs feature a *spell-checker* that will identify incorrect words and suggest correct spellings. If you are unsure how to use yours, consult the program's "help" function. Spell-checkers are not fool-proof; they will fail to catch misused homonyms like the words *your* and *you're.*

Step 5: Understand Basic Spelling Rules

Teaching Tip
You may want to quiz your students on these spelling rules.

Explained briefly here are three rules that may improve your spelling. While exceptions sometimes occur, these rules hold true most of the time.

1. **Changing *y* to *i***

   When a word ends in a consonant plus *y,* change *y* to *i* when you add an ending.

try	+ ed	= tried		marry	+ es	= marries
worry	+ es	= worries		lazy	+ ness	= laziness
lucky	+ ly	= luckily		silly	+ est	= silliest

2. **Dropping or keeping final silent e**

Drop a final *e* before an ending that starts with a vowel (the vowels are *a, e, i, o,* and *u*).

hope + ing = hoping   sense + ible = sensible

fine   + est = finest   hide   + ing   = hiding

Keep the final *e* before an ending that starts with a consonant.

use + ful = useful   care   + less = careless

life + like= lifelike   settle + ment = settlement

3. **Doubling a final consonant**

Double the final consonant of a word when all the following are true:

a. The word is one syllable or is accented on the last syllable.

b. The word ends in a single consonant preceded by a single vowel.

c. The ending you are adding starts with a vowel.

sob   + ing = sobbing   big   + est   = biggest

drop   + ed = dropped   omit   + ed   = omitted

admit + ing = admitting   begin + ing   = beginning

Combine the following words and endings by applying the three rules above.

1. carry   + ed = _Carried_   6. permit + ed   = _permitted_

2. revise   + ing = _revising_   7. glide   + ing = _gliding_

3. study   + es = _studies_   8. angry   + ly   = _angrily_

4. wrap   + ing = _wrapping_   9. rebel   + ing = _rebelling_

5. horrify + ed = _horrified_   10. grudge + es   = _grudges_

Step 6: Understand Plurals

Most words form their plurals by adding -*s* to the singular.

Singular	Plural
blanket	blankets
pencil	pencils
street	streets

Some words, however, form their plurals in special ways, as shown in the rules that follow.

1. Words ending in *-s, -ss, -z, -x, -sh,* or *-ch* usually form the plural by adding *-es.*

kiss	kisses	inch	inches
box	boxes	dish	dishes

2. Words ending in a consonant plus *y* form the plural by changing *y* to *i* and adding *-es.*

party	parties	county	counties
baby	babies	city	cities

3. Some words ending in *f* change the *f* to *v* and add *-es* in the plural.

leaf	leaves	life	lives
wife	wives	yourself	yourselves

4. Some words ending in *o* form their plurals by adding *-es.*

potato	potatoes	mosquito	mosquitoes
hero	heroes	tomato	tomatoes

5. Some words of foreign origin have irregular plurals. When in doubt, check your dictionary.

antenna	antennae	crisis	crises
criterion	criteria	medium	media

6. Some words form their plurals by changing letters within the word.

man	men	foot	feet
tooth	teeth	goose	geese

7. Combined words (words made up of two or more words) form their plurals by adding *-s* to the main word.

brother-in-law	brothers-in-law
passerby	passersby

Complete these sentences by filling in the plural of the word at the left.

bus

1. Nathan told his boss that the metro _____*buses*_____ were running late this morning.

patch

2. Jorge collects military insignia _____*patches*_____ from World War II.

therapy

3. The endocrinologist told Elisa about several new ___*therapies*___ for people with diabetes.

batch

4. I baked three ___*batches*___ of chocolate chip cookies for my son's sixth-grade graduation ceremony.

reef

5. The scuba divers explored the coral ___*reefs*___ on the island.

avocado

6. Tyler mashed three ripe ___*avocados*___ for the guacamole.

twenty

7. Jarik stopped at the ATM to withdraw two ___*twenties*___ but later wondered if he should have taken out an additional twenty.

knife

8. The security guard uses a hand-held metal detector to find concealed ___*knives*___ and other weapons.

daughter-in-law

9. Lynette wishes that at least one of her ___*daughters-in-law*___ will get pregnant so that she can become a grandmother.

thesis

10. I wrote several tentative ___*these*___ for my argument essay.

Step 7: Master a Basic Word List

Make sure you can spell all the words in the following list. They are some of the words used most often in English. Your instructor may assign twenty words for you to study at a time and give you a series of quizzes until you have mastered the words.

Teaching Tip
Encourage students to use these words in their writing.

ability	although	attention
absent	always	awful
accident	among	awkward
across	angry	balance
address	animal	bargain
advertise	another	beautiful
advice	answer **20**	because
after	anxious	become
again	apply	before
against	approve	begin
all right	argue	being
almost	around	believe
a lot	attempt	between

bottom   **40**
breathe
building
business
careful
careless
cereal
certain
change
cheap
chief
children
church
cigarette
clothing
collect
color
comfortable
company
condition
conversation   **60**
daily
danger
daughter
death
decide
deposit
describe
different
direction
distance
doubt
dozen
during
each
early
earth
education
either
English
enough   **80**
entrance
everything

examine
exercise
expect
family
flower
foreign
friend
garden
general
grocery
guess
happy
heard
heavy
height
himself
holiday
house   **100**
however
hundred
hungry
important
instead
intelligence
interest
interfere
kitchen
knowledge
labor
language
laugh
leave
length
lesson
letter
listen
loneliness
making   **120**
marry
match
matter
measure
medicine

middle
might
million
minute
mistake
money
month
morning
mountain
much
needle
neglect
newspaper
noise
none   **140**
nothing
number
ocean
offer
often
omit
only
operate
opportunity
original
ought
pain
paper
pencil
people
perfect
period
personal
picture
place   **160**
pocket
possible
potato
president
pretty
problem
promise
property

psychology
public
question
quick
raise
ready
really
reason
receive
recognize
remember
repeat   **180**
restaurant
ridiculous
said
same
sandwich
send
sentence
several
shoes
should
since
sleep

smoke
something
soul
started
state
straight
street
strong   **200**
student
studying
success
suffer
surprise
teach
telephone
theory
thought
thousand
through
ticket
tired
today
together
tomorrow

tongue
tonight
touch
travel   **220**
truly
understand
unity
until
upon
usual
value
vegetable
view
visitor
voice
warning
watch
welcome
window
would
writing
written
year
yesterday   **240**

Can you find the spelling mistake in the sign pictured here?

REVIEW TEST

Use the three spelling rules to spell the following words.

1. date + ing = *dating*
2. hurry + ed   = *hurried*
3. drive + able = *drivable*
4. try   + es   = *tries*
5. swim + ing = *swimming*
6. guide + ed   = *guided*
7. happy + est = *happiest*
8. bare + ly   = *barely*

Circle the correctly spelled plural in each pair.

9. gooses   **geese**
10. richs   **riches**
11. heros   **heroes**
12. wolfs   **wolves**
13. **pantries**   pantrys
14. lifes   **lives**

Circle the correctly spelled word (from the basic word list) in each pair.

15. dout   **doubt**
16. **written**   writen
17. **a lot**   alot
18. exercize   **exercise**
19. origenal   **original**
20. anser   **answer**

NAME: _____

DATE: _____

Spelling Improvement

Use the three spelling rules to spell the following words.

1. palate + able = *palatable*
2. silly + est = *silliest*
3. fate + ful = *fateful*
4. drag + ing = *dragging*
5. plan + er = *planner*
6. healthy + ly = *healthily*
7. cause + ing = *causing*
8. prefer + ed = *preferred*

Circle the correctly spelled plural in each pair.

9. (chiefs)   chievs   12. candys   (candies)

10. sandwichs   (sandwiches)   13. (vetoes)   vetos

11. yourselfs   (yourselves)   14. supplys   (supplies)

Circle the correctly spelled word (from the basic word list) in each pair.

15. compeny   (company)   18. (opportunity)   oppertunity

16. hieght   (height)   19. (restaurant)   restarant

17. (loneliness)   lonliness   20. importent   (important)

NAME: _____

DATE: _____

MASTERY TEST 2

Spelling Improvement

Use the three spelling rules to spell the following words.

1. drip   + ed   = *dripped*
2. merry   + ment = *merriment*
3. escape + ing   = *escaping*
4. expel   + ed   = *expelled*
5. finance + ing   = *financing*
6. accuse + er   = *accuser*
7. happy   + ness = *happiness*
8. spite   + ful   = *spiteful*

Circle the correctly spelled plural in each pair.

9. indexs   (indexes)   12. (babies)   babys
10. echos   (echoes)   13. lifes   (lives)
11. (gifts)   giftes   14. scratchs   (scratches)

Circle the correctly spelled word (from the basic word list) in each pair.

15. temorrow   (tomorrow)   18. straght   (straight)
16. truely   (truly)   19. (ready)   readdy
17. (vegetable)   vegetable   20. (condition)   condishun

Omitted Words and Letters

INTRODUCTORY ACTIVITY

See if you can find the six places in the passage below where letters or words have been dropped. Supply whatever is missing.

Two glass bottle_s of apple juice lie broken *in* the supermarket aisle. Suddenly, a toddler who has gotten away from his parents appears at the head of the aisle. He spots the broken bottles and begins to run toward them. His chubby body lurches along like *a* windup toy, and his arm_s move excitedly up and down. Luckily, *an* alert shopper quickly reacts to the impending disaster and blocks the toddler's path. Then the shopper waits with *the* crying, frustrated little boy until his parents show up.

Answers are on page 681.

Some people drop small connecting words such as *a, an, in, of,* or *the* when they write. They may also drop the *-s* endings of plural nouns. Be careful not to leave out words or letters when you write, as this may confuse and irritate your readers. They may not want to read what they regard as careless work.

Finding omitted words and letters, like finding many other sentence-skills mistakes, is a matter of careful proofreading. You must develop your ability to look carefully at a page to find places where mistakes may exist.

The exercises here will give you practice in finding omitted words and omitted *-s* endings on nouns. Another section of this book (pages 159–61) gives you practice in finding omitted *-s* endings on verbs.

PERSONALIZED LEARNING

Add the missing word (*a*, *an*, *the*, *of*, or *to*) as needed.

EXAMPLE

Some people regard television as ^a tranquilizer that provides temporary relief from ^the pain and anxiety ^of modern life.

1. In the rest room, Jeff impatiently rubbed his hands under ^the mechanical dryer, which blew out feeble puffs ^of cool air.

2. On February 10, 1935, the *New York Times* reported that ^an eight-foot alligator had been dragged out of ^a city sewer by three teenage boys.

3. Lionel dressed up as ^a stuffed olive for Halloween by wearing ^a green plastic garbage bag and a red knitted cap.

4. Mrs. Chan nearly fainted when she opened ^the health insurance bill and saw ^an enormous rate increase.

5. At 4 A.M., ^the all-night supermarket where I work hosts ^an assortment of strange shoppers.

6. With ^a loud hiss, ^the inflated beach ball suddenly shrank to ^the size of ^an orange.

7. The boiling milk bubbled over the sides ^of the pot, leaving a gluey white film on ^the stove top.

8. Nadja turned ^to the answer page of the crossword book, pretended ^to herself that she hadn't, and turned back to her puzzle.

9. In order ^to avoid stepping on the hot blacktop of ^the parking lot, the barefoot boy tiptoed along the cooler white lines.

10. The messy roommates used hubcaps for ashtrays ^and scribbled graffiti on their own bathroom walls.

The Omitted -s Ending

The plural form of regular nouns usually ends in -s. One common mistake that some people make with plurals is to omit this -s ending. People who drop the ending from plurals when speaking also tend to do it when writing. This tendency is especially noticeable when the meaning of the sentence shows that a word is plural.

> Jaya and Mikael pay eight hundred dollar a month for an apartment that has only two room.

The -s ending has been omitted from *dollars* and *rooms*.

The activities that follow will help you correct the habit of omitting the -s endings from plurals.

Add -s endings where needed.

EXAMPLE

> Kyle beat me at several game of darts.

1. Can you really get fifteen shave from one of those razor blade?

2. With perfect timing, the runner's powerful leg glided smoothly over a dozen hurdle.

3. One of the strangest fad of the 1950s was the promotion of chocolate-covered ant by candy manufacturers.

4. Because pet owner abandoned them, small bands of monkey are now living in southern Florida.

5. The photographer locked themselves in steel cages in order to film great white shark in their underwater environment.

6. The breeze blew dandelion spore and dry brown leave through the air.

7. Isaiah made twelve circular cage from chicken wire and set them around his growing tomato plant.

8. The special this week is three pound of grape for eighty-nine cent.

9. The rope sole on my summer shoe have begun to disintegrate.

10. The skinny man ordered two double cheeseburger and three vanilla shake.

ESL Tip
Nonnative speakers may omit -s endings because they often don't hear them in spoken English. In addition, some languages use determiners to form the plural.

PRACTICE 2

Teaching Tip
For this activity read each sentence aloud so students can "hear" omitted -s endings.

PRACTICE 3

Write sentences that use plural forms of the following pairs of words.

EXAMPLE

file, folder *I save my computer files in folders on the desktop.*

1. gambler, casino _____

_____

2. recycling bin, bottle _____

_____

3. diver, shark _____

_____

4. sports fan, game _____

_____

5. cherry, grape _____

_____

TIP People who drop the *-s* ending on nouns also tend to omit endings on verbs. Pages 159–61 will help you correct the habit of dropping endings on verbs.

REVIEW TEST 1

In each of the following sentences, two small connecting words are needed. Write them in the spaces provided, and write a caret (∧) at each place in the sentence where a connecting word should appear.

_____*a*_____
_____*to*_____ 1. Suffering from ∧ horrible head cold, Susan felt as though she were trying ∧ breathe under water.

_____*to*_____
_____*the*_____ 2. Because he forgot the key ∧ his padlock, Cam asked ∧ gym attendant to saw the lock off his locker.

_____*a*_____
_____*of*_____ 3. The store made ∧ mistake when it sent me a letter saying that I hadn't paid any ∧ my bills for six months.

_____the_____ 4. The children laughed with delight when ˄small dog jumped on ˄cir-
_____the_____   cus clown's back.

_____of_____   5. Dr. Marini recommends that my grandfather drink one glass ˄wine
_____his_____   every day to stimulate ˄appetite and improve his circulation.

REVIEW TEST 2

Correctly write the two words missing -s endings for each sentence.

_____vessels_____ 1. The whites of Sam's eyes were red from broken blood vessel, and
_____bruises_____   his forehead was a mass of purple bruise.

_____jobs_____   2. Raya has held five different job in four different cities in the past
_____years_____   two year.

_____specialists_____ 3. I've been to several specialist, but I still don't know what's causing
_____headaches_____   these terrible headache.

_____trees_____   4. Ian watched with dread as a bulldozer began knocking down tree
_____shrubs_____   and shrub in the patch of woods next door.

_____miles_____   5. Vance was driving eighty mile an hour when two police car
_____cars_____   stopped him.

NAME: _____

DATE: _____

Omitted Words and Letters

Part 1

In the spaces provided, write in the two short connecting words needed in each sentence. Use carets (∧) within the sentences to show where these words belong.

_____to_____
_____in_____

1. Returning∧her car, Sarah found she'd left the keys∧the ignition.

_____a_____
_____a_____

2. Tiara has∧superstitious habit of dribbling the ball exactly six times before he shoots∧free throw.

_____of_____
_____the_____

3. Carefully, Joe pasted small strips∧correction tape over each typing mistake on∧page.

_____an_____
_____the_____

4. I know∧easy way to get an A in that course—just agree with everything ∧instructor says.

_____the_____
_____the_____

5. Andy dreaded∧tests he would have to undergo even more than∧operation itself.

Part 2

Correctly write the two words missing -s endings for each sentence.

_____olives_____
_____pits_____

6. Marcy ate an entire jar of olive and left a pile of pit on the coffee table.

_____teenagers_____
_____bottles_____

7. Shards of green glass glittered on the pavement where those teenager had smashed a whole six-pack of empty beer bottle.

_____trays_____
_____cuts_____

8. Our supermarket's deli section sells tray of party cold cut.

_____holes_____
_____socks_____

9. Hector's tight-fitting new shoes have worn hole in all his sock.

_____rainstorms_____
_____plants_____

10 Those heavy rainstorm have flattened all my tomato plant.

NAME: _____

DATE: _____

Omitted Words and Letters

Part 1

In the spaces provided, write in the two short connecting words needed in each sentence. Use carets (∧) within the sentences to show where these words belong.

___*to*___
___*the*___ 1. This weekend, we're going ∧ replace all the shingles that have fallen off ∧ roof.

___*at (or in)*___
___*and*___ 2. My favorite appetizers ∧ this restaurant are the crispy baked-potato skins ∧ the marinated mushrooms.

___*the*___
___*the*___ 3. The eyes of ∧ woman on ∧ billboard seemed to follow me as I drove by.

___*my*___
___*the*___ 4. When I sat down, three quarters fell out of ∧ pants pocket and rolled under ∧ sofa.

___*a*___
___*the*___ 5. My pet turtles live in ∧ large, galvanized tin tub in ∧ garage.

Part 2

Correctly write the two words missing -s endings for each sentence.

___*books*___
___*sounds*___ 6. After I had read several horror book, I began listening for weird sound.

___*desserts*___
___*cones*___ 7. I love to eat exotic dessert, but my husband likes only vanilla ice cream cone.

___*neighbors*___
___*daffodils*___ 8. All the neighbor comment on my mother's garden of roses and daffodil.

___*chairs*___
___*cans*___ 9. I slowed the car when I noticed a pair of kitchen chair that had been set out along with three garbage can.

___*bags*___
___*cookies*___ 10. The old man sold me two bag of cookie from a homemade stand in front of his house.

415

CHAPTER

33

Commonly Confused Words

INTRODUCTORY ACTIVITY

This chapter will introduce you to words that people often confuse in their writing. Circle the five words that are misspelled in the following passage. Then write their correct spellings in the spaces provided.

If your a resident of a temperate climate, you may suffer from feelings of depression in the winter and early spring. Scientists are now studying people who's moods seem to worsen in winter, and there findings show that the amount of daylight a person receives is an important factor in seasonal depression. When a person gets to little sunlight, his or her mood darkens. Its fairly easy to treat severe cases of seasonal depression; the cure involves spending a few hours a day in front of full-spectrum fluorescent lights that contain all the components of natural light.

1. _you're_
2. _whose_
3. _their_
4. _too_
5. _It's_

Answers are on page 682.

Homonyms

The commonly confused words shown below are known as *homonyms;* they have the same sounds but different meanings and spellings. Complete the activities for each set of words, and check off and study the words that give you trouble.

Common Homonyms

all ready	knew	principal	to
already	new	principle	too
			two
brake	know	right	
break	no	write	wear
			where
coarse	pair	than	
course	pear	then	weather
			whether
hear	passed	their	
here	past	there	whose
		they're	who's
hole	peace		
whole	piece	threw	your
		through	you're
its	plain		
it's	plane		

all ready	completely prepared
already	previously, before

We were *all ready* to go, for we had eaten and packed *already* that morning.

Fill in the blanks: Eliza has _____*already*_____ phoned them twice to ask if they'll be _____*all ready*_____ to go by nine o'clock.

Write sentences using *all ready* and *already.*

_____

_____

Teaching Tip
You may want to ask students to complete these activities in pairs, and then go over some of the answers in class. Encourage students to identify words that still confuse them.

> **brake**   stop; device used to slow or cease movement
>
> **break**   come apart; an interruption

Sedalia slams the *brake* pedal so hard that I'm afraid I'll *break* my neck in her car.

Fill in the blanks: I hit the _____*brake*_____ pedal so hard that my car spun around on the slick highway; luckily, there was a _____*break*_____ in the traffic at that point.

Write sentences using *brake* and *break*.

_____

_____

> **coarse**   rough; crude in manners or language
>
> **course**   part of a meal; a school subject; direction; path; certainly (with *of*)

During the *course* of my career as a teacher, I've encountered some very *coarse* students.

Fill in the blanks: As her final project in the weaving _____*course*_____, Maria made a tablecloth out of _____*coarse*_____ fibers in shades of blue.

Write sentences using *coarse* and *course*.

_____

_____

hear	perceive with the ear
here	in this place

If I *hear* another insulting ethnic joke *here,* I'll leave.

Fill in the blanks: Do you want to _____*hear*_____ about what happened to the last visitors who stayed _____*here*_____ at the count's castle?

Write sentences using *hear* and *here.*

_____

_____

hole	an empty spot
whole	entire

If there is a *hole* in the tailpipe, I'm afraid we will have to replace the *whole* exhaust assembly.

Fill in the blanks: He walked the _____*whole*_____ way, despite the _____*hole*_____ in the sole of his right shoe.

Write sentences using *hole* and *whole.*

_____

_____

ESL Tip
Nonnative speakers may also confuse *its* and *it's*. Help them to distinguish the meaning of these two words. Generate some examples.

its	**belonging to it**
it's	**shortened form for *it is* or *it has***

The kitchen floor has lost *its* shine because *it's* been used as a roller skating rink by the children.

Fill in the blanks: _____*It's*_____ foolish to wear your flimsy jacket with _____*its*_____ thin hood in this downpour.

Write sentences using *its* and *it's*.

_____

_____

knew	**past tense of *know***
new	**not old**

We *knew* that the *new* television comedy would be canceled quickly.

Fill in the blanks: Georgia _____*knew*_____ that a _____*new*_____ 54″ screen would tempt the children to spend more hours parked in front of the TV.

Write sentences using *knew* and *new*.

_____

_____

know	**to understand**
no	**a negative**

I never *know* who might drop in, even though *no* one is expected.

Fill in the blanks: Now that we _____*know*_____ how the movie ends—thanks to you—there will be _____*no*_____ pleasure in watching it.

Write sentences using *know* and *no*.

_____

_____

| pair | a set of two |
| pear | a fruit |

The dessert consisted of a *pair* of thin biscuits topped with vanilla ice cream and poached *pear* halves.

Fill in the blanks: The _____*pair*_____ of infant overalls has a _____*pear*_____ embroidered on the bib.

Write sentences using *pair* and *pear.*

_____

_____

| passed | went by; succeeded in; handed to |
| past | a time before the present; by, as in "I drove past the house" |

After Emma *passed* the driver's test, she drove *past* all her friends' houses and honked the horn.

Fill in the blanks: As his mother _____*passed*_____ around her traditional Christmas cookies, Terry remembered all the times in the _____*past*_____ when he had left some of those very cookies on a plate for Santa Claus.

Write sentences using *passed* and *past.*

_____

_____

peace	calm
piece	a part

Archie went to bed with *peace* of mind after he completed the final *piece* of his research project.

Fill in the blanks: I won't give you any _____*peace*_____ unless you share that _____*piece*_____ of coconut cake with me.

Write sentences using *peace* and *piece.*

_____

_____

plain	simple
plane	aircraft

The *plain* box contained a very expensive model *plane* kit.

Fill in the blanks: The black-and-silver _____*plane*_____ on the runway looked unique next to the _____*plain*_____ ones surrounding it.

Write sentences using *plain* and *plane.*

_____

_____

| principal | main; a person in charge of a school; amount of money borrowed |
| principle | a law or standard |

My *principal* goal in child rearing is to give my daughter strong *principles* to live by.

Fill in the blanks: The _____*principal*_____ community program Gardens for Goodness was run by volunteers whose guiding _____*principle*_____ was community building.

Write sentences using *principal* and *principle.*

_____

_____

> **TIP** It might help to remember that the *le* in *principle* is also in *rule*—the meaning of *principle.*

| right | correct; opposite of *left;* privilege |
| write | to inscribe with language; to express in literary form |

It is my *right* to refuse to *write* my name on your petition.

Fill in the blanks: As I rested my fractured _____*right*_____ arm on his desk, I asked the doctor to _____*write*_____ out a prescription for a painkiller.

Write sentences using *right* and *write.*

_____

_____

ESL Tip
In addition
to confusing
than and *then,*
nonnative
speakers may
confuse *than*
and *that;* in
Spanish *que*
has both
meanings.

than	used in comparisons
then	at that time; next; in addition to

I glared angrily at my boss, and *then* I told him our problems were more serious *than* he suspected.

Fill in the blanks: Frankenstein's monster played peacefully with the little girl; _____*then*_____ he was chased by the villagers, who were more hysterical _____*than*_____ stampeding turkeys.

Write sentences using *than* and *then.*

_____

_____

TIP   It might help to remember that *then* is a time signal.

their	belonging to them
there	at that place; a neutral word used with verbs like *is, are, was, were, have,* and *had*
they're	shortened form of *they are*

The tenants *there* are complaining because *they're* being cheated by *their* landlords.

Fill in the blanks: _____*There*_____ has been an increase in burglaries in _____*their*_____ neighborhood, so _____*they're*_____ planning to install an alarm.

Write sentences using *their, there,* and *they're.*

_____

_____

_____

threw	**past tense of** *throw*
through	**from one side to the other; finished**

When a character in a movie *threw* a watermelon *through* the window, I had to close my eyes.

Fill in the blanks: As Liam picked _____*through*_____ the clothes in the dryer, he _____*threw*_____ the still-damp towels aside.

Write sentences using *threw* and *through*.

_____

_____

to	**a verb part, as in** *to smile;* **toward, as in "I'm going to heaven"**
too	**overly, as in "The pizza was too hot"; also as in "The coffee was hot, too"**
two	**the number 2**

Aiden drove *to* the store *to* get some ginger ale. (The first *to* means *toward;* the second *to* is a verb part that goes with *get.*)

The jacket is *too* tight; the pants are tight, *too.* (The first *too* means *overly;* the second *too* means *also.*)

The *two* basketball players leaped for the jump ball. (2)

Fill in the blanks: I don't know how _____*two*_____ such different people were attracted _____*to*_____ each other and made a happy marriage, _____*too*_____.

Write sentences using *to, too,* and *two.*

_____

_____

_____

wear	to have on
where	in what place

I work at a nuclear reactor, *where* one must *wear* a radiation-detection badge at all times.

Fill in the blanks: At the restaurant _____*where*_____ I work, the waiters _____*wear*_____ cowboy hats and Western snap-front shirts.

Write sentences using *wear* and *where*.

_____

_____

weather	atmospheric conditions
whether	if it happens that; in case; if

Because of the threatening *weather,* it's not certain *whether* the outdoor concert will take place.

Fill in the blanks: The _____*weather*_____ vane was once a valuable agricultural tool, indicating _____*whether*_____ the wind was coming from the north, south, east, or west.

Write sentences using *weather* and *whether.*

_____

_____

> **whose**   belonging to whom
>
> **who's**   shortened form for *who is* and *who has*

The nutritionist *who's* the author of the latest diet book is someone *whose* ability to cash in on the latest craze is well known.

Fill in the blanks: The substitute teacher, _____*whose*_____ lack of experience was obvious, asked, "_____*Who's*_____ the person who threw that spitball?"

Write sentences using *whose* and *who's.*

_____

_____

> **your**   belonging to you
>
> **you're**   shortened form of *you are*

Since *your* family has a history of heart disease, *you're* the kind of person who should take extra health precautions.

Fill in the blanks: I may not like _____*your*_____ opinion, but _____*you're*_____ certainly entitled to express it in this class.

Write sentences using *your* and *you're.*

_____

_____

Other Words Frequently Confused

Following is a list of other words that people frequently confuse. Complete the activities for each set of words, and check off and study the ones that give you trouble.

Commonly Confused Words

a	among	desert	learn
an	between	dessert	teach
accept	beside	does	loose
except	besides	dose	lose
advice	can	fewer	quiet
advise	may	less	quite
affect	clothes	former	though
effect	cloths	latter	thought

a	**Both *a* and *an* are used before other words to mean,**
an	**approximately, *one*.**

Generally, you should use *an* before words starting with a vowel (*a, e, i, o, u*):

   an absence   an exhibit   an idol   an offer   an upgrade

Generally, you should use *a* before words starting with a consonant (all other letters):

   a pen   a ride   a digital clock   a movie   a neighbor

Fill in the blanks: In _____*an*_____ instant, he realized that _____*a*_____ diamond-patterned snake was slithering over his foot.

Write sentences using *a* and *an*.

_____

_____

| accept | receive; agree to |
| except | exclude; but |

If I accept their loan, I'll lose out on all others *except* yours.

Fill in the blanks: The crowd couldn't _____ accept _____ the judges' decision; _____ except _____ for some minor mistakes, Jones had clearly won the competition.

Write sentences using *accept* and *except.*

_____

_____

| advice | noun meaning *an opinion* |
| advise | verb meaning *to counsel, to give advice* |

Jake never listened to his parents' *advice,* and he ended up listening to a cop *advise* him of his rights.

Fill in the blanks: I asked a plumber to _____ advise _____ me, since the _____ advice _____ in the do-it-yourself book had been disastrous.

Write sentences using *advice* and *advise.*

_____

_____

Teaching Tip
You may want to ask students to complete these activities in pairs, and then go over some of the answers in class. Encourage students to identify words that still confuse them.

affect	verb meaning *to influence*
effect	verb meaning *to bring about something or to create an impression;* noun meaning *result*

On Halloween, the Winters played scary music for added *effect*; but it didn't *affect* the trick-or-treaters.

Fill in the blanks: A dangerous flooding _____*effect*_____ is created when the full moon _____*affect*_____ s the tides in the spring.

Write sentences using *affect* and *effect*.

_____

_____

among	implies three or more
between	implies only two

We selfishly divided the box of candy *between* the two of us rather than *among* all the members of the family.

Fill in the blanks: _____*Among*_____ the heads of lettuce in the bin was one with a large insect nestled _____*between*_____ the wrapper and the outer leaf.

Write sentences using *among* and *between.*

_____

_____

beside	along the side of
besides	in addition to

Fred sat *beside* Teresa. *Besides* them, there were ten other people at the party.

Fill in the blanks: _____*Besides*_____ the broken leg, he suffered a deep cut _____*beside*_____ his mouth.

Write sentences using *beside* and *besides*.

_____

_____

can	the ability to do something
may	permission or possibility

If you *can* work overtime on Saturday, you *may* take Monday off.

Fill in the blanks: Although that mole _____*can*_____ be removed, it _____*may*_____ be better to leave it alone.

Write sentences using *can* and *may*.

_____

_____

clothes	articles of dress
cloths	pieces of fabric

I tore up some old *clothes* to use as polishing *cloths.*

Fill in the blanks: Maxine used inexpensive dust _____*cloths*_____ to make _____*clothes*_____ for her daughter's doll.

Write sentences using *clothes* and *cloths.*

_____

_____

desert	noun meaning *a stretch of dry land;* verb meaning *to abandon one's post or duty*
dessert	noun meaning *last part of a meal*

Don't *desert* us now; order a sinful *dessert* along with us.

Fill in the blanks: Guests began to _____*desert*_____ the banquet room after the strawberry shortcake _____*dessert*_____ had been cleared away.

Write sentences using *desert* and *dessert.*

_____

_____

does	form of the verb *do*
dose	amount of medicine

Elena *does* not realize that a *dose* of brandy is not the best medicine for the flu.

Fill in the blanks: If this ____*dose*____ of cough syrup ____*does*____ its work, I'll be able to give my speech.

Write sentences using *does* and *dose.*

_____

_____

fewer	used with things that can be counted
less	refers to amount, value, or degree

I missed *fewer* classes than Rafael, but I wrote *less* effectively than he did.

Fill in the blanks: Larry took ____*fewer*____ chances after the accident; he was ____*less*____ sure of his driving ability.

Write sentences using *fewer* and *less.*

_____

_____

ESL Tip

Nonnative speakers may need to learn to distinguish between what can be counted and what cannot in English. "Count" nouns are for people, places and things that can be counted and made into plurals. For a list of "non-count" nouns, see Appendix A, p. 608.

| former | refers to the first of two items named |
| latter | refers to the second of two items named |

I turned down both the service station job and the shipping clerk job; the *former* involved irregular hours and the *latter* offered very low pay.

Fill in the blanks: She eats lots of raisins and strawberries; the _____*former*_____ contain iron and the _____*latter*_____ are rich in vitamin C.

Write sentences using *former* and *latter.*

_____

_____

 TIP   Be sure to distinguish *latter* from *later* (meaning *after some time*).

| learn | to gain knowledge |
| teach | to give knowledge |

After Keisha *learns* the new dance, she is going to *teach* it to me.

Fill in the blanks: If Beth can _____*learn*_____ sign language, we can _____*teach*_____ her parents how to communicate with her.

Write sentences using *learn* and *teach.*

_____

_____

loose	not fastened; not tight-fitting
lose	misplace; fail to win

I am afraid I'll *lose* my ring: it's too *loose* on my finger.

Fill in the blanks: When he discovered that his pet turtles had gotten ___*loose*___,

he worried that he might ___*lose*___ some of them.

Write sentences using *loose* and *lose*.

_____

_____

quiet	peaceful
quite	entirely; really; rather

After a busy day, the children were still not *quiet,* and their parents were *quite* tired.

Fill in the blanks: Chuck couldn't keep ___*quiet*___ about the scholarship his

daughter had won; it was ___*quite*___ an honor.

Write sentences using *quiet* and *quite.*

_____

_____

ESL Tip
Nonnative speakers may also confuse *quiet* and *quite* (and perhaps *quit*). All three words are similar except for the vowel sounds.

though	**despite the fact that**
thought	**past tense of** *think*

Though I enjoyed the dance, I *thought* the cover charge of ten dollars was too high.

Fill in the blanks: _____*Though*_____ everyone claimed the silvery object was an airplane, I _____*thought*_____ it was a UFO.

Write sentences using *though* and *thought*.

_____

_____

Incorrect Word Forms

Following is a list of incorrect word forms that people sometimes use in their writing. Complete the activities for each word, and check off and study the words that give you trouble.

Incorrect Word Forms		
being that	could of	would of
can't hardly	must of	irregardless
couldn't hardly	should of	

being that	**Incorrect! Use** *because* **or** *since.*

Teaching Tip
You may want
to do these
activities as an
entire class.

I'm going to bed now ~~being that~~ *because* I must get up early tomorrow.

Correct the following sentences.

1. ~~Being that~~ *Because* the boss heard my remark, I doubt if I'll get the promotion.
2. I'll have more cake, ~~being that~~ *because* my diet is officially over.
3. Peter knows a lot about cars, ~~being that~~ *because* his dad is a mechanic.

| can't hardly | Incorrect! Use *can hardly* or *could hardly*. |
| couldn't hardly | |

Small store owners ~~can't~~ *can* hardly afford to offer large discounts.

Correct the following sentences.

1. I ~~couldn't~~ *could* hardly enjoy myself at the theater because my brother gave me a play-by-play account of the entire movie, which he had seen three times.

2. I ~~can't~~ *can* hardly believe that I spent over 100 dollars on gasoline to fill up my SUV.

3. By one o'clock in the afternoon, everyone ~~can't~~ *can* hardly keep from falling asleep in class.

could of	
must of	Incorrect! Use *could have, must have,*
should of	*should have, would have.*
would of	

I should ~~of~~ *have* applied for a loan when my credit was good.

Correct the following sentences.

1. Shoshanna must ~~of~~ *have* painted the walls by herself.

2. You should ~~of~~ *have* left the tip on the table.

3. I would ~~of~~ *have* been glad to help if you had asked politely.

4. No one could ~~of~~ *have* predicted that accident.

> | irregardless | **Incorrect! Use *regardless*.** |

Regardless
~~Irregardless~~ of what anyone says, he will not change his mind.

Correct the following sentences.

Regardless
1. ~~Irregardless~~ of what anybody else does, I'm wearing jeans to the meeting.
Regardless
2. ~~Irregardless~~ of the weather, the parade will go on as scheduled.
Regardless
3. ~~Irregardless~~ of what my parents say, I will continue to see Elena.

REVIEW TEST 1

These sentences check your understanding of *its, it's; there, their, they're; to, too, two;* and *your, you're.* Underline the correct word in the parentheses. Rather than guess, look back at the explanations of the words when necessary.

1. As I walked (to, <u>too</u>, two) the car, I stepped in the freshly laid cement that (to, too, <u>two</u>) workers had just smoothed over.

2. (Its, <u>It's</u>) safe (<u>to</u>, too, two) park (<u>your</u>, you're) car over (<u>there</u>, their, they're).

3. "(Your, <u>You're</u>) wearing (<u>your</u>, you're) shoes on the wrong feet," Carla whispered to her little sister.

4. (There, Their, <u>They're</u>) are more secrets about (there, <u>their</u>, they're) past than (there, their, <u>they're</u>) willing to share.

5. The (to, too, <u>two</u>) of us plan to go to (<u>your</u>, you're) party, (to, <u>too</u>, two).

6. (Its, <u>It's</u>) been a long time since (<u>your</u>, you're) car has had (<u>its</u>, it's) transmission checked.

7. (<u>To</u>, Too, Two) get into the dance, (<u>your</u>, you're) friend will have to pay, (to, <u>too</u>, two).

8. (Its, <u>It's</u>) a shame that (your, <u>you're</u>) being laid off from your job (<u>there</u>, their, they're).

9. (Its, <u>It's</u>) rumored that the team has lost (<u>its</u>, it's) best pitcher for the rest of the season.

10. (There, Their, <u>They're</u>) is a mistake on (there, <u>their</u>, they're) check, so they are speaking (<u>to</u>, too, two) the manager.

The sentences that follow check your understanding of a variety of commonly confused words. Underline the correct word in the parentheses. Rather than guess, look back at the explanations of the words when necessary.

1. My sister is better at math (<u>than</u>, then) I am, but I (right, <u>write</u>) more easily.

2. I was (<u>all ready</u>, already) (<u>to</u>, too, two) sign up for (<u>your</u>, you're) (coarse, <u>course</u>) when I discovered it had (all ready, <u>already</u>) closed.

3. He is the kind of person who (<u>accepts</u>, excepts) any (<u>advice</u>, advise) he is given, even if (its, <u>it's</u>) bad.

4. I (<u>know</u>, no) you want to (<u>hear</u>, here) the (hole, <u>whole</u>) story.

5. (<u>There</u>, Their, They're) is no (<u>plain</u>, plane) paper in the house, only a (<u>pair</u>, pear) of lined notebooks.

6. Our team got a real (brake, <u>break</u>) when Pete's pop fly fell (among, <u>between</u>) (to, too, <u>two</u>) infielders for a base hit.

7. I (can't hardly, <u>can hardly</u>) (<u>hear</u>, here) the instructor in that (coarse, <u>course</u>) without making (a, <u>an</u>) effort.

8. If (your, <u>you're</u>) going to have (desert, <u>dessert</u>), pick something with (<u>fewer</u>, less) calories than chocolate cheesecake.

9. Looking (threw, <u>through</u>) his front window, Felipe could see a (<u>pair</u>, pear) of squirrels getting (there, <u>their</u>, they're) food ready for the cold (<u>weather</u>, whether) to come.

10. When I (learn, <u>teach</u>) you to drive a stick-shift, we'll go (<u>to</u>, too, two) a (<u>quiet</u>, quite) country road where (<u>there</u>, their, they're) won't be much traffic.

On separate paper, write short sentences using the ten words shown below.

there	then	you're	affect	who's
past	advise	too (meaning *also*)	its	break

NAME: _____

DATE: _____

Commonly Confused Words

For each sentence, choose the correct words and write them in the spaces provided.

you're *right*	1. When (you're, your) looking for the (right, write) career, it's helpful to talk to other people about their jobs.
pair *loose*	2. Carol keeps a special (pair, pear) of (lose, loose) trousers with tough patches on the knees to wear while gardening.
They're *right*	3. (There, Their, They're) the (right, write) size, but these screws still don't fit.
principle *whole*	4. "It's a matter of (principal, principle)," the editor said. "I won't publish anything unless it's the (hole, whole) truth."
past *all ready*	5. By twenty (passed, past) eight o'clock, I was (all ready, already) for my ten o'clock interview.
through *two*	6. We went (through, threw) the entrance to the amusement park's haunted house and were met by (to, too, two) scary-looking creatures.
passed *except*	7. We all (past, passed) the midterm exam, (accept, except) for the student who had shown up for only three classes.
can hardly *through*	8. I (can hardly, can't hardly) see (through, threw) my windshield, since it's covered with squashed bugs and grit.
Whether *loses*	9. (Weather, Whether) or not Duane (loses, looses) his license depends on the outcome of the court hearing.
effect *brakes*	10. The tragic (affect, effect) of one car's faulty (brakes, breaks) was a six-car pileup.

Commonly Confused Words

For each sentence, choose the correct words and write them in the spaces provided.

know
principles

1. We were expected to (know, no) the (principals, principles) of photosynthesis for the biology test.

You're
write

2. (You're, Your) the first professor to ask me to (right, write) a sixty-page term paper.

course
two

3. I took a (coarse, course) in speed-reading and can now read (to, too, two) books in the time it once took to read one.

already
here

4. "It's (all ready, already) eight o'clock, and nobody's (hear, here) yet," Aliyah complained.

quite
dessert

5. I ate so much that I was (quiet, quite) full before (desert, dessert) arrived.

Among
thought

6. (Among, Between) the three of us, we (though, thought) we could scrape up enough money for a large pizza.

should have
piece

7. You (should of, should have) saved the last (peace, piece) of chicken for me.

clothes
pair

8. At the back of my (cloths, clothes) closet, I discovered a (pair, pear) of old, mildewed sneakers.

Who's
beside

9. (Whose, Who's) willing to sit (beside, besides) me in the back seat?

plain
fewer

10. The (plain, plane) truth is that (fewer, less) Americans feel financially secure these days.

NAME: _____

DATE: _____

Commonly Confused Words

Cross out the two mistakes in usage in each sentence. Then write the correct words in the spaces provided.

Does
whose

1. Dose anyone know who's glasses these are?

You're
than

2. Your a lot taller then I was when I was your age.

_to_
_an_

3. Taylor went too the mall for one item but came home with a armful of packages.

accept
advice

4. I told my brother that he should except my advise on all matters.

break
coarse

5. With his fingers, Ryan attempted to brake off a piece of the crusty, course bread.

plane
Then

6. In August 1945, a lone plain passed over the city of Hiroshima. Than a living hell began for the city's inhabitants.

who's
accepted

7. Marilyn, a stay-at-home mom whose returning to college, has been excepted in the medical technicians' program.

its
among

8. We divided the huge hero sandwich, with it's layers of salami and cheese, between the three of us.

Regardless
could have

9. Irregardless of the rumors, nobody could of guessed that the business would close.

There
threw

10. Their go the obnoxious fans who through bottles onto the field.

NAME: _____

DATE: _____

SCORE
Number Correct

_____/10

_____%

MASTERY TEST 4

Commonly Confused Words

Cross out the two mistakes in usage in each sentence. Then write the correct words in the spaces provided.

_____*too*_____ _____*it's*_____	1. As soon as my jeans get ~~to~~ tight, I know ~~its~~ time to cut down on sugar.
_____*must have*_____ _____*could*_____	2. I ~~must of~~ read the assignment five times, but I ~~couldn't~~ hardly make any sense out of it.
_____*past*_____ _____*knew*_____	3. After we drove ~~passed~~ the same diner for the third time, we ~~new~~ we were lost.
_____*since*_____ _____*lose*_____	4. I put my paycheck under my pillow, ~~being that~~ I was afraid I was going to ~~loose~~ it.
_____*through*_____ _____*whether*_____	5. As the wind blew ~~threw~~ the rafters, we wondered ~~weather~~ or not the old boathouse would survive the storm.
_____*two*_____ _____*wear*_____	6. I couldn't decide on which of the ~~too~~ costumes to ~~where~~ to the party.
_____*New*_____ _____*deserts*_____	7. ~~Knew~~ ~~desserts~~ are being created all over the world by the careless destruction of trees.
_____*plain*_____ _____*than*_____	8. The ~~plane~~ brown pears in the fruit bowl are sweeter ~~then~~ they look.
_____*hear*_____ _____*its*_____	9. Although I could ~~here~~ ~~it's~~ pitiful cries, I couldn't reach the animal caught under the caved-in shed.
_____*course*_____ _____*break*_____	10. Before I took this writing ~~coarse~~, I would ~~brake~~ into a cold sweat every time I picked up a pen.

CHAPTER 34
Effective Word Choice

Teaching Tip
You may want to use this activity to assess your students' understanding of effective word choice.

INTRODUCTORY ACTIVITY

Place a check mark beside the sentence in each pair that makes more effective and appropriate use of words.

1. _____ After a bummer of a movie, we pigged out on a pizza.
   ✓ _____ After a disappointing movie, we devoured a pizza.

2. _____ Feeling blue about the death of his best buddy, Tennyson wrote the tearjerker "In Memoriam."
   ✓ _____ Mourning the death of his best friend, Tennyson wrote the moving poem "In Memoriam."

3. _____ The personality adjustment inventories will be administered on Wednesday in the Student Center.
   ✓ _____ Psychological tests will be given on Wednesday in the Student Center.

4. _____ The referee in the game, in my personal opinion, made the right decision in the situation.
   ✓ _____ I think the referee made the right decision.

Now see if you can circle the correct number in each case:

Pair (**1**, 2, 3, 4) contains a sentence with slang; pair (1, **2**, 3, 4) contains a sentence with a cliché; pair (1, 2, **3**, 4) contains a sentence with pretentious words; and pair (1, 2, 3, **4**) contains a wordy sentence.

Answers are on page 683.

Choose your words carefully when you write. Always take the time to think about your word choices, rather than simply using the first word that comes to mind. You want to develop the habit of selecting words that are appropriate and exact for your purposes. One way you can show sensitivity to language is by avoiding slang, clichés, pretentious words, and wordiness.

Slang

We often use slang expressions when we talk, because they are so vivid and colorful. However, slang is usually out of place in formal writing. Here are some examples of slang expressions:

Last night's party was a *hot mess.*

I don't want to *lay a guilt trip* on you.

My boss *dissed* me last night.

Dad *flipped out* when he learned that Jan had *totaled* the car.

Someone *ganked* Jay's new running shoes from his locker.

After the game, we *stuffed our faces* at the diner.

I finally told my parents to *get off my case.*

The movie really *grossed me out.*

Slang expressions have a number of drawbacks. They go out of date quickly, they become tiresome if used excessively in writing, and they may communicate clearly to some readers but not to others. Also, the use of slang can be an evasion of the specific details that are often needed to make one's meaning clear in writing. For example, in "Last night's party was a hot mess," the writer has not provided the specific details about the party necessary for us to understand the statement clearly. Was it the setting, the food and drink (or lack of them), the guests, the music, or the hosts that made the party such a dreadful experience? In general, you should avoid slang in your writing. If you are in doubt about whether an expression is slang, it may help to check a recently published hardbound dictionary.

Rewrite the following sentences, replacing the italicized slang words with more formal ones.

PRACTICE 1

EXAMPLE

I was *so bummed* when my teacher *got on my case.*

I was discouraged when my teacher scolded me.

1. When I confronted my ex-boyfriend about *two-timing* me, he simply shrugged and said, "*My bad.*"

When I confronted my ex-boyfriend about cheating on me, he simply shrugged and said, "It was my fault."

Teaching Tip Get students to use slang in class. They will probably hesitate, which underscores why they should avoid using slang in their writing.

ESL Tip Many nonnative speakers have learned English from their American peers. Assist these students in substituting more formal language that is more appropriate in academic writing.

2. My friend thinks that Chantel is *fly,* but I think she's too *emo.*

   My friend thinks that Chantel is attractive, but I think she's too emotional.

3. Rayna is on her cell phone *24-7,* but *it's all good.*

   Rayna is on her cell phone all the time, but that's fine.

4. Joe wanted to *blow off* the family dinner so that he could *hook up* with his friends.

   Joe wanted to quickly leave the family dinner so that he could meet his friends.

5. They were *psyched* about the party, but they knew they'd have to *bail* early.

   They were excited about the party, but they knew they'd have to leave early.

Clichés

Clichés are expressions that have been worn out through constant use. Some typical clichés are listed below.

Teaching Tip
Ask students
to offer other
clichés.

Common Clichés

all work and no play	sad but true
at a loss for words	saw the light
better late than never	short and sweet
drop in the bucket	sigh of relief
easier said than done	singing the blues
had a hard time of it	taking a big chance
in the nick of time	time and time again
in this day and age	too close for comfort
it dawned on me	too little, too late
it goes without saying	took a turn for the worse
last but not least	under the weather
make ends meet	where he (*or* she) is coming from
needless to say	word to the wise
on top of the world	work like a dog

Clichés are common in speech but make your writing seem tired and stale. Also, they are often an evasion of the specific details that you must work to provide in your writing. You should, then, avoid clichés and try to express your meaning in fresh, original ways.

Underline the cliché in each of the following sentences. Then substitute specific, fresh words for the trite expression.

EXAMPLE

My parents supported me through some <u>trying times</u>.
rough years

1. Salespeople who are rude <u>make my blood boil</u>.
   make me very angry

2. Doug has been <u>down in the dumps</u> ever since his girlfriend broke up with him.
   depressed

3. That new secretary is <u>one in a million</u>.
   extraordinary

4. We decided to hire a hall and <u>roll out the red carpet</u> in honor of our parents' silver wedding anniversary.
   have a celebration

5. The minute classes let out for the summer, I felt <u>free as a bird</u>.
   free

Write a short paragraph describing the kind of day you had. Try to put as many clichés as possible into your writing. For example, "I had a long, hard day. I had a lot to get done, and I kept my nose to the grindstone." By making yourself aware of clichés in this way, you should lessen the chance that they will appear in your writing.

Pretentious Words

Some people feel they can improve their writing by using fancy, elevated words rather than more simple, natural words. They use artificial and stilted language that more often obscures their meaning than communicates it clearly. Here are some unnatural-sounding sentences:

The football combatants left the gridiron.

His instructional technique is peerless.

PRACTICE 2

Answers will vary.

Teaching Tip
You may want to do this activity as an entire class.

PRACTICE 3

Teaching Tip
Explain what the word *pretentious* means.

Teaching Tip
Get students to talk about why they use pretentious words in their writing.

ESL Tip
What might appear pretentious or wordy in English might actually be a translation from the primary language. Help nonnative speakers use correct idiomatic English. These students can also ask a native speaker in the class to help them.

Teaching Tip
Ask students to offer other inflated words.

At the counter, we inquired about the arrival time of the aircraft.

I observed the perpetrator of the robbery depart from the retail establishment.

The same thoughts can be expressed more clearly and effectively by using plain, natural language:

The football players left the field.

He is a good instructor.

At the counter, we asked when the plane would arrive.

I saw the robber leave the store.

Following is a list of some other inflated words and the simple words that could replace them.

Inflated Words	Simpler Words
component	part
delineate	describe
facilitate	help
finalize	finish
initiate	begin
manifested	shown
subsequent to	after
endeavor	try
transmit	send

PRACTICE 4

Cross out the two pretentious words in each sentence. Then substitute clear, simple language for the pretentious words.

EXAMPLE

Yiyun was ~~terminated~~ from her ~~employment~~.

Yiyun was fired from her job.

Answers may vary.

1. I do not ~~comprehend~~ that ~~individual's~~ behavior.
   I do not understand that person's behavior.

2. He ~~eradicated~~ all the ~~imperfections~~ in his notes.
   He erased all the mistakes in his notes.

3. She ~~contemplated~~ his ~~utterance~~.
   She thought about what he said.

4 . The police officer ~~halted~~ the ~~vehicle~~.

The police officer stopped the car.

5. Inez told the counselor about her ~~vocational aspirations~~.

Inez told the counselor about her career hopes.

Wordiness

Wordiness—using more words than necessary to express a meaning—is often a sign of lazy or careless writing. Your readers may resent the extra time and energy they must spend when you have not done the work needed to make your writing direct and concise.

Here is a list of some wordy expressions that could be reduced to single words.

Wordy Form	Short Form
a large number of	many
a period of a week	a week
arrive at an agreement	agree
at an earlier point in time	before
at the present time	now
big in size	big
due to the fact that	because
during the time that	while
five in number	five
for the reason that	because
good benefit	benefit
in every instance	always
in my opinion	I think
in the event that	if
in the near future	soon
in this day and age	today
is able to	can
large in size	large
plan ahead for the future	plan
postponed until later	postponed
red in color	red
return back	return

Teaching Tip
Ask your students to cover the right column with a sheet of paper. Then ask them to replace the wordy expressions with single words.

Here are examples of wordy sentences:

> At this point in time in our country, the amount of violence seems to be increasing every day.

> I called to the children repeatedly to get their attention, but my shouts did not get any response from them.

Omitting needless words improves these sentences:

> Violence is increasing in our country.

> I called to the children repeatedly, but they didn't respond.

Rewrite the following sentences, omitting needless words.

EXAMPLE

> Starting as of the month of June, I will be working at the store on a full-time basis.
>
> *As of June, I will be working at the store full-time.*

1. In light of the fact that I am a vegetarian, I don't eat meat.
   I am a vegetarian.

2. On Tuesday of last week, I started going to college classes on a full-time basis.
   Last Tuesday, I started going to college full-time.

3. On account of the fact that all my money is gone and I am broke, I can't go to the movies.
   Since I'm broke, I can't go to the movies.

4. I repeated over and over again that I refused to go under any circumstances, no matter what.
   I repeated that I wouldn't go.

5. Regardless of what I say, regardless of what I do, my father is annoyed by my words and behavior.
   Everything I say and do annoys my father.

Certain words are italicized in the following sentences. In the space provided, identify whether the words are slang (*S*), clichés (*C*), or pretentious words (*PW*). Then replace them with more effective words.

_____C_____ 1. The sight of the car crash *sent chills down my spine.*

terrified me

_____PW_____ 2. That garbage *receptacle is at maximum capacity.*

can is full

_____S_____ 3. He thinks his apartment is *all that,* but it's in a *sketchy* part of town.

great . . . dangerous

_____S_____ 4. The town *cheapskate* finally *kicked the bucket* and left all his money to charity.

miser . . . died

_____C_____ 5. I left work ten minutes early and made it home *in no time flat.*

very quickly

_____PW_____ 6. Phyllis *lamented* her grandmother's *demise.*

mourned . . . death

_____PW_____ 7. The pitcher *hurled* the *sphere* toward the batter.

threw . . . ball

_____C_____ 8. When she got her first paycheck, Kwan was *sitting on top of the world.*

extremely proud

_____S_____ 9. After studying for three hours, we *packed it in* and *cruised over* to the pizza parlor.

stopped . . . went

_____C_____ 10. Last year's popular television star turned out to be *a flash in the pan.*

short-lived

REVIEW TEST 2

Rewrite the following sentences, omitting needless words.

1. Before I woke up this morning, while I was still asleep, I had a dream about being a celebrity.

   Before I woke up this morning, I dreamed about being a celebrity.

   _____

2. Tamika lifted up the empty suitcase, which had nothing in it, and tossed it onto the unmade bed covered with messy sheets and blankets.

   Tamika lifted the empty suitcase and tossed it onto the unmade bed.

   _____

3. While he glared at me with an unfriendly face, I just sat there silently, not saying a word.

   While he glared at me, I sat silently.

   _____

4. Whereas some people feel that athletes are worth their salaries, I feel that the value of professional sports players in this country is vastly overrated moneywise.

   I feel that professional athletes are overpaid.

   _____

5. I don't like reading the historical type of novel because this kind of book is much too long and, in addition, tends to be boring and uninteresting.

   I find historical novels long and boring.

   _____

NAME: _____

DATE: _____

Effective Word Choice

Certain words are italicized in the following sentences. In the spaces at the left, identify whether these words are slang (S), clichés (C), or pretentious words (PW). Then, in the spaces below, replace the words with more effective diction.

Answers may vary for rewritten portions.

1. After she received an A, Barbara spent the rest of the day *walking on air.*   *C*

   happy

2. A *wheeler-dealer* salesman sold Jim a *lemon.*   *S*

   fast-talking   *unreliable car*

3. Robert's *rain garment was saturated.*   *PW*

   raincoat   *soaked*

4. He is inhumane to *members of the animal kingdom.*   *PW*

   animals

5. I have a lot of studying to do, but *my brain is out to lunch.*   *S*

   I can't keep my mind on my work

6. After moving the furniture, James lay down on the couch and *went out like a light.*   *C*

   fell asleep immediately

7. My parents *hit the roof* when they saw the dented car.   *S*

   became angry

8. If I had known you were *broke,* I would have lent you the *dough.*   *S*

   lacking funds   *money*

9. I *retired my mobile telephonic device* before boarding the *aircraft.*   *PW*

   cell phone   *plane*

10. Darlene gave the collection agency a *buzz* and asked to speak to the *head honcho.*   *S*

    call   *person in charge*

NAME: _____

DATE: _____

Effective Word Choice

Answers may vary for rewritten portions.

Certain words are italicized in the following sentences. In the spaces at the left, identify whether these words are slang (S), clichés (C), or pretentious words (PW). Then, in the spaces below, replace the words with more effective diction.

_____PW_____   1. The professor *perceived* that the students *had a negative response to the idea.*

     realized   disagreed

_____S_____   2. The movie was *a total downer.*

     depressing

_____PW_____   3. At nursery school, my child is learning to *interact in a positive manner* with her *peers.*

     get along   age group

_____C_____   4. Carlos felt *like a fish out of water* at the party.

     out of place

_____C_____   5. I talked to my daughter until I was *blue in the face,* but my words *went in one ear and out the other.*

     exhausted   were ignored

_____S_____   6. Leon *stuffed his face with* so much *grub* that he felt sick.

     ate   food

_____PW_____   7. Charlene *asserted* that her story was not a *fabrication.*

     said   lie

_____S_____   8. I tried to *get some z's* for a while, but some *dimwit* kept calling my number by mistake.

     sleep   stupid person

_____c_____ 9. Teresa grabbed the rolls out of the oven *in the nick of time*.

just in time

_____s_____ 10. *Lay off* or you'll get *decked*.

Don't touch me   *smacked*

NAME: _____

DATE: _____

Effective Word Choice

The following sentences include examples of wordiness. Rewrite the sentences in the space provided, omitting needless words.

1. Because of the fact that a time span of only five seconds separates the lightning from the thunder, we may safely conclude that the storm is directly overhead.

   Since the lightning and the thunder are only five seconds apart, the storm must be

   overhead.

2. After his long twelve-mile hike, Ruben was so exhausted that, when he walked into his living room, he staggered.

   After the twelve-mile hike, Ruben staggered into his living room.

3. My mouth dropped open in amazement when I heard the startling news that Loralei had just adopted three kittens and a dog last month.

   Loralei adopted three kittens and a dog.

4. Julia was convinced in her heart that she was doing the very best thing for herself when she decided to go to art school.

   Julia felt she was doing the right thing when she decided to go to art school.

5. A sad-eyed, mournful-looking little dog, no bigger than a puppy, followed my son home and walked behind him into the house.

   A small, sad-eyed dog followed my son home.

Effective Word Choice

The following sentences include examples of wordiness. Rewrite the sentences in the space provided, omitting needless words.

Answers will vary.

1. My overflowing closet is filled to capacity with piles of useless junk that I no longer need.

    My overly stuffed closet is filled with junk.

    _____

2. The leaky faucet that wouldn't stop dripping annoyed and bothered me all night long.

    The dripping faucet annoyed me all night.

    _____

3. If you are having difficulties with your schoolwork and are not keeping up with your assignments, you should budget your time so that you stick to a schedule.

    If you are having trouble keeping up with your studies, you should budget your time.

    _____

4. The main idea that I am trying to get across in this essay is that no driver of a motor vehicle should be permitted to drive while handling a phone and texting.

    Drivers should not text and drive.

    _____

5. When we looked as if we didn't believe him, Frank got upset and indignant and insisted that his story was a true incident that had really happened.

    When we looked skeptical, Frank insisted that his story was true.

457

Reinforcement of the Skills

PART 3

Introduction

To reinforce the sentence skills presented in Part Two, this part of the book—Part Three—provides combined mastery tests, editing and proofreading tests, and combined editing tests. The *combined mastery tests* will strengthen your understanding of important related skills. *Editing and proofreading tests* offer practice in finding and correcting one kind of error in a brief passage. *Combined editing tests* then offer similar practice—except that each contains a variety of mistakes. Five of these tests feature "real-world" documents—résumés, cover letters, and a job application—so you can apply your skills to situations you are likely to encounter outside the classroom. The tests in Part Three will help you become a skilled editor and proofreader. All too often, students can correct mistakes in practice sentences but are unable to do so in their own writing. You must learn to look carefully for sentence-skills errors and to make close checking a habit.

Write a paragraph in which you describe the advertisement shown here to someone who has never seen it. Don't forget to proofread your paragraph for sentence-skills mistakes. Use the Checklist for Sentence Skills on the inside back cover of your book.

Combined Mastery Tests

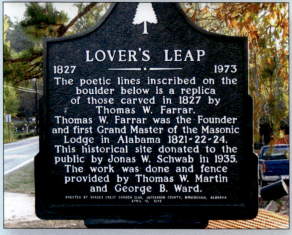

Teaching Tip
Ask students to complete these writing prompts in class.

Can you find the sentence-skills errors in the two signs above? Rewrite the wording of each sign so that it is grammatically correct. Would you pay less attention to a sign that was confusing or grammatically incorrect? Why or why not?

Fragments and Run-Ons

Each of the word groups below is numbered. In the space provided, write C if a word group is a complete sentence, write F if it is a fragment, and write R-O if it is a run-on.

1. _C_
2. _F_
3. _R-O_
4. _F_
5. _C_
6. _F_
7. _C_
8. _F_
9. _R-O_
10. _C_
11. _F_
12. _C_
13. _R-O_
14. _F_
15. _C_
16. _C_
17. _F_
18. _R-O_
19. _C_
20. _F_

[1]A few years ago, an experiment was conducted in Germany. [2]To determine how dependent people are on their televisions. [3]The researchers chose 184 volunteers these people were paid to give up watching television for one year. [4]During the first months of the experiment. [5]Most of the subjects did not suffer any ill effects. [6]Or complain that they were missing anything important. [7]The volunteers said they had more free time, and they were grateful for the extra hours. [8]Spending them on reading, paying attention to their children, or visiting friends. [9]Another month went by, suddenly things took a turn for the worse. [10]The subjects became tense and restless. [11]In addition, quarreled frequently with other family members. [12]Their tension continued until the subjects were permitted to watch television again. [13]Nobody in the experiment survived an entire year without televisions, in fact, the longest anyone lasted was five months. [14]As soon as the televisions were turned on again. [15]The symptoms of anxiety disappeared. [16]This experiment suggests a conclusion. [17]Which would be dangerous to ignore. [18]Television is habit-forming it may be even more habit-forming than cigarettes or drugs. [19]Perhaps the screen should carry a warning label. [20]That says, "Caution—This Product May Be Hazardous to Your Health."

NAME: _____

DATE: _____

NAME: _____

DATE: _____

Fragments and Run-Ons

In the space provided, indicate whether each item below contains a fragment (F) or a run-on (R-O). Then correct the error.

_____F_____ 1. Eleni's excitement grew. As she approached the door to her sister's apartment. She knew she was walking into a surprise party.

_____R-O_____ 2. Doug tried to grasp his new soft contact lens; it was like trying to pick up a drop of water. The slippery little lens escaped from his fingers again and again.

_____F_____ 3. Wearing huge, bright-blue sunglasses with gold wires, the new instructor strolled into class. One student whispered that she looked like a human dragonfly.

_____F_____ 4. Because Sara carried a large tote bag when she went shopping, store security guards regarded her with suspicion. They had been trained to watch out for shoplifters with extra-large purses.

_____R-O_____ 5. I watched my sister put away the produce. First she washed all the apples and grapes, and then she rubbed the onions with a towel.

_____F_____ 6. The crowd became silent. Then, while the drums rolled, the acrobat attempted a triple somersault in midair.

_____R-O_____ 7. Irene peeled off the itchy wool knee socks; she stared at the vertical red ridges the tight socks had left on the tender skin. With a sigh, she massaged her sore shins.

_____F_____ 8. Although they sip nectar for energy, butterflies never eat anything substantial. They have no need to because their bodies don't grow. Their only function is to mate.

_____R-O_____ 9. When he smelled the acrid odor, Lee rushed to the kitchen. He popped up the smoking bread, but something was still aflame in the toaster's crumb tray.

_____F_____ 10. Joanne painted her fingernails with pale-pink nail polish and put a slightly deeper shade of pink on her toenails. Her fingertips and toes looked as if they were blushing.

SCORE
Number Correct
_____/10
_____%

COMBINED MASTERY TEST 1

Verbs

Each sentence contains a mistake involving (1) standard English or irregular verb forms, (2) subject-verb agreement, or (3) consistent verb tense. Cross out the incorrect verb and write the correct form in the space provided.

_____*torn*_____ 1. The razor-sharp coral had ~~tore~~ a hole in the hull of the flimsy boat.

_____*warn*_____ 2. The signs in the park ~~warns~~ that litterers will be fined.

_____*start*_____ 3. I cringe in embarrassment every time I ~~started~~ my car because its broken exhaust makes it sound like a person wheezing.

_____*keeps*_____ 4. Somebody in the dorm ~~keep~~ the radio on all night long.

_____*hesitates*_____ 5. Mike wants to overcome his shyness but ~~hesitated~~ to meet new people because he fears he won't have anything interesting to say.

_____*expects*_____ 6. Each of my professors ~~expect~~ a term paper to be turned in before the holidays.

_____*sworn*_____ 7. The judge reminded the witness that she had ~~swore~~ to tell the truth.

_____*was*_____ 8. There ~~were~~ a heavy load of soggy clothes to be washed when Janet got home from camp.

_____*typed*_____ 9. Jenny ~~type~~ the final word and fell back in her chair; her report was finished at last.

_____*bitten*_____ 10. Someone called Elaine at the office to tell her that her son had been ~~bit~~ by a stray dog.

NAME: _____

DATE: _____

COMBINED MASTERY TEST 2

Verbs

Each sentence contains a mistake involving (1) standard English or irregular verb forms, (2) subject-verb agreement, or (3) consistent verb tense. Cross out the incorrect verb and write the correct form in the space provided.

___hidden___   1. Karen searched for the fifty-dollar bill she had ~~hid~~ in the thick book.

___feel___   2. After I leave the dentist's office, my jaw and mouth ~~feels~~ numb.

___reeled___   3. After he stirred the thick paint for several minutes, Walt ~~reels~~ backward as the strong fumes made his head spin.

___grown___   4. My nephew must have ~~grew~~ a foot since I last saw him.

___were___   5. Hovering overhead at the scene of the accident ~~was~~ several traffic helicopters.

___stung___   6. When the nurse gave him the injection, Alfonso felt as if a huge bee had just ~~stinged~~ him.

___talked___   7. When I caught my little boy pulling the dog's ears, I sat him down and ~~talk~~ to him about being kind to animals.

___sold___   8. McDonald's has ~~selled~~ enough hamburgers to reach to the moon.

___motioned___   9. When he noticed Helen holding only a quart of milk, the man ahead of her in the checkout line ~~motions~~ for Helen to take his place.

___were___   10. Leaping out of the patrol car ~~was~~ two police officers with their guns drawn.

NAME: _____

DATE: _____

Pronouns

Choose the sentence in each pair that uses pronouns correctly. Then write the letter of that sentence in the space provided.

_____*b*_____ 1. a. If anyone wants to try out for the women's softball team, they should go to the practice field today after class.

b. If anyone wants to try out for the women's softball team, she should go to the practice field today after class.

_____*b*_____ 2. a. At the hardware store, they told me I would need specially treated lumber to build an outdoor deck.

b. At the hardware store, the clerks told me I would need specially treated lumber to build an outdoor deck.

_____*a*_____ 3. a. Those greedy squirrels ate all the sunflower seeds in the bird feeder.

b. Them greedy squirrels ate all the sunflower seeds in the bird feeder.

_____*b*_____ 4. a. Each of the student waiters had to write a report about their employment experience.

b. Each of the student waiters had to write a report about his employment experience.

_____*b*_____ 5. a. We liked the price of the house, but you would have to do too much work to make it livable.

b. We liked the price of the house, but we would have to do too much work to make it livable.

NAME: _____

DATE: _____

COMBINED MASTERY TEST 2

Pronouns

In the spaces provided, write PE *for each of the nine sentences that contain pronoun errors. Write* C *for the sentence that uses pronouns correctly. Then cross out each pronoun error and write the correction above it.*

_____PE_____ 1. Jason, Nimi, and ~~me~~ *I* are studying for the math test together.

_____PE_____ 2. Someone in the women's Pilates class complained that ~~their~~ *her* back was sore.

_____PE_____ 3. If I fail the final exam, does that mean that ~~you~~ *I* automatically fail the course?

_____C_____ 4. Each of the twins had her name printed on her sweatshirt.

_____PE_____ 5. I enjoy my word-processing work, but ~~you~~ *I* tend to have eyestrain by the end

of the day.

_____PE_____ 6. When Juanita got her job as a waitress, ~~they~~ *the manager* told her she would have to buy

her own uniforms.

_____PE_____ 7. Tom read the paper while eating his lunch and then threw the rest of ~~it~~ *the paper* away.

_____PE_____ 8. At the minicar racetrack, I proved that my reaction time was quicker than

~~her's~~ *hers*.

_____PE_____ 9. If anyone walks to the cafeteria, will ~~they~~ *he or she* bring me a cup of coffee?

_____PE_____ 10. Since I've been up until two o'clock the last few nights and feel fine, I'm

convinced that ~~you~~ *I* need only six hours of sleep.

NAME: _____

DATE: _____

Faulty Modifiers and Parallelism

In the spaces provided, indicate whether each sentence contains a misplaced modifier (MM), a dangling modifier (DM), or faulty parallelism (FP). Then correct the error in the space under the sentence.

Rewritten sentences may vary.

_____FP_____ 1. Before she went to bed, Ameera brushed her teeth, took out her contact lenses, and was setting the alarm for six o'clock.

set the alarm for six o'clock.

_____DM_____ 2. After enjoying the fabulous meal, the bill dampened our spirits.

After we had enjoyed the fabulous meal,

_____MM_____ 3. Carmen read an article about exploring outer space in the dentist's office.

In the dentist's office, Carmen read an article about exploring outer space.

_____DM_____ 4. While watching my favorite show, the smoke detector emitted a whistle.

While I was watching my favorite show,

_____FP_____ 5. The wind blew over the table, and the cups and plates were scattered.

and scattered the cups and plates.

_____DM_____ 6. Backfiring and stalling, we realized that the car needed a tune-up.

We realized that the car, which was backfiring and stalling, needed a tune-up.

_____DM_____ 7. Being left-handed, scissors seem upside down to me.

Since I am left-handed,

_____MM_____ 8. A month ago, the Wallaces moved into the house next door from Ohio.

A month ago, the Wallaces moved from Ohio into the house next door.

_____MM_____ 9. I found an antique necklace in the old carton worn by my grandmother.

In the carton, I found an antique necklace worn by my grandmother.

_____FP_____ 10. The salesperson said we could pay for the furniture with cash, a credit card, or writing a check.

or a check.

467

NAME: _____

DATE: _____

COMBINED MASTERY TEST 2

Faulty Modifiers and Parallelism

Rewritten
sentences
may vary.

In the spaces provided, indicate whether each sentence contains a misplaced modifier (MM), a dangling modifier (DM), or faulty parallelism (FP). Then correct the error in the space under the sentence.

_____DM_____ 1. Working in her vegetable garden, a bee stung Erika on the shoulder.

Working in her vegetable garden, Erika was stung on the shoulder by a bee.

_____FP_____ 2. Our boss is smart and with plenty of dedication but coldhearted.

dedicated

_____MM_____ 3. Mr. Harris said he would be leaving the company during the meeting.

During the meeting, Mr. Harris said he would be leaving the company.

_____MM_____ 4. The delivery boy placed the pizza on the couch with anchovies.

The delivery boy placed the pizza with anchovies on the couch.

_____DM_____ 5. Covered with wavy lines, the technician suggested that our flatscreen needed adjusting.

The technician suggested that our flatscreen, which was covered with wavy lines,

needed adjusting.

_____DM_____ 6. Twisted in several places, Karl straightened out the garden hose.

Karl straightened out the garden hose, which was twisted in several places.

_____FP_____ 7. As I waited, the assistant typed, filed, and was talking on the telephone.

talked on the telephone

_____MM_____ 8. Jasmin saw a dress she was dying to wear in the department store window.

In the department store window, Jasmin saw a dress she was dying to wear.

_____DM_____ 9. Weighing three tons, my neighbor pays an added registration fee for his truck.

My neighbor pays an added registration fee for his truck, which weighs three tons.

_____MM_____ 10. While sitting in the traffic jam, I almost read the entire newspaper.

While sitting in the traffic jam, I read almost the entire newspaper.

NAME: _____

DATE: _____

Capital Letters and Punctuation

Each of the following sentences contains an error in capitalization or punctuation. Refer to the box below and write, in the space provided, the letter identifying the error. Then correct the error.

a. missing capital letter	c. missing quotation marks
b. missing apostrophe	d. missing comma

_____d_____ 1. The elevator was stuck for more than an hour, but all the passengers stayed calm.

_____c_____ 2. "When I step onto dry land after weeks at sea," said the sailor, "I feel as if I'm standing on a sponge."

_____a_____ 3. He doesn't talk about it much, but my uncle has been a member of Alcoholics Anonymous for ten years.

_____b_____ 4. My parents always ask me where I'm going and when I'll be home.

_____d_____ 5. Whenever Paul eats peanuts, he leaves a pile of shells on the table.

_____b_____ 6. In the school's "food band," the children used pumpkins for drums and bags of pretzels for shakers.

_____c_____ 7. "Stop making a fool of yourself," said Emily, "and put that sword back on the wall."

_____d_____ 8. The sweating, straining horses neared the finish line.

_____d_____ 9. The children, a costumed horde of Halloween pirates and zombies, fanned out through the neighborhood.

_____a_____ 10. I decided to drink a glass of milk rather than order a Pepsi.

469

NAME: _____

DATE: _____

Capital Letters and Punctuation

Each of the following sentences contains an error in capitalization or punctuation. Refer to the box below and write, in the space provided, the letter identifying the error. Then correct the error.

a. missing capital letter	c. missing quotation marks
b. missing apostrophe	d. missing comma

__a, d__ 1. During their cross-country trip to the ~~w~~est ~~c~~oast, Mariah and Latham decided to stop at the Grand ~~c~~anyon.

__b__ 2. The schools' janitor received nothing but a plaque for his loyal service.

__c__ 3. "Using these plastic chopsticks," said Lauren, "is like trying to eat soup with a fork."

__a__ 4. Some people don't know that ~~m~~anhattan is an island.

__d__ 5. Wanting to make a good impression, Bill shaved twice before his date.

__a__ 6. Crumpled sheets of paper and a spilled bottle of ~~a~~dvil littered Laurie's desk.

__c__ 7. "German," said the history instructor, "came within one vote of being named the official language of the United States."

__b__ 8. My mother's checks are printed with pictures of endangered wild animals.

__d__ 9. Feeling brave and silly at the same time, Art volunteered to go onstage and help the magician.

__a__ 10. My Uncle Tyrone fought in the Battle of the Bulge during World ~~w~~ar II.

NAME: _____

DATE: _____

SCORE
Number Correct
_____/10
_____%

Word Use

Each of the following sentences contains a mistake, identified in the left-hand margin. Underline the mistake and then correct it in the space provided.

Rewritten versions may vary.

Slang

1. At 50 percent off, this suit is a real steal.
   bargain _____

Wordiness

2. Although Yvette was on a reducing diet to lose weight, she splurged on some ice cream.
   diet _____

Cliché

3. Dan knew his friends would be green with envy when they saw his new car.
   envious _____

Pretentious language

4. The director's cinematographic repertoire was sublime.
   range of film was inspiring _____

Adverb error

5. I tied the knot slow, making sure it wouldn't come loose again.
   slowly _____

Error in comparison

6. I felt more thirstier than I ever had in my life.
   thirstier _____

Confused word

7. "Its the tallest building in the world," the guide said.
   It's _____

Confused word

8. There parking the car in one of those enclosed garages.
   They're _____

Confused word

9. Who's car alarm keeps going off?
   whose _____

Confused word

10. If you keep your wallet sticking out of a rear pocket, your bound to lose it to a pickpocket.
    you're _____

NAME: _____

DATE: _____

Word Use

Rewritten versions may vary.

Each of the following sentences contains a mistake, identified in the left-hand margin. Underline the mistake and then correct it in the space provided.

Slang

1. After her workout at the gym, Moira was too <u>wiped out</u> to walk home.
   tired

Wordiness

2. I asked the attendant at the gas station to fill up <u>my tank with gas as far as possible.</u>
   my gas tank

Cliché

3. I try to <u>turn the other cheek</u> instead of getting angry.
   stay calm

Pretentious language

4. The autumn <u>hues signified the commencement</u> of another academic year.
   The fall means the start of another school year.

Adverb error

5. Zander didn't think he did <u>good</u> on the final.
   well

Error in comparison

6. Sharon was <u>more happier</u> after she quit her job.
   happier

Confused word

7. Charles knew he was <u>all ready</u> late for the interview, so he ran up the steps.
   already

Confused word

8. Michael's <u>principle</u> fault is his tendency to lose his temper.
   principal

Confused word

9. The rabbi tried to <u>advice</u> the confused teenager.
   advise

Confused word

10. Before the operation, the surgeon will carefully study <u>you're</u> x-rays.
    your

472

Editing and Proofreading Tests

---

holiday plans

hollygl_49@ccemail.com

To: sbecker@workemail.net

hi mom

i may have to work during the holidays. its real busy & they said they can't spare any of us so im not sure when ill be able to come down to visit. will talk to my manager tomorrow & see if i can get a 1/2 day. no promises. if i cant make it please save a piece of Dad's pecan pie for me. and some of your stuffing!!?!

love

H

---

re: holiday plans

sbecker@workemail.net

To: hollygl_49@ccemail.com

That's ok sweetie I understand. Try not to work to hard. I know you need the money but we're all worried your burning the candle at both ends :(Of course i'll save you some stuffing there should be plenty of leftovers. If you cant come Dad will send you a whole pie. :P

xoxo
Mom

How many sentence-skills errors can you locate in the e-mail correspondence shown above? Why do you think it is common for people to pay less attention to sentence skills when writing e-mails?

Teaching Tip
Ask students to complete this writing prompt in class.

The passages in this section can be used in either of two ways: as editing tests or as guided composition activities.

As Editing Tests

Each passage contains a number of mistakes involving a single sentence skill. For example, the first passage (on page 473) contains five fragments. Your instructor may ask you to proofread the passage to locate the five fragments. Spaces are provided at the bottom of the passage for you to indicate which word groups are fragments. Your instructor may also have you correct the errors, either in the text itself or separately. Depending on how well you do, you may also be asked to edit the second passage for fragments.

There are two passages for each skill area, and there are twelve skills covered in all. Here is a list of the skill areas:

Test 1	Fragments
Test 2	Fragments
Test 3	Run-Ons (Fused Sentences)
Test 4	Run-Ons (Comma Splices)
Test 5	Standard English Verbs
Test 6	Irregular Verbs
Test 7	Faulty Parallelism
Test 8	Capital Letters
Test 9	Apostrophes
Test 10	Quotation Marks
Test 11	Commas
Test 12	Commonly Confused Words

As Guided Composition Activities

To give practice in proofreading as well, your instructor may ask you to do more than correct the skill mistakes in each passage. You may be asked to rewrite the passage, correcting it for skill mistakes *and* copying the rest of the passage perfectly. Should you miss one skill mistake or make even one copying mistake (for example, omitting a word, dropping a verb ending, misspelling a word, or misplacing an apostrophe), you may be asked to rewrite a different passage that deals with the same skill.

Here is how you will proceed. You will start with fragments, rewriting the first passage, proofreading your paper carefully, and then showing it to your instructor. He or she will check it quickly to see that all the fragments have been corrected and that you have made no copying mistakes. If the passage is error-free, you can proceed to run-ons.

If you have made even a single mistake, the instructor may question you briefly to see if you recognize and understand it. (Perhaps he or she will put a check mark beside the line in which the mistake appears and then ask if you can correct it.) You may then be asked to write the second passage under a particular skill.

You will complete the program in guided composition when you have successfully worked through all twelve skills. Completing the twelve skills will strengthen your understanding of the skills, increase your ability to transfer the skills to actual writing situations, and markedly improve your proofreading.

In working on the passages, note the following points:

a. For each skill, you will be told how many mistakes appear in the passages. If you have trouble finding the mistakes, turn back and review the pages in this book that explain the skill in question.

b. Here is an effective way to go about correcting a passage: First, read it over quickly. Look for and mark off mistakes in the skill area involved. For example, in your first reading of a passage that has five fragments, you may locate and mark only three fragments. Next, reread the passage carefully so you can find the remaining errors in the skill in question. Finally, make notes in the margin about how to correct each mistake. Only at this point should you begin to rewrite the passage.

c. Be sure to proofread with care after you finish a passage. Go over your writing word for word, looking for careless errors. Remember that you may be asked to do another passage involving the same skill if you make even one mistake.

NAME: _____

DATE: _____

Fragments

Mistakes in each passage: 5

Passage A

[1]During the year I spent cleaning pools for a living. [2]I found that dogs could be either the joy or the terror of my workdays. [3]I particularly enjoyed seeing Bugsy. [4]A Jack Russell terrier who loved chasing water as it squirted from the garden hose. [5]I also looked forward to seeing the twin chocolate Labrador retrievers Butch and Sundance. [6]Every week, they would take turns dropping tennis balls at my feet. [7]Then bounding away, sometimes into the pool. [8]Unfortunately, some of the pets on my route were not so welcoming. [9]One day, while I was cleaning a filter. [10]A German shepherd surprised me by stepping through a hole in the screened-in porch. [11]I turned to face the dog and spoke to it in low, soothing tones. [12]Suddenly, the dog bared its huge, yellow teeth and lunged at me. [13]Fueled by adrenaline. [14]I managed to leap over the chain-link fence in a single bound. [15]From then on, I asked to be formally introduced to family watchdogs before I set foot in their backyard.

Word groups with fragments: ___1___ ___4___ ___7___ ___9___ ___13___

Corrections (wording may vary):

Passage A

During the year I spent cleaning pools for a living, I found that dogs . . .

I particularly enjoyed seeing Bugsy, a Jack Russell terrier . . .

Every week, they would take turns dropping tennis balls at my feet, then bounding away . . .

One day, while I was cleaning a filter, a German shepherd . . .

Fueled by adrenaline, I managed to leap over . . .

Passage B

[1]Walter won't admit that he is out of a job. [2]Last month, Walter was laid off by the insurance company. [3]Where he had been working as a salesperson. [4]But Walter hasn't told anyone. [5]And continues to go downtown every morning. [6]Waiting at the bus stop with his newspaper folded under his arm and his briefcase on the sidewalk beside him. [7]He looks at his watch as if he were worried about being late. [8]When he gets downtown. [9]Walter goes to an arcade. [10]He plays video games for an hour or two. [11]Then he visits the public library. [12]To lose himself in the latest mystery novel. [13]At five o'clock, Walter catches the bus for home. [14]His newspaper is still folded under his arm. [15]He has not opened the paper to look at the want ads. [16]I feel sorry for Walter, but I understand his desire to live in a fantasy world.

Word groups with fragments: ___3___ ___5___ ___6___ ___8___ ___12___

Corrections (wording may vary):

Passage B

Last month, Walter was laid off by the insurance company where he had been . . .

But Walter hasn't told anyone and continues to go downtown every morning.

Waiting at the bus stop with his newspaper folded under his arm and his briefcase on the sidewalk beside him, he looks at his watch . . .

When he gets downtown, Walter goes to an arcade.

Then he visits the public library to lose himself in the latest mystery novel.

NAME: _____

DATE: _____

Fragments

Mistakes in each passage: 5

Passage A

¹Are you experiencing car trouble? ²Is your transmission acting up or your muffler rattling? ³By tuning in to your radio. ⁴You can find help. ⁵A weekly program mixing serious car advice and humor. ⁶Has become popular all over the country. ⁷The show began in Boston when a radio station invited a number of mechanics to take live calls on car problems. ⁸Although a large group of mechanics was expected. ⁹Only Tom and Ray showed up. ¹⁰Tom and Ray are brothers who liked fixing cars in their spare time. ¹¹And had opened a garage. ¹²The response to the show was so great that it became a weekly event. ¹³With no advance preparation, Tom and Ray take all car questions that the audience asks. ¹⁴They delight listeners with their wit, their down-to-earth philosophy, and their good car sense.

Word groups with fragments: ___3___ ___5___ ___6___ ___8___ ___11___

Corrections:

Passage A

> *By tuning in to your radio, you can find . . .*

> *A weekly program mixing serious car advice and humor has become . . .*

> *Although a large group of mechanics was expected, only Tom and Ray . . .*

> *Tom and Ray are brothers who liked fixing cars in their spare time and had opened . . .*

Passage B

¹For thousands of years. ²Humans have used certain animals to carry heavy loads. ³The ox, the elephant, the donkey, and the mule are examples of these "beasts of burden." ⁴Although they have a reputation for being stubborn at times. ⁵These animals normally work very hard for long hours. ⁶One beast of burden, however, refuses to be overworked. ⁷The llama, a South American animal much like the camel, has very definite ideas of what it's willing to do. ⁸Knowing just how much it can carry comfortably, the llama will sit down and refuse to budge. ⁹If even an extra half pound is placed on its back. ¹⁰In addition, the llama will carry a burden only a certain distance. ¹¹For example, nothing will persuade it to continue. ¹²After it travels twenty miles. ¹³Sometimes its owner tries to prod the llama with a stick once the animal has decided to quit. ¹⁴When it is disturbed in this fashion. ¹⁵The llama has an unusual way of striking back. ¹⁶It puckers its lips and spits in its owner's face.

Word groups with fragments: _____1_____ _____4_____ _____9_____ _____12_____ _____14_____

Corrections:

Passage B

For thousands of years, humans have . . .

Although they have a reputation for being stubborn at times, these animals . . .

Knowing just how much it can carry comfortably, the llama will sit down and refuse to budge if even an extra half pound . . .

For example, nothing will persuade it to continue after it travels . . .

When it is disturbed in this fashion, the llama has . . .

NAME: _____

DATE: _____

TEST 3

Run-Ons (Fused Sentences)

Mistakes in each passage: 5

Passage A

[1]How would you like to live in the most expensive part of New York City without paying any rent? [2]Recently, a fifty-five-year-old man did just that he set up residence on a thirty-five-foot-long traffic island in the middle of the FDR Drive. [3]His furniture was made from storage crates his stove was an oil drum. [4]His only protection from the weather was the elevated highway overhead. [5]People waved to him as they drove by some even donated food and beer. [6]Local television stations soon began to feature this unusual resident. [7]He was pictured relaxed and reading a book the traffic streamed by on both sides of him. [8]Social workers wanted to put him in a city shelter he refused, saying it was a pigpen. [9]Finally, the police took him away, but not before he had become a hero. [10]He had achieved the ultimate American dream; for a little while, he had beaten the system.

Sentences with run-ons: ___2___ ___3___ ___5___ ___7___ ___8___

Corrections (wording may vary):

Passage A

Recently, a fifty-five-year-old man did just that. He . . .

His furniture was made from storage crates; his . . .

People waved to him as they drove by, and some . . .

He was pictured relaxed and reading a book. The . . .

Social workers wanted to put him in a city shelter, but he . . .

Passage B

[1]Many common expressions have interesting origins one of these is the phrase "the real McCoy." [2]In fact, the real McCoy was not really named McCoy he was a farmer's son from Indiana named Norman Selby who got tired of farming and left home around 1890. [3]One year later, he began a boxing career, using the name Kid McCoy soon he was fighting every month. [4]He was willing to meet any opponent anywhere in the country. [5]He soon had a long string of victories most of them were knockouts. [6]A number of other fighters began calling themselves "Kid McCoy," thinking the name would get them more boxing matches and more money. [7]However, on March 24, 1899, the Kid defeated another great champion the fight lasted twenty rounds and cost the Kid three broken ribs. [8]In his report of the fight, the *San Francisco Examiner*'s sportswriter wrote, "Now you've seen the real McCoy!" [9]From them on, people have said "the real McCoy" whenever they have meant that something is not a fake.

Sentences with run-ons: ___1___ ___2___ ___3___ ___5___ ___7___

Corrections (wording may vary):

Passage B

Many common expressions have interesting origins. One . . .

In fact, the real McCoy was not really named McCoy. He . . .

One year later, he began a boxing career, using the name Kid McCoy, and soon . . .

He soon had a long string of victories; most . . .

However, on March 24, 1899, the Kid defeated another great champion. The . . .

NAME: _____

DATE: _____

Run-Ons (Comma Splices)

Mistakes in each passage: 5

Passage A

[1]One evening, a group of friends got together for a dinner party, after dinner they began telling stories. [2]As the evening wore on, the stories got wilder and wilder. [3]Some of the stories involved unusual scientific experiments, others were about strange creatures, such as werewolves and vampires. [4]The friends competed to see who could tell the most exciting story. [5]In the group was a young woman named Mary, who had recently been married. [6]When Mary went to bed that night, she had a frightening dream. [7]In her dream, a hideous monster came to life, she saw it bending over her. [8]The next morning, Mary told her dream to her new husband, Percy, he persuaded her to write it down. [9]After he read her account, Percy was so impressed that he urged her to expand it into a book. [10]The novel that Mary Shelley finally wrote, *Frankenstein,* is probably the most famous horror story of all time, hundreds of monster movies have been inspired by it.

Sentences with run-ons: ___1___ ___3___ ___7___ ___8___ ___10___

Corrections (wording may vary):

Passage A

One evening, a group of friends got together for a dinner party, and after . . .

Some of the stories involved unusual scientific experiments; others . . .

In her dream, a hideous monster came to life, and . . .

The next morning, Mary told her dream to her new husband, Percy. He . . .

The novel that Mary Shelley finally wrote, <u>Frankenstein,</u> is probably the most famous horror story of all time. Hundreds . . .

Passage B

[1]One of the coldest, snowiest, windiest places on earth is not in the Himalayas or the Arctic, it is on Mount Washington in the pleasant state of New Hampshire. [2]The top of this rather small mountain experiences hurricane-force winds, they slice through human beings like razors. [3]The world's highest wind speed was recorded on the mountain one April day in 1934, that speed was 231 miles per hour! [4]Snow is always possible, even in summer. [5]Supercooled fog, called *rime,* hugs the mountain, there is almost no visibility 55 percent of the time. [6]At least sixty people have lost their lives on Mount Washington in the last hundred years. [7]However, people continue to climb to the top, some take the auto route, open only in the summer. [8]The more foolish attempt to climb the mountain at other times of the year. [9]A warning sign on the mountain reads "People don't die on this mountain. They perish."

Sentences with run-ons: __1__ __2__ __3__ __5__ __7__

Corrections (wording may vary):

Passage B

One of the coldest, snowiest, windiest places on earth is not in the Himalayas or the Arctic; it . . .

The top of this rather small mountain experiences hurricane-force winds, which slice . . .

The world's highest wind speed was recorded on the mountain one April day in 1934. That . . .

Supercooled fog, called <u>rime,</u> hugs the mountain, and there . . .

However, people continue to climb to the top. Some . . .

NAME: _____

DATE: _____

TEST 5

Standard English Verbs

Mistakes in each passage: 5

Passage A

¹The scenes of flood damage on the network news tonight were horrible. ²Two weeks of steady, heavy rains had ~~raise~~ *raised* the waters of several midwestern rivers past the levels of their banks, and they had ~~overflow~~ *overflowed* onto the surrounding houses and fields. ³Extensive damage had resulted, with some buildings actually torn from their foundations and ~~suck~~ *sucked* helplessly into the swirling flood waters. ⁴Here and there a rooftop could be seen as it ~~float~~ *floated* by with one or two frightened survivors clinging to it. ⁵Many people's lives had been disrupted, and many millions of dollars' worth of damage had been ~~cause~~ *caused*. ⁶It would be several days yet until the waters receded. ⁷They say that "into every life some rain must fall," but no one could have predicted all this.

Sentences with nonstandard verbs (write the number of a sentence twice if it contains two nonstandard verbs):

___2___ ___2___ ___3___ ___4___ ___5___

Passage B

[1]I read an odd item in the newspaper about a pet snail that nearly ~~frighten~~ *frightened* its owner to death. [2]Actually, the owner did not even know that he had been keeping a pet. [3]The snail, which was very fancy, had been ~~varnish~~ *varnished* and made into an ornament. [4]Its owner had bought the snail at a gift shop and ~~place~~ *placed* it on his desk. [5]Apparently the snail was not really dead but had been ~~seal~~ *sealed* into hibernation by the varnish and was just asleep. [6]Three years later, when its owner accidentally ~~knock~~ *knocked* the ornament off his desk, chipping the varnish, the snail woke up. [7]It began moving across the desk as the owner was writing a letter and startled him so much that he jumped out of his chair. [8]The owner is feeding his former ornament on cabbage before taking it back to the seashore, where it belongs.

Sentences with nonstandard verbs: __*1*__ __*3*__ __*4*__ __*5*__ __*6*__

NAME: _____

DATE: _____

TEST 6

Irregular Verbs

Mistakes in each passage: 10

Passage A

[1]Vince ~~choosed~~ *chose* a job as a supermarket cashier because he liked people. [2]After what happened yesterday, though, he isn't so sure. [3]First, after he had ~~rang~~ *rung* up her entire order, a woman ~~throwed~~ *threw* a handful of coupons at him. [4]Then she ~~give~~ *gave* him a hard time when he ~~shown~~ *showed* her that a few had expired. [5]She ~~begun~~ *began* making nasty comments about stupid supermarket help. [6]The next person in line thought Vince had put the eggs on the bottom and would not leave until Vince had ~~took~~ *taken* everything out of the bag and repacked it. [7]Later, two teenagers ~~fighted~~ *fought* with Vince over the price of a bag of candy, saying that it could never have ~~rose~~ *risen* so high in one week. [8]Vince ~~gone~~ *went* home in a terrible mood, wondering how he would ever force himself to go in the next day.

Sentences with irregular verbs (write the number of a sentence twice if it contains two irregular verbs):

___1___ ___3___ ___3___ ___4___ ___4___

___5___ ___6___ ___7___ ___7___ ___8___

486

Passage B

[1] A college professor has ~~wrote~~ *written* a book about what he calls "urban legends." [2] These are folktales that have ~~spreaded~~ *spread* all over the country. [3] They usually have a moral to teach or touch on a basic fear ~~holded~~ *held* by many Americans. [4] In one of the more gruesome legends, a young couple parked on a lovers' lane ~~heared~~ *heard* a report on the car radio about a one-armed killer stalking the area. [5] The couple ~~leaved~~ *left*; after they ~~gotten~~ *got* home, they ~~seen~~ *saw* a bloody hook hanging on the car's door handle. [6] The moral of this urban legend? [7] Don't park on lovers' lanes! [8] In another story, a man ~~finded~~ *found* pieces of fried rat mixed in with his take-out fried chicken. [9] The professor has ~~sayed~~ *said* that this story is related to the American consumer's fear of being contaminated with some dreadful substance. [10] No one can find a factual basis for any of these stories, although many tellers have ~~swore~~ *sworn* they are true.

Sentences with irregular verbs (write the number of a sentence twice or more if it contains two or more irregular verbs):

1	2	3	4	5
5	5	8	9	10

NAME: _____

DATE: _____

Faulty Parallelism

Mistakes in each passage: 5

Passage A

¹Some people today are "survivalists." ²These people, because they fear some great disaster in the near future (like economic collapse or nuclear war), are preparing for a catastrophe. ³Hoarding food, stockpiling weapons, and the achievement of self-sufficiency are some of the activities of survivalists. ⁴In Arkansas, for example, one group has built a mountain fortress to defend its supplies and staying safe. ⁵Arkansas, the group feels, is the best place to be for several reasons: it is an unlikely target for nuclear attack; it offers plentiful supplies of food and water; a good climate. ⁶Some Americans feel that the attitude of survivalists is selfish and greed. ⁷These people say that such a philosophy turns society into a "dog-eat-dog" race for life. ⁸Other people believe that, after a nuclear war, the world, with radiation and where there would be disease, wouldn't be worth living in.

Sentences with faulty parallelism: ___3___ ___4___ ___5___ ___6___ ___8___

Corrections:

Passage A

    achieving self-sufficiency

    to stay

    it has a good climate

    greedy

    with radiation and disease

Passage B

[1]Doing your own painting is easy, inexpensive, and you will enjoy it, if you know what you're doing. [2]First, you must properly prepare the surface you are going to paint. [3]This means removing dirt, rust, or mildew. [4]Also, you should get rid of loose paint and to fill any cracks with spackling compound. [5]Primers or sealers should be used on bare wood or over stains. [6]Another important rule to follow is to buy the right amount of paint. [7]Some painters guess how much paint they need and are failing to measure accurately. [8]Then they might buy too little or an excessive amount of paint for the job. [9]The result is making an extra trip to the hardware store or to have a lot of paint left over. [10]Finally, before you begin to paint, read the directions on the container. [11]These hints will save you time and money.

Sentences with faulty parallelism: ___1___ ___4___ ___7___ ___8___ ___9___

Corrections:

Passage B

  enjoyable
  and fill
  and fail
  too much paint
  or having

NAME: _____

DATE: _____

TEST 8

Capital Letters

Mistakes in each passage: 10

Passage A

¹Last november, joanne fisher put her turkey in the oven and drove into town to see the thanksgiving day parade. ²Parking downtown was almost impossible. ³Joanne saw the sign warning visitors not to park on the private lot at Tenth street, but she thought that, since it was a holiday, nobody would mind. ⁴When she returned after the parade, her nissan was missing. ⁵It had been towed to a lot in a faraway section of the city. ⁶When Joanne finally got to the lot, the owner insisted on a cash payment and refused to accept a check for fifty dollars. ⁷Joanne lost her temper and screamed, "all right, go ahead and call the police, but I'm going to drive out of here!" ⁸A police car arrived immediately, and Joanne had visions of spending the next month in jail. ⁹But the officer, sgt. Roberts of the Sixteenth precinct, agreed to cash her check so she could pay the fine. ¹⁰Joanne was delighted until she got home and found that her turkey had burned to a crisp.

Sentences with missing capitals (write the number of a sentence as many times as it contains capitalization mistakes):

____1____ ____1____ ____1____ ____1____ ____1____

____3____ ____4____ ____7____ ____9____ ____9____

490

Passage B

¹Liza never realized how expensive it was going to be to have a baby. ²Before the birth, Liza visited dr. willis, her obstetrician, eleven times. ³After her baby was born, a multiple-page bill from valley hospital arrived. ⁴There were charges not only from Liza's own doctor but also from a Dr. David, the anesthesiologist, and a Dr. Ripley, the hospital pediatrician. ⁵After she had brought the baby home, Liza found herself visiting the supermarket more often. ⁶She loaded her cart with boxes of expensive pampers, dozens of cans of E enfamil formula, and lots of smaller items like johnson's baby powder and oil. ⁷Liza realized that she would have to return to her job at richmond insurance company if she were going to make ends meet.

Sentences with missing capitals (write the number of a sentence as many times as it contains capitalization mistakes):

2	2	3	3	6
6	6	7	7	7

NAME: _____

DATE: _____

TEST 9

Apostrophes

Mistakes in each passage: 10

Passage A

[1]Two Minnesota brothers, Ed and Norman, are engaged in a war. [2]It all started when Ed's wife gave him a pair of pants that didn't fit. [3]Ed wrapped up the pants and put them under Norman's Christmas tree. [4]When Norman opened the box, he recognized the unwanted pants. [5]The next year, he gave them back to Ed, sealed in a heavy carton tied with knotted ropes. [6]The War of the Pants was on. [7]Each year, on one of the brother's birthdays, or on Christmas, the dreaded pants reappear. [8]The war has escalated, however, with each brother trying to top the other's pants delivery of the previous year. [9]Two years ago, Norman bought an old safe, put the pants in it, welded it shut, and delivered it to Ed's house. [10]Somehow, Ed retrieved the pants (one of the war's rules is that the pants must not be damaged). [11]Last year, Ed went to an auto junkyard. [12]The pants were placed in an ancient Ford's backseat, and the car went through the huge auto crusher. [13]On his birthday, Norman found a four-foot square of smashed metal on his doorstep; he knew it could only be Ed's doing and the pants must be inside. [14]Norman is still trying to get at the pants and prepare next year's "topper."

Sentences with missing apostrophes (write the number of a sentence twice if it contains two missing apostrophes):

2	2	3	7	8
9	10	12	13	14

Passage B

[1]Sometimes I wish the telephone hadn't been invented. [2]When I come home after class or work, all I'm interested in is lying down for an hour's nap. [3]Typically, five minutes after I've closed my eyes, the phone rings. [4]Someone I've never met is trying to sell me a subscription to *Newsweek*. [5]Or I may have just begun to mix up some hamburger when I hear the phone's insistent ringing. [6]It won't stop, so I wipe the ground meat off my hands and run to answer it. [7]Yesterday, when this happened, it was my mother's best friend. [8]She'd found some clothes in her attic. [9]And she wanted to know if I could use an old evening gown. [10]Even if it's someone I want to talk to, the phone call always seems to come at a bad time.

Sentences with missing apostrophes (write the number of a sentence twice if it contains two missing apostrophes):

1	2	2	3	4
5	6	7	8	10

NAME: _____

DATE: _____

Quotation Marks

Quotation marks needed in each passage: 10 pairs

Passage A

¹Malik and Lucinda were driving home from the movies when they saw a man staggering along the street. ²"I wonder if he's all right," Malik said.

³"Let's stop and find out," Lucinda suggested. ⁴They caught up to the man, who was leaning against a tree.

⁵"Are you OK?" Lucinda asked. ⁶"Is there anything we can do?"

⁷"There's nothing the matter," the man answered. ⁸"I guess I had a few too many after work. ⁹Now I can't seem to find my front door."

¹⁰Malik steadied the man and asked, "Do you live anywhere near here?"

¹¹He responded, "Yes, if this is Forrest Avenue, I live at 3619."

¹²Malik and Lucinda walked the man to his door, where he fumbled in his pockets, took out a key, and began to stab wildly with it at the lock.

¹³"Let me hold your key, and I'll let you in," Malik offered.

¹⁴The man refused, saying, "Oh, no, I'll hold the key—you hold the house."

Sentences or sentence groups with missing quotation marks:

2	3	5	6	7
8–9	10	11	13	14

Passage B

[1]When Martin found a large dent in his new Nissan, he took it back to the agency. [2]"We can fix that," the smiling mechanic said. [3]"Just leave it for a few days."

[4]Martin waited three days and then called. [5]"Is my car ready yet?" he asked.

[6]"Not yet," the mechanic said. [7]"Try the end of the week."

[8]The following Monday, Martin called again. [9]"Is my car ready?"

[10]The mechanic sounded apologetic. [11]"Not yet. [12]We'll have it Friday for sure."

[13]On Friday, when Martin picked up his car, he noticed a new cigarette burn in the upholstery. [14]"We'll fix that, but it takes a week to match the material," the manager said.

[15]Martin took the bus home, fuming. [16]A few minutes later, the phone rang. [17]It was the mechanic. [18]"You left your owner's card here. [19]Want us to mail it?"

[20]Martin said, "You may as well keep it. [21]You're using the car more than I am."

Sentences or sentence groups with missing quotation marks:

2	3	5	6	7
9	11–12	14	18–19	20–21

NAME: _____

DATE: _____

Commas

Mistakes in each passage: 10

Passage A

¹Eben has a hard time studying,so he plays little games to get himself to finish his assignments. ²He will begin by saying to himself, "Whenever I finish an as-signment,I'll give myself a prize." ³Eben has all kinds of prizes; his favorites are watching a detective show on television,drinking a cold beer, and spending an hour with his partner. ⁴Of course,too many of these rewards will mean that Eben won't get much else done. ⁵So Eben uses other strategies. ⁶He will,for example,set the stove timer for one hour. ⁷Then he will work at the kitchen table until the timer buzzes. ⁸Also,he puts a paper clip on every tenth page of the book he is studying. ⁹As soon as he reaches the clip,he can take a five-minute break.

Sentences with missing commas (write the number of a sentence as many times as it contains comma mistakes):

1	2	2	3	3
4	6	6	8	9

Passage B

[1] When Andrei gets bored at his receptionist job, he has a whole assortment of things to do to pass the time until five o'clock. [2] First, he cleans out his desk. [3] Desk drawers, he has found, contain all sorts of hidden treasure. [4] Andrei found an old CD belonging to the temp who had previously worked from his desk, a faded Bart Simpson keychain, and a couple of dog-eared Terry Pratchett novels the last time he "cleaned house." [5] The books kept him occupied during lunch break for a week. [6] He has also become a master at fixing paper jams in the company's ancient, temperamental copy machine. [7] On particularly slow days, Andrei checks his e-mails or posts entries on his blog. [8] Lately, however, he has had to deactivate his Skype account in order to actually get work done.

Sentences with missing commas (write the number of a sentence as many times as it contains comma mistakes):

1	2	3	3	4
4	6	7	8	8

NAME: _____

DATE: _____

Commonly Confused Words

Mistakes in each passage: 10

Passage A

[1]Did you know that until, May 5 of every year, ~~your~~ *you're* not really working for yourself? [2]A group in Washington, D.C., has learned that it takes workers an average of four months and four days to earn enough to pay ~~there~~ *their* taxes. [3]The group found in ~~it's~~ *its* study that taxes eat up 34 percent of all the income in the United States. [4]So, if workers used their entire income for taxes, they would not be ~~threw~~ *through* paying them until May. [5]~~Being that~~ *Because* May 5 is the first day people really work for themselves, the study group has some ~~advise~~ *advice*. [6]It would like a bill ~~past~~ *passed* naming May 5 "Tax Freedom Day." [7]On that day, you would give yourself a ~~brake~~ *break*, ~~irregardless~~ *regardless* of how hard you worked. [8]For, from May 5 on, you would finally be your own boss.

Sentences with commonly confused words (write the number of a sentence twice if it contains two commonly confused words):

1	*2*	*3*	*4*	*4*
5	*5*	*6*	*7*	*7*

Passage B

¹Did you ever daydream about writing ~~you're~~ *your* life story? ²Do you think that your life is ~~to~~ *too* dull, or you can't ~~right~~ *write* ? ³Everyone's life story is filled with fascinating events, and writing them down in the best way you know can give you a sense of accomplishment and, perhaps, leave a valuable inheritance to your family. ⁴The first thing to do is to buy a ~~lose~~ *loose*-leaf notebook. ⁵Each page of the book should be titled with a significant milestone in your life—from your first dog to your proudest moment. ⁶You should ~~than~~ *then* jot down a few key words in the book whenever a memory comes back to you. ⁷The idea is *not* to begin with "I was born . . ." and try to write a chronological history of your ~~hole~~ *whole* life. ⁸Just delve into your ~~passed~~ *past* at random; one memory will trigger another. ⁹Writing will become ~~quiet~~ *quite* easy after a while. ¹⁰~~Its~~ *It's* also important to write in your own language. ¹¹~~Plane~~ *Plain*, honest writing is the goal.

Sentences with commonly confused words (write the number of a sentence twice if it contains two commonly confused words):

1	*2*	*2*	*4*	*6*
7	*8*	*9*	*10*	*11*

Combined Editing Tests

Did you grow up in a rural, suburban, or urban area? Write down some of the advantages and disadvantages of living in that environment, and then use the most interesting or important ideas to develop a paragraph about your home town or city.

Editing for Sentence-Skills Mistakes

The seventeen editing tests in this section will give you practice in finding a variety of sentence-skills mistakes. People often find it hard to edit a paper carefully. They have put so much work, or so little work, into their writing that it's almost painful for them to look at it one more time. You may simply have to *force* yourself to edit. Remember that eliminating sentence-skills mistakes will improve an average paper and help ensure a high grade on a good paper. Further, as you get into the habit of editing your papers, you will get into the habit of using the sentence skills consistently. They are a basic part of clear, effective writing.

NAME: _____

DATE: _____

COMBINED EDITING TEST 1

Identify the five mistakes in paper format in the student paper that follows. From the box below, choose the letter that describes each mistake and write it in the space provided.

> a. The title should not be underlined.
>
> b. The title should not be set off in quotation marks.
>
> c. There should not be a period at the end of a title.
>
> d. All the major words in a title should be capitalized.
>
> e. The title should just be several words and not a complete sentence.
>
> f. The first sentence of a paper should stand independent of the title.
>
> g. A line should be skipped between the title and the first line of the paper.
>
> h. The first line of a paper should be indented.
>
> i. The left *and* right margins should be one-inch wide.
>
> j. Hyphenation should occur only between syllables.

> ### "Noise in quiet places"
>
> The quietest places make the most noise. A library is one example. If you crinkle a bag of potato chips in a quiet library, people will stare at you as if you had lit a firecracker under their feet. But you could drop a food tray in a noisy cafeteria and nobody would pay much attention to you. Then, there's the cough in church. A muffled cough bounces off the stained glass windows like a sonic boom. But you could cough up a storm at a rock concert and not one head would turn. Finally, elevators are hushed places. If you ask someone for the time in an elevator, everyone will look at his or her watch. Ask the same question on a busy city street, and chances are that no one will hear you. It takes a quiet place for sound to be really heard.

1. ___*b*___   2. ___*d*___   3. ___*g*___   4. ___*h*___   5. ___*i*___

NAME: _____

DATE: _____

COMBINED EDITING TEST 2

Identify the five mistakes in paper format in the student paper that follows. From the box below, choose the letter that describes each mistake and write it in the space provided.

> a. The title should not be underlined.
>
> b. The title should not be set off in quotation marks.
>
> c. There should not be a period at the end of a title.
>
> d. All the major words in a title should be capitalized.
>
> e. The title should just be several words and not a complete sentence.
>
> f. The first sentence of a paper should stand independent of the title.
>
> g. A line should be skipped between the title and the first line of the paper.
>
> h. The first line of a paper should be indented.
>
> i. The left *and* right margins should be one-inch wide.
>
> j. Hyphenation should occur only between syllables.

"Bus Travel"

It is the worst way to get to work or school in the morning. First, the weather is unpredictable. Many bus stops are not sheltered, and the rider must wait in rain, cold, and heat. Another unpleasant thing about bus riding is the wait. It seems that buses are on time only when you're running late. Next, there is the matter of having exact change. If you try to enter without the right change, the driver looks at you as if your hair is on fire. Last, there's the problem of finding a seat. The elderly folks are saving seats for their friends, and most people look as if they will bite your nose if you sit next to them. Chances are that the only seat open will be next to a strange-smelling person with a wild look in his eye.

1. ___*a*___   2. ___*b*___   3. ___*f*___   4. ___*g*___   5. ___*j*___

503

NAME: _____

DATE: _____

COMBINED EDITING TEST 3

Identify the sentence-skills mistakes at the underlined spots in the selection that follows. From the box below, choose the letter that describes each mistake and write it in the space provided. (The same mistake may appear more than once.) Then, in the spaces provided between the lines, correct each mistake.

> a. fragment
>
> b. run-on
>
> c. dropped verb ending
>
> d. misplaced modifier
>
> e. incorrect end mark
>
> f. missing apostrophe
>
> g. missing comma

Methods of correction may vary.

When I was little, I really *hated* hate visiting Aunt Martha. She was my *father's* fathers sister and
   (1)   (2)

had never married. Since she had no children of her own, she *didn't* didnt know what to do

with me. I remember the *sofa, which was dark brown and filled with horsehair,* sofa in her living room, which was dark brown. And filled
   (3)   (4)   (5)

with horsehair. Every time I sat on it, I got stabbed by the stuffing. I had to plump up
   (5)

the cushion when I got *up. Otherwise* up otherwise, she would frown at me. She would sit opposite
   (6)

me with a stiff smile on her face and ask me what I was *learning* learn in school or if I had been
   (7)

good. good? *They were things* Things that I didn't want to talk about. I couldn't wait to say *good-bye, plump* good-bye plump
   (8)   (9)   (10)

up the cushion, and escape.

1. ___c___   3. ___f___   5. ___a___   7. ___c___   9. ___a___

2. ___f___   4. ___d___   6. ___b___   8. ___e___   10. ___g___

COMBINED EDITING TEST 4

Identify the sentence-skills mistakes at the underlined spots in the selection that follows. From the box below, choose the letter that describes each mistake and write it in the space provided. The same mistake may appear more than once. Then, in the space provided between the lines, correct each mistake. In one case, there is no mistake.

a. fragment	f. missing capital letter
b. run-on	g. missing quotation marks
c. dropped verb ending	h. missing comma
d. irregular verb mistake	i. no mistake
e. dangling modifier	

In the unending war of people versus machines, a blow was ~~striked~~ by a *[struck]* man in ~~pennsylvania~~ *[Pennsylvania]* who had a run-in with an ATM. At about ten o'clock one night, he approached the machine to make a withdrawal. After he inserted his ~~card the~~ *[card, the]* machine spat it back at him. The same thing then ~~happen~~ *[happened]* a second time. He put his card in ~~again, this~~ *[again. This]* time the machine kept the ~~card. And~~ *[card and]* did not give him the money he had requested. By now the customer was totally disgusted. ~~Hitting~~ the machine with all his strength, *[Even after he hit]* the card still did not come back. This was the last ~~straw he~~ *[straw. He]* grabbed a metal trash can and proceeded to beat up the machine. Unfortunately, the machine still had his card, and the man was later arrested and charged with causing $2,500 worth of damage. He didn't mind. "I've always had such trouble with ~~ATMs, he~~ *[ATMs," he]* said, "that it was time for me to get even."

Methods of correction may vary.

1. __d__   3. __h__   5. __b__   7. __e__   9. __i__

2. __f__   4. __c__   6. __a__   8. __b__   10. __g__

NAME: _____

DATE: _____

COMBINED EDITING TEST 5

Identify the sentence-skills mistakes at the underlined spots in the selection that follows. From the box below, choose the letter that describes each mistake and write it in the space provided. The same mistake may appear more than once. Then, in the space provided between the lines, correct each mistake. In one case, there is no mistake.

a. fragment	e. missing capital letter
b. run-on	f. mistake in subject-verb agreement
c. omitted word	g. irregular verb mistake
d. misplaced modifier	h. no mistake

Methods of correction may vary.

asked to name

If you were ~~asked name~~ our most dangerous insects or animals, which ones
1

would you list? You might jot down black widow spiders, rattlesnakes, and

scorpions, just

~~scorpions. Just~~ to list a few. However, our Public Enemy Number One is the
2

bee. More

~~bee, more~~ people die from bee and wasp stings every year than are killed by
3

New

animals. Not too long ago in Camden, ~~new~~ Jersey, over twenty-seven people
4

taken   *after being*

were ~~took~~ to hospitals ~~who had been~~ stung by a runaway swarm of bees. The
5   6

were

bees, which had escaped from a hive that had fallen off a truck, ~~was~~ maddened
7

by what they thought was an attack on their hive and would have destroyed

hive, bees

anyone who came near them. If there is no threat to their ~~hive. Bees~~ will usually not
8   6

sting, for once they lose their stingers, they die. Wasps and yellow jackets, how-

are

ever, ~~is~~ able to sting repeatedly with no danger to themselves. For that 1 percent of
10

the population allergic to insect stings, such attacks can be fatal.

1. __c__   3. __b__   5. __g__   7. __f__   9. __a__

2. __a__   4. __e__   6. __d__   8. __h__   10. __f__

NAME: _____

DATE: _____

COMBINED EDITING TEST 6

Identify the sentence-skills mistakes at the underlined spots in the selection that follows. From the box below, choose the letter that describes each mistake and write it in the space provided. The same mistake may appear more than once. Then, in the space provided between the lines, correct each mistake. In one case, there is no mistake.

a. fragment	e. mistake in parallelism
b. run-on	f. apostrophe mistake
c. irregular verb mistake	g. missing comma
d. inconsistent verb tense	h. no mistake

                                          room,
As she walked into the dimly lit ~~room.~~ Julie was more nervous than usual.
                              1   *gone*
This was the first time she had ever ~~went~~ to a singles bar, and she wasn't sure
                         2   *eyes'*
how she should behave. She stood near the back wall and waited for her ~~eyes~~ to
                                   3   4
adjust to the darkness. In a minute or so, she could see what was going on. Several
                              bar. Nearby,
women were sipping drinks at the ~~bar, nearby~~ unattached men were whispering
                                  5   *tables,*
and glancing at the women. Seated at small ~~tables~~ pairs of men and women were
                              smiling   6
talking animatedly and ~~smiled~~ at each other. They looked as if they were having a
                 watched   7   *ladies'*
good time. Julie ~~watches~~ for a few minutes and then went to find the ~~ladies~~ room.
                  8   *thought, could*   9
Joining the singles scene, she ~~thought could~~ wait just a little longer.
                                10

Methods of correction may vary.

1. __a__   3. __h__   5. __b__   7. __e__   9. __f__

2. __c__   4. __f__   6. __g__   8. __d__   10. __g__

507

NAME: _____

DATE: _____

COMBINED EDITING TEST 7

Identify the sentence-skills mistakes at the underlined spots in the selection that follows. From the box below, choose the letter that describes each mistake and write it in the space provided. The same mistake may appear more than once. Then, in the space provided between the lines, correct each mistake. In one case, there is no mistake.

a. fragment	f. mistake in parallelism
b. run-on	g. missing comma
c. mistake in pronoun reference	h. missing quotation marks
d. mistake in subject-verb agreement	i. no mistake
e. dangling modifier	

Methods of correction may vary.

Recently, a friend of mine has been on a crusade to reinvent the modern office. "Every day," she says "I *says,"I* 1feel as though my soul has been sucked out through a straw. *straw."* One of her pet peeves are *is* fluorescent lighting. Fluttering and faintly blue, *Because it is fluttering and faintly blue,* she complains that the lighting in her office leaves her drained and practically hypnotized. She also rails against her cubicle workspace. Which *workspace, which* is so cramped that she feels claustrophobic after only an hour or two at work. At the same time, it don't *doesn't* provide any meaningful privacy, she *privacy; she* can still hear every conversation within a twenty-foot radius. Worst of all, they *her employers* have no intention of remodeling the office, even though workers in more modern, ergonomic, and ecologically friendlier *friendly* workplaces tend to be more productive.

1. __g__   3. __d__   5. __i__   7. __d__   9. __c__

2. __h__   4. __e__   6. __a__   8. __b__   10. __f__

NAME: _____

DATE: _____

COMBINED EDITING TEST 8

Identify the sentence-skills mistakes at the underlined spots in the selection that follows. From the box below, choose the letter that describes each mistake and write it in the space provided. The same mistake may appear more than once. Then, in the space provided between the lines, correct each mistake. In one case, there is no mistake.

a. fragment	e. apostrophe mistake
b. run-on	f. missing comma
c. mistake in parallelism	g. dropped -*ly* ending (adverb mistake)
d. missing capital letter	h. no mistake

What would you do if you were driving to work during the morning rush hour and you saw a family of geese blocking the road? The adult ~~canada~~ *Canada* goose¹ and her goslings had been standing on the west side of River Drive, looking at the water on the other side. When a slight break in traffic ~~occurred the~~ *occurred, the*² mother started across. Traffic ~~slowed brakes~~ *slowed, brakes*³ squealed, and all the babies except one made it to the other side. That one stood right in the middle of the ~~highway. Blocking~~ *highway, blocking* one of the lanes.⁴ Meanwhile, the mother goose honked ~~helpless~~ *helplessly*⁵ from the safety of the riverbank. Not a single car moved as all the ~~driver's~~ *drivers*⁶ waited for the gosling to cross. Then, ~~just~~⁷ as one driver opened his door to get out and rescue the little ~~one the~~ *one, the*⁸ mother gave a deafening ~~honk. the~~ *honk. The*⁹ gosling quickly hurried over to join her. The drivers restarted their motors and ~~were continuing~~ *continued*¹⁰ on their way, proud that they had helped save a life.

Methods of correction may vary.

1. __d__   3. __f__   5. __g__   7. __h__   9. __b__

2. __f__   4. __a__   6. __e__   8. __f__   10. __c__

509

NAME: _____

DATE: _____

COMBINED EDITING TEST 9

Locate and correct the ten sentence-skills mistakes in the following passage. The mistakes are listed in the box below. As you locate each mistake, write the number of the word group containing it in the space provided. Then, in the spaces between the lines, correct each mistake.

> 2 fragments ___7___ ___15___
>
> 2 run-ons ___4___ ___6___
>
> 1 irregular verb mistake ___2___
>
> 1 dangling modifier ___4___
>
> 1 missing comma after a quotation ___25___
>
> 2 missing apostrophes ___10___ ___17___
>
> 1 missing quotation mark ___12___

¹Our daughter was a happy, pleasant child until she reached the age of two. ²Then, she ~~begun~~ *began* having tantrums—and not just any tantrums. ³No, Tasha would thrash on the floor, knock her head against the wall, and let out a bloodcurdling scream that pierced our eardrums like an ice pick. ⁴Consulting our child care books, ~~the decision was made~~ *we decided* to ignore the ~~screams, Tasha's~~ *screams. Tasha's* attempts to capture our attention might then stop. ⁵Have you ever tried to ignore a toddler whose howls and moans make the walls shake? ⁶We had to think of something before Tasha drove us to a pair of padded ~~cells, it~~ *cells. It* was then that I came up with a notion of a "screaming place." ⁷The next time that Tasha started the low, sirenlike wail that preceded a full-fledged ~~scream.~~ *scream, I* ⁸I carried her to the bathroom. ⁹I said, "Tasha, this is your screaming place. ¹⁰It's small, so ~~youll~~ *you'll* hear your screams nice and loud. ¹¹You can

roll around on the soft carpet. 12You can even get a drink if your throat feels ~~dry.~~ *dry."*

13Tasha came barreling out of the bathroom in about ten seconds—screaming—and I gently pushed her back in. 14When she came out the next time, she had stopped screaming. 15After a few more episodes like ~~this.~~ *this, Tasha's* 16~~Tasha's~~ tantrums started to subside. 17Apparently, the private screaming place ~~wasnt~~ *wasn't* as much fun as the more public parts of the house. 18I knew my system had triumphed when, one day, I passed Tasha's room and heard some muffled moans. 19I poked my head in the door and asked her why she was crying. 20"I'm not crying, Daddy," she said. 21"Brownie's crying." 22Brownie is the name of Tasha's teddy bear. 23"But where is Brownie?" I asked. 24Tasha walked over to the closet and opened it, revealing a rather lonely stuffed bear. 25"He's in his screaming ~~place"~~ *place,"* she replied.

NAME: _____

DATE: _____

COMBINED EDITING TEST 10

Locate and correct the ten sentence-skills mistakes in the following passage. The mistakes are listed in the box below. As you locate each mistake, write the number of the word group containing it in the space provided. Then, in the spaces between the lines, correct each mistake.

> 2 fragments ____4____ ____9____
>
> 2 run-ons ____8____ ____15____
>
> 1 dropped verb ending ____12____
>
> 1 irregular verb mistake ____17____
>
> 1 dangling modifier ____6____
>
> 1 apostrophe mistake ____18____
>
> 1 mistake in parallelism ____15____
>
> 1 missing capital letter ____5____

¹In 1940, an unusual young man was buried in a custom-built ten-foot-long casket. ²The young man needed such a gigantic casket because he himself was a giant. ³He was just a shade under nine feet ~~tall.~~ *tall and* ⁴~~And~~ weighed almost five hundred pounds. ⁵Robert Wadlow, an ~~american~~ *American* born in 1918, lived a tragic, pain-filled life. ⁶Weighing eight pounds at birth, *Robert was a* ~~Robert's mother had given birth to a~~ normal infant. ⁷But by the age of five, Robert stood over five feet tall. ⁸His exceptional growth never ~~stopped he~~ *stopped; he* grew three inches every year until he died. ⁹Because a human's internal organs can't support an excessively large ~~body.~~ *body, Robert* ¹⁰~~Robert~~ was doomed to an early death. ¹¹Just before he died, he was fitted with ankle braces to

help support his enormous weight. ¹²One of the braces cut into an ankle, triggering an infection that ~~overload~~ *overloaded* his already strained immune system.

¹³The Wadlow family's reaction to Robert's plight was an intelligent and loving one. ¹⁴They refused to let him be exploited, turning down offers from freak shows and greedy promoters. ¹⁵Robert's parents attempted to give him a normal ~~life they~~ *life. They* encouraged him to read, to join the Boy Scouts, and ~~playing sports.~~ *to play sports.* ¹⁶When the company that made Robert's shoes offered to employ him as a traveling representative, Mr. Wadlow drove his son more than 300,000 miles—all over the United States—on behalf of the shoe company. ¹⁷The Wadlows helped Robert to stay cheerful and avoid the depression and gloom he could so easily have ~~sinked~~ *sunk* into. ¹⁸Robert's life is an example of tremendous courage and persistence in the face of incredible ~~handicap's.~~ *handicaps.*

NAME: _____

DATE: _____

COMBINED EDITING TEST 11

Locate and correct the ten sentence-skills mistakes in the following passage. The mistakes are listed in the box below. As you locate each mistake, write the number of the word group containing it in the space provided. Then, in the spaces between the lines, correct each mistake.

1 fragments ___18___

1 run-on ___2___

1 mistake in subject-verb agreement ___1___

2 missing commas around an interrupter ___8___ ___8___

1 missing comma after introductory words ___16___

2 clichés ___1___ ___12___

1 mistake in parallelism ___11___

1 irregular verb mistake ___5___

¹Everyone ~~suffer~~ *suffers* from an occasional bad mood, but I get ~~down in the dumps~~ *depressed* more often than other people. ²As a result, I've developed a list of helpful hints for dealing with ~~depression, one~~ *depression. One* thing I've learned to do is to keep a mood diary. ³About four times a day, I jot down a one-word description of my mood at that moment—sad, tired, frustrated, happy, and so on. ⁴Then I ask myself questions like "What event preceded this mood? ⁵Have I just eaten a lot of junk food or ~~drank~~ *drunk* a lot of coffee? ⁶Have I felt this way before?" ⁷After keeping this diary for a while, I've begun to see patterns in my moods. ⁸I've ~~found for example that~~ *found, for example, that* consuming a lot of salty foods like chips or pretzels makes me feel tense. ⁹Another way I've found to control my moods is to exercise every day. ¹⁰Exercise seems to prevent

depression; it also helps me to sleep better. [11]Any type of exercise works, including running, yoga, and even ~~just to walk~~ *just walking* around the block. [12]I can also overcome depression by giving myself a small treat at those times when my spirits ~~are under the weather~~ *are low*. [13]For instance, I might go to a movie, listen to music, or buy a new shirt. [14]Finally, I try not to go to sleep in a bad mood. [15]I find that I will probably wake up in the same mood that I fell asleep in. [16]Before getting into ~~bed I'll~~ *bed, I'll* do some relaxation techniques like deep breathing or stretching exercises. [17]Sometimes, I'll try soaking in a warm ~~bath.~~ *bath, which* [18]~~Which~~ seems to ease the tension in my muscles. [19]If I still feel miserable, I try to remain hopeful, for no bad mood lasts forever.

NAME: _____

DATE: _____

COMBINED EDITING TEST 12

Locate and correct the ten sentence-skills mistakes in the following passage. The mistakes are listed in the box below. As you locate each mistake, write the number of the word group containing it in the space provided. Then, in the spaces between the lines, correct each mistake.

> 2 fragments ___4___ ___18___
>
> 1 run-on ___15___
>
> 1 dropped verb ending ___1___
>
> 1 mistake in subject-verb agreement ___13___
>
> 1 mistake in pronoun agreement ___6___
>
> 1 missing capital letter ___10___
>
> 2 missing commas around an interrupter ___12___ ___12___
>
> 1 apostrophe mistake ___17___

¹A former advertising copywriter named Paul Stevens ~~explain~~ *explains* in a book called *I Can Sell You Anything* how advertisers use "weasel words" to persuade people to buy. ²Weasel words are slippery, sneaky words that may not really mean what they imply. ³Some of them make you believe things that have never been stated. ⁴~~For example,~~ *Take, for example,* the weasel words *help* and *like*. ⁵How many ads can you think of that include the phrase *helps stop, helps prevent,* or *helps fight*? ⁶A toothpaste company couldn't possibly say that ~~their~~ *its* product will "stop cavities forever," so that weasel word *helps* is put in front of the claim. ⁷Now the ad sounds ~~impressive.~~ *impressive but* ⁸~~But~~ doesn't actually guarantee anything. ⁹The same is true of *like*. ¹⁰~~if~~ *If* a household cleanser claims that it cleans "like a white tornado," are

516

you impressed? [11]The image of a powerful, dirt-sucking whirlwind may have gripped your mind. [12]~~However if~~ *However, if* you think about ~~it a~~ *it, a* tornado springing out of a bottle is clearly impossible. [13]Then there ~~is~~ *are* the weasel words that don't have any particular meaning. [14]Words like *taste, flavor,* and *good looks* are all based on subjective standards that vary with each individual. [15]The truth is that every cigarette in the world can "taste ~~best" every~~ *best." Every* car manufacturer can claim the "most advanced design." [16]There's just no scientific way to measure qualities like these.

[17]Advertisers, using weasel words, manipulate language to win the trust (and the cash) of ~~consumer's.~~ *consumers.*

NAME: _____

DATE: _____

COMBINED EDITING TEST 13

Each numbered box in the application below contains a sentence-skills mistake. Identify each of the ten mistakes. Write the type of mistake you found, followed by the corrected entry, in the space provided. The first one has been done for you.

1. *missing comma: August 15, 2012*

2. *missing capital letters: Carson City*

3. *unnecessary quotation marks: Food Server*

4. *spelling error: Tomorrow*

5. *missing capital: Kennedy High School*

6. *homonym mistake: Course*

7. *missing capital: Outlet*

8. *missing comma: Carson City, NV 89706*

9. *apostrophe mistake: Sales Clerk*

10. *fragment: I also stock shelves.*

DT Food Services Ltd. • Employment Application

1. Date of Application
August 15 2012

Social Security #	Last Name	First Name	Middle Initial
123-45-6789	Lee-Thomas	Leona	F.

Address (Street number and name)	2. City, State, and Zip Code
550 Tenth Avenue	carson city, NV 89706

3. Desired Position	4. Date Available to Start	Home Phone	Business Phone
"Food Server"	Tommorrow		

EDUCATION

	Schools	Name and Location	Dates Attended (mo/yr) From: To:	Grad?	Major/Minor Course Work	Type of Degree
High School	5. Kennedy High school		9/00 to 6/04	YES X NO		
College or University		Washoe Community College	9/04 to 6/05	YES NO X		
Other Training or Education	6. Coarse in CSS			YES X NO		

WORK HISTORY (include volunteer experience. Use additional sheets if necessary.)

7. Current or Last Employer:	8. Address:
Grocery outlet	120 South Carson Street Carson City NV 89706

9. Job Title:	Supervisor's Name and Title	Telephone Number
Sales' Clerk	Julie Leroy, Manager	

Dates Employed (mo/yr–mo/yr)	Starting Salary	Ending or Current Salary	Reason for Leaving
10/05 to present	$ 6.00/hour	$ 7.50/hour	

10. List major duties in order of their importance in the job:

I operate the cash register. Also stock shelves.

NAME: _____

DATE: _____

COMBINED EDITING TEST 14

Each underlined area in the cover letter below contains a sentence-skills mistake. Identify the mistake and write its item number in the appropriate space in the box below. Then correct the mistake in the space above each error.

Missing colon: __1__   Homonym mistake: __5__ __9__

Missing apostrophe: __2__   Dangling modifier: __3__

Wrong verb tense: __4__   Fragment: __6__

Missing word: __7__   Run-on: __8__

Missing comma: __10__

Karen Sanchez

Personnel Officer

Bay Adventures

Tampa, FL 33619

Dear Ms. Sanchez:
        1

I am replying to your ad in last *Sunday's* Sundays newspaper that indicated an opening
                2   *Since I am athletic and outgoing,*
in Bay Adventures for a recreational activities coordinator. Athletic and outgoing,
                                3
the position seems ideal for me.
        spent   *where*
I spend the past two years working at an after-school program wear I devel-
        4   5
oped fun activities for children in grades K–6. My job required me to think of
                                fitness and to
creative yet safe ways to promote physical fitness. And encourage teamwork and

cooperation among the kids.
        6   *at the University*
Also, I took several physical education classes at University of Tampa. I learned
                        psychology. I even   7
about sports psychology, I even took a class on exercise techniques. Right now, I hope
                                                        8
to apply what I have learned, which is why I am very interested in your job.
                                                        your
Please feel free to call or e-mail me for an interview. Thank you for you're
                                                        9
consideration.

Sincerely,
        10
Mark Rankins

519

NAME: _____

DATE: _____

COMBINED EDITING TEST 15

Each underlined area in the cover letter below contains a sentence-skills mistake. Identify the mistake and write its item number in the appropriate space in the box below. Then correct the mistake in the space above each error.

Missing period: __1__   Spelling error: __10__

Homonym mistake: __3__   Slang: __4__

Faulty parallelism: __6__   Fragment: __5__ __7__

Run-on: __8__   Apostrophe mistake: __9__

Missing colon: __2__

August 15, 2012

Mr. Gordon

~~Mr Gordon~~ Hebling
   1

Western Savings Bank

122 Mijo Way

Tucson, AZ 85706

Dear Mr. Hebling:
       2

    I attended a career fair last week at the Tucson Convention Center and discov-

       your   *representative*

ered that you're company is hiring part-time and relief tellers. A guy I spoke to
         3   4

told me that I would be ideal for the position because of my experience working

as a cashier.

                                                    store, but I

    I currently work as a cashier at an electronics store. But would like to start a
                                                        5

career in banking. My job requires me to be responsible and accurate. I understand

                                         good communication.

the importance of customer service and am good at communicating.
                                                    6

In addition to my work experience. *experience, I* I am able to do some programming and web
_____7_____
design, I have used CSS in WordPress. If I am hired, I can work at various banks
*design, and I*_____8_____
because I have a valid drivers' lisense and my own car.
driver's license
_____9_____10_____

Please feel free to call me at (520) 222-2222. I hope that I will have an oppor-

tunity to talk with you in person.

Sincerely,

Monique Williamson

NAME: _____

DATE: _____

COMBINED EDITING TEST 16

Each underlined area in the résumé excerpt below contains a sentence-skills mistake. Identify the mistake and write its item number in the appropriate space in the box below. Then correct the mistake in the space above each error.

Missing capital letter: ___1___ ___10___

Dangling modifier: ___4___

Faulty parallelism: ___3___

Fragment: ___5___ ___6___

Inconsistent verb tense: ___7___

Run-on: ___9___

Apostrophe mistake: ___8___

Missing comma: ___2___

Alyssa Leong

      Bagley

597 bagley Street

Torrance, CA 1

Torrance CA 90501

      2

Phone: (310) 555-5555

OBJECTIVE: I hope to find a position as a certified nurse assistant at a nursing

                                 full-time hours

facility that will offer me rewarding work, hours that are full time, and medical

                                         3

benefits.

                                      working, I have experience

QUALIFICATIONS: Caring, competent, and hard working, my experience

caring for people.

caring for people is present. Having volunteered at an adult residential care

                      4

             two years, I

home for two years. I am aware of the responsibilities for providing basic care.

            5 *home, I*

At the care home. I helped staff members and sometimes fed, bathed, and dress

        6   *dressed*

                                                                             7

clients. My supervisors' encouraged me to enroll in a certified nursing assis-

8

training, and I

tant program. In 2012, I completed a six-month training, I also received my

CNA certification.

9

EDUCATION:

2000–2004   Diploma, Roosevelt High School

2012   Certified Nursing Assistance Program, Los Angeles Adult
              Community School

WORK HISTORY:

Central Adult Residential

Volunteer. South central adult residential Care Home, (9/2005 to 6/2012)

10

Assisted clients with personal hygiene and recreational activities.

Provided companionship.

NAME: _____

DATE: _____

COMBINED EDITING TEST 17

Each numbered line in the résumé below contains a sentence-skills mistake. Identify the mistake and write its item number in the appropriate space in the box below. Then correct the mistake in the space above each error.

Missing capital letter: __1__ __10__

Spelling error: __3__

Missing comma: __2__

Inconsistent verb tense: __7__

Homonym mistake: __8__

Missing -s ending: __4__ __6__

Apostrophe error: __5__ __9__

Kalani Bowers

Avenue
[1]203 Mahogany avenue
Louis, MO
[2]St. Louis MO 63103

Phone: (314) 777-7777

opportunity
[3]**Objective:** I wish to find a full-time sales position with an oportunity for advancement and personal growth.

Work History:

Inventory Clerk at Dave's TV & Appliance • St. Louis, MO • 2004 to present

Responsibilities:

[4] • Used a computer system to catalog and monitor inventory (electronics
appliances
and appliance)

524

5 • Conducted quarterly physical inventories'   *inventories*

Data Entry Clerk at CPK Trading Company • St. Louis, MO • 2001 to 2004

6 • Processed payments and invoice   *invoices*

7 • Maintain and audited numerous databases   *Maintained*

8 • Entered daily sales receipts for too branch locations   *two*

9 • Generated reports' and memoranda   *reports*

Education:

St. Anthony's High School • Columbia, MO

• Graduated June 2001

Special Skills:

• Experienced with Windows, Word, and Excel

10 • c.p.r. Certified   *C.P.R.*

Readings for Writing

Introduction

Part Four provides a series of reading selections that should both capture your interest and enlarge your understanding. This part of the book begins by explaining the format of each selection, the four kinds of comprehension questions that accompany each reading, and four hints that can make for effective reading. After you read each selection, work through the reading comprehension, technique, and discussion questions that follow. They will help you understand, appreciate, and think about the selection. Then write a paragraph or an essay on one of the three writing assignments provided.

   As you work on a paper, refer as needed to the guidelines for effective writing in Part One and the rules of grammar, punctuation, and usage in Part Two. Doing so will help make these basic rules an everyday part of your writing.

What was your favorite thing to read when you were younger? What about now? (It doesn't have to be a book; it could be a magazine, comic book, newspaper, blog, or website.) Has it changed since you were younger? Why or why not?

Introduction to the Readings

This part of the book will help you become a better reader as well as a stronger writer. Reading and writing are closely connected skills—so practicing one skill helps develop the other. Included here are ten high-interest reading selections that provide inspiration for a wide range of paragraph and essay writing assignments.

The Format of Each Selection

To help you read the selections effectively—and write about them effectively—the following features are included.

Preview

A short preview introduces you to each reading selection and its author. These previews will help you start thinking about a selection even before you begin to read it.

"Words to Watch"

A list of difficult words with their paragraph numbers and their meanings as they are used in the reading precedes each selection. You may find it helpful to read through "Words to Watch" to remind yourself of meanings or to learn new ones. Within the reading itself, each listed word is marked with a small bullet (•). When you're reading, if you are not sure of the definition of a word marked with this bullet, go back and look it up in "Words to Watch."

Reading Comprehension Questions

Following each selection, a series of questions gives you practice in four reading skills widely recognized as important to comprehension. These skills have to do with (1) vocabulary, (2) main and central ideas, (3) key details, and (4) inferences.

1 Understanding Vocabulary in Context The *context* of a word consists of the words that surround it. We learn many words by guessing their meanings from their context. For example, look at the sentence below. Can you figure out the meaning of the italicized word? After reading the sentence, try to answer the multiple-choice item.

> Karen was *euphoric* when the college that was her first choice accepted her.
>
> The word *euphoric* in the above sentence means
>
> a. puzzled.
>
> b. angry.
>
> c. overjoyed.
>
> d. sad.

You can figure out the meaning of *euphoric* on the basis of its context. Since Karen was accepted by the college that was her first choice, we can assume that she was overjoyed (*c*) rather than puzzled, angry, or sad. Understanding vocabulary in context is a very useful skill to develop, since we often meet new words in our reading. If we pay attention to their context, we may not need a dictionary to figure out what they mean.

2 Determining Main Ideas and the Central Idea As you learned in Part One of this book, a paragraph is about a point, or main idea, which is often expressed in a topic sentence; and in an essay, there is an overall main idea, often called the central idea. While the reading selections here are longer than the essays you write for your classes, they follow this same pattern. Sometimes the author of a selection states the central idea directly in one or more sentences; sometimes the reader must figure it out. In either case, to know what an author is really saying, readers must determine the central idea and the main ideas that support it.

3 Recognizing Key Supporting Details Supporting details are reasons, examples, and other kinds of information that help explain or clarify main ideas and the central idea. Recognizing key supporting details is an important part of understanding an author's message.

4 Making Inferences Often, an author does not state a point directly. Instead, he or she only suggests the point, and the reader must *infer* it—in other words, figure it out. We make inferences every day, basing them on our understanding and experience. For example, suppose you take your seat in a lecture class in which the instructor always reads from notes in a boring tone of voice. A fellow student comments, "Well, this should be another thrilling lecture." You readily infer—you conclude from the circumstances—that your classmate is not saying what he or she means. The meaning is really the opposite of what was said.

Here is another example of inference. Consider the sentence below. What can you infer from it? Circle the letter of the most logical inference.

Two elderly men silently played chess on a park bench, ignoring both the hot July sun and a fortyish woman who held a red umbrella over her head while watching their game.

The sentence suggests that

a.   the men disliked the woman.

b.   the woman was related to one of the men.

c.   it was raining heavily.

d.   the woman wanted to protect herself from the sun.

If the men were concentrating on their game, they would be likely to ignore their surroundings, including the woman, so nothing in the sentence suggests that they disliked her, and *a* is therefore not a logical inference. Also, nothing in the sentence suggests that the men knew the woman, so *b* is not a logical inference, either. And *c* is also incorrect, since the sentence mentions only the sun: if it were sunny and raining at the same time, the sentence would surely note such an unusual situation. That leaves only *d* as the correct inference—that the woman was using the umbrella to protect herself from the "hot July sun."

Making inferences like these is often necessary for a full understanding of an author's point.

Technique Questions

Questions about *technique* point to methods writers have used to present their material effectively. In particular, technique questions make you aware of directly stated central ideas, methods of organization, transition words, and vivid details that help writers make their ideas come alive for the reader. Focusing on such techniques will help you use them in your own writing.

Discussion Questions

The discussion questions help you think in detail about ideas raised by the selection and make connections between the selection and your own life. They will help you look closely at what you value, whom you respect, and how you react to people and situations.

Writing Assignments

The writing assignments following each selection are based specifically on that selection. Many assignments provide guidelines on how to proceed, including suggestions about prewriting, possible topic sentences and thesis statements, and methods of development.

Hints for Effective Reading

Effective reading, like effective writing, does not happen all at once. Rather, it is a process. Often you begin with a general impression of what something means, and then, by rereading, you move to a deeper level of understanding of the material.

Here are some hints for becoming a better reader:

1. **Read in the right place.**   Ideally, you should get settled in a quiet spot that encourages concentration. If you can focus your attention while lying on a bed or curled up in a chair, that's fine. But if you find that being very comfortable leads to daydreaming or dozing off rather than reading, then avoid getting too relaxed. You might find that sitting in an upright chair promotes concentration and keeps your mind alert.

2. **Preview the selection.**   Begin by reading the overview that precedes the selection. Then think for a minute about the title. A good title often hints at a selection's central idea, giving you insight into the piece even before you read it. For example, you can deduce from the title of Alice Walker's essay "My Daughter Smokes" that Walker is going to offer commentary about her daughter's habit.

3. **Read the selection through for pleasure.**   Allow yourself to be drawn into the world that the author has created. Don't slow down or turn back. Instead, just read to understand as much as you can the first time through. After this reading, sit back for a moment and think about what you enjoyed in the piece.

4. **Deepen your sense of the selection.**   Go back and reread it, or at least reread the passages that were not clear the first time through. Look up any words that you cannot figure out from context, and write their meanings in the margin. Then ask yourself the following questions:

   - What is the central idea of the piece?
   - What are the main supporting points for the central idea?
   - How does the author explain and illustrate these main supporting points?

Reread carefully the parts of the selection that seem most relevant to answering these questions. By asking yourself the questions and by rereading, you will gradually deepen your understanding of the material.

The Importance of Regular Reading

Chances are that you are not as good a reader as you should be to do well in college. If so, it's not surprising. You live in a culture where people watch an average of almost five hours of television and spend an average of two hours online every day! This does not allow much time for reading. Reading is a skill that must be actively practiced. The simple fact is that people who do not read very often are not likely to be strong readers.

Another reason for not reading much is that you may have a lot of responsibilities. You may be going to school and working at the same time, and you may have many family duties as well. Given a hectic schedule, you're not going to have much opportunity to read. When you have free time, you may be exhausted and find it easier to turn on the TV than to open a book.

A third reason for not reading is that our public school system may have soured you on it. One government study after another has said that our schools have not done a good job of turning people on to the rewards of reading. If you had to read a lot of uninteresting and irrelevant material in grade school and high school, you may have decided (mistakenly) that reading in general is not for you.

These reasons may help explain why you are not in the habit of regular reading. For people who are unpracticed readers, there is one overall key to becoming a better reader. That key, simple as it may sound, is to do a great deal of reading. The truth of the matter is that *reading is like any other skill. The more you practice, the better you get.*

Regular reading is a habit with many rewards. Research has shown that frequent reading improves vocabulary, spelling, reading speed, and comprehension, as well as grammar and writing style. All of these language and thinking skills develop in an almost painless way for the person who becomes a habitual reader.

The question to ask, then, is "What steps can I take to become a regular reader?" The first step is to develop the right attitude. Recognize that a person who can read well has more potential and more power than a person who cannot. Reading is a source of extraordinary power. Consider the experience of Wayne Lionel Aponte, on pages 538–40, about the challenges of maintaining his true "speaking self." And of Ben Carson, as told on pages 545–51. After he started reading two books a week, at his mother's insistence, his entire world changed. He moved from the bottom of his class to the head of his class, and he went on to become a world-famous surgeon. Increasingly in today's world, jobs involve processing information. More than ever, words are the tools of our trades. The better your command of words, the more success you are likely to have. And nothing else will give you a command of words like regular reading.

A second step toward becoming a regular reader is to subscribe to a daily newspaper and, every day, read the sections that interest you. Remember that it is not what you read that matters—for example, you should not feel obliged to read the editorial section if opinion columns are not your interest. Instead, what matters is *the very fact that you read.* Your favorite section may be the comics, or fashion, or sports, or movie reviews, or the front page. Feel perfectly free to read whatever you decide you want to read.

A third step is to subscribe to one or more magazines. On many college bulletin boards, you'll see displays offering a wide variety of magazines at discount rates for college students. You may want to consider a weekly newsmagazine, such as *Newsweek* or *Time,* or a weekly general-interest magazine, such as *People*. You will also be able to choose from a wide variety of monthly magazines, some of which will suit your interests. You can subscribe to print, electronic, tablet, and/ or mobile editions. You may also want to look over the magazine section at any newsstand or bookstore. Most magazines contain postage-paid subscriber cards, which you can send in to start a subscription, or you can easily do so online. Many magazines make select articles available for free online or even offer exclusive online-only articles, as well as video and audio content. Finally, you may want to visit the library on a regular basis to just sit and read for an hour or so.

A fourth step to regular reading is to create a half hour of reading in your daily schedule. That time might be during your lunch hour, or late afternoon before dinner, or the half hour or so before you turn off your light at night. Find a time that is possible for you and make reading then a habit. The result will be both recreation and personal growth.

A fifth step is to read aloud to your children if you're a parent, or to your younger siblings if you have them. This practice will benefit both them and you.

The most important step on the road to becoming a regular reader is to read on your own and get hooked on reading. Reading is most valuable and most enjoyable when you get drawn into the special world created by a book. You can travel in that world for hours or days, unmindful for a while of everyday concerns. In that timeless zone, you will come to experience the joy of reading. You will also add depth to your life and make more sense out of the world.

Browse a bookstore, a library, a reading center, or any other place with a large number of reading options. Amazon, Goodreads, and Chinaberry Books (Chinaberry.com) are also great resources. Or read the short descriptions of the widely popular books in the list that follows. Find something you like and begin your reading journey. If you stick to it and become a regular reader, you may find that you have done nothing less than change your life.

A List of Interesting Books

Autobiographies and Other Nonfiction

I Know Why the Caged Bird Sings, Maya Angelou

The author writes with love, humor, and honesty about her childhood and what it is like to grow up black and female.

Alicia: My Story, Alicia Appleman-Jurman

Alicia was a Jewish girl living with her family in Poland when the Germans invaded in 1941. Her utterly compelling and heartbreaking story shows some of the best and worst of humankind .

Growing Up, Russell Baker

Russell Baker's mother, a giant presence in his life, insisted that he make something of himself. In his autobiography, the prizewinning journalist shows that he did with an engrossing account of his own family and growing up.

In Cold Blood, Truman Capote

This book, a frightening true story about the murder of a family, is also an examination of what made their killers tick. Many books today tell gripping stories of real-life crimes. *In Cold Blood* was the first book of this type and may still be the best.

Gifted Hands, Ben Carson

In this inspiring autobiography, Ben Carson tells the story of how he grew up from being an inner-city child with poor grades and little motivation to a world-famous neurosurgeon at one of the best hospitals in the world.

Move On, Linda Ellerbee

A well-known television journalist writes about the ups and downs of her life, including her stay at the Betty Ford Center for treatment of her alcoholism.

Bossypants, Tina Fey

Formerly a starring member of the ensemble cast of *Saturday Night Live* and praised for her spot-on impression of former vice-presidential candidate Sarah Palin, Tina Fey describes in this witty autobiography her road to television comedy fame. Even in writing, Fey's unique brand of humor shines through.

The Diary of a Young Girl, Anne Frank

To escape the Nazi death camps, Anne Frank and her family hid for years in an attic. Her journal tells a story of love, fear, and courage.

Man's Search for Meaning, Viktor Frankl

How do people go on when they have been stripped of everything, including human dignity? In this short but moving book, the author describes his time in a concentration camp and what he learned there about survival.

The Woman Warrior, Maxine Hong Kingston

In this five-part memoir—each part representing the voice of a woman who has influenced her life—Kingston shares the challenges and successes, pain, and pride of growing up in two distinct worlds: the Chinese and the American. Using the narrative technique of "talk story," Kingston describes the myth, tradition, and family that have helped shape her uniquely Chinese American female identity.

The Autobiography of Malcolm X, Malcolm X and Alex Haley

Malcolm X, the controversial black leader who was assassinated by one of his followers, writes about the experiences that drove him to a leadership role in the Black Muslims.

Makes Me Wanna Holler, Nathan McCall

A dramatic first-person account of how a bright young black man was lured into— and then ultimately rose from—a life of crime to enjoy a successful journalism career at the *Washington Post.*

Angela's Ashes, Frank McCourt

This widely popular autobiography tells the story of an Irish boy whose father was a drunkard and whose mother tried desperately to hold her family together. The poverty described is heartbreaking, and yet the book is wonderfully moving and often funny. You'll shake your head in disbelief at all the hardships, but at other times you'll laugh out loud at the comic touches.

Down These Mean Streets, Piri Thomas

Life in a Puerto Rican ghetto is described vividly and with understanding by one who experienced it.

Fiction

The Cradle Will Fall, Mary Higgins Clark

A county prosecutor uncovers evidence that a famous doctor is killing women, not realizing that she herself is becoming his next target. One typical comment by a reviewer about Clark's books is that they are "a ticket to ride the roller coaster . . . once on the track, we're there until the ride is over."

The Hunger Games, Suzanne Collins

This trilogy is a young-adult novel series written in the voice of sixteen-year-old Katniss Everdeen, a sixteen-year-old girl living in the post-apocalytpic nation of Panem. Panem comprises twelve districts, and every year via lottery one boy and one girl between the ages of twelve and eighteen are selected from each of these districts to battle in the Hunger Games. These games are televised and the children selected are expected to fight to their deaths. In 2008, the first novel in the series was selected by *Publisher's Weekly* as one of the year's best books.

Deliverance, James Dickey

Several men go rafting down a wild river in Georgia and encounter beauty, violence, and self-knowledge.

Pillars of the Earth, Ken Follett

Although Follett is better known for his works of international suspense, this novel is a historical epic about the building of a twelfth-century Gothic cathedral—and the impact it has on the three men most intimately involved in its construction. The story spans forty years, covering not only the social and political upheaval of twelfth-century England but also the conflict and corruption of church politics and its leaders.

Lord of the Flies, William Golding

Could a group of children, none older than twelve, survive by themselves on a tropical island in the midst of World War Three? In this modern classic, Golding shows us that the real danger is not the war outside but "the beast" within each of us.

Snow Falling on Cedars, David Guterson

This is a unique murder mystery. The story is set in the 1950s in an island community, where a fisherman is found dead on his boat and another fisherman is quickly blamed for the death. The accused man is so proud that he refuses to defend himself for a crime he says he did not commit. Like all great stories, this one is about more than itself. It becomes a celebration of the mystery of the human heart.

Flowers for Algernon, Daniel Keyes

A scientific experiment turns a mentally challenged man into a genius. But the results are a mixture of joy and heartbreak.

The Shining, Stephen King

A haunted hotel, a little boy with extrasensory perception, and an insane father—they're all together in a horror tale of isolation and insanity. One review says, "Be prepared to be scared out of your mind. . . . Don't read this book when you are home alone. If you dare—once you get past a certain point, there's no stopping."

Watchers, Dean Koontz

An incredibly suspenseful story about two dogs that undergo lab experiments. One dog becomes a monster programmed to kill, and it seeks to track down the couple who know its secret.

To Kill a Mockingbird, Harper Lee

A controversial trial, involving a black man accused of raping a white woman, is the centerpiece of this story about adolescence, bigotry, and justice. One review described the book as "a novel of great sweetness, humor, compassion, and mystery carefully sustained."

The Natural, Bernard Malamud

An aging player makes a comeback that stuns the baseball world.

Gone with the Wind, Margaret Mitchell

The characters and places in this book—Scarlett O'Hara, Rhett Butler, Tara—have become part of our culture because they are unforgettable.

A Day No Pigs Would Die, Robert Peck

A boy raises a pig that is intelligent and affectionate. Will the boy follow orders and send the animal off to be slaughtered? Read this short novel to find out.

Harry Potter and the Sorcerer's Stone, J. K. Rowling

The first in a series of award-winning stories that have captured the hearts of young and old alike around the world. These funny, action-packed, touching books are about a likable boy who is mistreated by the relatives who take him in after his parents are killed. Then Harry discovers that he is a wizard, and his extraordinary adventures begin.

The Catcher in the Rye, J. D. Salinger

The frustrations and turmoil of being an adolescent have never been captured so well as in this book. The main character, Holden Caulfield, is honest, funny, affectionate, obnoxious, and tormented at the same time.

Push, Sapphire

This is the debut novel written by New York-based writer Sapphire. Its protagonist is Claireece "Precious" Jones, a sixteen-year-old obese and illiterate young woman from Harlem who has had to endure and survive the horrendous abuse of her parents. Although all odds seem against her, Precious finds the strength and courage to rise above and triumph from her situation. Thirteen years after its publication, *Push* became the basis of the 2009 film titled *Precious,* which earned two Academy Awards that year.

The Joy Luck Club, Amy Tan

In this moving novel about four Chinese mothers and their daughters, Amy Tan describes with exquisite detail the sometimes painful, often challenging, yet deeply felt connection between mothers and their daughters.

The Lord of the Rings, J. R. R. Tolkien

Enter an amazing world of little creatures known as Hobbits; you, like thousands of other readers, may never want to leave.

Charlotte's Web, E. B. White

This best-loved story, for children and adults, is about a little pig named Wilbur and his best friend, a spider named Charlotte. Wilbur is being fattened in order to be killed for a holiday meal; Charlotte must come up with a plan to save him.

Talkin' White

Wayne Lionel Aponte

PREVIEW

How often have people attempted to identify where you're from based on your accent, patterns of speech, or turns of phrases? In the essay that follows, Wayne Lionel Aponte describes his experience growing up in a black community where speaking grammatically correct English was not only frowned upon but also considered by other black community members as an attempt to "sound white."

WORDS TO WATCH

showboating (2): impressing

elocution (2): manner of speaking

oratory (3); the art of public speaking

marginal (5): on the outside

polylingual (5): ability to speak many languages

matriculated (9): admitted as a student

Recently, during a conversation on film at a dinner party, when I was using my best college-educated English, I was asked where I was born. I received a curious look when I replied, with pride, "Harlem." The questioner, whom I had met through a mutual friend, looked at me as if I were a brother from another planet and immediately wanted to know whether I'd lived in Harlem all my life. When I responded, "Yeah, man, I been cold chillin' on Lenox Avenue ever since I was rockin' my fly diapers," he laughed, and I realized his was a nervous laughter, the kind folks use to mask their thoughts. Has he really lived in Harlem all his life? He talks white was the thought behind his laughter, and the follow-up question asked after my departure.   1

While growing up in Harlem during my not-so-long-ago elementary and middle-school days, I often encountered the phrase "talkin' white." It was usually thrust on people who were noticed because they were speaking grammatically correct English in a community that did not. I've also heard the term applied to people who place themselves above others by verbally showboating• with the elocution• of a Lionel Trilling or a Sir Laurence Olivier.   2

Nevertheless, I've always loved those folks who have mastered the art of manipulating words. Eloquent oratory• and masterful writing have stimulated my mind for as long as I can remember. I took great pride in my ability to mimic and to   3 slowly transform the styles of my favorite writers and orators into my own voice. In this sense language is a form of intellectual play for me.

When I was a child, my reaction to the question "Why do you talk so white?" **4** was to alter my spoken English drastically (once "Ask yo mama" became less effective and after I ran out of money for candy bribes to make the kids like me). Like most children, I wanted to be liked and wanted to blend into each new social circle. But speaking as I did make blending difficult since it brought favorable attention from teachers that, outside the classroom, evoked fierce verbal attacks from my peers. I never could quite understand how talking slang proved I was Black. Nor did I understand why I couldn't be accepted as a full-fledged, card-holding member of the group by speaking my natural way.

Hearing the laughter, though, and being the butt of "proper" and "Oreo" jokes hurt **5** me. Being criticized made me feel marginal•—and verbally impotent in the sense that I had little ammunition to stop the frequent lunchtime attacks. So I did what was necessary to fit in, whether that meant cursing excessively or signifying [goading, often good-naturedly]. Ultimately I somehow learned to be polylingual• and to become sensitive linguistically in the way animals are able to sense the danger of bad weather.

The need to defend myself led me to use language as a weapon to deflect jokes **6** about the "whiteness" of my spoken English and to launch harsh verbal counterattacks. Simultaneously language served as a mask to hide the hurt I often felt in the process. Though over time my ability to "talk that talk"—slang—gained me a new respect from my peers, I didn't want to go through life using slang to prove I am Black. So I decided "I yam what I yam," and to take pride in myself. I am my speaking self, but this doesn't mean that I'm turning my back on Black people. There are various shades of Blackness; I don't have to talk like Paul Laurence Dunbar's dialect poems to prove I'm Black. I don't appreciate anyone's trying to take away the range of person I can be.

"Nevertheless, I've always loved those folks who have mastered the art of manipulating words. Eloquent oratory and masterful writing have stimulated my mind for as long as I can remember."

"Talkin' white" implies that the English language is a closed system owned **7** exclusively by whites. But my white friends from Chattanooga, Ventura, California, and New York City don't all speak the same way. Nor do the millions of poor whites working below the poverty line "talk white," as that phrase is interpreted.

But the primary reason I question this peculiar euphemism for "speaking well" **8** is that it has been used tyrannically to push to the periphery of the race people who grew up in the West Indies and attended English schools or who lived in predominantly white environments: They are perceived as not being Black enough, or as somehow being anti-Black.

It hurts to know that many people judge me and others on whether or not we **9** break verbs. If we follow this line of thought, maybe we'll also say that W. E. B. DuBois wasn't Black because he matriculated• at Harvard and studied at the

University of Berlin. Or perhaps that Alain Leroy Locke wasn't Black because he earned a degree from Oxford University. Or, to transfer the logic, maybe we're not all of African descent since we don't speak Swahili and some "real" Africans do.

If we can take pride in the visual diversity of the race, then surely we can 10 transfer this diversity and appreciation to spoken English. Because all of us don't be talkin' alike—ya know what I'm sayin'?

READING COMPREHENSION QUESTIONS

1. The word *curious* in "I received a curious look when I replied, with pride, 'Harlem'" (paragraph 1) means
   a. insulting.
   b. questioning.
   c. shocked.
   d. annoyed.

2. The word *impotent* in "Being criticized made me feel marginal—and verbally impotent in the sense that I had little ammunition to stop the frequent lunch-time attacks" means
   a. ineffective.
   b. witty.
   c. nonviolent.
   d. weak.

3. Which sentence best describes the central idea of the selection?
   a. It is disrespectful to speak a language that goes against the common language of your community.
   b. The phrase "talkin' white" makes assumptions about what it means to be "black."
   c. When a black person speaks grammatically correct English, it means that the person is trying to deny his or her true race.
   d. In order to be identified as "white," one should speak grammatically correct English.

4. Which sentence best expresses the main idea of paragraphs 3 and 4?
   a. Aponte alienated his black community by refusing to speak proper English.
   b. Aponte always felt bothered by the fact that he was never accepted as being fully "black" for speaking grammatically correct English.
   c. Aponte alienated the white community by refusing to speak proper English.
   d. Speaking grammatically correct English was not Aponte's natural way of speaking; he spoke this way because he wanted to feel like he belonged.

5. Which sentence best expresses the main idea of paragraphs 6 and 7?

    a. Feeling so alienated from his black community, the author decided to hide his true "speaking self" by using only slang.

    b. The author became so self-conscious of his "speaking self" that he resorted to writing poetry as a way to express his feelings about being black.

    (c.) The author learned to take pride in his true "speaking self" and used language to his advantage.

    d. The author believes that there is no such thing as a true "speaking self" and that one's race determines one's language.

6. One of the most challenging things for Aponte while growing up in Harlem was

    a. learning to speak the local slang.

    b. learning to speak grammatically correct English.

    c. learning how to fit in, despite his language.

    (d.) learning how to recognize when to alter his speaking behavior.

7. To defend against the jokes that made him feel like he was doing something wrong for speaking the way he did, Aponte

    a. engaged in a lot of verbal fights.

    b. learned several languages to emphasize the fact that he was different.

    (c.) began to speak the way his peers spoke in order to earn their respect and to fit-in.

    d. avoided the situation altogether and focused his time on his writing.

8. Aponte finds the phrase "talkin' white" to be

    (a.) a condemnation of individuals who choose not to speak slang or improper English in order to prove their "blackness."

    b. an accurate synonym for "speaking well."

    c. relevant only to white individuals in various parts of the country who speak their own dialect of English.

    d. a euphemism for well educated and elite.

9. When Aponte criticizes the phrase "talkin' white" as a euphemism for "speaking well," he is suggesting that

    a. you will be more respected by your peers only if you speak and behave as a white person.

    b. only whites can speak English properly.

    (c.) all black people will be pushed to the fringes of society strictly for their language habits.

    d. all people who do not speak English properly will be pushed to the fringes of society.

10. In the final paragraph, Aponte implies that

   a. there is no true acceptance of racial diversity in the United States.

   b. race has nothing to do with language.

   c. we are being hypocritical if we can accept one another for the color of our skin but not for the color of our spoken English.

   d. language has no color.

TECHNIQUE QUESTIONS

1. Aponte uses flashbacks in his essay to help the reader experience the impact that speaking grammatically correct English has had on his life. Select one of those flashbacks and list the words he uses to draw you into the scene with him. Are these action words, description words, or both? Is his choice of words effective? Why or why not?

   Answers will vary.

   _____

   _____

   _____

   _____

2. In paragraph 6, the author introduces the phrase "speaking self." Why do you think he introduces it at this point in the essay, as opposed to the beginning or the conclusion? What is the context for the introduction of this phrase?

   After discussing how uncomfortable the phrase "talkin white" makes the author and how

   he would alter his language to fit in, he then explains how eventually he comes to

   embraces his true "speaking self."

   _____

3. Aponte references several black scholars throughout his essay. List those scholars below. What point is the author trying to make by referencing them?

   Paul Laurence Dunbar, W.E.B DuBois, Alain Leroy Locke. Aponte purposefully references

   these scholars because they are well spoken, educated, and black.

   _____

   _____

DISCUSSION QUESTIONS

1. The focus in this essay is as much about language as it is about fitting in. As Aponte writes, "When I was a child, my reaction to the question 'Why do you talk so white?' was to alter my spoken English drastically (once 'Ask yo mama' became less effective and after I ran out of money for candy bribes to make the kids like me). Like most children, I wanted to be liked and wanted to blend into each new social circle." Can you recall a time when you altered your language, or some other aspect of yourself, to fit in? What did you do? Do you think your actions were effective?

2. The author's phrase "speaking self" is very much about staying true to who you are and speaking the English language that comes naturally to you. Do you agree or disagree with this statement? What other "selves" can you think of to which you feel that people should stay true?

3. Aponte talks about being judged for the way he spoke English; can you think of a time when you felt you were being judged for something you could not help? How did you feel, and what did you do in response to this judgment?

WRITING ASSIGNMENTS

1. In paragraph 4, Aponte writes, "I never could quite understand how talking slang proved I was Black. Nor did I understand why I couldn't be accepted as a full-fledged, card-holding member of my group by speaking my natural way." Do you use slang when you speak? If so, in what context(s) do you use it and how are you treated when you do speak slang? When you use slang, do you feel that you are more or less a part of your culture, race, or community? Write a paragraph in which you describe one incident when you did not use the language of your group or community and how people reacted to you. Include specific examples of expressions you used, as Aponte does in his essay. Make sure you include a clear topic sentence and concrete details to help your reader experience what you experienced.

2. Aponte introduces several main ideas in his essay. Following are statements for some of those main ideas:

   • Some people use the phrase "talkin' white" as a synonym for "speaking well."

   • Racial and cultural groups define themselves by the type of English they speak.

   • People who speak grammatically correct English are sometimes looked down upon by certain segments of society.

Pick one of these main idea statements and write an essay that either agrees or disagrees with the claim that is being made. Start by creating an outline to guide your writing. For each paragraph, remember to include a topic sentence, supporting details, and concrete examples. Be sure to include transition statements in between your paragraphs, as well.

3. In paragraph 6, Aponte writes, "There are various shades of Blackness; I don't have to talk like Paul Laurence Dunbar's dialect poems to prove I'm Black. I don't appreciate anyone's trying to take away the range of person I can be." What does the author mean by "various shades of Blackness"? Reread the essay and write a paragraph about a time during which you, too, felt you had to prove you belonged to a certain group—whether it was your racial group, cultural group, social group, or other group. Be sure to include a clear topic sentence and specific examples to demonstrate how the shades of your larger racial, cultural, or social identity can be varied yet accepted.

Do It Better!

Ben Carson, M.D., with Cecil Murphey

PREVIEW

If you suspect that you are now as "smart" as you'll ever be, then read the following selection, taken from the book *Think Big*. It is about Dr. Ben Carson, who was sure he was "the dumbest kid in the class" in school. Carson tells how he turned his life around from what was a sure path to failure. Today he is a famous neurosurgeon at Johns Hopkins University Hospital in Baltimore, Maryland.

WORDS TO WATCH

inasmuch as (13): since

potential (18): capacity for development and progress

solely (20): alone

rebellious (46): resisting authority

indifferent (58): uninterested

startled (75): surprised

astonished (81): surprised

"Benjamin, is this your report card?" my mother asked as she picked up the 1
folded white card from the table.

"Uh, yeah," I said, trying to sound casual. Too ashamed to hand it to her, I had 2
dropped it on the table, hoping that she wouldn't notice until after I went to bed.

It was the first report card I had received from Higgins Elementary School 3
since we had moved back from Boston to Detroit, only a few months earlier.

I had been in the fifth grade not even two weeks before everyone considered 4
me the dumbest kid in the class and frequently made jokes about me. Before long
I too began to feel as though I really was the most stupid kid in fifth grade. Despite
Mother's frequently saying, "You're smart, Bennie. You can do anything you want
to do," I did not believe her.

No one else in school thought I was smart, either. 5

Now, as Mother examined my report card, she asked, "What's this grade in 6
reading?" (Her tone of voice told me that I was in trouble.) Although I was embarrassed, I did not think too much about it. Mother knew that I wasn't doing well in
math, but she did not know I was doing so poorly in every subject.

While she slowly read my report card, reading everything one word at a time, I 7
hurried into my room and started to get ready for bed. A few minutes later, Mother
came into my bedroom.

"Benjamin," she said, "are these your grades?" She held the card in front of me 8
as if I hadn't seen it before.

"Oh, yeah, but you know, it doesn't mean much."   9

"No, that's not true, Bennie. It means a lot."   10

"Just a report card."   11

"But it's more than that."   12

Knowing I was in for it now, I prepared to listen, yet I was not all that inter- 13
ested. I did not like school very much and there was no reason why I should. Inasmuch as• I was the dumbest kid in the class, what did I have to look forward to?
The others laughed at me and made jokes about me every day.

"Education is the only way you're ever going to escape poverty," she said. 14
"It's the only way you're ever going to get ahead in life and be successful. Do you
understand that?"

"Yes, Mother," I mumbled.   15

"If you keep on getting these kinds of grades you're going to spend the rest of 16
your life on skid row, or at best sweeping floors in a factory. That's not the kind of
life that I want for you. That's not the kind of life that God wants for you."

I hung my head, genuinely ashamed. My mother had been raising me and my 17
older brother, Curtis, by herself. Having only a third-grade education herself, she
knew the value of what she did not have. Daily she drummed into Curtis and me
that we had to do our best in school.

"You're just not living up to your potential•," she said. "I've got two mighty 18
smart boys and I know they can do better."

I had done my best—at least I had when I first started at Higgins Elementary 19
School. How could I do much when I did not understand anything going on in our
class?

In Boston we had attended a parochial school, but I hadn't learned much be- 20
cause of a teacher who seemed more interested in talking to another female teacher
than in teaching us. Possibly, this teacher was not solely• to blame—perhaps I
wasn't emotionally able to learn much. My parents had separated just before we
went to Boston, when I was eight years old. I loved both my mother and my father
and went through considerable trauma over their separating. For months afterward,
I kept thinking that my parents would get back together, that my daddy would
come home again the way he used to, and that we could be the same old family
again—but he never came back. Consequently, we moved to Boston and lived with
Aunt Jean and Uncle William Avery in a tenement building for two years until
Mother had saved enough money to bring us back to Detroit.

Mother kept shaking the report card at me as she sat on the side of my bed. 21
"You have to work harder. You have to use that good brain that God gave you, Bennie. Do you understand that?"

"Yes, Mother." Each time she paused, I would dutifully say those words.   22

"I work among rich people, people who are educated," she said. "I watch how 23 they act, and I know they can do anything they want to do. And so can you." She put her arm on my shoulder. "Bennie, you can do anything they can do—only you can do it better!"

Mother had said those words before. Often. At the time, they did not mean 24 much to me. Why should they? I really believed that I was the dumbest kid in fifth grade, but of course, I never told her that.

"I just don't know what to do about you boys," she said. "I'm going to talk to 25 God about you and Curtis." She paused, stared into space, then said (more to herself than to me), "I need the Lord's guidance on what to do. You just can't bring in any more report cards like this."

As far as I was concerned, the report card matter was over.   26

The next day was like the previous ones—just another bad day in school, an- 27 other day of being laughed at because I did not get a single problem right in arithmetic and couldn't get any words right on the spelling test. As soon as I came home from school, I changed into play clothes and ran outside. Most of the boys my age played softball, or the game I liked best, "Tip the Top."

We played Tip the Top by placing a bottle cap on one of the sidewalk cracks. 28 Then taking a ball—any kind that bounced—we'd stand on a line and take turns throwing the ball at the bottle top, trying to flip it over. Whoever succeeded got two points. If anyone actually moved the cap more than a few inches, he won five points. Ten points came if he flipped it into the air and it landed on the other side.

When it grew dark or we got tired, Curtis and I would finally go inside and 29 watch TV. The set stayed on until we went to bed. Because Mother worked long hours, she was never home until just before we went to bed. Sometimes I would awaken when I heard her unlocking the door.

Two evenings after the incident with the report card, Mother came home about 30 an hour before our bedtime. Curtis and I were sprawled out, watching TV. She walked across the room, snapped off the set, and faced both of us. "Boys," she said, "you're wasting too much of your time in front of that television. You don't get an education from staring at television all the time."

Before either of us could make a protest, she told us that she had been praying 31 for wisdom. "The Lord's told me what to do," she said. "So from now on, you will not watch television, except for two preselected programs each week."

"Just *two* programs?" I could hardly believe she would say such a terrible 32 thing. "That's not—"

"And *only* after you've done your homework. Furthermore, you don't play 33 outside after school, either, until you've done all your homework."

"Everybody else plays outside right after school," I said, unable to think of 34 anything except how bad it would be if I couldn't play with my friends. "I won't have any friends if I stay in the house all the time—"

"That may be," Mother said, "but everybody else is not going to be as success- 35
ful as you are—"

"But, Mother—" 36

"This is what we're going to do. I asked God for wisdom, and this is the answer 37
I got."

I tried to offer several other arguments, but Mother was firm. I glanced at 38
Curtis, expecting him to speak up, but he did not say anything. He lay on the floor,
staring at his feet.

"Don't worry about everybody else. The whole world is full of 'everybody 39
else,' you know that? But only a few make a significant achievement."

The loss of TV and play time was bad enough. I got up off the floor, feeling as 40
if everything was against me. Mother wasn't going to let me play with my friends,
and there would be no more television—almost none, anyway. She was stopping
me from having any fun in life.

"And that isn't all," she said. "Come back, Bennie." 41

I turned around, wondering what else there could be. 42

"In addition," she said, "to doing your homework, you have to read two books 43
from the library each week. Every single week."

"Two books? Two?" Even though I was in fifth grade, I had never read a whole 44
book in my life.

"Yes, two. When you finish reading them, you must write me a book report 45
just like you do at school. You're not living up to your potential, so I'm going to
see that you do."

Usually Curtis, who was two years older, was the more rebellious•. But this 46
time he seemed to grasp the wisdom of what Mother said. He did not say one word.

She stared at Curtis. "You understand?" 47

He nodded. 48

"Bennie, is it clear?" 49

"Yes, Mother." I agreed to do what Mother told me—it wouldn't have occurred 50
to me not to obey—but I did not like it. Mother was being unfair and demanding
more of us than other parents did.

The following day was Thursday. After school, Curtis and I walked to the local 51
branch of the library. I did not like it much, but then I had not spent that much time
in any library.

We both wandered around a little in the children's section, not having any idea 52
about how to select books or which books we wanted to check out.

The librarian came over to us and asked if she could help. We explained that 53
both of us wanted to check out two books.

"What kind of books would you like to read?" the librarian asked. 54

"Animals," I said after thinking about it. "Something about animals." 55

"I'm sure we have several that you'd like." She led me over to a section of 56
books. She left me and guided Curtis to another section of the room. I flipped
through the row of books until I found two that looked easy enough for me to read.

One of them, *Chip, the Dam Builder*—about a beaver—was the first one I had ever checked out. As soon as I got home, I started to read it. It was the first book I ever read all the way through even though it took me two nights. Reluctantly I admitted afterward to Mother that I really had liked reading about Chip.

Within a month I could find my way around the children's section like some-   57
one who had gone there all his life. By then the library staff knew Curtis and me and the kind of books we chose. They often made suggestions. "Here's a delightful book about a squirrel," I remember one of them telling me.

As she told me part of the story, I tried to appear indifferent•, but as soon as   58
she handed it to me, I opened the book and started to read.

Best of all, we became favorites of the librarians. When new books came in   59
that they thought either of us would enjoy, they held them for us. Soon I became fascinated as I realized that the library had so many books—and about so many different subjects.

After the book about the beaver, I chose others about animals—all types of   60
animals. I read every animal story I could get my hands on. I read books about wolves, wild dogs, several about squirrels, and a variety of animals that lived in other countries. Once I had gone through the animal books, I started reading about plants, then minerals, and finally rocks.

My reading books about rocks was the first time the information ever became   61
practical to me. We lived near the railroad tracks, and when Curtis and I took the route to school that crossed by the tracks, I began paying attention to the crushed rock that I noticed between the ties.

As I continued to read more about rocks, I would walk along the tracks, search-   62
ing for different kinds of stones, and then see if I could identify them.

Often I would take a book with me to make sure that I had labeled each stone   63
correctly.

"Agate," I said as I threw the stone. Curtis got tired of my picking up stones   64
and identifying them, but I did not care because I kept finding new stones all the time. Soon it became my favorite game to walk along the tracks and identify the varieties of stones. Although I did not realize it, within a very short period of time, I was actually becoming an expert on rocks.

"That day—for the first time—I realized that Mother had been right. Reading is the way out of ignorance, and the road to achievement. I did not have to be the class dummy anymore."

Two things happened in the second half of fifth grade that convinced me of the   65
importance of reading books.

First, our teacher, Mrs. Williamson, had a spelling bee every Friday afternoon.   66
We'd go through all the words we'd had so far that year. Sometimes she also called out words that we were supposed to have learned in fourth grade. Without fail, I always went down on the first word.

One Friday, though, Bobby Farmer, whom everyone acknowledged as the 67 smartest kid in our class, had to spell "agriculture" as his final word. As soon as the teacher pronounced his word, I thought, I can spell that word. Just the day before, I had learned it from reading one of my library books. I spelled it under my breath, and it was just the way Bobby spelled it.

If I can spell "agriculture," I'll bet I can learn to spell any other word in the 68 *world. I'll bet I can learn to spell better than Bobby Farmer.*

Just that single word, "agriculture," was enough to give me hope.   69

The following week, a second thing happened that forever changed my life. 70 When Mr. Jaeck, the science teacher, was teaching us about volcanoes, he held up an object that looked like a piece of black, glass-like rock. "Does anybody know what this is? What does it have to do with volcanoes?"

Immediately, because of my reading, I recognized the stone. I waited, but none 71 of my classmates raised their hands. I thought, *This is strange. Not even the smart kids are raising their hands.* I raised my hand.

"Yes, Benjamin," he said.   72

I heard snickers around me. The other kids probably thought it was a joke, or 73 that I was going to say something stupid.

"Obsidian," I said.   74

"That's right!" He tried not to look startled•, but it was obvious he hadn't 75 expected me to give the correct answer.

"That's obsidian," I said, "and it's formed by the supercooling of lava when it 76 hits the water." Once I had their attention and realized I knew information no other student had learned, I began to tell them everything I knew about the subject of obsidian, lava, lava flow, supercooling, and compacting of the elements.

When I finally paused, a voice behind me whispered, "Is that Bennie Carson?" 77

"You're absolutely correct," Mr. Jaeck said, and he smiled at me. If he had an- 78 nounced that I'd won a million-dollar lottery, I couldn't have been more pleased and excited.

"Benjamin, that's absolutely, absolutely right," he repeated with enthusiasm 79 in his voice. He turned to the others and said, "That is wonderful! Class, this is a tremendous piece of information Benjamin has just given us. I'm very proud to hear him say this."

For a few moments, I tasted the thrill of achievement. I recall thinking, *Wow,* 80 *look at them. They're all looking at me with admiration. Me, the dummy! The one everybody thinks is stupid. They're looking at me to see if this is really me speaking.*

Maybe, though, it was I who was the most astonished• one in the class. Although 81 I had been reading two books a week because Mother told me to, I had not realized how much knowledge I was accumulating. True, I had learned to enjoy reading, but until then I hadn't realized how it connected with my schoolwork. That day—for the first time—I realized that Mother had been right. Reading is the way out of ignorance, and the road to achievement. I did not have to be the class dummy anymore.

For the next few days, I felt like a hero at school. The jokes about me stopped. 82 The kids started to listen to me. *I'm starting to have fun with this stuff.*

As my grades improved in every subject, I asked myself, "Ben, is there any rea- 83 son you can't be the smartest kid in the class? If you can learn about obsidian, you can learn about social studies and geography and math and science and everything."

That single moment of triumph pushed me to want to read more. From then 84 on, it was as though I could not read enough books. Whenever anyone looked for me after school, they could usually find me in my bedroom—curled up, reading a library book—for a long time, the only thing I wanted to do. I had stopped caring about the TV programs I was missing; I no longer cared about playing Tip the Top or baseball anymore. I just wanted to read.

In a year and a half—by the middle of sixth grade—I had moved to the top of 85 the class.

READING COMPREHENSION QUESTIONS

1. The word *trauma* in "I loved both my mother and my father and went through considerable trauma over their separating. For months afterward, I kept thinking that my parents would get back together, . . . but he never came back" (paragraph 20) means

   a. love.

   b. knowledge.

   c. distance.

   d. suffering.

2. The word *acknowledged* in "One Friday, though, Bobby Farmer, whom everyone acknowledged as the smartest kid in our class, had to spell 'agriculture' as his final word" (paragraph 67) means

   a. denied.

   b. recognized.

   c. forgot.

   d. interrupted.

3. Which sentence best expresses the central idea of the selection?

   a. Children who grow up in single-parent homes may spend large amounts of time home alone.

   b. Because of parental guidance that led to a love of reading, the author was able to go from academic failure to success.

   c. Parents should stay committed to their marriage when their children are young.

   d. Today's young people watch too much television day after day.

4. Which sentence best expresses the main idea of paragraph 56?

  a. Bennie's first experience with a library book was positive.

  b. The first book that Bennie ever checked out at a library was about a beaver.

  c. The librarian was very helpful to Bennie and Curtis.

  d. At first, Bennie could not read most of the animal books at the library.

5. Which sentence best expresses the main idea of paragraphs 61–64?

  a. Books about rocks gave the author his first practical benefits from reading.

  b. Curtis took little interest in what his brother had learned about rocks.

  c. The author found a piece of agate by the railroad tracks.

  d. Studying rocks can be a fascinating experience.

6. In Boston, Bennie

  a. had an excellent teacher.

  b. attended a public school.

  c. longed for his parents to get together again.

  d. lived with his father in a tenement building.

7. To get her sons to do better in school, Mrs. Carson insisted that they

  a. watch educational TV.

  b. finish their homework before playing.

  c. read one library book every month.

  d. all of the above.

8. We can conclude that Mrs. Carson believed

  a. education leads to success.

  b. her sons needed to be forced to live up to their potential.

  c. socializing was less important to her sons than a good education.

  d. all of the above.

9. We can infer that Bennie Carson believed he was dumb because

  a. in Boston he had gotten behind in school.

  b. other students laughed at him.

  c. he had done his best when he first started at Higgins Elementary School, but he still got poor grades.

  d. all of the above.

10. From paragraphs 70–80, we can infer that

  a. Bennie thought his classmates were stupid because they did not know about obsidian.

  b. Mr. Jaeck knew less about rocks than Bennie did.

   c. this was the first time Bennie had answered a difficult question correctly in class.

   d. Mr. Jaeck thought that Bennie had taken too much class time explaining about obsidian.

TECHNIQUE QUESTIONS

1. Instead of pausing to describe Bennie's mother, the author reveals her character through the specific details of her actions and words. For example, what does paragraph 25 tell us about Mrs. Carson?

   Paragraph 25 reveals Mrs. Carson's extreme concern about and devotion to her sons.

   It also illustrates her wisdom (regarding the value of education) and her powerful

   spirituality.

2. What is the main order in which the details of this reading are organized—time order or listing order? Locate and write down three of the many transitions that are used as part of that order.

   Time order. Answers include: first, Before long, Now, later, before, afterward, next, then,

   finally, after, until, following, within a month, soon, In a year and a half.

3. The author states in paragraph 65, "Two things happened in the second half of fifth grade that convinced me of the importance of reading books." In paragraph 66, the first of those two events is introduced with a listing transition. In paragraph 70, the second event is introduced with another listing transition. Write those two transitions on the lines below.

       first   *second*

DISCUSSION QUESTIONS

1. The author recalls his failure in the classroom as an eight-year-old child by writing "Perhaps I wasn't emotionally able to learn much." Why does he make this statement? In general, what things in a child's home or social life might interfere with his or her education?

2. Part of Mrs. Carson's plan for helping her sons do better in school was limiting them to two television shows a week. How much of a role do you think this limit played in the success of her plan? Do you agree with her that unrestricted television can be harmful to children? Explain.

3. Reading on a regular basis helped turn Carson's life around. Think about your daily schedule. If you were to do regular reading, where in your day could you find time to relax for half an hour and just read? What would you choose to read? How do you think you might benefit from becoming a regular reader?

WRITING ASSIGNMENTS

1. The reading tells about some of Carson's key school experiences, both positive and negative. Write a paragraph about one of your key experiences in school. Use concrete details—actions, comments, reactions, and so on—to help your readers picture what happened. (To see how Carson used details to bring classroom scenes to life, look at paragraphs 65–82.)

   To select an event to write about, try asking yourself the following questions:

   • Which teachers or events in school influenced how I felt about myself?

   • What specific incidents stand out in my mind as I think back to elementary school?

   Once you know which experience you'll write about, use freewriting to help you remember and record the details. Here is one student's freewriting for this assignment:

   > In second grade, Richard L. sat next to me. A really good artist. He would draw something, and it really looked like something. He was so good at choosing colors. Good at crayons, good at water paint. His pictures were always picked by teacher. They were shown on bulletin board. I remember his drawing of a circus and acrobats and animals and clowns. Many colors and details. I felt pretty bad in art. But I loved it and couldn't wait for art in class. One day the teacher read a story about a boy who looked at the mountains and wondered what was on the other side, the mountains were huge, dark. After the reading the teacher said "Paint something from the story." I painted those mountains, big purple brown mountains. Watercolor dripped to show slopes and a colored sunset, at the top of the picture a thin slice of blue sky. Next day I sat down in my desk in the morning. Then I saw my picture was on the bulletin board! Later teacher passed by me and put a hand on my shoulder and whispered good job, lovely picture. Made me feel really proud. The feeling lasted a long time.

   After the details of the experience are on paper, you will be free to concentrate on a more carefully constructed version of the event. The author of the freewriting above, for instance, needed to think of a topic sentence. So when writing the first draft, she began with this sentence: "A seemingly small experience in elementary school encouraged me greatly." Writing drafts is also the time to add any persuasive details you may have missed at first. When working on her second draft, the author of the above added at the end. "I felt very proud, which gave me confidence to work harder in all my school subjects."

Before writing out your final version, remember to check for grammar, punctuation, and spelling errors.

2. Reading helped Bennie, and it can do a lot for adults, too. Most of us, however, don't have someone around to insist that we do a certain amount of personal reading every week. In addition, many of us don't have the amount of free time that Bennie and Curtis had. How can adults find time to read more? Write a paragraph listing several ways adults can add more reading to their lives.

A good prewriting strategy for this assignment is making a list. Simply write out as many ways as you can think of. Don't worry about putting them in any special order. You will select and organize the strategies you wish to include in your paper after accumulating as many ideas as you can. Here is an example of a prewriting list for this paper:

<u>Ways adults can increase the amount of time they spend reading:</u>

on the bus to and from work/school

while eating breakfast

instead of watching some TV

choose motivating materials (articles, books about hobbies, problems, etc.)

Feel free to use items from this list, but add at least one or two of your own points to include in your paper.

3. "Do It Better!" suggests that television can interfere with children's academic progress. Write a paragraph on what you believe is another unfortunate effect of television. You may feel that television includes too much violence, that TV advertising encourages children to want to buy too much, or that TV sitcoms promote poor family values. After deciding what effect you wish to write about, make a list of possible points of support. You may find it helpful to spend a few sessions in front of the TV with a notebook. Following, for instance, is part of a list of notes that can be used to support the point "TV advertising promotes poor nutrition."

<u>During kids' cartoon show:</u>

In a sugary chocolate cereal, marshmallow ghosts appear once milk is added. Children are pictured enjoying these ghosts' appearances and loving the cereal.

Chocolate-dipped cookies are included in boxes of another chocolate cereal. Appealing cartoon characters invite children to look for these boxes.

<u>During talk show:</u>

Ad for soda (empty calories) shows symbols of Christmas, making the soda seem like a healthy holiday drink.

An ad for corn chips (high fat) shows happy, healthy faces finishing a huge bowl of the chips.

Lost Years, Found Dreams

Regina Ruiz

PREVIEW

Divorced, far from home, with three children, not very fluent in English—Regina Ruiz could easily have become a sad statistic, a woman sunk in despair after a failed marriage. But Ruiz decided she had given up enough years of her life; she would reclaim the rest. Her story is hardly a fairy tale with a magical happy ending. But it is perhaps even better; it is the story of a courageous, life-loving commitment to a new and meaningful future.

WORDS TO WATCH

regal (2): royal

haze (3): confused state of mind

intervened (7): came in to change a situation

bleak (8): not hopeful

bleary-eyed (18): with blurry vision

preoccupation (18): extreme concern with something

Morpheus (20): the god of dreams in Greek mythology

I feel funny. So very funny, telling you about my life, my feelings, my secrets. 1
I do not know how to welcome you into my heart and soul. You see, nobody ever asked me what I thought or how I felt about life's challenges. Or, maybe, nobody ever really cared about what I thought.

My journey to Burlington County College began many years ago in Caracas, 2
Venezuela, where I was born and grew to be a young lady full of energy and life. My parents called me Regina because there was something regal• about the sound. They had high hopes of my marrying a local boy from a good, wealthy family. You know the kind—slick, black hair, long sideburns, driving a sports car. The kind who brings you flowers on every date and swears his undying love for you three days a week, and the other days he is sleeping with Maria, the local social worker.

To get even, or because I was in a romantic haze,• I met and married a U.S. 3
Marine from Des Moines, Iowa, who was stationed at our local embassy, where I also worked.

Marriage, a home in America, and three beautiful children occupied twenty- 4
five years of my life.

Where did my life go? It went somewhere. But there is no lost-and-found 5
department for lost years.

The marriage was bad. It was so bad that I cried every night for all those years. **6** I would tell myself, "You are in a strange country—maybe the customs are different. The children need you, and you cannot admit failure to your parents back in Venezuela."

As luck would have it, fate intervened.• My ex-Marine husband found some- **7** one new and left me and the children with no money, very hurt and depressed.

I quickly took an inventory—foreign-born, with not a great command of the **8** English language, no money, no job training, and two kids in college. The future looked bleak.•

But it did not stop. My father died. I loved him so much, and he was always my **9** source of strength in need. Mother became ill.

I felt very hurt, lonely, angry, and very sorry for myself. **10**

However, I remembered a saying my Dad would quote to me when things were **11** going wrong and the future looked black. He may have gotten this quotation from the Spanish edition of *Reader's Digest*. He would say, "My dear, it is always the darkest when you are fresh out of matches."

"Dad, I am out of matches." Or so I thought. **12**

I decided to make my life something worthwhile by helping people. I wanted **13** to help and heal and maybe, at the same time, heal myself.

I appeared before the college doors with my knees shaking and full of doubt. **14** I wanted to be a nurse.

I enrolled in college. I was proud of myself for not falling into the garbage pit **15** waiting so close by.

Then the fun began—subjects which were very hard for me. **16**

In order to survive, I managed to get two jobs to keep up with house payments **17** and food. The kids found college money by working and by appealing to their father. I met my challenges on a daily basis.

Now, my days are very active and long. Before the sun makes its appearance, **18** I stumble bleary-eyed• to the shower and afterward select the day's outfit. After a quick check in the mirror, I make my way downstairs to prepare a quick breakfast along with my lunch, feed the cat (who happens to be my alarm clock), and do what seem like a million other small chores. Then I drive for forty-five minutes to the Pemberton Campus, while studying my chemistry key notes on index cards before a test. I do this with tears in my eyes. You see, at the same time I am worrying about the situation with my water heater that slowly but surely is leaking and may not last until the new one can be installed. In addition, I am anxious to schedule my exterminator's visit to treat the termites discovered in my basement. My preoccupation• with such household woes is due to a canceled appointment to have my furnace cleaned, which resulted in a periodic spray of soot.

After a hectic morning of classes, I rush to my car for a hurried thirty-minute **19** ride to the office, where a desk piled high with import documents is waiting for me, along with innumerable phone calls from the brokers, customs officials, and suppliers. Meanwhile, an impatient boss wants to know the precise location of one of the fifty containers traveling between eastern Europe and Burlington, New Jersey.

As the clock winds toward 5 P.M., I get ready to travel back to the Cinnaminson Campus for another round of classes. As I arrive on campus, I waste another thirty minutes searching for that nonexistent parking spot. My class continues until ten o'clock in the evening, and I praise the Lord it doesn't last longer. By that time, I am beginning to see double. I slowly make my way to the car and begin the long commute home, counting in my mind how many customers I will see as a result of my second job—hairdressing. On evenings when I have no classes scheduled, I take appointments to cut hair or give permanents. As I arrive home, I find a hungry son and starving cat, both waiting to be fed. I usually cook something simple for us, then proceed to do the few dishes because I hate the thought of adding one more chore to my early-morning schedule. By the time I finish getting ready for bed, it is midnight; I look up and see the stairway leading to the bedroom, which by then seems longer than the one outside the Philadelphia Museum of Art, and proceed to crawl in bed and into the arms of Morpheus.• 20

> "I decided to make my life something worthwhile by helping people. I wanted to help and heal and maybe, at the same time, heal myself."

On many nights, I do not stay there long. At 3 A.M., maybe 4 A.M., my eyes pop open. The thought, "Am I ready for the test? Do I understand the material?" makes me sit upright in a panic. Rather than toss and turn uneasily for the rest of the night, I get out of bed and open my textbooks for a couple of hours. If fatigue finally wins, I may fall back into bed before getting up for the day. 21

Without long luxurious stretches of time to study, I must constantly search out such little windows of opportunity to prepare for class. When the laundry is washing, I study. While supper is simmering on the stove, I study. When a customer cancels her appointment for a haircut, I thank the Lord for a free hour, and I study. "Mom, if I studied half as hard as you, I'd be a straight-A student," says my son. But he understands that the life of a working mother is not designed to make going to college easy. If I do not budget my time carefully, I will fail. 22

People question the wisdom of my studying to be a nurse. It may take four or five years. 23

"You will never last," they tell me. 24

"You will be too old to lift a bedpan," they mock. 25

But I am not discouraged. There are twenty more courses ahead of me before I get into the nursing area. While all these things challenge me, the greatest of all is to be able to hold my head high. 26

Somehow, just somehow, I think it might be all worth it—if I can hold the hand of someone dying all alone in a cold hospital ward and whisper in the patient's ear, "You are not alone, I am here, I am here, I will never leave you." 27

Maybe, just maybe, I will find that life that was lost. It is out there somewhere. 28

But I know one thing—I am in charge, and I will never let go again. Never. 29

An Update

Regina Ruiz successfully completed her registered nurse degree and is only a few credits away from earning her bachelor's degree at Jefferson University in Philadelphia. She is a nurse at Voorhees Pediatric Rehabilitation Hospital in New Jersey. 30

At the hospital, Regina's patients range in age from newborns to eighteen-year-olds. As she grows attached to particular patients, she requests that they be assigned to her daily shift, giving "extra love" to children battling illness, fear, and loneliness. "To see tiny preemies and children who are so sick grow and get better and be released to their families—it is wonderful to be part of that. School was very difficult, and nursing is a demanding profession, but when I am at work I am in heaven." 31

When she is not working, she takes pride in keeping her home beautiful. "After my divorce and through all those long difficult years, I worried so much about not being able to keep up with things," she said. "The roof leaked so badly at one point I had trash cans sitting in the living room. So I had to learn to budget my money as well as my time. When I had three jobs, one was for tuition and food, and the others were for repairs—a roof, siding, new windows, everything. Now I can look at the house and feel so good. A little neighbor boy told me the other day, 'Mrs. Ruiz, you have the nicest house on the street.'" 32

She still does hair for a handful of longtime clients. "They were my friends for so many years," she said. "When I'd come home from a test crying because I was sure I'd failed, they'd be the ones to say, 'No, Regina! You're going to make it.' Now, maybe I don't have to cut hair anymore to earn a living," she says with a chuckle, "but how can I tell them to go jump in the lake?" 33

READING COMPREHENSION QUESTIONS

1. The words *took an inventory* in "I quickly took an inventory—foreign-born, with not a great command of the English language, no money, no job training, and two kids in college" (paragraph 8) mean

   a. fell asleep.

   b. made a detailed list.

   c. formed a plan of action.

   d. got a job.

2. The word *appealing* in "The kids found college money by working and by appealing to their father" (paragraph 17) means

   a. pretending.

   b. refusing.

    c. suggesting an alternative.

    (d.) making a request.

3. Which sentence best expresses the central idea of the selection?

    a. Ruiz could not tell her parents back in Venezuela that her marriage was unhappy.

    b. Ruiz should not have married the Marine and moved so far from home.

    (c.) After a bad marriage, Ruiz successfully took charge of her own life and future.

    d. Ruiz is often exhausted by her schedule of school and two jobs.

4. A main idea may cover more than one paragraph. Which sentence best expresses the main idea of paragraphs 11–13?

    a. Ruiz remembered a saying her father used to say.

    (b.) Ruiz at first saw no way out of a bad situation but then thought of a worthwhile path.

    c. Ruiz's father may have gotten inspiration from the Spanish edition of *Reader's Digest*.

    d. Ruiz thought helping people was a worthwhile goal.

5. Which sentence best expresses the main idea of paragraphs 21–22?

    a. Ruiz never has time to study, so she goes to class unprepared.

    b. Ruiz always chooses to sleep an extra hour or two rather than study for class.

    (c.) Ruiz values studying and uses every spare minute for schoolwork.

    d. Because of her excess leisure time, Ruiz always has enough opportunity for study.

6. Ruiz's marriage ended when

    a. she left her husband for another man.

    b. she enrolled in college and her husband divorced her.

    (c.) her husband left her for another woman.

    d. Ruiz's parents demanded that she come back to Venezuela.

7. According to the "Update," Ruiz now works as a(n)

    a. office worker and baby-sitter.

    (b.) nurse and occasional hairdresser.

    c. translator and cleaning woman.

    d. parking lot attendant and veterinarian's assistant.

8. We can infer that Ruiz

    a. wishes she had married "a local boy from a good, wealthy family."

    (b.) believes she married the U.S. Marine too quickly.

    c. regrets having three children.

    d. believes enrolling in the nursing program was not wise.

9. We can infer that in the passage below the author uses the word *matches* to refer to

    a. heat.

    (b.) solutions.

    c. the love between a child and a parent.

    d. something that will light a cigarette.

He would say, "My dear, it is always the darkest when you are fresh out of matches." "Dad, I am out of matches." Or so I thought. (Paragraphs 11–12)

10. We can conclude one reason Ruiz wanted to become a nurse was that

    (a.) she believed that helping other people would help her, too.

    b. Venezuela needed more nurses.

    c. her father always wanted her to be a nurse.

    d. nursing was the easiest course offered by the college she attended.

TECHNIQUE QUESTIONS

1. In paragraph 5, Regina asks the question "Where did my life go?" Where in the essay does she return to the image of her "lost life"? Write here the number of the paragraph in which she returns to this image: __28__. What is the difference between how she discusses her lost life in paragraph 5 and in the later paragraph?

   In paragraph 28, she is optimistic about finding her lost life again.

2. Ruiz begins her essay by describing a series of disappointments and her resulting depression. Later, she describes her decision to make something good out of her life and what her life has been like since then. In what paragraph of her essay does she make the transition between those two sections, and what word marks that transition?

   Paragraph 11; the transition word is "However."

3. Who wrote paragraphs 1–29 of the reading? Was the update written by the same person? What evidence supports your answers to these questions?

Paragraphs 1–29 were written by Ruiz herself; this is indicated by the use of "I."

The update was written by someone else—probably the editor of her story or this

textbook. This is indicated by the use of "she."

DISCUSSION QUESTIONS

1. Ruiz stayed with an unhappy marriage for twenty-five years. During those years, she told herself, "You are in a strange country—maybe the customs are different. The children need you, and you cannot admit failure to your parents back in Venezuela." Judging from your own experience and observations of people around you, are these typical reasons for remaining in an unhappy relationship? Are they *good* reasons?

2. Like Ruiz, adults who return to college often have a difficult time balancing the demands of their work, family, and classes. What challenges do you face as a student? What ways have you found to deal with them?

3. Ruiz briefly explains her decision to become a nurse. Why have you chosen your own course of study? What about it interests you? What do you hope it will offer you after college?

WRITING ASSIGNMENTS

1. Ruiz and her parents had very different ideas about whom she should marry. How well have your plans for your life conformed to your parents' hopes for you? Write a paragraph about a decision in your life on which you and your parents have either clashed or agreed. In your paragraph, include concrete details that show exactly what your parents had in mind and how they communicated their hopes to you. Also, explain clearly your decision and the reasons for it. Here are some sample topic sentences for this assignment:

> Although my parents urged me to become a teacher, I am studying to be a veterinary assistant.
>
> My parents did not want me to marry my high school girlfriend, and I surprised them—and myself—by doing what they wanted.

2. In paragraph 18, Regina writes about her typical morning, from stumbling out of bed to getting to and through school. She includes various specific details about getting ready in the morning, studying for a test while driving to school, and thinking about the "household woes" that plague her all the while. Do some

freewriting or write a list of details you can use for a descriptive paragraph of what a typical morning is like for you. After accumulating enough information about a typical morning, think of a topic sentence that will cover all of the details you will write about. Here, for instance, is one possible topic sentence:

> A typical morning in my life starts slowly before developing into some very hectic but productive hours.

Before writing your final draft, double-check your topic sentence to see if it still covers the details in your paragraph or if it needs adjusting. (Perhaps, for example, you realize that your morning doesn't start so slowly after all.) Also, use a few time transitions to make the sequence of events clear to your reader. You could write, for example, "First I hear my alarm go off at 6 A.M. Then I take a shower, ending with a few seconds of ice-cold water to wake up my body and my brain."

3. Ruiz was proud of herself for taking control of her life and enrolling in college, rather than getting stuck in depression and self-pity after her marriage ended. When have you taken an action that you are proud of? Write an essay about such a time.

In your first paragraph, state your central idea. Here are some possibilities:

> I am proud of myself for quitting smoking.
>
> I am proud of myself for leaving an abusive marriage and getting my life together afterward.
>
> I am proud of myself for confronting a friend about her drinking problem.
>
> I am proud of myself for earning my high school diploma.

Then continue by explaining the situation you faced, how you decided to take the course of action you did, and what the results have been.

Below is a sample scratch outline for this paper.

> Central idea: I am proud of myself for confronting a friend about her drinking problem.
> 1. Lana's drinking and its effect on her family and job performance
> 2. The day I told Lana she was hurting herself and her children
> 3. Lana's decision to join a twelve-step program

A great deal of specific detail would be needed to support each general point in this outline. Freewriting or making a list, or both, would help generate the necessary specific details.

The introduction of the outlined essay might begin with an anecdote dramatizing Lana's problem. The conclusion could restate the central idea and include a brief explanation of how Lana is doing now.

My Two Moms

Zach Wahls

PREVIEW

In this selection, Zach Wahls describes each characteristic that makes his family unlike the average family in America. However, he also explains how, despite these differences—including the fact that he was raised by a same-sex couple—not once has he ever felt anything less than "normal."

WORDS TO WATCH

homogenous (1): the same or similar

disparaged (3): belittled

renders (3): causes

inciting (6): provoking

aesthetic (6): visual

discerning (7): showing insight and understanding

immutable (9): unchangeable

While this is a reality I was at first hesitant to acknowledge, ultimately, there is no 1 doubt that I have always been different. Folks from all walks of life have been informing and reminding me of this difference since I was a young child, and they continue to do so today. But it is on rare occasion that they explicitly define what this difference is, and I suspect the hesitancy to do so is the result of a culture that by and large craves conformity whenever possible and finds comfort in its largely homogenous° nature.

I am different insofar as I am defined by a number of traits I do not share with 2 the majority of my peers. Among many things, I am the son of a same-sex couple, was conceived using assistive reproductive technology, and scored in the 99th percentile of the ACT. I am also an Eagle Scout, a small-business owner, a Unitarian Universalist, and a state championship-winning debater.

My family, too, is undeniably different from the American mean. Two moms 3 is a familial construct that was considered novel until only recently, though it is still disparaged° as invalid by a shrinking—though increasingly shrill—minority. That minority would have you believe that this difference is all defining, that it disqualifies my mothers from access to civil marriage (though the Iowa constitution would beg to differ), and that it renders° my family undeserving of all the rights, privileges, and protections enjoyed every day by "straight" families.

Yet my moms' same-sex relationship is just one difference among many that 4 are found in families of all shapes and sizes.

At a young age, my family experienced the cruel reality of a chronic autoim- **5** mune disease. My mom Terry was diagnosed with multiple sclerosis at the age of forty-four, a development that, at nine years old, I could not even begin to under- stand, And, as a result, there is another significant difference between the Reger- Wahls household and the rest of America; After twelve years of struggling with multiple sclerosis, the one treatment that has worked for my mom is a radical change to her diet, so you'll find no gluten-based foods in our cupboards and no dairy products in our refrigerator. Though—and don't mention this to her—you'll find plenty to both at my apartment.

Yes, I can certainly see my family's differences—and I can acknowledge my **6** own—but I must confess, however, that I am unable to actually *feel* those differ- ences. I have, after all, no control group against which I may compare the experi- ences of my life, no memories of a more "normal," one-mom-and-one-dad past against which to weigh the present Though society regularly informs me that my family structure is different, I feel as though I'm being told that I am wearing dif- ferent colored socks. Yes, you might not like how they look, but beyond inciting• the occasional bout of aesthetic• displeasure, how does it affect your life?

I know mixing socks is purely a visual example. Being raised by a lesbian cou- **7** ple is substantively different from being raised by a straight, mixed-gender couple. But I suspect you would find yourself incapable of discerning• either the sex of my parents or color of my socks from simply shaking my hand and having a conversa- tion over coffee. In fact, though twenty years is hardly an impressive range of time upon which to make bold proclamations, I will proclaim that, to date, not once has anyone ever confronted me, having realized independently that I was raised by a gay couple. Not once. And I'll be surprised if that changes over the next twenty.

> "Yes, I can certainly see my family's differences—and I can acknowledge
> my own—but I must confess, however, that I am unable to actually *feel* those
> differences."

But besides the obvious, what were these substantive differences? Well, **8** I learned how to shave from my best friend's dad and how to tie a tie from an article in *Playboy.* I had to carefully explain to an Indian visa officer that I left the "Name of Father" space blank on my visa application because I don't know it—I've never met the man, nor do I plan to. The sexuality of my parents, and the rejection they felt from the Christian faith in which they were both raised, led them to embrace the more accepting teachings of Unitarian Universalism, another meaningful and substantive difference from the American mean.

Yet when I declared before the Iowa House Judiciary Committee during that **9** hearing on House Joint Resolution 6, that "the sexuality of my parents has had zero effect on the content of my character," I was not bearing falsehood. I believe this with all my heart to be true. After all, one's sexuality does not determine a person's response to discrimination. That response is informed not by the color of your skin, your gender identity, your sexuality, or any other immutable• characteristic, but by the beliefs you hold and the values you prize—*the content of your character.*

READING COMPREHENSION QUESTIONS

1. The word *mean* in "My family, too, is undeniably different from the American mean" (paragraph 3) means
   a. cruelty.
   b. model.
   c. standard.
   d. ideal.

2. The word *construct* in "Two moms is a familial construct that was considered novel until only recently, though it is still disparaged as invalid by a shrinking—though increasingly shrill—minority" (paragraph 3) means
   a. structure.
   b. marriage.
   c. agreement.
   d. movement.

3. Which sentence expresses the central idea of the selection?
   a. The author feels that he and his family are no different from the average American family.
   b. The author does not believe that being different invites discrimination.
   c. Just because a family does not conform to the standard mold, it should not be denied the rights, privileges, and protections that everyday "straight" families enjoy.
   d. Same-sex marriage should be legalized.

4. Which sentence best expresses the main idea of paragraph 6?
   a. The author compares his family structure to a pair of socks: although some people may not like the "look" of it, it bears no direct impact on their lives.
   b. The author wishes he knew what it was like to grow up with a mother and a father.
   c. The author believes the differences that make his family unique also make it difficult for him to adjust to everyday life.
   d. The author agrees that his family is not normal.

5. Which sentence best expresses the main idea of paragraph 9?
   a. Discrimination is solely about the color of one's skin.
   b. Same-sex couples should not be parents.
   c. If a parent teaches his or her child good values, it does not matter whether that parent is gay or straight.
   d. The content of one's character has little to do with how one responds to discrimination.

6. The author cites several characteristics that make his family "meaningfully different" from other American families; three of those characteristics concern
   a. religion, diet, and wealth.
   b. social status, economic status, and occupational status.
   c. social status, religion, and wealth.
   d. religion, parental structure, and diet.

7. Zach Wahls's mother Terry became sick with
   a. multiple sclerosis at the age of forty-four.
   b. a wheat allergy and had to restrict her diet.
   c. a serious illness that could not be treated.
   d. multiple sclerosis for nine years.

8. The author compares his parents' relationship to a pair of socks because he believes that
   a. parents must come in pairs.
   b. same-sex parents can relate better to their children.
   c. as long as parents do what they're supposed to do for their children it doesn't matter if they are the same sex or not—much like mismatched socks that keep the feet warm.
   d. no one cares what kinds of socks one wears; neither does anyone care who one's parents are.

9. Based on the reading, we can infer that Zach believes in the following:
   a. People embrace "differences" only insofar as they conform to their own notions of "normal."
   b. Children of gay couples develop healthier outlooks on life than children of straight couples.
   c. Parents raise their children to embrace value systems that only conform to those of the rest of society.
   d. His family is fundamentally no different from any other family in the world.

10. Zach's final line hearkens back to Martin Luther King Jr.'s speech "I Have a Dream" in the effort to
   a. gain sympathy.
   b. rally another March on Washington.
   c. remind others that one's values and belief systems are based on one's character.
   d. draw attention to his cause.

TECHNIQUE QUESTIONS

1. Wahls uses several literary techniques to drive home some key points about being different and what that ultimately means to him. Provide an example for each of the techniques listed below and explain whether you think the techniques he chose are effective and why.

   Repetition:

   Different, difference - effective because the more the author emphasizes difference, the more we see that difference is not abnormal.

   Analogy:

   A pair of socks to his same-sex parents - effective because like a pair of matching socks that keep the feet warm, so can same-sex parents care for their children.

   Rhetorical questioning:

   "But, besides the obvious, what were these substantive differences?"—effective because it forces the reader to consider what some of these answers might be before they make any judgements.

2. The author makes a point to differentiate between "differences" and "substantive differences." Why do you think he makes this distinction? What are some examples he identifies as "differences" and some he identifies as "substantive differences"?

   Some differences are just superficial; but even the substantive differences don't matter.

   Example of differences: The author's physical traits are different from the traits of others.

   Substantive differences: His familial construct does not follow the standard.

3. The author's thesis statement appears in the final paragraph of the selection. What is that thesis statement, and why do you think he chose to introduce it in the final paragraph instead of the first? What impact does this have on the reader?

   One's sexuality does not determine a person's response to discrimination. He introduces it at the end of the essay to further emphasize the fact that differences does not make one deserving of discrimination, and differences do not shape one's reaction to discrimination--overall values and character do.

DISCUSSION QUESTIONS

1. Throughout the selection, Wahls talks very openly about the things that make him "different" and how those differences make him feel. In what ways are you different from others, and how have you felt about those differences?

2. Wahls grew up with two mothers, and this did not hinder him from learning important life lessons, achieving certain goals, or developing a strong character. Given that, do you think it matters whether a child is raised by a straight couple or a gay couple?

3. The author's family structure does not conform with the societal norm, yet it is still a family structure—just a *different* one. He feels that, as such, his family should not be denied the rights, privileges, and protections afforded to the more standard family structures. Do you agree or disagree? Why?

WRITING ASSIGNMENTS

1. Wahls shares a number of personal experiences that he feels has set him apart from others. Write a paragraph about a personal or family experience that you feel makes you unique. Use concrete details, vivid images, and clear language to help your readers visualize the event or situation. (To see how Wahls used details to bring his personal experiences to life, look at paragraph 5.)

   To select an experience to write about, try answering the following questions:

   • Wahls mentions in paragraph 2 that he was a "state championship–winning debater." Was there any one thing you particularly excelled at in school that set you apart from others? What influenced that success?

   • What do you know about your parents' childhoods? How did their upbringing affect your own?

   Once you've decided on an experience or situation to write about, freewrite to jar your memory. Remember not to worry about punctuation, grammar, or complete sentences. The goal is to write whatever comes to mind about this experience and to get your ideas flowing. Following is a freewriting example for this assignment:

   > I remember watching my brother play guitar and thinking that I wanted to play, too. He taught himself when he was in junior high. but I wasn't good at teaching myself things like that. Too lazy? Couldn't focus. Music not my thing but wanted it to be. Oldest brother played violin. Big sister great at sports. When I was in fifth grade, school hosted a drawing contest. I always liked to draw. Doodled all the time. Liked making faces especially, drawing people when they're not looking. One day watching brother playing guitar I drew him. Didn't think it was so bad and for fun, thought I'd enter it in the contest. I did. I won first place for my grade! Been drawing ever since. I've had a few of my drawings displayed at local cafes. Sold a few. One local gallery owner took me under her wing. She's my mentor and helps me to expand my talents. I'm now learning watercolor. I have my own studio, that gallery owner, Inna, pays for. Everyone tells me I'm talented for someone so you. Hope to be famous one day. Art school first! Maybe one day will learn to play guitar. Nowadays, I draw them instead.

2. In paragraph 1, Wahls writes, "But it is on rare occasion that they explicitly define what this difference is, and I suspect the hesitancy to do so is the result of a culture that by and large craves conformity whenever possible and finds comfort in its largely homogenous nature." Write an essay that either supports or disagrees with this premise. Use an informal outline to help organize your essay. Your outline could look something like this:

Central idea: People crave conformity because it is comforting.

Thesis statement: I agree that people crave conformity because they find it is familiar, it is predictable, and it helps maintain order.

1. Topic sentence about familiarity.
   - Supporting detail.
   - Supporting detail.
   - Supporting detail.
2. Topic sentence about predictability.
   - Supporting detail.
   - Supporting detail.
   - Supporting detail.
3. Topic sentence about maintaining order.
   - Supporting detail.
   - Supporting detail.
   - Supporting detail.

Conclusion.

Be sure to include concrete details, examples, and transitional statements between each paragraph.

3. In this essay, Wahls openly talks about being raised by two mothers and the outcomes of his upbringing. Write an essay in which you compare and contrast the outcomes of being raised by your parents with those of Wahls. Think critically about whether your parents' sexuality had anything to do with the differences or similarities. Use a prewriting strategy such as clustering to help you come up with topics for each of your main and supporting ideas.

All the Good Things

Sister Helen Mrosla

PREVIEW

Teachers must often wonder if their efforts on behalf of their students are appreciated—or even noticed. In this article, Sister Helen Mrosla, a Franciscan nun from Little Falls, Minnesota, tells the story of a moment when she learned the answer to that question in a bittersweet way. This powerful account of a true incident in her life has been reprinted many times, as well as widely circulated on the Internet.

WORDS TO WATCH

mischievousness (1): minor misbehavior

accustomed (2): used to

novice (3): new

deliberately (5): slowly and on purpose

accomplished (12): been successful at

lull (13): brief silence

sheepishly (20): with embarrassment

frazzled (20): worn-out; ragged

1   He was in the first third-grade class I taught at Saint Mary's School in Morris, Minnesota. All thirty-four of my students were dear to me, but Mark Eklund was one in a million. He was very neat in appearance but had that happy-to-be-alive attitude that made even his occasional mischievousness• delightful.

2   Mark talked incessantly. I had to remind him again and again that talking without permission was not acceptable. What impressed me so much, though, was his sincere response every time I had to correct him for misbehaving—"Thank you for correcting me, Sister!" I didn't know what to make of it at first, but before long I became accustomed• to hearing it many times a day.

3   One morning my patience was growing thin when Mark talked once too often, and then I made a novice• teacher's mistake. I looked at him and said, "If you say one more word, I am going to tape your mouth shut!"

4   It wasn't ten seconds later when Chuck blurted out, "Mark is talking again." I hadn't asked any of the students to help me watch Mark, but since I had stated the punishment in front of the class, I had to act on it.

I remember the scene as if it had occurred this morning. I walked to my desk, 5
very deliberately• opened my drawer, and took out a roll of masking tape. Without
saying a word, I proceeded to Mark's desk, tore off two pieces of tape, and made
a big X with them over his mouth. I then returned to the front of the room. As I
glanced at Mark to see how he was doing, he winked at me.

That did it! I started laughing. The class cheered as I walked back to Mark's 6
desk, removed the tape, and shrugged my shoulders. His first words were, "Thank
you for correcting me, Sister."

At the end of the year I was asked to teach junior-high math. The years flew 7
by, and before I knew it Mark was in my classroom again. He was more handsome
than ever and just as polite. Since he had to listen carefully to my instruction in the
"new math," he did not talk as much in ninth grade as he had talked in the third.

One Friday, things just didn't feel right. We had worked hard on a new concept 8
all week, and I sensed that the students were frowning, frustrated with themselves—
and edgy with one another. I had to stop this crankiness before it got out of hand.
So I asked them to list the names of the other students in the room on two sheets of
paper, leaving a space after each name. Then I told them to think of the nicest thing
they could say about each of their classmates and write it down.

It took the remainder of the class period to finish the assignment, and as the 9
students left the room, each one handed me the papers. Charlie smiled. Mark said,
"Thank you for teaching me, Sister. Have a good weekend."

That Saturday, I wrote down the name of each student on a separate sheet of 10
paper, and I listed what everyone else had said about that individual.

On Monday I gave each student his or her list. Before long, the entire class 11
was smiling. "Really?" I heard whispered. "I never knew that meant anything to
anyone!" "I didn't know others liked me so much!"

*"I knew without looking that the papers were the ones on which I had listed all
the good things each of Mark's classmates had said about him."*

No one ever mentioned those papers in class again. I never knew if the students 12
discussed them after class or with their parents, but it didn't matter. The exercise
had accomplished• its purpose. The students were happy with themselves and one
another again.

That group of students moved on. Several years later, after I returned from 13
a vacation, my parents met me at the airport. As we were driving home, Mother
asked me the usual questions about the trip—the weather, my experiences in general. There was a slight lull• in the conversation. Mother gave Dad a sideways
glance and simply said, "Dad?" My father cleared his throat as he usually did
before something important. "The Eklunds called last night," he began. "Really?"
I said. "I haven't heard from them in years. I wonder how Mark is."

Dad responded quietly. "Mark was killed in Vietnam," he said. "The funeral is 14
tomorrow, and his parents would like it if you could attend." To this day I can still
point to the exact spot on I-494 where Dad told me about Mark.

I had never seen a serviceman in a military coffin before. Mark looked so hand- 15
some, so mature. All I could think at that moment was, Mark, I would give all the
masking tape in the world if only you would talk to me.

The church was packed with Mark's friends. Chuck's sister sang "The Battle 16
Hymn of the Republic." Why did it have to rain on the day of the funeral? It was
difficult enough at the graveside. The pastor said the usual prayers, and the bugler
played taps. One by one those who loved Mark took a last walk by the coffin and
sprinkled it with holy water.

I was the last one to bless the coffin. As I stood there, one of the soldiers 17
who had acted as pallbearer came up to me. "Were you Mark's math teacher?"
he asked. I nodded as I continued to stare at the coffin. "Mark talked about you
a lot," he said.

After the funeral, most of Mark's former classmates headed to Chuck's farm- 18
house for lunch. Mark's mother and father were there, obviously waiting for me.
"We want to show you something," his father said, taking a wallet out of his
pocket. "They found this on Mark when he was killed. We thought you might
recognize it."

Opening the billfold, he carefully removed two worn pieces of notebook paper 19
that had obviously been taped, folded, and refolded many times. I knew without
looking that the papers were the ones on which I had listed all the good things each
of Mark's classmates had said about him. "Thank you so much for doing that,"
Mark's mother said. "As you can see, Mark treasured it."

Mark's classmates started to gather around us. Charlie smiled rather sheep- 20
ishly• and said, "I still have my list. It's in the top drawer of my desk at home."
Chuck's wife said, "Chuck asked me to put his list in our wedding album." "I have
mine too," Marilyn said. "It's in my diary." Then Vicki, another classmate, reached
into her pocketbook, took out her wallet, and showed her worn and frazzled• list to
the group. "I carry this with me at all times," Vicki said without batting an eyelash.
"I think we all saved our lists."

That's when I finally sat down and cried. I cried for Mark and for all his friends 21
who would never see him again.

READING COMPREHENSION QUESTIONS

1. The word *incessantly* in "Mark talked incessantly. I had to remind him again
   and again that talking without permission was not acceptable" (paragraph 2)
   means

   a. slowly.

   b. quietly.

   c. constantly.

   d. pleasantly.

2. The words *blurted out* in "It wasn't ten seconds later when Chuck blurted out, 'Mark is talking again'" (paragraph 4) mean

   a. said suddenly.

   b. ran away.

   c. watched for.

   d. looked at.

3. Which sentence best expresses the central idea of the selection?

   a. Mark Eklund was a charming, talkative student who appreciated Sister Helen's efforts to teach him.

   b. Sister Helen found out that an assignment she had given years ago had been very important to a beloved former student and his classmates.

   c. When Sister Helen was a young teacher, she had some unusual classroom techniques.

   d. The Vietnam War was a historical tragedy that took the life of one of Sister Helen's former students.

4. Which sentence best expresses the main idea of paragraphs 1–2?

   a. Mark Eklund was in the first third-grade class Sister Helen taught at Saint Mary's School.

   b. Mark Eklund was the most talkative of all Sister Helen's students.

   c. Despite misbehaving in class, Mark Eklund was a very likable person.

   d. Although Sister Helen kept reminding Mark that talking without permission was not permitted, she was unable to stop him from talking.

5. Which sentence best expresses the main idea of paragraphs 8–12?

   a. A difficult math concept had made Sister Helen's students irritable.

   b. The "good things" assignment made the students feel happy with themselves and others.

   c. Sister Helen gave up part of her weekend to write out a list of good things about each student.

   d. At the end of Friday's class, both Charlie and Mark seemed to be in good moods.

6. When the students didn't mention the lists after the day they received them, Sister Helen

   a. assumed that the assignment had been a failure.

   b. didn't mind, because the assignment had done what she hoped.

   c. called a few students to ask what they thought of the lists.

   d. felt angry that the students didn't appreciate what she had done.

7. Sister Helen learned of Mark's death
   a. when her parents called her while she was on vacation.
   b. from Chuck, Mark's old friend.
   c. from her father as they drove home from the airport.
   d. from a story in the local newspaper.

8. In paragraph 3, the author implies
   a. a more experienced teacher would not have threatened Mark with tape.
   b. her decision to tape Mark's mouth shut was a good one.
   c. Mark was trying to annoy her by talking more often than usual.
   d. in order to correct Mark's behavior, she should have been more strict.

9. The author implies that
   a. she had known all along how important the lists were to her students.
   b. she did not support the war in Vietnam.
   c. the lists meant more to the students than she had ever realized.
   d. Mark's parents were jealous of her relationship with him.

10. It is reasonable to conclude that Mark
    a. cared as much for Sister Helen as she cared for him.
    b. never talked much about his past.
    c. planned to become a math teacher himself.
    d. had not stayed in touch with his classmates.

TECHNIQUE QUESTIONS

1. Although Mark is described as someone who talks a lot, the author chooses to include Mark's spoken words just three times in her essay. Look at these three instances. What do they share? Why do you think Sister Helen chose to include these quotes?

   All three examples are of Mark thanking Sister Helen. By only showing him thanking her, the author is able to convey to readers how special and nice Mark was. Also, by including these quotes, the author supports her point that Mark was "one in a million."

2. How does Sister Helen present most of the information in her essay—in listing order or in time order? Find three examples from the essay that support your answer.

   Time order. Answers will vary for examples but may include: one morning, later, since, as, end of the year, after, finally.

_____

_____

3. In paragraph 20, the author introduces a number of people who had not appeared elsewhere in the essay. What does Sister Helen accomplish by including these people at the end of her story?

By bringing these people in at the end, the author shows just how much everyone was

moved by the "good things" assignment. In addition, the inclusion of others at the end of

the story works to surprise the reader, just as Sister Helen was surprised. This technique

allows the reader to share the author's emotional experience and feel, as she did,

the sorrow for the loss of Mark.

DISCUSSION QUESTIONS

1. In this story, we read of two classroom incidents involving Sister Helen and her students. In one, she briefly taped a third-grader's mouth closed. In another, she encouraged junior-high students to think of things they liked about one another. In your opinion, what do these two incidents tell about Sister Helen? What kind of teacher was she? What kind of person?

2. At the end of the story, Sister Helen tells us that she "cried for Mark and for all his friends who would never see him again." Do you think she might have been crying for other reasons, too? Explain what they might be.

3. "All the Good Things" has literally traveled around the world. Not only has it been reprinted in numerous publications, but many readers have sent it out over the Internet for others to read. Why do you think so many people love this story? Why do they want to share it with others?

WRITING ASSIGNMENTS

1. Do you have any souvenir that, like Sister Helen's lists, you have kept for years? Write a paragraph about that souvenir. Start your paragraph with a topic sentence such as "_____ is one of my oldest and most-loved possessions." Then describe what the item is, how you originally obtained it, and where you keep it now. Most importantly, explain why the souvenir is precious to you.

2. Although Sister Helen didn't want to do it, she felt she had to tape Mark's mouth shut after announcing that she would do so. When have you done something you didn't really want to do because others expected it? Write a

paragraph about that incident. Explain why you didn't want to do it, why you felt pressure to do it, and how you felt about yourself afterward. Here are sample topic sentences for such a paragraph:

> Even though I knew it was wrong, I told my friend's parents a lie to keep my friend out of trouble.
>
> Last year, I pretended I didn't like a girl that I really did like because my friends convinced me she wasn't cool enough.

3. Mark Eklund obviously stood out in Sister Helen's memory. She paints a vivid "word portrait" of Mark as a third-grader. Write an essay about three fellow students who, for positive or negative reasons, you have always remembered. The three may have been your classmates at any point in your life. Your essay should focus on your memories of those students in the classroom—not on the playground, in the cafeteria, or outside of school. As you describe your memories of those three classmates in that setting, include details that appeal to as many senses as possible—hearing, sight, touch, smell—to make your readers picture those individuals and that time and place in your history.

   Alternatively, you may write an essay about three teachers whom you will always remember.

Responsibility

M. Scott Peck

PREVIEW

The Road Less Traveled, a well-known book by psychiatrist and author M. Scott Peck, begins with this famous line: "Life is difficult." Peck encourages people to embrace the messy difficulties that make up life, stressing that growth and development are achieved only through hard work. The following excerpt from *The Road Less Traveled* emphasizes one of Peck's favorite themes: personal responsibility.

WORDS TO WATCH

self-evident (1): not requiring any explanation

ludicrous (2): laughable because of being obviously ridiculous

inquired (11): asked

clarified (19): made clear

amenable (23): agreeable

glared (37): stared angrily

We cannot solve life's problems except by solving them. This statement may seem idiotically self-evident•, yet it is seemingly beyond the comprehension of much of the human race. This is because we must accept responsibility for a problem before we can solve it. We cannot solve a problem by saying, "It's not my problem." We cannot solve a problem by hoping that someone else will solve it for us. I can solve a problem only when I say, "This is my problem and it's up to me to solve it." But many, so many, seek to avoid the pain of their problems by saying to themselves: "This problem was caused by other people, or by social circumstances beyond my control, and therefore it is up to other people or society to solve this problem for me. It is not really my personal problem." 1

The extent to which people will go psychologically to avoid assuming responsibility for personal problems, while always sad, is sometimes almost ludicrous•. A career sergeant in the army, stationed in Okinawa and in serious trouble because of his excessive drinking, was referred for psychiatric evaluation and, if possible, assistance. He denied that he was an alcoholic, or even that his use of alcohol was a personal problem, saying, "There's nothing else to do in the evenings in Okinawa except drink." 2

"Do you like to read?" I asked. 3

"Oh yes, I like to read, sure." 4

"Then why don't you read in the evening instead of drinking?" 5

"It's too noisy to read in the barracks." 6

"Well, then, why don't you go to the library?" 7

"The library is too far away." 8

"Is the library farther away than the bar you go to?" 9

"Well, I'm not much of a reader. That's not where my interests lie." 10

"Do you like to fish?" I then inquired•. 11

"Sure, I love to fish." 12

"Why not go fishing instead of drinking?" 13

"Because I have to work all day long." 14

"Can't you go fishing at night?" 15

"No, there isn't any night fishing in Okinawa." 16

"But there is," I said. "I know several organizations that fish at night here. 17 Would you like me to put you in touch with them?"

"Well, I really don't like to fish." 18

"What I hear you saying," I clarified•, "is that there are other things to do in 19 Okinawa except drink, but the thing you like to do most in Okinawa is drink."

"Yeah, I guess so." 20

"But your drinking is getting you in trouble, so you're faced with a real prob- 21 lem, aren't you?"

"This damn island would drive anyone to drink." 22

I kept trying for a while, but the sergeant was not the least bit interested in 23 seeing his drinking as a personal problem which he could solve either with or without help, and I regretfully told his commander that he was not amenable• to assistance. His drinking continued, and he was separated from the service in mid-career.

"I can solve a problem only when I say, 'This is my problem and it's up to me to solve it.'"

A young wife, also in Okinawa, cut her wrist lightly with a razor blade and was 24 brought to the emergency room, where I saw her. I asked her why she had done this to herself.

"To kill myself, of course." 25

"Why do you want to kill yourself?" 26

"Because I can't stand it on this dumb island. You have to send me back to the 27 States. I'm going to kill myself if I have to stay here any longer."

"What is it about living on Okinawa that's so painful for you?" I asked. 28

She began to cry in a whining sort of way. "I don't have any friends here, and 29 I'm alone all the time."

"That's too bad. How come you haven't been able to make any friends?" 30

"Because I have to live in a stupid Okinawan housing area, and none of my 31 neighbors speak English."

"Why don't you drive over to the American housing area or to the wives' club 32
during the day so you can make some friends?"

"Because my husband has to drive the car to work." 33

"Can't you drive him to work, since you're alone and bored all day?" I asked. 34

"No. It's a stick-shift car, and I don't know how to drive a stick-shift car, only 35
an automatic."

"Why don't you learn how to drive a stick-shift car?" 36

She glared° at me. "On these roads? You must be crazy." 37

READING COMPREHENSION QUESTIONS

1. The word *comprehension* in "This statement . . . is seemingly beyond the comprehension of much of the human race" (paragraph 1) means

   a. definition.

   b. understanding.

   c. confusion.

   d. absence.

2. The word *excessive* in "A career sergeant . . . in serious trouble because of his
excessive drinking" (paragraph 2) means

   a. good-natured.

   b. unwilling.

   c. moderate.

   d. beyond what is normal.

3. Which sentence best expresses the central point of the entire selection?

   a. In Okinawa, Peck met two people who refused to take responsibility for
   their own problems.

   b. People demonstrate healthy creativity in the excuses they make for their
   irresponsibility.

   c. Many people, like the sergeant and the young wife, don't solve their problems because they refuse to take responsibility for them.

   d. The sergeant and the young wife would rather see their careers and lives
   ruined than take responsibility for their problems.

4. Which sentence best expresses the main idea of paragraphs 2–22?

   a. A career sergeant was in trouble because of his drinking.

   b. The sergeant denied that he had a problem with alcohol.

   c. Peck was expected to evaluate the sergeant and, if possible, help him.

   d. People will go to ridiculous lengths to avoid responsibility for their
   problems.

5. Which sentence best expresses the main idea of paragraph 23?

    a. Peck tried for some time to help the sergeant.

    b. Drinking has destroyed the lives of many people.

    c. The sergeant had a number of different resources to help him with his drinking problem.

    (d.) Despite Peck's efforts, the sergeant refused to take responsibility for his drinking problem.

6. Which of the following activities did Peck suggest to the sergeant to stop him from drinking?

    a. writing

    b. driving

    c. walking

    (d.) reading

7. The young wife first saw Peck because she

    a. was drinking too much.

    (b.) had cut her wrist.

    c. had tried to return to the States.

    d. wanted to learn to drive.

8. The young wife said she could not drive to the wives' club because

    a. she and her husband did not own a car.

    b. she had to be away at work all day.

    c. none of the other wives spoke English.

    (d.) she could not drive a stick-shift car.

9. We can infer that the sergeant and the young wife

    (a.) wanted someone else to take responsibility for their problems.

    b. knew each other.

    c. were good at taking responsibility for themselves back in the States.

    d. became happier and better adjusted after their meetings with Peck.

10. We can infer that the author probably believes that

    a. the sergeant and the young wife had no difficulties when they lived in the United States.

    b. the United States should increase the amount of support it gives to military families forced to live abroad.

    (c.) he cannot provide much help to people until they first accept responsibility for their problems.

    d. Okinawa is to blame for the problems of the sergeant and the young wife.

TECHNIQUE QUESTIONS

1. What kind of evidence does Peck use to support the main idea in his essay—
   that people cannot solve their problems unless they first accept responsibility
   for them?

   Peck uses two real examples—the sergeant and the young wife—to support his main

   idea. He includes their actual words to show the lengths people go to to avoid taking

   responsibility.

2. In trying to help the sergeant and the young wife, the author asks a series of
   questions. What does he accomplish by including all these questions in his
   essay?

   The author includes the questions and the responses to show just how determined people

   are to avoid taking positive actions to help themselves. Including the questions and

   answers illustrates the author's main point—that people who refuse to take responsibility

   will not solve their problems.

3. How does the author conclude his essay? What about this particular ending
   makes it effective?

   The author concludes his essay with a quote from the young wife. Her words stand out

   because she claims that driving is dangerous and crazy. But she says this right after she

   has sliced her wrist and tried to kill herself. It is ironic that a person who wants to end

   her life would be afraid of getting hurt. In this instance, her refusal to face her problem

   is so strong that she doesn't realize how crazy she sounds—more proof of the author's

   point.

DISCUSSION QUESTIONS

1. Peck refers to the "ludicrous"—that is, ridiculous—lengths people will go to
   to avoid taking responsibility for their problems. What do you think he finds
   ludicrous about the sergeant's behavior? The young wife's? Do you find their
   behavior ridiculous? Why or why not?

2. What do you think was Peck's goal in his conversation with the young wife
   and the sergeant? Why is his method of treatment effective, or why is it not
   effective?

3. Why do you think so many people find it difficult to take responsibility for
   their own problems? How might they be helped to do so?

WRITING ASSIGNMENTS

1. Write a paragraph about a time you have seen someone avoiding responsibility for his or her own problem. Begin with this topic sentence:

   > Just like M. Scott Peck, I have seen someone refuse to take responsibility for his (or her) own problem.

   Then go on to develop your paper by explaining who the person is, what the person's problem was, how he or she helped create it, and how he or she blamed others or circumstances rather than accepted responsibility. Be sure to include, as Peck does, specific details, such as direct quotes or vivid descriptions, so readers can see the person and the situation you've chosen to write about.

2. Peck draws examples of irresponsible behavior from his practice as a military psychiatrist. But you can find examples of people dodging responsibility everywhere. What kinds of responsibility do students often avoid? Write a paragraph giving details about two or three ways students try to escape their responsibilities. In your paragraph, explain what kind of excuses they frequently make for their behavior. Using Peck's essay as a model, you may even choose to present a series of questions and answers between a student and an instructor to illustrate your main point.

3. Peck explains that the only way to solve a problem is to solve it—in other words, to take responsibility for the problem and find a solution. Write an essay about a time in your own life when you had to accept responsibility for a problem and figure out a solution for it. As you decide on a topic, you might list areas in which you have experienced problems. Here is one imaginary student's list:

   - Getting along with parents
   - Breaking off with friends who were a bad influence
   - Managing money
   - Holding a job
   - Keeping up with schoolwork

   Once you have decided on a topic to write about, you might begin with a statement like this:

   > After blaming my teachers for my problems in school, I finally accepted responsibility for my own poor grades.

   Alternatively, write about two or three problems you've had to face and solve.

The Most Hateful Words

Amy Tan

PREVIEW

For years, a painful exchange with her mother lay like a heavy stone on Amy Tan's heart. In the following essay, Tan, author of best-selling novels, including *The Joy Luck Club* and *The Kitchen God's Wife*, tells the story of how that weight was finally lifted. This essay is from her memoir, *The Opposite of Fate*.

WORDS TO WATCH

tormented (3): hurt or tortured

forbade (3): would not allow

impenetrable (3): impossible to get inside

frantically (9): excitedly, with great worry

1   The most hateful words I have ever said to another human being were to my mother. I was sixteen at the time. They rose from the storm in my chest and I let them fall in a fury of hailstones: "I hate you. I wish I were dead. . . ."

2   I waited for her to collapse, stricken by what I had just said. She was still standing upright, her chin tilted, her lips stretched in a crazy smile. "Okay, maybe I die too," she said between huffs. "Then I no longer be your mother!" We had many similar exchanges. Sometimes she actually tried to kill herself by running into the street, holding a knife to her throat. She too had storms in her chest. And what she aimed at me was as fast and deadly as a lightning bolt.

3   For days after our arguments, she would not speak to me. She tormented° me, acted as if she had no feelings for me whatsoever. I was lost to her. And because of that, I lost, battle after battle, all of them: the times she criticized me, humiliated me in front of others, forbade° me to do this or that without even listening to one good reason why it should be the other way. I swore to myself I would never forget these injustices. I would store them, harden my heart, make myself as impenetrable° as she was.

4   I remember this now, because I am also remembering another time, just a few years ago. I was forty-seven, had become a different person by then, had become a fiction writer, someone who uses memory and imagination. In fact, I was writing a story about a girl and her mother, when the phone rang.

5   It was my mother, and this surprised me. Had someone helped her make the call? For a few years now, she had been losing her mind through Alzheimer's

disease. Early on, she forgot to lock her door. Then she forgot where she lived. She forgot who many people were and what they had meant to her. Lately, she could no longer remember many of her worries and sorrows.

"Amy-ah," she said, and she began to speak quickly in Chinese. "Something is wrong with my mind. I think I'm going crazy." **6**

I caught my breath. Usually she could barely speak more than two words at a time. "Don't worry," I started to say. **7**

"It's true," she went on. "I feel like I can't remember many things. I can't remember what I did yesterday. I can't remember what happened a long time ago, what I did to you. . . ." She spoke as a drowning person might if she had bobbed to the surface with the force of will to live, only to see how far she had already drifted, how impossibly far she was from the shore. **8**

She spoke frantically•: "I know I did something to hurt you." **9**

"You didn't," I said. "Don't worry." **10**

"I did terrible things. But now I can't remember what. . . . And I just want to tell you . . . I hope you can forget, just as I've forgotten." **11**

I tried to laugh so she would not notice the cracks in my voice. "Really, don't worry." **12**

"Okay, I just wanted you to know." **13**

After we hung up, I cried, both happy and sad. I was again that sixteen-year-old, but the storm in my chest was gone. **14**

My mother died six months later. By then she had bequeathed to me her most healing words, as open and eternal as a clear blue sky. Together we knew in our hearts what we should remember, what we can forget. **15**

READING COMPREHENSION QUESTIONS

1. The word *stricken* in "I waited for her to collapse, stricken by what I had just said" (paragraph 2) means
   a. wounded.
   b. amused.
   c. annoyed.
   d. bored.

2. The word *bequeathed* in "By then she had bequeathed to me her most healing words, as open and eternal as a clear blue sky" (paragraph 15) means
   a. denied.
   b. sold.
   c. given.
   d. cursed.

3. Which sentence best expresses the central idea of the selection?

    a. Because of Alzheimer's disease, the author's mother forgot harsh words the two of them had said to one another.

    b. Amy Tan had a difficult relationship with her mother that worsened over the years.

    (c.) Years after a painful childhood with her mother, Amy Tan was able to realize peace and forgiveness.

    d. Despite her Alzheimer's disease, Amy Tan's mother was able to apologize to her daughter for hurting her.

4. Which sentence best expresses the main idea of paragraphs 1–2?

    a. Amy Tan's mother was sometimes suicidal.

    b. Amy Tan wanted to use words to hurt her mother.

    c. It is not unusual for teenagers and their parents to argue.

    (d.) Amy Tan and her mother had a very hurtful relationship.

5. Which sentence best expresses the main idea of paragraphs 8–9?

    (a.) The author's mother was deeply disturbed by the thought that she had hurt her daughter.

    b. Alzheimer's disease causes people to become confused and unable to remember things clearly.

    c. The author's mother could not even remember what she had done the day before.

    d. The author's mother had changed very little from what she was like when Tan was a child.

6. After arguing with her daughter, the author's mother would

    a. say nice things about her to others.

    b. immediately forget they had argued.

    (c.) refuse to speak to her.

    d. apologize.

7. When she was a young girl, the author swore that she would

    (a.) never forget her mother's harsh words.

    b. never be like her mother.

    c. publicly embarrass her mother by writing about her.

    d. never have children.

8. The first sign that the author's mother had Alzheimer's disease was

    a. she forgot where she lived.

    b. she could speak only two or three words at a time.

c. she forgot people's identities.

(d.) she forgot to lock her door.

9. We can infer from paragraph 2 that

   a. the author wished her mother was dead.

   b. the author immediately felt guilty for the way she spoke to her mother.

   (c.) the author's mother was emotionally unstable.

   d. the author's mother was physically abusive.

10. The author implies, in paragraphs 9–15, that

   a. she was pleased her mother realized how badly she had hurt her.

   (b.) her love and pity for her mother were stronger than her anger.

   c. she did not recall what her mother was talking about.

   d. she was annoyed by her mother's confusion.

TECHNIQUE QUESTIONS

1. Tan begins her essay from the perspective of a sixteen-year-old girl but finishes it from the perspective of a woman in her late forties. Where in the essay does Tan make the transition between those two perspectives? What words does she use to signal the change?

   She makes the transition in paragraph 4, with the words "I remember this now,

   because I am also remembering another time, just a few years ago. I was

   forty-seven . . ."

2. In paragraph 2, the author quotes her mother speaking in English, her second language. What features stand out in her mother's speech? Why do you think Tan chose to include her mother's actual words rather than rewrite them into standard English?

   Her mother's sentences are short and grammatically incorrect. Using her actual

   words makes the story more vivid and real.

3. Tan uses weather images throughout her essay. Find three instances in which Tan mentions weather and list them below. What does she accomplish with this technique?

   Paragraph 1: Tan has a storm in her chest, hailstones

   Paragraph 2: Her mother has storms too, sends out lightning bolts

Paragraph 15: words as open as a clear blue sky

_____

_____

Storm imagery allows Tan to convey the fury and violence of her relationship with

her mother. Later, the description of the blue sky allows Tan to show readers that

the pain of the past has gone away.

_____

DISCUSSION QUESTIONS

1. Tan recalls "the times [my mother] criticized me, humiliated me in front of others, forbade me to do this or that without even listening to one good reason why it should be the other way." Did you have a difficult relationship with one or both of your parents? Were problems the result of your teenage behavior or of their behavior?

2. This essay brings to mind the phrase "Forgive and forget." But is this advice always fair or realistic? Are there times when it is better to hold someone accountable than to forgive and forget? Explain.

3. In Tan's discussion with her mother at the end of the essay, Tan chooses to hide her emotions. Why do you think she does this?

WRITING ASSIGNMENTS

1. Despite being an adult, Tan recalls feeling like "the same sixteen-year-old" girl when she speaks to her mother. Think about something in your life that has the power to reconnect you to a vivid memory. Write a paragraph in which you describe your memory and the trigger that "takes you back" to it. Begin your paragraph with a topic sentence that makes it clear to readers what you are going to discuss. Then provide specific details so readers can understand your memory. Here are sample topic sentences:

    Whenever I see swings, I remember the day in second grade when I got into my first fist fight.

    The smell of cotton candy takes me back to the day my grandfather took me to my first baseball game.

    I can't pass St. Joseph's Hospital without remembering the day, ten years ago, when my brother was shot.

2. In this essay, we see that Tan's relationship with her mother was very complicated. Who is a person with whom you have a complex relationship—maybe one you'd describe as "love/hate" or "difficult"? Write a paragraph about that

relationship. Be sure to give examples or details that show readers why you have such difficulties with that person.

Your topic sentence should introduce the person you plan to discuss:

> My mother-in-law and I have contrasting points of view on several issues.
>
> While I respect my boss, he is simply a very difficult person.
>
> Even though I love my sister, I can't stand to be around her.

Be sure to provide specific examples or details to help your reader understand why the relationship is so difficult for you. For example, if you decide to write about your brother, you will want to describe things he does that lead you to consider him to be so "difficult."

3. Like Tan's mother, most of us have done something in our lives we wish we could undo. If you could have a chance to revisit your past and change one of your actions, what would it be? Write an essay in which you describe something you would like to undo.

In your first paragraph, introduce exactly what you did. Here are three thesis statements that students might have written:

> I wish I could undo the night I decided to drive my car while I was drunk.
>
> If I could undo any moment in my life, it would be the day I decided to drop out of high school.
>
> One moment from my life I would like to change is the time I picked on an unpopular kid in sixth grade.

Be sure to provide details and, if appropriate, actual words that were spoken, so that your readers can "see and hear" what happened. Once you've described the moment that you wish to take back, write three reasons you feel the way you do. Below is a scratch outline for the first topic.

> I wish I could undo the night I decided to drive my car while I was drunk.
>
> 1. Caused an accident that hurt others
> 2. Lost my license, my car, and my job
> 3. Affected the way others treat me

In order to write an effective essay, you will need to provide specific details to explain each of the reasons you identify. For instance, to support the third reason above, you might detail possible new feelings of guilt and anger you have about yourself, as well as provide examples of how individual people now treat you differently. To end your essay, you might describe what you would do today if you could replay what happened.

My Daughter Smokes

Alice Walker

PREVIEW

Alice Walker is a famous writer, probably best known for her novel *The Color Purple*. In "My Daughter Smokes," her daughter's habit is a stepping-stone to a broader discussion of smoking than the title suggests. She goes on to tell of her father's experience with tobacco and from there slips into a discussion of tobacco that moves through the centuries and across continents.

WORDS TO WATCH

consort (2): spouse

pungent (3): having a sharp, bitter taste

dapper (4): stylishly dressed

perennially (6): continually

ritual (12): activity done regularly

emaciated (13): thin

futility (16): uselessness

empathy (17): understanding

denatured (17): changed from its natural state

mono-cropping (17): growing of single crops apart from other crops

suppressed (18): kept down

redeem (18): restore the honor of

cajole (20): gently urge

My daughter smokes. While she is doing her homework, her feet on the 1
bench in front of her and her calculator clicking out answers to her algebra
problems, I am looking at the half-empty package of Camels tossed carelessly
close at hand. Camels. I pick them up, take them into the kitchen, where the
light is better, and study them—they're filtered, for which I am grateful. My
heart feels terrible. I want to weep. In fact, I do weep a little, standing there
by the stove holding one of the instruments, so white, so precisely rolled, that
could cause my daughter's death. When she smoked Marlboros and Players
I hardened myself against feeling so bad; nobody I knew ever smoked these
brands.

She doesn't know this, but it was Camels that my father, her grandfather, smoked. 2 But before he smoked "ready-mades"—when he was very young and very poor, with eyes like lanterns—he smoked Prince Albert tobacco in cigarettes he rolled himself. I remember the bright-red tobacco tin, with a picture of Queen Victoria's consort,• Prince Albert, dressed in a black frock coat and carrying a cane.

The tobacco was dark brown, pungent,• slightly bitter. I tasted it more than 3 once as a child, and the discarded tins could be used for a number of things: to keep buttons and shoelaces in, to store seeds, and best of all, to hold worms for the rare times my father took us fishing.

By the late forties and early fifties no one rolled his own anymore (and few 4 women smoked) in my hometown, Eatonton, Georgia. The tobacco industry, coupled with Hollywood movies in which both hero and heroine smoked like chimneys, won over completely people like my father, who were hopelessly addicted to cigarettes. He never looked as dapper• as Prince Albert, though; he continued to look like a poor, overweight, overworked colored man with too large a family; black, with a very white cigarette stuck in his mouth.

I do not remember when he started to cough. Perhaps it was unnoticeable at 5 first. A little hacking in the morning as he lit his first cigarette upon getting out of bed. By the time I was my daughter's age, his breath was a wheeze, embarrassing to hear; he could not climb stairs without resting every third or fourth step. It was not unusual for him to cough for an hour.

It is hard to believe there was a time when people did not understand that 6 cigarette smoking is an addiction. I wondered aloud once to my sister—who is perennially• trying to quit—whether our father realized this. I wonder how she, a smoker since high school, viewed her own habit.

It was our father who gave her her first cigarette, one day when she had taken 7 water to him in the fields.

"I always wondered why he did that," she said, puzzled, and with some 8 bitterness.

"What did he say?" I asked. 9

"That he didn't want me to go to anyone else for them," she said, "which never 10 really crossed my mind."

So he was aware it was addictive, I thought, though as annoyed as she that he 11 assumed she would be interested.

I began smoking in eleventh grade, also the year I drank numerous bottles of 12 terrible sweet, very cheap wine. My friends and I, all boys for this venture, bought our supplies from a man who ran a segregated bar and liquor store on the outskirts of town. Over the entrance there was a large sign that said COLORED. We were not permitted to drink here, only to buy. I smoked Kools, because my sister did. By then I thought her toxic darkened lips and gums glamorous. However, my body simply would not tolerate smoke. After six months I had a chronic sore throat. I gave up smoking, gladly. Because it was a ritual• with my buddies—Murl, Leon, and "Dog" Farley—I continued to drink wine.

My father died from "the poor man's friend," pneumonia, one hard winter 13 when his bronchitis and emphysema had left him low. I doubt he had much lung left at all, after coughing for so many years. He had so little breath that, during his last years, he was always leaning on something. I remembered once, at a family reunion, when my daughter was two, that my father picked her up for a minute—long enough for me to photograph them—but the effort was obvious. Near the very end of his life, and largely because he had no more lungs, he quit smoking. He gained a couple of pounds, but by then he was so emaciated• no one noticed.

When I travel to Third World countries I see many people like my father and 14 daughter. There are large billboards directed at them both: the tough, "take-charge," or dapper older man, the glamorous, "worldly" young woman, both puffing away. In these poor countries, as in American ghettos and on reservations, money that should be spent for food goes instead to the tobacco companies; over time, people starve themselves of both food and air, effectively weakening and addicting their children, eventually eradicating themselves. I read in the newspaper and in my gardening magazine that cigarette butts are so toxic that if a baby swallows one, it is likely to die, and that the boiled water from a bunch of them makes an effective insecticide.

> "It is hard to believe there was a time when people did not understand that cigarette smoking is an addiction."

My daughter would like to quit, she says. We both know the statistics are 15 against her; most people who try to quit smoking do not succeed.*

There is a deep hurt that I feel as a mother. Some days it is a feeling of futil- 16 ity.• I remember how carefully I ate when I was pregnant, how patiently I taught my daughter how to cross a street safely. For what, I sometimes wonder; so that she can wheeze through most of her life feeling half her strength, and then die of self-poisoning, as her grandfather did?

But, finally, one must feel empathy• for the tobacco plant itself. For thousands 17 of years, it has been venerated by Native Americans as a sacred medicine. They have used it extensively—its juices, its leaves, its roots, its (holy) smoke—to heal wounds and cure diseases, and in ceremonies of prayer and peace. And though the plant as most of us know it has been poisoned by chemicals and denatured• by intensive mono-cropping• and is therefore hardly the plant it was, still, to some modern Indians it remains a plant of positive power. I learned this when my Native American friends, Bill Wahpepah and his family, visited with me for a few days and the first thing he did was sow a few tobacco seeds in my garden.

Perhaps we can liberate tobacco from those who have captured and abused it, en- 18 slaving the plant on large plantations, keeping it from freedom and its kin, and forcing it to enslave the world. Its true nature suppressed,• no wonder it has become deadly. Maybe by sowing a few seeds of tobacco in our gardens and treating the plant with the reverence it deserves, we can redeem• tobacco's soul and restore its self-respect.

---

*Three months after reading this essay, my daughter stopped smoking.

Besides, how grim, if one is a smoker, to realize one is smoking a slave.   19

There is a slogan from a battered women's shelter that I especially like: "Peace 20 on earth begins at home." I believe everything does. I think of a slogan for people trying to stop smoking: "Every home a smoke-free zone." Smoking is a form of self-battering that also batters those who must sit by, occasionally cajole• or complain, and helplessly watch. I realize now that as a child I sat by, through the years, and literally watched my father kill himself; surely one such victory in my family, for the rich white men who own the tobacco companies, is enough.

READING COMPREHENSION QUESTIONS

1. The word *eradicating* in "over time, people starve themselves of both food and air, effectively weakening and addicting their children, eventually eradicating themselves" (paragraph 14) means

   a. curing.

   b. feeding.

   c. destroying.

   d. controlling.

2. The word *venerated* in "For thousands of years, it has been venerated by Native Americans as a sacred medicine. They have used it extensively" (paragraph 17) means

   a. honored.

   b. ignored.

   c. ridiculed.

   d. forgotten.

3. Which of the following sentences best expresses the central idea of the essay?

   a. Most people who try to quit smoking are not successful.

   b. Pained by her daughter's cigarette addiction and the misdeeds of the tobacco companies, Walker urges people to stop smoking.

   c. Native Americans have used the tobacco plant for thousands of years as a sacred medicine and in ceremonies of prayer and peace.

   d. Tobacco advertisements that show healthy, attractive people are misleading.

4. Which sentence best expresses the main idea of paragraph 4?

   a. For Walker's father and others, the reality of smoking was very different from the images shown in ads and movies.

   b. Walker's father smoked because he wanted to be as stylish as Prince Albert.

   c. No one rolled his or her own cigarettes by the 1950s.

   d. Walker's father was poor, overweight, and overworked.

5. Which sentence best expresses the main idea of paragraph 5?

    a. Walker does not know when her father began to cough.

    b. When Walker was her daughter's age, she was embarrassed to hear her father wheezing.

    (c.) Walker's father's cough began quietly but grew to become a major problem.

    d. Walker's father had great difficulty climbing stairs.

6. Walker is especially upset that her daughter smokes Camel cigarettes because

    a. she believes Camels to be especially bad for people's health.

    b. Camels are the brand that Walker herself smoked as a teenager.

    (c.) Walker's father, who died as a result of smoking, smoked Camels.

    d. Camels' advertisements are glamorous and misleading.

7. When Walker's father picked up his granddaughter at a family reunion, he

    a. burned the child with his cigarette.

    b. put her down quickly so he could have another cigarette.

    c. warned her against smoking.

    (d.) was too weak to hold her for long.

8. We can infer that Walker

    (a.) believes people who are poor, uneducated, and nonwhite have been especially victimized by the tobacco industry.

    b. believes that tobacco should be made illegal.

    c. blames her father for her daughter's decision to smoke.

    d. believes Native Americans were wrong to honor the tobacco plant.

9. We can infer that, for Walker, smoking as a teenager

    a. was strictly forbidden by her parents.

    (b.) was an exciting experiment.

    c. was quickly habit-forming.

    d. was the end of her friendship with Murl, Leon, and "Dog" Farley.

10. We can infer that Walker's daughter

    a. did not care that her mother was concerned about her smoking.

    (b.) may have been helped to quit smoking by her mother's essay.

    c. remembered her grandfather well.

    d. did not believe that smoking was harmful to people's health.

TECHNIQUE QUESTIONS

1. In which parts of her essay does Walker use time order? _Paragraphs 2–5 and 12–13_

2. Write down what you think are two of the most vivid images in Walker's essay. Then explain how each helps further her central idea.

   (Answers will vary.)

   _____

   _____

3. How does Walker enlarge the significance of her essay so that it becomes more than the story of her daughter's smoking?

   She moves from her daughter's use of Camels to her father, then her and her sister's

   smoking. In paragraph 14, she uses her daughter and father as a transition to a discussion

   of Third World countries. Finally, she moves from her feelings for her daughter (16) to

   feelings for the tobacco plant itself (17). (Wording of answers will vary.)

   _____

   _____

DISCUSSION QUESTIONS

1. How would you deal with a friend who engaged in self-destructive behavior, such as smoking, drinking excessively, or using drugs? Would you ignore the behavior or try to educate the friend about its dangers? Is letting a friend know you are concerned worth risking the friendship?

2. The dangers of smoking are well documented. Study after study shows that smoking leads to a variety of illnesses, including cancer, emphysema, and heart disease. Secondhand smoke—smoke that nonsmokers breathe when they are around smokers—is dangerous as well. If you had the power to do so, would you make smoking illegal? Or do you believe that smoking should continue to be an individual's right?

3. Imagine learning that your sixteen-year-old child has begun smoking or drinking or has become sexually active. Which discovery would worry you most? Would it make a difference if the child were a girl or a boy? What fears would each of these discoveries raise in you? How would you respond to your child?

WRITING ASSIGNMENTS

1. Write a paragraph in which you try to persuade a friend to quit smoking. Explain in detail three reasons you think he or she should quit. Use transitions such as *first of all, second, another,* and *finally* as you list the three reasons.

2. In her essay, Walker is critical of the glamorous, healthy image presented by cigarette advertisements. Write a paragraph in which you describe what you

think an honest cigarette advertisement would look like. Who would appear in the ad? What would they be doing? What would they be saying? Use the following as a topic sentence, or write one of your own.

> The elements of an honest cigarette "advertisement" would tempt people not to smoke.

In preparation for this assignment, you might go online and research some old-time cigarette ads (for example, for Camels, Lucky Strikes) and use them as inspiration for this assignment. Use the name of a real cigarette or make up a name.

3. What bad habits do *you* have? Write an essay explaining how you believe you acquired one of those habits, how you think it harms you, and how you could rid yourself of it. You might begin by making a list or questioning to help you find a bad habit you wish to write about. (We all have plenty of bad habits, such as smoking, drinking too much, spending money impulsively, biting our nails, eating too much food, and so on.)

Remember to write an informal outline to guide you in your writing. Here, for example, is one possible outline for this assignment:

> Central idea: A bad habit I intend to change is studying for tests at the last minute.
>
> (1) I acquired the habit in high school, where studying at the last minute was often good enough.
>   For example, I studied for spelling tests in the hallway on the way to class.
>   Even history tests were easy to study for because our teacher demanded so little.
>
> (2) I've learned the hard way that last-minute studying doesn't work well in college.
>   During my first quarter, I got the first D I've ever gotten.
>   I thought memorizing a few names would get me through my first business class, but was I ever wrong.
>
> (3) I took a study skills course, and what I learned is helping me get on the right track.
>   I learned the benefits of taking class notes, and I'm trying to get better at getting down a written record of each lecture.
>   I also learned that keeping up with readings and taking notes on a regular basis are needed for some classes.

The writer of this outline still has to come up with many more details to expand each of her points. For instance, why did she get the D, and how did that help motivate her to improve her study habits? Also, what techniques is she experimenting with in her effort to improve her note-taking? She could add such details to her outline, or she could begin working them into her essay when she starts writing.

Wonder in the Air

Jeff Gammage

PREVIEW

Here is a chance to apply your understanding of addition and time relationships to a full-length reading. The following story tells about a loving father
who decides never to lie to his child—and then has to deal with Santa Claus.
Read it and then answer the relationship questions that follow. There are also
questions on understanding vocabulary in context, finding main ideas, and
identifying supporting details.

WORDS TO WATCH

innumerable (3): too many to count

leprechauns (5): Irish elves

by osmosis (7): like a sponge

allegedly and purportedly (7): supposedly

deceived (8): misled

literal (9): factual

weasel words (9): deliberately misleading language

prevalent (14): widely held

stark (17): plain

ponder (23): think over

subtleties (24): less obvious details

When my wife and I had our first child, we established one firm parental rule: 1
No lies.   2

Our daughter, Jin Yu, spent her first two years in an orphanage in China, and 3
we knew that as she grew, she would ask innumerable° questions about her life
there. We wanted to be able to answer from an established position of truth-telling.

For me, the "All the truth, all the time" policy extended onto the symbols and 4
myths of the holidays.

Every April, I gladly helped fill a basket with candy rabbits and colored eggs 5
for our daughter, and then for her new sister, but skipped the story of the Easter
bunny. I avoided any mention of leprechauns°, tried to ignore the tooth fairy.

Most of all, I was adamant about not telling Jin Yu tales about a certain red- 6
suited fat man who spends every December 24 breaking into people's homes.

Of course, like the Grinch, I couldn't stop Christmas—or Santa Claus—from 7 coming. Jin Yu absorbed a belief in Santa as if by osmosis•. By age 4 she knew who he (allegedly•) was, how he (purportedly•) looked, and what he (supposedly) did.

I didn't want to ruin her fun, but also didn't want her to feel deceived• later on. 8

So, I responded to her questions about the big man with what I liked to think 9 of as precise and technically accurate versions of the literal• truth—and what she would no doubt characterize as weasel words•.

At the mall, we'd walk past a jolly Santa sitting upon a velvet throne.   10

"Is that really Santa?" my daughter would ask.   11

I'd reply with a lawyerly, "The people in line must think so."   12

The worst was when she wondered if Santa truly kept lists of children who 13 behaved and misbehaved.

"That's the prevalent• belief," I said.   14

By last Christmas Eve, I had done such an expert job of parenting, made such 15 a successful effort to be truthful, that as I tucked my daughter into bed, she was confused and near tears.

"Daddy, will Santa"—here her voice almost broke—"bring me any presents?" 16

This was it, the question squarely placed, a moment that offered a stark• choice 17 between fable and fact, that demanded a reasoned response from a father grounded in principle. I looked at my adored child, her dark brown eyes threatening to over-flow, knowing there was but one choice, and I made it:

I lied.   18

On Christmas Eve, the holy of holy nights, I lied to my 5-year-old daughter so 19 fully, so deliberately, and in such compelling detail that I nearly believed it myself.

"Darling, of course Santa is going to bring you presents. He would never over- 20 look you. You're such a good girl [that part was true] that I know Santa will stop here. Listen, do you hear that sound outside? I think it's jingle bells! It must be his sleigh!"

Jin Yu turned to the window, hoping to glimpse a team of reindeer in flight, 21 then lay back and drifted off, content, or at least relieved.

The next morning, she awoke to find that, sure enough, Santa had visited her 22 home, proving his existence by magically delivering a wardrobe of princess gowns and dress-up shoes in exactly her size.

I think he left something for me as well: The power of a child's belief. A re- 23 minder that the best things in life cannot be seen with the naked eye. And that while there will be plenty of time for my daughter to ponder• cold and painful truths, her time of wonder should be savored.

This year, fully 6, Jin Yu is happily preparing for Santa by drawing crayon 24 snowscapes and discussing his impending arrival with friends. She counsels her 3-year-old sister, Zhao Gu, on the subtleties• of naughty and nice.

Last week Jin Yu came to me with a very specific Christmas question, the sort 25 that once again required a father's sure guidance: What kind of cookies should she leave for Santa on Christmas Eve?

I was firm in my response: Chocolate chip. Definitely, I told her, Santa likes 26 chocolate chip.

READING COMPREHENSION QUESTIONS

1. The word *adamant* in "Most of all, I was adamant about not telling Jin Yu tales about a certain red-suited fat man who spends every December 24 breaking into people's homes" (paragraph 6) means

   a. hysterical.

   b. glad.

   c. unwavering.

   d. dishonest.

2. The phrase *drifted off* in "Jin Yu turned to the window, hoping to glimpse a team of reindeer in flight, then lay back and drifted off, content, or at least relieved" (paragraph 21) means

   a. fell asleep.

   b. floated.

   c. daydreamed.

   d. sighed.

3. The word *impending* in "This year, fully 6, Jin Yu is happily preparing for Santa by drawing crayon snowscapes and discussing his impending arrival with friends" (paragraph 24) means

   a. late.

   b. soon to take place.

   c. surprising.

   d. possible.

4. Which sentence best expresses the central point of the selection?

   a. Holiday myths are so common in our culture that it is impossible to always tell the truth to children.

   b. If a child wants to believe in Santa Claus, there is little a parent can do to stop her.

   c. The author reluctantly goes along with his daughter's belief in Santa Claus.

   d. When he sees how important a belief in Santa Claus is to his daughter, the author comes to understand that all children should be permitted their time of wonder.

5. The main idea of paragraphs 1–5 is that

   a. the author's daughter was adopted from an orphanage in China as a two-year-old.

   b. the author knew that his adopted daughter would ask questions about her first two years in China.

c. the author and his wife vowed never to lie to their adopted daughter, even about holiday symbols and myths.

d. the author allowed his daughter to celebrate holidays but skipped telling her holiday myths.

6. The author breaks his vow never to lie to his daughter

a. when they see a Santa at the shopping mall.

b. a few days before Easter.

c. on Christmas Eve.

d. when she asks him what kind of cookies she should leave for Santa on Christmas Eve.

7. For Jin Yu, Santa's existence is proven when

a. she sees him at the shopping mall.

b. she finds that he has eaten all the chocolate chip cookies she left him on Christmas Eve.

c. she finds that he has magically delivered princess gowns and dress-up shoes in exactly her size.

d. all her friends tell her that he exists.

8. Paragraph 23 suggests that the author

a. regrets Jin Yu's belief in Santa Claus.

b. appreciates children's sense of wonder.

c. intends to tell Jin Yu that Santa isn't real.

d. thinks Jin Yu suspects the truth.

9. *True or false?* __*T*__ Paragraph 24 suggests that Jin Yu is passing her belief in Santa Claus on to her sister.

10. Gammage implies that

a. encouraging children to believe in stories is a harmless form of lying.

b. he continues to feel guilty about his deception.

c. Jin Yu will be heartbroken when he tells her the truth.

d. he never believed in Santa Claus.

DISCUSSION QUESTIONS

1. Was the author right to lie to his daughter? Why or why not?

2. When or if you have children, will you encourage them to believe in Santa, the Easter Bunny, and the tooth fairy? Why or why not?

3. The author and his wife decided that "no lies" would be their "one firm parental rule." What do you think are some other good parental rules?

WRITING ASSIGNMENTS

1. In explaining why he refused at first to encourage his daughter's belief in Santa Claus, Gammage states that he wanted to be able to answer his daughter's questions about China "from an established position of truth-telling." Do you think Jin Yu will later doubt her father because he "lied" to her about Santa Claus? Or will it make a difference? Write a paragraph that explains your thinking, drawing on an incident in your own life in which a parent or another authority figure either lied or told you a half-truth.

2. Write a paragraph that supports one of the following main ideas: "I believe that parents should encourage their children to believe in Santa Claus, the Easter Bunny, and the tooth fairy" or "I believe that it is important for parents to discourage their children's belief in Santa Claus, the Easter Bunny, and the tooth fairy." Explain your thinking, giving specific examples from your life experiences and comparing or contrasting them with Gammage's observations in the article.

3. Although Gammage and his wife decided that "no lies" would be their one firm parental rule, they eventually come to realize that the rule is not realistic. What do you think are two or three good (and realistic) parental rules? Write an essay in which you state and then discuss each rule.

   Your topic sentence should name the three rules you will write about. Here is such a topic sentence:

   > Kindness, fairness, and patience should be the guiding principles of any loving parent.

   The first sentence of your main paragraphs should then specify what makes each of these "rules," or guidelines, important—for example,

   > Kindness demands patience and understanding from the parent and sets an example for the child of how to treat others.

Such a main idea sentence would then be followed by a description of your own parent's kindness (or unkindness) in a specific incident in your life, as well as an explanation of what you learned from the experience. Repeat this process for each of the three rules you are writing about.

Don't Hang Up, That's My Mom Calling

Bobbi Buchanan

PREVIEW

Have you ever been awoken early in the morning or interrupted during dinner by a telemarketing call? As annoying as these calls may be, the people who make them are hardworking Americans who rely on telemarketing to earn a living. In the following selection, Bobbi Buchanan describes her mother as one of those people.

WORDS TO WATCH

supplement (1): add on to

nuisance (1): annoyance

viable (3): practical

exempts (4): excuses

impervious (5): incapable of being injured

1   The next time an annoying sales call interrupts your dinner, think of my 71-year-old mother, LaVerne, who works as a part-time telemarketer to supplement° her Social Security income. To those Americans who have signed up for the new national do-not-call list, my mother is a pest, a nuisance°, an invader of privacy. To others, she's just another anonymous voice on the other end of the line. But to those who know her, she's someone struggling to make a buck, to feed herself and pay her utilities—someone who personifies the great American way.

2   In our family, we think of my mother as a pillar of strength. She's survived two heart surgeries and lung cancer. She stayed at home her whole life to raise the seven of us kids. She entered the job market unskilled and physically limited after my father's death in 1998, which ended his pension benefits.

3   Telemarketing is a viable° option for my mother and the more than six million other Americans who work in the industry. According to the American Teleservices Association, the telemarketing work force is mostly women; 26 percent are single mothers. More than 60 percent are minorities; about 5 percent are disabled; 95 percent are not college graduates; more than 30 percent have been on welfare or public assistance. This is clearly a job for those used to hardship.

4   Interestingly enough, the federal list exempts° calls from politicians, pollsters and charities, and companies that have existing business relationships with customers can keep calling. Put this in perspective. Are they not the bulk of your annoying calls? Telemarketing giants won't be as affected by the list but smaller businesses that rely

on this less costly means of sales will. The giants will resort to other, more expensive forms of advertisement and pass those costs along to you, the consumer.

"In our family, we think of my mother as a pillar of strength."

My mother doesn't blame people for wanting to be placed on the do-not-call list. 5 She doesn't argue the fairness of its existence or take offense when potential clients cut her off in mid-sentence. All her parenting experience has made her impervious• to rude behavior and snide remarks, and she is not discouraged by hang-ups or busy signals. What worries my mother is that she doesn't know whether she can do anything else at her age. As it is, sales are down and her paycheck is shrinking.

So when the phone rings at your house during dinnertime and you can't resist 6 picking it up, relax, breathe deeply and take a silent oath to be polite. Try these three painless words: "No, thank you."

Think of the caller this way: a hard-working, first-generation American; the 7 daughter of a Pittsburgh steelworker; a survivor of the Great Depression; the widow of a World War II veteran; a mother of seven, grandmother of eight, great-grandmother of three. It's my mother calling.

READING COMPREHENSION QUESTIONS

1. The expression "pillar of strength" in "In our family, we think of my mother as a pillar of strength" (paragraph 2) means
   a. the person upon whom the family can rely for support and comfort during difficult times.
   b. the person who serves as the primary vehicle of communication for all the family members.
   c. the person who refuses to compromise.
   d. the person who argues the most.

2. The word *bulk* in "Are they not the bulk of your annoying calls?" (paragraph 4) means
   a. source.
   b. cause.
   c. majority.
   d. minority.

3. Which sentence best expresses the central idea of the selection?
   a. Telemarketing calls are made by hardworking Americans seeking to earn a living.
   b. If you do not want to receive telemarketing calls, then sign up for the do-not-call list.
   c. Avoid being rude to telemarketers.
   d. Telemarketing is a dying industry.

4. The main idea of paragraph 3 is
   a. telemarketing is not a viable industry.
   b. telemarketing is an industry comprising mainly minorities, women, single mothers, and people with disabilities.
   c. telemarketing is designed only for people who have been on welfare or public assistance.
   d. telemarketing is not ideal for those who have been used to hardship.

5. The main idea of paragraph 4 is
   a. do-not-call lists hurt the smaller businesses that rely on telemarketing to maintain sales.
   b. do-not-call lists are ineffective means of controlling the number of telemarketing calls a household receives.
   c. do-not-call lists apply only to politicians, charities, and big businesses.
   d. do-not-call lists do not apply to small businesses.

6. Telemarketing is an ideal job for people who have not been consistently part of the workforce because
   a. it pays well.
   b. it is flexible.
   c. it doesn't require a specific skill set.
   d. it is easy.

7. Buchanan's mother took the job as a telemarketer when
   a. she was forced to go on welfare.
   b. she ceased receiving any Social Security income.
   c. she decided she wanted to come out of retirement.
   d. her husband passed away and his pension benefits ceased.

8. The fact that mostly women—60% of whom are minorities and 26% of whom are single mothers—constitute the telemarketing industry suggests that
   a. many may be new immigrants seeking a way to earn an honest living for their families.
   b. many have endured hardships and telemarketing is a way for these women to earn an honest living without a college degree or specific skill set.
   c. many women are stay-at-home mothers.
   d. women are better telemarketers than men.

9. The fact that telemarketing giants will not be negatively affected by the do-not-call lists indicates that smaller businesses will, because
   a. the giants have the power and the funding to override the list.
   b. the smaller companies will need to resort to more costly means of sales and advertising that can put them out of business.

   c. the giants can buy out the smaller businesses.

   d. the smaller businesses will no longer be able to conduct their sales operations.

10. We can infer from this selection that Buchanan

   a. understands that telemarketing calls can be annoying.

   b. believes telemarketing as an industry is on a downward spiral.

   c. respects telemarketers as hardworking Americans trying to make ends meet.

   d. finds the telemarketing industry to be a scam.

TECHNIQUE QUESTIONS

1. "Don't Hang Up, That's My Mom Calling" is a persuasive essay about tele-marketing. What persuasive techniques does Buchanan use to persuade you to support her opinion about telemarketing as an industry? List those techniques here, and identify specific examples from the essay.

   Answers will vary, but one technique the author uses is eliciting sympathy from readers.

   See, for example, paragraph 2 where the author explains how his hard-working mother

   survived two heart surgeries and lung cancer.

   _____

2. In paragraph 3, Buchanan introduces statistical data from the American Tele-services Association. Why do you think she does this? How does bringing in this data help further her central idea?

   The author brings in actual data to make her argument credible, and to support with

   evidence the value of telemarketing as a form of employment for certain demographics.

   _____

   _____

3. The title of any written piece is often just as important as the written piece itself. Do you think the title that Buchanan chose is appropriate and effective? Would you have chosen a different title? Why or why not?

   Answers will vary. _____

   _____

   _____

   _____

DISCUSSION QUESTIONS

1. Buchanan describes some common reactions people have to telemarketers. How do you respond to telemarketers? Why do you think they tend to call at such odd hours? What can telemarketers do to avoid rude hang-ups or verbal insults?

2. One of the reasons Buchanan's mother started working again was to supplement her Social Security income. What do you think should be done for seniors whose Social Security income is not enough to allow them to buy food, pay for their utility and medical bills, and in some cases pay rent? Do you think they should find a job, or should the government provide them with additional services and support?

3. Given that so much selling and buying, and likewise advertising, is done online, it is not a surprise that Buchanan's mother sees her telemarketing sales going down and her paycheck shrinking. Do you think the telemarketing industry will survive? Why or why not?

WRITING ASSIGNMENTS

1. Buchanan describes her mother as her family's "pillar of strength" and the personification of "the great American way." What does "the great American way" mean for you? Write a descriptive paragraph about someone you admire who you feel represents both a "pillar of strength" and the personification of "the great American way." Identify this person in your topic sentence.

2. Have you ever registered your phone number with a do-not-call list? Has it helped cut down the number of telemarketing calls you receive? Write an essay that describes how you would cut down on or eliminate the number of telemarketing calls you receive. Start by brainstorming different ideas, and then choose three to write about. Next, create an informal outline that includes your central idea, main idea statements, supporting details, and transitions. Try to come up with a clever title for your piece as well.

3. In paragraph 5 of the selection, Buchanan states that her mother is less bothered by how her clients treat her than by the prospect of finding another job at her age (seventy-one). Write an essay about one industry or role that you feel would be ideal for seniors who still need to work to supplement their Social Security incomes. What makes the job especially ideal? What skills and experience, if any, are required? Do some research online to locate data that will support your claim.

ESL Pointers

This section covers rules that most native speakers of English take for granted but that are useful for speakers of English as a second language (ESL).

Articles

Types of Articles

An *article* is a noun marker—it signals that a noun will follow. There are two kinds of articles: indefinite and definite. The indefinite articles are *a* and *an*. Use *a* before a word that begins with a consonant sound:

a desk, **a p**hotograph, **a u**nicycle
(*A* is used before *unicycle* because the *u* in that word sounds like the consonant *y* plus *u,* not a vowel sound.)

Use *an* before a word beginning with a vowel sound:

an error, **an o**bject, **an h**onest woman
(*Honest* begins with a vowel sound because the *h* is silent.)

The definite article is *the:*

the sofa, **the** cup

An article may come right before a noun:

a magazine, **the** candle

Or an article may be separated from the noun by words that describe the noun:

a popular magazine, **the** fat red candle

> TIP   There are various other noun markers, including quantity words (*a few, many, a lot of*), numerals (*one, thirteen, 710*), demonstrative adjectives (*this, these*), possessive adjectives (*my, your, our*), and possessive nouns (*Raoul's, the school's*).

Articles with Count and Noncount Nouns

To know whether to use an article with a noun and which article to use, you must recognize count and noncount nouns. (A *noun* is a word used to name something—a person, a place, a thing, or an idea.)

Count nouns name people, places, things, or ideas that can be counted and made into plurals, such as *pillow, heater,* and *mail carrier* (*one pillow, two heaters, three mail carriers*).

Noncount nouns refer to things or ideas that cannot be counted and therefore cannot be made into plurals, such as *sunshine, gold,* and *toast.* The box below lists and illustrates common types of noncount nouns.

Common Types of Noncount Nouns

Abstractions and emotions: **justice, tenderness, courage, knowledge, embarrassment**

Activities: **jogging, thinking, wondering, golf, hoping, sleep**

Foods: **oil, rice, pie, butter, spaghetti, broccoli**

Gases and vapors: **carbon dioxide, oxygen, smoke, steam, air**

Languages and areas of study: **Korean, Italian, geology, arithmetic, history**

Liquids: **coffee, kerosene, lemonade, tea, water, bleach**

Materials that come in bulk or mass form: **straw, firewood, sawdust, cat litter, cement**

Natural occurrences: **gravity, sleet, rain, lightning**

Other things that cannot be counted: **clothing, experience, trash, luggage, room, furniture, homework, machinery, cash, news, transportation, work**

The quantity of a noncount noun can be expressed with a word or words called *qualifiers,* such as *some, more,* or *a unit of.* In the following two examples, the qualifiers are shown in *italic* type, and the noncount nouns are shown in **boldface** type.

How *much* **experience** have you had as a salesclerk?

Our tiny kitchen doesn't have *enough* **room** for a table and chairs.

Some words can be either count or noncount nouns depending on whether they refer to one or more individual items or to something in general:

Three **chickens** are running around our neighbor's yard.
(This sentence refers to particular chickens; *chicken* in this case is a count noun.)

Would you like some more **chicken**?
(This sentence refers to chicken in general; in this case, *chicken* is a noncount noun.)

Using a or an *with Nonspecific Singular Count Nouns*

Use *a* or *an* with singular nouns that are nonspecific. A noun is nonspecific when the reader doesn't know its specific identity.

A photograph can be almost magical. It saves a moment's image for many years.
(The sentence refers to any photograph, not a specific one.)

An article I read online today made me laugh.
(The reader isn't familiar with the article. This is the first time it is mentioned.)

Using the *with Specific Nouns*

In general, use *the* with all specific nouns—specific singular, plural, and noncount nouns. A noun is specific—and therefore requires the article *the*—in the following cases:

- When it has already been mentioned once:

  An article I read online today made me laugh. **The** article was about a talking parrot that frightened away a thief.
  (*The* is used with the second mention of *article*.)

- When it is identified by a word or phrase in the sentence:

  The song that is playing now is a favorite of mine.
  (*Song* is identified by the words *that is playing now*.)

- When its identity is suggested by the general context:

  The service at Joe's Bar and Grill is never fast.
  (*Service* is identified by the words *at Joe's Bar and Grill*.)

- When it is unique:

  Some people see a man's face in **the** moon, while others see a rabbit.
  (Earth has only one moon.)

- When it comes after a superlative adjective (for example, *best, biggest,* or *wisest*):

    The funniest movie I've seen is *Young Frankenstein.*

Omitting Articles

Omit articles with nonspecific plurals and nonspecific noncount nouns. Plurals and noncount nouns are nonspecific when they refer to something in general.

Stories are popular with most children.

Service is almost as important as food to a restaurant's success.

Movies can be rented from many supermarkets as well as public libraries.

Using the *with Proper Nouns*

Proper nouns name particular people, places, things, or ideas and are always capitalized. Most proper nouns do not require articles; those that do, however, require *the.* Following are general guidelines about when not to use *the* and when to use *the.*

Do not use *the* for most singular proper nouns, including names of the following:

- *People and animals* (Stephen Colbert, Fluffy)
- *Continents, states, cities, streets, and parks* (South America, Utah, Boston, Baker Street, People's Park)
- *Most countries* (Cuba, Indonesia, Ireland)
- *Individual bodies of water, islands, and mountains* (Lake Michigan, Captiva Island, Mount McKinley)

Use *the* for the following types of proper nouns:

- *Plural proper nouns* (the Philadelphia Eagles, the Marshall Islands, the Netherlands, the Atlas Mountains)
- *Names of large geographic areas, deserts, oceans, seas, and rivers* (the Midwest, the Kalahari Desert, the Pacific Ocean, the Sargasso Sea, the Nile River)
- *Names with the format* "the _____ of _____" (the Strait of Gibraltar, the University of Illinois)

PRACTICE 1

Underline the correct word or words in parentheses.

1. (<u>Indiana</u>, The Indiana) is a state where basketball is extremely popular.

2. (<u>Dictionaries</u>, The dictionaries) provide both the spelling and the definition of words.

3. On Friday, I'll be going to (<u>a birthday party</u>, the birthday party).

4. (A birthday party, <u>The birthday party</u>) will be held at an Italian restaurant.

5. Theo spends all his spare time playing (<u>soccer</u>, the soccer).

6. Rice, coconuts, and pineapples are some important products of (Philippines, <u>the Philippines</u>).

7. (Amazon River, <u>The Amazon River</u>) carries more water than any other river in the world.

8. (Lucky man, <u>The lucky man</u>) won a two-week trip to Paris.

9. The name of (<u>the National Organization for Women</u>, National Organization for Women) is often abbreviated as NOW.

10. (Cereal, <u>The cereal</u>) my sister likes has tiny blue and pink marshmallows in it.

Subjects and Verbs

Avoiding Repeated Subjects

In English, a particular subject can be used only once in a word group with a subject and a verb (that is, a clause). Don't repeat a subject in the same word group by following a noun with a pronoun.

> Incorrect: My *parents they* live in Miami.
> Correct: My **parents** live in Miami.
> Correct: **They** live in Miami.

Even when the subject and verb are separated by several words, the subject cannot be repeated in the same word group.

> Incorrect: The *windstorm* that happened last night *it* damaged our roof.
> Correct: The **windstorm** that happened last night **damaged** our roof.

Including Pronoun Subjects and Linking Verbs

Some languages omit a subject that is a pronoun, but in English, every sentence other than a command must have a subject. In a command, the subject *you* is understood: (You) Hand in your papers now.

> Incorrect: The soup tastes terrible. *Is* much too salty.
> Correct: The soup tastes terrible. **It is** much too salty.

Every English sentence must also have a verb, even when the meaning of the sentence is clear without the verb.

> Incorrect: The table covered with old newspapers.
>
> Correct: The table **is** covered with old newspapers.

Including *There* and *Here* at the Beginning of Sentences

Some English sentences begin with *there* or *here* plus a linking verb (usually a form of *to be: is, are,* and so on). In such sentences, the verb comes before the subject.

> **There are** ants all over the kitchen counter.
> (The subject is the plural noun *ants,* so the plural verb *are* is used.)
>
> **Here is** the bug spray.
> (The subject is the singular noun *spray,* so the singular verb *is* is used.)

In sentences like those above, remember not to omit *there* or *here*.

> Incorrect: *Are* several tests scheduled for Friday.
>
> Correct: **There are** several tests scheduled for Friday.

Not Using the Progressive Tense of Certain Verbs

The progressive tenses are made up of forms of *be* plus the *-ing* form of the main verb. They express actions or conditions still in progress at a particular time.

> The garden **will be blooming** when you visit me in June.

However, verbs for mental states, the senses, possession, and inclusion are normally not used in the progressive tense.

> Incorrect: I **am knowing** a lot about auto mechanics.
>
> Correct: I **know** a lot about auto mechanics.

> Incorrect: Gerald **is having** a job as a supermarket cashier.
>
> Correct: Gerald **has** a job as a supermarket cashier.

The following box lists the common verbs not generally used in the progressive tense.

Common Verbs Not Generally Used in the Progressive

Verbs relating to thoughts, attitudes, and desires: **agree, believe, imagine, know, like, love, prefer, think, understand, want, wish**

Verbs showing sense perceptions: **hear, see, smell, taste**

Verbs relating to appearances: **appear, seem, look**

Verbs showing possession: **belong, have, own, possess**

Verbs showing inclusion: **contain, include**

Using Gerunds and Infinitives after Verbs

Before learning the rules about gerunds and infinitives, you must understand what they are. A *gerund* is the *-ing* form of a verb that is used as a noun:

> **Reading** is a good way to improve one's vocabulary.
> (*Reading* is the subject of the sentence.)

An *infinitive* is *to* plus the basic form of the verb (the form in which the verb is listed in the dictionary), as in **to eat.** The infinitive can function as an adverb, an adjective, or a noun.

> On weekends, Betsy works at a convenience store **to make** some extra money.
> (*To make some extra money* functions as an adverb that describes the verb *works*.)

> I need a pencil **to write down** your phone number.
> (*To write down your phone number* functions as an adjective describing the noun *pencil*.)

> **To forgive** can be a relief.
> (*To forgive* functions as a noun—it is the subject of the verb *can be*.)

Some verbs can be followed by only a gerund or only an infinitive; other verbs can be followed by either. Examples are given in the following lists. There are many others; watch for them in your reading.

Verb + gerund (*enjoy + skiing*)
Verb + preposition + gerund (*think + about + coming*)

Some verbs can be followed by a gerund but not by an infinitive. In many cases, there is a preposition (such as *for, in,* or *of*) between the verb and the gerund. Some verbs and verb-preposition combinations that can be followed by gerunds but not by infinitives are listed below:

admit	believe in	feel like	practice
apologize for	deny	finish	suspect of
appreciate	discuss	insist on	talk about
approve of	dislike	look forward to	thank for
avoid	enjoy	postpone	think about
be used to			

Incorrect: The governor *avoids to make* enemies.
Correct: The governor **avoids making** enemies.

Incorrect: I *enjoy to go* to movies alone.
Correct: I **enjoy going** to movies alone.

Verb + infinitive (*agree + to leave*)

Common verbs that can be followed by an infinitive but not by a gerund are

agree	decide	manage
arrange	expect	refuse
claim	have	wait

Incorrect: I *arranged paying* my uncle's bills while he was ill.
Correct: I **arranged to pay** my uncle's bills while he was ill.

Verb + noun or pronoun + infinitive (*cause + them + to flee*)

Common verbs that are followed first by a noun or pronoun and then by an infinitive, not a gerund, are

cause	force	remind
command	persuade	warn

Incorrect: The flood *forced them leaving their home.*
Correct: The flood **forced them to leave their home.**

Following are common verbs that can be followed either by an infinitive alone or by a noun or pronoun and an infinitive:

ask	need	want
expect	promise	would like

Rita **expects to go** to college.
Rita's parents **expect her to go** to college.

Verb + gerund or infinitive
(*begin* + *packing* or *begin* + *to pack*)

Following are verbs that can be followed by either a gerund or an infinitive:

begin	hate	prefer
continue	love	start

The meaning of each of the verbs above remains the same or almost the same whether a gerund or an infinitive is used.

I love **to sleep** late.
I love **sleeping** late.

With the verbs below, the gerunds and the infinitives have very different meanings.

forget	remember	stop

Yuri **forgot putting money** in the parking meter.
(He put money in the parking meter, but then he forgot that he had done so.)

Yuri **forgot to put money** in the parking meter.
(He neglected to put money in the parking meter.)

PRACTICE 2

Underline the correct word or words in parentheses.

1. The waitress (she looks, <u>looks</u>) grumpy, but she is really quite pleasant.

2. Our picnic will have to be put off until another day. (Is raining, <u>It is raining</u>) too hard to go.

3. (Are, <u>There are</u>) some good articles in this magazine.

4. A very famous writer (coming, <u>is coming</u>) to talk to our class on Friday.

5. I (<u>have</u>, am having) a few questions to ask you.

6. Lila's mother (<u>prefers</u>, is preferring) that we call her by her first name.

7. If your boss is so unpleasant, you should think about (<u>getting</u>, to get) another job.

8. Standing in front of the mirror, Omar practiced (to give, <u>giving</u>) his speech for hours.

9. Because she was angry at her boyfriend, Delores refused (going, <u>to go</u>) to the movies with him.

10. Now that he's done it for several weeks, Sergei is used to (ride, <u>riding</u>) the city buses.

Adjectives

Following the Order of Adjectives in English

Adjectives describe nouns and pronouns. In English, an adjective usually comes directly before the word it describes or after a linking verb (a form of *be* or a "sense" verb such as *look, seem,* or *taste*), in which case it modifies the subject of the sentence. In each of the following two sentences, the adjective is **boldfaced** and the noun it describes is *italicized*.

> Marta has **beautiful** *eyes*.
> Marta's *eyes* are **beautiful**.

When more than one adjective modifies the same noun, the adjectives are usually stated in a certain order, though there are often exceptions. The box at the top of the next page lists the typical order of English adjectives.

Typical Order of Adjectives in a Series

1. Article or other noun marker: a, an, the, Helen's, this, seven, your

2. Opinion adjective: rude, enjoyable, surprising, easy

3. Size: tall, huge, small, compact

4. Shape: triangular, oval, round, square

5. Age: ancient, new, old, young

6. Color: gray, blue, pink, green

7. Nationality: Greek, Thai, Korean, Ethiopian

8. Religion: Hindu, Methodist, Jewish, Muslim

9. Material: fur, copper, stone, velvet

10. Noun used as an adjective: book (as in *book report*), picture (as in *picture frame*), tea (as in *tea bag*)

Here are some examples of the order of adjectives:

an exciting new movie

the petite young Irish woman

my favorite Chinese restaurant

Greta's long brown leather coat

In general, use no more than two or three adjectives after the article or other noun marker. Numerous adjectives in a series can be awkward: **that comfortable big old green velvet** couch.

Using the Present and Past Participles as Adjectives

The present participle ends in *-ing*. Past participles of regular verbs end in *-ed* or *-d;* a list of the past participles of many common irregular verbs appears on pages 173–75. Both types of participles may be used as adjectives. A participle used as an adjective may come before the word it describes:

There was a **frowning** *security guard.*

A participle used as an adjective may also follow a linking verb and describe the subject of the sentence:

The *security guard* was **frowning.**

While both present and past participles of a particular verb may be used as adjectives, their meanings differ. Use the present participle to describe whoever or whatever causes a feeling:

> a **disappointing** *date*
>
> (The date *caused* the disappointment.)

Use the past participle to describe whoever or whatever experiences the feeling:

> the **disappointed** *neighbor*
>
> (The neighbor *is* disappointed.)

Here are two more sentences that illustrate the differing meanings of present and past participles.

> The waiter was **irritating.**
>
> The diners were **irritated.**
>
> (The waiter caused the irritation; the diners experienced the irritation.)

Following are pairs of present and past participles with similar distinctions.

annoying, annoyed	**exhausting, exhausted**
boring, bored	**fascinating, fascinated**
confusing, confused	**surprising, surprised**
depressing, depressed	**tiring, tired**
exciting, excited	

PRACTICE 3

Underline the correct word or wording in parentheses.

1. We were glad to find such a (young helpful, <u>helpful young</u>) guide to show us the new city.

2. The children spent hours stacking the (<u>little square yellow</u>, yellow little square) blocks into different arrangements.

3. Our family attends the (old Orthodox Greek, <u>old Greek Orthodox</u>) church on Maple Avenue.

4. After his long workday, Ezra is often very (<u>tired</u>, tiring).

5. The (tired, <u>tiring</u>) journey lasted for almost five days.

Prepositions Used for Time and Place

The use of a preposition in English is often not based on the preposition's common meaning, and there are many exceptions to general rules. As a result, the correct use of prepositions must be learned gradually through experience. Following is a chart showing how three of the most common prepositions are used in some customary references to time and place:

Use of *on*, *in*, and *at* to Refer to Time and Place

Time

On *a specific day:* on Wednesday, on January 11, on Halloween

In *a part of a day:* in the morning, in the daytime (but *at* night)

In *a month or a year:* in October, in 1776

In *a period of time:* in a second, in a few days, in a little while

At *a specific time:* at 11 P.M., at midnight, at sunset, at lunchtime

Place

On *a surface:* on the shelf, on the sidewalk, on the roof

In *a place that is enclosed:* in the bathroom, in the closet, in the drawer

At *a specific location:* at the restaurant, at the zoo, at the school

---

Underline the correct preposition in parentheses.

PRACTICE 4

1. Kids like to play tricks (on, at) April Fool's Day.

2. The baby usually takes a nap (on, in) the afternoon.

3. (In, At) a few minutes, the show will begin.

4. You'll find paper clips (on, in) the cup on my desk.

5. I didn't see anyone I knew (on, at) the party.

Underline the correct word or words in parentheses.

1. At the beach, the children enjoyed playing in the (<u>sand</u>, sands).

2. (Are, <u>There are</u>) more stars in the sky tonight than I have ever seen.

3. Doesn't watching such a sad movie make you feel (<u>depressed</u>, depressing)?

4. On my way to the restaurant I had a (sobered, <u>sobering</u>) thought: I had no money.

5. I'll never throw away my (<u>favorite old denim</u>, old favorite denim) jacket.

6. The girl's parents suspect her of (to use, <u>using</u>) drugs.

7. The elderly woman carefully hung the picture of her grandchildren (in, <u>on</u>) the wall.

8. That umbrella by the door (<u>belongs</u>, is belonging) to my uncle.

9. (<u>Happiness</u>, The happiness) is something everyone hopes to find in life.

10. Many people dislike (to wait, <u>waiting</u>) in a long line.

Sentence-Skills Diagnostic Test

Part 1

This diagnostic test will check your knowledge of a number of sentence skills. In each item below, certain words are underlined. Write *X* in the answer space if you think a mistake appears at the underlined part. Write *C* in the answer space if you think the underlined part is correct.

The headings within the test ("Fragments," "Run-Ons," and so on) will give you clues to the mistakes to look for. However, you do not have to understand the heading to find a mistake. What you are checking is your own sense of effective written English.

Teaching Tip
You may want to have your students take the sentence-skills diagnostic test at the start of the semester. Encourage them to set sentence-skill goals for themselves.

Fragments

__*X*__ 1. Because I didn't want to get wet. I waited for a break in the downpour. Then I ran for the car like an Olympic sprinter.

__*C*__ 2. The baby birds chirped loudly, especially when their mother brought food to them. Their mouths gaped open hungrily.

__*X*__ 3. Trying to avoid running into anyone. Cal wheeled his baby around the crowded market. He wished that strollers came equipped with flashing hazard lights.

__*X*__ 4. The elderly woman combed out her long, gray hair. She twisted it into two thick braids. And wrapped them around her head like a crown.

Run-Ons

__*X*__ 5. Irene packed fruits and healthy sandwiches for her lunch, she went to a Mexican restaurant instead.

__*X*__ 6. Angie's dark eyes were the color of mink they matched her glowing complexion.

__*C*__ 7. My nutritionist keeps sending me bottles of vitamins, but I keep forgetting to take them.

_X_   8. The little boy watched the line of ants march across the <u>ground, he</u> made a wall of Popsicle sticks to halt the ants' advance.

Standard English Verbs

_C_   9. When she's stressed, Aurelia <u>goes</u> out for a five-mile run.

_X_   10. The street musician counted the coins in his donations basket and <u>pack</u> his trumpet in its case.

_X_   11. I tried to pull off my rings, but they <u>was</u> stuck on my swollen fingers.

_X_   12. Bella's car <u>have</u> a horn that plays six different tunes.

Irregular Verbs

_X_   13. I've <u>swam</u> in this lake for years, and I've never seen it so shallow.

_X_   14. The phone <u>rung</u> once and then stopped.

_C_   15. Five different people had <u>brought</u> huge bowls of potato salad to the barbecue.

_C_   16. The metal ice cube trays <u>froze</u> to the bottom of the freezer.

Subject-Verb Agreement

_X_   17. The Blu-rays in my collection <u>is</u> arranged in alphabetical order.

_C_   18. There <u>was</u> only one burner working on the old gas stove.

_X_   19. My aunt and uncle <u>gives</u> a party every Groundhog Day.

_X_   20. One of my sweaters <u>have</u> moth holes in the sleeves.

Consistent Verb Tense

_C_   21. After I turned off the ignition, the engine <u>continued</u> to sputter for several minutes.

_X_   22. Before cleaning the oven, I lined the kitchen floor with newspapers, <u>open</u> the windows, and shook the can of aerosol foam.

Pronoun Reference, Agreement, and Point of View

_C_   23. All visitors should stay in <u>their</u> cars while driving through the wild animal park.

_X_   24. At the library, <u>they</u> showed me how to use the interlibrary exchange program.

_X_   25. As I slowed down at the scene of the accident, <u>you</u> could see long, black skid marks on the highway.

Pronoun Types

_____X_____ 26. My husband is more sentimental than <u>me</u>.

_____C_____ 27. Andy and <u>I</u> like to go hiking together.

Adjectives and Adverbs

_____X_____ 28. Brian drives so <u>reckless</u> that no one will join his car pool.

_____C_____ 29. Miriam pulled <u>impatiently</u> at the rusty zipper.

_____X_____ 30. I am <u>more happier</u> with myself now that I earn my own money.

_____C_____ 31. The last screw on the license plate was the <u>most worn</u> one of all.

Misplaced Modifiers

_____X_____ 32. Skylar stretched out on the lounge chair <u>wearing shorts and a T-shirt</u>.

_____X_____ 33. I replaced the shingle on the roof <u>that was loose</u>.

Dangling Modifiers

_____X_____ 34. <u>While doing the dishes</u>, a glass shattered in the soapy water.

_____C_____ 35. <u>Pedaling as fast as possible</u>, Todd tried to outrace the snapping dog.

Faulty Parallelism

_____X_____ 36. Before I could take a bath, I had to pick up the damp towels off the floor, gather up the loose toys in the room, and <u>the tub had to be scrubbed out</u>.

_____X_____ 37. I've tried several cures for my headaches, including drugs, meditation, exercise, and <u>massaging my head</u>.

Capital Letters

_____C_____ 38. This <u>fall</u> we plan to visit Cape Cod.

_____X_____ 39. Vern ordered a set of tools from the <u>spiegel</u> catalog.

_____C_____ 40. When my <u>aunt</u> visits us, she insists on doing all the cooking.

_____X_____ 41. Maureen asked, "<u>will</u> you split a piece of cheesecake with me?"

Numbers and Abbreviations

_____X_____ 42. Before I could stop myself, I had eaten <u>6</u> glazed doughnuts.

_____C_____ 43. At <u>10:45 A.M.</u>, a partial eclipse of the sun will begin.

_____X_____ 44. Derrick, who is now over six <u>ft.</u> tall, can no longer sleep comfortably in a twin bed.

End Marks

_c_   45. Jane wondered if the blizzard would force the office to close.

_c_   46. Does that stew need some salt?

Apostrophe

_x_   47. Elizabeths quick wit makes her very popular.

_x_   48. I tried to see through the interesting envelope sent to my sister but couldnt.

_c_   49. Pam's heart almost stopped beating when Roger jumped out of the closet.

_x_   50. The logs' in the fireplace crumbled in a shower of sparks.

Quotation Marks

_c_   51. Someone once said, "A lie has no legs and cannot stand."

_x_   52. "This repair job could be expensive, the mechanic warned."

_c_   53. "My greatest childhood fear," said Sheila, "was being sucked down the bathtub drain."

_x_   54. "I was always afraid of everybody's father, said Midori, except my own."

Comma

_x_   55. The restaurant's "sundae bar" featured bowls of whipped cream chopped nuts and chocolate sprinkles.

_c_   56. My sister, who studies karate, installed large practice mirrors in our basement.

_x_   57. When I remove my thick eyeglasses the world turns into an out-of-focus movie.

_c_   58. Gloria wrapped her son's presents in pages from the comics section, and she glued a small toy car atop each gift.

Spelling

_x_   59. When Terry practises scales on the piano, her whole family wears earplugs.

_x_   60. I wondered if it was alright to wear sneakers with my three-piece suit.

_x_   61. The essay test question asked us to describe two different theorys of evolution.

_x_   62. A theif stole several large hanging plants from Marlo's porch.

Omitted Words and Letters

_c_   63. After dark, I'm afraid to look in the closets or under the bed.

_x_   64. I turned on the television, but baseball game had been rained out.

_x_   65. Polar bear cubs stay with their mother for two year.

Commonly Confused Words

_x_   66. Before your about to start the car, press the gas pedal to the floor once.

_x_   67. The frog flicked it's tongue out and caught the fly.

_x_   68. I was to lonely to enjoy the party.

_c_   69. The bats folded their wings around them like leather overcoats.

Effective Word Choice

_x_   70. If the professor gives me a break, I might pass the final exam.

_x_   71. Harry worked like a dog all summer to save money for his tuition.

_x_   72. Because Monday is a holiday, sanitation engineers will pick up your trash on Tuesday.

_c_   73. Our family's softball game ended in an argument, as usual.

_x_   74. As for my own opinion, I feel that nuclear weapons should be banned.

_x_   75. This law is, for all intents and purposes, a failure.

Part 2 (Optional)

Do the following at your instructor's request. This second part of the test will provide more detailed information about skills you need to know. On a separate sheet of paper or in a separate file, number and correct all the items in Part 1 of the test that you marked with an *X*. For example, suppose you marked the word groups below with an *X*. (Note that the following four examples were not taken from the actual test.)

4. When I picked up the tire. Something in my back snapped. I could not stand up straight as a result.

7. The phone started ringing, then the doorbell sounded as well.

15. Marks goal is to save enough money to attend graduate school next year.

29. Without checking the rearview mirror the driver pulled out into the passing lane.

Here is how you should write your corrections:

Many answers will vary; see Instructor's Manual for corrected sentences.

4. When I picked up the tire, something in my back snapped.

7. The phone started ringing, and then the doorbell sounded as well.

15. Mark's

29. mirror, the

There are over forty corrections to make in all.

Sentence-Skills Achievement Test

Teaching Tip

You may want to have your students take the sentence-skills achievement test at the end of the semester. Encourage them to reflect on the improvements that they have made as writers.

Part 1

This achievement test will help you check your mastery of a number of sentence skills. In each item below, certain words are underlined. Write *X* in the answer space if you think a mistake appears at the underlined part. Write *C* in the answer space if you think the underlined part is correct.

The headings within the test ("Fragments," "Run-Ons," and so on) will give you clues to the mistakes to look for.

Fragments

_____ *X* _____	1. When the town hero died. Hundreds of people went to his funeral. They wanted to pay their respects.
_____ *C* _____	2. Suzanne adores junk foods, especially onion-flavored potato chips. She can eat an entire bag at one sitting.
_____ *X* _____	3. My brother stayed up all night. Studying the rules in his driver's manual. He wanted to get his license on the first try.
_____ *X* _____	4. Hector decided to take a study break. He turned on the TV. And scrolled through the onscreen guide to find that night's listings.

Run-Ons

_____ *X* _____	5. Ron leaned forward in his seat, he could not hear what the instructor was saying.
_____ *X* _____	6. Our laptop obviously needs repairs the hard drive keeps freezing.
_____ *C* _____	7. Nick and Fran enjoyed their trip to Chicago, but they couldn't wait to get home.
_____ *X* _____	8. I checked the weather forecast online, I had to decide what to wear.

Standard English Verbs

_c_   9. My sister Louise <u>walks</u> a mile to the bus stop every day.

_X_   10. The play was ruined when the quarterback <u>fumble</u> the handoff.

_X_   11. When the last guests left our party, we <u>was</u> exhausted but happy.

_X_   12. I don't think my mother <u>have</u> gone out to a movie in years.

Irregular Verbs

_X_   13. My roommate and I <u>seen</u> a double feature this weekend.

_X_   14. My nephew must have <u>growed</u> six inches since last summer.

_c_   15. I should have <u>brought</u> a gift to the office holiday party.

_c_   16. After playing basketball all afternoon, Al <u>drank</u> a quart of Gatorade.

Subject-Verb Agreement

_X_   17. The cost of those new tires <u>are</u> more than I can afford.

_c_   18. Jin and Max <u>give</u> a New Year's Eve party every year.

_X_   19. There <u>was</u> only two slices of cake left on the plate.

_X_   20. Each of the fast-food restaurants <u>have</u> a breakfast special.

Consistent Verb Tense

_c_   21. After I folded the towels in the basket, I <u>remembered</u> that I hadn't washed them yet.

_X_   22. Before she decided to buy the eyeglass frames, Joanne <u>tries</u> on several other pairs.

Pronoun Reference, Agreement, and Point of View

_c_   23. All drivers should try <u>their</u> best to be courteous during rush hour.

_X_   24. When Rob went to the bank for a home improvement loan, <u>they</u> asked him for three credit references.

_X_   25. I like to shop at factory outlets because <u>you</u> can always get brand names at a discount.

Pronoun Types

_X_   26. My brother writes much more neatly than <u>me</u>.

_c_   27. Vonnie and <u>I</u> are both taking Introduction to Business this semester.

Adjectives and Adverbs

x 28. When the elevator doors closed sudden, three people were trapped inside.

c 29. The homeless woman glared angrily at me when I offered her a dollar bill.

x 30. Frank couldn't decide which vacation he liked best, a bicycle trip or a week at the beach.

c 31. I find proofreading a paper much more difficult than writing one.

Misplaced Modifiers

x 32. The car was parked along the side of the road with a flat tire.

x 33. We bought speakers at an electronics store that can be mounted on a wall.

Dangling Modifiers

x 34. While looking for bargains at Sears, an exercise bike caught my eye.

c 35. Hurrying to catch the bus, Tori fell and twisted her ankle.

Faulty Parallelism

x 36. Before she leaves for work, Ana makes her lunch, does fifteen minutes on the elliptical, and her two cats have to be fed.

x 37. Three remedies for insomnia are warm milk, taking a hot bath, and sleeping pills.

Capital Letters

c 38. Every Saturday I get up early, even though I can sleep in late.

x 39. We stopped at the drugstore for some crest toothpaste.

c 40. Rows of crocuses appear in my front yard every spring.

x 41. The attendant said, "sorry, but children under three are not allowed in this theater."

Numbers and Abbreviations

x 42. Our train finally arrived—2 hours late.

c 43. Answers to the chapter questions start on page 633.

x 44. Three yrs. from now, my new car will finally be paid off.

End Marks

_c_   45. I had no idea who was inside the gorilla suit at the costume party.

_x_   46. Are you taking the make-up exam.

Apostrophe

_x_   47. My fathers favorite book is *To Kill a Mockingbird*.

_x_   48. I couldnt understand a word of that lecture.

_c_   49. My dentist's recommendation was that I floss after brushing my teeth.

_x_   50. Three house's on our street are up for sale.

Quotation Marks

_c_   51. In the movie *The Godfather*, Don Corleone says, "I made him an offer he can't refuse."

_x_   52. "This restaurant does not accept credit cards, the waiter said."

_x_   53. Two foods that may prevent cancer," said the scientist, "are those old standbys spinach and carrots."

_x_   54. "I can't get anything done," Dad complained, if you two insist on making all that noise."

Comma

_x_   55. The snack bar offered overdone hamburgers rubbery hot dogs and soggy pizza.

_c_   56. My sister, who regards every living creature as a holy thing, cannot even swat a housefly.

_x_   57. When I smelled something burning I realized I hadn't turned off the oven.

_c_   58. Marge plays the xylophone at parties, and her husband does Dracula imitations.

Spelling

_x_   59. No one will be admited without a valid student identification card.

_x_   60. Trisha carrys a full course load in addition to working as the night manager at a supermarket.

_x_   61. Did you feel alright after eating Rodolfo's special chili?

_x_   62. My parents were disappointed when I didn't enter the family busines.

Omitted Words and Letters

_c_ 63. Both high schools in my hometown offer evening classes for adults.

_x_ 64. I opened new bottle of ketchup and then couldn't find the cap.

_x_ 65. Visiting hour for patients at this hospital are from noon to eight.

Commonly Confused Words

_x_ 66. Shelley has always been to self-conscious to speak up in class.

_x_ 67. Its not easy to return to college after raising a family.

_x_ 68. "Thank you for you're generous contribution," the letter began.

_c_ 69. Nobody knew whose body had been found floating in the swimming pool.

Effective Word Choice

_x_ 70. My roommate keeps getting on my case about leaving clothing on the floor.

_x_ 71. Karla decided to take the bull by the horns and ask her boss for a raise.

_x_ 72. Although Lamont accelerated his vehicle, he was unable to pass the truck.

_c_ 73. When the movie ended suddenly, I felt I had been cheated.

_x_ 74. In light of the fact that I am on a diet, I have stopped eating between meals.

_x_ 75. Personally, I do not think that everyone should be allowed to vote.

Part 2 (Optional)

Do the following at your instructor's request. This second part of the test will provide more detailed information about which skills you need to know. On a separate
sheet of paper or in a separate file, number and correct all the items in Part 1 of the
test that you marked with an *X*. For example, suppose you marked the word groups
below with an *X*. (Note that the following four examples were not taken from the
actual test.)

4. When I picked up the tire. Something in my back snapped. I could not
    stand up straight as a result.

7. The phone started ringing, then the doorbell sounded as well.

15. Marks goal is to save enough money to attend graduate school next year.

29. Without checking the rearview mirror the driver pulled out into the
    passing lane.

Here is how you should write your corrections:

4. When I picked up the tire, something in my back snapped.

7. The phone started ringing, and then the doorbell sounded as well.

15. Mark's

29. mirror, the driver

There are more than forty corrections to make in all.

Answers to Introductory Activities and Practice Exercises in Part Two

APPENDIX D

This answer key can help you teach yourself. Use it to find out why you got some answers wrong—to uncover any weak spots in your understanding of a skill. By using the answer key in an honest and thoughtful way, you will master each skill and prepare yourself for many tests in this book that have no answer key.

SUBJECTS AND VERBS

Introductory Activity (85)

Answers will vary.

Practice 1 (87)

1. Rachel poured
2. company offered
3. host introduced
4. Taryn adjusted
5. butt burned
6. bathroom is
7. Royden tripped
8. drink quenched
9. trimmer tossed
10. Volunteers collected

Practice 2 (88)

1. shows . . . were
2. burp is
3. sunglasses . . . look
4. voice sounds
5. Tamika became
6. lotion smells
7. Visitors . . . appear
8. vibrations are
9. cold feels
10. change . . . seems

Practice 3 (88)

1. light glowed
2. kite soared
3. Manuel caught
4. skaters shadowed
5. lights emphasized
6. Tracy reads
7. glasses slipped
8. Jane gave
9. squirrel jumped
10. Carpenters constructed

Practice 4 (89)

1. Stripes of sunlight glowed on the kitchen floor.
2. The black panther draped its powerful body along the thick tree branch.
3. A line of impatient people snaked from the box office to the street.
4. At noon, every tornado siren in town wails for fifteen minutes.
5. The tops of my Bic pens always disappear after a day or two.
6. Joanne removed the lint from her black socks with Scotch tape.
7. The mirrored walls of the skyscraper reflected the passing clouds.
8. Debris from the accident littered the intersection.
9. Above the heads of the crowd, a woman swayed on a narrow ledge.
10. The squashed grapes in the bottom of the vegetable bin oozed sticky, purple juice.

Practice 5 (91)

1. Einstein could have passed
2. She could have been killed
3. children did not recognize
4. strikers have been fasting
5. I could not see
6. People may be wearing
7. He should have studied
8. Rosa has been soaking
9. lines . . . were flying
10. brother can ask

633

Practice 6 *(91)*

1. trees creaked and shuddered
2. girl fell . . . and landed
3. I will vacuum . . . and change
4. sun shone . . . and turned
5. Sam and Billy greased
6. man and . . . friend rode
7. sister and I . . . race
8. Nia breathed and . . . began
9. Phil draped . . . and pretended
10. wrestler and opponent strutted . . . and pounded

FRAGMENTS

Introductory Activity *(97)*

1. verb
2. subject
3. subject . . . verb
4. express a complete thought

Practice 1 *(100)*

Answers will vary.

Practice 2 *(101)*

NOTE: The underlined part shows the fragment (or that part of the original fragment not changed during correction).

1. Since she was afraid of muggers, Barbara carried a small can of pepper spray on her key ring.
2. When I began watching the movie, I remembered that I had seen it before.
3. Tulips had only begun to bloom when a freakish spring snowstorm blanketed the garden.
4. Whenever I'm in the basement and the landline rings, I don't run up to answer it. If the message is important, the person will call back.
5. Since she is a new student, Carla feels shy and insecure. She thinks she is the only person who doesn't know anyone else.

Practice 3 *(103)*

1. Julie spent an hour at her desk, staring at a blank piece of paper.
2. Rummaging around in the kitchen drawer, Tyrone found the key he had misplaced a year ago.
3. As a result, I lost my place in the checkout line.

Practice 4 *(104)*

Rewritten versions may vary.

1. I tossed and turned for hours. *Or:* Tossing and turning for hours, I felt like a blanket being tumbled dry.
2. It fluffed its feathers to keep itself warm. *Or:* A sparrow landed on the icy windowsill, fluffing its feathers to keep itself warm.
3. The reason was that she had to work the next day. *Or:* Alma left the party early, the reason being that she had to work the next day.
4. Grasping the balance beam with her powdered hands, the gymnast executed a handstand.
5. To cover his bald spot, Walt combed long strands of hair over the top of his head.

Practice 5 *(106)*

1. For instance, he folds a strip of paper into the shape of an accordion.
2. Marco stuffed the large green peppers with hamburger meat, cooked rice, and chopped parsley.
3. For example, he craves Bugles and Doritos.

Practice 6 *(107)*

Rewritten versions may vary.

1. For instance, he has his faded sweatshirt from high school.
2. For example, she borrows my sweaters.
3. To improve her singing, Amber practiced some odd exercises, such as flapping her tongue and fluttering her lips.
4. For example, she had put on forty pounds.
5. Stanley wanted a big birthday cake with candles spelling out STAN.

Practice 7 *(108)*

Rewritten answers may vary.

1. Then she quickly folded her raggedy towels and faded sheets.
2. Michael took his wool sweaters out of storage and found them full of moth holes.
3. Also, she is learning two computer languages.
4. Then he hides under the bed.
5. A tiny bug crawled across my paper and sat down in the middle of a sentence.

RUN-ONS

Introductory Activity (121)

1. period
2. but
3. semicolon
4. although

Practice 1 (123)

1. coffee. His
2. way. She
3. coughing. A
4. me. It
5. time. The
6. machine. We
7. closely. They
8. Lauren. She
9. victims. They
10. late. The

Practice 2 (124)

1. cockroaches. Both
2. blood. The
3. counselor. She's
4. death. He
5. seen. One
6. beautiful. Now
7. penalty. The
8. down. It
9. Germany. In
10. request. He

Practice 3 (125)

Answers will vary.

Practice 4 (126)

1. drawer, but
2. paper, for
3. therapy, so
4. drive, and
5. on, and
6. summer, so
7. truck, so
8. break, but
9. faded, and
10. fit, so

Practice 5 (127)

Answers will vary.

Practice 6 (128)

1. backward; his
2. indestructible; it
3. cards; she
4. moth; it
5. book; it

Practice 7 (129)

Answers may vary.

1. month; on the other hand, they (*or* however)
2. sick; therefore, she (*or* consequently *or* as a result *or* thus)
3. hydrant; however, she

4. guests; furthermore, he (*or* also *or* moreover *or* in addition)
5. money; consequently, she (*or* therefore *or* as a result *or* thus)

Practice 8 (129)

1. wait; however, she
2. computers; as a result, she
3. abused; moreover, many
4. smoking; otherwise, I
5. carefully; nevertheless, the

Practice 9 (130)

Answers may vary.

1. After
2. before
3. When
4. If
5. until

Practice 10 (131)

1. Even though I had a campus map and a smartphone, I still could not find my classroom building.
2. When a cat food commercial came on, Marie started to sing along with the jingle.
3. Since the phone in the next apartment rings all the time, I'm beginning to get used to the sound.
4. After Michael gulped two cups of coffee, his heart began to flutter.
5. As a car sped around the corner, it sprayed slush all over the pedestrians.

SENTENCE VARIETY I

The Simple Sentence
Practice 1 (142)

Answers will vary.

The Compound Sentence
Practice 2 (142)

Answers may vary.

1. I am majoring in digital media arts, for I hope to find a job doing video-game animation.
2. My children were spending too much time in front of the TV and computer, so I signed up my entire family for a one-year gym membership.

3. Nicole's skin was blemished and sun damaged, so she consulted with a dermatologist about skin cancer concerns.

4. Riley insists on buying certified-organic fruits and vegetables, but I cannot distinguish organic from conventionally grown produce.

5. I was recently promoted to shift manager at work, so I need to drop down to part-time status at school next semester.

Practice 3 (144)

Answers will vary.

The Complex Sentence
Practice 4 (145)

Answers may vary.

1. Because the movie disgusted Dena, she walked out after twenty minutes.

2. After the house had been burglarized, Dave couldn't sleep soundly for several months.

3. When my vision begins to fade, I know I'd better get some sleep.

4. Since the family would need a place to sleep, Fred told the movers to unload the mattresses first.

5. When the hurricane hit the coast, we crisscrossed our windows with strong tape.

Practice 5 (146)

Answers may vary.

1. Although the muffler shop advertised same-day service, my car wasn't ready for three days.

2. Because the hypertension medication produced dangerous side effects, the government banned it.

3. While Phil lopped dead branches off the tree, Michelle stacked them into piles on the ground below.

4. Anne wedged her handbag tightly under her arm because she was afraid of muggers.

5. Although Ellen counted the cash three times, the total still didn't tally with the amount on the register tape.

Practice 6 (147)

Answers may vary.

1. The boy who limps was in a motorcycle accident.

2. Raquel, who is my neighbor, is a champion weight lifter.

3. The two screws that held the bicycle frame together were missing from the assembly kit.

4. The letter that arrived today is from my ex-wife.

5. The tall hedge that surrounded the house muffled the highway noise.

Practice 7 (148)

Answers will vary.

The Compound-Complex Sentence
Practice 8 (149)

Answers will vary.

1. Since . . . for
2. When . . . and
3. until . . . so
4. When . . . or
5. but . . . because

Practice 9 (149)

Answers will vary.

Review of Coordination and Subordination
Practice 10 (150)

Answers will vary.

1. I needed butter to make the cookie batter, but I couldn't find any, so I used vegetable oil instead.

2. Although Tess had worn glasses for fifteen years, she decided to get LASIK surgery. She would be able to see without glasses or corrective lenses, and she would save money in the end.

3. When the children at the day care center took their naps, they unrolled their sleeping mats, and they piled their shoes and sneakers in a corner.

4. When Jerry dialed the police emergency number, he received a busy signal. He dropped his phone and ran because he didn't have time to turn back.

5. Louise disliked walking home from the bus stop because the street had no overhead lights, and it was lined with abandoned buildings.

6. When the rain hit the hot pavement, plumes of steam rose from the blacktop. Cars slowed to a crawl, for the fog obscured the drivers' vision.

7. While his car went through the automated car wash, Harry watched from the sidelines. Floppy brushes slapped the car's doors, and sprays of water squirted onto the roof.

8. Since the pipes had frozen and the heat had gone off, we phoned the plumber. He couldn't come

for days because he had been swamped with emergency calls.

9. When my car developed an annoying rattle, I took it to the service station. The mechanic looked under the hood, but he couldn't find what was wrong.

10. The childproof cap on the aspirin bottle would not budge even though the arrows on the bottleneck and cap were lined up. When I pried the cap with my fingernails, one nail snapped off, and the cap still adhered tightly to the bottle.

STANDARD ENGLISH VERBS

Introductory Activity (159)

played . . . plays

hoped . . . hopes

juggled . . . juggles

1. past time . . . -ed or -d

2. present time . . . -s

Practice 1 (161)

1. wears	6. distributes
2. says	7. C
3. subscribes	8. feeds
4. believes	9. overcooks
5. sees	10. polishes

Practice 2 (161)

Jon works for a company that delivers singing telegrams. Sometimes he puts on a sequined tuxedo or wears a Cupid costume. He composes his own songs for birthdays, anniversaries, bachelor parties, and other occasions. Then he shows up at a certain place and surprises the victim. He sings a song that includes personal details, which he gets in advance, about the recipient of the telegram. Jon loves the astonished looks on other people's faces; he also enjoys earning money by making people happy on special days.

Practice 3 (162)

1. turned	6. washed
2. bounced	7. cracked
3. paged	8. collected
4. crushed	9. pulled
5. C	10. lacked

Practice 4 (162)

Brad hated working long hours, but he needed money to support his growing family and to pay for school. He started working at the auto body shop when he graduated from high school because he liked cars, but the job bored him. He wished that he could spend more time at home with his wife and new baby girl. He also wanted to dedicate more time to his homework. Brad knew that he had made his own choices, so he decided to appreciate his job, his family, and his chance to move ahead in life.

Practice 5 (165)

1. is	6. was
2. has	7. had
3. is	8. was
4. does	9. did
5. did	10. was

Practice 6 (165)

1. is	6. do
2. has	7. do
3. has	8. has
4. are	9. does
5. are	10. are

Practice 7 (166)

My friend Tyrell is a real bargain-hunter. If a store has a sale, he runs right over and buys two or three things, whether or not they are things he needs. Tyrell does his best, also, to get something for nothing. Last week, he was reading the paper and saw that the First National Bank's new downtown offices were offering gifts for new accounts. "Those freebies sure do look good," Tyrell said. So he went downtown, opened an account, and had the manager give him a Big Ben alarm clock. When he got back with the clock, he was smiling. "I am a very busy man," he told me, "and I really need the free time."

IRREGULAR VERBS

Introductory Activity (172)

1. R . . . screamed . . . screamed

2. I . . . wrote . . . written

3. I . . . stole . . . stolen

4. R . . . asked . . . asked

5. R . . . kissed . . . kissed

6. I . . . chose . . . chosen

7. I . . . rode . . . ridden

8. R . . . chewed . . . chewed

9. I . . . thought . . . thought

10. R . . . danced . . . danced

Practice 1 (175)

1. took
2. chosen
3. caught
4. stolen
5. saw
6. gone
7. fallen
8. sworn
9. shrunk
10. spoken

Practice 2 (176)

1. (a) loses
   (b) lost
   (c) lost
2. (a) brings
   (b) brought
   (c) brought
3. (a) swim
   (b) swam
   (c) swum
4. (a) goes
   (b) went
   (c) gone
5. (a) begins
   (b) began
   (c) begun
6. (a) hides
   (b) hid
   (c) hidden
7. (a) choose
   (b) chose
   (c) chosen
8. (a) speak
   (b) spoke
   (c) spoken
9. (a) takes
   (b) took
   (c) taken
10. (a) wake
    (b) woke
    (c) woken

Practice 3 (179)

1. laid
2. lay
3. laid
4. lying
5. lay

Practice 4 (180)

1. set
2. set
3. sit
4. set
5. setting

Practice 5 (181)

1. rise
2. raised
3. raised
4. rose
5. raised

SUBJECT–VERB AGREEMENT

Introductory Activity (187)

Correct: There were many applicants for the position.

Correct: The pictures in that magazine are very controversial.

Correct: Everybody usually watches the lighted numbers in an elevator.

1. applicants . . . pictures
2. singular . . . singular

Practice 1 (189)

1. leaders of the union have
2. One of Omar's pencil sketches hangs
3. days of anxious waiting finally end
4. members of the car pool chip
5. woman with the teased, sprayed hairdo looks
6. addition of heavy shades to my sunny windows allows
7. houses in the old whaling village have
8. stack of baseball cards in my little brother's bedroom is
9. puddles of egg white spread
10. box of Raisinets sells

Practice 2 (190)

1. were . . . trucks
2. are . . . coyotes
3. are rows
4. are . . . boots
5. was . . . boy
6. was . . . animal
7. is . . . shampooer
8. was . . . stream
9. is . . . box
10. is . . . sign

Practice 3 (191)

1. is
2. remembers
3. fit
4. has
5. wanders
6. needs
7. keeps
8. sneaks
9. is
10. eats

Practice 4 (192)

1. seem
2. is
3. are
4. help
5. impresses

Practice 5 (192)

1. roam
2. begins
3. thunder
4. fear
5. tastes

CONSISTENT VERB TENSE

Introductory Activity (201)

Mistakes in verb tense: Alex discovers . . . calls a . . . present . . . past

Practice 1 (202)

1. prepares
2. filled
3. found
4. began
5. are
6. separated
7. send
8. sells
9. said
10. likes

ADDITIONAL INFORMATION ABOUT VERBS

Practice 1 (210)

1. had watched
2. has written
3. am taking
4. had lifted
5. has improved
6. are protesting
7. have dreaded
8. has vowed *or* is vowing
9. were peeking
10. are getting *or* have gotten

Practice 2 (211)

1. P
2. G
3. I
4. G
5. I
6. P
7. P
8. P
9. G
10. I

Practice 3 (213)

Answers may vary.

1. The beautician snipped off Carla's long hair.
2. The parents protested the teachers' strike.
3. The alert bank teller tripped the silent alarm.
4. Relentless bloodhounds tracked the escaped convicts.
5. A famous entertainer donated the new PET scanner to the hospital.
6. A stock clerk dropped a gallon glass jar of pickles in the supermarket aisle.
7. A car struck the deer as it crossed the highway.
8. My doctor referred me to a specialist in hearing problems.
9. Family photographs cover one wall of my living room.
10. Fear gripped the town during the accident at the nuclear power plant.

PRONOUN REFERENCE, AGREEMENT, AND POINT OF VIEW

Introductory Activity (217)

1. b
2. b
3. b

Practice 1 (219)

Answers will vary. Rewritten sentences may have meanings different from the answers provided.

1. When we pulled into the gas station, the attendant told us one of our tires looked soft.
2. Nora broke the heavy platter when she dropped it on her foot.
3. Vicky asked for a grade transcript at the registrar's office, and the clerk told her it would cost three dollars.
4. Don't touch the freshly painted walls with your hands unless the walls are dry.
5. Maurice's habit of staying up half the night watching *Chiller Theater* really annoys his wife.
6. Robin went to the store's personnel office to be interviewed for a sales position.
7. Leon told his brother, "You need to lose some weight."

8. I wrote to the insurance company but haven't received an answer.

9. I went to the doctor to see what he could do about my itchy, bloodshot eyes.

10. I took the loose pillows off the chairs and sat on the pillows.
    Or: I sat on the loose pillows, which I had taken off the chairs.

Practice 2 (221)

1. them
2. their
3. they
4. them
5. it

Practice 3 (223)

1. her
2. he
3. her
4. his
5. she
6. its
7. her
8. his
9. their
10. his

Practice 4 (225)

1. we see
2. I can buy
3. we were given
4. we relax
5. they serve
6. I get depressed
7. I save
8. he or she could make
9. she can buy
10. I can stop

PRONOUN TYPES

Introductory Activity (232)

Correct sentences:

Ali and I enrolled in a computer course.

The police officer pointed to my sister and me.

Elle prefers men who take pride in their bodies.

The players are confident that the league championship is theirs.

Those concert tickets are too expensive.

Our parents should spend some money on themselves for a change.

Practice 1 (235)

2. I (*S*)
3. her (*O*)
4. me (*O*)
5. her and him (*O*)
6. I (*can* is understood) (*S*)
7. We (*S*)
8. she (*S*)
9. me (*O*)
10. he (*S*)

Practice 2 (235)

Answers will vary.

2. me *or* her *or* him *or* them
3. I *or* she *or* he
4. I *or* she *or* he *or* they
5. me *or* him *or* her *or* them
6. I *or* he *or* she *or* they
7. them
8. him *or* her *or* them
9. I *or* he *or* she
10. she *or* he

Practice 3 (238)

1. who
2. which
3. whom
4. who
5. who

Practice 4 (238)

Answers will vary.

Practice 5 (239)

1. hers
2. mine
3. ours
4. its
5. their

Practice 6 (241)

1. This
2. Those
3. These
4. Those
5. that

Practice 7 (241)

Answers will vary.

Practice 8 (243)

1. ourselves
2. himself
3. themselves
4. yourself
5. ourselves

ADJECTIVES AND ADVERBS

Introductory Activity (247)

Answers will vary for 1–4.

adjective . . . adverb . . . *ly* . . . *er* . . . *est*

Practice 1 (250)

1. kinder . . . kindest
2. more ambitious . . . most ambitious
3. more generous . . . most generous
4. finer . . . finest
5. more likable . . . most likable

Practice 2 (250)

1. thickest
2. lazier
3. harshest
4. more flexible
5. worse
6. best
7. less
8. less vulnerable
9. most wasteful
10. shinier

Practice 3 (251)

1. hesitantly
2. easily
3. sharply
4. abruptly
5. aggressive
6. regretfully
7. quickly
8. messily
9. envious
10. terribly

Practice 4 (252)

1. good
2. good
3. well
4. well
5. well

MISPLACED MODIFIERS

Introductory Activity (257)

1. Intended: The farmers were wearing masks.
   Unintended: The apple trees were wearing masks.
2. Intended: The woman had a terminal disease.
   Unintended: The faith healer had a terminal disease.

Practice 1 (258)

NOTE: In the corrections below, the underlined part shows what had been a misplaced modifier. In some cases, other corrections are possible.

1. Driving along the wooded road, we noticed several dead animals.
2. In her mind, Maya envisioned the flowers that would bloom.
3. In my tuxedo, I watched my closest friends being married.
4. Zoe carried her new coat, which was trimmed with fake fur, on her arm.
5. We just heard on the radio that all major highways were flooded.
6. Fresh-picked blueberries covered almost the entire kitchen counter.
7. Making sounds of contentment, Betty licked the homemade peach ice cream.
   Or: Betty, making sounds of contentment, licked the homemade peach ice cream.
8. With a grin, the salesman demonstrated the Roomba vacuum cleaner.
9. Dressed in a top hat and tails, Natasha is delivering pizzas.
10. The local drama group badly needs people to build scenery.

Practice 2 (259)

1. Using caution, I rolled down my car window only a few inches for the police officer.
2. Gossip blogs all over the world publish unflattering photos of celebrities who are arrested for drunk driving or for possession of illicit drugs.
3. The mongoose, which resembles the ferret, was brought to Hawaii to kill rats but has since destroyed much of the native plant life.
4. Led Zeppelin's fourth album sold almost 33 million copies.
5. Elisa decided to undergo laser eye surgery at the university medical center to correct her astigmatism.

DANGLING MODIFIERS
Introductory Activity (257)

1. Intended: The giraffe was munching leaves.
   Unintended: The children were munching leaves.

2. Intended: Michael was arriving home. . . .
   Unintended: The neighbors were arriving home. . . .

Practice 1 (258)

1. The shelter had the stray, which was foaming at the mouth, put to sleep.

2. Marian finally found her slippers, which had been kicked carelessly under the bed.

3. I tried out the old swing set, which was rusty with disuse.

4. The manager decided to replace his starting pitcher, who had given up four straight hits.

5. The farmers lost their entire tomato crop, which had frozen on the vines.

6. C

7. The audience cheered wildly as the elephants, which were dancing on their hind legs, paraded by.

8. Marta took the overdone meat loaf, which was burned beyond all recognition, from the oven.

9. We decided to replace the dining room wallpaper, which was tattered, faded, and hanging in shreds.

10. A person can keep membership cards clean by sealing them in plastic.
    Or: When sealed in plastic, membership cards can be kept clean.

Practice 2 (259)
Answers will vary.

FAULTY PARALLELISM
Introductory Activity (273)
Correct sentences:

I use my computer to write papers, chat with friends, and to play games.

One option the employees had was to take a cut in pay; the other was to work longer hours.

Dad's favorite chair has a torn cushion, a stained armrest, and a musty odor.

Practice 1 (274)

1. waved pennants
2. to stay indoors
3. make a cream sauce
4. turn down the heat
5. overdone hamburgers
6. coughed
7. demanding
8. drinking two milk shakes
9. puts a frozen waffle into the toaster
10. to leave the company

Practice 2 (275)
Answers will vary.

SENTENCE VARIETY II
-ing Word Groups
Practice 1 (282)
Answers may vary.

1. Fluffing out its feathers, the sparrow tried to keep warm.

2. Squeezing the tube as hard as I could, I managed to get enough toothpaste on my brush.

3. Checking the glass-faced gauges, the janitor started up the enormous boiler.

4. Staring straight ahead, the runner set his feet into the starting blocks.

5. The produce clerk, chatting with each customer, cheerfully weighed bags of fruit and vegetables.

Practice 2 (283)
Answers will vary.

-ed Word Groups
Practice 3 (283)
Answers may vary.

1. Bored with the talk show, I dozed off.

2. Crinkled with age, the old dollar bill felt like tissue paper.

3. Crowded into a tiny, windowless room, the students acted nervous and edgy.

4. Loaded down with heavy bags of groceries, I waited for someone to open the door.

5. Tired of his conservative wardrobe, Ron bought a green-striped suit.

Practice 4 (284)
Answers will vary.

-ly Openers
Practice 5 (285)
1. Abruptly, Clarissa hung up on the telemarketer.
2. Casually, the thief slipped one of the watches into her coat sleeve.
3. Swiftly, I tugged on my shoes and pants as the doorbell rang.
4. Gruffly, the defense lawyer cross-examined the witnesses.
5. Carefully, Estelle poked the corner of a handkerchief into her eye.

Practice 6 (286)
Answers will vary.

To Openers
Practice 7 (287)
1. To anchor the flapping tablecloth, we set bricks on the ends of the picnic table.
2. To break up the coating of ice, Darryl scraped the windshield with a credit card.
3. To make the basketball game more even, we gave our opponents a ten-point advantage.
4. To give my wife a rest, I offered to drive the next five hundred miles.
5. To feed the unexpected guests, Ashaki added Hamburger Helper to the ground beef.

Practice 8 (287)
Answers will vary.

Prepositional Phrase Openers
Practice 9 (288)
Answers may vary.
1. On the bus, the old man wrote down my address with a stubby pencil.
2. During the day, special bulletins about the election returns interrupted regular programs.

3. At 6:00 A.M., my clock radio turned itself on with a loud blast of '90s music.
4. At the concert, the security guard looked in Aly's bag for concealed bottles.
5. On the highway, a plodding turtle crawled toward the grassy shoulder of the road.

Practice 10 (289)
Answers will vary.

Series of Items: Adjectives
Practice 11 (290)
1. Impatient and excited, the child gazed at the large, mysterious gift box.
2. Sticky juice squirted out of the fuzzy crushed caterpillar.
3. The battered car dangled from the gigantic yellow crane.
4. Patty squeezed her swollen, tender, sunburned feet into the tight shoes.
5. The tall, white-aproned cook flipped the thick, juicy hamburgers on the grooved metal grill.

Practice 12 (291)
Answers will vary.

Series of Items: Verbs
Practice 13 (291)
1. In the sports bar, Dave placed a bet on his favorite basketball team, took a swig from his bottle of Budweiser, and sat back to watch the NBA playoff semifinals.
2. The robber scanned the liquor store for a surveillance camera, fidgeted with his dark sunglasses and baseball cap, and signaled to the clerk behind the counter that he had a handgun.
3. The phlebotomist pressed down on Logan's forearm, slid the needle into his arm, and let out a heavy sigh as the needle missed his vein.
4. The comedy hypnotist invited a volunteer to the stage, quickly brought her into a trance, and offered her a clove of garlic, which she thought was a cashew nut.
5. The paparazzo stalked the Hollywood actor on vacation, adjusted his lens, and snapped hundreds of candid photos.

Practice 14 *(293)*

Answers will vary.

PAPER FORMAT

Introductory Activity *(298)*

In "A," the title is capitalized and centered and has no quotation marks around it; there is a blank line between the title and the body of the paper; the first line is indented; there are left and right margins around the body of the paper; no words are incorrectly hyphenated.

Practice 1 *(299)*

1. Do not use quotation marks around the title.
2. Capitalize the major words in the title (Too Small to Fight Back).
3. Skip a line between the title and the first line of the paper.
4. Indent the first line of the paper.
5. Keep margins on both sides of the paper.

Practice 2 *(300)*

Answers will vary.

1. My First-Grade Teacher
2. My Hardest Year
3. My Father's Sense of Humor
4. Ways to Conserve Energy
5. Violence in the Movies

Practice 3 *(301)*

1. Effective communication is often the key to a healthy relationship.
2. Reality TV shows are popular for several reasons.
3. Correct
4. The best vacation I ever had began when my friends from high school booked a one-week trip to Cancun, Mexico.
5. Most professional athletes say that they don't use steroids to enhance athletic performance.

CAPITAL LETTERS

Introductory Activity *(305)*

1–13: Answers will vary, but all should be capitalized.
14–16: On . . . Let's . . . I

Practice 1 *(308)*

1. Fourth . . . July . . . Veterans' Day
2. When . . . I
3. Toyota . . . Long Island Expressway
4. *Entertainment Weekly* . . . *Sixty Minutes*
5. National Bank . . . Samsung
6. Melrose Diner . . . Business Institute
7. A Sound . . . Thunder
8. Pacific School . . . Cosmetology
9. Sears . . . Ninth Street
10. Slim–Fast . . . Boca

Practice 2 *(311)*

1. Uncle David
2. Motorola Razr . . . Bluetooth
3. United States President Barack Obama . . . Nobel Peace Prize
4. Pacific Islander . . . Samoa . . . East Coast
5. Principles . . . Marketing

Practice 3 *(311)*

1. high school . . . principal . . . discipline
2. father . . . witch . . . play
3. skull . . . hair . . . bones
4. monument . . . settlers' . . . plague . . . locusts
5. motorcycle . . . tractor-trailer . . . motel

NUMBERS AND ABBREVIATIONS

Introductory Activity *(319)*

Correct choices:
First sentence: 8:55 . . . 65 percent
Second sentence: Nine . . . forty-five
Second sentence: brothers . . . mountain
Second sentence: hours . . . English

Practice 1 *(321)*

1. five
2. eleven . . . seventy-seven
3. five . . . five
4. 2:30
5. 15

6. 206

7. 15

8. two hundred

9. July 7, 2007,

10. *The Artist*

Practice 2 *(322)*

1. department . . . purchase

2. Interstate . . . Pennsylvania

3. America . . . pounds

4. pair . . . inch

5. appointment . . . doctor . . . month

6. library . . . minutes . . . Facebook

7. teaspoon . . . French

8. license . . . driving . . . road

9. finish . . . assignment . . . point

10. limit . . . senator . . . representative

END MARKS

Introductory Activity *(326)*

1. weather.   3. parked.

2. paper?   4. control!

Practice 1 *(327)*

1. door?   6. Gotcha!"

2. massage.   7. ads.

3. jerk!"   8. storm.

4. shocked.   9. think?"

5. psychology.   10. officer.

APOSTROPHE

Introductory Activity *(331)*

1. To show ownership or possession

2. To indicate missing letters and shortened spellings

3. Because *families* signals a plural noun, while *family's* indicates ownership or possession

Apostrophe in Contractions
Practice 1 *(332)*

1. shouldn't   6. can't

2. doesn't   7. who's

3. isn't   8. wouldn't

4. won't   9. aren't

5. they're

Practice 2 *(333)*

1. you'll . . . it's   4. I'm . . . I'm

2. hadn't . . . couldn't 5. Where's . . . who's

3. isn't . . . doesn't

Practice 3 *(333)*

Answers will vary.

Practice 4 *(334)*

1. It's . . . it's

2. they're . . . their

3. You're . . . your

4. whose . . . who's

5. it's . . . your . . . who's

Apostrophe to Show Ownership or Possession
Practice 5 *(335)*

1. The assassin's rifle

2. his mother's inheritance

3. Ali's throat

4. Sam's parking space

5. The chef's hat

6. the president's wife

7. The mugger's hand

8. Harry's briefcase

9. Sandy's handbag

10. The dog's leash

Practice 6 *(336)*

2. instructor's   7. Brian's

3. astrologer's   8. Nita's

4. Ellen's   9. Ted's

5. lemonade's   10. hypnotist's

6. sister's

Practice 7 (336)

Sentences will vary.

2. bus's
3. computer's
4. Ross's
5. pizza's

Apostrophe versus Simple Plurals
Practice 8 (338)

1. restaurant: restaurant's, meaning "the hamburgers of the restaurant"
   hamburgers: simple plural, meaning more than one hamburger
   steaks: simple plural meaning more than one steak

2. San Franciscos: San Francisco's, meaning "the cable cars of San Francisco"
   cars: simple plural, meaning more than one car
   hills: simple plural, meaning more than one hill

3. brothers: brother's, meaning "the collection of my brother"
   cards: simple plural, meaning more than one card
   boxes: simple plural, meaning more than one box

4. toothpicks: simple plural, meaning more than one toothpick
   years: year's, meaning "the fashions of this year"
   fashions: simple plural, meaning more than one fashion

5. Pedros: Pedro's, meaning "the blood pressure of Pedro"
   minutes: simple plural, meaning more than one minute
   spaces: simple plural, meaning more than one space

6. write-ups: simple plural, meaning more than one write-up
   Rubys: Ruby's, meaning "the promotion of Ruby"
   co-workers: simple plural, meaning more than one co-worker

7. sons: son's, meaning "the fort of my son"
   pieces: simple plural, meaning more than one piece
   nails: simple plural, meaning more than one nail
   shingles: simple plural, meaning more than one shingle

8. mayors: mayor's, meaning "the double-talk of the mayor"
   reporters: simple plural, meaning more than one reporter
   heads: simple plural, meaning more than one head

notebooks: simple plural, meaning more than one notebook

9. cuts: simple plural, meaning more than one cut
   boxers: boxer's, meaning "the left eye of the boxer"
   rounds: simple plural, meaning more than one round

10. cafeterias: cafeteria's, meaning "the loudspeakers of the cafeteria"
    loudspeakers: simple plural, meaning more than one loudspeaker
    exams: simple plural, meaning more than one exam

Apostrophe with Plural Words Ending in -s
Practice 9 (332)

1. stores'
2. friends'
3. Cowboys'
4. students'
5. voters'

QUOTATION MARKS

Introductory Activity (348)

1. Quotation marks set off the exact words of a speaker.
2. They go inside the quotation marks.

Practice 1 (350)

1. "This is the tenth commercial in a row," complained Niko.

2. The police officer said sleepily, "I could really use a cup of coffee."

3. My boss asked me to step into his office and said, "Joanne, how would you like a raise?"

4. "I'm out of work again," Miriam sighed.

5. "I didn't know this movie was R-rated!" Lorrine gasped.

6. "Why does my dog always wait until it rains before he wants to go out?" Donovon asked.

7. A sign over the box office read "Please form a single line and be patient."

8. "Unless I run three miles a day," Marty said, "my legs feel like lumpy oatmeal."

9. "I had an uncle who knew when he was going to die," claimed Dan. "He saw the date in a dream."

10. The unusual ad on Craigslist read "Young farmer would be pleased to hear from young lady with tractor. Send photograph of tractor."

Practice 2 (350)

1. The firefighter asked the neighbors, "Is there anyone still in the building?"

2. "You'll have to remove your sunglasses," the security guard reminded the customers at the bank.

3. Upon eating a few drops of Horacio's homemade habanero sauce, Trudy yelped, "That's hot!"

4. "Good things come to those who wait," Zhao told himself as he waited in line for hours to buy the new iPhone.

5. "If at first you don't succeed," my wife joked, "you should read the directions."

Practice 3 (351)

Answers will vary.

Practice 4 (352)

2. Marian said, "It was the worst day of my life."

3. Luis said, "Tell me all about it."

4. Marian insisted, "You wouldn't understand my job problems."

5. Luis said, "I will certainly try."

Practice 5 (353)

1. He said that he needed a vacation.

2. Gretchen said that purple was her favorite color.

3. She asked the handsome stranger if she could buy him a drink.

4. My brother asked if anyone had seen his frog.

5. Françoise complained that she married a man who falls asleep during horror movies.

Practice 6 (354)

1. My recently divorced sister refused to be in the talent show when she was told she'd have to sing "Love Is a Many-Splendored Thing."

2. Disgusted by the constant dripping noise, Brian opened his copy of Handy Home Repairs to the chapter titled "Everything about the Kitchen Sink."

3. My little brother has seen Avengers at least eight times.

4. Before they bought new car tires, Nick and Fran studied the article "Testing Tires" in the February 2012 issue of Consumer Reviews.

5. Many people mistakenly think that Huckleberry Finn and The Adventures of Tom Sawyer are children's books only.

6. I just found out that the musical My Fair Lady is based on a play by George Bernard Shaw called Pygmalion.

7. The ending of Shirley Jackson's story "The Lottery" really surprised me.

8. I sang the song "Mack the Knife" in our high school production of The Threepenny Opera.

9. Unless he's studied the TV Guide listings thoroughly, my father won't turn on his television.

10. Stanley dreamed that both Time and Newsweek had decided to use him in their feature article "Person of the Year."

COMMA

Introductory Activity (362)

1. a.   4. d.
2. b.   5. e.
3. c.   6. f.

Practice 1 (364)

1. sunglasses, a bottle of water, and a recent issue

2. check e-mail, play games, look at friends' photos on Facebook, down-load music, and send instant messages

3. igloo-shaped doghouse, several plastic toys, trampled flowers, and a cracked ceramic gnome

Practice 2 (364)

1. A metal tape measure, a pencil, a ruler, and a hammer dangled from the carpenter's pockets.

2. The fortune-teller uncovered the crystal ball, peered into it, and began to predict my future.

3. That hair stylist is well known for her flat blowouts, butchered haircuts, and brassy hair colorings.

Practice 3 (365)

1. hands,

2. storm,

3. help,

Practice 4 (365)

1. In order to work at that fast-food restaurant, you have to wear a cowboy hat and six-shooters. In addition, you have to shout "Yippee!" every time someone orders the special Western-style double burger.

2. Barely awake, the woman slowly rocked her crying infant. While the baby softly cooed, the woman fell asleep.

3. When I painted the kitchen, I remembered to cover the floor with newspapers. Therefore, I was able to save the floor from looking as if someone had thrown confetti on it.

Practice 5 (367)

1. gadget, ladies and gentlemen,

2. Tigers, because they eat people,

3. dummy, its straw-filled "hands" tied with rope,

Practice 6 (367)

1. My brother, who likes only natural foods, would rather eat a soybean patty than a cheeseburger.

2. That room, with its filthy rug and broken dishwasher, is the nicest one in the building.

3. My aunt, who claims she is an artist, painted her living room ceiling to look like the sky at midnight.

Practice 7 (368)

1. hour, or	6. *C*
2. fine, but	7. housecleaning, and
3. releases, and	8. melted, and
4. one, but	9. telephone, but
5. *C*	10. *C*

Practice 8 (369)

1. asked, "Do

2. wrote, "2

3. of," said Richie, "is

Practice 9 (369)

1. "Could you spare six dollars," the boy asked passersby in the mall, "for train fare?"

2. "Man does not live by words alone," wrote Adlai Stevenson, "despite the fact that sometimes he has to eat them."

3. "That actress," said Velma, "has promoted everything from denture cleaner to shoelaces."

Practice 10 (370)

1. sorry, sir, but

2. May 6, 1954, Roger

3. June 30, 2010, will

4. Seven Seas, P.O. Box 760, El Paso, TX

5. Leo, turn

Practice 11 (371)

1. A new bulletproof material has been developed that is very lightweight.

2. The vet's bill included charges for a distemper shot.

3. Since the firehouse is directly behind Ken's home, the sound of its siren pierces his walls.

4. Hard sausages and net-covered hams hung above the delicatessen counter.

5. The students in the 1980s dance class were dressed in a variety of bright tights, baggy sweatshirts, and woolly leg warmers.

6. A woman in the ladies' room asked me if she could borrow a safety pin.

7. Books, broken pencils, and scraps of paper littered the reporter's desk.

8. The frenzied crowd at the game cheered and whistled.

9. Splitting along the seams, the old mattress spilled its stuffing on the ground.

10. To satisfy his hunger, Enrique chewed on a piece of dry rye bread.

OTHER PUNCTUATION MARKS

Introductory Activity (380)

1. list:	4. track;
2. life-size	5. breathing—but alive.
3. (1856–1939)	

Practice 1 (381)

1. follows:

2. things:

3. life:

Practice 2 *(382)*

1. outlets; otherwise,
2. spider; he
3. 9 A.M.; . . . 10:00;

Practice 3 *(382)*

1. well—
2. see—
3. hoped—no, I prayed—

Practice 4 *(383)*

1. hole-in-the-wall . . . hoity-toity
2. rabbit-ear . . . high-definition
3. hard-working . . . out-of-towners

Practice 5 *(384)*

1. prices (fifty to ninety dollars) made
2. election (the April primary), only
3. you (1) two sharpened pencils and (2) an eraser.

DICTIONARY USE

Introductory Activity *(387)*

1. fortutious (fortuitous)
2. hi/er/o/glyph/ics
3. be
4. oc/to/ge/nar9/i/an
5. (1) an identifying mark on the ear of a domestic animal
   (2) an identifying feature or characteristic

Answers to the activities are in your dictionary. Check with your instructor if you have any problems.

SPELLING IMPROVEMENT

Introductory Activity *(399)*

Misspellings:

akward . . . exercize . . . buisness . . . worryed . . .
shamful . . . begining . . . partys . . . sandwichs . . . heros

Practice 1 *(401)*

1. carried	6. permitted
2. revising	7. gliding
3. studies	8. angrily
4. wrapping	9. rebelling
5. horrified	10. grudges

Practice 2 *(402)*

1. buses	6. avocados
2. patches	7. twenties
3. therapies	8. knives
4. batches	9. daughters-in-law
5. reefs	10. theses

OMITTED WORDS AND LETTERS

Introductory Activity *(409)*

bottles . . . in the supermarket . . . like a windup toy . . .
his arms . . . an alert shopper . . . with the crying

Practice 1 *(410)*

1. In the rest room, Jeff impatiently rubbed his hands under the mechanical dryer, which blew out feeble puffs of cool air.
2. On February 10, 1935, the *New York Times* reported that an eight-foot alligator had been dragged out of a city sewer by three teenage boys.
3. Lionel dressed up as a stuffed olive for Halloween by wearing a green plastic garbage bag and a red knitted cap.
4. Mrs. Chan nearly fainted when she opened the health insurance bill and saw an enormous rate increase.
5. At 4 A.M., the all-night supermarket where I work hosts an assortment of strange shoppers.
6. With a loud hiss, the inflated beach ball suddenly shrank to the size of an orange.
7. The boiling milk bubbled over the sides of the pot, leaving a gluey white film on the stove top.
8. Nadja turned to the answer page of the crossword book, pretended to herself that she hadn't, and turned back to her puzzle.
9. In order to avoid stepping on the hot blacktop of the parking lot, the barefoot boy tiptoed along the cooler white lines.

10. The messy roommates used hubcaps for ashtrays and <u>scribbled</u> graffiti on their own bathroom walls.

Practice 2 *(411)*

1. shaves . . . blades
2. legs . . . hurdles
3. fads . . . ants
4. owners . . . monkeys
5. photographers . . . sharks
6. spores . . . leaves
7. cages . . . plants
8. pounds . . . grapes . . . cents
9. soles . . . shoes
10. cheeseburgers . . . shakes

Practice 3 *(412)*
Answers will vary.

COMMONLY CONFUSED WORDS
Introductory Activity *(416)*

1. Incorrect: your   Correct: you're
2. Incorrect: who's   Correct: whose
3. Incorrect: there   Correct: their
4. Incorrect: to   Correct: too
5. Incorrect: Its   Correct: It's

Homonyms *(417)*
Answers will vary for sentences only.

already . . . all ready
brake . . . break
course . . . coarse
hear . . . here
whole . . . hole
It's . . . its
knew . . . new
know . . . no
pair . . . pear
passed . . . past
peace . . . piece
plane . . . plain

principal . . . principle
right . . . write
then . . . than
There . . . their . . . they're
through . . . threw
two . . . to . . . too
where . . . wear
weather . . . whether
whose . . . Who's
your . . . you're

Other Words Frequently Confused *(428)*
Answers will vary for sentences only.

an . . . a
accept . . . except
advise . . . advice
effect . . . affect
Among . . . between
Besides . . . beside
can . . . may
cloths . . . clothes
desert . . . dessert
dose . . . does
fewer . . . less
former . . . latter
learn . . . teach
loose . . . lose
quiet . . . quite
Though . . . thought

Incorrect Word Forms *(436)*
being that *(436)*

1. Because the boss heard my remark,
2. because my diet
3. since his dad

can't hardly, couldn't hardly *(437)*

1. I could hardly
2. I can hardly
3. everyone can hardly

could of, must of, should of, would of *(437)*

1. Shoshanna must have
2. You should have
3. I would have
4. No one could have

irregardless *(438)*

1. Regardless of what anybody else does,
2. Regardless of the weather,
3. Regardless of what my parents say,

EFFECTIVE WORD CHOICE

Introductory Activity *(444)*

Correct sentences:

1. After a disappointing movie, we devoured a pizza.
2. Mourning the death of his best friend, Tennyson wrote the moving poem "In Memoriam."
3. Psychological tests will be given on Wednesday.
4. I think the referee made the right decision.
   1 . . . 2 . . . 3 . . . 4

NOTE: The answers may vary for all of the following word-choice practices.

Practice 1 *(445)*

EXAMPLE

1. When I confronted my ex-boyfriend about cheating on me, he simply shrugged and said, "It was my fault."
2. My friend thinks that Chantel is attractive, but I think she's too emotional.
3. Rayna is on her cell phone all the time, but that's fine.
4. Joe wanted to quickly leave the family dinner so that he could meet his friends.

5. They were excited about the party, but they knew they'd have to leave early.

Practice 2 *(447)*

1. Substitute <u>make me very angry</u> for <u>make my blood boil.</u>
2. Substitute <u>depressed</u> for <u>down in the dumps.</u>
3. Substitute <u>extraordinary</u> for <u>one in a million.</u>
4. Substitute <u>have a celebration</u> for <u>roll out the red carpet.</u>
5. Substitute <u>free</u> for <u>free as a bird.</u>

NOTE: The above answers are examples of how the clichés could be corrected. Other answers are possible.

Practice 3 *(447)*

Answers will vary.

Practice 4 *(448)*

Answers may vary.

1. I do not understand that person's behavior.
2. He erased all the mistakes in his notes.
3. She thought about what he had said.
4. The police officer stopped the car.
5. Inez told the counselor about her career hopes.

Practice 5 *(450)*

Answers will vary.

1. I am a vegetarian.
2. Last Tuesday, I started going to college full-time.
3. Since I'm broke, I can't go to the movies.
4. I repeated that I wouldn't go.
5. Everything I say and do annoys my father.

CREDITS

Photo Credits

Part 1 Opener: © Arthur Tilley/Getty Images; page 13: © Design Pics/Don Hammond RF © Huntstock/ Getty Images RF; p. 44: © Peter M. Fisher/Corbis; Part 2 Opener: © Design Pics/Don Hammond RF; p. 76: © Diane Collins and Jordan Hollender/Getty Images RF; p. 77: © DreamPictures/Blend Images LLC RF; p. 110: © Dann Tardif/LWA/Corbis; p. 144: © Flying Colours Ltd/Getty Images RF; p. 194: © Sean De Burca/Corbis; p. 241: © The McGraw-Hill Companies, Inc./John Flournoy, photographer RF; p. 248: © Erich Lessing/Art Resource, NY; p. 307: © Mike Kemp/In Pictures/ Corbis; p. 327: © Alan Schein Photography/Corbis; p. 337: © Colin Underhill/Alamy; p. 373: © H. Schmid/Corbis; p. 405: © Janet Fekete/Getty Images; Part 3 Opener: © Seam Yeh/AFP/GettyImages; p. 460 (top): © Chris Leslie Smith/PhotoEdit; p. 460 (bottom): © Natalie Hummel; p. 500 (top): © Peter Finger/Corbis RF; p. 500 (middle): © Alan Schein Photography/Corbis; p. 500 (bottom): © Lee Snider/Photo Images/Corbis; Part 4 Opener: © Digital Vision/PunchStock RF.

Text Credits

Aponte, Wayne Lionel. "Say Brother: 'Talkin' White' ", Essence (January 1989): 11.

Buchanan, Bobbi, "Don't Hang Up, That's my Mom Calling", from the New York Times, December 8, 2003. Reprinted by permission of the author.

Carson, Ben, M.D., and Cecil Murphey, "Do It Better!" from *Think Big*. Copyright © 1996 by Zondervan Publishing House. Reprinted with permission.

Gammage, Jeff. "Wonder in the Air." Copyright 2006 by the Philadelphia Inquirer. Reprinted with permission.

Mrosla, Sister Helen P., "All the Good Things." Originally published in Proteus, Spring 1991. Reprinted by permission as edited and published by *Reader's Digest* in October, 1991.

Peck, Scott, M., M.D., "Responsibility;" from *The Road Less Traveled*. Copyright © 1978 by M. Scott Peck. Reprinted with permission of Simon and Schuster Inc.

Ruiz, Regina, "Taking Charge of My Life." Copyright © 1994, 2000 by Townsend Press. Reprinted by permission.

Tan, Amy. "The Most Hateful Words". Copyright © 2003 Amy Tan. First appeared in THE NEW YORKER. Reprinted by permission of the author and the Sandra Dijkstra Literary Agency.

Wahls, Zach and Bruce Littlefield. "Introduction", from MY TWO MOMS, copyright © 2012 by Zach Wahls LLC. Used by permission of Gotham Books, an imprint of Penguin Group (USA) Inc.

Walker, Alice. "My Daughter Smokes;' from *LIVING BY THE WORD: Essays by Alice Walker. Copyright © 1987 by Alice Walker.* Reprinted by permission of Houghton Mifflin Harcourt Publishing Company. All rights reserved.

INDEX